The Great American Countryside

VAL LANDI

Drawings by Liz Shugart

The Great

A Traveller's Companion

American Countryside

Field Notes on Animals,
Plants, Historic Sites, and
the Natural Environment

COLLIER BOOKS
A Division of Macmillan Publishing Co., Inc.
New York
COLLIER MACMILLAN PUBLISHERS
London

Macmillan Publishing Co., Inc.
866 Third Avenue, New York, N.Y. 10022
Collier Macmillan Canada, Inc.

Library of Congress Cataloging in Publication Data

Landi, Val.
   The great American countryside, a traveller's
companion.

      1. Natural history—United States—Guide-books.
2. United States—Description and travel—1960-
—Guide-books.   I. Title.
QH104.L27   917.304927   82-2195
ISBN 0-02-567840-X   AACR2
ISBN 0-02-097900-2 (pbk)

First Collier Books edition 1982

The Great American Countryside is also published in a hardcover edition by Macmillan
Publishing Co., Inc.

PRINTED IN THE UNITED STATES OF AMERICA

Designed by Antler & Baldwin, Inc.

Contents

Acknowledgments

I AM deeply indebted to the Historic Buildings Survey of the U.S. Department of the Interior for their kind assistance and for material submitted and used in the historic sites entries throughout the book; to the National Park Service Superintendent's Offices and their staff naturalists and rangers for their gracious assistance and for material submitted and used in entries on the national parks and monuments, flora and fauna, fall aspen foliage, Upper Missouri River, Grand Teton National Park life zones, whooping cranes of Grand Teton National Park, snow accumulation areas, mountain tundra, Badlands of South Dakota, the Great Divide, elk bugling, plant zones of Yellowstone Park, Yellowstone wildlife areas, Yellowstone bison herd, elk or wapiti, Grasshopper Glacier, Newberry Caldera and the Glass Buttes, Mono Craters and Jeffrey pine, glaciers of Olympic National Park, Mt. Rainier life zones, glaciers of Mt. Rainier, historic features of the Pacific Crest Trail, Rogue River pioneer sites and wildlife habitats, Yosemite Valley, giant sequoias, Buffalo Na-

tional River, Isle Royale, vegetation zones of Pictured Rocks National Lakeshore, Great Lakes climates, vegetation zones and wildlife habitats of Sleeping Bear National Lakeshore, pioneer artifacts of the Sleeping Bear Dunes, life zones of Acadia National Park, Mt. Desert Island and its eroding shore, and the sunken forest at Fire Island National Seashore; and to the U.S. Geological Survey for material submitted and used on Mt. St. Helens and the Gros Ventre Slide.

Special thanks go to Chip Rawlins of the Bridger-Teton National Forest Office in Pinedale, Wyoming, for his hospitality and superb contributions on alpine habitats, the Western ranch, range fences, and Rocky Mountain and Colorado Plateau climates; to Fran Barnes of Moab, Utah, for his contributions to the Colorado Plateau introduction and on Colorado River canyons and Colorado River dams; to Dr. Peter W. Dunwiddie of the University of Washington Quaternary Research Center for his contribution on tree-ring dating; to Kevin Schafer of Seattle for his contributions on the Grand Coulee and Olympic rain forests;

to Louis Borie of the University of Michigan for his contributions on Pictured Rocks National Lakeshore, Sleeping Bear Dunes, features of the Great Lakes coastline, white pines, northern bogs, alpine habitats of New England, Michigan's prairie remnants, and the Kirtland's warbler; to Dr. Robert A. Brown of Wake Forest University for his contributions on balds of the Southern Appalachians, high-peak fir forests, ancient cove forests, and Cades Cove Pioneer Area; and to Kevin Proescholdt for his contributions on the Voyageurs Highway and Indian pictographs.

Thanks go to Marge Dalechek of the U.S. Geological Survey Photo Library in Denver; to Jonathan Arms of the National Park Service Photo Library in Washington, D.C., for his help and patience; and to the staff of the U.S. Forest Service Photo Library in Arlington, Virginia, for their time and assistance.

Acknowledgments go to John Muir's *The Mountains of California* (New York: Century Co., 1904), for historical information used in entries on Yosemite Valley and the Sierra Nevada; to William Wright's *The Big Bonanza* (New York: Alfred A. Knopf, 1947) for information used in Sierra Nevada gold-rush sites entries; to Bernard A. DeVoto's *Across the Wide Missouri* (Boston: Houghton Mifflin Co., 1964) and *The Course of Empire* (Boston: Houghton Mifflin Co., 1952), for invaluable background on Western frontier sites and history; to J. Arnold Bolz's *Portage into the Past* (Minneapolis: University of Minnesota Press, 1960) for historical information on the Boundary Waters Canoe Area and Canadian Shield; to Samuel Eliot Morison's *The Story of Mount Desert Island* (Boston: Little, Brown and Co., 1960), for historical background on the Acadia National Park area; to the *Federal Writers' Project* guides—*California: A Guide to the Golden State* (New York: Hastings House, 1939), *Oregon: End of the Trail* (Portland, OR: Binfords & Mort, 1940), *Washington: A Guide to the Evergreen State* (Portland, OR: Binfords & Mort, 1941), *Colorado: A Guide to the Highest State* (New York: Hastings House, 1941), *Idaho: A Guide in Word and Picture* (Caldwell, ID: Caxton Printers, 1938), *Montana: A State Guide Book* (New York: Viking Press, 1939), *Utah: A Guide to the State* (New York: Hastings House, 1941), *Wyoming: A Guide to Its History, Highways and People* (New York: Oxford University Press, 1941), *Arizona: A State Guide* (New York: Hastings House, 1940), *Oklahoma: A Guide to the Sooner State* (Oklahoma City: Tribune Publishing Co., 1938), *Texas: A Guide to the Lone Star State* (New York: Hastings House, 1940), *Kansas: A Guide to the Sunflower State* (New York: Viking Press, 1939), *Michigan: A Guide to the Wolverine State* (New York: Oxford University Press, 1941), *Maine: A Guide "Down East"* (Boston: Houghton Mifflin Co., 1937)—for material used in entries on rain-shadow climate, Rocky Mountain weather systems and rendezvous sites, ponderosa pine, Indian rock writings, north-country logging camps, Great Divide country, Death Valley, Indian copper mines, Colorado Front Range, Great Plains of Texas, High Sierra and Rocky Mountain life zones, Keweenaw Peninsula, Maine's mountains and aboriginal Indians, Cross Timbers, High Plains of Kansas, the roundup, adobes of the Southwest, Colorado's mountain parks, chaparral, Uinta Basin, Colorado's High Plains, birds of the Maine coast, Rocky Mountain pioneer homesteads and mining camps, plants of the Pacific Northwest seashores, and Wyoming's Spanish Diggings and Red Canyon country. Acknowledgment also goes to Nevin M. Fenneman for his superb studies, *Physiography of the Western United States* (New York: McGraw-Hill Book Company, Inc., 1931) and *Physiography of the Eastern United States* (New York: McGraw-Hill Book Company, Inc., 1948); and to W.W. Atwood's *The Physiographic Provinces of North America* (Boston: Ginn and Company, 1940).

Last, but by no means least, my thanks and gratitude go to Charles Levine, Macmillan's Director of General Reference Books, to Gladys Villegas, his assistant, and to Mary Donchez, the copyeditor, for their unfailing support and good cheer, and to Liz Shugart for her marvelous drawings.

Val Landi

PART ONE

Western United States

1. Great Plains

THE vast grasslands of the Great Plains sweep down the United States from Canada through western North Dakota, South Dakota, Kansas, Oklahoma and Texas and eastern Montana, Wyoming, Colorado and New Mexico—flanked on the east by the tall-grass prairies of the Central Lowlands, and on the west by the towering ramparts of the Rocky Mountains.

Traveling west from the tall-grass prairies of the Central Lowlands through the transition zone of the mixed-grass prairies between the 98th and 100th meridians—the famed winter wheat region, where little bluestem, June grass, and wheat grass grow not in a tall, waving carpet, but in clumps—you come to the arid short-grass country of the High Plains, lying in the rain shadow of the Rocky Mountains, as the elevation of the land increases some 1,500 feet and the amount of annual rainfall decreases sharply.

The Sixteen-Inch Isohyet—
A Meteorological Transition Zone

Winding and shifting through the Great Plains is the 16-inch isohyet—a meteorologists' line indicating areas with 16 inches or more annual rainfall. The gradual increase in elevation as one moves westward from the Mississippi to the Rocky Mountains and the decrease in rainfall create a dramatic biological transition zone around the isohyet, between the 98th and 100th meridians, where plants tend to grow taller east of the line and shorter to the west. In this zone of mixed-grass prairie, tall bunches of needle-and-thread grass and sand reed grass grow near short, tufted bushy squirreltail grass, buffalo grass, and blue gramma.

In this transition zone lies the great winter wheat region of the Great Plains; the central lowlands to the east make up the corn belt (formerly tall-grass prairie), while the land to the west, in the rain shadow of the Rockies, is home to the short grasses of the High Plains.

Grasslands of the Great Plains

The fields of the mixed-grass zone of the Great Plains—with golden Indian grass, sand dropseed, Canada wild rye, prickly needle-and-thread or porcupine grass, leafy big bluestem and little bluestem, and

2

Key to Sites

1. Giant Springs
2. Fort Benton
3. Medicine Rocks
4. Fort Union Trading Post
5. Fort Buford
6. Little Missouri National Grassland
7. Theodore Roosevelt National Park
8. Elkhorn Ranch
9. Grand River National Grassland
10. Geographical Center of the United States
11. Bear Butte
12. Deadwood Historic Goldrush District
13. Fort Meade
14. Black Hills
15. Wind Cave National Park
16. Badlands National Monument
17. Wounded Knee Battlefield
18. Devil's Tower National Monument
19. Agate Fossil Beds National Monument
20. Fossil Beds
21. Sand Hills
22. Scottsbluff on the Oregon Trail
23. Chimney Rock National Historic Site
24. Midway Stage and Pony Express Station
25. Museum of the High Plains
26. Fort Kearney on the Oregon Trail
27. Great Plains Apache Village
28. Pawnee Indian Village Site
29. Home on the Range Cabin
30. Cottonwood Pony Express Station
31. Mt. Sunflower (4,039 ft)
32. Council Grove Historic District
33. Pawnee Rock on the Santa Fe Trail
34. Fort Larned National Historic Site
35. Santa Fe Trail Remnants
36. Wagon Bed Springs on the Cimarron Cutoff

37. Pawnee National Grasslands and Buttes
38. Great Plains Reservoirs
39. Bent's Old Fort on the Santa Fe Trail
40. Comanche National Grassland
41. Spanish Peaks
42. Raton Region
43. Bell Ranch
44. Lincoln Historic District
45. Bottomless Lakes
46. Great Salt Plains
47. Osage Hills
48. Pioneer Sod House
49. Fort Supply
50. Black Kettle National Grassland
51. Wichita Mountains
52. Museum of the Great Plains
53. Fort Reno
54. Museum of the Western Prairie at Altus
55. Cross Timbers National Grassland
56. Alibates Flint Quarries and Lake Meredith
57. Odessa Meteor Crater
58. Monahans Sandhills
59. Fort Davis National Historic Site

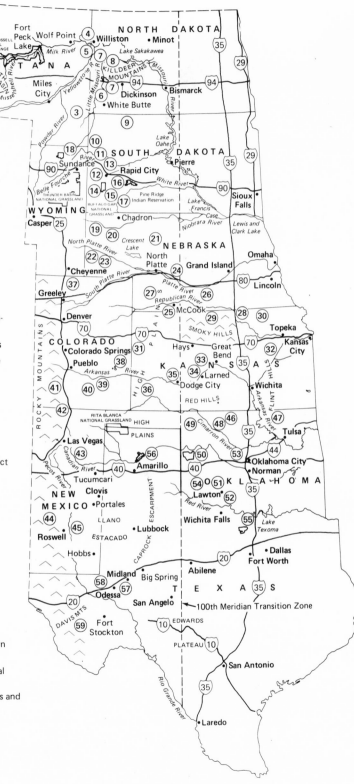

Medicine Rocks—wind-eroded formations common to Montana's High Plains

Buffalo Grass and Blue Gramma of the Short-Grass Prairies

The tight turf formed by this short grass of the High Plains conserves the rainfall and shelters it from the drying winds of the Rocky Mountain rain shadow. Both buffalo grass and blue gramma curl close to the arid soil, creating a resilient mat about four inches thick.

Little Bluestem Grass

The hardy little bluestem, a native bunchgrass often found with big bluestem, is usually from one to three feet tall, with wide, flat blades. More drought-resistant than big bluestem, its leaves roll up during dry spells, lowering the rate of evaporation and conserving its store of water. Little bluestem is the dominant native grass in the Flint Hills of Kansas and Oklahoma.

Big Bluestem Grass

Waving six-foot-high fields of big bluestem abounded on the prairies of the Great Plains before the arrival of the homesteaders. Its long root system helped anchor the virgin prairies against the constant erosion of wind and rain. Today, its dark-green two-

gramma and buffalo grass—dominate the landscape and anchor the soil. The grasses are the lifeblood of the region. The grasses here rarely grow higher than two or three feet tall, unlike the tall-grass country to the east, where once grasses that grew eight feet tall stretched from the forest margins of Indiana into Iowa. To the west of the mixed-grass country is the higher and drier short-grass country of the High Plains, merging into the sagebrush country. The constantly waving prairies of mixed-grass country appear in a hundred shades of green mixed with pale yellow, reddish brown, and a silvery purple.

Field of crested wheat on the mixed-grass prairies

Big bluestem and little bluestem—common grasses of the mixed-grass prairies

foot-high stalks grow only in random patches. The wispy, hairlike growth on its blades baffles the dry winds, slowing the rate of evaporation and conserving its moisture. Its purplish flowers grow at the tip of erect stems that often branch into three parts and resemble a turkey foot.

Needle-and-Thread Grass

Windblown fields of needle-and-thread grass are a common sight on the prairies of the Great Plains. Also known as porcupine grass, it has barbed seeds that grow at the end of each tendril.

Prickly Pear Cactus

This extremely tough cactus often marks the border between the grasslands and rocky, arid wastelands of the Great Plains. Identified by its long, spreading branches, the prickly pear often lives for 25 years or more.

Buffalo Bur

The prickly-stemmed buffalo bur borders the roadways and ranchlands of the Great Plains. These hardy, drought-resistant annuals have tiny yellow flowers.

Russian Thistle—A Tumbleweed of the Great Plains

Clumps of wiry, reddish-stemmed Russian thistle sprinkle the arid, desertlike areas, fields, and railroad embankments and roads of the Great Plains. Reaching a height of up to three feet, with branching stems that form a large, loose ball, often breaking loose to form a tumbleweed, this hardy survivor of drought conditions was introduced from the steppes of Russia around 1880, when they were accidentally planted by a homesteader in South Dakota.

Winds of the Western Prairie

One of the most noticeable and constant features of the Great Plains is the dry western wind that blows down from the Rockies without interruption for 11 or 12 months of the year. It is the dominant natural force that has kept the Western prairies treeless. These dry winds have dropped their moisture as they crossed the mountain ramparts and quickly evaporate the moisture from the open prairies.

Windmills of the Northern Plains

The traveller in the wide-open spaces of the northern plains will see a landscape studded with tens of thousands of windmills that tap down into the greatest known aquifer on the North American continent. This vast underlying layer of porous rock in large portions of eastern Montana, Wyoming, Nebraska, and Kansas absorbs the tremendous runoff of water from the slopes of the Front Range of the Rockies, the Big Horn Mountains, and the Black Hills, building up pressure against the overlying cap

Windmill tapping the greatest aquifer in North America

of impermeable rock. When this cap is pierced, an artesian well flows. In recent years, the rock cap of the arid northern plains has been tapped by an ever-increasing number of wells for water—the West's most precious resource—pumped out by the windmills to irrigate the prairies. The result has been that the water pressure of this great aquifer has been drastically reduced.

The Missouri Plateau

The rugged Missouri Plateau embraces the Great Plains north of Nebraska, separated from the High

The honeycombs in South Dakota's Long Pine Hills

Plains to the south by the north-facing 1,000-foot Pine Ridge, and from the Central Lowlands by the 500-foot Missouri River Escarpment on its eastern boundary. The region includes the Coteau du Missouri, an area of swales and sharp ridges and drainage channels formed by glaciers, and is separated from the main portion of the Missouri Plateau by the Missouri River Trench, a deep and narrow valley of the Missouri River along its course across South Dakota and North Dakota. The vast Missouri Plateau includes the Badlands carved by the White River east of the Black Hills, between the Cheyenne and White Rivers in South Dakota and along the Little Missouri River in southwestern North Dakota and the isolated spur ranges of the Rocky Mountains—the Black Hills in northeastern Wyoming and South Dakota and along the Upper Missouri River in eastern Montana.

Upper Missouri River

The Upper Missouri River, which in preglacial ages flowed into Hudson Bay, today flows from its headwaters high in the Rocky Mountains across Montana to about latitude 48° north in west-central North Dakota, where it makes a sharp southward bend and becomes what is called the Middle Missouri.

The 2,466-mile-long Missouri—believed to have been named for a tribe of Sioux called *Emessourita*, meaning "dwellers on the Big Muddy," living near the river—forms a wild, untamed stretch, designated as a national wild and scenic river in eastern Montana, between historic Fort Benton and the huge Fort Peck Reservoir. It flows through the rugged White Cliffs area of the Missouri River Breaks—between the Little Rockies and Bearpaw and Highwood mountains—with their spectacular, colorful eroded sandstone formations.

A boat trip down the "wild" Missouri passes through ancient Indian hunting grounds marked by tepee rings and "Pishkin," or buffalo jumps, along the high cliffs and bluffs. Historic landmarks note the passing of the Hudson's Bay Company and Northwest Company trappers, the Lewis and Clark Expedition, Manuel Lisa and John Colter, and countless other explorers, fur traders, mountain men, and adventurers. Five boater campsites are situated at intervals on the Missouri between Virgelle and James Kipp State Recreation Area in Charlie Russell country at Coal Banks Landing, Cow Island Landing, Judith Landing, Hole-in-the-Wall, and Slaughter River on the route of Lewis and Clark.

Downstream from Fort Benton—once the major supply depot of the American Fur Company for camp traders in Montana, Idaho, and Canada and outfitting

Missouri River Breaks in Montana, a celebrated frontier-era landmark

center for thousands of tenderfeet heading into the gold-rush country—are the faint remains of historic Fort McKenzie near the mouth of the Marias River, and Fort Cook, Fort Clagett, and Fort Chardon near the mouth of the Judith River. The Fort Benton Museum contains a reproduction of an early keel boat of the type used by Lewis and Clark during their arduous upstream exploration of the Missouri. Boaters on the "wild" river stretch may see golden eagles, pelicans, cliff swallows, elk, and bighorn sheep.

Charles Russell House and Studio

In Great Falls, Montana, stands the house occupied by Charles M. Russell from 1900 until his death in 1926. His log studio was added in 1903. Russell's work in this studio brought him full recognition as a Western artist. Among his best-known paintings on Western life are "Waiting for a Chinook" and "Father De Smet Relating the Story of Christ to the Flatheads." During the last decade of his life, his canvasses brought the highest sum ever paid to a living American painter. His two-story frame house has undergone almost no changes. The log studio has a recent addition on the west side.

The house and studio are in Great Falls at 1217–1219 4th Avenue North in Cascade County, Montana.

Great Falls Portage on the Missouri

On June 13, 1805 Meriwether Lewis and a small party reached the Great Falls of the Missouri while travelling overland on foot. They were the first white men to view the falls. The 18-mile portage necessitated by the falls, a 31-day trip, was one of the greatest ordeals endured by the Lewis and Clark Expedition on its way to the Pacific coast. The Great Falls have since been harnessed for hydroelectric power, and only a small amount of water flows over them. The great escarpment of jagged rocks and the general landscape remain.

The portage area is southwest of Great Falls at the junction of U.S. Highways 87, 89, and 91 in Cascade County, Montana.

Fort Benton and the Upper Missouri Steamboat Era

Fort Benton commemorates the steamboat era on the upper Missouri River. Although established earlier as a fur trading center, the fort's real prosperity dates from 1859, when the first steamboat arrived. Discovery of gold in 1862 made Fort Benton an overland transportation connection with the river steamers. An invasion of free fur traders in the late 1860s ended

Missouri River paddlewheel steamers carried supplies during the gold rush of the late 1800s.

Old ferry in the Badlands section of the Missouri River

monopoly of the Indian trade by the American Fur Company and the Hudson's Bay Company, but the free traders established an empire over the Northwest that centered at Fort Benton. After the advent of the railroads the town of Fort Benton and the river traffic rapidly declined. A blockhouse and a portion of the fort's adobe walls still stand, and the riverfront seems unchanged.

Fort Benton is in Chouteau County, Montana.

Hagen Site—Crow Indian Earth Lodge Village

The Hagen Site is a late prehistoric earth lodge village believed to represent a settlement of the Crow Indians during the 1600s before they became fully nomadic bison hunters. The Crow, who split off from the Hidatsa, were village farmers of the middle Missouri River area. Partial excavation of the site in 1938 revealed a middle area covering more than ten acres. Within it were many storage pits, a small circular house, and a low mound which contained fragments of human skeletons. Bison shoulder-blade hoes and the general semi-sedentary character of the site attest to the practice of farming. Archeologists believe that shortly after they lived at this site, the Crow forsook agriculture in favor of a nomadic, buffalo-hunting way of life.

The site is located in Montana's Dawson County, five miles southeast of Glendive on a secondary road.

Fort Union Trading Post

As the principal Upper Missouri fur trade depot, Fort Union Trading Post afforded northern plains tribes their first long contact with the alien white culture. Built in 1828, it marked the opening of John Jacob Astor's campaign to secure the Upper Missouri and Rocky Mountain fur trade for the American Fur Company. The extensive, well-built post lasted until 1866, when the Army purchased it and used its materials to build its nearby post, Fort Buford. Little surface evidence of the site remains today.

The post was located west of present-day Buford in North Dakota's Williams County.

The Black Hills

The Black Hills of southwestern South Dakota, the easternmost outpost of the Rocky Mountains, were so named by the early pioneers because from a distance the pine and spruce forests on their rocky slopes appear dark in contrast to the grasslands from which they rise. The range is 150 miles long and 75 miles wide, rising from 3,000 to 3,500 feet above the plains. Most of the peaks in the central Black Hills attain altitudes between 5,000 and 6,600 feet, culminating at 7,242-foot Harney Peak, an immense peak of pink granite in the central dome.

The Black Hills have several distinct areas: the central core of peaks encircled by a limestone plateau; the striking Red Valley that surrounds the Black Hills; Hogback Ridge, which forms the outer rim of the range; and the peaks at the northern edge formed by Bear Butte, an igneous plug, Elkhorn Peak, Crow Peak, Sundance Mountain, and Citadel Peak.

The forests of the Black Hills form a biological transition zone. Trees from Canada such as white birch and white spruce dominate the high elevations, and lodgepole pine and ponderosa pine from the Rockies cover the lower slopes, and Eastern species such as oak, elm, and ash form scrub forests on the lowlands.

The Ancient Black Hills

The Black Hills existed long before the Alps, when the site of the Himalayas was still a marsh, and they were ages old before the Rocky Mountains were uplifted. The great dome or latholith of the Black Hills, 150 by 75 miles in area, gradually rose over several million years. The oldest and deepest rocks now stand as the highest. Each layer or stratum of rock runs at about the same level in a concentric ring around the Black Hills, in a band of red here, a band of yellow there, forming cliffs facing the highest and innermost central core of granite. The slender pinnacles known as the Needles, worn by ages of wind and water, are remnants of this ancient central core. The encircling cliffs slope downward and outward toward the plains in successive strata or layers of sandstone, limestone and shale like shingles on a roof.

Inyan Kara Mountain

Inyan Kara mountain—6,368 feet above sea level—covers an area of about one square mile and has been associated with the Indians from the earliest times. According to one Sioux legend it was the temporary resting place for the dead warriors en route to the final hunting ground. The name means "stone made" and refers to the outcropping that appears at the mountain's peak, an important link in the Indian chain of communication as it connected their eastern and

Ancient Needles of the Black Hills predate even the Himalayas.

western Black Hills territory. The mountain has been a landmark for white travellers and settlers and was the objective of the Custer Expedition of 1874, which resulted in discovery of gold and a dispute with the Indians over jurisdiction of the mountain and the surrounding Black Hills.

The mountain is about 15 miles south of Sundance in the Black Hills National Forest in Crook County, Wyoming.

Bear Butte

From its discovery by the Verendrye Expedition in 1743 through the period of white settlement, Bear Butte remained a landmark for military expeditions,

Rock outcroppings in the Black Hills—aptly named by the pioneers for the dark forests on their slopes

stage routes, and wagon trails, as well as being of strategic military importance. Located in the northwest area of the Black Hills, the 1,200-foot-high rock formation could be seen for miles by prospectors, miners, and army scouts travelling from Bismarck. The Butte also played a major role as an icon in the religions of the Cheyenne, Sioux, and Mandan.

Bear Butte is near Sturgis, in South Dakota's Meade County.

Deadwood Historic Gold-rush District

The Deadwood Gulch area of the Black Hills was the site of a rich gold strike in the fall of 1875. Soon after the discovery of gold, people poured into the mining camp, and by summer 25,000 had settled in what became Deadwood. The town itself has one main street, and houses are built above it on both sides of the steep gulch. Today Deadwood still retains its mining-town atmosphere, and many original buildings have survived, including the No. 10 Saloon where Jack McCall shot Wild Bill Hickok. Three miles from Deadwood is Lead, site of the Homestake, the largest gold mine in the United States.

Deadwood is located in South Dakota's Laurence County.

Fort Meade in the Black Hills Mining District

Fort Meade was established in 1878 to control the Sioux and to protect the Black Hills mining district. In 1890 it was the key command post during the Sioux unrest that culminated in the Battle of Wounded Knee. Development of the fort took place over four periods during which time original frame structures were gradually replaced by stone and brick buildings. Four frame buildings survive in their original condition; others survive from the first period of rebuilding and are veneered with fieldstone. The most impressive structures, dating from the building effort of 1910, include the headquarters building, the guardhouse, four barracks, three stables, and various other military structures.

Fort Meade is in Meade County, South Dakota.

Wind Cave National Park

Wind Cave, discovered in 1881, is on the southeastern flank of the Black Hills. This huge limestone cavern, named for the strong currents of air that blow in and out of the cave, contains a series of "boxwork" subterranean passages and rooms, some lined with colorful calcite crystal formations. About 32 miles of the cave have been explored; the rest remains uncharted.

This 44-square-mile park is a prime example of the mixed-grass prairie composed of both true prairie and short-grass plains. The true prairie is dominated by prairie June grass, bluestems, and needlegrasses, the short-grass plains by buffalo grass and grammas. The great expanses of grassy plain form a transition zone between the deciduous forests to the east, Rocky Mountain forests to the west, and the desert vegetation of the southwest. Like the rest of the Black Hills, the Wind Cave country has bur oak and American elm from the east; yucca, cactus, and cottonwood from the arid southwestern plateaus; and ponderosa pine and juniper from the Rocky Mountains. The park contains remnants of the prairie dog towns that once covered the Great Plains, as well as a bison herd. Other inhabitants of the grassy plains include the pronghorn, with its tan-and-white coat and conspicuous white rump, elk, deer, badger, coyote, and raccoon. Commonly sighted birds include meadowlarks, sharp-tailed grouse, kingbirds, and magpies.

Devil's Tower in the Black Hills

Stump-shaped Devil's Tower, located near the old pioneer town of Sundance in northeastern Wyoming, is the most conspicuous geological feature in the Black Hills. It rises 600 feet above a rounded ridge of sedimentary rock, which itself rises 600 feet above the

Devil's Tower—the Indians' sacred Mateo Tipi, *or Grizzly Bear Lodge*

Prairie dog—the chien de la prairie *of the explorers.*

Belle Fourche River. Its nearly flat top is elliptical, with a diameter of 60 to 100 feet. The base of the tower, about 1,700 feet in diameter, is surrounded by solid bench rock extending outward 30 to 40 feet. The tower is composed of phonolite, a volcanic rock similar to granite. When the Black Hills uplift occurred more than 20 million years ago, the upswelling lava formed a blister, or laccolith. The giant columns of Devil's Tower are massive prisms formed during the lava's rapid cooling.

The tower was known to the Sioux Indians as *Mateo Tipi*, or Grizzly Bear Lodge, and was used by the Rocky Mountain trappers and pioneers as a landmark. During the Indian wars in Sioux and Crow country, military leaders of the U.S. Seventh Cavalry used the tower, which is visible in some directions for 100 miles, as a beacon to direct their marches.

In the countryside surrounding the tower, the pine forests of the Black Hills merge with the grasslands of the high plains. The Tower Trail that encircles the national monument winds past huge fallen columns of volcanic rock and talus slopes and through stands of ponderosa pine, juniper, and quaking aspen.

About one-half mile from the tower entrance is an active prairie dog colony. These little ground squirrels, named *chiens de la prairie* by French voyagers because of their doglike bark, once ranged southward across the Great Plains from southern Saskatchewan to central Texas and westward across the High Plains to Arizona, New Mexico, Colorado, Wyoming, and Montana. At the turn of the century, one prairie dog

town in Texas was estimated to support 800 million inhabitants within a 25,000-acre area. They live today in protected areas in the Badlands and the Black Hills, in underground dens with deeply burrowed entrances, identified by their surface mounds. Their close relative, the white-tailed prairie dog (the plains prairie dog has a distinctive black tail), inhabits the higher elevations in the foothills and valleys of the Rocky Mountains to the west.

Theodore Roosevelt National Park and the Little Badlands

Theodore Roosevelt National Memorial Park includes the site of the former president's Maltese Cross Ranch, one of the nation's first open-range cattle ranches, and the rugged badlands that straddle the final 200 miles of the Little Missouri River in southwestern North Dakota, which carved out this valley, one of many cut into the ancient preglacial plains. Starting about 6,000 to 3,000 years ago and continuing to the present day, grass fires and lightning periodically ignite exposed veins of lignite in the buttes, tablelands, and valleys formed on the ancient plains by the Little Missouri and its tributaries. The heat from these fires bakes the surrounding sand and clay to a natural, red-brick material, known locally as "scoria."

Scenic drives in the wild northern unit of the park provide access to a small herd of longhorn steers, which were trail-driven north from Texas along the Long X Trail that crosses the park; badland coulees (dry water gulches) and "breaks" in the grassy plains at Caprock Coulee; a prairie dog town on the Buckhorn Trail; and the oxbow of the Little Missouri at

Little Missouri River country at Theodore Roosevelt National Park, noted for its reddish rock, or "scoria"

Bison herd at Theodore Roosevelt National Park, a protected remnant of the once great herds

Sperati Point, where the river, blocked during the Ice Age, broke through the gap at this point and the Achenback Hills on the other side.

In the southern unit, scenic drives and trails provide access to a restored Maltese Cross Cabin, used by Roosevelt on his visits; a small herd of feral horses in the area east of Painted Canyon; massive bluffs capped with red scoria at Scoria Point; scoria-covered hummocks at Paddock Creek; Wind Canyon over the graceful oxbow of the Little Missouri; the petrified forest; and the site of Roosevelt's second ranch, the Elkhorn.

The badlands are inhabited by bighorn sheep, bison, antelope, coyote, and golden eagles. The north-facing slopes, which get less sun and therefore have less evaporation, are covered with green ash and junipers, while the south-facing slopes, which are warmer and much drier, nurture semiarid species such as yucca, greasewood, and cactus. Groves of cottonwoods mark the course of the park's rivers and streams.

Great Lakes of the Missouri

The Missouri River, which flows through western North Dakota and central South Dakota from north to south, marks the western edge of the vast ice sheet that in prehistoric times covered the north central portion of the United States. The Missouri, forced out of its original course by the ice cap, cut through the height of land and created the high bluffs for almost its entire course in which it now flows through the two states. Its powerful current is still cutting a channel, and its present course is so young that it has not created a wide valley. The land bordering the river on both sides is a mixture of farm and ranch land, reaching westward to the semiarid cattle-ranching country.

The Dakotas' portion of the Missouri has been almost entirely dammed by a series of great impoundments creating, from north to south, Lake Sakakawea, Lake Oahe, Lake Sharpe, Lake Francis Case, and

Little Badlands and bighorn sheep "pastures"

Lewis and Clark Lake. The semiarid, thinly populated country to the west of these lakes is a region of "gumbo," buttes, and badlands.

Big Badlands of South Dakota

Known to the Dakota Indians as *mako* (land) *sica* (bad), the battered, eroded monuments of the South Dakota Badlands cover a 6,000-square-mile tract. Over the past 20 million years rivers carved them out of the great grassland plain that sweeps across the middle of the continent. This awesome tract of natural devastation is some 20 to 50 miles wide and stretches for 100 miles from west of the Missouri River to just east and north of the Black Hills. It takes in the country of the White River Basin northward to the upland prairies on the south bank of the Bad River.

Described by General George A. Custer as "a part of hell with the fire burned out," the Badlands are dominated by the Great Wall: a range of grasslands and eroded multicolored peaks of gray, tan, buff, olive, deep rose, and cream. It is a barren country of ghostly peaks, lofty pinnacles, terraces, and cathedral-like spires that rise above eroded, rounded domes, with washed-out gaps forming natural windows. The Fossil Trail winds through an ancient region once roamed by giant saber-toothed tigers, dog-sized camels, titanotheres, and hyracodons. Historic Big Foot Pass lies in the heart of the Badlands. It was through this opening that Indian Chief Big Foot, with his band of 400 warriors, eluded the U. S. Cavalry. After his escape from the Badlands, Big Foot and his braves met their gruesome fate at the Battle of Wounded Knee—the last conflict between the whites and the Indians that culminated in the Messiah War.

Big Badlands of South Dakota, described by Custer as "a part of hell with the fire burned out"

Rivers of the Badlands—Nature's Sculptor

The breathtaking natural features of the Badlands were carved by the rivers that gouged, ripped, and washed away the original prairie. Ancient streams born in the newly formed Black Hills and Rocky Mountains first created the plain by washing down countless tons of limestone, sandstone, and granite. Newer rivers then carved out the grass-covered prairie into what we call the Badlands. The process continues today, and in some distant time, the area will again be worn down into a flat grassland prairie.

The three major river systems that have carved through the ancient sandstone and clay outwash from the Black Hills and the Badlands of South Dakota are the often-torrential White River, the milky, clay-laden master carver that flows through a network of braided channels on its course to the Missouri; the Bad River, which meanders across a grass plain on the northern boundary; and the peaceful Cheyenne River, flanked by hills along the northwestern boundary.

Great Wall of the Badlands

The Great Wall of the Badlands looks like nature gone berserk: a huge, jagged slope of river-eroded rock carved into an incredible chaos of gullies, buttes, and towering pinnacles. The colorful 200-foot-high Great Wall that bisects the Badlands is actually the northern flank of the White River Basin that has been sculptured out of the upper grassland plain stretching above it to the north and east.

Flats and bluffs, formed by rivers that carved the Badlands

Rock Humps

The crumbling humps of rock, an ancient uplift known to geologists as the Chadron Arch commonly sighted in the Badlands, were formed from mud deposits left by the ancestral rivers that dried into clay which was overlaid by rock that has since washed away.

Sod Tables

The tough, hardy grasses of the Great Plains have created the striking sod tables that rise like a staircase above the eroded rock of the Badlands. Actually remnants of the prairie, these terraces were saved from the eroding torrents for a hundred to a thousand years by the anchoring effect of their grass-covered crown. The mesa known as Sheep Table Mountain, once inhabited by Audubon bighorn sheep, is crowned by a green sod table, but it continues to shrink each year as numerous small streams add to its maze of gullies, washing away its rock and clay foundation.

Gumbo Slopes

The rounded and gullied hummocks of gumbo slopes in the Badlands, made of clay deposited by ancient rivers more than 30 million years ago, are a distinct hazard when hiking through the region. They become extremely slick and dangerous during rainstorms—much like walking on greased glass—and they often crumble and break when dry.

Mudstone and Siltstone Hills of the Badlands

The eroded mudstone and siltstone hills of the Badlands were deposited by the ancestral rivers during the Ice Age. Easily broken by water, many Badland Hills are being washed away at the rate of about a half an inch a year. In the past 5 million years the Badlands have been eroded and sculpted by torrential rains and swollen rivers into a maze of gullies, ravines, rock pinnacles, buttes, and escarpments. The colored bands of the Badland hills reveal the area's geological history. The dark striations of mudstone were deposited during the dry periods; the light-colored bands of siltstone were deposited during the wet periods. The geological drama of the Badlands will reach its climax a few million years in the future, when the hills will be worn away by the ravaging

forces of erosion down to the Pierre shale formations that underlie the region.

Dikes

Rock formations known as vertical dikes are a common sight in the Badlands. The dikes are formed when the water and wind erode the soft siltstone and mudstone, exposing knifelike vertical edges of thin rock layers that jut from the surface.

Haystacks

Domed mounds called haystacks are a common sight throughout the Badlands region of the Great Plains. The mounds are formed when the moisture-soaked clay is sucked down by gravity over the dry core of the interior rock layers.

Prehistoric Fossils of the Black Hills and Badlands

About 40 million years ago during the Mesozoic era (the age of reptiles), huge dinosaurs wallowed along the shores of tropical swamps of western South Dakota. In the area surrounding the Black Hills the lumbering triceratops, resembling a blend of an elephant and rhinoceros, waged combat with the swift, kangaroo-like tyrannosaurus rex. The 15-ton bronto-

Red-tailed hawk, often sighted soaring over open country in search of prey

Prairie dog, the little ground squirrel named by French-Canadian explorers for its doglike bark

saurus, largest of all prehistoric reptiles, often watched above the battle, its long neck supporting a two-ounce brain in a head rising 30 feet above the shore. In the Badlands National monument, fossilized bones and teeth have been found in the eroded claybanks of the three-toed horse, a tiny camel, a giant pig, saber-toothed tiger, and the giant rhinoceros.

Wildflowers of the Badlands and Black Hills

Native to the Missouri River breaks and the arid Badlands to the west is the soft waxlike gumbo lily, growing out of the bare clay gumbo. The yucca, also called Spanish bayonet and soapweed, is often sighted, with its sharp spears and white flowers blossoming on a tall spike. The cactus plant has waxy flowers flecked with pink which may brighten an entire hillside. In the Black Hills are scores of wildflowers, in-

Badger in the High Plains

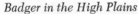

Colorado blue columbine—a common wildflower of the Black Hills and Badlands

cluding the blue-flag or fleur-de-lis, wood orchid, baby's breath, shooting star, bog-violet, larkspur, yellow lady slipper, monkshood, woodland star, and forget-me-not. Buffalo berry bushes grow thick in the draws throughout the region. In spring the purplish pasque and pink prairie rose are common on the grasslands, as are sunflower and goldenrod in fall.

Badger

The powerful grizzled gray-and-black-colored badger is common throughout the arid prairies and grasslands of the Great Plains and High Plains to the west. It reaches an adult length of 30 inches and weighs up to 25 pounds. It uses its powerful forefeet and claws to dig ground squirrels from their burrows. Although a badger can swim and climb, it is a master digger, often digging a new burrow each day. Its young are born in May in a large, grass-lined nest at the end of a burrow, usually about eight feet from the entrance. The badger is ferocious when attacked or cornered.

Black-footed Ferret

The black-footed ferret, an endangered species, is native to the Great Plains region from northern Montana and western North Dakota south to Texas, but it has become extinct over much of its original range. It lives in prairie dog towns and will often exterminate a town's inhabitants. The rare ferret, identified by its yellowish-brown body, masked eyes, and white face, throat, and underparts, may be sighted occasionally, slithering into the prairie dog burrows at the 44-acre prairie dog town near Sage Creek in Badlands National Monument.

Wounded Knee Battlefield in the South Dakota Badlands

The battle at Wounded Knee on December 29, 1890, marked the end of the Ghost War, the last major armed clash between Indians and soldiers in North America. When hunger, disease, loss of reservation lands, and the slaughter of the once great herds of buffalo doomed the Plains Indian culture, an attempt at revival was made with the religious movement known as the Ghost Dance. The Indians believed that the trancelike ritual of the Ghost Dance, which first appeared in 1870 among the Piaute Indians of Nevada, would result in the return of their dead ancestors and

the buffalo, the disappearance of the white man, the return of their ancestral lands, and a life free of death and disease. But the massacre at Wounded Knee, in which U.S. soldiers killed more than 200 Sioux men, women, and children, removed even this last hope. The military campaign waged by the Federal troops forced the Sioux to abandon the Ghost Dance religion and accept the reality of life on the reservation.

The battlefield is located 11 miles west of Batesland, South Dakota, in the badlands of the Pine Ridge Indian Reservation just north of the Nebraska state line.

The High Plains

The monotonous, arid, flat barrens of the High Plains section of the Great Plains extend from southern South Dakota through portions of western Nebraska, Kansas, Oklahoma, and through Texas and eastern Wyoming, Colorado, and New Mexico to the Rio Grande River in west-central Texas. One of the most interesting features of these short-grass plains is the existence of innumerable depressions, ranging in size from a foot deep and 10 feet in diameter to some 60 feet deep and several miles wide, many of which have lakes in them. The nearly 37,000 of these depressions in the High Plains region of Texas are believed

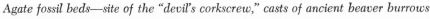

Agate fossil beds—site of the "devil's corkscrew," casts of ancient beaver burrows

to have been created by wind erosion. Depressions such as Big Basin and Jacob's Well in Clark County, Kansas, are collapse sinks formed where ancient salt beds underlie the High Plains.

Agate Fossil Beds

The grass-covered hills that form the Agate Fossil Beds National Monument are located along the meaders of the Niobrara River in northwestern Nebraska. Agate fossil deposits are found in sedimentary rock formed during the Miocene epoch, which spanned the period from 25 to 13 million years ago. The area contains the "devil's corkscrews"—casts of ancient beaver burrows—and quarries dominated by the fossils of such animals as the diceratherium, a two-horned rhinoceros that was smaller than a Shetland pony and roamed the plains in numbers as great as those of our bison before 1850; moropus, a large, heavily built animal with a horselike head, a neck like a giraffe, a torso like a tapir, the front legs of a rhinoceros, and bearlike hind legs with huge claws; and dinohyus, or "terrible pig," which stood 7 feet tall at the shoulders and about 10 feet long and had a massive head with large tusks and a small brain.

The grasslands surrounding the quarries are dominated by prairie sandreed, blue gramma, little bluestem, needle-and-thread grass, and colorful wildflowers such as lupine, western wallflower, spiderwort, and sunflower flanked by stands of cottonwoods and willows along the stream banks.

Nebraska's Goshen Hole and Sand Hills

Not all the vast High Plains short-grass region is flatland. North of the Platte River valley is the Goshen Hole Lowland, a widening of the North Platte valley in western Nebraska that has a width of 50 miles. Northeast of Goshen Hole are the mazelike sand dunes, anchored by prairie grasses, and the ridges, ephemeral lakes of the Sand Hills region that covers 24,000 square miles in the western part of the state.

Sunflowers

There is a vivid contrast between the eastern tall-grass prairie and the short-grass prairies of the western High Plains that is illustrated if one observes the growth patterns of both the wild and garden sunflower as one moves westward toward the Rocky Mountain foothills from the rolling hills and farmlands of eastern Kansas. Kansas, known as the Sun-

Sunflowers of the Great Plains decrease in size as one moves up into the arid High Plains

flower State, is a vast tableland tilted upward toward the west, where its elevation is 3,000 feet higher at the Colorado boundary than at the Missouri boundary on the east. In the eastern portion of the state sunflowers up to 15 feet tall brighten the countryside. As the traveller moves west and up in elevation past the break in the plains at the 100th meridian toward the arid High Plains of the Rocky Mountains, the sunflowers progressively shrink in height and in the size of their yellow-bordered brown or purple disks. In the arid, short-grass region of Colorado, they grow as little wildflowers because of the decreasing amounts of annual rainfall—a result of the rain shadow effect caused by the Rocky Mountain Front Range.

Plains Pocket Mouse

The small, two-inch plains pocket mouse is pale yellow with a white belly, which distinguishes it from its relative, the Wyoming pocket mouse, which has an olive-gray coloration with pale yellow on its ears and along the sides of its back. Both are found in open prairie areas with sparse vegetation.

The *Bertrand*—Missouri River Steamboat

In the early 19th century an increasing amount of steamboat traffic passed along Nebraska's segment

Frontier-era paddlewheel steamer plying through Missouri River Breaks

has been located near the Iowa border through the use of metal detectors, but thus far only the front section of the deck has been uncovered. The original superstructure above the deck was apparently carried away when the boat sank.

Scotts Bluff National Monument

Scotts Bluff, once part of the ancient High Plains, is a massive promontory that rises 800 feet above the valley of the North Platte River. It was once the dominant landmark and campground for thousands of overland migrants along the Great Platte River Road section of the Oregon Trail to the Far West. Today it is a monument to those who moved America westward—on foot, on horseback, and in covered wagons. In 1830, fur traders Jedediah Smith, William Sublette, and David Jackson took the first wagons past Scotts Bluff. In 1843, the first large migration to Oregon passed this spot. Among those who followed were Brigham Young and his band of Mormons. The greatest wave of migration occurred in the years following the discovery of gold in California's Mother Lode country in 1848. Today the ruts of the trail, worn by iron-rimmed wagon wheels and a quarter of a million emigrants, can still be seen from the transmonument highway. In the late 1870s and early 1880s, Scotts Bluff was the geographical center of the open-range cattle industry, the last great romantic episode of the frontier.

of the Missouri River. This traffic reached its peak in 1859 during the Colorado gold rush and declined in the 1860s because of the Civil War and competition from the railroads. The 160-by-30 foot stern-wheeler *Bertrand*, owned by the Montana and Idaho Steamship Lines, was one of the largest steamboats to ply the Missouri River north of the Platte. It reportedly hit a snag in the Missouri River north of Omaha and sank in April 1865. A cargo of 35,000 pounds of mercury was believed to have gone down with the ship. The mercury was to have been used in mining operations in Montana or the Dakotas. Large quantities of whiskey and gold may also have been on board at the time of the disaster. The current value of the entire cargo has been estimated at $250,000. The wreck

Scotts Bluff on the Old Oregon Trail—a massive promontory rising 800 feet above the North Platte River

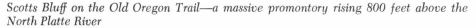

Robidoux Pass on the Old Oregon Trail

Robidoux Pass was a natural landmark on the old Oregon Trail. The great migrations of the 1840s passed through it, and from its crest westwardbound travellers had their first view of Laramie Peak in Wyoming's great basin desert. Joseph and Antoine Robidoux established a trading post here in 1849 and gave the place its name. After the Mitchell Pass route eastward was opened to travel in 1850, the Robidoux Pass fell into disuse. Extensive remains of the Oregon-California Trail of the pre-1850 period have survived.

The pass is nine miles west of Gering in Nebraska's Scotts Bluff County.

Chimney Rock

Chimney Rock was a famous natural landmark and campsite on the Oregon Trail. Towering 500 feet above the North Platte River valley, the rock quickly became a guidepost for Rocky Mountain traders and trappers on their seasonal migrations between the Rockies and the Missouri River trading marts. It was a welcome campsite because of the excellent spring nearby.

The landmark is three miles southwest of Bayard in Nebraska's Morrill County.

Midway Stage and Pony Express Station

The Midway Stage Station is one of 36 Nebraska buildings that served as Pony Express stations in 1860 and 1861. Three of these stations are extant: one at Cozad, one at Gothenburg, and the Midway Station. The Midway Station is the least altered of the three and the only one remaining on its original site. In 1859 the Leavenworth and Pikes Peak Express Company built 15 stage and mail stations across Nebraska to link the Missouri River with Denver and Salt Lake City. The freighting firm of Russell, Majors, and Waddell soon acquired the stations and built 21 more the following year, all to be used by the Pony Express. Originally known as U. S. Mail Station No. 17, Midway acquired its name because it was approximately halfway between Atchison, Kansas, and Denver. Eventually Midway was used to house riders as well as their horses. After the Pony Express was put out of business by the telegraph, Midway became a supply and stage station on the heavily traveled Oregon Trail. Midway is a long, low, one-story cabin built of heavy, squared, handhewn cedar logs. Two log sections were added at a later day on the east side of the original structure.

Chimney Rock on the Oregon Trail—popular campsite of Rocky Mountain traders and trappers

The station is located south of Gothenburg in Nebraska's Dawson County.

Grand Pawnee Indian Villages and Burial Grounds

Situated at the southern end of an embaymentlike arm of the Platte River valley, this site contains the remains of two or three Grand Pawnee Indian villages and burial grounds. The most recent habitation area was evidently confined to a low-level portion in the northeast half of the site, whereas the older occupations occurred about 20 feet higher on a terrace remnant in the southwestern section. Bounding these areas on the south and east are steep, 80-foot bluffs. The burial grounds are located along the riverine edge of the bluff tops. This site was the last village to be occupied by the Grand Pawnee as a distinct cultural entity before their agreement in 1857 to move to a reservation.

The site is southwest of Linwood on Nebraska Highway 115, in Butler County.

Great Plains Apache Village

The Lovett site, one of the largest Plains Apache villages in Nebraska, probably was occupied a portion of each year while the Indians tended their small fields of corn and other crops. Partial excavation of the site has revealed that the inhabitants lived in semipermanent structures that were supported by five foundation posts set in a circle about 15 feet in diameter. These posts were topped with lintels from which rafters radiated outward and downward to the ground to a domelike frame. The framework was then covered with brush and grass. Tree-ring studies of wood from the site indicate that it was occupied about 1700.

The village site is 12 miles north of Wauneta on U. S. Highway 6, in Nebraska's Chase County.

Pawnee Indian Village Site

A Republican Pawnee village was located on this site in the 1820s and 1830s. The village contained an estimated 30 or 40 earth lodges which were round, domelike structures with heavy timber framework covered by sod. These lodges measured 30 to 40 feet in diameter. As many as 1,000 people may have occupied the village site. A museum and interpretive center were built in 1967. This site is the only major Pawnee village location in the Central Plains to be preserved and the only such site in Kansas to have been excavated.

The village site is on Kansas Highway 266 and the Republican River, eight miles north of U. S. Highway 36.

Starke Great Plains Round Barn

The Starke Great Plains round barn is the largest round barn in Nebraska. The three-story barn has a bottom level for animals, a second level for machinery, and a third for hay. A central silo, of brick and mortar construction, stands 65 feet high. In the early 1960s the original horizontal wood siding was covered with corrugated iron sheets that also covered a continuous band of windows which originally encircled the lower level.

The barn is four-and-a-half miles east of Red Cloud on U. S. Highway 136, in Nebraska's Webster County.

Forb—a common prairie flower

Great Plains farmstead abandoned during the dust storms of the 1930s

High Plains and Prairies of Kansas

The uplands of eastern Kansas are rolling, interspersed with limestone cliffs. The most prominent of these are the Flint Hills, extending from the Oklahoma to the Nebraska lines. Bluestem grasses grow here, making it a grazing region unlike any other in the country except for the Osage section of Oklahoma which is an extension of the Bluestem Belt. Rainfall is sufficient to permit the growth of timber in the plains and valley slopes, and even the hills in the northeastern part are heavily wooded.

In the central portion of the state, north of the Great Bend Prairie, lie the Smoky Hills Upland and the Blue Hills Upland. South of the prairie area are the Cimarron Breaks, heavily eroded cliffs and terraces bordering the Cimarron River. Only in the western High Plains third of the state is the terrain comparatively monotonous and treeless. They were formed by ancient streams that flowed eastward from the Rocky Mountains carrying an enormous load of gravel, sand, and silt which was deposited to a depth of many feet along a wide belt extending from Canada to Texas. Two streams that cross the High Plains of Kansas, the Arkansas and the Smoky Hill, have excavated their valleys below the base of the prehistoric river deposits, exposing the older underlying rock.

The Smoky Hill River, cutting through the sand and silt deposits of the High Plains, has laid bare expanses of white, yellow, and orange chalk formations. Water and wind erosion have exposed fossil beds containing specimens of extinct species of fish, flying reptiles, and prehistoric birds. Castle Rock, a chalk

spire in western Gove County, rises to 70 feet and is visible for miles. Also in this area are the Monument Rocks or "pyramids," and a chalk pile that wind and water have carved into a likeness of a sphinx.

Other unusual formations are Kansas' natural bridge and a cave cut through gypsum rock, both in Barber County. The mesas and buttes found in this area are not unlike those that dot the landscape in New Mexico. The cap rock is of white gypsum, and the slopes are of red shale or sandstone. Nearby, in Comanche County, is Hell's Half Acre, a spot of unique beauty, and in Clark County is the Little Basin, one of Kansas' sink holes or sinks, as they are most commonly called.

The Break of the Plains

The boundary between the Great Plains and the Central Lowlands has been gradually receding westward. The accepted boundary has been the Flint Hills cuesta, a prominent east-facing escarpment in eastern Kansas known popularly as the Break of the Plains.

Council Grove Historic District

Because of its water, abundant grass, and timber, Council Grove was an important way station on the Santa Fe Trail. The town, incorporated in 1858, was named for a treaty negotiation with the Osage Indians in 1825. Later, other councils were held here as caravans organized themselves to cross the area inhabited

Council Grove Historic District—an important way station on the old Santa Fe freight trail

by hostile Indians. Within the town a number of landmarks survive: the Last Chance Store (1857); the Old Kew Mission (1850–1851); the Post Office Oak; the Hays Tavern; and the Council Oak Site.

The historic district of Council Grove is in Morris County, Oklahoma.

Cottonwood Pony Express Station

Built by George Hollenberg, the Cottonwood Pony Express Station is perhaps the only surviving unmoved and unaltered Pony Express station. An important stop on the Oregon-California Trail, it served as a relay station for both the Overland Mail (1858–1869) and the Pony Express (1860–1861). Built originally as part of a ranch, it later included a store, post office, kitchen, dining room, and sleeping quarters. The station is one-and-a-half miles east of Hanover on a secondary road in Washington County, Kansas.

Pawnee Rock on the Old Santa Fe Freight Trail

Pawnee Rock, a landmark on the old Santa Fe Trail—a freighting trail between Missouri and old Santa Fe, New Mexico—was used by Comanche, Kiowa, Arapahoe, Cheyenne, and Pawnee Indians for tribal council meetings years before the white man arrived in Kansas. The prominence rises 50 or 60 feet above the prairie and is reputed to have been twice that size, but homesteaders and railroad men removed

considerable portions to build homes and to lay the Santa Fe Railroad bed. Freighting wagons pulled by oxen or mules travelled the trail, which passes within 100 yards of Pawnee Rock, until the 1880s when the companies were put out of business by the completion of the railroad. Caravans often camped in the shelter of the rock, and traders, soldiers, and emigrants chiseled their names on its sandstone surface.

The landmark is just north of Pawnee Rock off U.S. Highway 46.

Fort Larned National Historic Site

In the 1860s and early 1870s Fort Larned, built near the confluence of the Pawnee and Arkansas rivers in south-central Kansas, was among the more important forts that helped guard the eastern leg of the Santa Fe Trail and played a significant role in the opening of the trans-Mississippi West. In addition, it served as a base of operations against hostile Indians on the central plains. The fort's final mission was to guard the construction crews laying the tracks of the Santa Fe Railroad westward across the plains. The post, abandoned in 1878, remains one of the best preserved mid-19th-century Western military posts. Among its extant buildings, constructed in 1867 and 1868, are three officers' quarters, the commissary storehouse, quartermaster warehouse, workshops, and two stone barracks.

The fort is five miles west of Larned in Kansas' Pawnee County.

Blacksmith shop at Fort Larned—one of the best preserved early Western military posts

Old stage station on the Santa Fe Trail, which annually carried millions of dollars in commercial traffic

Santa Fe Trail Remnants

The longest continuous remnant of clearly identified rut from the old Santa Fe freighting trail in Kansas, which annually carried millions of dollars in commercial traffic between Independence, Missouri, and Santa Fe, is preserved in rough, unplowed upland. These remains, on a hill overlooking the Arkansas River valley, form a two-mile arc intersecting U. S. Highway 50. Except where a long-abandoned irrigation ditch winds across the trail at several points, many clear stretches remain, some 300 to 400 feet wide. This site derives additional significance from the fact that the trail divided 10 to 20 miles upstream at the Cimarron Crossing, at which point some travellers followed the Arkansas River while others took the shorter Cimarron Cutoff route.

The trail ruts are located nine miles west of Dodge City on U. S. Highway 50.

Wagon Bed Springs on the Santa Fe Trail

Sometimes called Lower Cimarron Springs, Wagon Bed Springs was an oasis on the dry 60-mile stretch of the Cimarron Cutoff route of the Santa Fe Trail. After travellers crossed the Arkansas River, this spring was their objective, a welcome stopping place. The physical integrity of the spring has been little impaired by the passage of time; the ruts of the Santa Fe Trail are still evident in its vicinity.

The springs are 12 miles south of Ulysses on U. S. Highway 270.

Colorado Piedmont—The Denver Basin

The Colorado Piedmont includes the hogbacks of the Rocky Mountain foothills, a few dikes such as the Valmont Butte east of Boulder and the Ralston dike

near Golden, and the eastward-dipping Denver Basin. The surface of the Colorado Piedmont slopes eastward from elevations in the foothills between 5,000 feet and 7,000 feet on the divide between the Arkansas and Platte rivers to 4,000 feet near the High Plains at the Colorado-Kansas boundary to the east. The piedmont area was eroded by two river networks that rise to the west in the Front Range of the Rockies and flow eastward through deeply cut valleys.

Eroded rock formation on the High Plains

Bent's Fort on the Santa Fe Trail

From 1833 until the outbreak of the Mexican War in 1846, Bent's Old Fort was a principal outpost of American civilization and commercial penetration on the southwestern plains. The fort was strategically located for trade in relation to southern Plains Indians on the mountain branch of the Santa Fe Trail. Built by Charles and William Bent and Ceran St. Vrain, the post was the hub of a trading empire stretching from Texas into Wyoming and from the Rockies to central Kansas. The success of Bent and St. Vrain depended on friendly relations with the Indians and the suppression of competition. A sharp decline in trade with Indians followed the influx of Americans after the Mexican War. The adobe fort was composed of a series of adjoining compartments forming a hollow square. Round tower bastions on the northwest and southeast corners constituted the flanking protection arrangements. Only the foundations remain today.

The fort is eight miles west of Las Animas on Colorado Highway 194.

Raton Region—Mesas, Plateaus, and the Spanish Peaks

The lava-capped mesas, plateaus, and deep canyons of Raton region in southeastern Colorado and northeastern New Mexico are bounded on the north by the Colorado plateau, on the east by the High Plains, on the west by the eastern slope of the Sangre de Cristo Range and on the south by the Pecos Valley. The main steplike swath of lava-capped mesas stretches

Pioneer homestead in the Denver Basin

from Trinidad, Colorado to Raton, New Mexico and east to the High Plains and the Oklahoma boundary, rising from 5,000 on the east to 9,600 feet on the west. In addition to the laval flows, the area has countless volcanic plugs along the north side of the mesas, volcanic pills in the Park Plateau, and dikes, especially in the Spanish Peaks area.

The Spanish Peaks, among the most important landmarks of the West for the Indians and early Spanish and French explorers, lie on the north side of the Park Plateau in southern Colorado. The peaks rise abruptly out of the Great Plains, their great dikes and ridges radiating out like the spokes of a wheel. These dikes were once intrusions of volcanic material into the overlying sediment. Erosion eventually wore away the softer sedimentary rocks, leaving the impressive morphology of the Spanish Peaks.

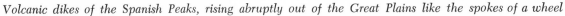

Volcanic dikes of the Spanish Peaks, rising abruptly out of the Great Plains like the spokes of a wheel

Adobe church on the Santa Fe Trail in the Pecos Valley

Long before the first Spanish explorer saw these mountains, Indians had revered them. The sudden summer thunderstorms that erupt over the peaks were thought by the Ute, Apache, and Comanche to mark the home of the rain god. The Indians named the mountains *Wahatova*, or Breasts of the World. The first known Spanish explorer to pass by the peaks was Juan de Ulibarri, who reached the area from Santa Fe in 1706. After him came many others, including Gov. Juan Bautista de Anza, founder of San Francisco and conqueror of the Comanches. Lt. Zebulon Pike explored the newly acquired area for the United States after the Louisiana Purchase in 1803.

Bell Ranch Headquarters

The original Bell Ranch was made up of the Pablo Montoya grant (1824), the overlapping Baca Location No. 2, and other small properties. An Englishman, Wilson Waddingham, began consolidating the land, and in 1875 he recorded the Bell Grant. The brand and the ranch name came from a natural landmark in the country, a small, bell-shaped hill called La Campana. Waddingham encountered financial difficulties, so his backers took over the property, acquired more land, and formed the Red River Valley Company (719,000 acres). Today the Bell Ranch encompasses 130,855 acres. The original ranch building, the center of the main house, consists of two adobe-walled rooms built about 1860. Adjoining rooms of brick date from 1873. The southwest wing was added in 1914. All these parts form a well-integrated, shallow, U-shaped structure measuring 204 feet across by 76 feet deep. Other buildings in the immediate vicinity are a post office, the ranch manager's office, the commissary, mess hall, kitchen, barns, and corrals. Pablo Montoya, recipient of the earlier grant, was alcalde of Santa Fe.

The ranch is north and east of the Conchas Reservoir in San Miguel County, New Mexico.

The Pecos Valley

The semiarid Pecos Valley of New Mexico and Texas is a broad, north-south depression between the Staked Plains on the east and the Guadalupe and Sacramento Mountains of the Basin and Range on the west. This trough was eroded by the Pecos River, which rises at the southern end of the Sangre de Cristo Range to the west at the 13,101-foot Truchas Peak.

Lincoln Historic District—A Frontier Cow Town

The Lincoln County War of 1878, one of the famous feuds of the cattle frontier, reached its climax in Lincoln. Fought between the rival Murphy-Dolan and Trunstall-McSween factions, the disturbance involved cattle baron John H. Chisum; General Lew Wallace, territorial governor of New Mexico; and William H. Bonney, better known as Billy the Kid. Aside from its dramatic history and its importance to the cattle industry, Lincoln is among the best preserved of the frontier cow towns. A considerable part of the town of 1878 remains comparatively unchanged. Still standing are the headquarters of the two rival factions, the adobe brick Murphy-Dolan store and the Trunstall-McSween store.

The district is located in New Mexico's Lincoln County.

Oklahoma's Cross Timbers Country— A Great Plains Transition Zone

Oklahoma's Cross Timbers country is a north-and-south-trending strip of rough country varying from 5 to 30 miles in width across the central part of the state. From Washington Irving's *A Tour on the Prairies* on through the accounts of such trail-makers as Randolph B. Marcy, who escorted gold-seekers to California over the southern route in 1849, this belt of matted, tangled undergrowth, stiff-branched blackjacks, shinnery, briars, and scions of fire-killed larger trees made a deep and unfavorable impression. It was a region of tumbled rocks and thin soil gashed by ravines and difficult to cross; it roughly marked the dividing line between the bluestem prairies of the eastern half of the state and the buffalo-grass plains of the western section.

Pronghorn, or antelope, often sighted racing at speeds up to 20 m.p.h.

Red Beds of Oklahoma

The red beds extend from the Kansas border to the Red River, from almost the center of Oklahoma to within 40 miles of the western line. Composed of shales and soft sandstones 1,200 to 1,600 feet thick, they get their color from iron oxide. Some of the state's most fertile farmland lies within this gently rolling region.

The western part of the red beds contains several ledges of gypsum, and here, particularly along the Cimarron River, the red and white combination makes picturesque scenery. The numerous gypsum strata differ in thickness and composition, some being nearly pure and hard, others softer and interbedded with shale. The hard layers topping the buttes of the Blaine Escarpment make these low mesas impressive, because of both their color and location on otherwise flat plains. One form of gypsum, selenite, is crystalline and breaks into pieces resembling fragments of glass or mica.

The Gyp Hills Region

The Glass (or Gloss) Mountains, an outlier of the Blaine Escarpment, are so called because their sides are littered with flakes of selenite that glisten in the sun. The gypsum area makes a rough triangle, its base a wide arc north of the Wichita Mountains and its apex at the Kansas border. Wheat, corn, sorghum, and livestock are the principal farming products of the gyp hills region.

Great Salt Plains

The Great Salt Plains near Cherokee and other salt plains in central northern Oklahoma near the Kansas border have been formed by springs of salt-water that, saturated from a deep-lying stratum, seeps through the red beds and gypsum formations. Of little commercial importance, these salt deposits are striking in appearance. The northwestern section of the state and the Panhandle, in the High Plains region, are level grassland, treeless except for elms, cottonwoods, and willows along the streams.

Fort Supply Historic District

This fort was established as Camp Supply in November 1868 by General Alfred Sully. It was constructed as an advance base of operations for General Phil Sheridan's campaign against the Cheyenne and Arapaho. The installation had nearly 100 buildings,

Prairie falcon

Pioneer sod house in 1901—a common dwelling of the homesteaders

all of wood except for the guardhouse, which was brick. There were nine double houses of 16 rooms each, seven barracks, 25 six-room cottages, a hospital, an entertainment hall, and 50 additional houses, including the commandant's residence. Several of the buildings remain, including one of the double houses (1879), the guardhouse, and a cabin (early 1870s), believed to be the oldest extant structure. After the military abandoned the installation in 1893 it was turned over to the Oklahoma Territory. In 1903 it became the Western State Hospital.

Ringing the Wild Horse Site

From a vantage point on a section of Nine Mile Flat beside the North Canadian River, Washington Irving observed and later recorded an attempted roundup of wild horses. This account became a chapter in his book *A Tour on the Prairies.* Irving, in company with Charles J. Latrobe (an Englishman), Count Albert de Pourtales (a Swiss), and Henry L. Ellsworth (a government emissary) left Fort Gibson, Oklahoma, in early October 1832. They joined a detachment of rangers on a scouting expedition into the center of present-day Oklahoma. Irving described in his book the deployment of men to encircle a grazing band of wild horses, how one man broke the ring before it was completed, and the resulting stampede of men and animals. Today, the site is ordinary meadowland without indications of its literary past.

The site is near Jones in Oklahoma County.

Fort Reno

Indian unrest, principally among the Cheyenne, prompted construction of Fort Reno in 1875. Northern Cheyenne, numbering over 900, were resettled here following the massacre of Lieutenant Colonel G. A. Custer and his immediate command at the Little Big Horn (June 1876). The 40-acre site contains a military cemetery and 1876 officers' quarters, barracks, a guardhouse, an 1878 school and chapel, a bakery, an ordnance magazine, and a storehouse. Most of the structures are brick, and those named date from the 1890s. The post was active militarily until 1949, when it became a U. S. Department of Agriculture experimental station.

The fort is three miles west and two miles north of El Reno in Oklahoma's Canadian County.

Pioneer Sod House

Marshall McCully staked a claim to the quarter section on which the Pioneer Sod House now stands in September 1893, shortly after the Cherokee Outlet was opened. He built his two-room sod dwelling the following August and lived in it until 1909. At that time the McCully family moved into a larger frame house nearby. The Oklahoma Historical Society acquired the house in 1963, and it is now believed to be the only extant example of this type of construction in the state. The walls were smoothed on the inside

High Plains of the Texas Panhandle—the Llano Estacado, or "Staked Plains," today a land of cowboys and gas refineries

with plaster, and the original dirt floor was covered with wood in 1895. A sheet-iron cover has been put over the house for protection, and the sod roof has been replaced. The furnishings inside are representative of the homesteading period.

The homestead is about four miles north of Cleo Springs in Oklahoma's Alfalfa County.

Great Plains of Texas and the Llano Estacado

The semiarid Central Plains of Texas are an extension of the lower part of the Great Plains below the Red River to the Pecos River and from the Balcones Escarpment northwestward to the limestone Cap Rock country. Altitudes range from 800 feet on the east to 3,000 feet at the western margins. There are four major divisions of this central plain: north of the Colorado River and immediately west of the Balcones Escarpment, a region of low hills and broad valleys, called the Grand Prairie; south of the Colorado River and bounded on the east and south by the Balcones Escarpment, a deeply eroded country of low, treeless hills, cedar breaks, and very narrow stream valleys fed by limestone springs, called the Edwards Plateau; the broad plain west of the Grand Prairie; and the uplift of the Central Mineral Region, a smaller area surrounded by the other three subregions and consisting of rugged hill country along the Colorado and its tributary, the Llano River.

The chaparral country of the western High Plains, noted for its violent windstorms and thunderstorms, is bounded on the east by the Cap Rock—an abrupt white-limestone escarpment with a zone of broken

country below called the breaks. It extends west to the New Mexico line and southward from the northernmost limit of the Panhandle to the Pecos Valley. Altitudes along the southern margin are 3,000 feet and at the northwest corner of the Panhandle reach 4,700 feet. These high plains, dominated by mesquite and cactus, are in two parts, locally called the Panhandle High Plains or "Staked Plains," which occupy all the Texas Panhandle except the extreme eastern tier of its counties, and the South Plains, below the Palo Duro Canyon and other draws tributary to the Red River.

In the Panhandle the High Plains are crossed by the deep valley of the Canadian River. Elsewhere they are a flat, gently sloping, treeless region covered with

Sharp-tailed grouse

mesquite, prickly pear, yucca and grasses, with more or less frequent depressions or sinks, known locally as "lakes"—which they usually are after heavy rainfall. The cactus and mesquite country of the Panhandle High Plains, once thought to be a desert, was called the Staked Plains, or Llano Estacado.

The Llano Estacado, today a land of cowboys and gas refineries, is a plain as flat as any surface in the world. Across this dry, windswept plain the Canadian River flows along its ancient course, carving deep canyons crowned with white-limestone cap rock and flanked by scenic buttes, pinnacles, and reddish-brown coves. Most of this great canyon section of the Canadian River has been filled by sprawling Lake Meredith. Trails and drives above the reservoir provide access to remote canyons, river flats, and historic sites, such as McBride House, on the site of an early Panhandle ranch. Cottonwoods, soapberry, and sandbar willows flourish along the river flats and in sheltered creek beds.

Alibates Prehistoric Flint Quarries on the Canadian River Breaks

Archeologists have found ancient stone tools throughout the Great Plains and Southwest made of flint from the Alibates Quarries, a small section of the Texas Panhandle around Lake Meredith on the breaks of the Canadian River. The flint, in a layer up to six feet deep, usually lies just below the surface at ridge level. For thousands of years these bluffs and ridges were quarried for flint to make stone tools and weapons. The Stone-Age craftsmen seemed to have preferred flint that was red, white, blue, or banded, but nearly every color in the rainbow is found in Alibates flint and no two pieces are alike. From 10,000 B.C. to as

Fort Davis, on the Old California Overland Trail, played an important role in the last Indian war in Texas.

Indian arrowhead quarried from Alibates flint

late as the 1870s, Alibates flint was distributed widely over the High Plains country. Most of the tribes who used it were nomads—hunters who followed the game trails and never built permanent homes. But between A.D. 1200 and 1450, the Alibates area was settled permanently by the people of the Panhandle Pueblo culture, primarily farmers, who also quarried the flint and bartered it for pottery, pipestones from Minnesota, seashells, and obsidian from the Yellowstone country. The houses of these Plains Village Indians show the influence of pueblo-style houses in the Southwest.

Fort Davis on the California Overland Trail

Fort Davis was established at a strategic spot in the Davis Mountains in 1854 to protect travellers on the road between San Antonio and El Paso, a section of the Overland Trail to California. With the outbreak of the Civil War it was occupied for a few months by a small Confederate garrison and then abandoned. Reoccupied by federal troops in 1867 and rebuilt afterward, Fort Davis rose to peak strength and significance between 1879 and 1885. Although the men stationed there performed mostly routine duties such as patrolling, scouting, and escorting wagon trains and stagecoaches, they played an important part in the 1879–1881 campaign against Chief Victorio and his Warm Springs Apaches—the last Indian war in Texas. The National Park Service has identified over 50 structures and sites, and portions of about 30 buildings have been either restored or stabilized. Seven of the surviving buildings are of cut red stone, the rest of adobe.

Fort Davis is at the junction of Texas Highways 17 and 118 in Fort Davis, Jeff Davis County.

2. Southern Rockies

THE massive ramparts of the Southern Rocky Mountains rise abruptly from the Great Plains on the east and dominate the landscape from the Sangre de Cristo Range in north-central New Mexico northward along the Continental Divide in the volcanic San Juan Mountains and the Colorado Front Range, to the northern end of the Laramie Mountains, south of Casper, Wyoming. The Southern Rockies are the highest of the Rocky Mountains, with at least 46 snow-capped peaks soaring to heights of 14,000 feet in Colorado.

The ranges of the Southern Rockies fall into two general north-south belts separated by four intermountain basins or "parks": North Park, Middle Park, South Park, and the Wet Mountain Valley flanked on the east, from north to south, by the Laramie Mountains, Colorado Front Range, and the Wet Mountains, and on the west by the Park Range, Gore, Mosquito, Sawatch, and Sangre de Cristo mountains. The San Luis Valley is a similar park dividing the Sangre de Cristo Range from the San Juan Mountains to the west.

Formation of the Rockies—The Uplift of the Laramide Revolution

As you travel from east to west across the high plains, the massive front of the Rockies looms in the distance like dark sentinels, with peak after snow-covered peak rising to heights of nearly 8,000 feet above the level of the plains, many towering more than 14,000 feet above sea level. How did they come to be? And how, high among the spires of Wyoming's Wind River Range and Colorado's Front Range, were nearly flat summits that look like an ancient plain formed? The awesome peaks and valleys of the Rocky Mountains as we see them today are part of an on-going story that began 600 million years ago when part of western North America began to sag downward to form an elongated trough. This downwarping process continued until the trough was filled with an ancient, shallow sea that extended from the Arctic Ocean to the Gulf of Mexico. Great masses of silt and sand poured down the rivers into the sea and slowly

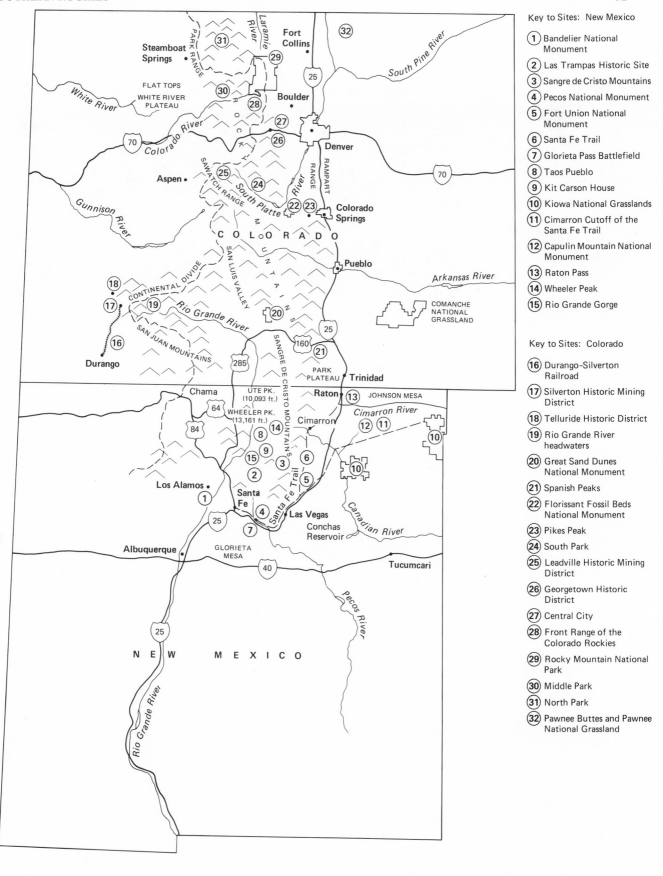

Tundra zone above 10,000 feet in New Mexico's Sangre de Cristo Mountains

transformed to sedimentary rock, which accumulated and was then compressed so that the rocks were folded and broken. Large masses of molten materials appeared in the cores of the folded and broken rock, eventually solidifying into granite.

This gradual uplift from the bed of the ancient sea reached its climax about 60 million years ago in the massive crustal movement known as the Laramide revolution of the Rocky Mountain geosyncline. This great period of uplift, which continued on and off for 30 million years, accompanied the folding and faulting caused by tremendous internal forces that buckled the earth's crust into immense wrinkles of rock bulging upward above the ancient seabed. When the rocks emerged from the sea, they were sculptured by extensive intervals of erosion, followed by intermittent periods of uplift, which renewed the power of stream erosion and were followed by the glaciers of the Ice Age, which carved the valleys and formed the peaks and lake basins of the Rockies.

Rocky Mountain Weather Systems

The high elevations of the Rocky Mountains exert a noticeable effect on the climate of the region, shifting the direction of the wind and cooling the air that passes over their crests. Since the westerly wind's moisture is condensed and dropped before reaching the Great Plains, the region as a whole has a cool, dry climate.

The mountains, with their heavy forest cover, provide a storage place for the winter snows that, in summer, feed the lakes and streams. Electrical storms, cloudbursts, whirlwinds, and fearsome hail storms occur during the summer; cyclones are rare. Although the prevailing winds blow from the west, the presence of the mountains and foothills influences their direction in different areas. On the Laramie Plains in southern Wyoming, for example, the prevailing winds, from the southwest during winter and southeast in summer, often attain a velocity of 40 miles per hour, sometimes reaching 60 miles per hour. The chinook, a drying wind from over the Rockies, is often the salvation of the Western ranchers. When feed for the cattle and game is covered with hardpacked snow on the range, it is not unusual for a chinook wind to melt snowbanks two and three feet deep almost as quickly as if a blast from a furnace had been turned on them. These winter winds change conditions in a few hours from freezing cold to mild spring weather. The mirage is another phenomenon that often occurs on the plains regions.

Winter blizzards are a common hazard of the mountain high country. Because of the shape of the country, a small amount of snow can be driven with such force and fury by a 40- to 60-mile-an-hour gale that any living thing caught in it will perish. A blizzard is sometimes caused by a high wind whipping apart old drifts in subzero weather, and sometimes by a combination of old and new snow carried by a high-speed wind. A common Rocky Mountain country saying is that snow doesn't melt, it's just blown away.

Rocky Mountain Life Zones—From Sagebrush Flats to Arctic Tundra

The journey up through the distinct life zones of the Rocky Mountain country will transport the traveller from the low sagebrush and greasewood flats to the rolling, grassy High Plains and pine-clad foothills, up through the broad, U-shaped glacial valleys with their meandering streams and elk meadows surrounded by slopes covered with stands of Douglas fir and spruce, on up to the stunted, gale-swept rocky world at the timberline to the treeless arcticlike crest of the Great Divide—a fragile tundra

Prickly pear cactus on the arid Low Plains

world of dwarf vegetation where grasses, mosses, primitive lichens, and bright-blossoming plants create colorful patterns of endless variety.

In the Rocky Mountains from New Mexico north to British Columbia are an Upper Sonoran zone in the valleys and plains; a transition zone of the High Plains and lower foothills; a Canadian zone, covering the middle slopes and highest foothills; the narrow band of the wind-swept Hudsonian zone at timberline; and the eerie, treeless Arctic-alpine zone along the crest of the Rockies above the timberline.

Upper Sonoran Zone—
Low Plains and Sagebrush Deserts

Covering nearly a third of the Rocky Mountain country is the semiarid upper Sonoran zone; a warm climate, rich soils, and a long growing season make this low country the chief zone of crop production and cattle grazing. Streams and rivers wind through this grass plain and desert land, their meandering courses marked by colorful stands and thickets of cottonwoods, willows, box elders, and balsam poplars with their red blossoms and olive-yellow leaves.

On the dry hillsides and plains, cactus and rabbitbrush alternate with gray and black sage. Purple cactus, named for the colorful hue of its flower, spreads in bunches over the prairies and hills to altitudes of 4,000 and 5,000 feet. Greasewood, a low,

Wind-eroded rock formations dot the sagebrush desert

branching, thorny shrub with thick bright-green leaves, is found in the moist alkali flats near the bases of the mountains. For the Hopi Indians, greasewood provided a ready source of quick-burning fuel. The ever-present common sagebrush, also known as black sage, a scrubby, heavily branched small shrub, is the symbol of the cattle country. During winter, sheep and cattle that range over the arid areas eat its leaves. The mountain valleys and plains are also inhabited by dark-green aromatic sagebrush with its tufted stems. The sprawling gray Eaton sagebrush with its yellow spikelike blossoms grows in the alkali flats. In May and June, when rainfall is frequent, hundreds of wild-flowers provide a bright splash of color in the sun-warmed pockets amid the barren rocks and brown sod of the prairies—whitish-purple thimbleweed, wind-flower, sour dock, evening star, miner's candle, sunflowers, fireweed, and flax.

Wildlife commonly sighted on the low, dry plains are the buff-and-white antelope, or pronghorn, often recognized in the distance by its flashing white rump as it runs across the prairies at speeds of up to 40 m.p.h., ground squirrels, yellow pocket gophers, ferrets, Wyoming kangaroo rats, and grasshopper mice. High above the broad plains soar the winged predators—red-tailed hawks, golden eagles, shrikes, and prairie falcons. Along the waterways and marshes of the plains is occasionally heard the "stump-knocking" booming of the bittern, also known as the "bog bull" or "thunder pumper." The bittern is usually unseen because of its protective camouflage as it stands in the high grass. Other commonly sighted birds of the low plains are the orange-breasted and black-winged Bullock orioles, buff-and-gray western grasshopper

Coyote stalking its prey on the High Plains

sparrows, bronzed grackles, brown mourning doves, Arkansas kingbirds, and brownish-white lark sparrows, with their purring song.

An extended hike through the dry prairies and plains may also reveal the burrows and signs of field and pocket mice, pygmy pocket gophers, Wyoming cottontails, and white-tailed jackrabbits among the rabbitbrush, Wyoming and Uinta ground squirrels, white-tailed prairie dogs, and the sharp-nosed northern plains skunk. The sagebrush and greasewood flats are also inhabited by the plains rattlesnake, blue racer, scaly lizard, prairie bull snake, and the desert horned lizard.

Transition Zone—The High Plains and Foothills

As you travel from the dry flats to the high peaks you will notice changes in the plant life, due largely to increasing moisture, exposure, and coolness. From the Upper Sonoran zone you will move into the transition zone of the High Plains, an open and tree-less area that covers about half the Rocky Mountain

Red Rocks country near Denver

Junco, or "snowbird," of the high-country pine forests

number of rushes and sages. Bluestem grass is the staple range plant, along with wheat grass, which grows in clumps that sometimes reach heights of three feet, tufted fescues, and retops, the latter found along the moist meadows and wet stream banks.

The foothills and rangelands provide a rich habitat for a great variety of birds, including the sage hen, sharp-shinned hawk, Rocky Mountain and pygmy nuthatches, willow thrush, white-throated swift, bluish-gray pinon jay, sawwhet owl, and the commonly sighted noisy magpies, which raise a clamor over the plains as they hunt in groups for insects and small rodents.

Canadian Zone—The High Country

The Canadian zone extends from the base of the Rocky Mountains up to an elevation of 9,000 or 10,000 feet. At the lower elevations, below 9,000 feet, where the climate is relatively warm and dry, open stands of ponderosa pine and juniper grow on the slopes facing the sun; on the cooler north-facing slopes they are mixed with stands of Douglas fir. Elsewhere grow dense armies of lodgepole pines and along the stream banks are cottonwoods, mountain alder, and beautiful Colorado blue spruce. Along the forest borders and ravines are glades of quaking aspen, with their silvery trunks, which turn a shimmering golden yellow in autumn. The meadows and glades are carpeted with Rocky Mountain iris, plains erysimum, or "western wallflower," pestemon, and American pasqueflower.

Above 9,000 feet or so, forests of Engelmann spruce, subalpine fir, and limber pine take over. Open-

country and is characterized by sagebrush flats, vast grassy plains, high plateaus, and pine-clad foothills. Along the stream banks near the base of the mountains are thickets of diamond willow, black and red haws, white-flowered hawthorn, wild gooseberry and serviceberry. Rocky mountain cedars, wind-blown and twisted on the higher ridges, grow straight and tall on the shady northern slopes and in the river valleys. Vivid junipers grow in large, matlike clusters on the hillsides and forest floor.

Perhaps the dominant feature of the transition zone is the presence of vast cattle rangelands, made up of more than 150 types of grasses and an equal

Sagebrush plains, foothills, and the Front Range

ings in these cool, dark forests produce wildflower meadows of striking beauty. Here the Colorado columbine reaches its peak. As the traveller approaches the upper limits of this zone, he will notice that where the cold winds blow, the trees suddenly begin to decrease in size and become increasingly twisted and grotesque.

Hudsonian Zone—At Timberline

The uppermost edge of the Canadian zone along the timberline is known as the Hudsonian zone, a land of wind-whipped, stunted timber that girdles the peaks of the high mountain ranges. This zone varies in width from a few hundred feet to more than a thousand feet, broadest in cold saddles and at its most narrow on unsheltered ridges. Snowfields and drifts that withstand the summer sun prevail year-round, bordered by a few stunted, ragged mats of Engelmann spruce and juniper. On the upper slopes of the zone lives the alpine fir, with its thin, silvery-white to light brown bark and violet-purple and indigo-blue blossoms that appear in June. Along the alpine meadows at lower altitudes the alpine fir grows in tall, symmetrical spires;

Thick orange bark of the ponderosa pine, noted for its vanilla fragrance

Glacial valley in the Canadian zone of the San Juan Mountains

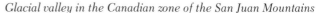

near the timberline it shrinks to a small shrub that clings to rocks and crevices. For a brief season in July and August, globeflowers, mountain cowslip, Jacob's ladder, shooting star, buttercup, and other wildflowers bend and nod with the mountain gales. Summer brings wildlife of the Canadian zone forests up into the timberline areas. Elk, coyotes, snowshoe hares, red foxes, marmots, ground and red squirrels make a brief summer appearance among the rocky boulder fields and ledges.

Alpine-Tundra Zone—Land Above the Trees

Above the timberline the trees disappear and you are in alpine tundra—broken, open expanses of dwarf vegetation like that in arctic regions, interrupted by fingers of the Canadian-zone valleys. Wyoming's Wind River Range in the Middle Rockies contains the most continuous of the arctic-alpine areas in the Rockies. Deep snowfields, intermittent rain, sleet storms, and arctic temperatures are common in all seasons. Ice fields are found throughout the year in the high canyons and gorges scoured out among the granite peaks.

Here plant growth hugs the ground, an adaptation to the fury of the high-altitude winds, and produces seeds quickly, an adaptation to the brief, fleeting

Ptarmigan feeding in a tundra boulder field

Whistling marmot in its rocky timberline habitat

"Wind timber" in an alpine meadow

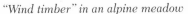

summers. From the middle of May until August, the usually barren slopes are carpeted with brightly tinted buttercups, lupine, dwarf gentians, golden rod, saxifrage, and alpine forget-me-nots. Grasses, mosses, and lichens spread at random where the soil can support their growth, providing forage for bighorn sheep and pika.

Along the crest of the Rockies the brownish-yellow pika, or cony, makes its home among the jumbles of shale and frost- and heat-cracked rock masses. The pika, noted for its sharp, squeaking cry, is tailless and has smaller ears than the hare, as well as shorter legs. The tiny pika, also known as the little chief hare, rock rabbit, or whistling hare, is about seven or eight inches long. A hike along the crest of the Continental Divide will usually reveal small piles of "hay" stacked between the jagged rocks by the pika, which it allows to dry out in the sun and gathers in the fall, storing the hay in its underground den.

Flat Tops and an alpine meadow

Sangre de Cristo Range

The Sangre de Cristo Range, the frontal range at the southern end of the Rocky Mountains, extends for 140 miles in a great arc from near Salida in southern Colorado south to Santa Fe, New Mexico. The range, as one might expect, takes in some of the most spectacular high country in the Southwest, including the Wheeler Peak Wilderness, dominated by 13,160-foot Wheeler Peak, and the Pecos Wilderness at the headwaters of the Pecos River.

Hypoxia—The Rocky Mountain High

The shortness of breath and euphoria you may experience as a newcomer among the alpine peaks and meadows of the Rockies has a name, hypoxia, or oxygen shortage. At the higher mountain altitudes the air is thinner, and the air pressure drops from its sea-level measure of 15 pounds per square inch or 1.2 ounces per cubic foot to 0.8 ounces per cubic foot. To compensate for this loss of oxygen the body works harder; the bone marrow produces more red corpuscles, and the pulse rate increases to more than 100 beats per minute. The result is often an intoxicating euphoria, or with those less fortunate, dizziness, nausea, or headaches. It usually takes about three months for the body to adjust to the high altitudes of the mountain country.

Alpine Meadows

Alpine meadows make up the largest part of the tundra regions of the Western mountains. Most mountain meadows began thousands of years ago as lakes gradually became bogs that filled up with decayed vegetable matter and soil. These well-drained, wind-swept meadows, free of snow in winter, are characterized by a great variety of miniature perennial plants, predominantly sedges and forbs. Numerous mosses and lichens can be found among the flowering plants. The most commonly sighted species found in the alpine meadows include alpine avens, alpine forget-me-not, rydbergia, sky pilot, twisted-pod draba, American bistort, mountain candytuft, birdfoot buttercup, alpine wallflower, mountain harebell, pinnate-leaved daisy, alp lily, arctic gentian, kings crown, moss gentian, alpine anemone, alpine primrose, snowball saxifrage, western yellow paintbrush, northern rockjasmine, and alpine androsace.

Mountain Cottontail

The mountain cottontail is a 12-to-14-inch-long hare similar to the Eastern cottontail but paler in coloration. It is usually the only cottontail found in most of its range in the Western mountains, where it is usually sighted among the loose rocks and cliffs, thickets, and high sagebrush areas.

Pecos Pueblo National Monument

The ancient pueblo of Pecos, a multistoried, quadrangular pueblo built in 1450 by the Pecos Valley Indians around a central plaza on a rocky ridge, was a landmark to the early Spanish explorers and one of the largest structures of its kind in 17th-century New Mexico. The pueblo was the point of departure for Francisco Coronado's expedition in 1540 from New Mexico to search for treasure in the legendary Quivira—the City of Gold. By the 1620s the Spanish mission of Nuestra Señora de los Angeles de Porcincula had been completed, only to be destroyed during the 1680 Pueblo Indian rebellion. The mission included a church and a convento containing a carpenter shop, weaving rooms, tanneries, and living quarters. After the massive church at Pecos was destroyed, the Indians built a kiva in the courtyard of the convento from adobe bricks salvaged from the burned church.

Pecos began to decline in the mid-18th century after being besieged by disease and hostile Indians. Today the adobe walls of the new mission, built in the early 1700s following the Spanish reconquest, rise as high as 50 feet above the foundations of the earlier church. Both the mission complex and the pueblo have been partially excavated.

The Pecos Ruins Trail, which begins at the visitor center, winds through the convento to the kiva, one of the many underground Indian religious ceremonial rooms found at Pecos, and on to the defensive wall used by the Indians as a village boundary, the mission churches, and the north pueblo, unexcavated mounds that were once a massive, five-story rectangular village that housed an estimated 2,500 Pueblo Indians.

The pueblo is located south of Pecos on New Mexico Highway 63 in San Miguel County.

Glorieta Pass Battlefield

The battle of Glorieta Pass, March 26–28, 1862, ended a Confederate invasion of New Mexico that

Pecos Pueblo National Monument

Indian kiva at Pecos—an underground religious ceremonial room

Taos pueblo

for many of the Western and Southwestern fur trappers. Kit Carson was one of the most renowned of these mountain men. His fame as a guide for exploring expeditions and as an army officer in the Southwest Indian wars equaled his earlier reputation as a trapper and mountain man. Carson bought this house in 1843 when he married Josefa Jaramillo. It became their permanent home until their deaths in 1868. The house was restored to its historic appearance after 1910 and stands today as a symbol and museum of the fur trade, the mountain men, and the free trappers of the Southwest.

Taos Pueblo

The Pueblo of Taos, still active today, commemorates Indian resistance to Spanish rule in the 17th century. This terraced pueblo of the Tigua was well known to Spanish explorers as early as 1540. The mission of San Geronimo, one of the earliest in New Mexico, was built near Taos Pueblo in the early 17th century. It was twice destroyed and rebuilt prior to the uprising of 1680. Fourteen years passed before Spanish rule was restored and the mission re-established. Though another revolt occurred in 1696, the mission continued until 1847, when it was bombarded by an American force under Colonel Sterling Price during the Taos Rebellion.

The pueblo is located three miles north of Taos.

attempted to seize a large portion of the Southwest and its resources. Brigadier General Henry H. Sibley's Confederate command achieved success in driving back Brigadier General E. S. Canby's forces, but a Union flanking column succeeded in destroying the Confederate wagon train and supplies from the rear, thus forcing Confederate withdrawal from New Mexico. The building of a highway and one railroad line through the pass has impaired the integrity of the scene, but most key positions of the battle are identifiable.

The battlefield is located 10 miles southeast of Santa Fe on U.S. Highway 84–85.

Seton Village

Ernest Thompson Seton informed three generations of Americans concerning the world of nature through his paintings, writings, and lectures. Present-day conservation philosophy was partially shaped by people influenced by his ideas. He was chairman of the committee that brought the Boy Scout movement to the United States. On his ranch he built a 45-room "castle"—a combination home, museum, art gallery, and institute for people in the creative disciplines. The community known as Seton Village grew up around the house, which until recently contained many of his paintings, books, mammal and bird specimens, and Indian artifacts.

The village is located six miles south of Santa Fe off U.S. Highway 84–85.

Kit Carson House at Taos

During the second quarter of the 19th century Taos was the rendezvous point and winter quarters

Prehistoric "Cavate" ruins at Bandelier National Monument

Las Trampas Historic District

The village of Las Trampas, a Spanish-American agricultural community, preserves its 18th-century heritage in both appearance and culture. It is situated near the western slopes of the Sangre de Cristo Mountains below Truchas Peak, and tradition still guides its agrarian life, which until World War II was almost untouched by Anglo-American influence and modern techniques. The church of San Jose de Garcia de Las Trampas, completed about 1780, is the center of village life. It is an important and well-preserved example of Spanish Colonial church architecture. Around the plaza and along the edges of the valley floor are several typical early Spanish colonial adobe houses.

Las Trampas is located about midway between Taos and Santa Fe on New Mexico Highway 76.

Bandelier Ruins on the Volcanic Pajarito Plateau

Bandelier National Monument covers 50 square miles on the volcanic, canyon-slashed slopes of the Pajarito Plateau in the Upper Rio Grande country near Los Alamos. The prehistoric ruins at Bandelier, which date from A.D. 1200, are surrounded by a rugged landscape of tan cliffs, forested mesas, and deep gorges. The Pajarito Plateau is made up of volcanic tuff and basaltic lava ejected thousands of years ago by a massive volcano. The saucer-shaped caldera was created by the collapsed summit of the volcano and forms the Jemez Mountains along its rim. This awesome caldera ranks among the largest in the world.

For centuries the Indian inhabitants lived in the deep canyons, where they built villages, honeycombed the cliffs with artificial caves, and cultivated crops on the mesa top and valleys. Their disappearance is believed to have been caused by a combination of factors—drought, disease, famine, and raiding by hostile tribes.

Maintained trails provide access to the cliff ruins, or talus villages, that extend along the base of the northern wall of Frijoles Canyon for nearly two miles; and to the Tsankawi section 11 miles north of Frijoles Canyon, which is a large unexcavated ruin on a high mesa with sweeping views of the Rio Grande valley, the Sangre de Cristo Mountains to the east, and the Jemez Mountains to the west. Other trails in the wild back-country areas provide access to the gorges of Alamo Canyon and Stone Lions Shrine, Painted Cave, the San Miguel and Yapashi pueblo ruins, and to the White Rock Canyon of the Rio Grande River.

Western Larch

The western larch is among the most majestic trees on earth. The larch may reach a height of 250

Aspens in autumn foliage create a hillside of brilliant yellows, reds, and oranges.

feet, growing at high elevations in the deep, moist soils of the mountain slopes and valleys. It is unlike any other conifer in that it has almost no foliage after it reaches some size and that it drops most of its leaves when winter comes. In summer a mature larch has a bushy top and a mighty spire of trunk as straight as a lodgepole. Very slow to grow, a larch only nine inches in diameter may be 50 years old; a tree with an 18-inch diameter may be 250 years old. Lined against the morning light, its foliage has a silken, spidery loveliness from its unsheathed needles, which grow in tufts or tiny spray brooms.

Quaking Aspen

The quaking aspen, also known as trembling aspen, popple, and squawstongue, is one of the most common nonevergreens found in the West, especially along the streams, in moist areas, and on burned-over areas. It is the first tree in the plant succession in the subalpine life zone. It often occurs in pure, dense stands, especially following a forest fire, where it often grows in association with fire cherry and fire-weed. It is found from Alaska to Newfoundland and has probably the widest range of any native North American tree. In autumn in the West whole hillsides are ablaze with the yellow to red-orange color of the aspen.

Quaking aspen—bark, leaves, and blossom

Fall Aspen Foliage

The brilliant yellows and oranges of the aspen as they turn in the fall are a major attraction of the Rocky Mountain country. Normally, the aspen leaves start changing color at lower elevations around mid-September, usually continuing for two to four weeks. However, weather conditions each year are the determining factor as to whether it will be a good year for color or a poor year.

When temperature, moisture, and light conditions change with the arrival of fall, so do the chemicals inside the leaves. As the leaf forms in the early weeks of spring, the chemical parts of the leaf appear, showing up as yellow, orange, and red pigments. These colors are masked by the abundant chlorophyll which carries on the major leaf function of converting sunshine into food energy (a process known as photosynthesis). The other colors are there through the summer, but are dominated by the green chlorophyll.

By late summer, when the days grow shorter and the temperatures begin to drop, the production of the chlorophyll begins to decrease as the trees get ready for their winter dormancy. As the chlorophyll gradually disappears from the leaf, the production of the colored pigments continues, with an increase in certain pigments (carotenoid) giving the leaf the yellow color which may gradually degrade into a reddish hue.

Another chemical in the leaf—anthocyanin pigment—begins to appear. This chemical is controlled by the production and movement of sugar which in turn is controlled by the amount of sunshine and night temperatures. Cool temperatures retard the transfer of these sugars from the leaves to the roots, allowing a concentration to build up in the leaves. Their color may range from brilliant red to nearly blue, depending on the acidity of the cell sap. The brilliant leaf colors will continue to a certain point, then diminish under falling temperatures and shorter days. The colors gradually become brown as the activity inside the leaf decreases and ends, or freezing temperatures kill the leaf. The most spectacular colors are produced when leaf growth continues well into fall under warm temperatures and rainfall, which delays the color process that would start if moisture in the soil becomes low. Coloring is brought on by a combination of short, dry days and cooler temperatures.

Watrous Wagon Train Rendezvous Site

The junction of the Mora and Sapello rivers was the rendezvous point for organizing wagon trains before the venture east into the hostile Indian territory of the open plain. Watrous, or LaJunta, was also the point at which the mountain and Cimarron Cutoff routes of the Santa Fe Trail divided. Extensive cultivation has obliterated much of the trail, but it is possible

Remains of officers' quarters at Fort Union

to trace its approximate route and to locate the main crossings of the two streams. Among the remaining buildings associated with the era are the Watrous Store and Ranch (1849), the Sapello Stage Station (1850s), and the Fort Union Corral (1850s).

The site is located at Watrous in New Mexico's Mora County on U.S. Highway 85.

Fort Union National Monument

Located near the point where the Santa Fe Trail's mountain route and Cimarron Cutoff joined together, Fort Union was the principal quartermaster depot supplying army operations in New Mexico. Soldiers at this post, the largest then guarding the Southwestern frontier, saw action against Apache, Ute, Kiowa, Navajo, and Comanche Indians. At the battle of Glorieta Pass, March 28, 1862, Union volunteers based at Fort Union turned back the Confederacy's only serious threat to New Mexico and Colorado. Today only melted adobe walls and a few chimneys rise above ground level.

The site is located east of the Rockies on New Mexico's Highway 477, nine miles north of Watrous in Mora County.

Wagon Mound on the Santa Fe Trail

Wagon Mound was the last great landmark of the High Plains section of the Cimarron Cutoff of the Santa Fe Trail. First visible from Point of Rocks, it was the guidepost for caravans moving westward from the rock crossing of the Canadian River to Santa Fe. Two miles northwest of Wagon Mound is Santa Clara Spring, an important watering point. Beginning in the late 1840s, these sites became the scene of frequent Indian ambushes. South and west of Wagon Mound are visible remains of the Santa Fe Trail.

The landmark is east of Wagon Mound and the Sangre de Cristo Range in the High Plains on U.S. 85 in New Mexico's Mora County.

Headwaters of the Rio Grande— From Timberline to Desert

The Rio Grande—called the Great River of the North by the Spanish conquistadors—rises high in the alpine wilderness of Colorado's upper Rio Grande wilderness in the San Juan Mountains and flows south through the San Luis Valley, entering the spectacular 70-mile-long Rio Grande Gorge, which begins just above the New Mexico–Colorado boundary and continues southward on its 2,200-mile journey to the sea.

Along its course the upper Rio Grande passes through an alpine zone of 14,000-foot peaks of the San Juan Mountains and the arid sagebrush flats of the San Luis Valley flanked by the Sangre de Cristo Range to the floor of the gorge, bordered by sheer, 800-foot, volcanic, lichen-covered canyon walls below a landscape of yellow bluffs, plains, and sagebrush benchlands. The bottom of the gorge is lined by black basalt formed from an ancient lava flow. Thickets of pinon, apache plume, yucca, sagebrush, small oaks and willows fringe the banks of the Rio Grande during its wild course through the canyon floor.

Capulin Mountain—A Volcanic Remnant on New Mexico's High Plains

Solitary Capulin Mountain, which rises 1,000 feet above the flat High Plains in northeastern New Mexico, is the cone of an extinct volcano formed about 10,000 years ago during the last great period of volcanic activity in North America. Nearby are scores of volcanic hills and peaks; the largest of these is the Sierra Grande, an extinct volcano rising some 2,200 feet above the surrounding plain, about 10 miles to the southeast of Capulin.

The rim of Capulin's crater is about one mile in circumference, with a depth of about 415 feet. A maze of ragged, lava-formed rocks juts out from the western base of the cone. The lower slopes are carpeted with ponderosa pine, juniper, and pinon pine. At the high

Volcanic peak near Capulin Mountain

"Baby Capulin" formed during the last phase of volcanic eruption

elevations, mountain mahogany, chokecherry, Gambel oak, and squawbush reach up over the crater's lip.

Capulin Mountain is in the heart of the ancient Kiowa and Comanche Indian hunting grounds and was a conspicuous landmark on the old Cimarron Cutoff of the Santa Fe Trail, the principal freight route between Forts Union, Dodge, and Leavenworth, which passed some 30 miles to the east and south.

Raton Pass on the Santa Fe Trail

The pass through the Raton Mountains was one of the most difficult on the mountain branch of the Santa Fe Trail. It became increasingly important as an invasion route during the Mexican War and during the Civil War, when hostilities with the southern Plains Indians almost halted traffic over the alternate Cimarron Cutoff route. From 1861 to 1865 much of the traffic to Santa Fe crossed Raton Pass.

The pass is on U.S. 85–87 on the Colorado–New Mexico border near Raton.

Cumbres and Toltec Narrow-Gauge Railroad

This railroad is a remnant of one of the most important sections of the Denver and Rio Grande Railroad. Because of the rugged terrain and low population density, this railroad was the major means of transportation into and out of this section of the

country for nearly half a century. This section of the railroad consists of 64 miles of narrow-gauge three-foot-wide track between Antonito, Colorado and Chama, New Mexico. In addition, there are nine coal-burning steam locomotives, 130 cars of various types, a railroad yard at Chama, and various sidings, water tanks, and related line-side structures.

Colorado's Great Sand Dunes

The Great Sand Dunes, established as a national monument by President Hoover in 1932, cover an area of 80 square miles along the abrupt western base of the Sangre de Cristo Range in south-central Colorado; to the west lie the volcanic San Juan Mountains. Rising more than 700 feet from the broad floor of the San Luis Valley, these changing mounds are large enough to cover all but the largest cities and their highest buildings. One explanation for their presence is that the sands once made up the bed of a great inland sea and were blown by the prevailing winds against the western wall of the Sangre de Cristo, where they piled higher and higher through the ages. Others ascribe them to the wear and tear on the sandstone of the so-called Santa Fe formation in this region, augmented by sand blown in from the valley or washed in by the Rio Grande and its tributaries. The sand of the dunes, for the most part, is of extremely fine grain. The only vegetation on the dunes —which are visible for 70 miles—are long, coarse grasses, a species of low pea plant, and sunflowers that grow in the shallows between hillocks. At the end of the road a river runs down from the base of the mountains at certain seasons of the year, skirting the dunes, only to sink suddenly from view in a dry expanse. A few miles to the west the river reappears at Indian Springs, once a water hole for game. When the river is dry, no bed marks its course.

Colorado's Great Natural Mountain "Parks"

Extending north-south down the middle of Colorado, behind the Front Range of the Rocky Mountains, stretches a chain of four large "parks," great, level expanses rimmed by snow-capped mountains flanked on the west by the Park, Gore, and Mosquito ranges. The headwaters of the North Platte are in North Park, a broad, flat-floored circular basin opening into Wyoming in the north-central part of the state. Directly south, separated by the east-west Rabbit Ears Range and the Continental Divide, is Middle Park, with a rougher landscape through which the Colorado, the state's largest river, flows westward toward the Pacific. Farther south, again across the Divide on the eastern slope, lies South Park, the 45-mile-long, 35-mile-wide *Bayou Salado* of the mountain men and a favorite hunting ground of the Ute, a broad and beautiful mountain meadow between 8,500 and 10,000 feet high at the source of the South Platte River. Most of the area is drained by the South Platte River, which leaves South Park through Eleven Mile Canyon in the Front Range. These grassy basins, with little or no timber, have been cut up into farms and ranches for the most part, and life here is in the plains rather than the mountain mode.

Midway along the southern boundary, traced by the Rio Grande as it flows sluggishly toward New Mexico, is a large, triangular, 50-mile-wide, 150-mile-long park known as the San Luis Valley, once the bed of an inland sea. One of the largest intermountain basins in the Southern Rockies, it lies between the Sangre de Cristo range on the east and the San Juan and Sawatch mountains on the west. It is open on the south, where it merges with the Rio Grande Valley. A naturally arid but widely irrigated area, its adobe villages and scattered jascals are the center of Spanish-American culture in the state. These villagers are descendants of the free Spanish settlers who followed the march of the conquistadors, or of the retainers brought along by the haciendos who divided up the Southwest in princely domains under the seal of the Spanish and Mexican governors at Santa Fe.

San Juan Mountains

Southwestern Colorado's San Juan Mountains are a sprawling, volcanic mass about 90 miles east to west and 70 miles north to south. Rugged and colorful, the pink-gray, red, mauve, charcoal, ivory, and buff rocks of the San Juans cover more than 10,000 square

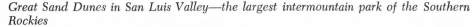

Great Sand Dunes in San Luis Valley—the largest intermountain park of the Southern Rockies

miles and form the largest single range in the United States Rockies. Formed by six distinctive periods of volcanic uplift, the range has numerous summits over 13,000 feet, culminating at Uncompahgre Peak, which exceeds 14,000 feet and is noted for its extensive rock glaciers, needlelike peaks, landslides of volcanic rock, and rock streams. The range encompasses the old gold and silver mining centers at Silverton and Telluride, the headwaters of the Rio Grande, and the vast alpine high country of the Weminuche and Uncompahgre wilderness area. In the rain shadow to the east is the outlying San Luis Valley, with its giant 700-foot sand dunes.

Silverton Historic Mining District

About 10 miles north of the jagged, billion-year-old pink-gray spires of the Grenedier Range in the topsy-turvy center of the San Juan Mountains is the old Rocky Mountain mining town of Silverton at a 9,302-foot elevation. It was founded in 1874 after the discovery of gold and later of silver in the gulches. During the 1870s the old way in to the remote outpost was by packhorse over a trail, a 50-mile backbreaking trek over the Continental Divide to the east. In winter the town was completely isolated for a six-month stretch until May, when the ice cleared, and pack trains hauled in food, supplies, and news of the outside world. In 1882 a narrow-gauge railroad, the Denver and Rio Grande was constructed along the rugged canyons of the Anemas River from Durango up through the San Juans for 46 miles north to Silverton. It hauled ores economically and efficiently from isolated mountain areas to points where smelters could operate. The Denver and Rio Grande is still in operation. From Durango at the edge of the plains the train

Old Placer Mine at Silverton Historic Mining District

climbs 3,000 feet pulled by an old coal-burning steam engine iron horse.

A few of the mines still operate in Silverton, which also has some extant early buildings. Among them are the Imperial Hotel (1882), the Congregational Church (1881), the City Hall (1908), and the Courthouse (1907).

Alpine Avens

Alpine avens, a yellow-flowered member of the rose family, is the most common and widespread alpine wildflower in the Rocky Mountains tundra. Its fernlike leaves belie its roselike flowers. It is found both in alpine meadows and in almost all areas above the timberline.

Eroded sandstone formations in the San Juan Mountains—the result of successive outpourings of volcanic ash and lava

Telluride Historic District

Gold claims were first staked in the Telluride area in 1875, and gold was later struck in Smuggler, uncovering a vein that assayed at $1200 per ton. Telluride grew slowly at first, but became one of the busiest gold camps in Colorado after the narrow-gauge railroad was built to it in 1890. Its prominence lasted only a few years, however, and only a few mines are still in operation. Several buildings dating from the late 19th and early 20th centuries still remain. Among them are the City Hall (1883), the Sheridan Hotel (1890s), the Opera House (c. 1900), and the Miner's Union Building (1902).

Telluride is located in the San Juan Mountains in the heart of the Uncompahgre National Forest at the end of an 18-mile serpentine box canyon formed by the San Miguel River.

Avalanche Lily

Called the avalanche lily by some, lamb's tongue by others, Easter bells in Utah, dog-toothed violet in the East, and trout lily by fishermen who have seen it blooming at the opening of the season, this flower is

Rocky Mountain foothills and the "Great Wall" of the Front Range—"the barrier that became a goal"

one of the commonest and loveliest in the mountain areas of the West. It pushes up at the edge of melting snow, rarely at altitudes below 4,000 feet, and flowers into yellow blooms of exquisite fragrance. Sometimes it is found with violets, buttercups, and spring beauties.

Colorado Front Range—The Shining Mountains

The prominent cirques, ridges, and deep glacial troughs and ancient crystalline peaks that are characteristic of the massive Colorado Front Range stretch for 185 miles from its southern end at the Arkansas River northward to the Colorado-Wyoming boundary where it merges into the Medicine Bow Mountains and Laramie Range. The Front Range is flanked on the east by the hogback ridges of the foothills that dip steeply into the Denver Basin and the Great Plains and on the west by the broad intermountain basins, North Park, Middle Park, and South Park.

The Front Range rises on the east on a plateau-like slope at 8,000 feet or so to a north-south line of towering, wind-swept crystalline peaks that reach their greatest height at Mount Evans (14,264 feet) and Long Peak (14,255 feet). Pikes Peak rises abruptly above the upland plateau, known as the Rocky Mountain peneplain, somewhat isolated east of the main ramparts of the Front Range. The Colorado Front Range contains some of the most spectacular alpine

Avalanche lily

wilderness found in the Rockies: the massive pyramid-shaped granite peaks, parks, beaver meadows, alpine lakes, and evergreen forests of the Ranah Wilderness at the headwaters of the Laramie River; the high peaks, valleys, and lake basins of Rocky Mountain National Park, which contains the headwaters of the Colorado River; the Gore Range–Eagles Nest Primitive Area and Indian Peaks, and the 14,000-foot peaks of the Maroon Bells–Snowmass Wilderness.

Rocky Mountain National Park— A Glacier-Carved Landscape

Rocky Mountain National Park preserves an awe-inspiring 410-square-mile alpine area of soaring peaks, glacial cirques, moraines, lake basins, valley troughs, and canyons along the massive Colorado Front Range. Bounded by the high peaks, 84 of which exceed 11,000 feet, is beautiful Grand Lake, Colorado's largest natural body of water and the headwaters of the Colorado River.

Features formed by the geological forces and Ice Age that shaped the Front Range are found throughout the park. Specimen Mountain, an extinct volcano, was created by ancient volcanic activity in the western part of the park, as was the lava flow exposed in the cliffs above Iceberg Lake and the volcanic cliffs in the Never Summer Range. The flat summits of Flattop and Deer mountains are remnants of past periods of erosion when the Front Range was worn down to a relatively flat plain, then uplifted

An alpine lake at Rocky Mountain National Park

during the Laramide revolution that created the Rockies about 60 million years ago.

Following this period of uplift, streams and massive valley glaciers carved the spectacular landscape we see today. Several small remnants of these once-mighty glaciers can be seen sheltered at the higher elevations. Remnants of the power of the valley glaciers are everywhere, from the horn-shaped peaks to the flat-bottomed glacial trough at Spruce Canyon, to the recessional moraine that formed a natural dam across a valley to create Dream Lake, to the ice-polished bedrock and giant boulders known as glacial erratics along the Bear Lake Nature Trail.

Vegetation in Rocky Mountain National Park ranges from that common to the relatively warm and dry climate of the montane or transition zone, dominated by yellow ponderosa pine and Douglas fir, up through the treeless, wind-swept tundra of the arctic-alpine zone up beyond the timberline. The Alpine Visitor Center on Trail Ridge Road at Fall River Pass is situated at a 11,976-foot elevation and offers interpretive exhibits and lectures on the tundra world of the Rockies.

Colorado Blue Spruce

Colorado blue spruce is found from 6,500 to 11,000 feet along stream banks from Wyoming, Utah, and Colorado south to northern New Mexico. It reaches heights of 150 feet and may live to 600 years. It has dull, blue-green, prickly needles that are a diamond shape in cross section. Its twigs are not hairy, and its cones are larger than those of the Engelmann spruce, about three and one-half inches long.

The massive ramparts of the Maroon Bells near Aspen

Rocky Mountain Juniper

Rocky Mountain juniper is found on the dry, rocky slopes of the Rocky Mountain foothills. A small, many-branched tree, its blue, fleshy, berrylike cones take two years to mature. Its foliage is scalelike.

The Great Divide

The Continental Divide—the barrier that became a goal—winds down the middle of Colorado, splitting it into two roughly equal sections, the eastern and western slopes of the Rocky Mountains. These are geographically and even economically distinct regions. South from Wyoming, the Continental Divide follows the crest of the Park Range, turns sharply eastward along the Rabbit Ears for 50 miles, then turns as sharply southward along the Front Range through Rocky Mountain National Park and the glacier country. Angling southwestward to the High Mosquitoes, "that highway of frozen death" in boom days, the Divide boxes in the headwaters of the Arkansas and follows the towering Sawatch and Collegiate ranges to the lower Cochetopa Hills, the watershed between the basins of the Pacific-bound Colorado River and the Gulf of Mexico–bound Rio Grande. Again ascending, it runs up and over the precipitous San Juans to descend along its lesser ridges into New Mexico. Pikes Peak, Longs Peak, and many other of Colorado's highest summits stand apart from the Divide.

Mountain goats

Rocky Mountain juniper, a dominant tree of the foothills

Stream Banks of the Rocky Mountain High Country—From Foothill Canyons to Timberline

Anyone who hikes along the streams of the Rocky Mountains will pass up through the narrow canyons of the foothills. There ponderosa pine, red cedar, and Douglas fir of the upland forests mix with water-loving cottonwoods and Colorado blue spruce, broken here and there by small meadows and thickets of alder, willow, and the deep, red bark of river birch. Large patches of wild plum, hawthorn, box elder, and choke-cherry are often seen along north-facing canyon slopes and in protected spots on southern exposures. On the broad floodplains above the foothills the stream banks are bordered by distinct belts of river birch, willow, and red alder separated from the upland forests by large meadows and stands of quaking aspen. In the glacier-carved U-shaped valleys high in the subalpine zone are meandering streams, beaver ponds,

The "Chinese Wall" in the Flat Top Range

and bogs dominated by thick tangles of willows and bog birch. Water shrews, beaver, raccoon, rabbits, great blue heron, sparrows, and dippers are often sighted along the high-country streams. Insect galls and the large, gossamer tents of the tent caterpillar moth larvae are common.

At many of the subalpine ponds, the traveller may see the slow transformation from pond to bog to alpine meadow, with sedge mats and floating moss growing out over the pond, followed by bog birch and willow growing in the sedge mats, which are in turn being invaded by evergreens.

Ponderosa or Yellow Pine

The western yellow pine is a titan of the Western forests and one of the most beautiful trees, with its golden bark, deep black seams, and straight stateliness. The most extensive pine forests in the world are the yellow pine forests of the American West. Hardier than most trees and amazingly adaptable to rigorous conditions, this tree grows to great size in arid foothills of volcanic origin, on mesas of the Southwest, where it is the chief source of timber, in the comparatively rainless areas of western Nebraska, on swampy slopes of the Cascade Range, and high in mountains against the timberline. Because of its huge size at maturity, it was called a bull pine by frontiersmen; because it is so heavy it will barely float in water, it was called ponderosa by the early lumbermen.

Golden Eagles

If there is one bird that symbolized the mountains, remote canyons and rangelands of the Rockies, it's the majestic golden eagle. Common throughout the West, from Alaska to Mexico, the adult has a wingspan of up to seven feet and a dark brown to black body, with a golden or yellow nape visible only at close distances. A golden eagle nest or aerie is a huge pile of sticks, usually built on rocky crags or at the top of tall trees in the upland forests. Aeries often measure as much as seven feet across and five feet high. Eagles feed largely on small mammals, especially jack rabbits and gophers.

Colorado's High Plains

Colorado, contrary to popular belief, is not entirely mountainous. Broken only by occasional sand hills and isolated buttes, vast stretches of the state are as smooth and level as a tidal flat, which is what they were, in fact, in the ancient past. Emerging gradually from the true prairies of Kansas and Nebraska, the High Plains slope gently upward some 200 miles to the base of the Rocky Mountain foothills. Northeast across these plains angles the South Platte; in the southeast, the Arkansas. Between their fertile and intensively cultivated valleys, bright green ribbons threading a brown expanse, lies a huge, dry farming area crisscrossed by thousands of miles of barbed wire, checkered with farms, dotted here and there with the green oasis of a prairie hamlet shading itself from the blistering sun under trees as carefully transplanted and lovingly tended as garden flowers.

Rainfall here is scant, seldom attaining the annual state average of 16.62 inches. Winds are high in spring, and now and again a tornado has whirled its terrifying course across these plains that were homesteaded by sturdy hopefuls four or five generations ago.

Mule Deer

Mule deer are inhabitants of the mountains and foothills. In summer they move to the higher elevations and timber until winter arrives and drives them back to warmer levels. The strongest characteristics of the mule deer are large, double-branched antlers, large broad ears, and rounded whitish tail with a brushlike black tip. Their summer coat is a rich, rusty red that becomes grayish brown in winter. Unlike the Eastern whitetails, mule deer have little protective caution and when frightened, bound high into the air, facing this way and that until, as the disturbance continues, they dash off with bounding leaps.

Hutchinson Ranch in the Upper Arkansas Valley

The ranch comprises a two-story frame farm house, believed to be the first frame structure in the upper Arkansas Valley, and various outbuildings, including log bunkhouses, a blacksmith shop and corrals. The structures are well preserved, and most of them contain original furnishings or equipment. Joseph S. Hutchinson, a captain in the 18th Indiana Volunteer Infantry Regiment in the Civil War, arrived in Colorado in 1866. He was superintendent of the Gall Mining Company and in 1873 became a member of the first territorial legislature.

The ranch is located two miles east of Poncha Springs on U.S. Highway 50. To the west are the peaks of the Sawatch Range.

Pikes Peak

Pikes Peak was discovered by Zebulon Pike in 1806, although it had been long familiar to the Indians and Spaniards. Set forward from the front range of the Rockies, this prominent landmark appears to rise much higher than its actual 14,110 feet. The ascent by automobile or cog railway affords the visitor a panorama of both mountain scenery and the eastern plains.

Pikes Peak is 15 miles west of Colorado Springs in the Pike National Forest.

Florissant Fossil Beds

Florissant Fossil Beds National Monument lies in the valley bed of ancient, sickle-shaped Lake Florissant,

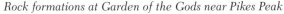

Rock formations at Garden of the Gods near Pikes Peak

Petrified stump of a giant sequoia tree at the Florissant Fossil Beds

formed during the Oligocene epoch about 26 to 38 million years ago, in an area of rolling, grassy hills and ridges covered with Douglas fir, ponderosa pine, and Colorado blue spruce 35 miles west of Colorado Springs and the snow-capped summit of Pikes Peak.

Lake Florissant was formed when massive lava flows from the ancient Thirtyninemile volcanic field, some 15 miles to the southwest, dammed the local streams. Mudflows buried great tracts of forest around the lake and petrified the sequoia stumps that may be seen today. With successive periods of volcanic activity, the lake itself was filled, forming fossil-rich shale beds beneath a hard volcanic cover. The fossil beds were discovered in 1874 by Dr. A. C. Peale of the U.S. Geological Survey. Since then scientists have removed over 80,000 specimens of fossil palm leaves, birches, willows, beeches, hickories, and needles from fir and giant sequoia trees, as well as fossil butterflies, birds, small mammals, fish, and insects. A self-guiding environmental study area and nature trail are located near the monument headquarters and museum.

Snowlover

The snowlover is found only high in the Rocky Mountains in snow accumulation areas of the alpine tundra. This white-flowered member of the fogwort family was first discovered in 1821 on Pikes Peak by Edwin James, a botanist on Major Long's expedition to the Rocky Mountains. Both the common name and scientific name, *Chionophila jamesii*, convey the ecology of this plant.

Junco

The junco, or snowbird, is a hardy member of the sparrow family that lives in the high pine forests and remains near its nest until late in the fall, when it descends to lower levels. There are numerous varieties of the junco, but their habits of nesting, feeding, and singing are similar. Their nests are built under grass roots or weeds and occasionally in rock crevices or upturned tree roots.

Rocky Mountain Mining Camps

The early Rocky Mountain mining camps were marked by structural forms as simple as those of the plains or mesa country. Because thick stands of pine covered the mountains, the first structures in the camps were of logs. Soon portable saw-mills were cutting slabs of green pine lumber, and frame construction began. Use of masonry in the camps was usually deferred until a reasonable degree of permanency seemed assured, but the miners' chronic optimism often induced disastrous illusions. This was the day of false-fronts, when rows of one-story buildings in every town were camouflaged to give an impression of far greater size. False-front buildings still characterize many mountain towns and small plains villages of Colorado, Wyoming, and Montana. Log houses have never gone out of style in the mountains, and such construction has reached elaborate proportions in "rustic" hotels and resort lodges.

Central City Historic Mining District

Heart of the first great mining boom in Colorado, Central City is well preserved in both appearance and atmosphere. It was the cradle of most of Colorado's mining laws. Most of the remaining buildings were constructed after the fire of 1874. They include the Teller House (1872), the Old Armory (1875), St. James Methodist Church (1872), and the Opera House (1878). During the 1870s and 1880s, the town was a cultural center, and in recent years dramatic and operatic productions have again become popular.

Georgetown–Silver Plume Historic District

The Georgetown–Silver Plume area is among the most scenic and historic in Colorado. The area flourished first as a gold- and silver-producing area and later as a recreational center. Next to Leadville, it was the most important silver camp in Colorado, and up to 1939 it produced more than 90 million dollars in gold, silver, lead, copper, and zinc. The still-active communities of Georgetown and Silver Plume have retained much of the boom town atmosphere, for many of the buildings have been preserved or restored. Among the surviving buildings in Georgetown are the Maxwell House (c. 1880), the Hamill House (1867), the Protestant Episcopal church (1869), and the Hotel de Paris (1875).

Ore Processing Mill and Dam

The Ore Processing Mill is a two-story wooden structure. Ore was carried by elevator from the first-floor receiving room to the second floor, where it was crushed by a jaw crusher, then sampled and sacked. According to newspaper accounts, the mill, patented in 1872, contained an automatic sampling system, considered quite innovative at the time. The horizontal water wheel used to drive the machinery now lies buried beneath an accumulation of earth and water; only the foundation of the dam is still visible. The mill is one of the few remaining structures of its type and size in Colorado.

The mill is located one mile southwest of Georgetown, adjacent to Interstate 70 and Clear Creek.

Leadville Historic Silver Mining District

Once the world's greatest silver camp, Leadville has yielded a greater number of minerals of total value over a longer period than any other place in the United States. It has been estimated that the district produced some $136,000,000 in silver between 1879 and 1889. Its first boom, however, was in gold, and after the collapse of silver prices in 1893, it was again a gold camp until the end of the century. Since that time

Mountain pass across the Southern Rockies' Great Divide

lead, zinc, manganese, and molybdenum have been mined in the district. Because of the area's stability, a relatively large number of early structures survive: the Elks Opera House, the Old Pioneer Bar, the Dexter Cabin, the Tabor Opera House, and the Healy House, now a museum.

Leadville is located in the Colorado Front Range on U.S. Highway 24.

Dexter Cabin at Leadville

James Viola Dexter, banker and mining magnate, built this cabin as a hunting lodge. The exterior of square-hewn logs chinked with plaster belies the luxury and elegance of the interior, which exhibits a multiplicity of texture, color, and pattern. Alternate light and dark boards are used for flooring, and the wall covering is Lincrusta-Walton, a hand-stamped paper board. Window blinds are hand painted, and Dexter's furniture included a Persian rug and a zinc-lined bathtub. The contrast between exterior and interior is striking.

Cripple Creek Historic District

One of the world's largest gold fields was discovered at Cripple Creek in the Colorado Front Range in 1891, and unlike so many boom areas, the district prospered for many years. During 1901, its peak year, almost $25 million was taken from the field, a record unequaled in the United States. Most of the original structures were destroyed by fire in 1906. The abandoned railroad depot now serves as a municipal museum. Other extant buildings include Johnny Nolan's Saloon and the Western Federation of Miners Building.

Mountain Passes

The narrow, steep-walled ridges along the alpine timberline, known as aretes, are formed where the backs of two glacial cirques meet. As the frost action erodes these ridges over the centuries, they become saw-toothed and eventually disintegrate, forming a mountain pass, also known as a col.

Rocky Mountain Red Cedar

The Rocky Mountain red cedar, a patriarch of the Western forests and very similar to the red cedar of the East, has been known to reach ages of up to 3,000 years. This lonely baron was a favorite with naturalist John Muir: "even when overgrown by avalanches, they refuse to lie at rest, leaning stubbornly on their big elbows." Often this tree is an ancient and wind-swept sentinel, standing alone on a rocky mountainside.

Bighorn Sheep

In summer, mountain sheep browse in small bands to the summits above the timberline until winter drives them down through the open timber and foothills. Rough ground is the typical range of these traditionally sure-footed sheep. They have thick, sharply curving horns. In color they are brownish-gray above, with a dark line along the middle of the back and white under-parts, buttocks, inside of legs, and upper throat. About five feet long, the mountain sheep moves quickly and easily for its size and weight and will bound from ledges 20 feet or more in height.

Alpine fir clinging to high slopes

Beaver dam in an alpine meadow

Alpine Tundra Plant Pioneers

The alpine tundra plants are rugged pioneers that seldom grow as members of plant communities but are found in places where there is little competition for light, water, or nutrients. They frequently colonize open surfaces, such as talus and scree slopes, rock crevices, or open frost scars. As their colonization progresses and the space becomes occupied, conditions are altered sufficiently for plants of the fellfield areas to invade, crowding such pioneers as the big-rooted springbeauty, alpine columbine, alpine kittentails, whiplash saxifrage, goldbloom saxifrage, and alpine sorrel.

Pika

This small, rat-sized cony, grayish or buff-colored, with short round ears and no visible tail is found among the rockslides and talus slopes, usually near timberline in the mountain regions of the West. It is usually found among the boulders of the fellfield areas, where small piles of fresh hay indicate its presence. It is a common sight among the talus slopes in the western national parks such as Yellowstone, Glacier, Crater Lake, and Yosemite.

Snow Accumulation Areas

Snow accumulation is the basic control of the pattern and distribution of alpine tundra plants. The interaction of wind and topography causes snow to begin accumulating in certain areas from autumn on. This snow usually does not melt until the following summer in mid-to-late July, providing a very short growing season, from 6 to 10 weeks, to which only a few plants are adapted. The snow cover areas afford plants considerable protection from the extreme alpine winters. Temperatures underneath a three-foot snowbank range around 27° F, great contrast to the −35° F temperatures above the snow. Common plant indicators of these areas include the snow lily, sibbaldia, snow buttercup, parry clover, arctic willow, snowlover, and black-headed daisy.

Arctic Willow

The tiny arctic willow with a lavender flower grows in slight depressions in the fellfield of mountain tundra, where a shallow snow cover develops in winter. The shrubby branches are completely prostrate and reduced to the size of string. It is one of the most common shrubs of the tundra and is also found around the North Pole.

Alpine Moist Areas

The lush islands of green the hiker may come across above the timberline are alpine moist areas. Water is one of the controlling factors of alpine tundra. Certain alpine plants are confined to these moist places, which are sharply limited and are a conspicuous green in autumn when the rest of the tundra is ochre, gold, and red. There is little free surface water in the tundra, and few flowing streams, even in these sites. Pools that develop behind terraces and ice masses that form in their soil supply these communities with water throughout the growing season. Typical alpine plants found in these moist areas include Nelson willow, white marshmarigold, rose crown, koenigia, and alpine lousewort.

Beaver Meadows

A common sight in the alpine parks of the Rockies are streams with a series of dams and ponds built by several generations of beavers and often stretching for a mile or more in the mountain-rimmed valleys.

A semiaquatic animal, the beaver is the craftsman of the Rockies. The dams are built to block the current to create small, still ponds for its lodge. Over the cut trunks it packs willow branches and mud far enough above water level to form a dry cavity in which a grass bed is laid. The entrance to this chamber is gained through a tunnel opening below the water surface. The beaver, the largest of the rodents, has close, thick, brown fur and is completely at home in the water. Large, strong teeth aid in tree cutting; webbed feet drive the sleek body through swift streams and rivers.

Subalpine Fir

The subalpine fir is a true fir of the Rocky Mountains noted for its purple cones from two to four inches long standing erect on the branch. The cones disintegrate at maturity, leaving a thin spike on the branch. Its needles leave a small, round, depressed scar when pulled from the stem. They are generally found above the 9,000-foot level.

Colorado's Pawnee Buttes

In the prairies of north-central Colorado, near the Wyoming boundary, rise the Pawnee Buttes, limestone cliffs carved by wind and rain, which from a distance resemble an eerie ship sailing across a hazy blue expanse. Their chief interest is the remains of animal life found in their strata. Some catastrophe of the Pliocene and Miocene ages caught innumerable plains animals here. An ancient sea laid over their remains a covering of mud and sand which in the course of centuries turned into limestone. Pawnee Buttes, known to scientists throughout the world, contain the fossilized remains of prehistoric horses and camels.

Pawnee Buttes of northern Colorado, ancient fossil beds surrounded by a vast expanse of national grassland

3. Great Gap in the Rockies— Wyoming Basin

THE vast stretches of sagebrush and alkali flats, sand dunes, and badlands of the Wyoming Basin are an extension of the Great Plains that forms a huge gap, separating the Southern and Central Rockies between the Laramie Range and Bighorn Mountains. Nearly surrounded by mountains, it includes the Great Divide Basin and the Green River Basin; to the north are the Wind River, Bighorn, and Powder River basins.

Laramie Range and Medicine Bow Mountains

Just south of the Colorado-Wyoming boundary the ramparts of the Front Range split along the Continental Divide into two ranges: the Laramie on the east and the Medicine Bow on the west, separated by the sagebrush flats of the Laramie Basin. The Laramie, with its steep eastern slope, is the northern continuation of Colorado's Front Range. Much more rugged are the Medicine Bow Mountains, a plateaulike mass of glacially carved peaks that rise dramatically in the Snowy Range above numerous alpine lake basins.

Fort Laramie National Historic Site

Fort Laramie was established as a center for trade with the Indians of the northern plains in 1834. Situated on the Laramie River Crossing of the California-Oregon Trail, it was purchased in 1849 for army use as a base for guarding the overland trails, controlling the Indians of the region, and extending American influence. A Pony Express station was located here in 1860–1861, and the post was a hub in the transportation and communications of the northern plains and mountains. Its troops were involved in numerous campaigns and treaties designed to pacify the northern Plains Indians. It was abandoned in 1890.

The fort is located in Wyoming's Goshen County about three miles southwest of the town of Fort Laramie.

Swan Land and Cattle Company Headquarters

The Swan Land and Cattle Company, established in 1883, was among the prominent foreign stock con-

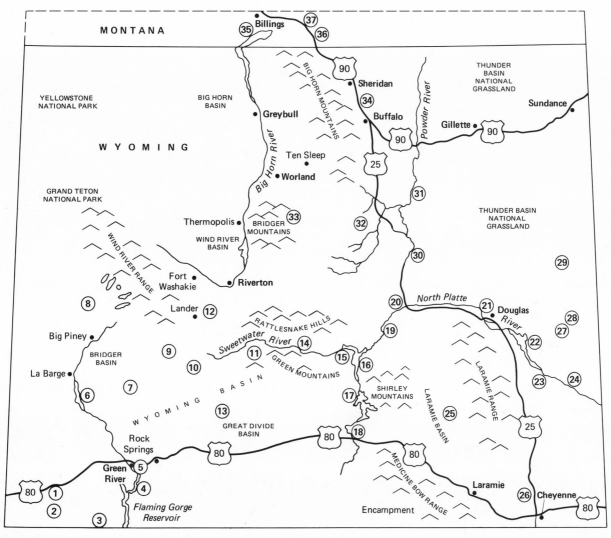

Key to Sites

1. Fort Bridger (1843)
2. Fort Supply Mormon Farms
3. Site of the first Rocky Mountain trappers' and traders' rendezvous, July 1825
4. Firehole Region
5. Expedition Island
6. Fontenelle Reservoir
7. Site of the historic "Big Sandy" Stage Station
8. Father De Smet's "Prairie Mass" site
9. South Pass City
10. South Pass on the Continental Divide (7,550 ft.)
11. Oregon Trail Crossing
12. Site of the first oil well drilled in Wyoming, 1884

13. Red Desert Basin and Sand Dunes
14. Independence Rock on the Oregon Trail
15. Old Sweetwater River Crossing on the Oregon Trail
16. Pathfinder Reservoir
17. Seminoe Reservoir on the North Platte River
18. Remains of Fort Steele
19. Red Buttes
20. Site of the Mormon Ferry on the North Platte, built by Brigham Young in 1847
21. Site of Fort Fetterman, 1867
22. Glendo Reservoir
23. Historic Warm Springs
24. Fort Laramie

25. Como Bluff Dinosaur Fossil Beds
26. Old Cheyenne to Deadwood Stage Road
27. Spanish Diggings Aboriginal Stone Quarries
28. Texas Trail to Montana, 1876-1897
29. Area where the famous "horned dinosaurs" were discovered
30. Teapot Dome
31. Powder River Crossing, 1878-1892
32. Red Canyon country and Hole-in-the-Wall
33. World's largest mineral hot springs
34. Fort Phil Kearney
35. Bighorn Canyon
36. Little Bighorn River
37. Custer Battlefield National Monument

cerns that flourished in the American West during the heyday of the range cattle industry. Organized in Scotland, the company grazed more than 113,000 head of cattle on more than a million acres of grassland within three years. Turning to sheep in 1911, the Swan Company built sizable herds, reaching a peak of 112,000 head. Surviving buildings associated with the early days of the operation include the ranch house and barn (1876) and a store housing the ranch commissary (1913).

The headquarters site is on private land on the east side of Chugwater in Wyoming's Platte County.

Wyoming's Gangplank Area

Cutting across the surface of the Laramie Range is the 8,500-foot ramp of the Gangplank area, a gently undulating surface covered with a thick mantle of weathered granite debris. Here, the alluvial deposits of the Great Plains were merged with the eruption of the granite core of the Front Range.

Elk browsing in the Medicine Bow Mountains

Fort Laramie—a frontier trading post and Pony Express station on Wyoming's High Plains

Badlands in the Great Divide Basin

Laramie Basin

The wind-swept sagebrush flats and rangelands of the Laramie Basin extend for 2,700 square miles in south-central Wyoming between the Medicine Bow Mountains on the west and the Laramie Range on the east. One of the most interesting features of the basin is Big Hollow, a blowout created by wind erosion that lies just west of Laramie and is about 300 feet deep, nine miles long, and three miles wide.

Fort Fetterman on the North Platte

Fort Fetterman was established as a military post in July 1867 on the North Platte River at the crossroads of the Bozeman Trail and earlier overland routes. The fort was intended to provide protection against hostile Indians. Its strategic location caused it to become a supply base, headquarters, and marshalling point for army expeditions against the Indians of the northern plains. The post was named for Lieutenant Colonel William J. Fetterman, who was killed in an Indian battle near Fort Phil Kearney in December 1866. Fort Fetterman was no longer needed once the power of the Indians was broken; it was abandoned in 1882. It still contains two original structures: a log officers' quarters (now used as a museum and caretaker's house) and a rammed earth ordnance warehouse. Only foundations of the other buildings remain.

The fort is located in Wyoming's Converse County on the Orpha County Road, one mile west of Orpha Road, seven miles north of Interstate 25.

Fort Steele—Frontier Outpost

Fort Steele was one of three forts set up to protect the railroad during its construction. It was also used as a supply post during the army's wars with the Plains Indians. The fort was established on June 30, 1868. The post was named for Maj. General Frederick Steele, a Civil War hero. Indian disturbances in the area were kept to a minimum, and Fort Steele exerted a stabilizing influence on the population. Abandoned by the army on August 7, 1886, the site became a small civilian community along the transcontinental railroad. The Union Pacific trains still pass through, but the town and the fort are largely deserted. Parts of the original fort still in existence are the commanding officer's quarters, two large warehouses, a powder magazine, and several smaller buildings.

The fort is located on the North Platte River in Wyoming's Carbon County at the point of the Union Pacific Railroad crossing.

Great Divide Basin—Land of the Mustang

The vast stretches of the Great Divide Basin cover 2.25 million acres of sagebrush country, dry creeks, sand dunes, alkali flats, buttes, badlands of rain-eroded honeycomb sandstone formations, and rolling hills in southwestern Wyoming where the Continental Divide cuts through the state. The high plains of the basin are inhabited by about 2,000 wild horses or mustangs, descended from once-domesticated stock and now protected by federal law; pronghorn antelope; and coyotes. Just north of the basin is South Pass, where the Continental Divide leaves the soaring spires of the massive Wind River Range, drops into the foothills, and meanders across the High Plains. The Oregon Trail crossed the Great Divide here and was the main route across the Rockies for emigrant wagon trains, stagecoaches, and Pony Express riders. Just

Mustangs in the Red Desert of the Great Divide Basin— home of some 2,000 wild horses

Short-grass prairies of Wyoming's High Plains lying in the dry Rocky Mountain rain shadow

south of the pass, at the northern rim of the Great Divide Basin, are the Oregon Buttes, where the Continental Divide splits in two, encircles the basin, and rejoins some 90 miles to the southwest near the Colorado border.

Pathfinder Dam

The Pathfinder Dam—named for the Pathfinder of the West, John Charles Fremont—was one of two built within the same 20-year period. Its twin is the Buffalo Bill Dam (see separate listing). Both dams were the physical outgrowth of scientist-engineer John Wesley Powell's theory of arid-lands reclamation; both gave evidence of the federal government's concern about national economic development, with particular emphasis on regional problems. These were the first large-scale masonry arch dams built by the Department of the Interior's Bureau of Reclamation. The water thus impounded serves large sections of Wyoming and Nebraska. The reservoir, located at the confluence of the North Platte and Sweetwater rivers in the Great Divide Basin, has a shoreline greater than 75 miles and a storage potential of more than 1 million acre-feet of water. Built of locally quarried granite blocks, the dam stands 214 feet high, has a crest of 432 feet, and tapers upward from a width of 87 feet to 11 feet.

The dam is located 45 miles southwest of Casper in Wyoming's Natrona County.

Tom Sun Ranch in Sweetwater Valley

The Tom Sun Ranch in the Sweetwater Valley of central Wyoming typifies the medium-sized ranching operations of the open-range period. Tom Sun, a French Canadian frontiersman, became a respected pioneer cattleman, establishing operations in 1872 on the Oregon Trail near Devil's Gate and Independence Rock. The present ranchhouse includes the original log building built by Sun and several outbuildings and corrals believed to be original.

The ranch is six miles west of Independence Rock on Wyoming Highway 220.

Range Fences

Along the road leading to the ranch, there is a stretch of buck-and-pole fence, weathered but standing firm. The rails dip gently from the weight of winter snow, and the wood is the gentle silver of aged lodgepole, with rust stains where rain has trickled over the heads of the spikes that hold it together. The work that went into the fence is obvious to the careful eye: neatly hewn notches in the poles, even, handsawn joints where the bucksticks cross, stout X-braces every fifth panel, all assembled with a rhythmic quality that distinguished craftsmanship. A few fresh-cut bucks and poles stand out where the fence crosses a willow bog and moisture rots the pine. The new poles are dry but still a tawny, unweathered beige.

Most of the fence in the West is barbed wire, which goes up fast and will hold cattle. It can also cut them up. A horse that gets a stray twist looped around a pastern is in serious trouble. So is a deer or elk calf that tries to leap a wire fence and gets a hind leg twined between the two upper strands, to be caught just as surely as if a trap had been intended. Death from shock and dehydration follows, and cowhands riding fence in the spring will come upon the remains, or whatever part the coyotes have left. A lot of people use barbed wire, but it comes in for a big share of cussing by those who string it or fix it. Like a lot of "improvements" it gets the job done without inspiring much affection.

There are other ways of holding stock that existed before Joseph Glidden invented barbed wire, and they all had this in common: they used native materials in such a manner as to get the best fence for the purpose with the least amount of labor. In rocky areas stones cleared from agricultural ground were piled into walls, accomplishing two tasks with one operation. In places where timber was plentiful, fencing methods grew out of the qualities of the timber, soil, topography and weather, and certain types of fence were specific to areas where they represented the most efficient type.

In the Eastern and Central United States, hardwood timber and easily dug soils produced the post and split-rail fence, often with tight mortise joints. In the Southwest deserts juniper and pinyon could be used for fence that was stacked as much as built of the gnarled trunks. In the high cattle range, lodgepole pine combined with hardpan or rocky soils made buck-and-pole fences useful, with log-and-block styles making use of heavier timber and zig-zag fences being built of aspen as well as the more common pine. In each case the builders generally used the easiest material available and put it together in a manner suited to the purpose in mind and the tools in hand.

"Buck-and-pole" fence—a common sight on the Rocky Mountain range

Besides local conditions, a source of variation in fencing styles is related to the needs each fence will serve. A corral for horse-breaking is a good example. The stout posts are set deep to resist the impact of a bronc crashing into the fence. The rails or planks are heavy and are placed on the inside so they cannot be kicked off; they are set close together so a horse's leg will not plunge between them during a fit of bucking. The overall shape is round or oval rather than square so that horses cannot bunch up in the corners where they are difficult to rope and so that a horse being ridden can be kept moving at a steady pace. These qualities are more than a matter of style: serious and sometimes fatal accidents have been the unhappy result of working stock in a poorly designed or built enclosure.

By contrast, a drift fence, which is used to hold or direct cattle over a much wider area, can be simpler in construction and more lightly built. Its purpose is to turn cattle, and a mama cow is not the most agile of creatures. A buck-and-pole fence, also known as jack fence, serves the purpose and lasts better than barbed wire on snow-covered ranges where drifting and freezing snaps strands of wire easily. Another advantage of buck-and-pole fences and timber fences in general is that they do not trap game like barbed wire. Also to be considered for those short of cash and long on muscle is that if timber is available, a hundred pounds of spikes fences more ground than a hundred pounds of wire, besides being easier to pack. A few common tools—ax, shovel, digging bar, hammer— and the ranch has got a fence.

The main types of timber fence in the West can be categorized (like the residents) by their means of support. Post fences have the uprights, usually pine or juniper, sunk into the ground with poles nailed or bolted between, the number dependent on the type of stock to be held. Buck fences have X-shaped supports that rest on the surface, making this type appropriate for hard or rocky ground. There can be between three and seven rails per panel, with diagonal bracing used for rigidity. A primitive type of fence similar to the buck fence is called rip-gut fence because of the upturned points of its propped and wedged rails which discourage climbing. Of striking appearance is the zig-zag fence, also descriptively titled worm or snake fence. It has no proper supports, the overlapped poles requiring only a pair of stays to hold them in alignment. A final type is the log-and-block fence which is constructed of heavier timber lengths laid perpendicular to short pieces—the blocks—and notched to fit, log-cabin style.

Most travellers on interstate highways will see little else but wire fence except when they pass a real-estate development or a tourist trap where timber fence is used to lend an aura of authenticity and picturesqueness. On less-travelled routes or mountain roads, timber fences will often line the right-of-way. National parks, remote ranches, and abandoned homesteads have an interesting variety of fences in conditions all the way from brand-new (not even any rust on the nailheads) to a state of disrepair somewhere between heap and mulch.

A log fence, weathered and gently settled under snow and gravity, fits gracefully into the landscape of the rural west. It follows the slope and contour of hills, wanders around boulders or patches of marsh, never exactly straight, reflecting the impartial judgment of seasons on the work of its builders as it ages with dignity, often seeming to have grown in place.

Coyotes

The coyote, or "little wolf," was a common sight on the Western prairies in earlier times, its nightly serenade ringing out from the summits of the buttes. In spite of persecution by man, the coyote is just as common today in many parts of its range. Coyotes were originally blamed for serious wildlife losses until the results of careful research showed that the chief diet of the coyote consists of marmots, picket-pins, mice, rabbits, and other small animals as well as carrion. It was customarily assumed that when coyotes were seen on a carcass that they were the cause of the death, when many of the animals died from other causes before coyotes found them.

Coyote—"little wolf" of the Western rangelands and high country

This rather small, slender animal resembles a shepherd dog in general appearance, with a fairly long and heavy coat that is coarsely grizzled, buffy, grayish and black (almost yellowish in some cases), with lighter underparts. Its tail is large and bushy. Its total length is from 3 and a half to 4 and a half feet and weighs between 35 and 45 pounds.

The coyote is found throughout the West at practically all elevations, but especially in open meadows and rangelands.

Oregon Trail Remnants and the South Pass

Wyoming's South Pass is a long, treeless valley in the Great Divide Basin; 25 miles wide, it is broken by low, flat-topped sagebrush hills and pyramidal sand dunes. Old wagon tracks of the Oregon Trail, which passed through here, were once so numerous that the valley resembled an old plowed field, grassed over before the furrows were pulverized. These wagon tracks and graves of emigrants have been preserved. The snow-capped peaks of the Wind River Mountains rise ahead. The incline on both approaches is so gradual that the early trappers and explorers topped the summit, unaware that they were crossing the Continental Divide. Even the explorer, Fremont, guided by Kit Carson, was in doubt about the highest point.

By 1843, wagon trains of emigrants were wearing deep tracks in the earth of South Pass, known as the Lander Cutoff of the Oregon Trail, toward the Pacific. During the next two decades it is estimated that some 300,000 pioneers—in covered wagons, on horseback, or pushing handcarts—crossed the pass. In the late 1850s, the stagecoach provided faster transportation. The Pony Express was inaugurated in 1860, and in 1861 the first telegraph line in the region wove through the pass.

Although Indian uprisings caused the shift of the freight and stage lines southward in 1862 to what became known as the Overland Trail, private wagon trains continued using the South Pass route because of its abundant grass and water. The wagons became fewer, however, as the Union Pacific Railroad advanced westward.

South Pass City—Frontier Gold Rush Town

South Pass City was laid out in 1867, when miners and adventurers began to pour into Wyoming's Sweetwater gold country. The town reached a peak of prosperity in 1870, but declined thereafter as mining activity petered out. During its heyday South Pass City served as county seat of Sweetwater County, and

South Pass City, frontier gold-rush town—view of the exchange bank, recorder's office, Grecian Bend Saloon, and the Idaho House

Wyoming's first female justice of the peace, Mrs. Esther Morris, presided over 34 cases there between February and November 1870. Original buildings still standing are a store, bar and hotel, former Wells Fargo office, a dugout, and a log dwelling.

The town is located about 10 miles northeast of South Pass (which see) in Wyoming's Fremont County.

Independence Rock on the Oregon Trail

Called the great registry of the desert, Independence Rock was a well-known natural landmark on the Oregon Trail. This oblong mass, over 1,900 feet long and 850 feet wide, lies near the Sweetwater River where the Oregon Trail first approaches it, making it a favorite stopping and resting place for travellers. The rock soon became famous because of the numerous names painted, carved, or written on its face. The landmark and its environs are little changed from that era.

Independence Rock is located in Wyoming's Natrona County, 60 miles southwest of Casper on State Highway 220.

Names Hill on the Oregon Trail

Names Hill on the Green River is one of three places (Register Cliff on the North Platte and Indedendence Rock on the Sweetwater) along the Oregon-California Trail where emigrants carved their names or left messages and greetings for those following. In 1844, Jim Bridger, famous trapper and mountain man,

left his name here. The earliest dated name is 1822, earlier than any dated inscription at either of the other two locations. Names Hill was a popular camping spot and was used frequently by westward-moving emigrants.

Names Hill is located in Wyoming's Lincoln County on the Green River, five miles south of the Town of La Barge and just west of U. S. Highway 189.

Oregon Trail markers guided about 300,000 pioneers across the South Pass toward the Pacific

Badlands

A common feature of the central Rocky Mountain basins are the grotesquely shaped wind- and water-sculptured areas of shale and sandstone. Two of the best examples of badland formations are the huge rain-eroded holes and crevasses of the 20,000-acre Honeycombs in the Great Divide Basin and Hell's Halfacre at the headwaters of the South Fork of the Powder River, about 40 miles west of Casper, Wyoming.

Jim Bridger's Pass on the Great Divide

During the period of America's westward migration, Bridger's Pass, named for trapper and army scout Jim Bridger, was one of the most important passes over the Continental Divide. Bridger guided Captain Howard Stansbury and his men over the pass in 1850. Stansbury had been sent out by the federal government in 1849 to explore and survey the valley of the Great Salt Lake. His crossing of the divide through Bridger's Pass helped publicize the route for overland travel, which increased steadily in the decade preceding the Civil War. In 1862 a section of the overland stage line was rerouted through Bridger's Pass, but, on completion of the transcontinental railroad (1869), the stage line was forced to suspend operations. The pass then reverted to its original quiet natural setting.

The pass is located near Rawlins in Wyoming's Carbon County.

Eroded rock formations, common in the Wyoming Basin

Cheyenne–Deadwood Stage Trail

The Cheyenne–Black Hills Stage route ran between Cheyenne, Wyoming, and Deadwood, South Dakota. Thousands of passengers, tons of freight and express, and millions of dollars in gold passed over this trail from 1876 to 1887, when the advent of the railroad drove the stage line out of business. Both the stage stations were typical of the road-ranches scattered throughout the west wherever stage lines existed. The Cheyenne-Deadwood Trail ran to Fort Laramie, then north to Rawhide Buttes and Running Water. It served as a main artery to the Black Hills goldfields. Rawhide Springs, between the two stage stations, possessed water and grass in quantity and so became a favorite camping spot along the trail. The Cheyenne–Black Hills Stage Company carried mail to the Black Hills, and numerous robberies of gold and mail by armed desperadoes occurred along the route. The coming of the railroad brought an influx of settlers, but it meant the end of the stage line. Today, the Running Water Station is marked only by stone ruins, but the Rawhide Buttes Station still stands and is used as a ranch.

The stage trail is located in Wyoming's Goshen County, one mile west to about 15 miles southwest of the town of Lusk.

Playas and Alkali Flats

The rainfall in the arid sagebrush basins of western Wyoming flows into small pockets known as playas or ephemeral lakes whose waters evaporate to form white alkali deposits on the basin floors.

Sand Dunes of the Rocky Mountain Basins

Sand dunes are found at scattered sites throughout the Wyoming Basin, as are silt dunes in the Great Divide Basin, which have been formed from the silt and mud washed into the areas' playas.

Green River Basin

The vast ranchlands, sagebrush flats, mesas, ridges, and buttes form the Green River Basin in southwestern Wyoming, some 170 miles long and 140 miles wide, flanked on the north by the glacier-carved summits of the Wind River Range and Gros Ventre Mountains, on the south by Utah's Uinta Mountains, on the west by the Wyoming Range, and on the east by the Rock Springs Uplift. The basin is drained by the upper

Pioneer ranch in the beautiful Wind River foothills of the Green River Valley

Green River, which flows from its headwaters high in the Bridger Wilderness section of the Wind River Range through the basin and the Lodore Canyon in the Uinta Mountains into the Uinta Basin of the Colorado Plateau.

Green River Rocky Mountain Trappers' Rendezvous Site

Of all the rendezvous sites connected with the Rocky Mountain fur trade, the most popular was that on the Green River. The rendezvous, instituted by General William Ashley, was an annual trading fair held each spring to which trappers, traders, and Indians came. The great supply caravans from St. Louis brought trade goods to exchange for the furs. Among the foremost figures who came were Kit Carson, Jedediah Smith, and Jim Bridger. The rendezvous area is in a natural state, almost unchanged from its condition when fur trappers gathered there.

The first gathering in the vicinity, conducted by Thomas Broken Hand Fitzpatrick, was small, with only the employees of William H. Ashley's Rocky Mountain Fur Company participating. The next year Ashley selected a spot on Henrys Fork of the Green River—and posted signs inviting all trappers to attend. After that, until the end of the free trapping era in the 1840s when beaver hats went out of fashion in London and Paris, the rendezvous was an annual event vital to the industry.

Trappers trekked in singly, in pairs, and in groups, to swap their catch for the powder, traps, and other things they needed. Rival companies competed with gusto—and not too many scruples—for pelts already taken and for the future services of trappers. Sometimes more than 1,500 men took part in the daily activities. Trading went on briskly at fixed hours, followed usually by target shooting, wrestling, horse racing, and gambling. By day men lounged in the shade of the cottonwood trees, while their animals fed on the lush valley grasses. At night the air vibrated with the pounding of tom-toms, the chanting of Indians, the barking of dogs, and the singing, cursing, and laughter of white men.

The site is located on the Green River above and below the town of Daniel in Wyoming's Sublette County.

Wardell Indian Buffalo Trap

Archeological investigation of the Wardell site was begun in June 1970. Outlines of an ancient fence near the end of a box canyon were uncovered. Animals were driven into the canyon from below. The site was found to be rich in artifact material, and three distinct periods of use were evident in the trap. Bone preservation varied from poor to good, and variations in butchering methods are beginning to appear under analysis. The actual butchering and processing area has been located. It contained food preparation pits, stone heating pits, and artifact material.

The buffalo trap is located six miles east and two miles north of Big Piney in Wyoming's Sublette County.

Father De Smet's Prairie Mass Site

On this site in 1840, Father Pierre-Jean De Smet celebrated the first recorded mass of the Roman Catholic Church in the northern Rocky Mountains. Father De Smet (1801–1873), a Belgian, came to America in 1821 and entered the novitiate of the Jesuit order. Ordained in 1827, he embarked upon his lifetime work as a missionary to the Indians 11 years later. The occasion for the prairie mass was the annual fur traders' rendezvous near present-day Daniel on the Upper Green River. A granite cross has been erected on the site, which is a broad, open plain atop a bluff overlooking the river valley. Father De Smet, affectionately called Blackrobe, became a well-known and trusted friend of the Plains and Pacific Northwest Indians and frequently acted as a mediator when trouble broke out between tribes or between red man and white.

Glenrock Indian Buffalo Jump

The Glenrock Buffalo Jump is partly situated on a large, flat plateau that has abundant grass and water and extends to the edge of a 40-foot bluff—the jump-off point. Below the bluff is a talus slope. A large number of bones have been found in the soil of the talus slope. The buffalo jump dates from the Late Prehistoric period. The butchering site is believed to be at the base of the talus slope, but the area has not been excavated. Buffalo herds were driven over the cliff without the aid of horses. First, a herd of sufficient size had to be gathered and carefully driven to a point where it could be stampeded toward the jump-off. Most buffalo jumps have been destroyed by the recovery of bones for commercial use, and few have had adequate archeological work performed. The Glenrock Buffalo Jump is unique in being undisturbed, and plans are being made to conduct proper archeological investigations.

The jump, which was in use from A.D. 500 to 1750, is located about two miles west of the Glenrock Interchange on Interstate 25 in Wyoming's Converse County.

Expedition Island on the Green River

The town of Green River, Wyoming, on the Union Pacific Railroad, was the starting point for the two expeditions down the Green and Colorado rivers led by Major John Wesley Powell in 1869 and 1871. On these expeditions, Powell completed the exploration of the last, large, unknown land area in the continental United States.

No conclusive information has been found to indicate the precise campsite or embarkation point of the first expedition, but the second camped on Expedition Island and left from there May 22, 1871. Here the men prepared their specially designed boats for the arduous voyage ahead. In the absence of positive information as to the 1869 campsite, Expedition Island is recognized as the appropriate site to commemorate both trips.

Fort Bridger on Black's Fork of the Green River

Fort Bridger may be considered as one of the two most important forts in this area of the country with regard to overland migration, the other being Fort Laramie. Fort Bridger was named for fur trapper and mountain man Jim Bridger, who opened a trading post on the site in 1843. As time passed, his trading post became a major resupply and oufitting point for emi-grants, gold seekers, adventurers, and explorers and a stopping place for friendly Indians. The Mormons acquired and held the fort from 1853 until 1857. In 1858 Fort Bridger became a U. S. Army post. During the 1860s, it served as a Pony Express, overland telegraph, and overland stage station. When the Indians were finally subdued, the protection offered by the fort was no longer needed, and the post was abandoned on October 1, 1880.

The fort is located near the town of Fort Bridger in Wyoming's Uinta County.

Wind River Basin

The Wind River Basin, a forbidding area of low, sagebrush-covered hills, ridges, and wind-carved badlands, is a broad depression in north-central Wyoming between the Wind River Mountains on the south and the volcanic crags of the Absaroka Range and Owl Mountains on the north.

Fort Washakie at the Wind River Indian Reservation

Fort Washakie was founded to protect the Bannock and Shoshone Indian reservations from attacks by wandering hostiles. It also served as a supply base for expeditions to Yellowstone National Park (which was established in 1872) and the Big Horn country. The fort was provided for in a treaty between the federal government and the Shoshone Indians signed at Fort Bridger on July 3, 1868. A series of camps at several locations were built before the permanent post was established on the present site in 1871. Originally called Camp Brown to honor Capt. Frederick H. Brown, killed at the Fetterman massacre (December 26, 1866), the post was renamed in December 1878 for the Shoshone chief Washakie. Chief Washakie is buried in the post cemetery. The post was abandoned early in 1909 and became the property of the U. S. Department of the Interior's Bureau of Indian Affairs. The Shoshone share the reservation lands with the Arapaho.

The reservation is on U. S. Highway 287, northeast of the Wind River Mountains in Wyoming's Fremont County.

Castle Gardens Indian Petroglyph Site

The cliffs on which the petroglyphs appear are six miles long and one mile wide, with drawings scattered all along the vertical face, which ranges from 10 to

Working cattle ranch in the Wind River Basin

100 feet high. A wide variety of forms appear, from simple to highly complex. The petroglyphs were executed with stone tools using techniques of pecking, rubbing, grinding, and fine-line incising. Particularly significant designs are figures of water turtles and recurrent circular shield motifs. All the numerous rock formations created by wind and water erosion, when combined with the natural landscape, give the impression of a medieval castle surrounded by gardens— hence the name. The age and specific meaning of these petroglyphs are not known.

The petroglyphs are located about 28 miles south of Moneta on U. S. Highway 20-26 in Wyoming's Fremont County.

Fort Phil Kearny on the Bozeman Trail

In and around Fort Phil Kearny the Sioux Indians fought successfully to prevent invasion of their hunting grounds by prospectors and wagon trains bound for the Montana gold fields. From 1866 to 1868 the fort was held under virtual siege as the focus of the Red Cloud War, which resulted in relinquishment of military control of the area and the abandonment of the Bozeman Trail. The natural setting of Fort Phil Kearny has suffered comparatively little encroachment.

In 1938 a peeled-log reproduction of an officers' quarters and a seven-foot slab stockade were erected here.

The fort is located in Wyoming's Johnson County on the secondary road west of U. S. Highway 87 near the town of Story.

Woodruff Frontier Cabin Site

The cabin of John Dwight Woodruff was the first recorded white man's dwelling in the Big Horn Basin, the entire northwestern corner of Wyoming. Only the cabin site remains today, marked by a rock-and-mortar monument. From pictures it has been estimated that the cabin measured 12 feet wide by 20 feet long, was constructed of logs, and was covered with several inches of dirt on the roof to absorb moisture. Woodruff used the cabin in the winter, spring, and early summer as a headquarters while trapping and prospecting. He eventually introduced both sheep and cattle into the area, and the cabin may have served as a ranch house. Woodruff sold his cabin in the early 1880s, and buildings of the Embar Ranch presently form a semicircle around the cabin site.

The site is 26 miles northwest of Thermopolis and 18 miles west on the County Route from the intersection with Wyoming Highway 120.

Wyoming's Red Canyon Country

Wyoming's Red Canyon, or Hole-in-the-Wall, is a jutting fault 35 miles long along the Middle Fork of the Powder River in the northeastern part of the state. The Red Wall country was long an Indian and pioneer hunting ground, and tributaries of the Big Horn and Powder rivers, which have their headwaters in this country, bear such names as Beartrap, Otter, and Buffalo. In 1876, after the Custer battle, Dull Knife and Little Wolf led the Cheyenne and Arapaho here. On the eve of November 26 General Mackenzie surrounded Dull Knife's camp on the Red Fork of the Powder. At dawn, with 1,100 troopers, he surprised the sleeping Cheyenne and drove them from their lodges. The

Indians rallied in the hills and fought until mid-afternoon, but Mackenzie destroyed their camp and supplies. Almost naked, the Cheyenne made their way to the Sioux camp of Crazy Horse, 70 miles away. Men, women, and children walked through deep snow, leaving a trail of blood. In the camp, the soldiers found many articles that had belonged to Custer's men.

The famous Hole-in-the-Wall, near the old Bozeman road and not two days' hard ride from the Union Pacific Railroad, was an outlaw hideout for half a century. In its 35-mile length there was only one eastern entrance, which a few armed men could easily defend, but on the west trails led to Montana, Idaho, Utah, and Colorado. It was used over the years by members of the James gang, Butch Cassidy and his wild bunch, Flat Nose George Curry, and Nate Champion. In the Red Canyon region today ranches sprawl along the green cottonwood bottoms beside Buffalo Creek and cattle and sheep graze among the hills.

Ruins of an old Army fort in the Bighorn Basin, built during the Indian scare of the 1890s

Sage hen on the arid Bighorn Basin flats

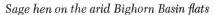

Wyoming's Spanish Diggings

The Spanish Diggings are located in northeastern Wyoming among the rugged hills, rocky gulches, and bare mesas of the Rawhide Range. Scattered prehistoric quarries and village sites and outcroppings of jasper, agate, and quartzite cover an area of 400 square miles. Before white traders introduced metals, the aboriginal Indian tribes used quartzite and jasper for arrow and spear heads, knives, and hide scrapers. The soil has drifted considerably, vegetation is scarce, and little molds cover the work pits and ancient refuse heaps. Partly filled quarries are 25 to 30 feet in diameter and 10 to 30 feet deep. Fine flakes or chips are rare, and rejected articles display a very rough handiwork. Identical materials have been found in the Indian mounds of the Ohio and Mississippi valleys, and it is assumed that these rough pieces were transported down the Platte and Mississippi rivers to Indian work sites. Stone knives, wedges, mauls, hammers, axes, grinders, and other implements are scattered over the diggings. Rough drawings of animals have been found in caves here, and a stone cross about 90 feet long, with 16-foot arms, lies on a northern slope. From the foot of the cross two parallel rows of cairns run northward for more than a mile. No Indian burial places have been found, however, and the only signs of habitation are old tepee rings. It is believed that the camps were maintained only while workmen quarried the raw material. It has been estimated that the quarries are from 250 to 5,000 years old.

The early range riders called the area the Mexican Mine. Two ranchers, assuming that the area had been worked by the Spanish conquistadores, prospected here in hopes of finding gold. Since 1893 several major universities have sent expeditions into the diggings.

Bighorn Basin and Pryor Mountain Wild Horse Range

Enclosed on the west and east by the Absaroka and Bighorn ranges and lesser mountains, the elliptical Bighorn Basin covers an area of the Great Plains about 150 miles long and 100 miles wide bisected by the Bighorn River in northwestern Wyoming and southwestern Montana. Ancient geological forces formed the immense walls, or anticlimes, surrounding the basin. The largest of these natural arches is the Bighorn, which extends south from Bighorn Lake and the Yellowtail Dam to form the Bighorn Mountains. The Bighorn River has cut a deep canyon through this great arch, exposing colorful towering cliffs and fossil-bearing rocks up to 500 million years old.

Beyond the western portion of the Bighorn Canyon National Recreation Area lie the sagebrush-covered foothills and flats of the 31,000-acre Pryor Mountain Wild Horse Area, established to preserve the natural habitat of more than 200 mustangs.

Custer Battlefield in the Little Bighorn River Valley

The clash between northern Plains Indians and the United States Army in the valley of the Little Bighorn River on June 25–26, 1876, is commemorated at Custer Battlefield National Monument. The battle was

Custer and Crow Indian scouts in 1873

"Battle of Little Bighorn," interpreted by Sioux Chief Red Horse

Bighorn Canyon with Pryor Mountain Wild Horse Range in background. The old Bozeman Trail, a shortcut to the gold fields of western Montana, passed through this area.

precipitated by shrinkage of Indian land and the government's ultimatum to come into the reservations by January 31, 1876. The Sioux and Cheyenne Indians instead rallied around the Sioux leader Sitting Bull, who advocated resistance. In the resulting battle, Lieutenant Colonel George A. Custer and every member of his immediate command of about 225 men were killed. The other seven companies of the regiment managed to defend themselves for about two days, five miles south of where the Custer contingent was annihilated.

The battlefield is located in Montana's Big Horn County, 15 miles south of Hardin.

4. Middle Rockies

THE Middle Rocky Mountains form an irregular area that encompasses a variety of mountain formations ranging from the broad, folded summits of the Bighorn, Beartooth, and Wind River ranges on the east to the fault-formed Uinta, Wasatch, and Teton ranges on the west to the volcano-formed Yellowstone Plateau and Absaroka Mountains on the north. The Middle Rockies are nearly broken on the south by the Wyoming Basin and on the north by the Yellowstone volcanic plateau and Snake River high lava plain.

Rocky Mountain Canyons— Rivers Across the Mountains

An unusual feature of the waterways in the Rocky Mountains is the large number of streams that flow directly across mountains through deep gorges. Examples of these streams that have been let down from a former mountain formation include the Wind River Canyon through the Owl Creek Mountains in north-central Wyoming, the Snake River Canyon south of Jackson Hole through the Teton Range, Devil's Gate of the Sweetwater River north of Wyoming's Medicine

Bow Mountains, the spectacular Bighorn Canyon through the Bighorn Mountains, the Shoshone River Canyon through the Absaroka Mountains near Cody, Wyoming, the Big Hole River through the Highland Range in southwestern Montana, the Royal Gorge of the Arkansas through Colorado's Front Range of the Rockies, and the Lodore Canyon of the Green River through the Uinta Mountains.

Fossil Butte National Monument— Remnant of an Ancient Subtropical Lake

The brightly colored red, purple, yellow, and gray base of Fossil Butte rises from the Cundrick Ridge in southwestern Wyoming, surrounded by arid rangelands of wild rye, Indian rice grass, and June grass, mixed with sagebrush, snowbush, greasewood, and rabbit brush. On the high north-facing slopes are scattered stands of Douglas fir and limber pine. At the lower elevations, willow thickets mark the course of the streams. In autumn, golden stands of aspen dot the ravines on the southwestern face of the ridge. Mule deer, elk, moose, pronghorn antelopes, coyotes, and golden eagles are commonly sighted residents of

70

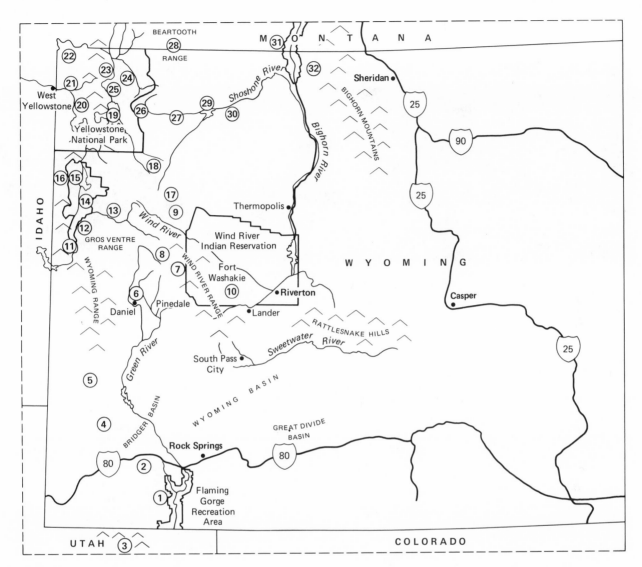

Key to Sites

1. Flaming Gorge Reservoir
2. Granger Stage Station on the Old Oregon Trail
3. Uinta Mountains
4. Fossil Butte
5. Absaroka Ridge
6. Rocky Mountain trappers' rendezvous site
7. Gannett Peak, at 13,804 ft., the highest point in the Middle Rockies
8. Squaretop Mountain
9. Dubois
10. Sacajawea's grave site
11. Snake River
12. Jackson and the National Elk Refuge
13. Gros Ventre River
14. Moose—Grand Teton National Park headquarters
15. Jackson Lake
16. Grand Teton National Park and Jackson Hole
17. The Ramshorn in the Washakie Wilderness
18. Thorofare Plateau—headwaters of the Yellowstone River
19. Yellowstone Lake
20. Old Faithful and the Finehole River Geyser Basin
21. Madison River
22. Gallatin Range
23. Mt. Washburn, 10,243 ft.
24. Mirror Plateau and Specimen Ridge
25. Grand Canyon of the Yellowstone
26. Hoodoo Basin Area of the Absaroka Range
27. Wapiti Valley
28. Beartooth Plateau and glaciers
29. Buffalo Bill Reservoir
30. Cody
31. Bighorn Canyon Recreation Area
32. Indian Medicine Wheel

A typical Rocky Mountain canyon, carved by rivers cutting across the uplands

this rugged Rocky Mountain landscape of western Wyoming.

Fossil Butte contains the most important record of freshwater fossil fish ever found in the United States. The butte is a portion of the bed of an ancient lake that existed during the Eocene epoch 50 million years ago. The fossil remains of this subtropical lake bed have been found in the upper buff-white layer of laminated limestone averaging 18 inches thick. The fossils discovered here include several varieties of perch as well as freshwater genera and several kinds of herring whose descendants now live in saltwater. Other fish fossils include those of paddlefish, stingray, and catfish. The underlying rock formation contains fossil fragments of primitive horses, tortoise shells, ancestral monkeys, snakes, birds, and crocodiles.

The Fossil Lake expanded and contracted several times during the Eocene epoch with changes in the climate. Fish died in great numbers and settled undisturbed into the lake bottom. Layers of sediment gradually turning to limestone kept intact their skeletons, delicate fins, tail rays, and even their scales.

A trail with interpretive wayside markers leads from the national monument visitor center near the town of Kemmerer up to the site of the old fossil quarries on the butte.

Granger Stage Station on the Oregon Trail

A great westward migration to California and Oregon began in the 1840s. Wagons, cattle, and settlers crossed the country in great numbers, and trails and river fords came into being almost overnight. Such a crossing was located on Black's Fork near the site of the Granger Stage Station. Eventually Pony

Express riders stopped here (1861–1862), and the Union Pacific Railroad laid tracks nearby in 1868. Only one original building remains today. It measures 56 feet by 22 feet, and the walls are stone and lime-sand mortar. None of the doors or windows is original.

The station is at Granger in Wyoming's Sweetwater County.

Old stage station on the Oregon Trail

Piedmont Charcoal Kilns

The Piedmont charcoal kilns were built to process charcoal for use in mining smelters. Union Pacific Railroad tracks were laid through the area in 1868, and Piedmont was a station on the line. Because of its proximity to Utah mines, the ease of transportation, and an abundant supply of timber, the site was an ideal location for a charcoal-processing operation. Five conical native limestone kilns were constructed (only three and part of a fourth remain) in 1869 by Moses Byrne. Measuring 30 feet in circumference and 30 feet from the ground to the peak of the roof dome, each has one arched entrance eight feet high. The walls are two feet thick. Wood was placed in the kilns, a fire started, and the kilns sealed in such a way that the heat could be regulated. The wood smoldered slowly for several days, then the fire was allowed to die out, and the wood cooled before handling.

The kilns are located 14 miles northeast of Hilliard in Wyoming's Uinta County.

Utah's Uinta and Wasatch Mountains

The 150-mile-long Uinta Mountains, the largest east-west range in the Rockies, lie just south of the Wyoming border and reach for some 30 miles into northwestern Colorado. The crest of the 30-to-40-mile-wide range reaches an elevation of 13,528 feet at King's Peak and consists of a broad, plateaulike summit deeply carved, much like a scallop, by glacial canyons and cirques.

The Wasatch Range to the west is separated from the Uintas by a sag in the landscape known as the Kamas Prairie. The west side of this westernmost range of the Central Rockies is a bold, sheer fault scarp formation in contrast to the stream-cut rugged landscape of the eastern slope.

The high passes and canyons of the Uinta-Wasatch country were crossed into Kamas Prairie and Salt Lake Basin by the fabled Kit Carson, Jedediah Smith, and Jim Bridger, followed by the gold prospectors, Pony Express riders, and adventurers of every description. The 237,177-acre Uinta Primitive Area, once the hunting grounds of the Uinta Indians, straddles the crest of the range and is traversed by the High Uintas Highland Trail.

Emigration Canyon—Route of the Mormon Pioneers

Emigration Canyon forms the passage through the Wasatch Mountains to Salt Lake Valley traversed by Brigham Young and his Mormon followers in their

Utah's Uinta Mountains—fabled haunt of Rocky Mountain trappers and gold prospectors

journey from the Missouri Valley. From it, Brigham Young allegedly stated, "This is the place." He had seen the valley lying before him in a vision as the destined home for his people. Just north of the mouth of the canyon on a bench of land overlooking the valley the Mormons built Pioneer Monument in 1947 as a memorial to their forebears.

The canyon is located at the eastern edge of Salt Lake City on Utah Highway 65.

Flaming Gorge Dam on the Green River

In 1862 Flaming Gorge Dam was constructed where the Green River flows south from Wyoming's arid Green River Basin through the Uinta Mountains via a sheer-walled, red canyon named Flaming Gorge by Major John Wesley Powell. The impounded waters of the lake extend north for 91 miles across the Utah-Wyoming boundary and are inhabited by giant brown, rainbow, and lake trout. Below the dam the Green River flows through the remaining portion of the Red Canyon and Brown's Park, a long, mountain-rimmed valley once a winter retreat of the Rocky Mountain trappers during the 1800s. Old frontier cabins situated here once provided a place of refuge for Butch Cassidy's wild bunch.

Flaming Gorge Reservoir, home of giant brown and rainbow trout

Desolation Canyon of the Green River

John Wesley Powell (1834–1902) was born in New York State and spent most of his early life in Illinois. He attended Wheaton College (Illinois) and Oberlin College (Ohio) without receiving a degree. As a young man he developed a curiosity about nature that led to solitary expeditions on the Mississippi and Ohio rivers for the purpose of observing and collecting specimens of nature. As the captain of an artillery company during the Civil War, Powell lost his right forearm from a wound received at Shiloh. After the war he turned to exploring and led two expeditions (1869 and 1871) down the Green and Colorado rivers. The 1869 expedition of 11 men and four boats started from the point on the Green River where it is crossed by the Union Pacific Railroad. In Desolation Canyon the men saw a heretofore unexplored area of the United States and were confronted by dangers and natural wonders, frightening and at the same time awe-inspiring. Here the men gave enduring names to mountains, rapids, streams, and other natural landmarks that had never before been seen by white men. Except for an occasional abandoned ranch, Desolation Canyon is virtually unchanged from its appearance in 1869.

Wyoming's Great Divide Country

West of Wyoming's Great Plains region rise the awesome mountain ranges that form the Continental Divide, the lofty ridge of the Rocky Mountains. These mountains—the Absaroka, Wind River, Teton, Gros Ventre, and the Sierra Madre ranges—extend southeastward from the northwest corner of Yellowstone Park across the southern boundary of the state into Colorado. The high peaks of this chain are crowned with perpetual glacier-forming snows, from which streams cascade down the slopes through forests and alpine meadows, carving canyons and forming waterfalls and lakes. On the crest of the Great Divide in the Wind River Range is Gannett Peak, 13,785 feet in altitude, the highest point in Wyoming. Spurs and elevations of the Wind River Range form the Rattlesnake and Seminoe mountains to the south along the Sweetwater River.

Two distinct breaks are made in the Divide: the first, resembling a plain more than an opening in the mountain, is South Pass, through which hundreds of thousands of emigrants made their way over the old Oregon Trail, which passed through here; the second is the Great Divide Basin, which includes the Red Desert, named for the color of its soil, a vast, treeless, and dry high plateau broken near its southern border

Alpine Timberline

The Western United States has a wide range of life zones occurring within relatively small areas. Arid desert valleys are overlooked by peaks where conditions approximate those of the arctic barrens, separated by only a few miles of steep incline. Springs and streams are bordered by lush vegetation in the midst of sunburnt sandstone plateaus. Forms of life adapted to the wide range of conditions occupy certain areas that are favorable to their survival. And many different life zones and microenvironments can be observed, even in the distance traversed in a half-day's hike.

One of the most visible boundaries between life zones is that of the timberline: anyone looking at a high Western mountain can see the forest thin out or entirely cease at a certain elevation. But few persons understand the complexity of factors that define the line above which trees cannot grow.

Timberline is a popular term which scientists have refined into several more precise ones, but in general the upper limit of tree growth follows the 10° isotherm. This means that the average temperature at the height of the growing season, say mid-July, averages no more than 10°C (50°F). When applied to the precise elevation of timberlines, this is an approximation, and other factors enter in. These include not only mean temperature but also the range of temperatures, atmospheric content, soil and air moisture, soil type, amount of solar radiation, and prevailing winds. The

Glacial stream and valley in the Bridger Wilderness of the Wind River Mountains

Gnarled, wind-stunted trees at timberline

by a spur of the Uinta Mountains. The area is not a complete waste, for its abundant salt sage forms a winter range for sheep.

All of Wyoming east of the Continental Divide slopes to the north and east, and all water sources drain in an easterly direction. Here three mountain ranges—the Sierra Madre, Medicine Bow, and Laramie ranges, with the Upper Platte and Laramie valleys in between—extend northward from Colorado into Wyoming. West of the Great Divide, except for a narrow fringe near the state boundary, all rivers drain to the south.

Three great river systems have their sources on the slopes of the Continental Divide in Wyoming—the Columbia, Colorado, and the Missouri. The Snake River and its tributaries, which has its headwaters in the Thorofare Plateau in the Yellowstone region, flows into the Columbia and hence into the Pacific; the Green River, with its alpine headwaters in the peaks of the Wind River Range, flows into the Colorado; the Yellowstone, Big Horn, and Wind rivers, the Belle Fourche in the northeast corner, and the Laramie, Sweetwater, and North Platte rivers all empty into the Missouri.

Mountain pass and snowfields among the high peaks of the Wind River Range, known to the Indians as "the crest of the world"

growth of trees at high elevations is limited by all these factors acting together to produce a total context for the area. To be successful in a given location, a tree must be able to grow from seed or by vegetative reproduction, carry on photosynthesis and respiration, resist climatic and physical damage, and reproduce itself. When any of these processes is prevented by conditions, trees do not exist except fortuitously in small numbers from windborne or animal-borne seed. In these severe, high altitudes other forms of plant life are found that have adapted and can carry on their life processes.

The more precisely descriptive terms for timberline are these: *Forest limit* is the highest elevation at which a closed forest—a dense mature stand of trees —can grow, which is the most commonly used sense of the term timberline. *Tree limit* is the upper zone beyond which individual trees are unable to survive, characterized by isolated pockets of trees in sheltered locations and individual trees with a habit of growth differing from that of trees in the closed forest, having twisted or windwept forms with a much higher proportion of deadwood in their makeup. *Krummholz limit* is the absolute limit of tree existence, *krummholz* being a German word meaning crooked wood or dwarf timber. These survivors are scattered in the lee of boulders

or ridges and can be related to the tall trees of the closed forest only by examination of the needles; the effect of the severe conditions on them is dramatically, almost painfully, evident. They are usually small in size and extremely slow in growth. A tree in the closed forest may be three feet in diameter after 300 years of growth, while a krummholz specimen of the same age has attained a diameter of three inches in the same time and a height of one or two feet. These trees may never achieve the margin of stored energy necessary to set seed; winds or animals carry the original seed from more hospitable elevations into this biological exile.

The margin of tree growth, however expressed, delineates the boundary between two major climatic zones, the temperate and the arctic. Above the trees is a kind of tundra defined by elevation and latitude, where small, specially adapted plants carry on lives under harsh constraint by cold and wind and thin air and massive doses of solar radiation. Higher still is the *firn line*—snow line—where snow and ice remain throughout the year and little grows but algae or lichens livings on the bare rocks that are exposed.

One noticeable quality of the timberline in the West is that the trees are uniformly conifers such as whitebark pine, limber pine, subalpine fir, Douglas fir, bristlecone pine, Engelmann spruce, and common juniper. These are all common at intermediate elevations with the ability to survive higher up where other trees cannot. Some explanations for this ability of conifers to withstand high alpine stresses include their woody leaves (needles) with less surface area, frost-resistant sap, a carryover of needles from year to year requiring less energy than complete regeneration of leaves, and a consequent ability to revive more quickly from dormancy when conditions are favorable for photosynthesis. The absolute elevation range of tree limit recedes as one travels north. In the Southern Rockies of Colorado, trees may grow at 11,500 or 12,000 feet, but in the Wind River and Teton ranges of Wyoming the tree limit is about 10,500 feet. In the Montana Rockies it dips to around 7,500 feet, and in the Olympic Range of Washington the tree limit is about 6,500 feet because of the heavy snowfall and intense storm activity. In all these locations there are variations in forest and tree limit owing to differences in aspect, winds, and the like that may be several hundred feet within a small area or a single drainage. The hiker on a high mountain should watch the changes when ascending. Meadows give way to climax forest and forest to scattered patriarchs, endurance graven in every whorl of snow-blasted wood, to the

tiny dwarf krummholz crouched in the protection of a boulder, old as 10 generations of mankind. And above tree limit, the unrestrained eye follows ridge and rockslide and snow up to a sky of piercing blue.

Wind River Range

The glacier-studded peaks and spires of the massive Wind River Range rise abruptly from the Great Divide Basin near South Pass and wind for more than 100 miles along the Continental Divide before they merge with the volcanic crags of the Absaroka Range to the northwest, beyond which lie the sagebrush flood plain of Jackson Hole and the headwaters of the Snake River.

The Winds, known to the Indians as the Crest of the World, contain about 4,000 granite-bound lakes surrounded by towering spires and glacial cirques, flat plateaus, barren crags, sheer river valleys, alpine meadows, and tundra inhabited by shiras moose, mule deer, coyotes, lynx, black bear, elk, and the nation's largest population of bighorn sheep.

The range, formed some 55 million years ago during the Laramide revolution (which see), reaches its highest point at 13,804-foot Gannett Peak and contains

The volcanic Ramshorn country east of the Wind River Mountains

the Bridger Wilderness, Popo Agie and Glacier primitive areas, and a portion of the Wind River Indian Reservation, the burial place of Sacajawea.

Sky Pilot

The sky pilot, a member of the phlox family, is the symbol of high-altitude tundra areas in mountain regions of the West. It grows vigorously in alpine meadow areas where the surface has been disturbed by gophers or road construction. Visible variations occur in this beautiful, blue-flowered plant from mountaintop to mountaintop.

Paternoster Lakes of the Great Divide

Scattered throughout the Rocky Mountain high country like blue jewels are countless thousands of small lakes, many of them still unnamed, whose beds were dug out of the granite core by the slow advance of the glaciers. A common feature of the timberline areas is a series of shallow interconnected lakes known as paternoster lakes, from the fact that they appear like beads strung along a watery thread on a rosary.

Unlike tarns, or cirque lakes, which lie isolated in bowls once occupied by glaciers, the paternoster lakes were formed where the ice sheet met a resistant chunk of rock and was forced to shift horizontally before heading downhill again. Some of the most striking examples of paternoster lakes are found high up in the Bridger Wilderness area of Wyoming's Wind River Range.

Squaretop Mountain of the Wind River Range

This legendary peak in the Wind River Range, a historic landmark of the early explorers and Rocky Mountain trappers, is an inelegant, eroded remnant of an ancient plateau. It has no snow and is the shape of a giant tree stump. Located at the headwaters of the Green River, Squaretop towers 11,695 feet above the surrounding countryside.

Yellowbellied Marmot

The high-pitched chirp of the yellowbellied marmot is often heard among the fellfields, talus slopes, valleys, and foothills in the mountains of the West. It

Glacially gouged "paternoster" lakes at timberline in the Wind River Range

is found up to 12,000 feet in elevation, from the foot-hills to the tundra. This thick-bodied, 14-to-19-inch yellowish-brown marmot has a yellow belly, with white between the eyes, conspicuous, buff-colored patches on the sides of the neck, and buff to dark brown feet. Its den is usually near a large boulder, which serves as a look-out station.

Sheepeater Indian Relics of the Wind River Range

Unlike their relatives of the high plains, the Shoshones, the Sheepeaters lived in the high country of the Central Rockies—the Big Horns, Absaroka Range, Tetons, Wind River Range, and the Yellowstone region—where they lived during the summer in the remote alpine meadows, hunting bighorn sheep, mule deer, elk, and mountain buffalo. Their flakes and

Squaretop Mountain—Rocky Mountain trappers' landmark

Historic photo of a Sheepeater Indian wickiup dwelling at Yellowstone Park

arrowhead points have been found along ancestral game trails through the high mountain passes, and remnants of long wooden fences used to corral game have been discovered in the Wind River Mountains.

Talus Creep and the Treeless Mountain Slopes

Talus creep is the slow, constant sliding of the talus slopes—the bare brownish hillsides seen throughout the Rocky Mountain country created by masses of ice-chipped rock fragments that are too unstable to support trees. The sharp fragmented boulders on a talus slope are caused by the cyclical warming and freezing of the mountain bedrock. The rising and setting of the sun expand and contract the rocks, opening minute fractures. Water seeps into these fractures, expanding as it freezes and cracking the rocks, creating the rugged talus slopes.

Union Pass on the Great Divide

Union Pass is a strategically located passage through the mountains of northwestern Wyoming. The pass location, at an altitude of 9,210 feet, is really a hub or core area from which three great Wyoming mountain ranges rise in gradually ascending elevations to heights of 13,000 feet or more—the Wind River Range to the southeast, the Gros Ventre Range to the west, and the Absaroka Range to the north. Union Pass, about 4,000 feet lower than the mountains surrounding it, offers an easy passageway among the headwaters of three great river systems—the Colorado, the Columbia, and the Missouri. On September 15, 1811 an overland expedition of John Jacob Astor's fur company led by Wilson Price Hunt became the first group of white men to cross the Continental Divide here. This expedition was travelling toward the mouth of the Columbia River. Prior to this time the pass had been used frequently by Indians, and it later became important in the Oregon fur trade.

The pass is reached by a gravel road 12 miles west-southwest of the Wind River Ranger Station in the Shoshone National Forest, 16 miles north-northeast of the Kendall Ranger Station in the Bridger National Forest, and 20 miles east-southeast of the Goose Wing Ranger Station in the Teton National Forest in Wyoming's Fremont and Sublette Counties.

Jackson Hole and the Teton Range— Mountains Without Foothills

Jackson Hole, one of the largest enclosed valleys in the Rocky Mountains, covers a lake-studded area

Grand Tetons and Jackson Lake from across Jackson Hole—an historic crossroads of the Western fur trade

of 400 square miles, varying in width from 6 to 12 miles and about 60 miles in a north-to-south direction. The sagebrush flats, cobblestone flood plains, wetlands, pioneer homesteads, lush hay meadows, and ranchlands of this mountain-bound valley are dissected by the upper Snake River and Jackson Lake, flanked on the west by the jagged, hornlike peaks of the Teton Range and on the east by the Gros Ventre and the Great Divide along the soaring peaks of the Wind River Range.

Jackson Hole was a historic crossroads of the Western fur trade, named after David Jackson, one of the original partners of the Rocky Mountain Fur Company. A hole in Western lingo traditionally refers to any sizeable mountain-girded valley, much as a park refers to a large alpine meadow.

The area has a varied wildlife population: during summer coyotes and sandhill cranes are a common sight on the sagebrush flats of the National Elk Refuge (which see); beaver dams and moose inhabit wetlands bordering the Snake River; pronghorn antelope dot the appropriately named Antelope Flats; and bald eagles, golden eagles, red-tailed hawks, osprey, trumpeter swans, white pelicans, and great blue herons are often sighted along the waterways and lakes.

Rising abruptly to the west are the wind-swept summits, snowfields, alpine meadows, and boulder-strewn parks of the Teton Range, a classic fault-block mountain formation reaching to heights of 13,770 feet at the horn peaks of the Trois Tetons, important landmarks for the early explorers and trappers. These great peaks were thrust upward along fracture zones near the eastern front of the range and gradually carved by wind, rain, massive valley glaciers and streams into towering spires.

The Teton Range and much of Jackson Hole lies preserved within the boundaries of Grand Teton National Park, with more than 220 miles of trails passing through evergreen forests, flats, and meadows to high-country tundra fields and lake basins.

Beaver dam and pond on one of the braided channels of the Snake River

Grand Teton National Park Life Zones

Grand Teton National Park is dominated by one of the most spectacular mountain ranges in the world. The striking beauty and grandeur of the Teton Range can easily overshadow the more subtle features of the park. The Jackson Hole Valley, a sagebrush flood plain, is prime habitat for a variety of flora and fauna of the Middle Rockies. These features are perhaps best understood when the park is separated into four major habitats, each with its own characteristic plant and animal life.

Riverbank Zone

The first zone, the riverbank or riparian environment, includes the Snake and Gros Ventre rivers, Cottonwood Creek, and the other creeks and streams. This relatively moist area supports willow and cottonwood trees. In winter these river corridors are critical habitat for moose, elk, bald eagles, and other wildlife. In summer this zone is the nesting area for bald eagles, osprey, great blue herons, geese, and other waterfowl. Beavers frequently dam up parts of the rivers, forming small ponds. Moose like to feed on the aquatic vegetation in these ponds and can often be seen at Blacktail Pond, Sawmill Pond, along the Moose-Wilson Road, and at the Oxbow Bend between the Buffalo Entrance and the Jackson Lake Dam. Trumpeter swans nest and can often be sighted at Christain Pond.

Coyote, commonly sighted searching for duck and goose eggs along the Snake River

Sagebrush flats, forests, and horn-shaped Teton peaks, rising abruptly more than 13,000 feet above Jackson Hole

Sagebrush Flats

The drier sagebrush flats, the second zone, are more than just a scenic foreground for the Teton Range. Sagebrush is the dominant plant, but there are more than 100 other plants growing among the sagebrush, including many wildflowers, such as arrow-leaf balsamroot, the yellow sunflowerlike plant with arrow-shaped leaves. Yellow fritillary or yellowbell is a common small plant with a yellow, bell-shaped flower. Scarlet gilia is one to three feet tall, with brilliant red trumpet-shaped flowers. Its nectar is the favorite food of the tiny calliope hummingbird. A main part of the sage grouse's diet is sagebrush. The sagebrush flats are also the summer habitat of pronghorn antelope. Pronghorn can be seen in small bands on Antelope Flats north of Kelly. They can also occasionally be seen along the Teton Park Road between Jenny Lake and Moose. The park bison herd of about 35 animals often roams in the vicinity of the Potholes area or along the Snake River near Moran Junction.

Forest Zone

The third zone, the forest of Grand Teton, is dominated by lodgepole pine at the lower elevations and Engelmann spruce and subalpine fir at higher elevations. Elk usually spend the day in this heavy timber. In the early morning and evening hours they move out into the open areas along the forest border to graze. Elk cows can often be seen near Burnt Ridge,

Signal Mountain, and Timbered Island. Gold-mantled ground squirrels, red squirrels, and chipmunks are commonly sighted forest residents. Some of the typical forest birds include the bright red and yellow western tanager, mountain and black-capped chickadees, Steller's jays and Clark's nutcrackers. Forest wildflowers include heartleaf arnica, calypso orchids, bluebell, and pipsissewea or prince's pine.

Mountain Zone

At first glance the mountains of the fourth zone look overpowering, and one might think hiking would be at best difficult and the trails steep. Surprisingly, trails into some of the mountain regions gain in elevation gradually and open into broad meadows not visible from the flats below. These alpine meadows and rocky slopes are inhabited by a wide variety of plants and animals, including pika or rock rabbit, bighorn sheep in the remote rocky reaches, yellowbellied marmots, and alpine wildflowers such as sky pilot, subalpine buttercup, alpine laurel, mountain heather, and alpine forget-me-nots.

Mountain Tundra

Alpine tundra is the wind-swept, treeless areas of the Western mountains found above the timberline. It's an area of violent contrasts, with intense sun one hour, blinding summer snowstorms the next. Much of the

Western larch in the Teton Range

Fellfield at timberline

tundra appears to be a high-altitude desert of barren rock, but the desert may be interspersed with marshes and alpine meadows. The tundra is similar to the high-latitude, treeless stretches of the northern Arctic and to the treeless Western plains, in that both areas are dominated by small herbs because the climate is too severe to support trees.

Animal and plant life in the mountain tundra is a miniature world of dwarf shrubs, cushion plants, and small forbs with brightly colored flowers and moist meadows of narrow-leaved sedges and grasses. The rocky surfaces are covered with thick mats of lichens and mosses. In the rocky, fellfield areas are found low, round mats of moss pink, alpine sandwort, alpine avens, alpine forget-me-nots, prostrate willows, and clovers. Tundra areas that have snow cover through the winter are dominated by bunch grass and tufted hairgrass, which forms lush meadows interspersed by flowering plants. Shallow depressions that hold snow until early summer are dominated by the purple-flowered Parry's clover, yellow-flowered snow butter-cups, and marsh marigold. On the moist soil of ridge slopes are different species of sedge, grass, rushes, lichen, and moss. The moist ridge terraces are dominated by marsh marigold, Rocky Mountain lousewort, and rose crown. Flat tundra marsh areas are dominated by willow and sedge hummocks broken by pools of water.

Several birds are found primarily on the alpine tundra. The brown-capped rosy finch nests on cliffs and forages on the permanent snowfields for insects.

The water pipit nests in the tundra meadows, as does the horned lark, which also nests in plains grasslands. The white-tailed ptarmigan is the only year-round resident. This chickenlike bird is a mottled brown in summer and pure white in winter. This natural camouflage compensates for its poor flying abilities.

The tundra is also the home of several mammals. The yellow-bellied marmot and pika, or rock rabbit, live in the rocky, fellfield areas. Northern pocket gophers are found in tundra turfs and meadows, where they dig their burrows. The tundra also serves as summer range for mule deer, elk, and bighorn sheep, as well as shrews, long-tailed weasels, white-tailed jackrabbits, ermine, coyotes, and bobcats.

One of the most interesting features of mountain tundra is its "gopher gardens," where moist soils tilled by the northern pocket gopher grow dense, tall plants with brilliant flowers such as alpine avens, sky pilot, bistort, and blue and purple grasses. The gophers can produce miles of burrows that push up the rocky soil and disrupt plant cover. Boreal sage dominates areas where the pocket gopher has burrowed through tufted hairgrass meadows. After the strong tundra winds have eroded the "gopher garden," it becomes an area of large rocks and cushion plants.

White-tailed ptarmigan in the high reaches of the Tetons

Hoary Marmot

The hoary marmot is usually heard before it is seen. Its high-pitched shrill whistle, from which it gets the name whistle pig, is usually heard among the alpine meadows and talus slopes in the high mountain country of the West, often above the timberline. This high-country dweller is from 18 to 21 inches long, with a black-and-white head and shoulders and grayish body tinged with yellow. Unlike the yellowbellied marmot, its feet are black and its belly a dirty white.

Hoary marmot, identified by its shrill, high-pitched whistle

Glacial Features of Jackson Hole

The fascinating glacial features of Jackson Hole were deposited by ancient mountain glaciers from the Teton Range flanking the valley on the west and an intermountain glacier, once a southward extension of the upper Yellowstone Glacier that crossed the Continental Divide from the present-day park area to the north. Glacial outwash from both Teton and intermontane glaciers is common throughout Jackson Hole: broad, sloped outwash terraces border the Snake River and the Potholes area just south of Jackson Lake is made up of basin-shaped depressions on the outwash plain known as kettles, formed by blocks of ice left buried by the retreating glacier, which then melted to form the pits you see today. Burned Ridge, just west of the Potholes, and Timbered Island, southeast of Jenny Lake, are both parts of end moraines deposited by the glaciers. Jackson Lake lies back of an end moraine left by the Yellowstone Glacier. Leigh, Jenny, and Phelps lakes to the south lie behind end moraines deposited by mountain glaciers that once covered the Teton Range.

Whooping crane, the tallest bird of North America

Whitetailed Prairie Dog

The whitetailed prairie dog, a denizen of the Western high country, is usually found among the junipers and pines and valleys of the Rocky Mountain country. This small prairie dog is similar in coloration to the blacktailed prairie dog (which see) but has a white-tipped tail and is from 11 to 12 inches in length.

Whooping Cranes of Grand Teton National Park

In recent years there have been reports of the rare and endangered whooping crane in Grand Teton National Park. Whooping cranes probably never occurred in great numbers, but by 1937 their population had declined to 29 birds in two flocks. The last remaining flock migrates from wintering grounds on the Arkansas National Wildlife Refuge in Texas to nest in Canada's Wood Buffalo National Park, a distance of 2,600 miles. The nesting area is so remote that it was not discovered until 1954.

Distinguishing characteristics of the whooping crane easily separate it from other birds. The adult whooping crane is pure white in color, with black outer wing feathers and a red cap. It is North America's tallest bird, standing four to four and a half

feet tall. Its voice is a vibrant trumpetlike call. Immature whoopers are fawn colored, but they, too, have black wing tips.

The sandhill crane, which is found in Grand Teton Park, is gray in color with a red cap and stands three to three and a half feet tall. Its voice is low pitched and sounds like a loud musical rattle.

The bird most commonly misidentified as a whooper is the white pelican, which is white with black wing tips. White pelicans are common in Grand Teton during spring migration but rare during the summer. Pelicans are short and keep their necks bent in an S shape. Cranes keep their necks stretched straight while standing or flying.

Menor's Frontier Ferry Across the Snake River

Bill Menor homesteaded in 1892 in the area of the present Menor's Ferry. He settled on the west bank of the Snake, whereas most settlers remained on the east side and used his ferry to reach the timber on the western bank. Menor was joined by his brother, Holiday, who assisted in the operation of the ferry. Both men had sold out and left the area by 1927. Two years later the ferry was acquired by the Rockefeller family. It was refurbished, placed in working order, and turned over to the National Park Service in 1953. The ferry itself is large enough to carry a fully loaded wagon of logs plus a four-horse team. It was formed of two sharp-prowed boats across which the carrying platform was set at right angles. The ferry swung from a cable by means of two lines, either one of which could be shortened while its opposite was lengthened by means of a windlass set on the platform and operated by the pilot. Thus the prow of the boat could be pointed at the angle desired, and the current itself carried the ferry across the stream.

The ferry is situated across the Snake River just above the Grant Teton National Park headquarters in Moose.

Cottonwoods

Cottonwoods are one of the dominant trees of the river valleys in the West. They reach heights of 30 to 50 feet, with ovate or lance-shaped leaves. In forest areas, especially in openings and clearings, it is associated with white spruce, birch, and aspen. Its close relative, the narrowleaf cottonwood, is found along low-elevation streams. In the fall its narrow, lance-shaped leaves turn a bright yellow-orange. The large black cottonwood reaches heights of up to 80 or 100 feet and develops a tall massive trunk and small, flat-

Elk herd wintering at the National Refuge in Jackson Hole, established in 1912

topped crown in maturity. The cottonwoods are common from Alaska through the Rocky Mountain region.

Jackson Hole National Elk Refuge

Jackson Hole, Wyoming had been the winter feeding grounds of the nation's largest band of elk, but pioneer fencing changed the yearly migration trek of the elk from the high country of Yellowstone and the Teton and Gros Ventre mountains down into the low sagebrush plains of Jackson Hole in winter. The elk still came to the lower levels for the winter, but finding their range fenced in, broke down barriers to get at the settler's haystacks. In 1912 the National Elk Refuge was established in Jackson Hole at the base of the Gros Ventre Mountains to provide a winter feeding area to prevent starvation of the large elk herd. In addition to its elk population, the refuge also serves as a winter range for bighorn sheep and trumpeter swans on its 37-mile terrain.

Elk Bugling

The visitor to the Rocky Mountain high country during September and early October is likely to hear the legendary bugling of the mature bull elk echoing throughout the hills and valleys. The bugling, although biologically a challenge or warning to other bulls, often appears to be simply an expression of sheer exuberance with the mating season. Beginning with a low-pitched note which is not often heard, the call quickly rises to the high, drawn-out bugle and suddenly drops to a low cough or grunt which may be repeated several times. The elk is a polygamous animal, and each bull will attempt to gather and hold as

many cows as he can. Fights among bulls are common, but though some are violent, most involve only preliminary sparring. Generally, when harems are won or lost, it is by nothing more than a dominant bull shaking his head and pawing the ground.

Sandhill Cranes

This large, yard-tall bird is commonly sighted in the marshes and on the sagebrush prairies and fields of the West. The color of wet sand with a red cap on its forehead, it flies in V-formation in groups of 20 to 100, usually during the warm afternoon thermals, with outstretched neck and legs.

River Otter

This large, weasel-like animal is found along wilderness lakes and streams, where it feeds on fish, crayfish, frogs, and other aquatic invertebrates. It has webbed feet and a rich brown coat with a silvery sheen below. It builds its den in river or pond banks with the entrance below water and has a feeding range of 15 miles.

Gros Ventre Slide

About six miles up the Gros Ventre River, above the village of Kelly in Jackson Hole, is an example of a phenomenal geologic landslide, which occurred on June 23, 1925. The uppermost part of the slide broke loose about 2,000 feet above the river on the south side, carrying 50 million cubic yards of rock and earth debris across the valley and 400 feet up on the north

River otter, commonly sighted along the stream banks of the Middle Rockies

side of the valley. A natural dam, 225 feet high and nearly half a mile wide, was formed which completely blocked the Gros Ventre River and trapped the water in a 5-mile-long lake, known today as Lower Slide Lake. On May 18, 1927, heavy rains swept away the upper portion of this natural dam, causing a sudden and disastrous flood at Kelly and lowering the level of Lower Slide Lake approximately 50 feet. The original high-water mark can be seen on both sides of the present lake.

Miller Pioneer Homestead in Jackson Hole

Robert A. Miller settled on Flat Creek in 1885. His meadowland was well suited for hay production. Miller eventually helped to plan the town of Jackson. At the turn of the century, Yellowstone Timber Land Reserve was created, and Miller was made the chief administrator of the Teton division (one of four). Miller set up his headquarters at the cabin in 1903, two years before the establishment of the Forest Service within the U. S. Department of Agriculture. The cabin also served as the seat of administration for the first major federal refuge for a large species of North American wildlife—the wapiti elk—which was started on 2,000 acres of Miller's original homestead. The Miller Cabin is really two cabins, both constructed of logs and typical of home construction during frontier times in the forested mountain valleys of the Northwest. The two cabins are only a few feet apart and belong to a single homesite. The original cabin was the first home of Robert Miller and was used during the period connected with Miller's forest service. The larger, two-storied home was built later and was the headquarters for the wildlife refuge.

The Miller Cabin is about three miles east of Jackson's central square along Main Street; follow the northeast fork of the road for one mile beyond city limits.

The Cattle Ranch

Along some secondary roads there is nothing for miles except open grazing land bounded by a few stretches of fence and perhaps a power or telephone line. There may be a windmill with a small bunch of Hereford cattle gathered near a watering trough where the ground has been trodden to dust. From the road, rolling hills rise to timbered mountains that loom, far and blue, above the short-grass plains. The road takes a bend between two low, sage-covered hills, and a mailbox appears, lonesome and solitary next to a cattleguard and a dirt road meandering out of sight. The mailbox is wood, weathered by summer sun and wind-driven snow to a blend of buff and gold and gray. On one side a brand has been burned into the wood—Lazy Seven Bar T—and a painted legend reads Stuart Cattle Co.

If you followed the road, which you probably wouldn't unless you were a friend of the family or a cowhand looking for a job, you'd pass through the sagebrush hills, winding slowly higher and dodging ruts left after the last cloudburst, until the road struck a stream drainage and skirted clumps of willows through bottomland meadows. The road would cross a creek on a bridge of rough-sawn timber, and your car would shimmy across another cattleguard as a band of white-faced calves dashed off the track, hightailing it for mamma.

A half mile up the road, buildings would come

Buck-and-pole fence in Jackson Hole

Typical Rocky Mountain ranch headquarters with prairie barn, corral, and bunkhouses

in sight: a single-story house, painted a light gray; a stocky barn constructed of logs squared at the corners with a stained tin roof; a low bunkhouse of unpainted lumber with red-and-white checked gingham curtains visible through the small windows; a miscellany of sheds and pole corrals unsorted at first glance. Beyond the structures, hayfields lie along the wandering creek, with fenced stackyards protecting the winter supply of hay. Beyond, the range undulates, vast and rising first to aspen-covered benches, then to alpine peaks, an ocean of rolling country in which the ranch is a small island of habitation.

In the early days of the Western cattle business, the ranch was a loosely defined institution. Rich men from the East or even England or Scotland built palatial homes furnished on a grand scale from faraway sources while their cowhands existed in isolated line camps where necessities were the rule: a wood cookstove, a few bunks, a sooty coffeepot and wallpaper fancifully concocted from the pages of catalogs, maps, and advertisements. The line camps were needed to patrol huge expanses of unfenced range, often several days ride from the main ranch. Ranchers starting on a shoestring occupied quarters much like, or worse than, the line camps and tried to build up an outfit before they or their cattle fell victim to weather or disease or a foreclosing bank or the judgment of a nearby big outfit that they represented undesirable competition.

There was no organized law enforcement except in the towns, and disputes were settled by "cow custom"—the unwritten code of the range—or by force. It was a risky business and a fluid situation with cattle diffused over an area where grazing might be sparse and weather rapidly changeable, where the nearest shipping point might be 200 miles off or more, to be reached only by a grueling trail drive. The home ranch, whether mansion or dugout, was a center and a

sanctuary that give the rider a place to call home, even if he didn't sleep there for six months in a row.

The 1880s brought many large ranching ventures —which were entirely dependent on the grass produced by the open range and on their ability to claim and hold a large portion of it—crashing to an abrupt end. The Homestead Act had given political preference to the small farmer—nester or squatter in the cattleman's jargon—who began to break up the open range with fences and follow customs drawn from the agricultural towns of the East and Midwest that conflicted with the precedent of "cow custom." From then on, the ranchers fought a losing battle with means both political and direct, as in the famous Johnson County War of Wyoming. The severe winter of 1886–1887 froze and starved thousands of cattle on

Roundup of whiteface cattle

winter ranges and forced many outfits to go out of business, throwing cowhands out of jobs and forcing them, ironically, to become squatters or leave the country. Some ranches were rebuilt out of homesteads filed on by riders who worked for the brand and had no intention of becoming dirt-farmers, a role they considered quite beneath their dignity. If their job included bending the law a bit and foxing the government, so much the better.

The ranch changed to meet the new conditons, with owners trying to buy or file on land that controlled the water supply or could be used for winter range. Where winter range was unavailable, hay ground became necessary to the survival of herds, and ranchers found themselves growing hay like farmers. The ranch typically became more localized in scope and was progressively infected (or civilized, depending on one's point of view) by the culture of townsmen and small farmers, who, though ignoble, had a supply of daughters who were difficult for a cowboy to overlook.

The typical cattle ranch of the Western plains and the Rockies today resembles nothing so much as a feudal manor, without most of the negative connotations the word feudal raises in the modern mind. A large ranch is a relatively self-sufficient and self-contained social unit with a structure that, though fixed, is adapted to a kind of functional democracy. The ranch owner's or manager's family is the nobility. A rancher is a cattleman or stockman, but not a cowboy. The intermediate level of ranch society is the skilled hands who work as cooks or mechanics, foremen or farriers. They tend to stay with an outfit for long periods of time and are often married, with houses on or near the ranch. At the bottom in terms of pay and tenure, but certainly not of dignity, are the cowboys. Many of them are young and unmarried, often far from their natural families. Some drift from ranch to ranch, excellent workers but determined to be on the move, spending a season on one outfit and then loading up the pickup that has supplanted the "traveling pony" with their gear to try their luck over the hill.

A ranch must be a self-contained and self-sufficient unit materially as well as socially, particularly if it is remote. Although this quality tends to decrease with the degree of modernization, it is still notable. A ranch must provide for the needs of humans, horses, cattle, and machinery in all the seasons of the year. There are buildings to be made and maintained along with the corrals and fences for the stock, the buck rake and beaverslide of horse-drawn haying or the swathers, balers, sweeps and bobtails of a mechanized outfit. There are breakdowns and appendicitis when the ranch is snowed in and hurt feelings or grudges to resolve and unexpected vagaries of weather or bovine temper. It adds up to a complicated way to make a living, with a number of skills practiced by a few people. Under the roofs of barns and sheds are stored the necessities on which a whole way of life depends: saddles, ropes, hay, grain, baling and barbed wire, lumber, welding rod, horseshoes, bearings, antibiotics, etc., with spares for every conceivable emergency, sometimes neatly arranged, sometimes assorted by the logic of haste and overwork.

Still there is the land, and the tradition of a way

Ranch hands working the corral

of life that dies hard and much mourned: a legacy of courage and hard labor and horse sense with a feeling of independence and satisfaction out of proportion to the financial reward, a very personal sense of pride and responsibility that in much of urban America seems irrevocably damaged.

Magpie

The incessant chattering of the black-billed magpie, a large, black-and-white bird with a long tail that tapers half its length, is one of the most conspicuous indicators of the Western rangelands. A member of the crow family, it is 17 to 22 inches long with a black bill, head, breast, and underparts. The white markings on its shoulders, belly, and primaries are conspicuous in flight as white wing patches. Its common range is the open plains and brush-covered country and along streamside thickets from Alaska south to eastern California and east through the Western rangelands to the 100th meridian region. It is sometimes found living in colonies or nesting in scattered colonies in thickets or streamside trees. It lays 7 to 10 grayish or greenish blotched eggs in a strong nest the size of a bushel basket made of twigs and dry plants cemented together with mud.

Magpie, a noisy denizen of the rangelands and river thickets

Yellowstone National Park— A Mountain-Rimmed Plateau

The Yellowstone Country, known to the Indians as the Land of Evil Spirits and the Burning Moun-

Glacially carved valley in the Yellowstone Plateau

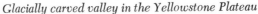

tains, is our largest and oldest national park and contains some of the most spectacular wilderness and natural phenomena in the Rocky Mountains within the boundaries of its 3,500 square miles: the hot springs, mud pots, and geysers along the Firehole River; the ancient fossil forests of the Mirror Plateau; Yellowstone Lake—the lake in the mountains; Grand Canyon of the Yellowstone River; waterfalls of the Cascade Corner; the eerie, lunar landscape and lava floors of the Pitchstone Plateau; and the wind-eroded, gnome-like rock spires that reach heights of up to 300 feet in the Hoodoo Basin. The park is not mountainous country, but rather a heavily glaciated volcanic plateau flanked on the east by the Absaroka Mountains, on the northeast by the Beartooth Mountains, on the northwest by the Gallatin Range of the Northern Rockies, on the west by the Snake River high plains, and on the south by the Teton Range in northwestern Wyoming.

Plant Zones of Yellowstone Park

Yellowstone Park is divided into three major vegetation zones and two smaller zones. A spruce fir forest zone covers the largest area, followed by a rather large lodgepole pine forest zone, and a smaller Douglas fir forest zone. Alpine tundra exists on areas above 10,000 feet and a small area, near Gardiner, Montana supports a Great Basin Desert vegetation.

Spruce-Fir Forest Zone

This zone is dominated by spruce-fir forests in successionally young to mature states. The young stands are characterized by fast-growing lodgepole pines, with a good representation of both spruce and fir, especially in the understory. The tall, mature stands are dominated by either spruce or fir, or a fairly even mixture of the two. Whitebark pine may also be a major tree in the mature forest of this zone, especially near the timberline, usually above the 8,400-foot elevation.

Lodgepole Pine Forest Zone

This zone is dominated by climax lodgepole pine forests with very little or no spruce or fir in the understory. The lodgepole are slower growing and may reach ages in excess of 300 years. Whitebark pine may also be present in areas near the timberline. Spruce and fir stands may be found in the lodgepole zone along stream banks, pond borders, and on north-facing slopes.

Douglas Fir Forest Zone

This zone may better be called the sagebrush zone. Douglas fir is the dominant forest tree here, but

Stand of Douglas fir on the Yellowstone Plateau, habitat of elk and bison

Pod of white pelicans at the Molly Island Rookery on Yellowstone Lake

the area is covered by big sagebrush and various grasses. The forest is characterized by very large, fire-scarred, well-scattered trees, with an understory of smaller Douglas fir. Aspen stands are also common in this zone, and small stands of spruce and fir are found along waterways. At old burns along the Yellowstone and Lamar river valleys the original Douglas fir forests are being replaced by lodgepole pines. This area lies between 6,000 and 7,600 feet in elevation and is underlain by glacial till from the granite and old Absaroka volcanoes found upstream. This area is also the winter range for 5,000 to 8,000 elk and a few hundred bison.

Great Basin Desert and Alpine Tundra Zones

Along the northern boundary of the park, near Gardiner, Montana, is a small area that has vegetation similar to that found throughout the Great Basin Desert: saltbush, greasewood, winterfat, blue gramma, and other species. These areas receive less than 15 inches annual precipitation and have heavy soils derived from shale deposits.

The alpine tundra zone is found above 10,000 feet elevation. Moss campion, mountan avens, native dandelions, and other alpine plants are found in these arctic islands throughout the park.

Hayden Valley and Pelican Valley are two large, treeless areas covered with grassland species. Both these areas are remnant lake beds from the Ice Age and are covered with thick deposits of lake sediment, which probably accounts for their treeless condition.

The two main forces that determine the zones of vegetation in Yellowstone are precipitation and bedrock type. The region of highest rainfall is the southwest corner, known as the Cascade Corner. This area is the first topographic rise met by the air masses from the west, and thus it receives most of the moisture. The rest of the park is in a rain-shadow region.

Yellowstone Wildlife Areas

Although much of Yellowstone Park's wildlife ranges throughout the park, certain species are found in distinct areas of their prime habitat. Animals such as grizzly, coyotes, black bears, martens, gray wolves, yellowbellied marmot, northern pocket gopher, mountain lion, lynx, and bobcat range throughout the park and its backcountry wilderness areas.

Pronghorn antelope, a typical animal of the plains and open rolling country, are most often sighted between Gardiner and Mammoth, on the Swan Lake Flats, from Mammoth to Tower Falls, along the

Yellowstone River below the canyon, and in the beautiful Lamar River valley and Slough Creek area. The park antelope population has been stable in recent years at about 150 to 200 animals. Mule deer, or black-tail deer, are well scattered over the park in summer and may be seen along the trails, at edges of open meadows, and along the roadside or near developed areas day or night. In the winter they drift down to the lower, more protected areas, but not in migratory herds as elk do.

The Yellowstone region has the largest number of elk or wapiti found in the world. There are smaller numbers in scattered places in the Rocky Mountains from northern New Mexico to Montana, Idaho, and Washington, with small introduced herds in other places such as northern Michigan.

In Yellowstone, elk migrate to the high alpine meadows during the summer, but some can usually be seen in the meadows along the Madison River, in the small meadows between Mammoth and Old Faithful, between Norris and the Grand Canyon of the Yellowstone River, and from Yellowstone Lake to the East Entrance. The summer park population usually exceeds 25,000 animals.

Black bears are found throughout the park, where they eat anything that comes their way: grass, fruit, berries, roots, mammals, birds, carrion, grubs, and ants, fish, frogs. The cinnamon and brown bears of the Yellowstone country are simply regional color phases of the black bear.

Bighorn Sheep are the inhabitants of the rugged, Rocky Mountain country and arctic alpine meadows. During summer they are found in the higher mountain ridges of Yellowstone, especially around Mount Washburn, Quadrant Mountain, and on Sepulchre Mountain. In winter they migrate down to the Mount Everts section between Mammoth and Gardiner. They are often seen in the vicinity of the junction of the Lamar and Yellowstone rivers, and occasionally near Oxbow Creek.

The shiras moose, which is found in Yellowstone and surrounding areas, is slightly smaller than the typical American moose found in the northern states east of the Rocky Mountains and north to the Arctic. In Yellowstone they are most likely to be seen in Swan Lake Flats and Willow Park between Mammoth and Norris, in the Dunraven Pass area, along the Lewis River above Lewis Canyon, and between Fishing Bridge and the East Entrance. Moose are active all day, but they are best seen early in the morning or in late afternoon and evening. They are also common in the Falls River Basin, Pelican Creek, Slough Creek, and along the Yellowstone River above the lake. The park moose population numbers about 1,000 animals.

Badgers are frequently seen throughout the sagebrush valleys of the northern portions of the park. River otters are found all along the major river systems, especially along the Yellowstone River in Hayden Valley, along the shoreline of Yellowstone Lake, and along the Gibbon River. Red Fox are occasionally seen along the Mammoth to Tower Road. Uinta ground squirrels are found in the open grassy areas of sagebrush plains.

White Pelicans of Yellowstone Lake

On Molly Island, sequestered in the southern arm of Yellowstone Lake, white pelicans, ungainly on land and superb in flight, thrive in undisturbed sanctuary. These birds have formed the only white-pelican breeding colony within the confines of a national park. Nearly five feet long and weighing about 17 pounds, the pelican has a wingspread of nine feet. A large pouch or bag hangs beneath the long bill. When contracted, the pouch is small, but it is distended as a

Majestic shiras, or "Yellowstone" moose, feeding along the Madison River

scoop for fishing or for feeding the young. Lake shores are the pelican's breeding grounds or rookeries; eggs are laid in nests built on the sand, where the youngsters waddle around on their large, webbed feet, their wings dragging like new crutches.

Yellowstone Lake, fed by the runoff from the snowfields of the volcanic Absaroka Range, is the largest lake in North America above 7,500 feet. Its clear, cold waters reach a maximum depth of 300 feet and an average depth of 30 feet. The lake, which sprawls across the center of the park, shaped like a gnarled old hand, is only three miles from the Continental Divide and has numerous hot springs that cause the surface water to become quite hot. The upper Yellowstone River country to the south is one of the park's prime grizzly habitats.

Volcanic Rocks

During the violent volcanic activity that transformed the Rocky Mountains in the Tertiary period, vast deposits of volcanic debris accumulated on the mountain-rimmed Yellowstone plateau. Evidence of this volcanic activity is found at the outcrops of yellowish rhyolite, a fine-grained solidified lava, along the walls of Gibbon River Canyon and the Grand Canyon

Petrified stump on Specimen Ridge, part of the world's largest fossil forest

of the Yellowstone, as well as layers of basalt, a dark, fine-grained hardened lava, and the glassy, black volcanic rock known as obsidian found at the 165-foot Obsidian Cliff, located about halfway between Norris Geyser Basin and the Mammoth Hot Springs.

Ancient Fossil Forests

The fossil forests of Yellowstone National Park are the most remarkable of their kind in the world. They occur in an area more extensive than any other known fossil forest, covering more than 40 square miles in the northeast portion of the park in the rugged uplands between the Yellowstone River and Lamar River valleys, some five to eight miles west and southeast of Tower Falls. The most accessible are those on Specimen Ridge, southwest of the Lamar River Valley. The great bulk of the fossil trees are still standing upright in the exact positions in which they originally grew. Most other known fossil forests of the world, including those of Arizona, California, and Egypt, are actually drifted logs and stumps, lying scattered at random in the enclosing rocks. The volcanic ridges in the Yellowstone fossil forests have yielded, in addition to hundreds of upright petrified trees, many thousands of beautifully preserved impressions of the leaves, twigs, needles, and cones of over 100 different species of plants. The fossil forest displays not just a single forest, but a vertical succession of 12 or more distinct forests of varying compositions, within a thickness of about 2,000 feet of volcanic ash, breccia, and mud glows.

Recent studies of the numerous plants from these fossil forests show that they were originally made up of a great variety of vegetation, including ferns, horsetail rushes, conifers, and broadleafed deciduous hardwoods. The forests were dominated by the presence of numerous ancient redwoods, or sequoias, very similar in all respects to the modern giant redwoods of western California and southwestern Oregon. In addition to the conifers, these ancient forests were dominated by species of deciduous trees and shrubs whose modern descendants are common in our living warm, temperate forests of the Appalachian Mountains: sycamores, walnuts, oaks, chestnuts, and ancestral beeches. Of unusual interest is the common occurrence of ancient relatives of the living katsura tree, which is no longer native to the North American continent, being restricted to eastern Asia. Of secondary importance in these ancient fossil forests were species of soapberries, maples, hickories, dogwoods, bayberries, and bay trees.

The climatic conditions of these ancient forests must have been very similar to those now found in

Eerie hoodoos resembling giant toadstools in the Absaroka Mountains on Yellowstone's Mirror Plateau

Virginia and the Carolinas—a genial warm-temperate climate with abundant rainfall of 40 to 60 inches a year. The Yellowstone area at that time is believed to have been one of low relief, lying less than 2,000 feet above sea level, compared with over 8,000 feet at the present time. In geological terms the fossil forests of Yellowstone extend back in time as far as the early part of the Eocene epoch of the Tertiary period about 55 million years ago.

Hoodoos

In the high, wind-swept valleys of the West are eroded rock structures known as hoodoos. In the rugged Mirror Plateau region of Yellowstone Park, for example, these eroded pinnacles rise like sentinels of rock and clay, each capped by sheets of rock, resembling giant toadstools.

Madison River Earthquake Area

Earth tremors have been recorded in Yellowstone since 1871, but the most severe on record was the Madison River Earthquake on the night of August 17, 1959. In the Madison River Canyon about 14 miles west of the park boundary, more than 80 million tons of rock were jolted from the canyon walls. This massive landslide extended a mile up the canyon and formed a natural dam, creating what is now known as Earthquake Lake. Seven miles to the east a strong oscillation, called a seiche, tilted the basin of Hebgen Lake and cracked its earthern dam. Fortunately, the dam held.

The violent tremors produced by this earthquake created considerable damage and loss of animal life. It also had a profound effect on Yellowstone Park's hydrothermal activities, releasing dormant geysers, creating new fumaroles, increasing the water temperature of the hot springs, and causing geysers such as Old Faithful to erupt at shorter intervals.

Glacial Drift

About 1 million years ago, glaciers plowed down the deep, V-shaped stream-cut canyons of Yellowstone and turned them into the wide, flat-floored U-shaped glacial valleys and deposited vast amounts of glacial

Lower Falls cascade 308 feet in the Grand Canyon of the Yellowstone River, twice the height of Niagara Falls.

debris as they melted, creating Twin Buttes and Porcupine Hills near the Lower Geyser Basin and Capitol Hill at Mammoth Hot Springs.

Grand Canyon of the Yellowstone River

The geologically young, V-shaped, stream-cut Grand Canyon of the Yellowstone River extends for 24 miles from the 109-foot Upper Falls. The 308-foot Lower Falls cascade a distance twice as high as Niagara. The steep-sided yellow walls of the canyon range from 800 to 1,200 feet high, and its floor is as much as 1,500 feet wide.

Geysers of Yellowstone Park

A geyser is a special kind of hot spring that from time to time spurts water above the ground. It differs

from most hot springs because it has periodic eruptions broken by intervals without flow of water. The temperature of the erupting water is generally nearly at boiling for pure water, or 212°F at sea level. Some geysers erupt every minute or so, but others are inactive for months or even years between eruptions. Contrary to popular opinion, most geysers are very irregular in their behavior. Among the major geysers, only a few such as Old Faithful are predictable enough to satisfy an impatient tourist; even Old Faithful varies from about 30 to 90 minutes between eruptions, with an average interval of about 65 minutes. In the hot springs that we call geysers, steam bubbles become too abundant to escape quietly through the water, and the steam lifts the water, sweeping it upward and out of the vent, lowering the pressure at deeper levels, increasing boiling, and starting a chain reaction that leads to eruption.

A tremendous supply of heat is essential for the geyser action. Recent measurements by the U. S. Geological Survey show that the total heat flowing from Yellowstone's Upper Geyser Basin is at least 800 times more than the heat flowing from a normal area of the same size. Geological studies also indicate that this tremendous flow of heat has continued for at least 40,000 years. This large outflow of heat over thousands of years is the major reason to believe that a large magma chamber exists below the circulating water of Yellowstone's geyser system.

Sharing the Upper Geyser Basin with Old Faithful are numerous geysers, including Riverside, Grand, Castle, and Beehive. Downstream along the Firehole River are the Midway and Lower Geyser basins. Boardwalk trails and side roads lead to points of interest in those areas. The Fountain Paint Pots Trail in the lower basin presents more varied hot water phenomena in a concentrated area than any other trail in the park.

The Norris Geyser Basin is Yellowstone's most active thermal area. Besides the numerous geysers, a variety of fumaroles and hot springs are found here. The Mammoth Hot Springs are quite different from other springs and geysers. Here the hot waters cascade over series of delicately colored rimstone pools. Limestone dissolved in the waters deep beneath the surface is deposited rapidly to form terraces and pools.

Remote back-country hot spring cauldrons and steam vents are also located at Shoshone Lake and Heart Lake.

Mud Thermals—Pots, Volcanoes, and Geysers

Among Yellowstone's most fascinating hydro-thermal phenomena are the gurgling, splashing, steaming mudpots, hot springs filled with boiling mud and small amounts of water. Most mud pots are quite shallow, but some reach depths of as much as 10 feet below the rim of the crater. The boiling, mineral-colored white, pink, and orange mud of some cauldrons known as paintpots are found in the Lower Geyser Basin and at West Thumb near the Fishing Cone. Small mud volcanoes and mud geysers are located on a scenic turnout on the Grand Loop Road between Canyon Village and Fishing Bridge.

Hot Springs

Yellowstone's thermal pools, or hot springs, are found in the geyser basins, with the exception of Mammoth Hot Springs, and deposit minerals that form colorful, algae-covered terraces, bowls, mounds, and rims. At Mammoth Hot Springs are found giant, staircaselike, brightly colored travertini terraces and snow-white "dead" terraces of extinct springs. Nearby is a 37-foot hot spring cone known as Liberty Cap. The most unusual hot spring in the park is the Fishing Cone, a hot spring in a cone-shaped mound in Yellowstone Lake at West Thumb.

Jupiter Terrace and hot springs

Firehole River and Geyser Basin

Historic 1913 photo of the sprinkler wagons at Yellowstone Park

Yellowstone's Fumaroles

Another type of thermal activity in the park is its fumaroles, or steam vents, found where there is a scarcity of groundwater. These vents, which produce sulfurous fumes that smell like rotten eggs, are most common in the Porcelain Basin at the Norris Geyser area and at Old Faithful. The steam produced by the Black Growler in the Porcelain Basin comes out with a roar and has been recorded to reach 284°F.

Sheepeater Cliffs of Yellowstone

On the remote Sheepeater Cliffs of the Gardiner River in Yellowstone Park are the picture writings, tribal emblems, and outlines of pygmy men and women cut in irregular semicircles by the ancient Sheepeater Indians, who were forced into the Yellowstone region by hostile tribes. The Yellowstone area was known to the Indians as the Land of Evil Spirits, which most of the tribes shunned except when gathering obsidian for arrowheads.

The Sheepeaters lived in the cliffs near the steaming fumaroles, hot springs, geysers, and bubbling paint pots avoided by the other tribes. They were skillful hunters of mountain sheep, their chief food, using bows made of ram's horns bound with sinew. Their dwellings were frames made of poles covered with cedar bark and moss cemented with pitch. Their arrowheads, of exquisite design, were made of obsidian. In their tribal ceremonies and songs the Sheepeaters told that their forebears had inhabited the geyser region from the beginning, and that a large part of the tribe had once been destroyed by a terrible convulsion of the earth in the Upper Geyser Basin, most likely an earthquake similar in magnitude to the one that changed the face of the nearby Madison River Canyon area in 1959.

The Yellowstone Park Bison Herd

The Yellowstone bison are unique in the United States. Only here have wild bison survived since primitive times, long before the establishment of the park in 1872. The park's present population derives from two bloodlines: the original population of moun-

Bison grazing at Yellowstone Park

tain bison and the plains bison introduced in 1902. The Yellowstone bison are wild, free-ranging, and unrestricted by boundary fences. The population numbers more than 1,500 animals.

Most bison calves are born in the wintering areas during the first two weeks of May. Reddish-tan at birth, the calves begin to darken at about two and a half to three months of age. Both sexes are horned. Adult bulls may weigh as much as 2,000 pounds; adult cows usually weigh half as much.

The bison may be seen eastward of Tower Junction along the Lamar River and northward. A herd on Pelican Creek, one ranging in Hayden Valley, and another in the Lower Geyser Basin may also be viewed. During the summer months small numbers may occasionally be noticed along the Gibbon River, Madison River, in the Lower Geyser Basin, in Hayden Valley, and along the east shore of Yellowstone Lake between Fishing Bridge and Lake Butte. The larger herds go into the high country during summer and are seldom seen.

Volcanic peaks of the Absaroka Range, one of the nation's last grizzly bear strongholds

Absaroka Mountains

The volcanic barren summits of the sparse forests and rocky crags of the Absaroka Mountains, a highly dissected plateau, are named after the Crow Indians who called themselves Absarokee, or the People of the Raven. The range is bounded on the south by the Wind River Mountains and basin, on the north by the Beartooth Plateau, on the west by the Yellowstone Plateau, and on the east by arid sagebrush basins. Formed by the alternating flows of lava and buildups of ash beds, the range lies within the Shoshone National Forest and contains the alpine lake basins, rocky summits, and thin forests of the North Absaroka Wilderness and the vast Washakie Wilderness in the southern portion of the range.

Buffalo Bill's Pahaska Tepee

Pahaska Tepee was conceived and built by Colonel William Frederick Cody—Buffalo Bill—as a pleasant place for his personal entertainment and to provide a means of income as a hostelry. The lodge is a two story building constructed of handsawn lodgepole pine and is 84 feet long covered with a corrugated-iron gabled roof. The lodge remains much the way it appeared when built.

Pahaska Tepee is located two miles east of the East Entrance to Yellowstone National Park on U. S. Highways 14/16/20.

Thorofare Plateau— Headwaters of the Yellowstone

At 12,165-foot Younts Peak on the western slope of the Absoraka Range in the Thorofare Plateau area of the 563,000-acre Teton Wilderness rise the headwaters of the Yellowstone River. To the west of the Yellowstone headwaters is 8,150-foot Two Ocean Pass on the Continental Divide, where in a small marshy area known as the "parting of the waters," a single stream divides, with a portion of its waters flowing to the Pacific Ocean via Pacific Creek and the Snake River and a portion flowing to the Atlantic Ocean via Atlantic Creek and the Yellowstone, Missouri, and Mississippi rivers—a distance of about 6,000 miles.

T E Ranch Headquarters

Following completion of the first road into Yellowstone National Park, Buffalo Bill Cody wanted to establish a place that would offer accommodations to travellers entering the park. The T E Ranch, which he acquired and stocked in 1895 upon his arrival in the area, was the first of these enterprises. The ranch was operated as a free dude ranch and offered packhorse camping trips and big game hunting expeditions. During his affluent years as a showman, Cody entertained notable guests from Europe and America at the ranch. Although additional log structures have been built on the ranch, the original single-story, white-painted log building still serves as ranch headquarters.

The ranch, under private ownership, is located 30 miles southwest of Cody in Wyoming's Park County on South Fork Road.

Wapiti Historic Ranger Station

Wapiti Ranger Station was the first to be erected, built in 1903, at federal expense. It is located within the area of the first national forest reserve, Yellowstone Timberland Reserve, which was established by President Benjamin Harrison in 1891. Built as a supervisory ranger station for the Shoshone division of the reserve, the original still stands, though incorporated into the present station.

The ranger station is located near Wapiti in the beautiful Wapiti Valley portion of the Shoshone National Forest in Wyoming's Park County.

Elk or Wapiti

Elk or wapiti are the largest of the deer family in North America, next to the moose. Bull elk weigh as much as 800 pounds; their head, neck, and under parts are dark brown, sometimes nearly black; the sides, back, and thighs are yellowish gray, shading to a tan patch on the rump and to white between the legs. Antlers attain their full size—about five feet in length from tip to burr—in late July or August, when the velvet dries and peels off or is rubbed off against tree trunks and branches. Rutting season is heralded by the bugling of the bulls, a sonorous call first heard as a guttural roaring. It passes through trumpet pitches to a shrill, screaming whistle that modulates abruptly to the guttural again, then breaks off to a grunt. A challenge as well as a mating call, the bugling is a frequent prelude to battle in which sharp antlers flash savagely at the charge. Occasionally, antlers interlock in battle, and the rivals die together.

Before settlers brought fences to the upland ranges of the West, elk wintered in the lower altitudes where snow was not too deep for foraging. When spring brought herds into the hills, the cows paused in the lower aspen groves for calving, and the bulls continued high into the heavier pine and spruce timber, where the growth of their antlers was completed by August. In the next month, the bulls began to seek out the cows. Then with snowfall, they drifted down to the winter range to browse on grass, brush, and twigs until spring.

American elk, or "wapiti," the largest member of the deer family in North America

Buffalo Bill Dam on the Shoshone River

John Wesley Powell, chief of the U. S. Geological Survey, sought federal financial backing for extensive reclamation of arid western lands. As a result of Powell's efforts, Theodore Roosevelt signed the Reclamation Act (June 17, 1902), creating this authority and the agency to administer it. Buffalo Bill Dam, one of the first two dams built by the new Bureau of Reclamation, is a concrete arch located near the head of the Shoshone River Canyon. The dam is 325 feet high and 108 feet wide at the base tapering to 10 feet at the top; the length of the crest is 200 feet. The reservoir thus created has a capacity of 439,800 acre-feet of water and a shoreline of about 20 miles. (Also see the section on the Pathfinder Dam.)

The dam is located seven miles west of Cody in Wyoming's Park County.

Beartooth Plateau

The bold eastern ramparts of the Beartooth Mountains rise abruptly from the Great Plains to the east and are bounded on the south by the Yellowstone Plateau and Absaroka Range and the Clark Fork of the Yellowstone River. The stark granite outcroppings of the Beartooths, some as old as 2.7 billion years, soar to 12,799 feet at Granite Peak, which dominates an icy alpine world of krummholz and perpetual snowfields. The summits gradually merge into the forested slopes of the Custer National Forest and then into rolling prairie country in the Long Pines region of eastern Montana. In the heart of the mountains is the 230,000-acre Beartooth Primitive Area, an alpine wilderness of rock-strewn plateaus, glaciers, cascades, sheer canyons, meadows, and hundreds of small, glacier-carved lakes. Many of the peaks in the area, such as Beartooth Mountain, are ochre-tinted granite. The northeast slopes of the range have been carved by valley glaciers and from a series of glacial troughs and small plateaulike areas. The southwest side slope, in contrast, was formed by a mountain icecap, and its unweathered bedrock, basins and lakes, ice-scoured rocks, and sheep rock formations resemble parts of the Canadian shield.

Grasshopper Glacier

Grasshopper Glacier, near Cooke City, Montana in the wilderness section of Custer National Forest, is a shrinking ice mass, which has probably lost more than half of its volume in the past 40 years. Scattered through it are the remains of thousands of grass-

Beartooth Plateau—a primitive world of ochre-tinted peaks, glaciers, and alpine lakes

hoppers blown up into the mountains by strong west winds. The grasshoppers originated in Nevada, Oregon, and possibly northern California. They were carried in air masses that swept over the mountains. As the wind velocity decreased along the mountain ridges, the grasshoppers fell to the earth where they died. Those that fell on the ice have been preserved. Grasshopper Glacier is not unique, as grasshopper remains are found in many glaciers of the Beartooth country.

This glacier and others of the Beartooth Mountains are quite small and are still shrinking. All are found on north and northeast-facing slopes, which offer maximum protection from the sun and at sites where the snows, blowing off exposed slopes, are dumped in drifts of unusual thickness by southwest winds. These glaciers are not remnants of the Pinedale Valley glaciers, which originated in the Beartooth Range 10,000 years ago and melted during the altithermal period that cleared all the Rocky Mountain cirques of ice. The existing Beartooth glaciers date from the "Little Ice Age," which followed the altithermal period.

The major scientific interest in the Beartooth glaciers is their importance as climatic indicators. Poised on the eastern front of the Rocky Mountains and far from other glacier-bearing ranges, they are sensitive indicators of climate changes in this part of the country.

Typical glacier in the Beartooths, formed 10,000 years ago during the "Little Ice Age"

Bighorn Mountains

The biscuitboard-like crest of the Bighorns rises gently in dip slopes from the sagebrush flats of the Bighorn Basin on the west and the Powder River Basin on the east. From the distance, it looks like a giant wall in the Great Plains, with snow-capped peaks ranging in height from 9,000 to more than 13,000 feet. In the heart of the range and the Bighorn National Forest are the alpine lakes, boulder fields, and elk meadows of the Cloud Peak Wilderness.

Indian Medicine Wheel in the Bighorns

On the top of Medicine Mountain in the snow-capped Bighorn Range about eight miles south of the Montana-Wyoming state line is the historic Indian medicine wheel, some 70 feet in diameter, with a 12-foot hub and 28 spokes. It resembles the ancient houses of dawn built by sunworshippers of Mexico and the Aztec religious structures. Archeologists have found evidence that aboriginal people lived near here, but no artifacts to identify them have been found. It is believed that the sonte cairns at the end of the medicine wheel spokes marked the beginning of the summer and winter solstices. Recently discovered timber,

Young sparrow hawks in the Bighorn Mountains

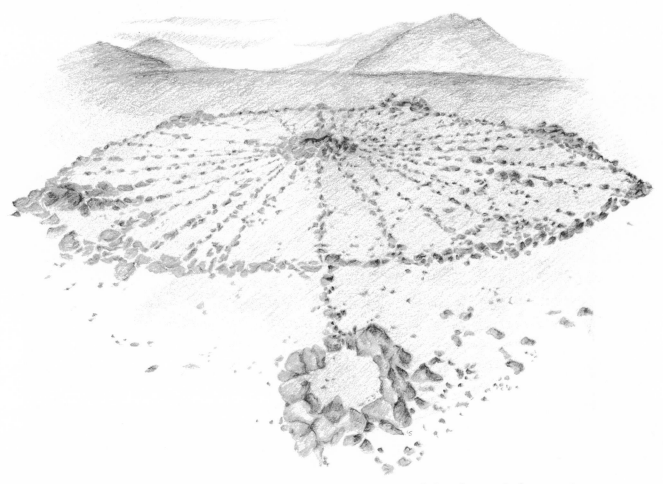

Sacred Indian medicine wheel in the Bighorn Mountains, believed to mark the start of the summer and winter solstices

which was imbedded in the rock cairns, have been carbon-dated to about 1770. The Crow Indian legend of Scarface relates to the medicine wheel. As a boy he fell face first into a fire pit, and his face was grotesquely scarred. Other children called him burnt face or scarface, and he ran away. Years later a hermit was found living in a cave on Medicine Mountain. It was Scarface. He returned to the Crow Camp near present-day Yellowtail Dam and built the medicine wheel found there.

The medicine wheel is located in Wyoming's Bighorn County, just north of U. S. 14 Alt., about 15 miles east of the town of Kane.

Buffalo Bill's Sheridan Inn

When the Chicago, Burlington, and Quincy Railroad tracks reached Sheridan, the company constructed the Sheridan Inn as a feature of its development program. Buffalo Bill operated the hotel from 1894 to 1896, catering principally to a large clientele of sportsmen bound for the Big Horn Mountain country. Still in use today, the frame building has a piazza extending around two sides and a Buffalo Bill bar which retains its original features. The inn is located in the town of Sheridan at Broadway and 5th Street.

5. Northern Rockies

EACHING northward into Canada from the Snake River lava plain and Yellowstone Plateau, the Northern Rockies are made up of three major and one minor group of mountains: (1) the broad central Idaho ranges of the central Idaho batholith, a sprawling mass of mountains north of the Snake River Plain and extending northward to the Lake Pend Oreille area; (2) the bold north-south mountains and valleys or trenches in northwestern Montana and the Idaho Panhandle, which include the Lewis Range, a frontal formation, on the east and the Selkirk Mountains on the west along the Idaho-Washington boundary; (3) the short ranges broken by broad valleys in southwestern Montana; and (4) the easternmost extension of the Northern Rockies at the edge of the Great Plains formed by the Big Belt and Little Belt mountains, Castle Mountains, and Crazy Mountains in south-central Montana.

Mountain Trenches of the Northern Rockies

One of the most unusual features of the Northern Rockies is the Rocky Mountain Trench on the east and the Purcell Trench on the west, separated from each other by great valleys running north and south. The Rocky Mountain Trench extends south from Flathead Lake in Montana through the beautiful Flathead and Bitterroot valleys and north from Flathead Lake for 800 miles east of the Rocky Mountain ramparts into Canada. The Purcell Trench lies 60 miles west of the Rocky Mountain Trench and extends northward from Lake Coeur d'Alene in Idaho for 220 miles, where it merges with the Rocky Mountain Trench.

The course of the Rocky Mountain Trench formed a major portion of the Great North Trail, the major emigration route for about 200 million years for animals and prehistoric tribes crossing the Bering Land Bridge from Asia into North America.

Rocky Mountain Pioneer Homesteads

Although the log cabin belongs to every pioneer era, the first log houses built by the early Rocky Mountain settlers differed in some respects from those of other regions. These differences were mainly due to the type of construction materials at hand and the

104

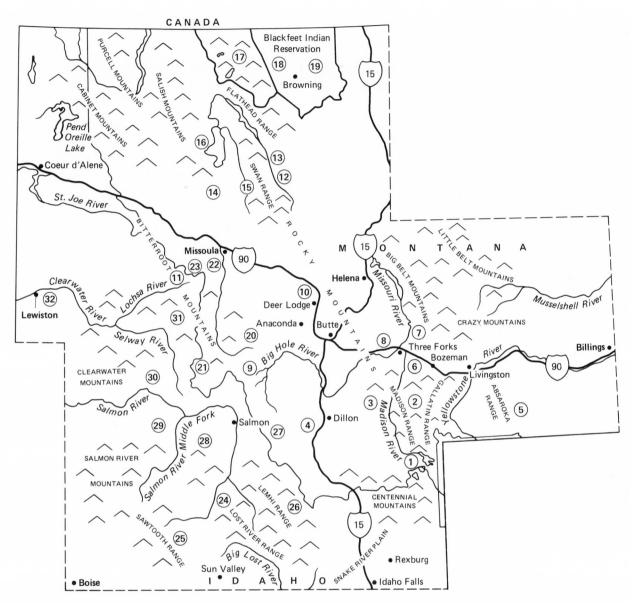

Key to Sites

1. Madison River Earthquake Area
2. Spanish Peaks
3. Virginia City
4. Bannack Historic District
5. Beartooth Primitive Area
6. Madison Buffalo Jump
7. Missouri River Headwaters
8. Lewis and Clark Caverns
9. Big Hole National Battlefield
10. Grant-Kohrs Ranch National Historic Site
11. Gates of the Mountains

12. Bob Marshall Wilderness
13. Chinese Wall
14. National Bison Range
15. Mission Mountains Wilderness
16. Flathead Lake
17. Glacier National Park
18. Indian Tepee Rings
19. Camp Disappointment
20. Anaconda Pintlar Wilderness
21. Nez Perce Pass
22. Traveler's Rest

23. Lolo Pass and Trail
24. Miniature Grand Canyon
25. Sawtooth National Recreation Area
26. Charcoal Kilns
27. Fort Lemhi
28. Sacajawea Monument
29. Idaho Primitive Area
30. Salmon River Breaks
31. Selway-Bitterroot Wilderness
32. Nez Perce National Historical Park

Alpine lake in the Northern Rockies, inhabited by native cutthroat trout

late date of construction. The logs used for Rocky Mountain cabins were seldom dressed down, and stone fireplaces were rarely built. Most of these early cabins, such as the ones that can be seen today in Montana and Idaho, were one-room, rectangular buildings about 12 by 15 feet, built by notching the logs and fitting them one above the other at the corners so that some six inches or more of each log projected. The joints between the logs were battened with large chips, over which a chinking of mud, clay, dung, or plaster was daubed. Some cabins were chinked first with mud or plaster and then stripped with lathes or lengths of crude lumber. There were no foundations, and earth was banked around the base to keep out the cold and wind. In some of the cabins of later construction the walls were built by cutting a groove in one log, filling the groove with oakum, and then laying over it a peeled log smoothed to fit the groove.

Most of the cabins had roofs made of small poles, brush, or rough slabs covered with about six inches of dirt, from which plants or weeds grew in season. Some of these roofs extended over the front of the houses, forming a porch. The porch roofs varied, some projecting in the form of a gable, others sloping over the door in the manner of a lean-to.

The cabins were for the most part low-ceilinged and had a door in the center of the front wall and a small window on each side. The windows were usually

of the barn-sash type—a single sash with four small panes—hung on hinges to open either in or out; if two sashes were used, they were constructed so that the sashes could be pushed back into a groove in the wall when the windows were opened. Windows and doors facing north were avoided, especially in the windswept open country and in areas where snowfall was heavy and slow to melt in the spring.

Since much of the Rocky Mountain country was not settled until after the coming of the railroads, stoves were usually cheaper and more convenient than stone fireplaces and flues. The stovepipe, collared by a piece of sheet iron or tin, projected above the roof.

The first cabins were built by trappers, hunters, or cattlemen without families. These men worked singly or in pairs and hence, being out in the mountains or on the range much of the time, did not need large living quarters. Later, when settlers arrived, their cabins grew with their families, the added rooms forming a rambling structure of no particular design. These paintless, weatherbeaten dwellings of natural logs gradually assumed the brown color of the hills and prairies.

A few of the early cabins had two compartments under one roof with a runway between. One half of the building was living quarters, and the other half served as a barn. A hewn-log building of this type is still standing today on the Goose Egg Ranch in Wyoming.

It was common on many of the early ranches that the living quarters and bunkhouses were comparatively small, while the barns, cattle sheds, outbuildings, and pole corrals for the livestock were extensive. As the ranchman's holdings increased, he built a larger and better house for his family. Since there was always

Montana ranch homestead built in the 1890s

Grizzly with cubs in high-country wilderness—this mountain hermit rules over a 20-square-mile terrain

plenty of space, he did not tear down the original cabin but merely built another one near it, using the first one for a bunkhouse or storehouse.

Grizzly Habitats of the Northern Rockies

The nation's last remaining grizzly habitats outside of Alaska are found in the northern wilderness reaches of the Rocky Mountains in Wyoming and Montana: in Yellowstone National Park and the adjoining Absaroka Mountains in Wyoming, in Montana's vast Bob Marshall Wilderness and Mission Mountains Wilderness, and in Glacier National Park.

The grizzly is the hermit of the mountains. A lumbering brute with low, swinging head and a flattened snout, the grizzly slouches through the forest, stopping now and then to gorge itself with berries or to warm its shaggy brownish-blonde coat in the open sunlight. The grizzly can kill anything in its domain, which usually exceeds a 20-square-mile territory, and its fighting supremacy is unquestioned among the crags, yet its common fare is usually limited to mice, insects, berries, wild plums, and green plants. Winters are passed in hibernation, for which the grizzly, like the black bear, prepares itself by gorging in fall. Its shelter varies: sometimes it is a cave among the rocks or a hole beneath the roots of an upturned tree. Winter snows cover the openings and make the den weathertight. Before the long Rocky Mountain winter is over, warm days may bring the big bear out for a short ramble in the sun.

Big Hole Battlefield

Big Hole Battlefield National Monument preserves a portion of the battlefield where on August 9–10, 1877, Colonel John Gibbon fought five bands of Nez Percé Indians who were attempting to escape to Canada after fleeing from Idaho. Gibbon's men were outnumbered two to one, but his attack weakened the Nez Percé, who were later forced to surrender within about 30 miles of their destination. Today in the battlefield area, remains of shallow, grass-grown trenches where Gibbon's men defended themselves and bullet-scarred trees are found in a natural setting similar to that of 1877.

The battlefield is located in Montana's Beaverhead County, 12 miles west of Wisdom.

Bannack Historic District

Bannack was the site of Montana's first gold discovery in 1862. Abandoned since 1938, Montana's oldest town and first territorial capital is a remarkable example of surviving frontier camps and boom towns. Most of the remaining buildings are of frame and log construction, and all are typical of a frontier boom town.

The district is located in Montana's Beaverhead County 22 miles from Dillon on a secondary road off State Highway 278.

Sacajawea's Beaverhead Rock

Beaverhead Rock was sighted by the Shoshone Indian woman Sacajawea on August 8, 1805. She recognized it as a landmark near the summer camping ground of her people and was then able to assure Captains Meriwether Lewis and William Clark, leaders of the transcontinental exploratory expedition (1804–1805), that her people were nearby. Shortly thereafter, Lewis and Clark encountered the Shoshone and obtained horses from them. Without these horses, the party would have been unable to cross the Bitterroot Mountains and reach the Pacific coast. Beaverhead Rock is located west of Dillon in Montana's Madison County.

Lewis and Clark's Traveller's Rest Campsite

Traveller's Rest is the campsite where Meriwether Lewis and William Clark stopped to prepare for the westward crossing of the Bitterroot Mountains on their way to the Pacific coast in 1805. On its return from the coast the following year, the expedition stopped here again. It was then that Lewis took a small party to explore the country between Traveller's Rest and the Great Falls of the Missouri. This was deemed essential in order to meet President Thomas Jefferson's instructions to find the shortest and most feasible route between the Missouri and Columbia rivers.

The site is located in Montana's Missoula County, one mile south of Lolo near U. S. Highway 93.

Big Hole Basin—
Valley of 10,000 Stacks

Montana's beautiful Big Hole Basin is a fertile floodplain formed by the meandering Big Hole River. The basin, named after the Rocky Mountain trapper's term for a large mountain valley, is the site of extensive ranchlands dotted in fall by thousands of haystacks.

The Roundup

A common sight during spring and early fall in the Rocky Mountain country is a large herd of cattle being "driven" across the rangelands by a few ranch hands. With the spring, or calf, roundup held in May or early June, the cowpunchers bring cows and calves in from the river bottoms and sheltered valleys where they have wintered. The calves are separated from their mothers and steers and are led into corral chutes where the cowpunchers brand them with a stamping iron. As in the old days, smoke goes up from branding fires and mingles with the fumes of burning hair. Some of the cows and steers are dehorned; the bull calves castrated; and all are checked for ticks and disease. The beef roundup is held in the fall.

Many of the large ranch outfits have grazing rights in adjacent national forest lands, and cattle may be stranded high in the surrounding alpine meadows where they have summered. In most cases the lead bulls will bring the young steers and cows down from the high country with the first snowfalls in September. The modern roundup is simplified by the freedom from cattle thieves and by the fact that railroad shipping pens are usually within a few days drive, and overnight camps can always be made at ranch buildings.

When the range was wild, the roundup crew went out in the spring, equipped for several weeks in the field. It always had one chuck wagon, sometimes several; a wagon for bedrolls and extra gear; and numerous horses. The cowboys scoured for cattle all the country between great natural boundaries, such as rivers and mountain ranges. What they gathered in a day or two they moved into a herd and held until they had covered a certain territory or had as many head as they could safely handle. Then, while some of the cowboys held the herd, others worked out the unbranded calves, cows, and steers, roped them, dragged them to a fire, and held them down by force while the branding iron was applied. The branded animals were kept apart from the unbranded until the entire herd had been worked; then the herd was sent back on grass, and the wagon went on to another part of the range.

Riders slept on the ground, ate food cooked in a dutch oven, and caught their horses in a flimsy rope corral improvised daily by the camp wrangler. Each man had to stand guard during part of the night, riding around the herd and singing to keep the cattle calm. During storms, when the herd was likely to stampede, the riders were sometimes in the saddle 24 hours at a stretch. Double roundups were held in the fall, one in September, and another, for beef, in October. Then came the drive to the railroad, with stampedes, swollen rivers, soaked blankets, and a cold supper all in a day's work. The cow puncher's monthly pay was $40 and grub.

"Gold-rush" artifacts at Virginia City—a classic Old West boom town that yielded $300 million in gold at its zenith

Virginia City Historic District—
Old West Gold Rush Town

Virginia City, located due west of Ennis in the southwestern portion of Montana, became the territorial capitol of the state after the discovery of gold at Alder Gulch in 1863. The yield was $300 million in gold at the height of the rush, which gave birth to a classic old-West boom town, with equally crowded saloons and a boot hill. The Virginia City buildings that have been restored include the old Wells Fargo Express Office, blacksmith shop, Gilbert Brewery, and the offices of the *Montana Post* territorial newspaper. Other features of this rough 'n ready gold rush town include the Bale of Hay Saloon, Nevada City Hotel, St. Paul's Episcopal Church with its Tiffany windows, and the gold camp artifacts on display at the Thompson-Hickman Memorial Museum. It has close association with one of the vigilante bands of the mining era, which was formed to do away with the infamous Henry Plummer gang. Nearby is the cemetery where the graves of several of the Plummer gang may be found.

Plains buffalo—a remnant of the herds slaughtered during the construction of the Great Northern Railroad

Butte Copper Mining Historic District

Butte is the center of the largest copper mining regions of the world. An area less than five miles square beneath Butte has produced more than $82 billion worth of mineral wealth since 1864. The town site of Butte was laid out in 1876. With the arrival of the first railroad in 1881, the first copper boom began. Surrounded by yellow and gray ore dumps and frames marking mine shafts, Butte is a living mining community whose era of production has not yet ceased.

Butte is located in the southwestern portion of Montana and is reached via Interstate Highways 90 and 15.

Madison River Indian Buffalo Jump

Before horses were introduced to the North American continent, the Plains Indians, on foot, drove large herds of buffalo over cliffs to their death. The technique was quite successful, and those animals not killed by the fall were quickly dispatched by arrows or lances at the bottom of the cliff. The Madison Buffalo Jump is located on a 30-foot limestone bluff above the Madison River Valley. A large grassy prairie covers the land above and behind the cliff, and the jump area includes an Indian village site, a slaughter site, an archeological site, Indian trail, gravesite, and lookout point.

The buffalo jump is located near Logan in Montana's Gallatin County.

Gates of the Mountains—
The Missouri River Canyon

The spectacular Gates of the Mountains of the Missouri River Canyon were named and described by Lewis and Clark in July of 1805 as "the most remarkable cliffs we have yet seen. . . ." rising "from the water's edge on either side to the height of 1,200 feet."

Three Forks—The Headwaters of the Missouri

Captain William Clark discovered the Three Forks in July 1805. He and Meriwether Lewis concluded that the Missouri River had its beginning at the point where the Three Forks joined. They named the three streams the Gallatin, the Madison, and the Jefferson rivers. The Three Forks is associated with the history of the first westward-moving Americans, for since those early days, numerous paths of commerce and communications have passed through this essential point.

The Missouri headwaters site is located in Montana's Gallatin County, northwest of Three Forks on the Missouri River.

Grant-Kohrs Ranch in the Deer Lodge Valley

One of Montana's first territorial ranches, the Grant-Kohrs Ranch National Historic Site, is located just north of Deer Lodge, off Interstate 90 midway between Glacier and Yellowstone national parks. This old-time 216-acre ranch preserves the history of the frontier cattle era and reflects the development of Montana from wilderness to territory to state. The ranch has more than 30 existing structures, including a 23-room ranch house crowded with Victoriana, a perfectly preserved bunkhouse, tack room, ice house, prairie barns, blacksmith shop, wagon collection, corrals, and livestock.

Terraces of Ancient Lake Missoula

Numerous traces of the shoreline of ancient Lake Missoula may be seen along the valley slopes at Missoula, Montana. The city is situated on the old lake terrace formed by Lake Missoula during the last Ice Age by the ice-damming of the Clark Fork of the Columbia River. This ancient lake once covered an area of 3,300 square miles, and its shoreline was 1,000 feet higher than the present-day city.

National Bison Range

The National Bison Range, located 29 miles south of Montana's Flathead Lake near Moiese off U. S. Highway 93, covers 29 square miles of High Plains country. Remnants of the region's once-great herds of plains bison slaughtered during the construction of the Union Pacific and Great Northern railroads roam this protected area of grassy hills and stands of quaking aspen and yellow ponderosa pine.

Flathead Lake—Gem of the Rockies

The beautiful glacier-gouged Flathead Valley, called the Park between the Mountains by the Kalispel Indians, was first explored by David Thompson of the Hudson's Bay Company, which established a trading post there in 1811. Flathead Lake, named after the Indians whose tepees once dotted its shores, is 28 miles long and 10 miles wide and is one of the largest natural freshwater lakes in the United States. The lake and valley are surrounded by the Flathead National Forest and the rugged Bob Marshall and Mission Mountains wilderness areas.

Frontier-era ranch barn and pole corral, still a common sight on Montana's ranches

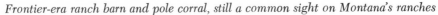

Bob Marshall Wilderness and the Chinese Wall

The vast Bob Marshall Wilderness, located east of Flathead Lake in northeast Montana, straddles the Continental Divide for 60 miles within the Flathead and Lewis and Clark national forests. An unusual feature of this rugged land of alpine lakes, valleys, and massive peaks is a 12-mile-long escarpment known as the Chinese Wall with its 1,000-foot-high sheer face through which there are only three passes. The cliffs of the wall are inhabited by numerous bands of mountain goats.

Limber Pine

The limber pine is a timberline tree, also known as Rocky Mountain white pine, found on dry, rocky, east-facing slopes, summits, tops of ridges, and foothills in the Rocky Mountains from Alberta and Montana to western Texas. Its key feature is five needles in a bundle from one to two and a half inches long. Its cones are three to six inches long, and the scales are not pointed. Its seeds are edible.

Limber pine cone and needles

Limber pine—a timberline tree of the dry, east-facing slopes

Sheer 1,000-foot-high Chinese Wall in the Bob Marshall Wilderness, frequent haunt of bands of mountain goats

Glacier National Park—From Prairies to Glaciers

Glacier National Park, often called the Crown of the Rockies, encompasses more than 1,500 square miles astride the Continental Divide in northwestern Montana. Although not as high as the ranges of the Southern and Central Rockies, the Lewis Range on the east and the Clark Range on the west contain some of the finest glacial landscape to be seen in the Rockies. The lower snowline here has created a monumental world of sculptured horn peaks, glacial cirques, and aretes along the high mountain crests to large trough lakes in the lower parts of the glacier-gouged valleys.

In the valleys along the west slope of the Continental Divide are forests associated with the moist Pacific winds, dominated by fir, larch, spruce, and lodgepole pine. The eastern slopes, exposed to cold winds and less rainfall, are much more open and sparse. On the meadows and slopes at the lower elevations are found Great Plains flora, including pasque-flower, prairie rose, asters, and Indian paintbrush. The Great Plains on the east provide an expansive view of rolling prairies and grassy meadows in stark contrast to the dark wall of peaks to the west.

Lewis Overthrust and the Formation of Glacier's Mountains

The spectacular peaks and summits of Glacier National Park were created by the glacial erosion of the Lewis Overthrust, one of the finest examples of this phenomenon in the world. The overthrust (a fault where rocks on one side are thrust over and above the other side, reversing the normal order of rock layers) was created millions of years ago when earth movements or forces from the west compressed and elevated the sedimentary deposits of an ancient seabed, causing the strata to wrinkle, fold, and fracture, eventually thrusting the great rock mass as much as 40 miles over on top of the rocks on the eastern side of the fault along the fault line. One of the best examples of the effects of the overthrust in the park can be seen along Chief Mountain International Road on Chief Mountain, an erosional remnant of the massive thrust sheet that was driven eastward, where Precambrian rocks hundreds of millions of years old are seen lying on top of cretaceous rocks that are only about 60 million years old.

Features of the Glacier-Carved Mountain Ranges

Much of the landscape of the Rocky Mountain high country is the result of the age-old battle between rock and ice during the series of ice ages that created the valley glaciers that ground their way down the mountain slopes. There are still scores of small glaciers in the Rockies that were formed during a mini-ice age 300 years ago. The major natural features created by the advance of the glaciers include numerous lake basins, boulder fields, U-shaped valleys and meandering streams, jagged hornlike peaks, sharp ridges known

Peaks on the Lewis Overthrust, Glacier National Park, expose Precambrian rocks over a billion years old.

Snowfields and lake on the continental divide in Glacier Park—where scores of small glaciers formed during a mini-Ice Age 300 years ago

as aretes, and cirques—deep amphitheater-shaped valley heads usually on the lee side of mountain slopes, hanging valleys, and glacier-formed ledges of resistant rock known as sheep rock, which have been smoothed, rounded and grooved by the ice and are steeper on the down-valley side where the ice has plucked frost-loosened rock fragments. Many of the region's cirques contain tarns, lakes that fill small rock basins gouged out of the cirques' floor. Curved ridges across the valley floors, created by rocks dropped where the glacier melted, are called moraines. Ridges running parallel to the glacier-carved valley are called lateral moraines; the ridge formed at the farthest point of the glacier's advance are called terminal moraines; ridges deposited up the valley during the glacier's retreat are recessional moraines.

Tall Blazing Star

The tall blazing star is a five-foot prairie plant with blue flowers. It is widely spread from Maine west to the Rocky Mountains. This beautiful plant of the open prairies is also known locally as blue feather, rattlesnake master, devil's bite (because of its finely barbed bristles), and blue blazing star.

White Bark Pine

The white bark pine, a strange tree which grows only in the central and northern Rocky Mountains, is one of the most unconquerable of alpine conifers. It grows at high altitudes, often rimming the world and often getting flattened into a mass of boughs and ice; even at lower altitudes, mountaineers sometimes build their beds of the wide flat branches lying on the earth. At their highest elevations these hardy trees are dwarfed and beaten down but seldom killed and often look like young trees when in fact they are remarkably old; trees only three feet tall have been reported to be 426 year of age. Usually found with it is the limber pine, a crooked, stunted tree that seeks dry, rocky hillsides and other severe sites.

Rock Tripe

Rock tripe, a leathery brown, shieldlike lichen, is common on overhanging cliffs, near streams and ponds, or on rocks and soil on the forest floor. It is flat and leaflike, from one to nine inches in diameter. It attaches its body by an umbilicus made up of plant tissue. It is often found exposed on rocks and talus slopes in the boreal or arctic-alpine regions. This edible plant, called *tripe de roche* by the Arctic explorers, has been credited with saving the lives of many north-country explorers.

Indian Tepee Rings

Tepee rings are circles of stone where Indian lodges once stood. A tepee was a conical tent of animal skins wrapped around three or more poles, with a ventilation hole at the top. The skins were weighted down with stones to retain heat and to prevent their flapping in the wind. Where villages of the Plains Indians stood, hundreds of these circles remain, sometimes on the surface, sometimes half-buried. In some sections of the plains pioneer farmers dug and hauled away innumerable tons of them in preparing the land for cultivation. An example of the tepee rings exists today near Browning, headquarters of the Blackfoot Indian Reservation.

Lewis and Clark's Camp Disappointment

Camp Disappointment, the northernmost point reached by the Lewis and Clark Expedition, was established by Meriwether Lewis and nine of his men on July 23, 1806, on the return trip from the Pacific. The purpose of this side trip was to explore an Indian trail, to determine if the Marias River extended north of the 49th parallel, and to determine if there was a short portage between the headwaters of the Marias and Saskatchewan rivers. These objectives were stated by President Thomas Jefferson in his instructions to Lewis. Unfortunately, there was no portage. The site is an undeveloped area used for livestock grazing, apparently little changed since 1806.

The site is located on private land 12 miles northeast of Browning on the Blackfoot Indian Reservation in Montana's Glacier County.

Bighorn sheep—a common sight on Glacier National Park's high crags

Canada geese during height of the spring migration

Alpine Kittentails

Alpine kittentails, dense spikes of lavender flowers two to three inches high, grow from a rosette of thick basal leaves nestled in rock crevices and are among the first alpine blossoms seen each summer. This plant, a member of the figwort family, is restricted to mountain tundra areas, although it has close relatives at lower elevations.

Chief Joseph Battleground at the Bearpaw Mountains

In June of 1877 the federal government attempted to remove the Nez Percé Indians from their home in Oregon's Wallowa River valley. Led by Chief Joseph, the Nez Percé resisted and fled northeast across Idaho and Montana en route to Canada. On the rolling prairie land at the base of the Bearpaw Mountains, the Indians were overtaken by soldiers led by General Nelson A. Miles. A battle was engaged that lasted from September 30 to October 5, but the Indians, exhausted by their long journey, hungry, and taken by surprise, finally surrendered. "From where the sun now stands, I will fight no more forever," said Chief Joseph. Eight years later, the Nez Percé were settled on the Lapwai Colville Reservation in western Idaho.

The Bearpaw Battleground is about 15 miles south of Chinook in Montana's Blaine County.

Moss Campion

Moss campion is a dominant and easy-to-recognize pink plant of the mountain fellfield areas forming discrete cushions among the upturned rocks. It grows in fellfields throughout the northern hemisphere, where its extensive taproot system enables it to live where the soils shift continuously. Its narrow, needle-like leaves gives it the appearance of a moss, hence the name.

Rock Flour

The milky blue waters of creeks fed by the run-off waters of glaciers are laden with powder-fine particles of rocks that have been pulverized by the advancing glacier.

Fellfields

The fellfield (*fell* means rock in Gaelic) is a typical high-mountain area covered with rocks, created by the action of frost churning the soil characteristic of alpine and arctic regions. This process pushes rocks to the surface and leaves many rocks on edge as it slows down. Since strong winds sweep across the fellfields most of the time, very little snow covers them in winter, and they become dry early in summer. Plants living in fellfields, which are above timberline and have an otherworldly look about them, must be well adapted to withstand severe conditions. This adaptation is accomplished by a cushion or mat form of growth with long taproots, which may reach several hundreds of years in age. The characteristic alpine plant life found on the high fellfields include moss campion, dwarf clover, alpine clover, alpine sandwort, Rocky Mountain nailwort, alpine phlox, round-leaved willow, yellowstone crop, pigmy bitterroot, and mountain dryad.

Alpine Krummholz Areas

Krummholz areas are islands of stunted, deformed trees, interspersed with patches of small shrubs and herbs, located at the uppermost boundary of mountain forests between the treeline and tundra. These broken and gnarled trees form dense clumps that are shaped by the fierce mountain winds and separated from each other by alpine meadows (which see). As one goes up in elevation through krummoholz areas and wind velocity increases, the flag trees, which have branches on one side of the erect trunk, are replaced by cushions of low-branching tree mats. The krummholz islands become increasingly oddly shaped at higher altitudes, until the trees are the size of small herbs, broken by meadows of tundra herbs and shrubs of increasing size. Krummholz aspen at high elevations may often

Krummholz area—alpine islands of stunted, gnarled trees

Bitterroot

The Flathead Indians of Montana who used bitterroot for food gave it the name later applied to the Bitterroot mountains, river, and valley in the western part of Montana. The bitterroot is a small plant, with a rosette of 12 to 18 leaves; its low-set pink blossoms turn white after a few days in the sun. The early pioneers called it Lewisia in honor of Captain Meriwether Lewis and rediviva (Latin for lives again) in recognition of its vitality. The gumbo lily is like the bitterroot, and even more beautiful, but it is not so commonly sighted.

Idaho's Salmon River Country

The Salmon River country encompasses about 16,000 square miles of large, sprawling mountains, narrow, gorgelike valleys and small basins, and wild rivers in a geological region known as the Idaho batholith. The major ranges of the region are the Bitterroot, Coeur d'Alene, Clearwater, Salmon River, and the jagged Sawtooth Mountains.

be more than 80 years old and less than one foot tall.

The dominant tree species in krummholz areas are Engelmann spruce and subalpine fir, limber pine, and small numbers of quaking aspen and lodgepole pine. The plants between the clumps of trees include willows, herbs, bog birch, and mosses. The krummholz areas form the primary habitat for white-tailed ptarmigan, white-crowned sparrow, and summer resting range for elk. The dense mats of tree needles and herbs provide both protective cover and browse.

Lemhi Pass in the Bitterroot Mountains

Lemhi Pass is associated with many events crucial to the success of the Lewis and Clark Expedition. It is the point where the party crossed the Continental Divide and where it left the United States as represented by the boundary of the Louisiana Purchase and entered Spanish territory. The success or failure of the expedition rested with the Shoshone Indians, who lived on either side of the crest of Lemhi Pass. The cooperation of these Indians in supplying horses, food, and guides made possible the overland journey of the party to the navigable waters of the Columbia River. Lemhi Pass, elevation 8,000 feet, has changed little in the intervening years.

The pass is located 12 miles east of the town of Tendoy, Idaho, off State Highway 28.

Idaho's Sawtooth Range—a favorite haunt of Ernest Hemingway, who lived near Sun Valley

The major features of this rugged high country include the sheer gorges, crags, and breaks along the wild Salmon, Middlefork of the Salmon, Clearwater, Selway, and Lochwa rivers; the 10,000-foot Bighorn Crags, alpine lakes, canyons, and rolling plateaus of the 1.2-million-acre Idaho Primitive Area; the craggy peaks and Stanley Basin area of the Sawtooth Wilderness at the headwaters of the Salmon River; and the vast wildlands of the Selway-Bitterroot Wilderness along the Idaho-Montana boundary.

Lolo Trail

The Lolo Trail is the 150-odd miles of the Nez Percé Indian Buffalo Trail that was followed by Lewis and Clark in their 1805 crossing of the Bitterroot Mountains to navigable waters of the Columbia River system. In general, the Lolo Trail travelled the high backbone of the mountain mass north of the Lochsa River. Today, the trail extends through wilderness country from 5,187-foot Lolo Pass over the Bitterroot Mountains westward to Weippe, Idaho.

Beginning near Lolo Hot Springs, Idaho, the trail runs parallel to U. S. Highway 12 along the ridges of the Bitterroot Mountains from Lolo Pass westward to Weippe Prairie. Information on the historic sites along the trail is available at the Forest Service's Lolo Pass Visitor Center and at the National Park Service headquarters in Spalding, Idaho.

Fort Lemhi—The Salmon River Mission

Thomas S. Smith, at the annual Mormon Conference in 1855, was appointed leader of an expedition to found a mission in the north among the Indians, and on June 15 the group selected this site. A fort, consisting of 25 cabins enclosed by a timber stockade and having an adobe-wall stock corral, was soon constructed. By 1857 plans were made to transform the mission into a permanent colony; however, a raid on the stock by the Bannock Indians the following year greatly discouraged the settlers, who shortly quit the fort and returned to Salt Lake City. All that remains on the site are remnants of the stock corral and an irrigation ditch.

The site is about 18 miles southeast of Salmon in Idaho's Lemhi County.

Mountain Hemlock

The mountain hemlock, which grows in association with the alpine larch, is sometimes called the

Pioneer marker on the wild Middle Fork of the Salmon River—named "River of No Return" by early prospectors and pioneers

black hemlock and is one of the most beautiful of the cone bearers in American forests. A mature tree may be four feet in diameter and 100 feet in height, with gracefully drooping branches, each with a feathery sheath of gently arching evergreen needles, and beautifully colored cones. It grows along the margins of alpine meadows, pushing the advance guard of the forest to the edge of glaciers. It is usually found near the upper tree limits of the mountains.

Alpine Sorrel

Throughout the Northern Hemisphere alpine sorrel, a member of the buckwheat family, is one of the first plants to invade gravel areas, especially in the wake of retreating glaciers. Its leaves taste pleasantly acid, resembling rhubarb and sheep sorrel. It provided essential vitamin C for early arctic explorers.

Salmon Charcoal Kilns

Discovered in 1881, the Viola mine became an important source of lead and silver from 1886 to 1888. Charcoal for a smelter was produced in 16 kilns here until low prices for lead and silver forced the smelter to shut down after 1889. The four extant kilns are beehive in shape, 20 feet high and 21.5 feet in diameter, with walls 14 inches thick. Although charcoal

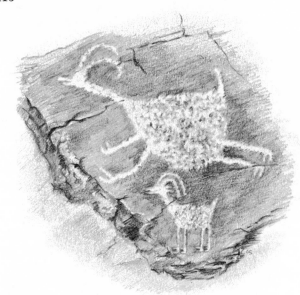

Indian petroglyph of bighorn sheep, carved with a sharp stone instrument

kilns were built for smelters in a number of Idaho mining areas in the late 19th century, these are some of the few remaining in the state.

The kilns are six miles west of Idaho Highway 28, midway between Salmon and Idaho Falls.

Indian Rock Writings

Indian pictographs (painted inscriptions) and petroglyphs (inscriptions carved with a sharp instrument) are found throughout the West. Their significance seems to be as records of visits of individuals, battles, hunting expeditions, game areas, religious ceremonies, dreams, warnings, and information about water or trails. Although most of them are very crude, they show varying artistic ability and seem to be the records of ancient but not primitive man.

The pictographs are most often found on walls under rock shelters or in caves, and some of them have lines so neatly executed that it is thought the paintings were sketched beforehand. In design the pictographs feature curvilinear and geometric elements with numerous dots and some triangles. The circular figure occurs in many combinations, with connected, concentric, and plain circles as well as some used in series or chains. Other representative characters are wavy lines, rakes, stars, rain symbols, ladders, deer, mountain sheep, birds, lizards, bear tracks and paws, sheep horns, hands, men on horses, and the sun. The paints, made by dissolving minerals with gum or resin from pine and fir trees, have glazed and become bright in color—mostly red—retaining that brightness many years. In a cave at Indian Head Gulch in Idaho, for

example, are drawings representing the hoop and pole game, which was probably a championship game between the Shoshone and Arapaho tribes.

Petroglyphs, made by abrasion, were usually placed on the southern exposure of the rocks, because the other sides were more likely to be covered with moss or lichens. The stones used to carve were of a very hard nature, often quartz. Some of the marks are barely visible, whereas others are as legible as though they were of recent date. In some instances writings of a later period were superimposed on the first writings.

Nez Percé National Historic Park

The vast stretch of Nez Percé Indian country in northern Idaho is the setting of a new kind of historical park. Scattered over 12,000 square miles are 18 separate historic sites, many privately owned, which preserve and interpret the history and culture of the Nez Percé Indians and of the whites who eventually engulfed them. Some of the sites, such as the Weippe Prairie, are merely scenic views recalling significant events. Others, such as Coyote's Fishnet and Ant and Yellow Jacket, are natural formations that figure in the religion and legends of the Nez Percé. A few consist of historic buildings, as at Fort Lapwai, that are now open to the public. Canoe Camp, where Lewis and Clark camped on their westward journey to the Pacific in the autumn of 1805, is about five miles west of Orofino on U.S. Highway 12. After building dugout canoes, caching their supplies for the return journey, and leaving their horses with the Nez Percé, they began their journey down the Snake River to the Columbia.

The park covers an area 90 miles south and 150 miles east of its headquarters at Spalding, Idaho, reached via U. S. Highway 95.

Lewis and Clark's "Canoe Campsite" during their journey to the Pacific guided by Sacajawea

Field of wild lupine, member of the bean family, in bloom

Camas Meadows

One of the most famous flowers in the records and legends of the early Western explorers and an important food of the Indians was the camas, which made many a meadow blue. Its blossoms spread in dense gardens in damp areas, which from a distance look like lakes of blue water. Its edible bulb was steamed for 24 hours or longer in a kind of fireless cooker of heated stones. Many an Indian war was fought for possession of camas meadows. The flowers, from 12 to 30 on a pedicel, are blue or white and bloom from April to July.

Weippe Prairie

On September 20, 1805, members of the Lewis and Clark Expedition emerged from the Bitterroot Mountains onto the Weippe Prairie, where they first encountered the Nez Percé Indians. Here at the western terminus of the Lolo Trail, Lewis and Clark established friendly relations with these Indians, a relationship which continued unbroken for 70 years. A few farmhouses and some fences are present on this upland plain of about 3,000 feet, but enough open areas still remain to suggest the unspoiled prairie seen by Lewis and Clark.

The area is south of the town of Weippe on Idaho Highway 11.

Idaho's St. Joe River—World's Highest Navigable River

Idaho's St. Joe River is the world's highest navigable waterway; at 2,128-foot elevation, tugboats can be seen pulling large rafts of logs to the lumber mills at Coeur d'Alene. Although the upper stretches of the river have 120 miles of free-flowing waters, the lower 6-mile portion meanders through natural cottonwood-lined levees and is known as the River through the Lakes. The levees are the summer rookeries of the largest osprey colony in North America.

Water Ouzel, or American Dipper

The water ouzel, or American dipper, builds its nest beside or behind a waterfall so that the spray will keep the moss lining green and fresh. Its body is chunky and about as large as the robin's. Its dull slate color is sometimes difficult to distinguish against the canyon rocks or in the brawling rapids, where it makes frequent plunges for underwater insects. Completely at home under water, it walks on the gravelly creek bottoms, unafraid of the swift current, protected from the cold by soft, thick plumage, sure-footed on the slippery rocks.

Idaho's Lake Pend Oreille

The glacier-formed waters of huge, 43-mile-long Lake Pend Oreille sprawl across the mountain-rimmed forests of Northern Idaho's Panhandle. The lake was once the fishing grounds of the Pend O'Reille Indians, who held the lake's islands sacred and used them as burial grounds, where they suspended their dead from trees. Northward of the lake, which reaches depths of 1,800 feet and is inhabited by the giant Kamloops strains of rainbow trout that reach weights of up to 37 pounds, stretch the rugged Selkirk Mountains.

American dipper, or water ouzel, a stocky, slate-colored bird of the mountain streams

6. Cactus and Sagebrush— The Great American Deserts

THE stark, mountain-studded deserts of the American West lie within the vast Basin and Range region—a 500-mile-wide area that lies between Utah's Wasatch Mountains and California's Sierra Nevada, narrows to about half that distance between the Grand Wash Cliffs of the Colorado Plateau and the Sierra Nevada at Owens Valley, then opens into the great Sonoran and Chihuahuan deserts for nearly 700 miles along the southern border of the United States to the Sacramento Mountains and the Big Bend of the Rio Grande in Texas.

The Basin and Range contains five distinct sections: the short mountain ranges and sagebrush country of the Great Basin, the saguaro-studded slopes and arid flats of the Sonoran Desert, the hot lowlands of the Salton Trough and Colorado River Desert, the high desert valleys and mountain ranges of the Chihuahuan Desert, and the plateaulike landscape of the Sacramento Mountain and Big Bend country.

The mountains of the Basin and Range, described as "an army of caterpillars crawling northward out of Mexico," are short and appear to rise abruptly from the surrounding landscape to heights of up to more

than 10,000 feet. Some were high enough to shelter glaciers during the Pleistocene Ice Age. There are more than 150 mountain ranges in the region, extending along a north-south axis.

The Great Basin

The vast 200,000-square-mile Great Basin is the largest desert on the North American continent. It occupies the ancient Ice Age lake basins between the Sierra Nevada and Rocky mountains, covering nearly all of Nevada and portions of southeastern Oregon, northeastern California, western Utah, arid portions of the Snake River country in southern Idaho, and Wyoming's Red Desert.

Shut off from the moist sea winds of the Pacific by the ramparts of the Sierra Nevada and other mountains bordering it on the west, this high, dry sagebrush country is made up of broad basins with gleaming flats of alkali salts, plateaus, valleys, and a succession of north-south mountain ranges, which rise abruptly from the parched plains like snow-covered alpine

Key to Sites

1. Joshua Tree National Monument
2. Pinto Basin
3. Salton Sea
4. Death Valley National Monument
5. Devils Hole
6. Ancient Bristlecone Pine Forest
7. Desert National Wildlife Range
8. Valley of Fire
9. Lake Mead National Recreation Area
10. Nevada Wild Horse Range
11. Wheeler Peak
12. Lehman Caves National Monument
13. Ward Charcoal Ovens
14. Ruby Marsh
15. Jarbidge Wilderness
16. Emigrant Pass on the Old California-Humboldt Trail
17. Charles Sheldon National Antelope Range
18. Black Rock Desert
19. Fortyniner Camp on the Applegate Cutoff of the California Trail
20. Pyramid Lake
21. Carson Sink

22. Eureka Historic Mining District
23. Cold Springs Pony Express Station
24. Hickison Indian Petroglyph Site
25. Comstock Lode at Virginia City
26. Singing Sand Mountain
27. Hart Mountain National Antelope Range
28. Malheur National Wildlife Refuge
29. Organ Pipe Cactus National Monument
30. Kofa Mountains and Game Range
31. Colorado River Indian Tribes Museum
32. Kitt Peak National Observatory
33. Saguaro National Monument—Tucson Mountain Unit
34. Saguaro National Monument—Rincon Mountain Unit
35. Ventana Cave
36. Casa Grande Ruins
37. Theodore Roosevelt Dam
38. Superstition Mountains
39. Tonto Cliff Dwellings

40. Snaketown, Prehistoric City State
41. Tombstone Historic District
42. Tumacacori National Monument
43. Coronado's Trail National Monument
44. Lehner Prehistoric Mammoth-Kill Site
45. Fort Bowie National Historic Site
46. Chiricahua Mountains
47. Gila Cliff Dwellings National Monument
48. Gila Wilderness Area
49. Sandia Cave and Mountains
50. Gran Quivira National Monument
51. Valley of Fires Lava Fields
52. White Sands National Monument
53. Carlsbad Caverns National Park
54. Guadalupe Mountains National Park
55. Big Bend National Park

Stark, mountain-studded desert of the 500-mile-wide Basin and Range region

islands. Within the natural boundaries of the region lie Death Valley and Great Salt Lake, a shallow remnant of ancient Lake Bonneville.

Great Basin Life Zones

Mountain

The mountain ranges of the 500-mile-wide Great Basin rise up from the arid plains at intervals of 20 to 30 miles. These beautiful alpine islands are usually from 40 to 80 miles long and reach heights of 10,000 feet. Their plant and animal life is similar to the Sierra Nevada and Rocky mountains. Among the wind-swept slopes and small lake basins high above the glimmering alkali flats and sagebrush-speckled plains the hiker will enter a world of gnarled bristlecone pines, junipers, and giant colorful fragmental rocks metamorphosed from sandstone millions of years ago. Here

Roadrunner, named by the pioneers for its curious habit of jogging alongside their spinning wagon wheels

and there are tangled, low-lying mats of mountain juniper; patches of bunch grass, dock, and low-lying flealane waving gently in the breeze; colorful glades of Oregon grape; and great stands of pine, spruce, and silver-trunked aspen.

Moving down in elevation from the world of the alpine lakes and big trees, the landscape opens up into a rocky mosaic of dwarf forests of twisted mountain mahogany, golden-flowered rabbit brush, bunch grasses, and a few sagebrush. Thickets of chokecherry fringe the small mountain streams.

On the rocky slopes approaching the high desert zone between 8,000 and 6,000 feet are stands of single-leafed pinyon pine and gnarled, shrubby Utah or desert junipers laden with silver berries, interspersed with golden carpets of rabbit brush, clumps of crested wheat grass, and sagebrush.

High Desert

The largely treeless zone of the high desert overlaps both the mountains and high plains at elevations varying from 5,000 to 10,000 feet. It is largely a world of arid sagebrush plains, broken here and there at the higher elevations by lonely stands of pinyon pine and juniper. It is a vast, monotonous world of sagebrush hummocks, mounds of greasewood, and springs surrounded by green meadows of tall bulrushes and salt grass, whirring horse flies, antelope, coyotes, mule deer, collared lizards, kit fox, badger, and sage hens. The alert traveller, through the seemingly endless expanses of broad, pebble-strewn, brush-covered basins flanked by the colorfully banded mountain ranges, may see the small sagebrush chipmunk gathering seeds in the tops of the bushes as well as gophers, kangaroo rats, the big-eared harvest mouse, buffy-gray canyon mouse, pack rats, coyotes, jack rabbits, rattlesnakes, sage thrasher and sage sparrow, and the spade-foot toad about the desert water holes.

Low Desert

The low desert, a sharply defined region of the Mohave Desert and Death Valley (which see), lies to the south of the Great Basin Desert and is dominated by the yellow-flowered creosote bush, cactus, and the many-branched Joshua tree.

Canyon Slopes of the Great Basin

The deep, hidden canyons of the Great Basin have interesting microclimates (which see) that relate directly to their exposure to sunlight. The north-facing canyon slopes, which receive little direct sunlight, tend to be moist and covered with green vegetation. The arid and sparsely covered south-facing slopes, however, receive direct sunlight during most of each day. In a similar fashion the softer, more porous and easily eroded andesite canyon slopes are generally green, whereas on the hard, black-slate-formed slopes of the Great Basin canyons are found only the most hardy, wind-resistant grasses and shrubs, such as Mormon Tea and sagebrush.

Sagebrush—symbol of the Great Basin Desert

Nevada's Great Basin Desert across from the White Mountains of California, dominated by 14,242-foot-high White Mountain Peak, site of the Ancient Bristlecone Pine Forest

Plant Coloration of Basin and Range

The greenish-brown patchwork of colors the traveller sees through the Great Basin region are formed by the region's dominant plant life. The green areas are created by big sagebrush; the dark green areas on the slopes by mountain mahogany; the brown areas by low sagebrush; and the pale green areas along the canyon floors by willow bushes and cottonwood.

Mountain Haze

One of the characteristic features of the mountain ranges of the Great Basin country is the murky haze that envelops the slopes and peaks. It is caused by the mixing of fine dust particles blown up from the arid basins with plants' natural hydrocarbon emissions, known as terpenes.

Mirage

The low blue haze that often appears on the distant surface throughout the Great Basin and desert areas of the West—and that often caused teams of oxen to stampede toward what looked like a lake during the westward trek of the pioneers—is a mirage, caused when the intense afternoon sun rays are reflected in heat waves, creating a mirrorlike reflection of the sky that shimmers along the basin floors.

Desert Varnish

The parched areas of desert floors that appear a shiny dark brown are known as desert varnish, gravel that has become coated by a film of iron and manganese oxide that has been brought to the surface by water seeps.

Dust Devil

A common occurrence along the desert floors of the Great Basin, dust devils are small, cyclone-shaped swirls of gray alkali dust, whipped into motion by the wind.

Graben

Valleys in the Great Basin that have been created by the faulting and uplifting of the earth's surface creating a sunken bowl surrounded by bordering

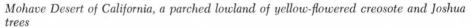

Mohave Desert of California, a parched lowland of yellow-flowered creosote and Joshua trees

Dry, south-facing slopes of the Great Basin, in direct sunlight most of the day and supporting only sparse plant life

mountains are called graben, German for trench. Death Valley is a perfect example of this unusual phenomenon. Yosemite Valley to the north is an example of the more common glacier-carved valley.

Gravel Terraces—Remnants of the Ancient Lakes

The high gravel terraces found throughout the ancient lake beds of the Great Basin mark the former beaches and shorelines of the once-great lakes. About 50 of these wave-carved terraces flank Great Salt Lake and mark the former boundaries of ancient Lake Bonneville. Bonneville Terrace, the highest in these prehistoric remnants, rises 1,000 feet above the surface of present-day Great Salt Lake.

Talus Slopes

The barren, jagged broken rock areas fractured and split by frost on the mountains of the West are known as talus slopes. Hikers should bear in mind that these slopes can be treacherous and should be avoided when possible.

Blowouts

Common throughout the sand dune areas of the Basin, blowouts are wind-gouged hollows or troughs usually dotted by the gnarled stems of half-buried mesquite trees and creosote bushes.

Playa Lakes

Playa lakes are temporary bodies of water fed by intermittent streams, that form only after rains in the low desert plains. Some have been known to disappear completely during years of little rainfall, suddenly to reappear after a heavy spate to cover vast areas of desert land. Playas with an extremely high salt content are known as *salinas*. A playa in Nevada's Black Rock Desert has been known to cover an area of more than 450 square miles under several inches of

Joshua tree of the Mohave Desert, named by Mormon pioneers because its armlike branches resemble an Old Testament prophet

water during the winter months, when the desert rains most often occur. These highly alkaline playas are inhabited by salt-resistant greasewood, tumbleweed, and salt grass.

Desert Pavement

A common feature of the arid playa lakes of the Great Basin, desert pavement, is a thin layer of wind- and water-polished pebbles that form a mosaic that looks like man-made inlaid cobblestones.

Rock Spires

Giant spires of rock, formed after the drying up of the huge prehistoric lakes that once flooded the

Great Basin, are commonly sighted along the canyon walls of the region. As the exposed rock dried, it contracted to form thin vertical crevices, which were widened and eroded over the succeeding centuries by rain and ice.

Mohave Desert

The ancient lake basins of the picturesque Mohave Desert are an upland area between the Great Basin Desert on the north and the Sonoran Desert on the south, dominated by the green creosote bush, burro bush, and other low shrubs. The Mohave Desert is the natural habitat of the Joshua tree (which see). The outermost limits of the tree's growth mark the natural boundaries of the region. Though most portions of the desert lie between 2,000 and 5,000 feet above sea level, one part, Death Valley, lies some 550 feet below sea level. Valleys of Joshua trees, the tree lily, are preserved in their natural state along the southern border of the desert in the 500,000-acre Joshua Tree National Monument, flanked by rugged pinyon-covered mountains. The sere basin of the Mohave, dotted by galleta grass, creosote bush, Mohave yucca, paper-bag bush, and deer-horn and larrel cactus are inhabited by the desert chipmunk, ground squirrels, lizards, Mohave rattlesnake, sidewinder, and a variety of desert birds. In autumn flocks of migrating turkey vultures are often sighted along the Mohave River.

Volcanic Features of the Mohave Desert

Evidence of the widespread volcanic activity of the Mohave Desert's recent past is found in the cinder caves, layers of volcanic ash, lava flows, and craters found near Little Lake at the southern end of Owens Valley.

Prehistoric Artifacts of the Mohave Desert

The caves and volcanic deposits of the Mohave Desert, once a lush land of forests, meandering rivers, and lake chains, have yielded fossils of the flora and fauna that once thrived here, including the camel and three-toed horse, mammoth, giant ground sloth that inhabited the area along with the primitive Pinto Basin man who roamed the lake country some 9,000 years ago. Artifacts of this spear-throwing nomad have been discovered at the Pinto Basin of the Joshua Tree National Monument and at Little Lake in the northeastern portion of the desert.

Joshua Tree—Indicator of the Mohave Desert

The Joshua tree was named by a colony of Mormon pioneers travelling in search of their new Jerusalem across the Mohave Desert because its armlike branches seemed to beckon them across the scorched plain like an Old Testament prophet. This strange tree, a yucca also known as the tree lily, grows to heights of 40 feet. It is found nowhere outside its natural range in the Mohave Desert. Its daggerlike leaves are crowded near the ends of stout, branching stems. Its lilylike flower may or may not appear each year, depending on the amount of rainfall and temperature. Its stem is the habitat of a boring beetle, butterfly larvae, and numerous other insects. The night lizard is completely dependent on the tree for food and shelter. Its branches serve as nesting platforms for a variety of desert birds. The area's Indian tribes used its thin red roots in basket weaving and its seeds for food. Several square miles of the Joshua tree's natural habitat have been preserved near Palm Springs as the Joshua Tree National Monument.

Joshua Tree National Monument

Near the southern boundary of the Mohave Desert, north of California's Salton Sea (see separate entry) lies the rugged desert landscape of the Joshua Tree National Monument. Few areas more vividly illustrate the contrast between the plant life of high and low desert. Below 3,000 feet the Colorado Desert, occupying the eastern half of the monument, is dominated by creosote bush, with small stands of spidery ocotillo and jumping cholla cactus. Above 3,000 feet is the slightly cooler, wetter Mohave Desert, the natural range of the Joshua tree, extensive stands of which dot the western half of the monument.

The monument's half million acres form a striking desert mosaic of rugged mountains, bajadas, desert varnish, arroyos, playas, alluvial fans, and exposed granite monoliths broken here and there by five fan-palm oases, which indicate those few areas where water appears naturally at or near the surface.

In prehistoric times, the area was inhabited by the Pinto Man, who hunted and gathered along a

Sand Dunes in Death Valley—named Tomesha by the Indians, meaning "ground afire"

meandering river that ran through the now dry Pinto Basin. Later, Indians travelled into the area to harvest pinyon nuts, acorns, cactus fruit, and mesquite beans, leaving behind rock paintings and pottery ollas as remnants of their passing. In the late 1800s, explorers, cattlemen, and miners invaded the desert landscape, building dams to create water tanks and tunneling deep-shaft mines in search of gold and silver. They left behind the Lost Horse and Desert Queen mines and the Desert Queen Ranch.

Death Valley

Death Valley at the outermost reaches of the Great Basin in southeastern California, established as a national monument in 1933, covers 2,981 square miles of the Mohave Desert, 500 of which are below sea level. The narrow, pearl-colored trough of the valley curves for 140 miles between steep mountains of naked rock that are striped and patched with vivid colors. The Panamint Range, rising 6,000 to 11,000 feet above sea level, gives the valley its western wall, and the Grapevine, Funeral, and Black mountains, rising 4,000 to 8,000 feet, form its eastern wall. The heavy rains that sometimes fall on the mountains run swiftly off the steep, barren slopes and cascade into the valley, where the water quickly vanishes. The valley floor, once the bed of ancient Lake Manly, is streaked with white salt, gray clay, and yellow sand; in the glimmering salt beds is the lowest spot in North America.

From June to September, while the days are a blaze of light and the rocks radiate stored heat at night, Death Valley is one of the hottest places in the world, reaching temperatures of 190°F. The Indian name for the valley was *Tomesha*—ground afire. Place names within and around the valley attest to the hardiness and suffering of the pioneers and forty-niners who braved its harsh environment: Hell's Gate, Devil's Cornfield, Coffin Canyon, Arsenic Spring, Last Chance Range. In the winter snow lies lightly on the ranges, except on Telescope Peak, which is white until May, and sunny days in the valley are delightful. The charm of the area lies in its magnificent range of color, which varies from hour to hour.

Geology

Death Valley contains rock of all the great divisions of geologic time. At one time this was probably a region of low mountains and wide valleys, with streams and lakes. Then followed a period of great earth disturbances accompanied by volcanic actions; Death Valley was formed by faulting. At the end of the glacial period the valley was a lake, but the waters gradually evaporated, and the land became a desert.

Vegetation

In a wet year, when from two to five inches of rain fall, canyons, washes, and even the valley floor are tinted with gray desert holly and green creosote bush, with cigarette plant, paperbag bush, sprucebush, saltbrush, brittle bush, and wetleaf. Two types of mesquite, willows, and cottonwoods are found. High on the Panamints and Grapevines are pinyon, juniper, mountain mahogany, Rocky Mountain maple, and bristlecone and limber pine. Six plant species in Death Valley are found nowhere else: rock midget, large-flowered sunray, yellow-flowered gelmania, holly-leafed spurge, death valley sage, and napkin-ring spidermat.

Wildlife

The desert animals include the Nelson bighorn sheep in the mountains, the desert coyote and kit fox, and wild burro. The bushy-tailed antelope, ground squirrel, and the trade and wood rat are often sighted. Among the birds that live in the valley year-round are black ravens, roadrunners, prairie falcons, the beautiful LeConte thrasher, and rock wrens. There are several varieties of lizards, including whip-tailed, gridiron, horned toads, and chackwalls. Rattlesnakes are rare. An inch-long pupfish, found at Cottonball Marsh, Salt Creek and Saratoga Springs, is a prehistoric remnant from the days when the valley was a lake.

Pupfish from Devil's Hole—a living prehistoric relic from the time Death Valley was submerged under a great lake

"Beehive" charcoal kilns in Death Valley. In 1870, 300 men cut juniper and pinyon pine and sledded it to these kilns. The charcoal product was carted by mule train to gold and silver smelters at the Modoc Mines west of Panamint Valley.

Rhyolite ghost town in Death Valley

Ruins of the Harmony Borax Works

Visible on a low bluff off the Death Valley highway are the old adobe walls of the first borax works in the valley. The refined borax was hauled by the famous mule teams through Wingate Pass to Mohave, 160 miles away. Each outfit consisted of a lead wagon and a trailer carrying 20 tons of borax, which were drawn by teams of 12 to 20 mules, guided by a check line 125 feet long. The works were closed in 1887 when the price of borax fell. A small museum exhibit of Death Valley history and natural history installed by the Pacific Coast Borax Company is at Furnace Creek Ranch.

Sand Dunes of Death Valley

Death Valley's wind-rippled sand dunes, often reaching heights of 100 feet, are formed by minute particles of eroded granite and sandstone that have been washed down from the surrounding mountains and piled up by the winds. In spring their lower reaches are often carpeted with brilliant displays of wildflowers, including blazing stars, yellow- and white-flowered evening primroses, and bush penstemon.

Great Salt Lake and Prehistoric Lake Remnants of the Great Basin

Utah's Great Salt Lake, a closed-basin lake with no outlets whose waters are now 10 times saltier than any ocean, is a remnant of ancient Lake Bonneville, once a vast inland sea formed during the retreat of the glaciers that covered most of southern Idaho, Utah, and eastern Nevada. The seven terraces that rise in the distance along the shoreline of the present-day lake, the largest lake west of the Mississippi, are remnants of the previous shoreline of Lake Bonneville, whose surface was 1,000 feet above the present-day lake. The evaporation of Lake Bonneville's water left a flat, sterile desert of white mineral salts. Elsewhere along the shoreline of Great Salt Lake, visitors will see sandbars, cliffs, and ancient beaches formed by the action of waves in the old lake. The cliffs and islands are nesting areas for a great variety of seabirds, including thousands of gulls, terns, and white pelicans. Other existing remnants of Lake Bonneville in the Great Basin are Little Salt, Sevier, and Utah lakes.

Historic photo before the Golden Spike ceremony when the Jupiter *met the last of the old covered-wagon trains near the shore of Great Salt Lake at Monument Point*

Lake Utah has remained a freshwater lake because its outlet into Great Salt Lake prevents excessive evaporation.

Other remnants of ancient lakes in the Great Basin desert include 30-mile-long Pyramid Lake and Walker Lake, the Carson and Humboldt sinks in Nevada, and Honey Lake in California. All were once part of Lake Lahontan in present-day Nevada and eastern California, which once covered an area the size of Lake Erie. The surface of Pyramid Lake, which has no outlet and is slowly receding from its former shoreline, is broken here and there by volcanic tufa islands, including 248-acre Anaho Island, which is inhabited by the West's largest rookery of pelicans.

Golden Spike National Historic Site

The Golden Spike National Historic Site at Promontory Point is north of Great Salt Lake, some 32 miles west of Brigham City, Utah. The site marks the historic joining of the tracks of the Union Pacific and Central Pacific railroads and the end of the great race to complete the construction of the transcontinental railroad. At 12:47 P.M. on May 10, 1869, the telegrapher's three dots—"Done"—flashed across the country from Promontory Point. The Golden Spike was symbolically driven and the rails from east and west were connected. The railroad soon fulfilled its objectives of eliminating the Indian menace to travel and settlement in the West, providing a way of transporting troops, supplies, and mail swiftly and cheaply, and serving as a physical connection to strengthen the political and commercial ties of California and the western territories with the rest of the nation.

In 1903, the Southern Pacific, which had absorbed the Central Pacific, began the Lucin Cutoff across

Great Salt Lake to shorten the line. When it was completed in 1904, almost all rail traffic used it, with only occasional traffic being routed through Promontory Point. About 1.7 miles of track have been relaid at Promontory Point on the original roadbed where the railroads were joined.

Lucin Cutoff of Great Salt Lake

The building of the transcontinental railroad was responsible for altering the natural form of Great Salt Lake. With the construction of the Lucin Cutoff in 1903 to avoid the mountainous terrain to the north, the lake was split into northern and southern segments. The cutoff, which required the back-breaking labor of 3,000 men, hundreds of tons of rock, and the timber of 38,000 trees, shaved 44 miles off the original route of the railroad.

White Pelicans of Great Salt Lake

Each spring the briny, island-dotted shallows of Great Salt Lake serve as a mecca for thousands of white pelicans that fly in to breed on Gunnison Island, which lies isolated in the northwestern portion of the lake by the man-made barrier formed by the Lucin Cutoff. Other islands in the lake serve as rookeries for vast flocks of California gulls, blue herons, caspian terns, and cormorants. The gulls, protected by state law, are known as the "Mormon Air Force" for their now legendary feat of having devoured the hordes of crickets that plagued the crops of Brigham Young's pioneers. The gulls thrive on the lake's teeming population of brine shrimp and brine flies, or buffalo gnats, as they are called locally.

Marshlands of the Great Basin

Like the mountain-flanked Ruby Marsh of eastern Nevada, the immense oasis of wet meadowlands, lakes, and ponds of the Malheur National Wildlife Refuge to the east of the Harney High Desert at the very edge of the sagebrush country of the Great Basin in southeastern Oregon is a surviving remnant of the ancient lakes formed after the last Ice Age some 10,000 years ago. The nutrient-rich, bulrush-bordered lakes and ponds of the marshlands sustain a wide variety of life, including geese, muskrats, great blue herons, American coot, jackrabbits, ground squirrels, and white-faced ibises. The oozy debris of the rotting plants and animals on the bottom of the marsh constantly replenish the food chain and keep its plant and animal community—from microscopic algae to deer—in balance.

Nevada's Wheeler Peak

Wheeler Peak rises 13,063 feet from a base on the desert floor in Humboldt National Forest through the high desert and subalpine life zones to its glacier-carved summit. This alpine island, like its neighbor Mount Moriah, is part of the Snake Range in northeastern Nevada and one of the highest peaks in the

Nevada's 13,063-foot Wheeler Peak—an alpine "island" in the Great Basin

Great Basin. During the Indian wars the top of Wheeler Peak was used by the U.S. Army as a heliograph point for flashing messages with mirror relays between Troy Peak in Nevada and Mount Nebo in Utah.

Lehman Caves at Wheeler Peak

The Lehman Caves National Monument lies in the pinyon-pine and juniper zone at 7,000 feet on the limestone eastern slope of 13,063-foot Wheeler Peak, one of the highest mountains in the Great Basin and the pinnacle of the Snake Range, on the eastern edge of Nevada. Eastward, beyond the flats of the Snake Valley, rise peak after peak of the awesome Basin and Range region.

The cave trail winds past a colorful subterranean world of huge, fluted columns that reach from floor to ceiling; past pools of water and terraced, miniature dams and weblike ridges of rock; past myriads of stalactites on the cave ceiling and stalagmites built up on the cavern floor; and on through giant rooms with high-arched ceilings colored buff, orange, red, chocolate, and creamy white.

Nevada's Ruby Range

The green and white steep-walled peaks of the 90-mile-long Ruby Range rise abruptly out of the

White pelicans at the Gunnison Island rookery in Great Salt Lake

brown sagebrush barrens of eastern Nevada like a giant, misplaced spur of the Rockies. The range, which culminates at 11,000-foot Ruby Dome, has sheer canyons rising 2,000 feet above the U-shaped valley floor, glacier-carved hollows and lake basins dotted by silver-dollar-shaped alpine ponds, hanging valleys, and waterfalls. It is flanked by ancient Precambrian rocks and ledges, snowbanks, and the solitary, wind-polished, and twisted glossy trunks of ancient bristlecone pines (which see). Adapted to the buffeting of the winds and snows at high altitudes, the bristlecone pines are the oldest living things on earth, some reaching ages of more than 4,000 years. In the basin floor of the Ruby Valley far below the summits, the long-stemmed tube bulrushes of the Ruby Marsh Wildlife Refuge provide a watery oasis for sandhill cranes, sage grouse, trumpeter swans, and waterfowl.

Oregon's Great Sandy Desert and Fossil Lake

The Great Sandy or, as it is also known, the Harney High Desert, covers an area about 150 miles long and 30 to 50 miles wide in south-central Oregon. It is a parched land of picturesque buttes and mesas and white-surfaced playas. To the east lie the hills, valleys, small craters, and canyons of the Snake River Plains. To the south in the bed of ancient Fork Rock Lake, once a feeder of the Pacific Ocean, is Fossil Lake, flanked in the distance by the wave-cut terraces of the ancient shoreline. The prehistoric lake bed has yielded intriguing fossils of ancient salmon, flamingo, and giant beaver.

Buckaroo Country of Northern Nevada

The vast ranchlands of northern Nevada are the last domain of the oldtime cowboy and of open range that is shared by the cattle of competing outfits. Unlike the rangelands of Wyoming, Montana, and other areas of the West that are divided by man-made barbed wire and buck-and-rail fences, the Buckaroo Country is largely unfenced, due primarily to the awesome acreage needed to support a single head of cattle on these arid, sagebrush plains, estimated in most cases to be from 40 to 60 acres.

Black Rock Desert

The shimmering, sun-baked pavement of the Black Rock Desert in northwestern Nevada, named for the finlike pyramids of black volcanic rock rising above its surface, contains a huge alkali flat which, with the spring rains, turns into a shallow, million-acre lake.

Nevada's Valley of Fire

The Valley of Fire, picturesque layered beds of bright-red sandstone, is a portion of an ancient desert whose sands were cemented together by the minerals of the prehistoric sea that once covered them. Similar formations are found in southwestern Utah and near Lake Mead.

Fort Rock in Oregon's Harney High Desert, marking the shoreline of an ancient lake rich in fossil deposits that have yielded giant prehistoric beaver, flamingo, and salmon. Fort Rock was a famous landmark along the old Oregon Trail.

Comstock Lode at Virginia City

The famous silver-bearing veins of the Comstock Lode were discovered in the Virginia Range of western Nevada in 1859 by several prospectors, one of them a Henry T. P. Comstock, known as Old Pancake. This richest of all silver strikes, climaxed in 1873 by the discovery of the Big Bonanza, gave birth to the boom town of Virginia City, which reached a population of 30,000 in its heyday and had declined to 2,700 by 1900. Many of the town's landmarks have been preserved, including the Church of St. Mary's in the Mountains, Miner's Union Hall, Piper's Opera House, and the Union Brewery. Near Dayton is the four-mile Sutro Tunnel, completed in 1878, which was designed to ventilate and drain the mines.

Wild Horse Range

Wide-ranging bands of hardy wild horses descended from the Andalusian horse of the Spanish conquistadors roam the sagebrush deserts and mountain wilds of the West—a magnificent symbol of our frontier heritage. From Wyoming's Pryor Wild Horse Range to the deserts of the Great Basin, some 16,000 of these gallant beasts thrive in the sagebrush flats in compact bands, each dominated by a stallion who engages in fierce combat for a harem of mares and rules it until his strength fails. The harem is usually made up of eight or more mares and their offspring, called foals or when older, colts or fillies. The stallion establishes a feed territory for his band and acts as their protector and sentinel, signaling danger by whistling, snorting, or sharply raising his head. With the first snows, the stallion leads his band up to the mountain slopes where the high winds expose the range grasses that they browse on. An odd fact of harem life is the stallion's selection of mares of a single shade of color.

Wild Burros

A descendant of the frontier prospectors' and miners' pack animals, the wild burro has adapted superbly to the desert wilderness areas of the Western states. Western naturalists estimate that their population has exploded to somewhere between 8,000 and 10,000 animals, with more than 1,500 living in Death Valley alone. The burro, whose voracious appetite has threatened the food supply and survival of the desert bighorn sheep, is extremely well adapted to its desert environment. They can withstand extremes of weather

Big sagebrush, the dominant plant of the Great Basin country

and can walk for more than 15 miles without water in temperatures well over 100°F.

Common Plants of the Great Basin

In the Great Basin the dominant brownish-green creosote bush of the southern deserts is replaced by the soft gray shades of the toothleaved sagebrush and the oval-leaved shadscale or sheep fat, a low-lying woody-stemmed salt bush common to the alkaline plains and mesas of the arid portions of the West. Other common plants of the desert flats are hop sage and mule fat and tough, alkali-resistant shrubs such as the grayish-green greasewood, salt grass, samphine, and mat salt bush, as well as yellow-flowered rabbit brushes on the large flats. The Great Basin cactus is a common sight along the Snake River in Idaho and in eastern Washington and Oregon.

Sagebrush

The dark, twisted stumps of dead sagebrush interspersed with the gray-green living sagebrush is the characteristic plant of the West's Great Basin country. The dominant big sagebrush has gray-green leaves bearing three short, wedge-shaped teeth at their tips. When crushed, its foliage has a tangy, sweet, sagelike odor. In alkaline-free areas it forms pure stands reaching heights of two to three feet over extremely large areas. In the volcanic, mineral-rich soils of southern Idaho and eastern Oregon, it develops extremely thick horse-high stems.

Bristlecone Pine—The Oldest Living Thing on Earth

Standing at the base of a coastal redwood tree in California—the tallest living things in the world—it is easy to imagine that they are the oldest trees as well. But in the plant world, big does not always mean old. Growing in a cool, moist climate, these towering giants have had a relatively easy life. They can grow for 1,500, 2,000, maybe even 3,000 years, with ample water to support their mammoth size. But just a few hundred miles to the east, after the Sierra Nevada Mountains have wrung most of the water from the westerly winds, grow the real ancients. High in the White Mountains of California, and on top of parched ranges in Nevada, a few gnarled bristlecone pines manage to survive much longer. With only a few branches bearing living foliage, they cling to life for up to 5,000 years, their growth nearly imperceptible to us short-lived humans.

The gnarled, twisted forms of the wind-glossed 10- to 30-foot-high bristlecone pines grow on the rocky, dry, wind-swept slopes of the Great Basin and eastern Sierra Nevada. The adversity of its environment slowed the growth of the bristlecone and forced it to adapt by producing a resin that helps the tree ward off decay and insect damage, thus prolonging this majestic pine's life. Its hardy, foxtail-shaped bunches of needles remain on the tree for 20 to 30 years, allowing it to withstand long periods of drought.

The oldest living bristlecone pine, named Methuselah and dated at 4,600 years, is in the rugged 28,000-acre Ancient Bristlecone Pine Forest in California's White Mountains, east of the High Sierras and Owens Valley, above 10,000 feet elevation. The area has two trails, the Pine Alpha Trail, which passes living driftwood stumps bleached, polished, and gnarled from centuries of wind, rain, and blowing sand, and the two-mile-long Methuselah Trail. At the north end of the forest is the Patriarch Grove,

Ghost of an ancient bristlecone pine high up in the White Mountains. In the background, living bristlecones march up the slopes and stop at the timberline on White Mountain Peak, which is only 254 feet lower than Mount Whitney, the highest peak in the continental United States.

named for the world's largest bristlecone pine, a giant more than 25 feet high and 37 feet in diameter.

Tree-Ring Dating

Bristlecone pine, the struggling but hardy survivors and others like them, are sought by dendrochronologists—scientists who study the patterns of the rings formed by the year-to-year growth of the trees. Using borers to extract pencil-thin cores from the trunks, they are able to record these sequences of wide and narrow rings with microscopes and specially designed measuring tools, without having to cut or otherwise damage the trees. And from this record, they are able to tell us a surprising amount about past rainfall, temperature, air pressure, even river flows, glacier movements, and catastrophic events in the distant past.

The bases for these diverse studies are the growth rings laid down each year by the trees. In most years a single layer will be formed under the bark, somewhat wider bands in favorable years, narrower ones when drought or cold temperatures slow the tree's growth. Because the climate is similar for most trees in a single area, similar patterns are recorded in the growth rings on different trees. By using cores collected from many trees in many different areas, scientists have reconstructed tree-growth patterns over much of western North America for several hundred years. Computers are necessary to analyze the large amount of data collected, and they have revealed a wealth of valuable additional information. Studies have shown, for example, that bristlecone pines found at high elevations are especially slow-growing when temperatures are cold. By using this information, scientists have identified colder periods during the last several thousand years from the tree-ring records. In some areas, trees grow best under wet conditions and form very narrow rings when droughts occur. These trees are useful in telling us how often prolonged dry periods may strike, such as the one during the 1930s. This information is valuable to farmers, hydroelectric companies, and others who depend on abundant water every year.

Another useful application of tree rings has been in dating archeological sites in the Southwest. By matching the patterns of living trees with those preserved in roof beams of houses, the year these logs were cut can be determined. Over several decades of work scientists have been able to date many Indian dwellings in Arizona and New Mexico that are many hundreds of years old. Near Sunset Crater in Arizona, a volcanic eruption that spread cinders over the forest nearby, and slowed tree growth for several years

Gnarled desert juniper on a south-facing slope

thereafter, was dated using tree rings to the year A.D. 1064.

Trees in many different environments have been studied, from immense Douglas firs in Washington to stunted subalpine firs in Wyoming, in an effort to learn more about past climates and events. New methods are continually being developed to extract more information from tree rings. Microscopic amounts of lead and other elements can provide clues about the buildup of pollutants in our environment. Studies of naturally occurring radioactive elements, called isotopes, that are preserved in the rings tell us about past changes in the earth's atmosphere, and perhaps even the sun. X-ray photographs of cores are being used to study past temperature and rainfall with even greater accuracy. As our understanding about the types of changes the earth has undergone in the past increases, we may be better able to anticipate, and perhaps even predict, future changes. It is a long step from a lonely, gnarled tree on the Nevada mountainside.

Creosote

The evergreen creosote bush, which reaches heights of up to 10 feet, is one of the most widely spread desert plants of North America. Its presence

Desert bighorn sheep roaming the high country of the Desert Wildlife Range

marks the division between the lower and upper Sonoran life zones. This sweet-smelling bush of the lower plains has large yellow flowers that appear suddenly with the first rains of April and May. Over large areas of the Mohave Desert (which see) it is found in pure stands. Its white fruit balls provide food for the desert rodents and birds.

Mesquite

A life source of the desert regions, the mesquite ranges from California to Texas. It reaches a height of 20 feet, with drooping branches that give it a rounded appearance and two sharp spines at the axils of the leaves. This common host for the desert mistletoe is often buried in sand, with only the top few feet visible, while the roots reach downward for 50 feet to water. It blossoms in flowered spikes up to five inches long from April to June. The mesquite provides cover, food, and nesting sites for a wide variety of desert animals, including jackrabbits, roadrunners, skunks, and coyotes.

Pinyon Pine

A hardy desert pine of the high mountain slopes, the single-leaf pinyon, often found in the company of yuccas, junipers, and cacti, produces an enormous

crop of cones that yield delicious oval pinyon nuts, prized by Navajo and other Indian tribes for their nutritional value.

Junipers

Large mats of mountain junipers, with their twisted, creeping boughs, are common in the alpine zones of the desert mountains, along with the desert or Utah juniper, a shrubby tree with ashy gray bark, stiff, low-lying branches, and small silver berries, that seldom exceeds 12 to 15 feet in height.

Insect Galls

Insect galls—round brownish or green bud-shaped objects often seen on juniper trees and sagebrush—are formed when an insect, often a midge fly, lays its eggs within the plant's tissue and secretes a chemical that causes the plant to form a growth or gall around its larvae.

Coyote Wells

The coyotes of the Great Basin region have developed a remarkable ability to locate water pockets concealed in a pit in the desert floor. Coyotes will often dig a diagonal tunnel several feet deep to reach these sand-collected remnants of flood runoffs. There are numerous accounts of prospectors who were saved from a parched death by these coyote wells.

Desert Bighorn Sheep

Some 3,500 desert bighorn sheep survive in the sagebrush country of the Great Basin, mostly in the high mountains of southern Nevada and Death Valley. One of the largest protected habitats for the desert bighorn are the sagebrush flats and high country of the Desert National Wildlife Range in the Mohave Desert northwest of Las Vegas. One of the major threats to the survival of the desert bighorn are the large bands of wild burros, whose incredible appetite for plants and water exerts tremendous competition on all other wildlife sharing its range. It is believed that this pressure from the wild burros has forced the once wide-roaming bighorn to retreat up into the isolated mountain crags. These largest of the desert mammals have distinctive, massive spiraled horns and white rump patch. The horns of the female are much smaller than those of the male.

Sage Hen

Over the high alkali and dry sagebrush stretches of the high plains, sometimes at altitudes of more than

Pronghorn antelope—a common sight on the open flats

Male sage hen of the open sagebrush country, noted for its elaborate mating dance

7,000 feet, sage hens—also known as sage grouse and prairie chickens—travel in packs in search of food. Strong wings carry the sage hen beyond the reach of its natural enemies. About 25 inches long, this endangered species has upper parts of black, brown, and yellowish white; beneath, they are brownish yellow. The mating season of the sage hen furnishes an unusual prairie scene. It is begun by a drumming or croaking song at dawn, voiced by the males as they gather on the mating ground—barren flats where 100 or more males flock together in February and March. In the early morning and at sunset the females also gather. Standing erect, the males lift their wings away from their sides and raise and spread the tail, as the air sacs on the sides of the neck are inflated to great size and the feathers surrounding them bristle out in all directions. The skin between the sacs is drawn in by a sucking motion, and the air is expelled from the throat with a grunting or croaking. Sounding their mating call, the cocks strut about, tail feathers erect, dancing or fighting. Sometimes they lower their breasts to the ground and push them along in the dust.

Pronghorn Antelope

The American antelope, or pronghorn, the only representative of the antelope goat family, wanders the dry open plains of the West seeking grass and sage. The pronghorn is about four and a half feet long and three feet high. The upper parts, sides, and legs are yellowish brown; the underparts and rump are white. Bucks gather their harem in September and October and join other herds in large winter migrations determined by weather and the presence of abundant food and water. Winter usually finds them in the sheltered hill valleys, from which they journey to the open plains and low foothills in spring.

Mohave Ground Squirrel

This cinnamon-gray squirrel with a short tail is found only among the scattered brush of the Mohave Desert. It is closely related to the white antelope squirrel, which has white stripes on its body and is most often sighted running with its tail over its back, exposing its white underface.

Eureka Historic Mining Boom Town

Eureka is one of Nevada's best-preserved mining boom towns. It became a boom town in 1869, and by the 1880s it was second in importance to Virginia City in the state. The main street is fronted by brick and stone commercial structures; the side streets are filled with small stone, frame, and brick houses typical of a mining community. Included in the district are the two-story brick Sadler House; the log Tannehill Cabin, reputed to be the first permanent building in the town; the opera house, the courthouse (1879); and 10 known smelter sites. The Eureka historic district is in Nevada's Eureka County.

Belmont Ghost Town

Belmont, now a ghost town, was settled as a result of a silver strike in 1865. Many substantial stone and brick buildings were erected soon after its establishment to provide houses and businesses for its 2,000 inhabitants. The town served as the county seat from 1867 to 1905 and became an important mining and milling area and trade center for settlements within a 100-mile radius. Five sawmills and three stamp mills served the area until 1887, when most of the mines were shut down. Some of the best remaining structures include the Courthouse (1874), the Cosmopolitan Saloon (c. 1870), and the smokestacks of the Monitor-Belmont Mill and the Combination Mill.

Belmont it 46 miles northeast of Tonapah via U.S. Highway 6 and Nevada Highways 8A and 82.

Cold Springs Pony Express Station

To supply the need for communication between the East and the gold and silver mining areas in California and Nevada, the Pony Express was established in 1860. The route crossed the Edwards Creek Valley, and a station was erected at Cold Springs. This station also became a stage stop for the central Overland Express Company, which began operating the same year. It served as a stage and freight station from 1861 to 1869, then only as a freight station until 1880 when the Nevada Central Railroad was completed and the large stage companies were abandoned. All that remains aboveground on the site are the stone ruins of the station and the stone foundation of a nearby Overland Telegraph repeater station.

The site is 51 miles west of Austin on U.S. Highway 50 in Nevada's Churchill County.

Salton Sea and the Colorado Desert

The vast Salton Sink, a great basin about 200 miles long and 50 miles wide, lies at the heart of the westernmost extension of the Sonoran Desert that surrounds the lower portion of the Colorado River. Known as the Colorado Desert, it lies to the south of the Mohave Desert and California's Joshua Tree National Monument. The Salton Sea, about 35 miles long and 20 miles wide, lies within the trough, more than 200 feet below sea level. The Salton Sea is a successor to Lake Cahuilla, which was formed behind a dam of silt deposited at the mouth of the Colorado River from the overflow of the Colorado along a now-dry channel known as the New River.

By 1900 Lake Cahuilla had evaporated to a small, saltwater lake. In 1906 the Colorado River overflowed, flooded the Salton Sink, and by 1920 formed the present-day lake, which like Utah's Great Salt Lake and Nevada's Pyramid Lake, has become a mecca for a host of sea birds, including pelicans, gulls, and terns.

The former shoreline of Lake Cahuilla encircles

Belmont ghost town, a thriving silver mining center in the late 1800s

Open spillways of Boulder Dam on the Lower Colorado River

the Imperial Valley and Coachella Valley of California in the Salton Sink 40 to 50 feet above sea level. On the east side of the Imperial Valley is the former beach, the Algodones Dunes, which extend for over 40 miles in a sandy swath three to six miles wide.

Lake Mead

This vast man-made lake extends for 115 miles at the southeastern edge of the Great Basin along the old course of the Colorado River from Hoover Dam to the Grand Canyon. Its 550-mile shoreline cuts through the colorful landscape of the Great Basin Desert along the Grand Wash Cliffs and the surrounding arid sagebrush plains. Surrounded by a desert country of creosote bush, Joshua tree and cacti, Lake Mead stretches southward from the base of Hoover Dam for 67 miles. Submerged under the waters of the lake are the ancient Lost City of Pueblo and the Virgin River salt quarries of the Pueblo Indian culture.

Sonoran Desert—The Big Cactus Country

The mountain-studded Sonoran Desert reaches up from Mexico, stretching through southeastern California and southwestern Arizona. It is a harsh, yet beautiful land of numerous mountain ranges, broad plains, and rugged valleys with water-storing cactus from the small two-inch-tall pincushion to the giant saguaros that stand 50 feet and more. Other characteristic plants of the gently undulating Sonoran Desert plain are the creosote bush, mesquite, lechuguilla, paloverde, brittlebush, and organ pipe cactus in southern Arizona. Beds of black or brownish lava are scattered throughout the desert, and some of them, such as the Pinacate Lava, cover several square miles. The region takes in the Salton Trough and a portion of the lower Colorado River, which is the only permanent stream in the region. The mountains of the desert are barren rock because of the violent desert rainstorms, which allow little soil to accumulate on the steep slopes.

Saguaro cactus—symbol of the Sonoran Desert

Saguaro—Symbol of the Southwest

This giant cactus, which reaches heights of up to 40 feet, is the dominant symbol and life force of the Sonoran Desert. It grows nowhere else. Its erect, cylindrical trunk and branches hold up to a ton of water, absorbed by a massive root system as much as 80 feet in diameter. The largest of these living reservoirs are believed to live as long as 200 years. Its fruit, a red or purple berry, holds as many as 2,000 seeds and was highly prized by the area Indian tribes. Its beautiful white or cream-colored blossom is the state flower of Arizona. During the wet season, the plant may be as much as 98 percent water, most of which is used up during the months of May and June. The saguaro is the focus of life in the Sonoran Desert. Its ribbed main trunk is inhabited by the Gila woodpecker and the golden flicker, as well as by silverfish, lizards, and numerous spiders. Pygmy owls nest in the holes burrowed in the massive trunk by the Gila woodpeckers and golden flickers. The original Indian tribes of the Sonoran region used heavy rods from the branches of the saguaro to build their shelters.

Saguaro Forests of the Bajada

Great forests of saguaro, some individual trees reaching ages of more than 150 years old and heights greater than 30 feet high, often cover the rocky slopes, known locally as bajada, in numerous areas of the Sonoran Desert, where they store the runoff from the spare rainfall and are sheltered from the desert winds. At the lower elevations near the arid desert flats the saguaros thin out, and mesquite and ironwood dominate the landscape.

Saguaro National Monument and Arizona-Sonoran Desert Museum

Two small, picturesque sections of the vast Sonoran Desert near Tucson, Arizona, have been preserved as the Saguaro National Monument. Excellent views of an aging saguaro forest are available in the Rincon Mountain Unit from the Cactus Forest Drive. Studding the desert floor are thousands of stately saguaros, with lesser plants forming a dense underbrush. In the distance, the pine- and fir-clad ridges of the Santa Catalina Mountains tower more than a mile above the surrounding desert flats. A hike up into the forests of the Rincon Mountains will take you through six distinct plant communities: through the desert scrub biotic community, which is the home of the saguaro and is found up to 1,200 feet; above that the desert grassland; the oak woodlands; then the oak-pine woodlands; the ponderosa pine forest; and, on the north-facing slopes below Mica Mountain and Rincon Peak, a Douglas fir/white fir forest. The mountain areas are inhabited by Mexican jays, Steller's jay, cliff chipmunks, white-tailed deer, rufous-sided towhee, and Mexican junco. The saguaro forests of the desert scrublands are inhabited by cactus wrens, the Gila woodpecker, desert tortoise, peccaries, coyotes, and the curve-billed thrasher.

The Arizona-Sonoran Desert Museum, adjacent to the 21,078-acre Tucson Mountain Unit, houses fascinating displays of living plants and animals of the Sonoran Desert.

Organ Pipe National Monument

Although not as striking as the giant saguaro, the single, unbranched column of the organ pipe cactus grows to heights of 10 to 15 feet, with spiny ribs and funnel-shaped flowers. Common in northwest Mexico, in the United States it grows only on south-facing slopes of Arizona's Sonoran Desert region.

The Organ Pipe National Monument covers a

510-square-mile area in the heart of the Sonoran Desert 100 miles west of Tucson, with stands of protected organ pipe cactus. Other major features of this mountain-studded land of volcanic rocks that rise 3,000 feet above the sea level and shimmering desert flats are the multicolored peaks of the Ajo Range, Dripping Springs, the granite hills and abandoned mines of the Senita Basin, old corrals and line cabins, the cottonwood oasis at Quitobaquito—a pond fed by natural springs inhabited by pupfish, a remnant of the great inland seas that disappeared a million years ago. Montezuma's Head, a 3,634-foot-high volcanic butte, dominates the landscape in the northeastern area of the national monument. One of the most striking landmarks is the Bull Pasture, a great shelf that juts out the side of Mount Ajo. This grassy basin, with waving fields of knee-high grass and yucca and ocotillo, is a natural corral hundreds of feet above the desert floor. Reached by a rugged trail that winds through a narrow canyon and along great yellow cliffs, the pasture once provided a lush grazing area for cattle.

Ventana Cave in the Sonoran Desert

Ventana Cave has a history of continuous Indian occupation in Arizona extending over a period of about 5,000 years. The earliest occupations were those of food-gathering peoples related in their way of life to inhabitants of southern California. The final occupation was by Indians who dwelt there in early historic times. The high, shallow caves lie at the base of a cliff on the southeast face of Castle Mountain. The cave, inhabited sporadically from 11,000 B.C., is 11 miles west of Santa Rosa at the Papago Indian Reservation.

Cactus Wren

A denizen of the cactus thickets of the Southwest, the cactus wren is the largest wren found in the United States. Its old and new nests protected among the spiny stands of jumping cholla, staghorn, and teddy bear cacti are a common sight.

Roadrunner

This nimble two-foot-long bird, which can run up to 18 mph, was aptly named by the pioneers crossing the desert and mesquite country of the American Southwest, because of its habit of jogging on the ground following the wagon wheels. This picturesque white-streaked, olive-brown character is a deadly foe of the rattlesnake, which it stuns with powerful thrusts of its beak. It survives on a wide variety of desert life, including lizards, scorpions, tarantulas, and insects. A solitary bird, the roadrunner, unlike most desert birds, does not migrate.

Chain Fruit Cholla

The treelike chain fruit cholla cactus is easily identified by its spiky, chainlike links of green fruit that grow in festoons, often reaching to the ground. Each link begins as a pink or purple flower that

Saguaro cactus—symbol of the Sonoran Desert, reaching heights of more than 45 feet and weighing more than 5 tons. The dots often seen are woodpecker holes.

withers away, leaving an egg-shaped green fruit, which the following year produces another flower and another linklike fruit. Chain fruit chollas grow up to 12 feet high. Chains of 12 to 14 linked fruits are frequently seen in the Sonoran Desert region.

Buckthorn Cholla

A common sight on the upland slopes and flats of the Sonoran Desert is the spiny, sprawling buckthorn cholla cactus, so named because of its antler-shaped water-storing branches. Unlike the bristling teddy bear, the buckthorn is lightly armed with spines and produces a beautiful red flower.

Teddy Bear Cholla

The furry clumps of teddy bear chollas are the prickliest plants in the cactus family. It gets its name from its brittle, straw-colored spines, which have the appearance of fur in the bright desert sun. The incredible spiny water-storing branches have inflicted painful wounds on many a desert traveller. These fiercely armed cholla clumps, which usually grow no more than four feet high, often serve as secure nesting places for the cactus wren.

Hedgehog Cactus

The sprawling, many-stemmed hedgehog cactus, named for its long, prickly spines, is noted for its magnificent satiny flowers, which range in color from pale green to white-yellow to pale lavender to a dark, almost black magenta. The low-lying hedgehog or strawberry cactus grows to a height of a few inches in the arid desert country of western New Mexico and southern Arizona.

Wild Palm Oasis of the Kofa Mountains

The rugged volcanic spires and turrets of the Kofa Mountains in southwest Arizona, named after an old gold mine there known as the King of Arizona, is the home of wild, stunted California fan palms. Outside of southern California and the Baja Peninsula, they grow only in this one area of the Sonoran Desert, where they thrive on the sheltered walls of the canyons and an ample supply of water, creating an oasis. The stunted palms of the Kofa Mountains, which in California grow as high as 50 feet, are believed to live for up to 200 years.

Desert Tortoise

Like the kangaroo rat, the desert tortoise is a master at conserving moisture. Also known as the gopher turtle, it thrives in the desert country of southwestern Arizona, Nevada, and southeastern California, where it lives on cactus and other low-growing desert plants. Although its upper shell reaches sizes up to 10 inches long, it is related to the giant Galapagos tortoise, which reaches lengths of up to four feet and weights of 500 pounds. During the daylight hours of the dry season it retreats to cool, moist dens.

Coatimundi

This desert relative of the raccoon lives in bands in the uplands of the desert country. Like the raccoon, the coatimundi, also known as the coati and in Arizona as the chulu, is a skilled climber and nocturnal feeder, preying on a wide variety of desert life, from insects to lizards, mice and berries.

Thick, squat barrel, or fishhook, cactus in bloom with beautiful yellow flowers

Coatimundi, a desert relative of the raccoon

Adobes of the Southwest

The structural use of clay in the form of adobe, practical only in arid climates, has been traced back some 2,000 years to the Basketmakers of the Southwest, who covered their pit dwellings with dome-shaped roofs fashioned with interlaced willow bows and plastered with adobe mud. Spanish priests taught the Indians to use adobe in the form of precast bricks, a superior type of construction to the aboriginal method of puddling. The traditional form of adobe dwelling predates the Spanish, however, and was adopted by them from the designs of the pueblos of the mesa country and the dwellings of the Aztecs and other people of Mexico. Adobe structures are beautiful in a setting of cliff walls and mesa, for their simple lines and soft coloring harmonize well with their background.

The true adobe house is simple in design, usually consisting of a single room, with walls of sun-dried brick about a foot long, six inches wide, and three inches thick, made of adobe and straw. The flat roof is also of adobe, supported by rafters called *vagas*, hewn from long logs; these are usually allowed to project beyond the walls at each end of the house. In some areas, such as Taos, New Mexico, the old single-room houses have been converted into large communal dwellings by adding bays of rooms or additional apartments to the sides of the original building as members of the family have married.

Desert Laboratory at Tucson

As part of the Carnegie Institution of Washington, the Desert Laboratory is recognized as having initiated the study of the ecology of arid regions. Of the many studies conducted there, the most important were those dealing with the influence of arid conditions on the evolution of plants and on their migration from humid zones. Operation of the laboratory for ecological studies ended in the late 1930s. The United States Forest Service used the site as an experiment station until 1958 when it was acquired by the University of Arizona for its geochronology program. Three major buildings dating from the period of the Desert Laboratory are still in use. The laboratory is on Tumamon Hill off West Anklam west of Tucson.

Indian Irrigation Sites at the Park of the Four Waters

Spanish explorers first found the Pima Indians of the Gila River irrigating their crops from canals and ditches of complex construction in 1687. Later archeological excavations have shown that other irrigation works were originally constructed by peoples of the Hohokam culture. The systems, built as communal efforts with hand tools, formed great networks extending over thousands of acres of land. Some of the canals are still in use today, tied in with contemporary irrigation systems of Indians and whites who currently farm the valley. These sites illustrate that both ancient and modern man have made similar adjustments to the arid environment of the Southwest. The sites, located at the Park of the Four Waters in Phoenix, were built between A.D. 1200 and 1400.

Pueblo Grande Ruin

Pueblo Grande Ruin is one of the few remaining large Hohokam village sites in the area. Its major feature is a large mound, standing some 20 feet above the desert floor, on and around which jacales and caliche-walled houses were located. The latter struc-

Casa Grande ruins, a 4-story earth tower built about 600 years ago

Casa Grande Ruins National Monument

Casa Grande or Big House is a four-story tower of packed earthen walls built over 600 years ago by Indian farmers of the Gila River valley. This building and others with thick walls of unreinforced clay were built by a people accustomed to constructing multistory dwellings. The site, which appears to be similar to structures found in Mexico, also contains Hohokam Indian remains dating from about A.D. 900. It served both as an astronomical observation tower and an apartment house. Early excavations of the Casa Grande ruins showed ordinary cooking and storage vessels, sleeping mats, and fragments of textiles. The monument covers 472 acres and is two miles north of Coolidge on Arizona Highway 87.

tures have been encroached on by modern developments, but four prehistoric canals are visible across the existing irrigation canal in the Park of the Four Waters. The above-ground structures, with the exception of the ball court, represent the final phase of occupation (A.D. 1150–1450), during which the cultures of two distinct peoples were fused. The ruin is at Pueblo Grande Park in Phoenix.

Roosevelt Dam on the Salt River

Roosevelt Dam was the first major project to be completed under the Reclamation Act of 1902. Its primary purpose was to provide adequate water storage for the Salt River Irrigation Complex, whose line of descent goes back to the ancient Hohokam irrigation projects, the historic Pima Indian projects, and the projects of 19th-century settlers in the area. The world's highest masonry dam, Roosevelt is 284 feet high, and 1,125 feet long. Roosevelt Lake, which is

Roosevelt Dam on the Salt River—the world's highest masonry dam

Weaver's Needle in the Superstition Mountains, the fabled landmark of the Lost Dutchman Gold Mine

impounded by the dam, irrigates over a quarter million acres of farmland.

The dam is 31 miles northwest of Globe on Arizona Highway 88.

Superstition Mountains and the Lost Dutchman Gold Mine

The Superstition Mountains rise from the flat, arid floor of the Sonoran Desert country east of Phoenix, forming a rugged wilderness of peaks, vast inner valleys, and dark canyons in the Tonto National Forest. One of the major features of this desert range is Weaver's Needle, a fabled landmark to the Lost Dutchman Gold Mine described by the Dutch prospector, Jacob Wolz, on his deathbed in the early 1900s. Thousands of prospectors since Wolz's death have used Weaver's Needle as the key landmark in their search for this legendary bonanza, but none has been successful.

Tonto Cliff Dwellings National Monument

Tonto National Monument comprises two of the most accessible and best-preserved cliff dwellings of southern Arizona. The dwellings, constructed of masonry and topped with pole and mud roofs, were built with primitive wooden and stone tools by Indians who farmed in the Salt River valley during the mid-1300s. The Lower Ruin has 16 or 17 ground-floor rooms with at least 4 second-story rooms. The Upper Ruin, with 32 ground-floor and 14 second-story rooms, is better preserved. That the Tonto cliff dwellers were excellent craftsmen is illustrated by artifacts found in the ruins. Decorated storage vessels with bold, complicated designs and plain utility vessels were the principal pottery forms. Also found were examples of textiles, jewelry, and weaponry. One of the largest collections of vegetal material in the Southwest has been recovered from these ruins.

The ruins are 28 miles northwest of Globe on Arizona Highway 88.

Snaketown—A City-State of Prehistoric Arizona

Snaketown was one of the large Hohokam Indian city-states of prehistoric Arizona. Excavations revealed that the Indians of southern Arizona were strongly influenced by the more highly developed cultures of Mexico. These cultures lifted the Indians into a pattern of living that contrasted sharply with the scattered rancherias of early Indian farmers in the region. The irrigation canal system and the large urban developments mark the highest achievement of Hohokam labor.

Snaketown, occupied from 300 B.C. to A.D. 1200, is 12 miles southwest of Chandler at the Gila River Indian Reservation.

Kinishba Indian Ruins in the White Mountains

A large pueblo consisting of two large and seven small masonry buildings, Kinishba Ruins could have housed up to 1,000 Indians. The culture of the inhabitants represents the climax period in the White Mountain area, a blend of Mogollon and Anasazi ancestry. The people depended primarily on agriculture for subsistence; pottery was manufactured for storage, table, and ceremonial use. A large rectangular building on the east has two enclosed courtyards, an architectural plan typical of this mountain region during the late 1200s and early 1300s. The pueblo was abandoned about 1400.

Tumacacori Mission, a northern outpost founded by Jesuit priests in the 17th century

The ruins are 15 miles west of Whiteriver via Arizona Highway 73 and a secondary road in Gila County.

Tombstone Historic District

Tombstone, which surrounded the mining claim of Ed Schieffelin, was widely known in the southwestern mining frontier. The site of rich silver mines, it attracted miners, gamblers, and gunmen, attaining a population of 7,000 by 1881. Its unrivaled reputation for lawlessness and violence is evidenced by the Earp-Clanton feud, which culminated in the gunfight at the OK Corral in 1881. The town declined as a mining center because of the entry of water into the mining shafts. Among the buildings illustrating the town's frontier flavor are the Bird Cage Theatre, the City Hall, and St. Paul's Episcopal Church.

Tumacacori National Monument

The mission of San José de Tumacacori was a northern outpost of the Sonora mission chain founded by Jesuit priests in the 17th century. This frontier mission church illustrates Spanish colonial endeavor and commemorates the introduction of Christianity into southern Arizona. Although the settlement was first visited by Father Kino in 1691, mission activity reached its peak between 1790 and the end of Spanish rule in 1821. The chapel still stands, partly in ruins, and a museum houses exhibits of early Indian and Spanish history.

The mission is 18 miles north of Nogales on Interstate Highway 19.

Coronado's Trail to the American Southwest

The Coronado National Memorial is located in the scenic Montezuma Canyon of the Huachuca Mountains along the International Boundary near the site where Coronado and his expedition entered the present-day United States in 1540 in search of the fabled Seven Cities of Cibola. His small force, weary and weak from hunger, reached the legendary Cibola—actually the Zuni Indian Pueblo of Hawikuh, near what is now Gallup, New Mexico—on July 7, 1540. Instead of a golden city, the rock-masonry pueblo was crowded with Indians ready to fight. The Spaniards attacked, drove the Indians back, and forced them to abandon the village. The pueblo served as Coronado's headquarters until November 1540. Although deemed a failure at the time, Coronado's expedition brought back knowledge of lands and peoples

Fort Bowie—a key stronghold during the Chiricahua Indian wars led by Apache chiefs Cochise and Geronimo

to the north and opened the way for later Spanish exploration, colonization, and the development of a distinctive Southwest culture.

The memorial is about 22 miles south of Sierra Vista, Arizona, 30 miles west of Bisbee, and just north of the Mexican state of Sonora. A foot trail leads to Coronado Peak, which provides a sweeping view of the route followed by Coronado's expedition.

Lehner Prehistoric Mammoth-Kill Site

The Lehner site is one of the outstanding mammoth-kill sites in the New World. The stone butchering tools found with Clovis fluted spear points expand the variety of tools known to have been used by these nomadic hunters. Radio-carbon dates for the artifacts and bones serve as a control for several scientific studies, including the most intensively analyzed pollen chronology of any alluvial site in the Southwest. The site, which remains largely in a natural state, is well preserved. The site, which was actively used around 11,000 B.C., is 10 miles west of Bisbee in Arizona's Cochise County.

Fort Bowie National Historic Site

Established by California Volunteers during the Civil War, Fort Bowie controlled a key water source in strategic Apache Pass. Its garrison, situated in the homeland of the Chiricahua Apache Indians, was ac-

tive during the 1860s, 1870s, and 1880s in the Chiricahua wars led by Cochise, Geronimo, and other Apache chieftains who spread terror throughout the Southwest. A major way station of cross-country travel in the Southwest, Apache Pass permitted crossing of the Chiricahua Mountains. It was considered the most dangerous point along the entire southern Overland Mail Route, which stretched from Tipton, Missouri, to San Francisco, California. Stone foundations and rock debris today mark the site of the Apache Pass Stage Station. The Butterfield Trail traverses the pass, and the natural historic setting remains intact. Stabilized adobe walls mark the fort site, which was abandoned by the Army in 1894.

The site covers 900 acres 13 miles southwest of Bowie, Arizona.

Chihuahuan Desert—The Mexican Highlands

The vast Chihuahuan Desert, also known as the Mexican Highland, lies to the east of the Sonoran Desert and to the south of the Colorado Plateau and covers portions of southern Arizona, New Mexico, and western Texas—an area almost as large as the Great Basin. The landscape of the region is characterized by arid, undulating plains, mountains, playa lakes, and extensive dunes of silica in southern New Mexico. In the famous White Sands area of southern New Mexico there are dunes of glistening white gypsum sand. Small beds and stark, isolated buttes of dark lava are scattered throughout the desert region. The plant life

Sotol and ocotillo plants—a common sight in the Chihuahuan Desert, which is dominated by low shrubs, small cactuses, yuccas, and agaves

of the desert is dominated by thorny shrubs, including mesquite on deep soils, a few cottonwoods along the intermittent streams, great areas of creosote bush, and ocotillo and lechugilla on the rocky slopes. Kangaroo rat mounds are commonly sighted throughout the desert region. The summer rains, usually local torrential storms, begin during July and continue through October.

The region is drained on the west by tributaries of the Colorado—the Gila, Williams, Salt, and Verde rivers—and on the east by the mighty Rio Grande, which flows through the Rio Grande Depression—dividing the southern end of the Rocky Mountains into the Sangre de Cristo Mountains on the east and the Conejos and Jemez mountains on the west—for 450 miles from Poncha Pass at the head of the San Luis Valley in Colorado to near El Paso in Texas.

Chirichua Mountains

The Chirichua Mountains rise steeply from the dry grasslands of southeastern Arizona and southwestern New Mexico, like a forested island in a sea of desert, forming rows of strange, massive spires, turrets, and battlements eroded out of ancient volcanic

rocks. The ancient lava masses were carved by millions of erosional channels into blocks of endless sizes and shapes, to be further sculpted by the elements. Shallow canyons became deeper and more rugged as time passed. Weathered rock formed soil, which collected in pockets; plants gained a foothold. Trails wind through beds of volcanic ash, indicating the power of the ancient eruptions. One trail is littered with volcanic hailstones weathered out of a ledge made of marblelike pellets, some firmly cemented into an unusual "peanut-brittle" rock.

The canyon floors of this desert island, long the home of the nomadic Apache Indians, are covered with red-stemmed manzanita and bark-shedding madrones, white-limbed sycamores and Arizona cypress with its feathery gray foliage. The cool, moister north-facing slopes covered by chaparral of scrub oak and ponderosa pine face the warm, southern slopes dotted by desert plants, such as beargrass, agave, yucca, alligator juniper, and Mexican pinyon.

Sidewinder

The sidewinder, a horned rattlesnake, inhabits the arid, sandy flats and bush-covered washes of the desert country from southern Nevada and southwestern Utah through Arizona and southern California. One of the smallest of the rattlesnakes, usually about 18 inches long, it gets its name from the S-shaped curve it forms when it is moving across the desert flats. Its parallel slash marks in the sand are a common sight, forming a J-shaped trail, particularly in the Mohave and Sonoran deserts. The nocturnal sidewinder hunts at night, preying on lizards, kangaroo rats, and other small rodents, killing the victim with its fast-working venom (which causes a fatal hemorrhage), then swallowing it whole.

Antelope Jackrabbit

This 19- to 21-inch jackrabbit is often sighted as a white flash among the giant cactus, mesquites, and catclaws of the Arizona and New Mexico deserts. It has huge, eight-inch-long ears and pale tannish-white or grayish sides and hips and is known to reach running speeds of 30 to 40 miles per hour. It feeds on common desert plants including cactus. Lacking sweat glands, its long ears serve as a natural air-conditioning unit, dissipating its body heat through the ears.

Desert hare, often sighted zigzagging among the cactus and mesquite

"Wilderness of Rocks" eroded out of volcanic lava in Chiricahua Mountains National Monument

Javelina, or desert pig, that uses its powerful snout to dig up cactus and roots

Javelina—The Desert Pig

One of the most fascinating animals of the desert country is the javelina, also known as the collared peccary, a distant relative of the domestic pig and wild boar. Found chiefly in southern Texas, southern Arizona, and parts of New Mexico, the javelina travels in herds of about 12 animals. It is known to kill rattlesnakes, and in herds may charge to drive off its foes. It uses its powerful snout to dig up its primary diet of cactus and roots.

Gila Monster

The low-slung, stubby Gila monster, the only poisonous lizard in the United States, is common in the vicinity of the Gila River in Arizona, but it ranges from southernmost Utah through the hot, desert country of Nevada and Arizona. An endangered species, the colorful Gila monster—irregular black or brown patterns on an orange, yellow, or pink body, covered with beadlike scales—reaches lengths of up to 24 inches and can strike with lightning speed. It chews its victims with its powerful jaws rather than biting them.

Kangaroo Rat

The diminutive kangaroo rat, named for its resemblance to the kangaroo, has small forelegs and long hind feet and an ability to leap eight feet at a jump to escape predators. It is admired by desert naturalists for its adaptation to arid, hot lands where coolness exists underground. A single square mile of desert country has been known to support 1,000 such animals, which dig underground tunnels and nests. This bluish-fawn white-bellied creature survives in the arid deserts by means of several amazing adaptations. It has no kidneys, secretes a pastelike substance rather than urine, and has nasal passages that create moisture by maintaining a lower temperature than the rest of its body.

Barrel Cactus

The thick, squat shapes of the barrel cactus—its various species are also known as mule or candy cactus, fishhook cactus for their long curved spines, or compass cactus, because of their tendency to lean toward the sun rays in the Southwest—grow throughout Arizona's Sonoran Desert and New Mexico's Chihuahuan Desert and on to El Paso, Texas. The ribbed, spiny barrel reaches heights to over six feet with beautiful yellow flowers. Desert legends to the contrary, the barrel is not filled with cool, clear, life-saving water. Its interior is filled with a soft, pulpy mass of tiny water storage cells that yield a bitter, sticky liquid.

Spiny, water-storing prickly pear cactus pads in bloom

Gila Cliff Dwellings high above a canyon floor date from A.D. *1,000.*

Prickly Pear Cactus

The incredibly hardy prickly pear cactus, which grows in the arid, sun-baked desert flats in the high rugged uplands, is readily identified by its linked succession of spiny water-storing pads which bear red fruit and colorful flowers. The prickly pear's efficient root system, which anchors the thin, arid soil of the Southwestern deserts, sends out a wide, shallow network of roots that absorb rainwater and swell up in winter, replacing the water-storing job of the pads during the months of subfreezing temperatures.

Gila Cliff Dwellings

The Gila Cliff Dwellings National Monument is located above the canyon floor of the West Fork of the Gila River in the Gila National Forest at the edge of the rugged Gila Wilderness Area. These prehistoric dwellings are reached by a short hike from the ranger station. The earliest ruin is a pithouse of a type made from about A.D. 100 to 400. The people of this period, referred to by archeologists as the Mogollon, grew corn and beans, hunted, and gathered wild plants. About A.D. 1,000, influences from the Pueblo peoples to the north began to affect the lives of these Indians. Cliff dwellings were erected during this period of influence from the north, and so were other pueblos on terraces overlooking the West Fork of the Gila River. Seven natural caves are found high in the southeast-facing cliff of a side canyon, and five of these caves

contain ruins of cliff dwellings—a total of about 40 rooms. All the timbers in the dwellings are originals. Tree-ring dates from these timbers date through the 1280s.

These small, artistic people lived in their cliff houses and riverside villages, tilling their fields with digging sticks, grinding cornmeal with metate and mano, fashioning their pottery and cloth, carrying on trade with Indians of other communities, hunting, and gathering wild plants and fruit. Sometime before 1400, they abandoned their homes and fields. Why they left and where they went are not known.

Nomadic bands of Apaches soon made this area their homeland. Later, Spanish colonists settled in the areas to the east and south of the monument, and many of their descendants still reside in the vicinity.

The Gila Cliff Dwellings and the wilderness area are a 44-mile drive north from Silver City, New Mexico, on State Highway 15.

San Juan Mesa Ruin

San Juan Mesa Ruin occupies an area 1,200 feet long by 300 feet wide along the eastern edge of San Juan Mesa. Portions of the site extend down the adjacent east slope of the mesa for a distance of several hundred feet. The site consists of several continuous, masonry-walled room blocks. Walls are made of large, roughly shaped pieces of volcanic tuff. Two depressions each in two of the central plazas show locations of subterranean kivas. Indigenous pottery at the site is

Gran Quivira early Spanish church ruins, built about 300 years ago near New Mexico's Valley of Fires

Jemez black-on-white. Intrusive pottery types include Rio Grande glaze. Pottery found at the site indicates that the greatest contact was with the prehistoric and historic period Indians in the vicinity of the present-day pueblo of Zia, to the south.

The ruin is located near Jemez Springs in Sandoval County, New Mexico.

Sandia Cave

Sandia Cave apparently represents one of the earliest occupations of the Americas. Excavations in 1936 yielded information on three distinct prehistoric groups, each separated from the other by a well-defined layer. The top level contained objects from the Pueblo occupation of New Mexico. The middle layer revealed artifacts of the Folsom bison hunter period, c. 9000–8000 B.C. The lowest layer contained the still older Sandia points, a type of early spearpoint notched on one side only. These points were associated with remains of extinct animals.

Sandia Cave is 11 miles east of Bernalillo on New Mexico Highway 44 in the Cibola National Forest.

Gran Quivira Church and Pueblo Ruins

The early Spanish church ruins, known as Gran Quivira, and numerous nearby Indian pueblo ruins lie atop Chupadera Mesa, a grassland area surrounded by pinyon pine and juniper, in central New Mexico. Also in the vicinity is the Valley of Fires, an area of ancient lava flows. The church is believed to have been built about 350 years ago by Spanish missionaries. The Indian pueblo it served, Pueblo de las Humanas, which had first been visited by Don Juan de Onate during his explorations only 31 years before the church was built, was the largest community in that part of the country and an important trading center. Within 85 to 87 years after Onate's visit, the pueblo and the church were abandoned. The reasons are complex and not fully understood. The immediate, primary cause was the severe drought of 1666–70, which was accompanied by famine and disease. Increasing raids by Apaches, who had become much more mobile with the introduction of the horse, also destroyed much of the population.

Gran Quivira is located 26 miles from Mountainair on New Mexico Highway 14.

White Sands National Monument

The famous salt flats and white sands that form the White Sands National Monument lie near the center of southern New Mexico's Tularosa Basin, which is enclosed by the Sacramento and San Andreas mountains and lacks external drainage. The gleaming white gypsum dunes of the monument are built up

to heights of 50 feet by tiny gypsum crystals eroded from the low rock ridges by frost and wind. The rounded gypsum hills of the White Sands area cover nearly 500 square miles, anchored by hardy salt-resistant dune plants, such as yucca and flowering salt-brush, a low, grayish shrub. Yuccas found here will often have stems as long as 30 feet. Other desert life found in this bleak environment include coyotes, jack-rabbits, and dune-adapted white spiders and white lizards.

Carlsbad Caverns in the Ancient Capitan Reef

Carlsbad Caverns National Park lies in south-eastern New Mexico in the subterranean portion of the ancient Capitan Reef, a remnant of a prehistoric sea formed 225 to 280 million years ago which also formed the Guadalupe Mountains to the south. Carlsbad Caverns are nearly a mile long and 350 feet high, forming a complex underground world linked by intricate passageways and shafts hollowed out of a limestone layer of the reef 1,400 feet thick. The caves were dis-

Gleaming gypsum dunes at White Sands National Monument covering a 500-square-mile area

Temple of the Sun at Carlsbad Caverns, discovered by a cowboy in 1901 who noticed bats swarming over a ground hole

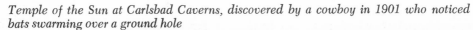

The 350-mile-long Capitan Reef—fossil remnant of an ancient inland sea

covered in 1901 when Jim White, a cowboy, was attracted by a swarm of bats to an opening in the earth's crust. His discovery was followed by an expedition sponsored by the National Geographic Society. To date, more than 32 miles of the caverns have been explored and three different levels discovered. Guided tours by park rangers take you through the dome-shaped entrance into a spectacular world, past Bat Cave, Whale's Mouth, huge domelike vaults, obelisks, giant limestone pillars, past emerald pools and Frozen Waterfalls, to the King's Palace 829 feet underground, the Polar Regions, Giant Domes, the Totem Pole, and Mirror Lake, a 700-foot-deep Bottomless Pit, and more. Bat Cave has one of the world's largest known concentrations of bats. The caverns are inhabited by five different species of bats, and their population has been estimated at between three to five million.

Guadalupe Mountains—An Island in the Desert

The Guadalupe Mountains resemble a giant wedge. Rising high above the desert in Texas, the "arms" reach northward into New Mexico. At the point

El Capitan in the Guadalupe Mountains, a sheer 2,000-foot-high cliff that was once an ancient barrier reef

The Rio Grande at Mariscal Canyon in Big Bend National Park—called "River of Ghosts" by early pioneers

of the "V" looms El Capitan, a sheer, 2,000-foot cliff that is a remnant of an ancient barrier reef built by lime-secreting algae and other organisms in an inland sea formed during the Permian period, 225 to 280 million years ago. A series of earth movements eventually raised the region dramatically, tilting its southwestern edge upward. The south face of the Guadalupes marks the location of the seaward face of Capitan Reef. The portion of the range reaching northward from the reef slope is made of sediments deposited in the ancient lagoon. The reef extends for 350 miles across western Texas and southeastern New Mexico, mostly far beneath the arid plain. The most extensive exposure is the 40-mile eastern Guadalupe escarpment, stretching northward through Guadalupe National Park through Carlsbad Caverns National Park. Within the 76,293 acres of Guadalupe National Park, the most dramatic cross section of Capitan Reef is at the 1,900-foot north wall of McKittrick Canyon.

The mountains, desert lowlands, and canyons at Guadalupe form a biological transition zone, where species from the Rocky Mountains reach their southern and eastern limit—and meet species from Mexico at the northern limit of their range. Plants and animals of the eastern and central plains also reach into the area. The low, arid deserts are covered with creosote bush, Parry agave, sotol, and yucca. The cooler high country contains a forest of ponderosa pine, Douglas fir, limber pine, and a few aspens—a relic of a forest that covered the Guadalupes thousands of years ago when the climate was cooler and the rainfall greater.

In the sheltered canyons, where moisture is more abundant, ferns, chokecherry, Texas madrone, bigtooth maple, and other species mix with vegetation from the higher and lower elevations.

Hiking trails and drives provide access to Guadalupe Peak, at 3,000 feet the highest point in Texas; to McKittrick Canyon; the Frijoles Historic site, an excellent example of the early ranching enterprises in the area; the Williams Ranch historic site; and to the "Pinery," the ruins of the Butterfield stagecoach station built in 1858.

Big Bend National Park and the Canyons of the Rio Grande

The Rio Grande—known to the early pioneers as the River of Ghosts—flows for 1,248 miles along the Texas-Mexico border through stunning, mountain-studded desert country and through a series of awesome canyons. The lower canyons of the Rio Grande, located near the eastern boundary of Big Bend National Park, form a turbulent group of rapids. Old Indian trails, rock paintings, and caves are found along the riverbank trails.

The deserts and mountains along the sweeping "Big Bend" of the Rio Grande form one of the wildest areas in mainland United States. The park's 708,221 acres encompass volcanic rock formations, deep canyons, and life zones ranging from cactus country up through Douglas fir stands in the rugged Chisos Mountains north of the Big Bend.

7. Canyons and Mesas —Colorado Plateau

THE Colorado Plateau is a unique geologic region that lies partly within each of four western states, Arizona, Colorado, New Mexico, and Utah. In shape it is an immense, rough oval that is centered on the Arizona-Utah border about 50 miles west of Four Corners, where these four states meet. The region has about the same total area as the state of New Mexico. It is essentially the drainage basin for the upper Colorado River, for which it was named by the first Old World explorers. In Spanish, Colorado means red or reddish, which conveys an idea of the region's most dominant and overpowering hue.

The Colorado Plateau is geologically unique in many ways, but one major difference is that within its boundaries the crust of the continent is 70 kilometers thick, about twice the average thickness of the rest of North America. Geologists are not certain how this came to be, but some believe that it is the result of one of the geologic processes associated with continental drift.

Whatever its original cause, the extraordinary thickness of the continental crust of the Colorado Plateau has protected it for at least the past half-billion years from the slow but powerful geologic forces that have distorted the western half of the North American continent during that time. Forces that have formed whole mountain ranges, overthrust wide belts of continental crust, and created vast fields of volcanic activity have left the Colorado Plateau relatively unscathed, although not totally unaffected.

These muted effects include a series of immense uplifts and eight relatively small but unusual mountain ranges, of a type found nowhere else in this continent. Among the uplifts are the Uncompahgre Uplift in western Colorado, the Kaibab Uplift in northwestern Arizona, the San Rafael Swell near central Utah, and the immense Monument Uplift that extends from northeastern Arizona into southeastern Utah. The unusual mountain ranges, called laccolithic by geologists, are the La Sal, Henry, Abajo, and Navajo mountains in Utah; the Carrizos in Arizona; and the Ute, Rico, and LaPlata ranges in Colorado.

Within the last 10 million years the entire western half of the North American continent has been lifted upward about one mile by some as yet unknown geologic force, again probably as part of some continental drift process. This drastic change in elevations caused

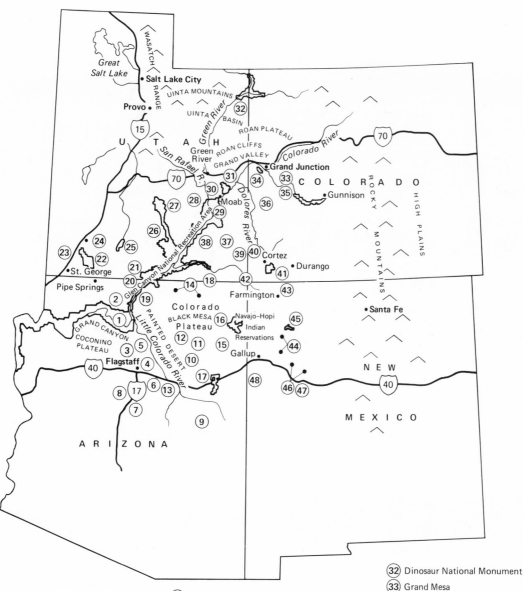

Key to Sites

1. Grand Canyon National Park
2. Kaibab Plateau
3. San Francisco Peaks
4. Sunset Crater
5. Wupatki National Monument
6. Walnut Canyon Cliff Dwellings
7. Montezuma Castle National Monument
8. Tuzigoot Ruins
9. Mogollon Rim
10. Hopi Buttes
11. Awatovi Ruins
12. Old Oraibi
13. Meteor Crater
14. Navajo National Monument
15. Hubbel Trading Post National Historic Site

16. Canyon de Chelly Pueblo Ruins
17. Petrified Forest National Park
18. Monument Valley
19. Marble Canyon of the Colorado River
20. Lees Ferry
21. Paria Canyon Primitive Area
22. Zion National Park
23. Old Irontown
24. Cedar Breaks National Monument
25. Bryce Canyon National Park
26. Anasazi Indian Village Site
27. Capitol Reef National Park
28. Horseshoe Canyon
29. Canyonlands National Park
30. Dead Horse Point
31. Arches National Park

32. Dinosaur National Monument
33. Grand Mesa
34. Colorado National Monument
35. Black Canyon of the Gunnison
36. Uncompahgre Plateau
37. Edge of the Cedars
38. Natural Bridges National Monument
39. Hovenweep Indian Ruins
40. Lowry Ruins
41. Mesa Verde National Park
42. Four Corners
43. Aztec Ruins National Monument
44. Chaco Canyon Ruins
45. Pueblo Bonito
46. Mt. Taylor Lava Fields
47. Acoma Pueblo
48. Hawikuh Pueblo—Cibola's City of Gold

The colorful Yampa River Canyon slashing through the ancient Colorado Plateau, part of a maze of deep river gorges unmatched in the world

a rapid increase in precipitation and erosion rates, especially within the relatively arid Colorado Plateau region. This rapid erosion, further accelerated by several major and minor glacial epochs, created the network of rivers that now drain the plateau and has removed thousands of feet of deposits from the region, carving from ancient geologic strata the fantastic maze of canyons, cliffs, and spires that typify the region today. Within this vast region spectacular erosional forms and breathtaking natural beauty are everywhere. Some of the highlight areas, either of outstanding natural beauty or of historic or prehistoric interest, have been protected by the establishment of national parks and monuments. Arches, Bryce Canyon, Canyonlands, Capitol Reef, Grand Canyon, Mesa Verde, Petrified Forest and Zion national parks all feature various erosional forms. Such national monuments as Colorado, Dinosaur, Hovenweep, Navajo, Canyon de Chelly, Wupatki, Sunset Crater, Montezuma Castle, Walnut Canyon, Pipe Springs, Rainbow Bridge, Cedar Breaks, Natural Bridges, Aztec Ruins, Chaco Canyon and El Morro all lie within the Colorado Plateau.

In addition to these federal parks and monuments the Colorado Plateau also contains huge Glen Canyon National Recreation Area, a number of special areas set aside by the Federal Bureau of Land Management, and numerous state parks. Because of its high, arid, extremely wild and broken terrain, the Colorado Plateau has had an unusual impact on human prehistory and history. Its prehistoric inhabitants had to be ex-

ceptionally adaptable to live there, and the region was the last on the continent to be explored by white men.

Settlement of the region was also late, and its development for human use would even now be very slow were it not for the presence of such minerals as uranium, vanadium, potash, coal, oil, natural gas, oil shale, and tar sands.

Since its initial creation in the dim Precambrian past, stupendous geologic forces and endless megayears of time have worked patiently together to build and shape the Colorado Plateau into the unique wonderland it is today. Exploring this wonderland can be highly rewarding to any who appreciate natural beauty or who have an interest in almost any aspect of natural or human history.

The Rocks—A Journey through Deep Time

The exposed layers of rocks of the Colorado Plateau's cliffs and canyons provide a rare opportunity to observe the evolution of the land reaching down and back hundreds of millions of years ago.

Known to the geologists as wedding cake geology, this layering of the rocks descends from the youngest strata of rock at the top of the canyons and cliffs to the oldest at the canyon floors, where the powerful Colorado and its tributaries have cut deeply into the earth's surface.

Red sandstone formations and volcanic necks in Monument Valley

The hardy traveller in this lonely maze of canyons and mesas can journey, to an extent unmatched elsewhere, down through what geologists call deep time to remnants of a massive mountain range formed nearly 2 billion years ago, exposed by the ancient Vishnu schists in the Grand Canyon; to the gypsum outcroppings in Cataract Canyon, formed about 300 million years ago when the region was submerged under a warm shallow sea; to the gray horizontal band of marine limestone, formed about 290 million years ago; to the commonly sighted bright red Halgait shale, formed some 280 million years ago from the mudbanks during the age of reptiles when the area was a vast coastal plain; to laminations of red sandstone pavement at the tops of the mesas and canyons, formed from the ancient sand dunes and offshore sandbars, called cedar mesa sandstone.

The Mesas

The typical flat-topped, steep-sided mesas that rise abruptly from the desert floor throughout the Colorado Plateau are the eroded river-carved remnants of the ancient sea bed of sedimentary rock that once stretched unbroken across the region. The mesas of the arid red rock country vary greatly in size, from small, low, flat-topped monoliths 600 to 1,000 feet high, sparsely covered with tough sagebrush and grasses, to massive sweeping uplands that are more similar to plateaus than mesas. Examples of the latter are the Grand Mesa in western Colorado, a lava-capped plateau that reaches up as much as 11,000 feet and contains some 400 glacier-carved lake basins and stands of ponderosa pine, pinyon, and juniper, and the vast, canyon-carved Cedar Mesa in southwestern Utah.

The arid, heat-scorched, wind-dried tops of the

Mesa and canyon country along the Colorado River Valley in Western Colorado

typical mesas are sparsely covered with tough, drought-resistant plants with roots that go deep into the cracks in the solid rock. Plants that are common throughout the red rock country tend to be much smaller and more widely spaced at the tops of the mesa—an area known as a tension zone where two life zones overlap and the species from both zones struggle to adapt to the dryness, heat, and cold.

The most commonly sighted species of the miniature plant world at the mesa tops are prince's plume, yucca, bottlebrush, gumweed, buckwheat, Indian rice grass, rabbit brush, stunted prickly pear, saltbush, single-leaf ash, barrel cactus, prickly pear cactus, lemonade bush, desert hackberry, stipa-grass, and blackbrush, which form small islands among the thin, wind-swept, red-brown sand. During the brief, fleeting periods of the spring runoff and summer thunderstorms, the colorful sunflower, lupine, and yellow bee plants blossom and brighten the harsh landscape.

Inhabited eons ago by dinosaurs, saber-toothed tigers, and prehistoric camels, the mesa world is the home of burrowing desert animals such as kangaroo rats and collared lizards.

Ancestral Rockies and the Scenery of the Colorado Plateau

About 280 million years ago the Colorado Plateau was a lush coastal plain, bounded on the west by an ancient ocean and on the northeast by the towering ramparts of the Ancestral Rockies that were worn away before the creation of the present-day Rockies. The vast amounts of slit, of fine sand and mud washed down from the mountains to the prehistoric coastal plain, where the Colorado River now meanders and roars through its giant gorges, was rich in iron. The iron oxidized and formed the bright red Halgait shale, which colors the present-day canyon walls and cliffs.

The Life Zones

The vast Colorado Plateau is a land of mesas and canyons. At the lower elevations is a zone of arid grassland dominated by sagebrush, cactus, and yucca, with cottonwood trees along the permanent streams. At higher elevations is the extensive zone dominated by open stands of pinyon and junipers. At the lower margins of this zone the trees are mostly confined to the walls of canyons and to other steep slopes. The mountain zone of the plateau is dominated by yellow pine, which most frequently grows in an open stand with an understory of grass or sagebrush and

Douglas fir, which grows in more sheltered situations and at higher elevations, with an open forest floor covered only by litter or shade-tolerant shrubs and herbs. The subalpine zone on the volcanic mountains of the plateau is dominated by Engelmann spruce and alpine fir. The treeless tundra zone is not extensive here, because only a few isolated peaks rise above timberline.

The Canyons

Until about 10 million years ago, the Colorado Plateau was much lower in elevation, more arid, and more gently contoured. It exhibited none of the stark, dramatic landscapes that are so typical of the region now, and no major rivers entered or crossed the vast, barren expanse. Then, a still-unexplained geologic event bodily uplifted most of western North America about 6,000 feet within a relatively short time. As this uplifting took place, precipitation steadily increased through the region, gradually creating a new system of winding streams and rivers, most of them draining into the broad lowlands from the mountainous areas to the north, east, and west.

At first, the waters from these meandering streams and rivers were swallowed entirely by the flat, arid Colorado Plateau lowlands. Then, as the uplift process continued and precipitation and runoff increased still further, the rushing waters gradually cut their twisting channels deeper into the land. One river, now called the Colorado, ultimately managed to make its way entirely across the plateau. It then carved deeply into the igneous and sedimentary strata to the southwest, ending its long journey by adding its water and sedi-

Young roadrunner—when full grown they can attain speeds up to 18 m.p.h.

Black Box Canyon on Utah's San Rafael River

ments to the Gulf of California. As the mighty Colorado River and its many major and minor tributaries slashed ever more deeply into ancient Colorado Plateau rock strata, the tumbling waters were confined within their river-gorge walls, following the same meandering, twisting courses they had first established when the land was gentle and flat. This created the spectacular "entrenched meanders" that are scenic highlights within the Colorado Plateau region.

Thus during the past 10 million years the Colorado Plateau region has changed gradually from low, fairly flat, arid plains, to high desert that is slashed by

Grand Canyon, offering a view of the Earth's history stretching back two billion years

a great twisting maze of appallingly deep, sheer-walled river gorges and tributary canyons.

Though the basic forces that created this vast labyrinth were continental uplift and erosion, the process was not always simple and straightforward. Smaller uplifts within and near the Colorado Plateau affected even major drainage patterns, as did massive sedimentation, faulting, and a strange erosional process called stream piracy. Together, these complications caused major rivers to change course, rearrange their tributaries, and even reverse their directions of flow. Ten million years ago there were no rivers entering or crossing the vast Colorado Plateau, and the several major rivers that now slash deeply through the region did not always flow exactly as they do today.

The principal river, of course, is the Colorado, which travels more than 1,000 miles from its origin near Rocky Mountain National Park in Colorado to where it joins the Gulf of California in northern Mexico. The Green River rivals the Colorado in size and flows from its origin in Wyoming's Wind River Range to its confluence with the Colorado in the heart of Canyonlands National Park.

The San Juan River flows from the Rockies that sprawl across the Colorado–New Mexico border to join the Colorado River in south-central Utah. The main tributaries of the Green River are the Yampa, Price, and San Rafael rivers. The major Colorado tributaries within the Colorado Plateau are the Gunnison, Dolores, Dirty Devil, Escalante, Paria, Little Colorado, and, of course, the San Juan and Green rivers.

These major rivers, together with literally thousands of their perennial and intermittent tributary streams, have created a maze of river gorges of a size, depth, complexity and sheer grandeur unmatched any-where else on this planet.

Grand Canyon of the Colorado River

The Grand Canyon of the Colorado River lies within the Colorado Plateau region in northern Arizona. Measured along the river, the canyon is 277 miles long, about one mile deep, and varies in width from 600 feet to 18 miles. The walls of the canyon provide a view of geological history that stretches back as far as 2,000 million years. Nowhere else on earth has such a geological record been so clearly exposed.

About 1,700 million years ago, during the Archean era, massive mountains were pushed up where the Grand Canyon is today. The high temperatures and pressures associated with the mountain-building changed the rocks into the dark granite and gneiss we see today in the Inner Gorge. Through another infinitely long period of time, these early mountains were eroded down to their roots, and where they once stood, crustal movements of the earth created a basin in which more than 12,000 feet of sediments and volcanic rocks were collected. About 800 million years ago this process was repeated. Between 570 and 225 million years ago, the region was once again covered by an ancient sea. The flat bands of sandstones, shales, and limestones that form the upper three-fourths of the canyon walls were collected in this basin, creating the bright red, brown, buff, and gray bands we see today.

During a long period of violent erosion, called the Great Denudation, several thousand feet of red shales and sandstones deposited in the Mesozoic era were stripped away. The only remnants of these rocks—which are widely spread today over the Painted Desert and form great cliffs in Utah—are Cedar Mountain and Red Butte.

About 65 million years ago the earth's crust in the Grand Canyon region began to rise above sea level, and the Colorado, swollen by the snow and rain falling on the newly formed Rocky Mountains, began digging a deeper channel to the sea. At some time between five and 25 million years ago, the river started to carve the Grand Canyon, slicing down through successive layers of geological time. From its junction with the Green River in Utah, the river drops more than 6,000 feet to the Gulf of Mexico, flowing through the Grand Canyon at speeds that vary from 2.5 to 20 m.p.h. Water, wind, and rapid changes in temperature have worn back the canyon walls and carved the colorful buttes. From the north and south rims of the canyon you can look down on the tops of mountains that reach up for 2,000 feet from the bases within the gorge.

Grand Canyon Microclimates and Life Zones

In addition to its vivid geological history, the Grand Canyon is a vast biological "museum." The great gorge and its innumerable side canyons are bounded by high plateaus that have cool north-facing slopes and hot south-facing slopes, perennial and intermittent streams, and great seasonal climatic changes. These microclimates support biological communities that range from arid desert conditions in the vast inner canyon and on the canyon walls, with summer temperatures exceeding 100°F, to the cool North Rim with its blue spruce and Douglas fir forests. Rising some 7,000 feet above sea level, the South Rim supports plants and animals adapted to a dry, cool climate, including pinyon pine, Utah juniper, and ponderosa pine. Above the rims, the surface of the land slopes from north to south. Water falling on the South Rim falls away from the canyon, while water falling on the North Rim flows toward the canyon, eroding the North Rim farther back from the river. The North Rim is 8,000 feet above sea level and the climate is cooler and wetter, supporting a conifer forest.

The diversification of wildlife in the park—naturalists have recorded 187 birds, more than 60 mammals, 29 reptiles, and 5 amphibians—is due not only to the differences in elevation, but also to the barrier created by the river and the canyon itself. The habitat of the Kaibab squirrel, a dark animal with a plumy white tail and tufted ears, is limited to the North Rim. The only other squirrel with tufted ears found in the United States is the abert squirrel of the South Rim; it is smaller than the Kaibab, has a red-brown body, and a gray tail. There are also wild burros, beavers, deer, bighorn sheep in the inner canyon, porcupines, a few mountain lions, some beautifully colored lizards and snakes, meadowlarks, mockingbirds, long-tailed chats, spurred towhees, water ouzels, and roadrunners.

Parks of the Kaibab Plateau

An unusual feature of the high Kaibab Plateau with its cool conifer forests just north of the Grand Canyon is the existence of many flat or undulating valleys, called parks. These valleys, thought to be ancient stream beds, become increasingly narrow as

Red sandstone pueblo ruins at Wupatki National Monument, built by a group of farming Indians between A.D. *1087 and 1197, after the great eruption at Sunset Crater. Wupatki, which means "long house" in the Hopi Indian language, is the most important ruin in the San Francisco Mountains area.*

one hikes down them, eventually becoming steep, V-shaped canyons.

San Francisco Volcanic Field

The San Francisco Plateau, the portion of the Grand Canyon region lying south of the Colorado River, comprises 2,000 to 3,000 square miles, with Flagstaff near its center. This area of ancient cinder cones and lava fields is dominated by the volcanic cone of San Francisco Mountain.

Life Zone Base Camp

Dr. Clinton Hart Merriam (1855–1942) made the investigations that led to his formulation of the life-zone concept, which was basic in the development of the science of ecology, at a base camp here. Merriam concluded that forms of life are peculiar to certain climatic zones or regions which are determined by the combination of altitude, exposure, and latitude. His so-called laws of temperature, delimiting life zones and life distribution are fundamental to the life-zone concept.

The campsite is 20 miles northwest of Flagstaff at Little Springs in the Coconino National Forest.

Lowell Observatory on Mars Hill

The broad program of astronomical research conducted by Lowell Observatory, founded by Dr. Percival Lowell, has contributed greatly to knowledge of the universe. Most significant of the observatory's discoveries was the first observable evidence of the expanding universe, made by Dr. V. M. Slipher in 1912. The observatory is also noted for intensive studies of Mars, the discovery of Pluto, and researches in zodiacal light and sunspot phenomena. The 24-inch Lowell refracting telescope, installed in 1896, is in operation today in its original housing.

The observatory is one mile west of Flagstaff.

Sunset Crater

Sunset Crater is an extinct volcano located on the San Francisco Plateau, an area of lava flows and volcanic cones covering from 2,000 to 3,000 square miles south of the Colorado River, with Flagstaff near its center. The crest of Sunset Crater rises 7,000 feet above sea level and 1,000 feet above the surrounding 3,000-acre national monument tract. It has a pit about 3,000 feet in diameter and 400 feet deep. The crater is bright yellow at the crest, shading into orange, red, and finally a fringe of black volcanic ash. Other fea-

Montezuma Castle—one of the best preserved cliff dwellings in the Southwest

tures of the area include the Bonito lava flow, which poured in four directions from a disrupted cone and piled up to a thickness of 300 feet; the ice caves, formed by the cold air of the protected intercone basin; and the fumarole, or spatter cone, near the ice caves.

Ancient Sandstone Pueblos at Wupatki

The red sandstone prehistoric pueblos of Wupatki were built by groups of farming Indians who settled here following a local environmental disturbance. These ruins constitute the tangible remains of an 11th-century Indian "land rush" that resulted from increased soil fertility caused by the eruption of Sunset Crater, a nearby volcano in the San Francisco Peaks, in 1065. Indians who had farmed around older cinder cones and those from neighboring regions moved into the area as word of the productive farmland spread. The Wupatki area—Wupatki is the Hopi word for "tall house"—became a cultural frontier and villages

were established throughout the area. Anasazi dry farmers from northeastern Arizona and Cohonino groups mingled with the original Sinagua people. The area includes several large pueblos, a stone-masonry ball court, and an open-air ceremonial amphitheatre. Nearly 800 sites are located within the monument boundaries.

The Wupatki National Monument is 30 miles north of Flagstaff off U.S. Highway 89.

Walnut Canyon Cliff Dwellings

Walnut Canyon National Monument preserves the remains of over 300 small cliff dwellings where prehistoric Indians built their one-room homes in recesses along canyon walls. Conditions in the area provided many inducements for choosing this site: sufficient water, protection from the elements and enemies, abundant fuel, and fertile soil. The inhabitants, who were farmers and pottery makers, were Stone Age people with no knowledge of metal. The site is important because it has yielded information concerning population shifts after the eruption of Sunset Crater in 1065, which spewed fine cinders and ash over an area of about 800 square miles. The porous cinder layer formed a moisture-retaining agent that transformed the area into rich farmland, luring prehistoric tribes from the east, north, and south.

The national monument is eight miles east of Flagstaff on U.S. Highway 66.

Montezuma Castle Cliff Dwellings

High in a limestone cliff above Beaver Creek in the Verde Valley is Montezuma Castle, one of the best-preserved cliff dwellings in the United States. The occupants were agrarian Indians who worked the farmland on a nearby river terrace. Overpopulation became a problem because drought in other areas brought more Indians to the site. The pueblo, a five-story building with 20 rooms, is largely intact. The monument also includes Montezuma Well, a large limestone sink, whose waters flow out at the rate of 1.5 million gallons a day and were used to irrigate the farmlands.

This national monument is 40 miles south of Flagstaff on Interstate Highway 17.

Jerome Historic Mining District

As a result of the large-scale production of high-grade copper ores at the United Verde Mine, Jerome was by 1907 the major mining town in Arizona and one of the greatest copper-producing centers in the world. The demand for copper during World War II led to intensive mining which depleted the known ore deposits, and Jerome is today virtually a ghost town. With its frame buildings propped on stilts and its narrow, steep streets, the town retains much of its original appearance and atmosphere. One of the original buildings, the James H. Douglas Mansion, houses a mining museum.

The district is at Jerome in Arizona's Yavapai County.

Tuzigoot Indian Ruins

The extensive ruin of Tuzigoot, meaning "crooked water" in the Apache language, is a significant example of the periodic additions made to late prehistoric pueblos of the Verde River valley. The hilltop pueblo of 110 clustered rooms is about 500 feet long and 100 feet across at its greatest width. There are few doors, as the rooms were entered through small openings in the roofs. Abandonment of the area occurred about A.D. 1400. Tuzigoot National Monument includes not only the pueblo ruins but also a museum housing the entire collection recovered during excavations.

This national monument is two miles east of Clarkdale in Arizona's Yavapai County.

Mogollon Rim

The Mogollon Rim extends in an east-west direction across Arizona south of the Grand Canyon. This great south-facing scarp divides the Grand Canyon region, the highest part of the Colorado Plateau, from the low-lying Basin and Range region.

Hopi Buttes Country

The volcanic necks, lava-capped mesas and buttes, and volcanic vents that flare at the top like giant funnels and tower over the surrounding desert of the Hopi Buttes Country form a portion of an 800-square-mile area of ancient volcanic flows in northeastern Arizona and northwestern New Mexico. This area includes the famous Shiprock, a volcanic neck shaped like an old sea-going schooner, that served as a landmark for the early explorers and pioneers.

Volcanic Necks

Volcanic necks, common in the Navajo area, east of the Grand Canyon and south of the Canyonlands, are the eroded remnants of the hardened molten magma that once filled the throats of the ancient volcanos. Two prominent examples of these ancient remnants eroded by frost, wind, and water are Shiprock

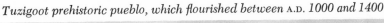

Tuzigoot prehistoric pueblo, which flourished between A.D. *1000 and 1400*

Keet Seel Ruin at Navajo National Monument, the largest known cliff dwelling in Arizona. Keet Seel, which means "broken pottery" in Navajo, has 160 rooms.

in northwestern New Mexico, towering 1,400 feet above the desert floor, and Agathla Peak in Monument Valley, rising 1,200 feet above the flatlands.

Awatovi Ruins on the Hopi Indian Reservation

In July 1540 Francisco Vasquez de Coronado dispatched Pedro de Tovar to investigate the Hopi Indian villages in the province colled *Tusayan* by the Spanish. His expedition became the first European visit to the Hopi pueblos. Awatovi, one of the largest and most important of the villages, was the first to be reached by the Spanish. During the period of missionary activity (1628 until the Pueblo Rebellion of 1680), Awatovi showed the highest number of converts. The pueblo was destroyed in 1700 by people in neighboring villages who resented its inhabitants' supposed sympathy to Christianity. Excavation of the site has uncovered much of the pueblo and three churches. Most of the material recovered was aboriginal, with only a few fragments of porcelain, metal, and other Spanish materials.

The ruins are eight miles south of Keams Canyon on the Hopi Indian Reservation in Navajo County, Arizona.

Old Oraibi—The Southwest's Oldest Continuously Inhabited Pueblo

Old Oraibi is probably the oldest continuously inhabited pueblo in the Southwest. The site consists of seven discontinuous north-south house rows, with most houses three to four stories high. There are thirteen ceremonial rooms (kivas) and a number of enclosed courts. The Hopi Indians were the only prehistoric pueblo culture in Arizona to survive into historic times. Studies at this site have produced invaluable data for tree-ring dating in the Southwest. The site indicates one of the least-changed Indian cultures in the United States, as well as numerous early contacts between the Hopis and European explorers.

The Oraibi pueblo is three miles west of Oraibi on Arizona Highway 264 on the Hopi Indian Reservation.

The Navajo Country

The Navajo country, south of the Canyonlands in southwestern Utah and northeastern Arizona, is a land of broad, open valleys, dry washes, hills, buttes, and mesas. The average elevation here is about 5,000 feet above sea level. The only permanent stream in Navajo country is the San Juan River, which rises in the San Juan Mountains of Colorado. One of the most interesting features of the region is the Painted Desert, a barren plateau broken by lone peaks, columns, and buttes of multicolored sandstone eroded into fantastic shapes. The Petrified Forest lies within the desert.

Navajo National Monument

Navajo National Monument in the canyon country of northeastern Arizona has three of the largest cliff dwellings of the prehistoric Pueblo Indians still extant. Betatakin, which means "Ledge House" in Navajo, is 450 feet long, with a maximum depth of 150 feet. Its towering red sandstone walls once held almost 135 rooms, including dwellings, ceremonial rooms (kivas), courts, storage areas, and grinding rooms. Keet Seel, meaning "Broken Pottery," one of the largest cliff ruins in Arizona, has about 160 rooms and was among the last in the Four Corners region to be abandoned. Inscription House, the smallest of the three, was built in 1274 and is notable for the date of 1661 carved on the plastered wall of one of the rooms.

The national monument is 30 miles southwest of Kayenta in Navajo County, Arizona.

Hubbel Trading Post

Built in 1878 by Don Lorenzo Hubbell, the Hubbell Trading Post became the most important trade center on the Navajo Indian Reservation. Through its influence rug weaving was revived and became an important means of livelihood among the Navajos. It has had an unbroken history of influence among the Navajos and is the oldest surviving post of its kind.

The trading post is on the west side of Gavado in the Navajo Indian Reservation in Apache County, Arizona.

Canyon de Chelly Pueblo Ruins

The awesome canyons along the Rio de Chelly in northwestern Arizona shelter prehistoric Pueblo Indian dwellings built at the base of sheer red cliffs or in caves in the canyon walls which served as an ancestral stronghold for the Navajo Indians. The Rio de Chelly rises near the Chuska Mountains close to the Arizona-New Mexico line in the Four Corners region and winds westward, emptying into the Chinle Wash just west of the monument. Except for the last few miles, the Rio de Chelly and its tributaries are enclosed by towering, vertical-walled canyons that range in depth

Four-stick hogan, a cone-shaped Indian house at Navajo National Monument

from 1,000 feet to only 30 feet at the mouth of Canyon de Chelly.

In the canyons are the ruins of several hundred prehistoric Indian villages, most of them built between A.D. 350 and 1300. About 1300, drought, and perhaps other causes, forced the people of Canyon de Chelly and other nearby pueblo centers to abandon their homes and scatter to other parts of the Southwest. About 1700 the aggressive Navajo Indians, related to the Apaches, began to occupy Canyon de Chelly, and present-day Navajo homes are scattered along the canyon floor. Their distinctive circular houses of logs and poles are called hogans.

The major features at Canyon de Chelly include Spider Rock, a massive spire of sandstone rising 800 feet above the canyon floor; White House Cliff Dwelling in Canyon de Chelly, named after a long wall in the upper part of the ruin that is covered with white plaster; Mummy Cave Ruin, in the Canyon del Muerto, or Canyon of the Dead, which includes a spectacular three-story tower house; Antelope House, also in the Canyon del Muerto, named for the pictures of antelope painted there by a Navajo artist 150 years ago. Indian pictographs may also be seen elsewhere in the canyons. Some date from the prehistoric Basketmaker and Pueblo periods, but the best are of Navajo origin. On the cliff face at Standing Cow Ruin, in the Canyon del Muerto, is a Navajo painting of a Spanish cavalry unit accompanied by a priest.

Meteor Crater

Arizona's famous Meteor Crater, believed to have been created some 40,000 years ago by the impact of a giant meteor from space, lies near the southeastern edge of the San Francisco Plateau. The crater averages about 570 feet across and some 600 feet deep from the highest point on the rim.

The Painted Desert and Petrified Forest

Yellow, magenta, red, and mauve terraces, mesas, hills, and buttes dominate the badlands of the Painted Desert of the Navajo country in northern Arizona. Eons of rain and wind have exposed the colorful

Spider Rock at Canyon de Chelly, where prehistoric Indian dwellings were built at the base of sheer red cliffs and in caves along the canyon walls

A Navajo pictograph at Canyon de Chelly

shales, marls, and sandstones of this area, which extends for 300 miles along the north bank of the Little Colorado River. The Petrified Forest National Park contains forests of petrified wood and lies within the Painted Desert. In the northern portion of the forest, where silica is the only mineral present, the trees are mostly white and gray; as one travels south, the amounts of manganese and copper in the logs increase, and their colors are more brilliant.

The major features of the national park include the Painted Desert; Puerco Indian Ruins, a site that was occupied before A.D. 1400 and is believed to have been a rectangular village of about 150 rooms enclosed in a large courtyard; prehistoric Indian rock at Newspaper Rock, pecked into the surface of a massive sandstone block; The Tepees, colorful bands of eroded clay; the elevated petrified logs, erosion gullies, and brightly banded clay hills at Blue Mesa; the 100-foot-long Agate Bridge petrified log spanning a 40-foot wide ravine; the great mass of petrified logs that litter the floor of Jasper Forest Mesa; the amethyst quartz crystal fossil logs at Crystal Forest; the massive Flat-Tops; and the large concentrations of petrified wood at the Rainbow Forest.

Geologists estimate that approximately 150 million years ago this area formed part of a valley that covered western Texas, New Mexico, eastern Utah, and northeastern Arizona. Araucaria-like trees (similar to Norfolk Island pine) covered the land and perched along banks of streams that slowly wound across the valley. (Fossilized ferns and bones of giant amphibians and reptiles have been found.) To the

west the ancestral Rocky Mountains formed a boundary, as did another ancient range to the southwest. Because there were no Sierra Nevada, a long plain sloped west to the Pacific. The network of streams occasionally rose to flood stage and from the surrounding uplands carried sediments that slowly filled the entire valley with sand and silt and covered the forest to a depth of nearly 3,000 feet. Before the trees had time to decay, minerals dissolved in the groundwater

Petrified Forest in the Painted Desert, which extends for 300 miles along the Little Colorado River

Badlands in the Rainbow Forest at Petrified National Park, once part of a subtropical valley that flourished 150 million years ago

seeped into the trunks until the wood cells were replaced by stone. (Some of the minerals found in the different stages of petrifaction are silica, iron, manganese, aluminum, copper, lithium, and carbon.) A shallow ocean spread over this region during the Cretaceous period, which ended about 60 million years ago when the mountain-making period began. The present range of Rocky Mountains uplifted and the interior basin of the Petrified Forest region consequently rose from 3,000 feet below sea level to 5,000 feet above, buried under a blanket of sand, silt, and limestone 3,000 feet deep. The petrified logs were uncovered as water carried the silty substance into the Puerco and Little Colorado rivers. The forest is still being exposed by this erosion. In the deep washes logs have been found 250 feet below the surrounding land surface.

Monument Valley in the Navajo Country

Monument Valley lies in the heart of Navajo Country and straddles the Arizona-Utah boundary. Although the larger part of the valley, which extends north to the San Juan River and west to the Segi Mesas, is in Arizona, some of its most spectacular features are in Utah. Scattered throughout the valley are wind-swept sand dunes and gnarled, dwarf cedars.

Outcrops of red sandstone several hundred feet high have been eroded by wind and rain over the eons into pillars, spires, buttes, huge rectangular blocks with grooved sides that resemble the ruins of immense Greek temples, and steplike talus slopes. At the southern end of the valley is Agathla Peak, an eroded volcanic neck with a spire that rises 1,255 feet above its sloping base.

Monument Valley Navajo Tribal Park

The park sprawls across the Utah-Arizona border, encompassing the wonders of Monument Valley, where maroon buttes and pinnacles soar upward to 1,000 feet above the red desert floor. Jeep tours of the valley may be arranged at Goulding's Lodge and Trading Post, founded in the 1930s by Harry Goulding, who was known to the Navajos as Long Sheep. The park visitor center is situated off U.S. 163 and provides information on self-guided tours.

Paria Canyon Primitive Area

The rugged Paria Canyon Primitive Area covers 12,726 acres in Arizona and 8,726 acres in Utah at the southwestern boundary of the canyon country. The

Paria flows through a deep gorge that reaches down 1,500 feet in the White Cliffs and Vermillion Cliffs for 45 miles just below Bryce Canyon to its confluence with the Colorado River at Lee's Ferry. Along its journey it cuts through the jagged East Kaibab Monocline, known locally as the Cockscomb, enters a deep gorge on the Paria Plateau, and runs through a spectacular course in Buckskin Gulch before joining the Colorado.

Lee's Ferry on the Colorado

Lee's Ferry is the historic crossroads in Cococino County, Arizona, between the upper and lower basins of the Colorado, where the river cuts through the Echo Cliffs and leaves the Glen Canyon as it briefly sweeps out into the open near the boulder delta formed at the mouth of the Paria River before it is again swallowed by the walls of Marble Canyon. It was here, in 1870, that Major John Wesley Powell and Jacob Hamblin built the first ferry, the *Canyon Maid*, and crossed the river. In 1872 John D. Lee, a wanted man for his involvement in the Mountain Meadows Mas-

sacre, arrived, built his ferryboat the *Colorado*, and established a new crossing site of the Colorado, replacing the historic crossing of upstream discovered by Dominguez and Escalante in 1776. Lee's Ferry was replaced as the major crossing of the Colorado in 1929 with the completion of Navajo Bridge across Marble Canyon six miles upstream.

The Arizona Strip and Pipe Spring Historic Site

The open country of the Arizona Strip lies to the west of Paria Canyon, between the Grand Canyon and the southern rim of Utah's High Plateaus.

Free-flowing Pipe Spring on the arid Arizona Strip in the Kaibab Indian Reservation in northwest Arizona has attracted Indians and settlers for centuries. Prehistoric Basketmaker and Pueblo Indians lived near the spring over a thousand years ago. Later Paiutes, nomadic Indians of the Great Basin, camped here during their spring migrations. The Paiutes were followed by the Spanish, and in October 1858 the spring was "discovered" by Mormon missionaries en

Navajo Bridge spanning the mighty Colorado River 500 feet above the entrance to Marble Canyon

route to the Hopi Pueblo to the southeast. Pipe Spring soon became an active church ranch and a popular stopover along the trail between the Virgin River towns and the Colorado River. The Mormons built Winsor Castle, the main fort and ranch house as well as barracks and juniper-post corrals that served as an oasis in the Arizona Strip. Winsor Castle has two rectangular, two-story houses with walls connecting their ends to form a courtyard. The stone was quarried from red sandstone cliffs to the west of the fort, and lumber was hauled from a nearby sawmill.

Microclimates

On the Paria Plateau, in southern Utah, bare sandstone stretches for miles. Under a summer sun the rock reflects heat and light from grains of silica bound in its matrix, dazzling the eye. The heat is intense, often over 100°F in the shade, if there were any, and there is little surface water: a pocket from the last rain, hidden between fins of rock, quickly evaporated by the brutal daytime heat. On the bald sandstone nothing grows. In cracks and patches of shadow, lichens pioneer the porous sandstone. Where wind- or water-borne sand has come to rest in crevices, a few wiry plants hang onto existence, covered with fine pubescence or a silvery, waxy sheen to reflect the

radiant heat and retain moisture. To put it mildly, it is tough country. With minimal vegetation or water to hold the day's heat, nighttime temperatures can plunge 40 or 50° from 75° to freezing, when the sun falls.

Splitting the plateau, in a narrow declivity, is the canyon of the Paria River, *Pah-reah* being the Paiute term for muddy water. The canyon is invisible from a distance. As one approaches, the line of rimrock is a brilliant skein of color above the deep shade and desert varnish of the defile. Looking down, down, down from the edge, the eye meets a surprise. There is green in the depths, abundant green. Plants crowd along the river's course. Tamarisk, ephedra thick as grass, scrub oak, the vibrant cottonwoods huge in contrast with the tiny plants of the plateau surface. A constricted thread of oasis that promises life: water, the cool of shadows even at high noon. If you could only get down, which for the most part, you can't. The Paria Narrows are inaccessible from the plateau above without rope and climbing gear—no place to lead a horse down to the water that gurgles almost a thousand feet below.

In most locales, the differences in microclimate and microenvironment are neither this extreme nor so striking, yet they are still important. Wild animals are intimately aware of them, because they mean the difference between life and death. Rabbits retreat to

Winsor Castle at Pipe Spring—a historic Mormon ranching center

deeper burrows to sit out spells of subzero cold. Bears sleep under the insulating cover of earth and deadfall while the air temperature drops to 40 below. Tiny spiders climb grass stems to escape the heat close to the ground. Frogs sit in mossy hollows by streams while sun on the sagebrush-covered slopes just a few yards away raises the temperature to a dry 90. Our ancestors, depending on the land more closely, had an awareness that one should not build a cabin in a stream bottom where chill air flows down from the heights, or found a town on a low, marshy ground where moisture rots wood and breeds mosquitoes. Fever ground, they called it.

Microclimate is a slippery term, based on so many interacting variables that several modern scientific disciplines must be brought to bear for even a partial understanding of it: meteorology, botany, topography, geology, physics, hydrology, zoology. Although the factors operating to determine microclimate are diverse and complex, the evidences of these operating together are easily observed. Look up a Western canyon: the south-facing slopes are sparsely covered with dry grass and junipers, but the north-facing slopes are thickly timbered with Douglas fir. On the south-facing slopes, limestone scree and lizards; on the north-facing, mushrooms and moss. In between, in the canyon bottom by flowing water, box elder and river birch and wild licorice and flowering dogwood, lushness bordering on the subtropical. That all these varied forms can exist in the same segment of a canyon and occupy a distinct space within it exhibits a kind of immemorial biological wisdom.

The evidence of plants and animals turns our eyes to the terrain. Both major and minor topographical features affect microclimate. A stunted limber pine grows in the shelter of a boulder at 11,000 feet. A valley glacier in Alaska, miles wide and grinding its way 20 miles to the sea, generates its own specific winds near its surface which are often in a direction opposite to the prevailing airflow. On some winter days, you'll rise to find the sun brilliant on new snow around the cabin, temperature 10 above, while the valley 500 feet below is swathed in icy fog trapped under an inversion, visibility 200 feet, temperature, 10 below zero. Some people have bought rural land in Wyoming where none of the early settlers had built before them. The hills crowd close along the river and the wind, constricted in its sweep over the open country, speeds up through the gap between the hills. In winter, the wind-chill factor is truly awesome.

The primary concept behind microclimate is thermodynamic. The earth receives a tremendous energy input from the sun in the form of radiant energy. Some of this energy is reflected while some is retained by the atmosphere, oceans, lakes, soil, and vegetation. Imbalances in heat lead to distribution of unequal heat through convective movements of air masses. Of this massive solar input, only a small part falls on plant life and of that small part only less than one percent is directly used by the plant for photosynthesis, the basic process on which earth's life depends. But the amount of energy involved in this process is staggering in itself. A single acre of corn can produce an aggregate 20,000 pounds of sugar. To do this, the plants absorb 144,000,000 Btu's of solar energy out of a total input of 15,000,000,000 Btu's. And a single acre of corn is lost in the fields of Iowa.

The differential heating and cooling of the earth's atmosphere and surface is a factor in causing local winds. In the Western mountain ranges, a basic pattern is downslope, downdrainage winds in the morning with a shift to upslope, updrainage winds later in the day when the valleys have been warmed. The behavior of forest fires illustrates this in a dramatic manner. A slowly burning fire caught by the shift in wind can suddenly make a roaring run up steep slopes. It is better not to be in the way, and most trained firefighters are alert to these local winds and react quickly to any change. Spot weather readings are taken on the fire site to supplement general forecasts with data for the microclimate.

The influence of slopes has already been cited. Terrain is another important variable in microclimate. A high range of western mountains wrings moisture from the air which must rise, lowering its temperature and pressure and consequently its ability to hold water vapor. The air that descends the eastern slope is much drier and precipitation is less likely, a phenomenon known as rain shadow. In winter topography influences the distribution of snowfall by causing turbulence that builds drifts and cornices in the lee of ridges and saddles. On shaded slopes, this snow melts slowly, retarding the growth of plants on the soil beneath while releasing life-giving water to the vegetation below, the adequacy and evenness of the water supply having much to do with the type of plants that can grow.

The Canyonlands— Rim Rock Country

The high, lonely, often spectacular Canyonlands embrace 32,000 square miles in the heart of the Colorado Plateau, cut and sculptured by the Marble Canyon, Glen Canyon, and Cataract Canyon of the Colorado River, the Labyrinth Canyon of the Green River, and the Canyon of the San Juan River. This desolate water-scarred land is like an ancient battlefield that has been plucked and gouged by nature. It is bounded

Slickrock—gray limestone, once an ancient seabed, that leaves a slippery, and often treacherous, polished sheen along the canyon waterways

on the west by the Aquarius Plateau, on the north by the Book Cliffs, on the east by the San Juan Mountains of the Southern Rockies, and on the south by the San Juan River. The western part of the Canyonlands is in southeastern Utah, with a small, narrow portion extending into Arizona along the Paria Canyon and Marble Canyon of the Colorado. The eastern part lies in southwestern Colorado.

The names on the map of the Canyonlands give an evocative sense of the colors, magnitude, and power of the place: Red Canyon, White Canyon, Rainbow Plateau, Forbidding Canyon, Valley of the Gods, Devil's Canyon, The Maze, Red Sea Flat, Upheaval Dome, Dead Horse Point, and Island in the Sky.

This land of deep canyons and huge mesas, plateaus, buttes and wind-worn pinnacles is a harsh, arid, desert country drained by the Colorado River and its tributaries, broken here and there by snow-capped mountains and forests of pine and juniper. Only the Colorado and its meandering feeders, the Green and San Juan rivers, flow year round.

Basalt Boulder Fields

Black basalt boulder fields, remnants of the volcanic fields that once formed portions of the Colorado Plateau, are often sighted near the ancient volcanic peaks, where they were washed down by long-extinct rivers.

Chert

The brick-red chunks of rock embedded in the limestone segments of the canyon walls are known as chert. Often packed with the fossils of minute marine animals, the chert was formed from soft masses of silica that were washed into the ancient sea by streams and were eventually surrounded by the limestone formations on the seabed.

Desert Varnish of the Canyon Walls

A common feature of the canyon walls in the Colorado Plateau are the dark streaks of desert varnish, formed when water, with a concentration of manganese and iron oxides, seeps through the sedimentary rocks and hardens into a varnishlike film as the water evaporates.

Slickrock

The gray limestone rock of the canyon and mesa country of the Colorado Plateau was formed from the marine life that once inhabited the ancient, shallow sea that covered the area some 290 million years ago. Where the limestone or shale created from the mudbanks of the former sea's shore has become polished and smoothed to a slippery, greaselike sheen along the canyon waterways, it is known as slickrock.

Canyon Wren

A denizen of the remote canyons of the Colorado Plateau country, the small canyon wren is identified by its rust-colored rump and tail, mottled brown body, and white throat and breast above its chestnut brown belly. It nests in rocky crevices, where its call, a loud *zieep*, may be heard.

Colorado River Dams

The enormous Colorado River system, with its thousands of miles of deep gorges, was the last to be fully explored in this country. Despite this late exploration, however, American exploitation of the region's rich resources began early. Following closely on the heels of official exploring parties, even preceding them in some cases, were the fur trappers and traders of Wyoming, Colorado, and Utah who ventured into the wilderness regions of the upper Green and Colorado rivers, and the intrepid paddlewheeler captains who explored and plied the lower Colorado, serving the farmers, miners, and stockmen who settled near the river. The first uses of the waters of the Colorado River drainage basin for agriculture were confined to the diversion of smaller streams and tributary rivers. Later attempts to divert the Colorado itself were less successful, because the river soon demolished the crude, earth-fill diversion structures and destructively flooded the laboriously cultivated lands.

Thus as civilization penetrated ever more deeply in the Four Corners states, political pressures grew for the control of Colorado River flooding, and for the diversion and use of its valuable, life-giving waters. The taming of the mighty Colorado really began with the National Reclamation Act of 1902, which led immediately to the construction of the Laguna Dam near Yuma. This dam was the first successful challenge to the Colorado. Others quickly followed, fueled by local and state enthusiasm and financed largely by the federal government. Some projects were on the Colorado, others on its major tributaries. Roosevelt Dam was built on the Salt River in Arizona in 1911. The Grand Valley Project on the Gunnison in Colorado and the Imperial Dam on the Colorado just above the Laguna soon followed. Then came Hoover Dam in 1935, with Parker Dam soon after. Davis Dam was completed in 1946, and in 1950 the Mexican government finished the Morelos Dam downriver from Yuma.

Dam building and diversions on the Colorado River and its tributaries have continued to the present, with some 26 major dams completed and others under construction, such as the McPhee Reservoir on the Dolores River in Colorado.

Since the very first dam on the lower Colorado curtailed riverboat commerce, dam construction on the Colorado and its tributaries has been very highly controversial, especially in recent years. Inevitably, for every gain made from a dam or diversion, there have been losses, some aesthetic, some cultural, some scientific, some economic. Though the arrival of the railroads did strike the first deadly blow to paddlewheel riverboat trade on the lower Colorado, the coup de grace was given by dam construction, which forever blocked navigation on the troublesome river. Other dams since that first one have caused massive losses of historic sites, mineral deposits, and archeological knowledge, not to mention outstanding scenic beauty and unique ecosystems.

Some of the dams completed in the Colorado River system within the last few decades are Glen Canyon Dam on the Colorado in Utah and Arizona, Blue Mesa and Morrow Point reservoirs on the Gunnison River in Colorado, Flaming Gorge Reservoir on the Green River in Wyoming and Utah, Fontenelle Reservoir on the Green in Wyoming, and Navajo Reservoir on the San Juan River in New Mexico. In addition to the major dams that now control the once-rampaging Colorado River, dozens of smaller dams and diversions on its hundreds of tributary rivers and streams add a final touch of civilization. The 10-million-year-old river that ran wild and free until barely 80 years ago is now little more than a steplike series of slender, calm, man-made lakes, confined between ancient walls of rock.

Glen Canyon National Recreation Area

The principal feature of the Glen Canyon National Recreation Area is Lake Powell, a body of water 186 miles long with 1,960 miles of canyon-indented shoreline. The lake was formed by the Glen Canyon Dam, built by the Bureau of Reclamation between 1956 and 1964 on the Colorado River in southern Utah. The rough canyon country of the Colorado Plateau has been known to various Indian tribes for 2,000 years. The name Glen Canyon was given to this area of the Colorado River by John Wesley Powell, who led explorations of the region in 1869 and 1871.

Lake Powell provides easy access to the Rainbow Bridge National Monument, which contains the largest natural stone bridge in the world. At Bridge Canyon, a foot trail about one half mile long leads to the natural bridge. Towering sandstone walls edge the river upstream from Lee's Ferry. Canyons easily accessible by boat from Waweap include Antelope, Navajo, Dungeon, Cathedral, Driftwood, and Cascade. The Rainbow Bridge National Monument, a spectacular natural bridge 309 feet high with a span of 278 feet, is reached by a one-day boat trip from Page, Arizona.

The Grand Staircase—
High Plateaus of Utah

The High Plateaus of Utah, ranging from 8,000 to 11,000 feet, form the divide between the Great Basin Desert and the Colorado River country. The plateaus rise between Grand Canyon and Bryce Canyon national parks along a "Grand Staircase" of south-

Rock formations along the "Grand Staircase" at the White Cliffs in Zion National Park

facing cliffs and rock terraces. The staircase is a series of cliffs, all retreating to the north as the superimposed rock layers of southern Utah are eroded. Some layers formed at the bottom of ancient seas and others on the prehistoric coastal plains adjacent to the shifting shorelines of the sea. These layers were uplifted and are now being slowly eroded by the action of water.

The capstone of the Grand Staircase is the Pink Cliffs, where Bryce Canyon was carved into a specular amphitheater by water and wind erosion in the 50- to 60-million-year-old rocks. Their color is caused by the presence of iron particles in the rock that oxidize. The 9,100-foot Pink Cliffs are the uppermost of five major steps formed by the eroding cliff faces of tilted sedimentary rock layers, each distinctive in color and character. Looking southward from Bryce Canyon National Park you will see the Grand Staircase stretching backward in time.

The rocks of the Gray Cliffs, formed about 120 to 135 million years ago, can be seen at the base of Bryce Canyon and are visible along the road between Bryce Canyon and Zion national parks. The Gray Cliffs are made up of such soft stone that their cliff faces are less sheer than those of adjacent formations.

South of the Gray Cliffs are the spectacular White Cliffs, where Zion Canyon has been carved. These formations range in age from 135 to 165 million years and are the tallest cliffs among the steps of the Grand Staircase. The cliffs are actually tan but appear white in sunlight. The brilliant dark red Vermilion Cliffs, the next south-facing step, range in age from 135 to 165 million years and are visible at the base of the canyon walls at Zion and along the road to the Grand Canyon. The next step in the staircase is the Chocolate, or Belted, Cliffs, which were formed 200 to 225 million years ago and are reddish-brown but have belts of other colors running through them. They are visible near the south entrance to Zion National Park. The bottom of the Grand Staircase is the North Rim of the Grand Canyon at the southern edge of the Kaibab Plateau. The Kaibab limestone at the top edge of the Grand Canyon is more than 225 million years old— but is one of the youngest formations you will see at the Grand Canyon.

Bryce Canyon in the
High Plateaus

Bryce Canyon National Park lies on the great line of plateaus, known as the High Plateaus—the natural divide between the Colorado River country and the Great Basin to the west. It is located on a huge uplifted block known as the Pink Cliffs of the Paunsaugunt Plateau that rises up 9,000 feet above sea

Bryce Canyon in the Pink Cliffs of the "Grand Staircase"—the divide between the Colorado Plateau and Great Basin Desert

level. The canyon is a spectacular maze of eroded pinnacles, turrets, deep canyons, and minarets cut by Bryce Creek, which flows after a short distance into the Paria River.

The Aquarius Plateau

North of Bryce Canyon lies the 11,000-foot-high lava-capped rim of the Aquarius Plateau, known locally as Boulder Mountain, the Table Cliff Plateau or Escalante Mountain. From its rim one can view a great portion of the Canyonlands—the buttes, red and white domes, and canyon-slashed plateaus.

Kaiparowits Plateau— The Fifty-Mile Mountain

South of the Aquarius Plateau are the long straight cliffs of the Kaiparowits Plateau, also known as Fifty-Mile Mountain. It stretches from the base of the Table Cliff Plateau for 50 miles to the Colorado River. To the north is the exquisitely sculptured, meandering canyon of the Escalante River.

Old Irontown

The development of Utah's iron and steel industry began in the fall of 1849, when an exploring party discovered Iron Mountain and the coal beds at nearby Cedar City. The Pioneer Iron Company and the Deseret Iron Company were founded to develop these resources. A third organization, the Union Iron Works, began operations in 1868 at the Old Irontown location on Pinto Creek. Several charcoal furnaces were built, one of which still remains. An "arastra" was constructed to prepare fine sand for furnace molds. This is also in fair condition. Stoves, irons, and milling equipment were made at the site. Reorganized in 1873 as the Great Western Iron and Manufacturing Company, the enterprise expanded to include an engine house, two furnaces, a foundry, a pattern shop, and offices. Today remnants of the foundry, a partial chimney, foundations, and walls are all the remaining evidence of a once-productive complex.

The site is about 22 miles west of Cedar City, three miles south of Utah Highway 56 in Iron County.

Capitol Reef and the Waterpocket Fold

The Waterpocket Fold, a high monoclinal ridge that extends for 80 miles from the Colorado River to Capitol Reef National Park, its northern extension, flanks the Aquarius Plateau on the east. Capitol Reef National Park, dominated by the white-capped domes of the great Capitol Reef, which extends for about 65 miles from Lake Powell to Thousand Lake Mountain, encompasses 241,671 acres and includes the Grand

The Needles at Canyonlands—a colorful area of slender spires, meadows, and parks

Wash, Great Curtain, the Fremont River Gorge, and red and gray pinnacles known as the Three Wise Owls and Capitol Gorge. The area is a maze of rock temples and cliffs, huge multicolored arches, and fossilized remains from the age of reptiles.

Green River Desert and Land's End Plateau

The Green River Desert, shaped like a parallelogram tilted toward the north, is a land of occasional sand dunes, low mesas and stone knobs, and extensive grassy areas between the Green and Colorado rivers on one side and the San Rafael Swell and Dirty Devil River on the other. The haunting Lands' End Plateau forms the southern half of the desert, where it descends, beyond Robber's Roost, on three sides down the Red Rim, the Black Rim, and White Rim for 3,000 feet into the great canyons of the Colorado and Dirty Devil rivers. This fantastically eroded area includes the Land of Standing Rocks and the Maze.

Canyonlands National Park—
Land of the Standing Rocks

The great twisting blue forks formed by the confluence of the Green and Colorado rivers in the heart of the Land of the Standing Rocks are surrounded by a labyrinth of upheaved domes, red and orange cliffs,

Indian ruins, deep red sandstone chasms, pinnacles, and needlelike spires of the awesome 337,258-acre Canyonlands National Park. The first trip through the Canyonlands on the Green and Colorado rivers was made by Denis Julien, a French trapper. He was followed by Major Powell's expedition in 1869 and the ill-fated Brown–Stanton expedition. The Green River flows through the deep, colorful Labyrinth and Stillwater canyons; surrounded by red buttes, spires, and mesas, this is the longest smooth-water stretch of the river. The major features of the Canyonlands include Butch Cassidy's Robber's Roost Canyon hideout on the Old Outlaw Trail, the roaring, foaming waters of Westwater Canyon, the Spur, Horsethief Point, the ancient cliff dwellings at the Island in the Sky, the Grabens, Orange Cliffs, the Needles, and the twisting waters and islands of the Colorado River.

The park has three natural divisions; the Maze district along the western boundary of the park, which takes in the Maze and Horseshoe Canyon and the Land of Standing Rocks; the 111,000-acre Needles region with its colorful spires, meadows, and parks; and the Island in the Sky, in the northern region.

Upheaval Dome

Upheaval Dome, one of the most unusual features of the Colorado Plateau, lies to the west of the Paradox Salt Basin between the confluence of the Green and Colorado rivers. This two-mile-wide conical salt dome, next to Gray's Pasture, is similar to those more common to the Gulf Coast Plain.

Horseshoe Canyon Indian Pictographs

There are several major pictograph panels scattered along the canyon in rock shelters and one deep cave. The most outstanding panel, the Great Gallery (200 feet long and 15 feet high in places), is a distinctive type and has become known as the Barrier Canyon Style. Huge mummylike anthropomorphic figures, varying in size from two to over seven feet, predominate. Some have intricate painted and incised designs within the bodies and around them; others have simple, tapered torsos lacking arms and legs. In addition, there are many small figures of animals, men, and geometric designs. Other panels along the canyon are much smaller and cruder than those in the Great Gallery. Evidence indicates that these pictographs were created by preagricultural people who were in the area before the distinctive cultural period known as Fremont (around A.D. 1000).

The pictographs are 43 miles south of Green River City in Utah's Wayne County.

Dead Horse Point

Dead Horse Point in Utah State Park overlooks the confluence of the Colorado and Green rivers 1,800 feet below the rim of the High Plateau. This magnificent overlook provides a panorama that sweeps across 5,000 square miles of red rock country: eastward to the snow-capped La Sal Mountains, south-

Arches National Park, shaped by wind, water, and frost over thousands of years

ward to the Abajo Mountain, southwest to the Henry Mountains, westward to the Aquarius Plateau, and below, in a canyon within a canyon flows the muddy Colorado through a maze of buttes and mesas.

Arches National Park

Arches National Park is sandwiched into a triangle of the Colorado River, Interstate 70, and U. S. 163 in the southeast corner of the state. The park was named for its many arches, the largest concentration of these natural wonders in the world, ranging from holes hardly large enough to crawl through to massive sandstone bridges. The arches were formed by wind, water, and frost erosion over thousands of years. Landscape Arch, with a span of 291 feet, is one of the world's largest natural arches. Foot trails lead to some of the park's most interesting features.

San Rafael Swell

The remarkable San Rafael Swell is an elongated, kidney-shaped dome about 30 miles wide that extends for 70 miles north and south in the northwest corner of the Canyonlands. This colorful limestone and sandstone uplift, or swell in the earth's surface, is completely encircled by hogback ridges or reefs consisting of cliffs up to 2,000 feet in height. Rising above the encircling reefs is a gently domed area of rocks, knobs, and low mesas known as the Sinbad.

Book Cliffs

The Book Cliffs, also known as the Tavaputs or Roan Plateau, wind for 215 miles like an inverted S from the northern boundary of canyon country where it reaches heights of up to 10,000 feet along its bold crest and forms a maze of cliffs, mesas, and steep canyons that open on broad valleys below, to its gradual descent to the Uinta Basin. The cliffs, often up to 15 miles across, run east to west from the Grand Mesa in Colorado to Castle Gate in Utah. The cliffs are cut midway by the 3,000-foot gorge of the Green River known as Desolation Canyon.

The Uinta Basin— Dinosaur Country

The Uinta Basin, which straddles the Utah-Colorado boundary, is the lowest part of the Colorado Plateau. Located south of the Uinta Range, this an-

Ancient fish fossil at Dinosaur National Monument

The huge domes that form the mountains of canyon country are made of volcanic masses of rock that uplifted the overlying sedimentary strata to great heights but never broke through them. These isolated ranges rise above the level landscape of the plateau and are referred to as island mountains.

Bear's Ears Plateau

To the west of the Abajo Mountains is the deeply carved Bear's Ears Plateau or, as it is also known, Elk Ridge. Named for the Bear's Ears, two huge buttes over 400 feet high on the south rim of the plateau, it stretches for 20 miles north and south above the depths of Dark Canyon and Gypsum Canyon.

Edge of the Cedars Indian Ruin

The Edge of the Cedars Indian Ruin contains stratigraphic structures from prehistoric and historic times. The numerous kivas (ceremonial chambers) unearthed indicate that the site may have been a Pueblo regional ceremonial center. Noticeable occupational remains are a series of rubble masonry mounds and circular depressions, either kivas or pit houses. Excavations were carried on in 1969 and 1970, and some stabilization and rebuilding of walls and roofing has occurred.

The ruins are just west of 4th North and 4th West streets in Blanding in Utah's San Juan County.

Natural Bridges National Monument

The Natural Bridges National Monument is located in a 7,600-acre area of spectacular eroded rock formations, including three water-carved natural bridges and several ancient cliff-dweller villages of the Anasazi Indians. This fantastic plateau country 51 miles west of Blanding with its box-walled canyons, gorges, whorls, windows, and turrets is cut by the meandering loops of the San Juan and Colorado river tributaries. The eight-mile Bridge View Loop Drive and hiking trails provide access and views of the natural bridges and cliff dwellings in White and Armstrong canyons. A visitor center and museum are in the Monument Headquarters Building.

Great Sage Plain

Utah's Great Sage Plain appears to be a broad, flat, barren plain extending east and south of the Abajo

cient east-west valley is bordered on the west by the Wasatch Mountains and High Plateaus, on the east by the White River Plateau and West Elk Mountains, and on the south by the Canyonlands.

Excavations in the Uinta Basin near Jensen since 1909 have uncovered a graveyard of dinosaur bones, and the site has been set aside as a national monument. In this region long ago was a flood plain, across which streams meandered. Upon the banks of these rivers and in the surrounding marshes the great reptiles lived. Some of them preyed on smaller dinosaurs and became masters of their primitive world; others, feeding on water plants, attained a length of 100 feet and a weight of 35 or 40 tons. When these mighty reptiles died their carcasses were borne away by floods and deposited on a bar, where the drifting sediments that covered them hardened into stone. The Jensen quarry, at Dinosaur National Monument, has yielded hundreds of dinosaur bones. Among them are the back and leg bones of the herbivorous brontosaurus and diplodocus, the bones of a flesh-eating allosaurus, and the complete skeleton of an immense brontosaurus 100 feet long and 20 feet high.

The Little Rockies—
The Island Mountains

The laccolithic peaks of the Henry Mountains in the western portion of the Canyonlands and their counterparts in the eastern portion—the Abajo Mountains, La Sal Mountains, and Navajo Mountains—form the highest elevations in the region. Long landmarks in the canyon and mesa country, they range up to over 11,000 feet in height. The isolated southern peaks of the Henry Mountains rise to 4,000 feet over the Colorado River near Glen Canyon and are known locally as the Little Rockies.

Mountains, broken only by the Ute Mountains of Colorado and Arizona's Carriyo Mountains. When viewed from a distance, this 1,200-square-mile area of the Canyonlands seems to be an endless sea of sagebrush. Actually, there are some 20 canyons from 100 to 500 feet deep that cut deeply into the surface of the plain.

Paradox Salt Basin

A strange region of valleys and flat-topped mesa-like areas created from masses of salt and gypsum, the Paradox Salt Basin is located in southwestern Colorado and southeastern Utah. It forms a rectangular tract about 150 miles long and 60 to 70 miles wide just west and parallel to the Uncompahgre Plateau. The major features of the basin are the Paradox, Salt, and Gypsum valleys.

New Mexico's Mount Taylor Volcanic Field

New Mexico's Mount Taylor volcanic field covers 2,000 square miles in the southern portion of the San Juan Basin. The major features of the area are the grotesquely shaped, eroded volcanic necks along the Puerco River valley and the lava capped Mount Taylor mesa, above which looms Mount Taylor at 11,390 feet elevation, an ancient volcanic cone.

Zuni Uplift

The Zuni Uplift on the southeastern edge of the Colorado Plateau is 75 miles long and 30 miles wide. Unlike the mountains of the Canyonlands region, the exposed crystalline core of this volcanic uplift, which reaches 9,000 feet elevation, has broken through the overlying layer of sedimentary rock. The uplift is encircled by valleys and mesas.

Hawikuh and the Cities of Cibola

The pueblo of Hawikuh was the largest of the "Cities of Cibola" and the first to be visited by Francisco Vasquez de Coronado. Conquered by the conquistador in 1540, it remained a Spanish headquarters for several months. It was visited frequently by sub-

Green River cutting through Dinosaur National Monument—the fossil quarries here yielded the skeleton of a giant brontosaurus.

sequent explorers. A few rock and adobe walls may still be seen in the ruin, which was excavated in 1917–1923.

The pueblo is 12 miles southwest of Zuni on the Zuni Indian Reservation in Valencia County, New Mexico.

Acoma Pueblo—The United States's Oldest Continuously Occupied Settlement

Acoma Pueblo is believed to be the oldest continuously occupied settlement in the United States. It was a familiar landmark in the period of Spanish exploration from 1540 until the 17th century. The Acoma Indians were generally successful in resisting the Spaniards because of their favorable location on a high mesa, but the San Estevan mission was finally established by the Franciscans in 1629. Though only a few families live at Acoma today, the tribe reassembles here for periodic festivals. The mission is among the least altered in New Mexico.

The Acoma Pueblo is 13 miles south of Casa Blanca on New Mexico's Highway 23.

Lowry Pueblo Ruins

Lowry Ruin is a pueblo of about 50 rooms. Its early masonry and associated pottery are closely related to those of the Chaco Canyon area to the south. Though originally a small unit similar to others in the area, it differs in having a great kiva. The great kiva, a large religious ceremonial structure, is more commonly found farther south in New Mexico and Arizona.

The Lowry Ruins is 30 miles northwest of Cortez via U.S. Highway 160 and a secondary road.

Aztec Ruins National Monument

In the Aztec Ruins National Monument in northern New Mexico's Animas River valley are preserved the ruins of one of the largest pre-Spanish Indian villages in the Southwest. The largest of these ruins, which has undergone excavation, was a three-story building with 500 rooms and a great kiva. Several unexcavated pueblos appear today as mounds with parts of masonry wall protruding from them. The term Aztec was mistakenly applied to these prehistoric people, for they were actually ancestors of the present-day Pueblo Indians.

The national monument is one mile north of Aztec on a secondary road in San Juan County, New Mexico.

Prehistoric wall and door at Chaco Canyon—once a major hub of Anasazi culture

Ruins at Chaco Canyon in New Mexico's San Juan Basin

Hovenweep Indian Ruins

Mesa Verde Cliff Dwellings—home of the Anasazi, the "ancient ones"

Chaco Canyon Ruins in New Mexico's San Juan Basin

At about A.D. 900 something happened at the Anasazi village at Chaco Canyon that lifted the community to prominence as the hub of culture in the San Juan Basin area of the Four Corners region. Between A.D. 900 and 1150, the Chaco Anasazi built 13 large towns in or near Chaco Canyon. Sandstone blocks were quarried and roof beams were transported into Chaco from 15 to 70 miles away without use of the wheel or draft animals. An irrigation system was constructed to support a peak population of about 5,600 people. Archeologists recently discovered a prehistoric road system radiating out of Chaco Canyon that connected upwards of 70 outlying Anasazi communities with the same planning and cored-masonry buildings as those found in the canyon.

The ruins, which include the Chetro Kettl, Pueblo del Arroyo, Casa Rinconada, and Pueblo Bonito, are preserved as a national historical park near Bloomfield, New Mexico.

Hovenweep Indian Ruins

Six groups of Anasazi ruins in the Four Corners region north of the San Juan River make up the Hovenweep National Monument: the Square Tower Canyon Cluster and the Cajon Group in Utah and the Holly Group, Hackberry Canyon Group, Cutthroat Castle, and Goodman Point in Colorado. The Colorado sites contain numerous towers and large pueblos. Goodman Point includes a large unexcavated pueblo and several smaller sites. The prehistoric inhabitants were Pueblo Indians, part of a farming group which occupied the Four Corners area from before A.D. 400 until almost 1300. Failing crops and diminishing water supplies forced them to abandon the area.

The national monument is northwest of Cortez, Colorado in Montezuma County.

Mesa Verde and the Prehistoric Indian Cultures of the Colorado Plateau

For more than 1,300 years the Colorado Plateau in the Four Corners region was occupied by Indians who were ancestors of today's numerous Pueblo groups. Archeologists call their civilization the Anasazi, from the Navajo word meaning "the ancient ones."

Earlier Indians, known as the Basketmakers because of their skill at weaving baskets, roamed the high Colorado Plateau country, hunting, trapping,

Anasazi ruins at Hovenweep National Monument in the Four Corners region

Long House at Mesa Verde—discovered in 1874 by two cowboys

The Cliff Palace, an apartmentlike building constructed in the 12th century

gathering nuts and seeds, and growing beans, squash, and corn, which was stored as dry kernels for later use as cornmeal. The dry kernels were pounded into cornmeal on a flat stone called a *metate*, using a smaller stone, a *mano*, that fitted easily into the hand. By A.D. 400 farming was becoming an increasingly central part of the economy and the Basketmakers began building pithouses dug into the ground.

Late in the 10th century, descendants of the Basketmakers began building their houses entirely above ground, grouping the rooms into small villages, or pueblos, the Spanish word for village. Archeologists have named these people Pueblo Indians.

As time went by, three major distinct cultural centers emerged: Mesa Verde in southwestern Colorado, Chaco Canyon in northwestern New Mexico, and Kayenta in the present-day Navajo country in northeastern Arizona.

In the 11th and 12th centuries the many small villages of the Four Corners region combined into fewer but much larger villages and cities. Their crafts reached a high point of decorative sophistication. The peak of cultural development at Chaco Canyon occurred in the 11th century; at Mesa Verde in the 12th century; and in the Kayenta area in the 13th century.

By A.D. 1300 the Ancient Ones of all three cultures had abandoned their homes, possibly because of severe drought and disease, soil erosion, too much concentration of population, and raids by enemy Indians on stored food supplies.

The inhabitants of Mesa Verde and Chaco Canyon migrated toward the Rio Grande with its rich farmlands, while the Kayentans moved south to Hopi territory. The Hopi in Arizona, carrying on their ancient traditions, offer a contemporary insight into the life of the Ancient Ones of early America.

The cliff dwellings at Mesa Verde, which means green table in Spanish, so called because of its pinyon–juniper woodlands, were discovered in 1874 by two cowboys who came upon Two-Story Cliff House. Before the year 1000, stone masonry began to replace the old pole-and-mud construction. Solid, compact, apartmentlike buildings were erected, and by the 12th century they were works of art. Built into steep cliffs below the mesa top some 2,000 feet above the canyon floors, some stood as high as three stories and contained more than 50 rooms, which were built around a courtyard that contained several underground rooms, called kivas, for religious ceremonies. The spectacular Cliff Palace, built of shaped sandstone and mortar, consists of eight levels that were joined by ladders from balconies and rooftops and housed over 400 people in separate apartments.

Colorado's Uncompahgre Plateau
Mesa and Canyon Country

West of Colorado's Rocky Mountains, which harbor the headwaters of the Colorado River, the land shelves off into the mesa and canyon country of the Uncompahgre Plateau that stretches away toward the purple sage flats along the Utah boundary, a beautiful but often sterile land inhospitable to man and beast. Through the mesa and canyon country flow the upper reaches of the Colorado and its chief tributary, the Gunnison, which cuts through the awesome walls of the 53-mile-long Black Canyon. Between them, almost at the point of their confluence in Grand Junction, looms the huge lake-dotted mass of Grand Mesa, rising 10,000 feet to form a vast tabletop, the largest in the United States. Remnant lava from ancient volcanic eruptions forms an erosion-resistant cap on the Grand Mesa. The lower surrounding mesas are heavily forested, for the most part, and on these and in the more remote valleys between them are the last true strongholds of Colorado's once-mighty cattle barons.

The Gunnison River has carved the awesome Black Canyon for 53 miles through the highlands of western Colorado. The most spectacular 12 miles of this gorge lie within the Black Canyon of the Gunnison National Monument. The name Black Canyon is derived from the fact that sunlight penetrates this deep and narrow canyon for only brief periods, leaving the canyon's dark gray walls shrouded in heavy shadows most of the day. The canyon's depths range from 1,730 to 2,700 feet. Two of the canyon's most striking features are its block islands and pinnacles, especially in the eastern portion, which were created by weathering and erosion.

Lizard Head in Colorado's Uncompahgre Plateau—a colorful eroded landscape of great mesas, spires, and deep canyons

To the west of the Black Canyon are the great mesas and rugged canyons of the Uncompahgre Highland. A portion of this beautifully eroded landscape is preserved at the Colorado National Monument near Grand Junction.

8. Snake River Country —Columbia Plateau

THE vast Columbia Plateau is a crazy-quilt volcanic land of craters and coulees, ancient dry falls, sheer canyons, giant springs, and mountains that are unified by the great Pacific-bound waters of the Snake and Columbia rivers. Embracing 200,000 square miles, it is flanked on the west by the snow-capped Cascade Range, on the east by the Rocky Mountains, and on the south by the Basin and Range region. The character of this country has been shaped by a succession of geological upheavals far distant in time, when wave after wave of massive lava flows issued from great fissures in the earth's surface, covering the land from the Cascades in Washington and Oregon across southern Idaho to the Grand Tetons of Wyoming from depths of a few feet to 5,000 feet or more. The lava cooled and contracted and was carved into the land we see today by the glacial meltwaters of the last Ice Age, by uplift, and by stream erosion.

Columbia Basin

The rolling plains of the arid Columbia Basin stretch eastward from the Cascade Mountains, flanked on the south by the Blue Mountains and on the east by the Northern Rockies. The basin is dissected by the Columbia and Spokane rivers and covers nearly two-thirds of eastern Washington. Within the Columbia Basin are the central plains, Yakima Folds, Waterville Plateau, Channelled Scablands, and the Palouse Hills (see separate listings).

The Columbia—The Great River of the West

The mighty Columbia, the long-sought "River of the West" discovered by Robert Gray of Boston in 1792, flows from its headwaters high in the Canadian Rockies, southward .in Washington State through Franklin D. Roosevelt Lake and the ancient lava plains of the Columbia Basin and forms the "Great Bend of the Columbia" at its confluence with the Snake River. The Columbia swings first southwest, then southeastward and then due west through the Great Gorge in the Cascades to the Pacific.

The spectacular Grand Coulee, 50 miles long, one-half to four-and-a-half miles wide, and nearly 1,000 feet deep at its head, was carved by the Columbia

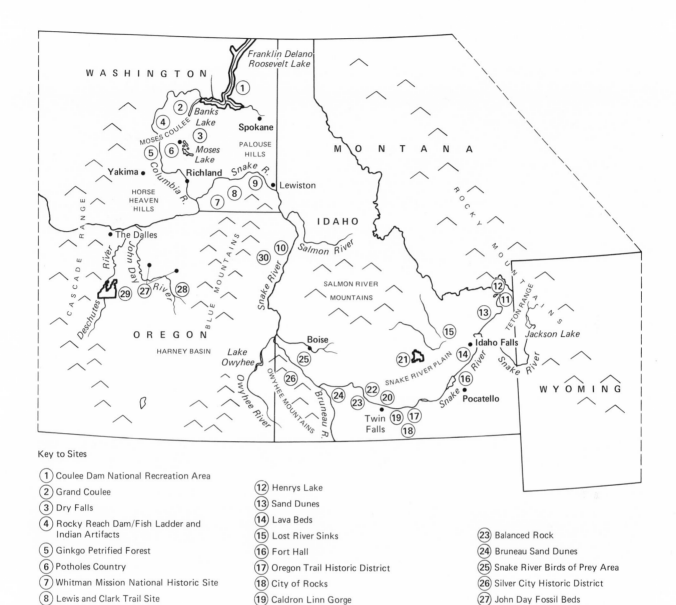

Key to Sites

① Coulee Dam National Recreation Area

② Grand Coulee

③ Dry Falls

④ Rocky Reach Dam/Fish Ladder and Indian Artifacts

⑤ Ginkgo Petrified Forest

⑥ Potholes Country

⑦ Whitman Mission National Historic Site

⑧ Lewis and Clark Trail Site

⑨ Snake River Canyon

⑩ Hells Canyon

⑪ Big Springs of the Henrys Fork

⑫ Henrys Lake

⑬ Sand Dunes

⑭ Lava Beds

⑮ Lost River Sinks

⑯ Fort Hall

⑰ Oregon Trail Historic District

⑱ City of Rocks

⑲ Caldron Linn Gorge

⑳ Shoshone Falls (212 ft.)

㉑ Craters of the Moon National Monument

㉒ Thousand Springs of the Snake River

㉓ Balanced Rock

㉔ Bruneau Sand Dunes

㉕ Snake River Birds of Prey Area

㉖ Silver City Historic District

㉗ John Day Fossil Beds

㉘ Picture Gorge of the John Day River

㉙ Crooked River National Grassland

㉚ Eagle Cap Wilderness

The Snake River—the "mad, accursed" waterway of the early French-Canadian explorers who attempted to canoe its violent rapids and canyons

during the last Ice Age, when the river was temporarily forced southeastward by the ice cap. This now-abandoned riverbed has numerous black mesas of exposed basalt, rock-rimmed lake basins, sheer mid-channel buttes, and dry waterfalls, including 400-foot high Dry Falls.

Great Terrace of the Columbia

The Great Terrace, one of several formed by the silt deposits in glacier-dammed lakes during the last ice age, extends downstream from the mouth of the Okanagan River to the southern end of Lake Chelan, rising at places several hundred feet above the Columbia River.

Rain-Shadow Climate of the Pacific Northwest

Eastward of the great ramparts of the Cascade Mountains are semiarid plateaus of rolling hills covered with sagebrush and bunch grass, the natural habitat of prairie dogs, rattlesnakes, and coyotes. In contrast to the humid, western slope of the range, with its dense fog-belt forests of Douglas fir, cedar, and hemlock, the drier eastern slopes are blanketed with forests of lodgepole and ponderosa pine, fir, and tamarack.

A hiker on a trail at the crest of the range will

sometimes notice a knife-edge break in the flora. High inland plateaus and basins stretch away to the eastern borders of Washington and Oregon, cut by deep river canyons, coulees and arroyos, sinks, potholes, and dunes and small mountain ranges. In this region low-growing sagebrush covers mile upon mile of brownish-red hills. Silvery gray, with small, wedge-shaped leaves and yellow bloom in spring, sagebrush emits a spicy, pungent odor. It is common in association with rabbit brush, antelope brush, and hop sage, and in the more alkaline soils, with greasewood. Tules, cattails, and yellow water lilies and green willows grow along the edges of sloughs and lakes. On rock ledges, serviceberry bushes bend their white towers in the wind, and spring-fed grassy slopes are dotted with yellow bells, sunflowers, grass flowers, and lupine. Along the bluffs of the Columbia River, wild clover covers the dry hillsides and distant fields have a purplish hue.

Chinook Wind

The chinook wind is the warm winter wind that sweeps off the Pacific from a southwesterly direction down the eastern slopes of the Cascade Range and Rocky Mountains, often melting depths of snow in a few hours. The Indians of the Pacific Northwest named the wind chinook because it came from the

Cheatgrass-covered hills along the Columbia River

direction of the Chinook tribe, who lived near the mouth of the Columbia River.

The chinook winds may be expected every winter through the eastern Cascade Range and Rocky Mountain regions. For days the country will be held in the iron grip of cold. Snow crackles underfoot, and at night the aurora borealis flashes overhead. Then, almost without warning, comes the chinook, usually at night. There is a low, moaning sound, like a prolonged sigh; the air seems alive. Water drips from the eves of houses, and icicles shatter below. When morning comes, the snow, which a few short hours before had glittered with blinding light, is sodden, turning to rivulets before the eyes. Sometimes, as suddenly as the temperature rose it drops again, as the wind veers from the west to the northeast. Then the melting snow is halted and the ice returns.

Central Plains of Washington's Columbia Basin

The low-lying central plains occupy the central area of the Columbia Basin and encompass the sand dunes country of the Quincy Basin in the north and Pecos Basin in the south, which are separated from each other by the Frenchman Hills and Saddle Mountain section of the Yakima Folds. Ancient Moses Lake lies in the southern portion of the Quincy Basin.

Yakima Folds

The high, broad ridges and valleys of the Yakima Folds area of the Columbia Basin lie west of the Central Plains. The area is cut by the Yakima River, which flows through several gorges in the ridges. The southernmost of the broad ridges is Horse Heaven Plateau, a broad, flat-topped ridge several miles wide, slashed by a narrow 1,000-foot-deep gorge, known as the Wallula Gap of the Columbia River.

Waterville Plateau

The Waterville Plateau lies at the northwest corner of the Columbia Basin and embraces a number of ancient coulees cut by the glacial runoff of the Wisconsin Ice Age, including the spectacular Grand Coulee and Moses Coulee.

Grand Coulee of the Columbia

Some 20 million years ago the dry open landscape to the east of the present-day Cascade Moun-

Ponderosa, or yellow, pine of the rain-shadow region—the bull pine of the frontiersmen

tains was a lush, humid hill country. Prehistoric rhinoceros and camels roamed swamp-filled forests of ginkgo, beech, and elm. Beginning suddenly and occurring repeatedly for several million years, immense lava flows poured from the earth and spread across the entire region.

These massive flows are believed to have erupted from long fissures in the earth's surface rather than from the volcanic summits that erupt with such fury in the Cascades. The lava, flowing like water, travelled at speeds of up to 30 miles an hour, with a single flow covering an area of 2,000 square miles in just a few hours—stretching eastward from the Cascades in Washington and Oregon across southern Idaho to the Grand Tetons of Wyoming. Individual flows ranged in thickness from a few feet to depths of 5,000 feet, cooling and contracting into tall basalt columns that are visible today in canyons and roadcuts.

Between the successive lava flows came periods of quiet, some lasting several thousands of years. Erosion created soil, followed by the return of wildlife and great forests. At Ginkgo Petrified Forest, near Vantage, Washington, the remains of an ancient forest lie scattered across the landscape. The forest, buried between separate lava flows, has opened a window on the past with over 200 species of prehistoric plants represented.

Eventually, nothing remained of the original landscape, buried in places under 10,000 feet of lava, the surface of which was a flat and featureless plain. This vast area is now known as the Columbia Plateau, named after the mighty river that borders it on two sides.

Driving across the plateau today in the summer heat, you may grow restless following roads as straight as rulers across seemingly endless expanses of land—that is, until the road comes abruptly to the brink of an enormous chasm, dropping away on both sides with sheer vertical rock walls 500 feet high.

This is the Grand Coulee, the greatest of the hundreds of riverless canyons that dissect the plateau, carved into the black basalt as if with a giant chisel. The story behind the coulees is as remarkable as the canyons themselves. During the last Ice Age, some 15,000 to 20,000 years ago, giant glaciers ground south from their sources in Canada. The ice, in places a mile thick, dammed rivers draining the mountains to the east, creating huge lakes that filled portions of what are now Idaho and Montana. One glacial lake, in the valley of the Clark Fork River, covered an area of 30,000 square miles, before the retreating ice released the water in a single catastrophic flood. Breaking through the melting ice dam the water rushed out onto the flat plateau, gouging out the myriad of coulees in what some authorities estimate was only a matter of two weeks.

Similar floods occurred several times during the retreat of the massive ice cap, leaving behind hundreds of dry canyons, plunge pools, and a landscape that geologists refer to as channeled scablands. Boulders the size of houses and sandbars 200 feet high are remnants of the immense flooding of the Columbia Plateau.

At Dry Falls State Park the floor of the Grand Coulee drops abruptly, the remnant of what was once a gigantic waterfall four times as high as Niagara and four miles wide. Like Niagara, the waterfall that once thundered here was cutting its way upstream when the Ice Age floods subsided, leaving the coulees as we see them today, dry testimonials to the awesome power of water.

Coulee Dam National Recreation Area

The Coulee Dam National Recreation Area includes the vast impounded waters of the Columbia River that form Franklin D. Roosevelt Lake, which extends northeastward behind the dam for almost 130 miles, and a narrow strip of surrounding lakeshore. A scenic highway parallels the lake through the Columbia Basin to rolling wheatlands, rain-shadow forests and mountains. Nearby is Dry Falls in the

Dry falls and channeled scablands

The 400-foot-high Dry Falls of the Grand Coulee, formed during the great floods at the end of the last Ice Age, was 4 miles wide and four times as high as Niagara Falls

Grand Coulee, west of Coulee City, a prehistoric skeleton of an ancient waterfall that once tumbled over an 800-foot lip near the Upper Coulee.

Channeled Scablands

The Channeled Scablands of the Columbia Basin are the exposed areas of the great mass of lavas that cover an area of some 200,000 square miles east of the Cascades. This eerie, forbidding area lies to the east of the Central Plains. The exposed basalt of the area was eroded by the glacial floods during the last Ice Age that formed scarlike channels of interconnected coulees, mesas, buttes, dry waterfalls and cataracts, and hanging channels above the main channels. Although the scablands were carved during the great Ice Age floods, there are no permanent streams and only a few lakes in rock-rimmed basins.

The Palouse Hills

The famous Palouse region southeast of the channeled scablands in southeastern Washington and northeastern Oregon is one of the nation's richest wheat-growing areas, producing millions of bushels annually. The Palouse, named after the Palus Indians who formerly occupied the low, hilly bunch-grass region of southeastern Washington and adjacent Idaho, is noted for its hot, nearly rainless summers and cool, foggy, rainy winters. Most of the original land has been plowed under, and there are only a few remains of the area's original flora on land too rocky for cultivation. The high, rolling hills that border the region are dominated by western yellow pine, western larch, and Douglas fir.

Central Highlands of the Columbia Plateau

The Central Highlands and intermontane valleys of the Columbia Plateau extend eastward from the Cascade Mountains to the Northern Rockies and includes the Blue Mountains in southern Washington, the ice- and water-carved ridges of the Wallowa Mountains in northeastern Oregon, the Seven Devils

Rolling Palouse Hills, one of the nation's richest wheat-growing areas

Seven Devils Range towering high above Hell's Canyon of the Snake River

along the Snake River Canyon in Idaho, and the high lava plateau to the south cut by the 2,000- to 4,000-foot-deep canyons of the Snake, Clearwater, lower Salmon, and Grand Ronde rivers.

Snake River High Lava Plain

The Snake River High Lava Plain covers a crescent-shaped area of about 14,000 squares miles in southern Idaho, northern Nevada, and northern Oregon. The Snake River bisects the eastern portion of the region for 350 miles, fed by giant springs where the upper Snake River canyons cut through the pillow lavas that trapped the waters of ancestral valleys. Many of these springs, such as Big Springs on the Henrys Fork, occur at the head of steep box canyons. An interesting feature of the Snake River as it flows through the High Lava Plains is the scarcity of northern tributaries, which is a direct result of the porous nature of the lava beds.

This is a region of "lost" rivers, which rush down from the Rockies to the north and vanish into the porous volcanic basalt, eventually joining the Snake through underground channels. The aptly named Big Lost River flows from its headwaters in the Lost River Range and vanishes at Lost River Sinks near Craters of the Moon, only to reappear some 100 miles distant at Thousand Springs near Twin Falls (which see).

The Snake—The Mad, Accursed River

The wide, crystal-clear water of the Snake River, known to the early French-Canadian trappers who plied its canyons and rapids as *la Maudite Riviere Enroyée*, rises high on Two Ocean Plateau, just south of Yellowstone National Park, and flows southward on

its turbulent journey to the Columbia River and Pacific Ocean through the sagebrush flats of Jackson Hole in Wyoming before it turns north and enters the eastern end of the Snake River Plain. At American Falls, Idaho the river gains in force and volume and flows through a series of waterfalls and cataracts cut into the old lava flows. The river drops 50 feet at American Falls, 180 feet at Twin Falls, and 200 feet at Shoshone Falls. It flows on some 600 feet below the lava plain before it turns to the northeast at Farewell Bend and enters the rugged 200-mile-long Snake River Canyon. The free-flowing 40-mile Hell's Canyon Stretch between the Seven Devils Mountains of Idaho and Wallowa Mountains of Oregon has cut through the black basalt to an average depth of 5,500 feet—deeper than the Grand Canyon of the Colorado.

Almost two-fifths of the once-free-flowing main stem of the Snake has been impounded by dams, from Jackson Lake in Wyoming to American Falls Reservoir in Idaho to Ice Harbor Dam near its confluence with the Columbia in southeastern Washington.

Idaho's Teton Basin and the Trapper's Rendezvous

Idaho's Teton Basin, formerly called Pierre's Hole during the days of the Rocky Mountain fur trade, lies just west of the spectacular Teton Mountains and

A typical box canyon on the Snake River

Wyoming's Jackson Hole. The basin was the site of an annual rendezvous in the early days for trappers and traders. Probably no spot in the West knew a larger congress of rascals and scoundrels. It was here that 42 adventurers encountered a roving band of Gros Ventre Indian men, women, and children and engaged in battle. Arrows, spear points, stone axes, and tomahawks are occasionally found near the site of the battle.

Idaho's Tiny Sahara Desert

Idaho's tiny Sahara Desert, created by wind and soil erosion, lies in a desolate volcanic area west of the Teton Mountains near the town of St. Anthony. These wind-swept sand dunes form a belt more than a mile wide and 30 miles long, with wind-drifted dunes that vary in height from 10 to 100 feet. From year to year and mile to mile they shift uncertainly under the sculpturing winds, never twice the same.

Big Springs of the Henrys Fork

The Big Springs, the source of the Henrys Fork of the Snake River in southeastern Idaho, gush out from the base of a mountain in such volume that a full-fledged river is formed within a hundred feet of the springs. They are the largest natural springs in the United States, with an average flow of 185 feet per second and a constant temperature of 52°F. The springs have been preserved as a breeding sanctuary for giant rainbow trout up to 20 pounds in weight. From its source at Big Springs, the Henrys Fork becomes the largest spring-fed river in the world.

Fort Hall on the Great Bend of the Snake River

Fort Hall, located on the great bend of the Snake River near its confluence with the Portneuf River, occupied one of the most strategic sites of the American West. Built by Nathaniel Wyeth at the division of the Oregon and California trails, the fort was importantly associated with the fur trade, the overland migration, and the transportation and supply network to the gold mines in both Idaho and Montana. The precise location of the fort was once lost because of flooding of the Snake River, but in 1916 the site was identified from artifacts taken from the ground at the presently established location. A group of low mounds encloses the site today.

The fort is 11 miles west of Fort Hall at the Fort Hall Indian Reservation in Bannock County, Idaho.

Sand dunes on Idaho's Snake River High Lava Plain

Oregon Trail Historic District

The 2,000-mile-long wagon path known as the Oregon Trail cut through the Snake River Plains country along its route from Independence, Missouri, to the mouth of the Columbia River on the Pacific Ocean. The trail had been explored by fur traders earlier in the century, but it was rarely used before "Oregon fever" began sweeping the country in 1842, the year the first large wagon train made the long trek. In the "Great Migration" the following year, waves of emigrant wagons crossed the plains and the western mountain ranges via South Pass through the Snake River country and the Blue Mountains to the Columbia River. By the 1850s, wagon travel had left the great road so deeply rutted that it remains visible in spots to this day.

The Oregon Trail Historic District includes two unaltered segments of the Oregon Trail. One segment, east of Register Rock, extends for about half a mile. Here the trail winds down into a ravine where wagons once had difficulty crossing. The other segment ascends a grade out of the Snake River shoreland west of Bonanza Bar and includes a small ridge covered with tracks where, again, wagons encountered trouble in crossing the incline. Undisturbed areas of

Oxen-powered covered wagon, or "prairie schooner," used during the "Great Migration" west along the 2,000-mile Oregon Trail

the trail are not common, and these two along the Snake River are among the best remaining in the state.

The historic district is southwest of American Falls along U.S. Highway 30N in Idaho's Power County.

City of Rocks on the Old California Trail

The City of Rocks, one of the natural landmarks of the California Trail, was probably first opened in 1842 by the Joseph B. Chiles party, which was exploring for a satisfactory route for the trail. The site received its name from the formations of rock found in the valley of Circle Creek. Here thousands of emigrants camped, some of whom carved their names in the curious rock formations. Visible tracks left by wagon trains still remain. The area is largely in the same condition as when the wagon trains were passing through this section of the country.

The landmark is in City of Rocks State Park near Almo, Idaho, in Cassia County.

Giant Sturgeon of the Snake River

The greatest of all the fish species in the Snake River is the white sturgeon, a prehistoric relic of the ancient seas that once covered vast portions of the Columbia Plateau some 300 million years ago. Its body is covered with rows of bony, armorlike scales. With a life span of up to 100 years, it reaches lengths of up to 12 feet and weighs up to 1,500 pounds.

Ice Age Boulders

The hiker along the flat lava floors of the Snake River canyons will often see huge, house-sized boulders—remnants of a great flood that occurred during an ice age about 30,000 years ago. At the time, the vast waters of prehistoric Lake Bonneville lay to the south. With the melting of the glaciers, the lake's surface rose and roared through a 400-foot mountain pass near Pocatello, Idaho with such force that it swept boulders from the slopes and carried them into the canyon floor.

Caldron Linn Gorge on the Snake River

Wilson Price Hunt's overland expedition to Astoria, a Pacific Fur Company post at the mouth of the Columbia River, explored much of southern Idaho and eastern Oregon in 1811. His belief that canoes could descend from the upper Snake River to Astoria was destroyed when the expedition encountered water too turbulent to cross near this site. The gorge, which they named Caldron Linn, symbolized the misfortunes encountered on their journey. Members of the expedition were forced to cache their supplies nearby, divide into three parties, and walk to the Pacific.

The gorge is two miles east of Murtaugh in Jerome County, Idaho.

Thousand Springs of the Snake River

Thousand Springs, on the north side of the Snake near Twin Falls, Idaho, is the largest of the basalt trapped surface water springs along the Snake River. These massive springs are among the largest in the United States, gushing an estimated 40,000 gallons of water per second from the pillow lavas at the base of ancient volcanic flows.

Prairie Falcons

A common sight soaring above the canyons of the Snake River country, the prairie falcon is identified by its call, a loud *kree, kree, kree*, often heard near its canyon aeries, and its body coloring—a light sandy brown above and creamy color below, with black wing tips. It feeds, along with its relative the peregrine falcon, on the ground squirrels, marmots, jackrabbits, and smaller birds that inhabit the austere sagebrush country surrounding the Snake River.

Spatter cones at Craters of the Moon along the 14-mile-long Great Rift

Cinder Cones of the Snake River Plain

The great lava flows that oozed from volcanic craters along gaping mile-long fissures in the earth that created the Snake River Plain formed the cinder cones and eerie volcanic devastation found scattered throughout the region. The most spectacular group of cinder cones are those extending in a northwest-to-southeast slash at Craters of the Moon along a 14-mile-long fracture called the Great Rift. Big Cinder Butte, the tallest cinder cone at Craters of the Moon, rises 800 feet above the plain. At one spot an awesome volcanic hole reaches a depth of 200 feet and is 660 feet across and 2,000 feet in circumference.

Craters of the Moon

The blackened, devastated landscape of the Craters of the Moon National Monument was formed within the last 100,000 years when three successive outpourings of boiling molten rock flowed from great cracks in the earth's surface over the Snake River Plain, engulfing all the plant life and creating tall cinder and ash cones. The national monument preserves 83 square miles of this lunarlike landscape. Bushes and scrub trees grow among the crater-studded lava fields, including rabbit brush, tansy bushes, sagebrush, mock orange, and antelope bitter brush; limber pine, aspen, and Douglas fir grow on the sides on the tall cones. In spring, wildflowers carpet areas of the blackened earth in pink, magenta, yellow, and bright blue.

Rabbit Brush and Dwarf Buckwheat

Dwarf buckwheat and bright clusters of rubber rabbit brush are typical of the hardy plants found along the desolate volcanic barrens of the Snake River Plain. These tenacious plants put down roots on the arid slopes and cinder fields that receive, at most, 17 inches of annual rainfall.

Wildlife of Craters of the Moon

Although apparently desolate, the bleak volcanic landscape of the Craters of the Moon is the natural habitat for several plant and animal species. Found here are western junipers, limber pines, and quaking aspens. Among wildflowers there are red or yellow eriogonums and white primroses; the most beautiful of all in the black wastes are the white blossoms of the bitterroot, the yellow blossoms of the sand lily, and the white sego lily. There are also cinquefoil, daisy and phlox, yarrow and aster and prairie pink. Among the craters and sagebrush wastes are several species of rabbit, gophers, chipmunks, porcupine, pack rats, skunks, coyotes, and bobcats. Moss Cave and Sunbear Cave were once the dens of bears, and several grizzlies were slain in the area some years ago. Skull remains show that mountain sheep, antelope, and deer used to roam here. Birds of the area include woodpeckers, hawks, ravens, crows, larks, sage grouse, and bald and golden eagles. There are no snakes because of the rough and jagged volcanic terrain.

Tree Molds at Trench Mortar Flat

The volcanic havoc created by the ancient lava flows at the Trench Mortar Flat area of the Craters of the Moon region is noted for formations that pock the landscape known as tree molds. These formations, which resemble Civil War trench mortars, were created when the trunks of trees, engulfed by lava, rotted, leaving their shapes cast in lava.

Breadcrust Bombs

Breadcrust bombs commonly sighted at Craters of the Moon are small blobs of lava that hardened in the air during eruption. These cracked, bomblike formations are often covered with colorful patches of primitive lichen.

Indian and Pioneer Sites at Craters of the Moon

An ancient Indian trail followed the Great Rift area of Craters of the Moon National Park. Caves along the route were used as temporary shelters and at times as strongholds against attacks from rival tribes. At Indian Tunnel the semicircular arrangements of stone indicate that they were used either for protection or as firebreaks. Arrowheads and other stone implements were previously found in this vicinity.

The lava fields and the general rugged landscape of the Craters of the Moon area have been barriers to westward migration and to local settlement. All early travellers avoided crossing this rough area. The old pioneer wagon road from Arco to Carney, Idaho, which skirted the lava flows, was 76 miles long. To-

Lava-twisted tree at Craters of the Moon, formed when molten lava flowed from great fissures over the Snake River Plain

day's route, crossing some of the most rugged parts of these flows, is only 43 miles long.

Arrowrock Dam on the Boise River

Arrowrock Dam was built by the Bureau of Reclamation to provide water storage for enlargement of the Boise project. At the time of its completion, it was the highest dam in the world. It took five years from planning to opening, and it impounds 280,000 acre-feet of water, creating a lake 17 miles long. The dam is 354 feet high and 223 feet thick at the base. It was renovated in 1936–1937; however, its appearance was not altered. The lower face of the dam is submerged when the lower reservoir is full because of another, more recently constructed dam.

The dam is about 10 miles east of Boise, Idaho, on U.S. Forest Service roads.

Snake River Birds of Prey Area

The rugged basalt cliffs along the Snake River Canyon south of Boise are the site of the 31,000-acre Birds of Prey Natural Area. This high desert landscape of sagebrush and greasewood attracts a greater concentration of raptorial (meat-eating) birds than any other area of comparable size in the United States. Golden eagles and great horned owls are found among the lava ledges and pinnacles of the canyon year round; the American rough-legged hawk, sparrow hawks, goshawks, osprey, and bald eagles arrive in January. The commonly sighted prairie falcons arrive here in February, after the owls and eagles have set up their nests and aeries. The birds of prey share the area with a wide variety of wildlife, including ground squirrels, marmots, jackrabbits, coyotes, mule deer, mink, and a variety of smaller birds.

Hell's Canyon National Recreation Area

This 130,000-acre national recreation area straddles the awesome Hell's Canyon of the Snake River at the Idaho-Oregon boundary. The sheer volcanic walls of the gorge reach down to a depth of 7,900 feet from the summit of He Devil Peak in the Seven Devils Mountains. It is the deepest and narrowest gorge on the North American continent.

Lewiston Depot

The arrival of the railroad was important to Lewiston, because of its strategic location on the Co-

Old hotel at the abandoned "Black Lake Mine" near Hell's Canyon

lumbia and Snake rivers, the heart of the grain and fruit belts and the mining and lumbering region. For several years the town was on a branch of the Northern Pacific. The Clearwater Valley railroad war between the Northern Pacific and Union Pacific was resolved by creation of the Camas Prairie Railroad, after which, this permanent depot was erected. It consists of a two-story central block of light-colored pressed brick flanked by long one-story wings.

The depot is at 13th and Main streets in Lewiston, Idaho.

Whitman Mission on the Old Oregon Trail

Whitman Mission National Historic Site east of the Blue Mountains, an important station overlooking the Walla Walla Valley on the Oregon Trail during the 1840s, is the place where Dr. and Mrs. Marcus Whitman ministered to the spiritual and physical needs of the Cayuse Indians until a handful of the Indians massacred them and three other whites in 1847. On their 1836 journey over the Oregon Trail, Narcissa Whitman and Eliza Spaulding became the first American women to cross the continent overland, a feat that encouraged the great migrations west that followed. The present site preserves the original mission grounds known as Waiilatpu—the "place of the people of the rye grass" in Cayuse—the millpond, and the graves of the Whitmans and other victims of

Grayish long-eared owl at the Snake River Birds of Prey area

Lava formations along the Deschutes, called the "River of Falls," like the Snake River fed by giant springs gushing up through the porous lava

the 1847 massacre.

The site is six miles west of Walla Walla, Washington, off U.S. Highway 410.

Sumpter Valley Gold Dredge in the Blue Mountains

Oregon's Blue Mountain region was the most important gold-bearing area in the state. In 1896 a big lode was found near Bourne, and Sumpter itself was booming between 1899 and 1903. This gold dredge, the third to operate in the valley, is the last one surviving in the state. It is moored in a pond amid miles of tailings near the entrance of the Cracker Creek into the Powder River. The dredge has a hull of coast fir and steel frame; its gravel stacker has a 36-inch belt, the bucket line has 72 buckets, and the digging line was powered by an electric motor. In 1938 the dredge was reported to have washed away as much as 10 acres of river bottom land in a month.

The gold dredge is southwest of Sumpter near Cracker Creek in Baker County, Oregon.

Mesa Region of the High Lava Plains

To the west of the relatively flat Snake River Plain is the middle portion of the High Lava Plains in eastern Oregon. This region is lower in altitude and more highly eroded than the plains to the east, with numerous mesalike areas.

Oregon's Harney High Desert

Similar in landscape to the Snake River Plain is the Harney High Desert, a portion of the High Lava Plains in south-central Oregon. The arid sagebrush flats, lava flows, cinder cones, ash deposits, and large ephemeral lakes form a transition zone to the Great Basin region to the south.

The most notable feature of the region is the Great Sandy Desert, a flat arid area of low volcanic cones extending for 150 miles southeastward in a swath 30 to 50 miles wide from Bend, Oregon. The "sand" of this desert is actually disintegrated volcanic pumice.

The Deschutes—The River of Falls

The beautiful Deschutes River, known to the early explorers and trappers as *Riviere des Chutes*, the river of falls, rises in the northwest corner of the Harney High Desert. Like its eastern counterpart, the Snake, the Deschutes is fed by giant springs from the porous volcanic lavas, fed by runoff from glaciers in the High Cascades to the west, and flows through a spectacular canyon.

The John Day Fossil Beds

The John Day River country in northwest Oregon, with its succession of startling contours, jagged skylines, eroded palisades, painted hills, sharp pinnacles rising from mountains of solid rock, and gashes through volcanic formations, often brilliantly red and buff colored, has great fascination. In this arid rangeland of sagebrush and juniper are the John Day Fossil Beds, a ridge where a layer of pale green calcareous deposit a thousand feet thick is exposed.

In these deposits are fossilized relics of the period when this high region of badlands, sagebrush plains, and wheatfields was a low tropical jungle inhabited by rhinoceroses, saber-toothed tigers, giant sloths, sheeplike oreodonts, miniature horses, and other ancestors of present-day animals, as well as curious and extinct species. As shown by great numbers of specimens—including agatized roots and leaves—palm, redwood, magnolia, fig, and ginkgo trees grew in profusion in an area where the hardy sagebrush now survives with difficulty. After the gigantic upheaval that resulted in the formation of the Coast Range, volcanic eruptions covered the land with lava and ash. Then came the great ice cap over the lands to the north and, later, the slow melting period during which some of the region's chief rivers were formed. As these rivers, including the John Day, cut down through the crust accumulated through the ages, they revealed the deposits that tell the story of the land's prehistoric life.

Oregon's Dry River

On the rugged bluffs of the bed of the Dry River in southwestern Oregon is one of the region's largest collections of Indian pictographs. These crude, prehistoric paintings of varying heights are applied to the canyon walls with colors that have grown dim with the ages. Dry River is a geological wonder in itself and can be traced across the central Oregon Plateau for 50 miles. At one time, it was a large river rising in the prehistoric lake region of central Oregon, and flowing northeast to empty into an ancient stream which followed the present-day course of the John Day River.

Owhyee Mountains and the Bruneau Sand Dunes

The dome-shaped, silver-bearing Owhyee Mountains, which occupy the southwest corner of Idaho and the southeastern corner of Oregon, are flanked on the west by the wild Owhyee River and on the east by the rugged canyons of the Bruneau River, both southern tributaries of the Snake River. This upland plateau rises some 5,000 feet above the younger Snake River High Lava Plain to the north. To the east of the mountains, near the confluence of the Bruneau and Snake rivers, are the ancient Bruneau Sand Dunes, swept into high mounds by the prevailing winds from the ramparts of the Cascade Range far to the west.

Silver City Historic District in the Owyhee Region

Discovery of gold in the Boise Basin brought mining to the Owyhee region in 1862, but the following year it became apparent that the Owyhee mines were primarily silver producers. The mines kept a number of stamp mills busy producing $2 million per year until the failure of the Bank of California (August 26, 1875) brought most work to a halt. A majority of the large companies shut down completely in 1912, and by 1942 Silver City had become a ghost town. The district includes Silver City, consisting of about 40 buildings dating from 1884, several smaller, closely related mining towns, and the major silver mines in the vicinity.

Silver City is in Owyhee County, Idaho.

9. Rim of Fire and Range of Light—High Cascades and Sierra Nevada

THE volcanic snow-capped peaks of the Cascade Range and the granite summits of the "Range of Light," the Sierra Nevada, form a nearly continuous mountain wall, stretching south for more than 2,000 miles from the Canadian border to the Mohave Desert near the Mexican border. This massive, cloud-wreathed crest is flanked on the west by the Coast Range Mountains and the wild, log-strewn beaches of the Pacific and on the east by the ancient lava fields of the Columbia Plateau and the arid sagebrush country of the Great Basin.

Cascade Range and the Rim of Fire

The massive snow-capped volcanic peaks of the Cascade Range dominate the landscape of the Pacific Northwest, sweeping south for 600 miles from Canada through Washington and Oregon to its southern terminus at Mount Lassen in northern California—the transition zone between the volcanic Cascades and the granite Sierra Nevada.

The volcanoes of the Cascade Range are part of the Rim of Fire that parallels the Pacific from Mount Lassen to Alaska's Mount Katmai with its eerie "ghost forests" and Valley of Ten Thousand Smokes. Seventy million years ago the Northwest was covered by a vast sea, which gradually receded. The continent emerged as awesome volcanic eruptions spread great flows of molten lava. The eruptions of the Cascade Range— less than 10 million years old—have continued to modern times from Mount St. Helens, to Mount Lassen, which erupted in 1921, to Mount Baker, which last erupted in 1870, to Mount St. Helens, which has been erupting since May 1980. Emissions of hydrogen sulfide gas and steaming fumaroles are common near the summits of several of the great peaks.

The great peaks of the range—which reach 14,408 feet at Mount Rainier and 12,307 feet at Mount Adams in Washington; 11,225 feet at Mount Hood and 10,499 feet at Mount Jefferson in Oregon; and 14,162 feet at Mount Shasta and 10,457 feet at Mount Lassen in California—are flanked on the east by the arid sagebrush country of the Columbia Plateau and Great Basin and on the west by a lowland trough formed by the Inland Passage, the Willamette Valley and Puget Sound lowland of Washington and Oregon,

200

Key to Sites

1. North Cascades National Park
2. Ross Lake National Recreation Area
3. Pasayten Wilderness
4. Mt. Baker Volcano
5. Bald Eagle Natural Area
6. Lake Chelan National Recreation Area
7. Glacier Peak
8. Stevens Pass
9. Snoqualmie Pass
10. Mt. Rainier National Park
11. White Pass
12. Goat Rocks Wilderness
13. Mt. Adams Volcano
14. Mt. St. Helens Volcano
15. Ice Caves
16. Columbia River Gorge
17. Horsethief Lake Indian Village
18. Mt. Hood
19. Barlow Pass
20. Mt. Jefferson
21. Crooked River National Grassland
22. Three Fingered Jack
23. Santiam Pass
24. Mt. Washington
25. McKenzie Pass and Lava Beds
26. Three Sisters Wilderness
27. Lava River Caves

28. Lava Cast Forest
29. Mt. Newberry Caldera and Glass Buttes
30. Fort Rock Valley
31. Crater Lake National Park
32. Gearhart Mountain Area
33. Abert Rim
34. Oregon Caves
35. Lava Beds National Monument
36. Mt. Shasta Volcano
37. Shasta Lake
38. Subway Caves
39. Weaverville
40. Eagle Lake
41. Honey Lake
42. Lassen Volcanic National Park
43. Donner Pass
44. Dutch Flat
45. Lake Tahoe
46. Sutter's Mill
47. Desolation Wilderness
48. Mokelumne Wilderness
49. Calaveras Big Trees
50. Emigrant Basin
51. Yosemite National Park
52. Mono Craters
53. Minarets Area
54. Devil's Postpile National Monument
55. Ancient Bristlecone Pine Forest
56. Owens Valley
57. Palisade Glacier
58. John Muir Wilderness
59. Kings Canyon and Sequoia national parks
60. Giant Forest
61. Mt. Whitney
62. Dome Land Area

Mount Baker, an active volcano on the "Rim of Fire" that stretches from northern California along the crest of the Cascades to Alaska and the Hawaiian Islands

and the Central Valley of California, all of which are bordered to the west by the dense coastal forests of the Olympic and Coast Range mountains of Washington, Oregon, and California.

A distinctive feature of the Cascades is its great line of young volcanic peaks that often rise several thousand feet above the general elevation of the range crest, which varies from 5,000 to 8,000 feet; yet the great volcanoes at Mount Rainier and Mount Shasta soar above 14,000 feet. These are the result of explosive volcanic activity from central vents, instead of having been poured out as vast lava flows as was the Columbia Plateau to the east. Although the Cascades are largely a massive pile of volcanic rocks, they have also undergone regional uplifting to reach their present height.

Together with the Sierra Nevada, they form an almost continuous rampart of snow-capped peaks that stretch for over 1,000 miles from southern Canada to the Mohave Desert in California, which only two rivers have cut through: the Columbia and the Pitt.

Indian and Pioneer Sites Along Washington's Cascade Crest Trail

The Pacific Crest Trail, known in Washington as the Cascade Crest Trail, was designated in October 1968 as one of the two national scenic trails (the

Appalachian Trail being the other). The trail follows the backbone of mountain ranges for 2,350 miles along ancient Indian footpaths from the Canadian border to the Mexican border.

The Cascade Crest Trail crosses historic routes travelled by trappers, miners, stockmen, and pioneers who blazed through the wilderness of the Cascades in the last century; at Hart's Pass, where Colonel Hart built a narrow-gauge wagon road in the 1890s to reach the Slate Creek Mines, where the old town of Barron sprang up; at Stevens Pass, selected by John F. Stevens, explorer for the Great Northern Railway, as a through route for the railroad in 1890; at Naches Pass, site of the crossing of the Cascade Range by the Citizens Road into western Washington and Puget Sound; and at Cispus Pass, where the old Klickitat Indian Trail is claimed to be the first trail between the east and west sides of the Cascades.

The North Cascades

In contrast to the great volcanic summits to the south, the North Cascades are more like the Sierra Nevada, having been built up gradually by the uplifting of sedimentary and metamorphic rocks. Except for Glacier Peak and Mount Baker, which are volcanic cones, most of the North Cascade peaks are granite, forming a plateaulike summit cut by hundreds of deep glacier-carved valleys and moraines, pocked by countless glacial cirques and tarns.

Hundreds of small glaciers cling to the high peaks. Awesome glacial troughs were carved during the Pleistocene Ice Age along the east slope of the North

Crater Mountain, a volcanic remnant in the North Cascades that erupted in prehistoric times. The lake is one of seven found on the old crater floor.

Wind-stunted Jeffrey pine, a relative of the ponderosa pine, that reaches maturity in 100 to 200 years

Campo, Mount Shuksan, the Picket Range and Eldorado Peaks are composed of granitic gneiss, forming a cloud-wreathed sea of spires, horns, peaks, and ridges. More than 300 glaciers cling to these crags, and hundreds of lakes lie in the glacial cirques below. Numerous trails follow the long valley bottoms, leading through thick rain forests on the western slopes and through open sunlit woodlands to the east, winding out of the forests at 4,000 to 5,000 feet over high passes, through beautiful alpine meadows, and on up along the glaciers clinging to the high peaks.

Bald Eagle Natural Area in the North Cascades

One of the largest concentrations of bald eagles in the Pacific Northwest congregates from December to March along the bottomlands and gravel bars on the Middle Fork of the Skagit River in the North Cascades between the old logging towns of Marblemont and Rockport. These huge raptors, with wingspans up to seven-and-one-half feet, gather here to feed on the great runs of spawning Pacific salmon. During the 17th and 18th centuries, "bald" was commonly used to signify white; the adult bird's head feathers are white, thus the name bald eagle. Bald eagles usually nest in the tops of old-growth Sitka spruce or hemlocks, often within a few hundred yards of the Pacific coast. The tall Sitka spruce trees, with wind-flattened tops, serve as natural platforms for the eagles' massive nests, which often attain tremendous size and weight and often survive the winter to be used successively for as long as 65 years.

Cascades. The great U-shaped valley filled by Lake Chelan, which is 60 miles long and some 1,500 feet deep, was scooped out by a glacier some 5,000 feet thick. At one time this portion of the Cascades was covered by an almost continuous sheet of ice, broken here and there by only the highest peaks.

North Cascades National Park encompasses 1,053 square miles in northern Washington State, south of the British Columbia boundary. A majestic alpine wilderness area, the park embraces heavily forested valleys, deep glaciated canyons, snowfields, fjordlike lakes, jagged peaks, and more than 150 glaciers. The summits of Mount Challenger, Three Fingers, Del

Abandoned mine in the Lake Chelan area of the North Cascades

Homestead ranch in the Cascade foothills, built by pioneers who travelled the Oregon Trail across the Rockies and the lava plains of the Columbia Plateau

Douglas Fir

The Douglas fir is the dominant tree in the forests of the Pacific Northwest. This majestic tree reaches heights of up to 200 feet, with thick gray bark often broken into oblong plates on the mature trees. Its natural range is eastward from the Pacific coast to the Rocky Mountains through a wide range of climatic conditions. Though not a true fir, it resembles a fir and is found in association with ponderosa and lodgepole pines in the lower elevations of the rain-shadow regions and Rocky Mountains. Its cones are pendant and three-pointed bracts showing beyond the scales look like the back feet and tails of mice crawling into the cone. Its needles leave a small, raised scar when pulled from the cone.

A Land of Glaciers

The Glacier Peak Wilderness lies to the south of the North Cascades National Park, straddling the

Active glacier world among the jagged granite peaks of the North Cascades

eastern and western slopes of the Cascades Range in Snoqualmie and Wenatchee national forests. This awesome 464,240-acre North Cascades area derives its name from Glacier Peak (10,436 feet), the fourth highest mountain in the state, with its more than 30 sister peaks and massive icefields, Dome Peak, Spire Peak, and Sentinel Peak, rising to 8,000 feet above the valleys. More than 90 glaciers lie within the area, creating a number of rivers.

The alpine glaciers that have carved the Cascades thrive on the massive amounts of water carried by the westerly winds from the Pacific Ocean, in some areas only 50 miles away, depositing the moisture in winter up to 50 feet deep on the high slopes. When more snow accumulates in winter than melts in spring and summer, it compresses under its own weight into layers of ice, adding to a glacier. Gravity pulls the glacier slowly down the mountainside, tearing and scraping chunks from the mountain's bedrock, creat-

Ross Dam in North Cascades National Park

Diablo Dam on the Upper Skagit River

Bald eagle hunting salmon spawning in a North Cascades river

South Cascades Glacier—formed from the massive amounts of snow created by the moisture-laden westerly winds from the Pacific

ing valleys, and depositing tons of debris as ridges or moraines. The melting, lower end of the glaciers form many of the great, wild rivers of the Cascades.

Glacier Streams and Rock Flour

The minute rock debris crushed and ground to a fine, powderlike composition by the glaciers of the Cascades turns the meltwaters and glacier-fed streams a milky white. Unlike a rain- and snow-fed river,

Douglas fir needles and cone

High Cascades wildflower meadow, a common feature along the rugged Pacific Crest Trail

which reaches its highest flow during the spring run-off, glacier-born streams rise as the summer heat increases the flow of meltwater.

Plants of the Glaciers and Alpine Meadows

In July and August great ponds of brilliant wild-flowers are found between the towering peaks and below the hanging glaciers of the Cascade Mountains. In the remote alpine meadows grow a profusion of pink valerian, painted cup, shooting star, monkey flower, mountain phlox, mertensia, and crimson penstemon. A riot of color is created by the white-green and pinkish-purple of the hellebore and giant helleborine, both touched with yellow and gold, mingled with the delicate white, blue, and purple of the mountain anemones; the cream-colored cat's-ear or mariposa lily, the pure pink dogtooth violet, and the red columbine. More fragile and isolated are the avalanche lily, alpine beauty, and the ghostly white of the spiraea.

Among the glaciers and rocks and the fellfields grow lupine and lace fern; red, white, and yellow heather; kinnikinnick, used as a tobacco by the Indians; mountain polypody, yellow mustard, white saxifrage, and broad, thick mats of partridgefoot. Rockbrake and the yellow stonecrop, with its leafy rosettes,

seem to grow everywhere. A reddish algae gives color even to the perennial snowbanks.

Balsam Fir

The balsam fir is a beautiful tree, broad and symmetrically branched, sometimes growing to more than 150 feet in height. The bluish-green foliage is often intensified by the bright indigo of the flowers. The purple cones complete the striking picture when left standing by loggers to reseed its half acre of home. Its bark yields a thick juice that Indians and old-timers used for the healing of bruises and cuts.

The Middle Cascades

The middle portion of the Cascades stretch from near Seattle, Washington to south of Crater Lake in Oregon, forming the great north-south line of volcanic cones dominated by the 10,000 to 14,000-foot summits of Mount Rainier, Mount Adams, Mount St. Helens, Mount Hood, Mount Jefferson and the Three Sisters. These striking peaks rise several thousand feet above the uniform plateau crest. These young volcanic peaks do not show the effects of glacial sculpturing as strikingly as the nonvolcanic peaks of the North Cascades, where nearly the entire range summit was buried during the Pleistocene Ice Age. This spectacular lake-dotted High Cascades segment of the range is broken where the Great Gorge of the Columbia River cuts through.

Enchantment Lakes Wilderness and the Lost World Plateau

The remote Enchantment Wilderness lies adjacent to the Alpine Lakes Area on the east. Known as the Lost World Plateau, the Enchantment Wilderness encompasses some 30,700 acres of jagged granite spires, glacially carved slopes, and scenic lake basins interspersed with mountain meadows at elevations ranging from 3,000 feet to 9,470 feet at Mount Stuart. The area is reached by an extremely steep and rugged trail from the Icicle River.

Pacific Tree Frog

The Pacific tree frog is usually found along waterways and moist, wet meadows, where it is often seen during the day. Its color varies—green, brown, gray, gold, or black—with a black eye stripe, and it can change colors within a few minutes. Its length is two inches. The Pacific tree frog is commonly heard peeping in the evening during spring and summer. It will breed in almost any pond or pool, and the eggs are laid in small jelly masses attached to debris in the water. Tadpoles transform into small frogs the first year.

Greenish-brown Pacific tree frog, often heard peeping during spring along the Cascades waterways

Mount Rainier

The glacier-studded peaks, alpine valleys, forests, and lakes of Mount Rainier National Park encompass 235,000 acres of the High Cascades. The area is dominated by the highest volcano in the Cascade Range, Mount Rainier (14,410 feet), known locally as "The Mountain," with its steep, unstable rock, heavily crevassed glaciers, and sudden devastating storms.

Before a series of violent volcanic explosions blasted 2,000 feet of rock from its summit, leaving a deep, jagged-edged crater, Mount Rainier was more than 16,000 feet high. Subsequent eruptions, the last in 1870, gradually filled the crater and formed its dome-shaped summit.

For most of the year, Mount Rainier lies under a blanket of snow, and even as late as July there may be eight-foot drifts in the sheltered coves. As the days grow warmer in the early summer months, the meadows become a brilliant sea of lupine, Indian paintbrush, marigold, and fawn lily. Then as summer turns to fall, the forests and fields mellow with the deep reds of huckleberry, maple, and mountain ash.

Mount Rainier Life Zones

The Mount Rainier National Park Area was first explored during a botany expedition in 1833 by Dr. William Fraser Tolmie of the Hudson's Bay Company. It has several distinct life zones, ranging from the transition zone up to the arctic-alpine zone.

Transition Zone

Within the park, the transition zone, characterized by heavy forest growth of Douglas fir, western hemlock, red cedar, and scatterings of maple, alder, western yew, and black cottonwood, reaches to elevations found at all the entrances and as far as Longmire

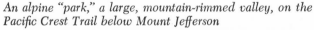

An alpine "park," a large, mountain-rimmed valley, on the Pacific Crest Trail below Mount Jefferson

Springs, White River Camp, and Ipsut Creek on the Carbon River Road. Ferns, devil's club, and skunk cabbage form a thick undergrowth, along with dogwood, trillium, white clintonia, and twinflower. The great forests provide a habitat for black bear, northern spotted owl, western winter wren, and the Cooper chipmunk.

Canadian Zone

The Canadian zone, merging with the Hudsonian above and the transition below, is the least distinct of all the park zones; yet certain points, such as Narada Falls on the Nisqually Road, Yakima Park on the east, and Mowich Lake on the northwest and the glacier bases mark its upper limits. The forest, although dense, has smaller trees, of which the western white pine is the most common. One of the most picturesque plants is the goatsbeard moss, which forms great tangles on the trees. The undergrowth here is thinner, dominated by red and blue huckleberries, rhododendron, kinnikinnick, everlasting, and minulus. The hoary or whistling marmot, Pacific beaver, snowshoe hare, Columbia blacktailed deer, and mountain beaver are common in both the transition and Canadian zones.

Hudsonian Zone

At the upper edge of the forest belt and extending to the timberline is the Hudsonian zone, supporting such hardy trees as the mountain hemlock, alpine fir, and white-barked pine. Flowered alpine meadows dominate here and carry right up around the glaciers.

Black bear crossing a daisy-covered meadow. These bears often vary in color from black to cinnamon.

Some 300 species of wildflowers grow in this scenic area, including the commonly sighted heathers, glacier and avalanche lilies, valerian, Indian basket grass, Indian paintbrush, western anemone, speedwells, asters, lupines, and buttercup. The Clark's nutcracker is one of the mostly commonly sighted birds, along with the sooty grouse, pine siskin, rufous hummingbird, and western bluebird. Hikers in the Hudsonian heights often encounter pika, pack rats, hoary marmots, jumping mice, weasels, and pine marten.

Alpine meadows at Mount Rainier—the highest peak in the Cascade Range at 14,410 feet

Band of nimble-footed mountain goats near timberline

Arctic-Alpine Zone

The arctic-alpine zone reaches up from timberline to the summit of Mount Rainier. In this region of wind-swept wastes and pumice fields, plant and animal life is limited to the most hardy, but the region is the habitat for a broad and interesting variety of herbaceous plants, among which are lupine and phlox, saxifrages, sedges, and grasses. A few juniper and arctic willow are found in sheltered locations. This treeless area is the habitat of the mountain goat, white-tailed ptarmigan, pipit, rosy finch, and pine siskin. Migratory visitors include the Cascade fox, coyote, marmot, weasel, pine marten, juncos, hawks, and eagles.

Northern Pocket Gopher

The northern pocket gopher is a creature of the high mountain country of the West, where its intricate burrows are found in the alpine meadows and fell-fields of the tundra. Other habitats include the grassy prairies, open pine forests, and brushy areas at lower elevations. It is a grayish or grayish-brown gopher with black patches behind its round ears.

Glaciers of Mount Rainier

Mount Rainier dominates this 337-square-mile preserve of rugged mountains, evergreens, valleys and mountain streams, alpine meadows, great cirques, and glaciers. The great dome of Mount Rainier, the third highest peak in the United States at 14,408 feet, covers almost one-fourth of the park area. Its great,

isolated height dwarfs the Cascade Range on the east. The mountain is a truncated cone, approximately 2,000 feet of its top having been lost through an eruption lost in time. When the top of the original 16,000-foot peak was blown off, a vast caldron more than three square miles in area was formed. Minor volcanic activity was reported here as late as 1843, 1858, and 1870. Fumaroles are still found on the heights, and there are several hot springs around the base.

Twenty-eight glaciers, sixteen of which have a downward flow, cling to the sides of Mount Rainier, forming one of the nation's most extensive glacier systems, with a spread of approximately 48 square miles. The six major glaciers originate in the summit névé; the five secondary glaciers are born in snow-filled cirques at levels between 12,000 and 10,000 feet. Between these major ice flows, which average from four to six miles in length, are found 17 smaller ice fields or what are called interglaciers. As the glaciers have melted back, at an average of 70 feet per year, weathering has broken down the sheer canyon walls, so that

Rhododendron thicket on the lush, moisture-rich western slope of the Cascades

Glacier field at Mount Rainier, born in the high, snow-filled cirques

is a typical interglacier, lying between Cowlitz Glacier on the east and Nisqually Glacier on the west. Relatively unshielded, the Paradise receives the full heat of the sun and melts at a perceptible rate. In early summer it is a white blaze in the sun, but as the hot season lengthens, grayish patches—old ice of past seasons—are exposed. Small streams tumble down crevasses in the glacier's sides and drop to the glacier bed below, and aided by the warm air currents, they carve new and fantastic caverns and grottoes at the glacier's base—the source of the Paradise River.

Mount Adams Volcano

The bold summit of Mount Adams, towering above a sea of forest, dominates 32,400-acre Mount Adams Wilderness, located on the west slope of the High Cascades in the Gifford Pinchot Forest adjacent to the Yakima Indian Reservation. Mount Adams, or *Pah-To* according to Indian legends, at 12,307 feet, is second only to Mount Rainier in height and bulk among Washington's peaks. The area is extremely rugged, having undergone successive volcanic convulsions. Mount Adams was formed by volcanic eruptions of ash and cinder accompanied by flows of basaltic and andesitic lava. Its largest glaciers and most severe examples of erosion are found on the northern and eastern flanks, where prevailing storm paths have caused large accumulations of snow and ice. The arctic-alpine zone near Mount Adams's summit includes many vents, blowholes, and caves. Hydrogen sulfide gas still issues from crevasses, and large deposits of sulfur cover the crater floor. The peak is adorned by the massive Mazama, Avalanche, White

the valleys below them broaden out and merge with the tablelands of the lower wedges. Here in high valleys and tablelands are found great alpine valleys noted for their profusion of wildflowers.

The Paradise Glacier Trail—
An Ice Laboratory

Paradise Glacier originates on the lower slope of Mount Rainier at an elevation of about 9,000 feet. It

Bold, glacier-studded summit of the Mount Adams volcano and nearby wildflower meadows

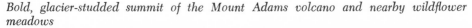

Little Mount Adams—a miniature volcano

grows in patches of hundreds, often thousands, of acres on high, cool mountain slopes throughout the West. The fruit hangs singly and not in clusters. Pilgrimages are made each August to gather the berries for preserving and for wine. The shrub that bears this fruit is widely scattered in the forests.

Indian Race Track and Huckleberry Fields

The Indian Race Track at the south end of the lake-dotted Indian Heaven wild country in the Gifford Pinchot National Forest was the site of pony races many years ago when the Indians hunted and camped in the area. A groove some 2,000 feet long and 10 feet wide, worn by the ponies' hooves, is still plainly visible. A portion of the large Twin Buttes huckleberry fields are reserved for the exclusive use of Indians in accordance with an old treaty agreement. Other historic huckleberry fields are located on the north side of Mount Adams, Nowich Butte-Bare Mountain Area, Mosquito Meadows, and Hamilton Mountain.

Salmon, and Klickitat glaciers, below which are lava crags and flows, alpine meadows, lakes, and forests of hemlock, pine, spruce, fir, and larch.

Goat Rocks of the High Cascades

The Goat Rocks Wilderness, totaling 82,680 acres of rocky crags, meadows, glaciers, alpine lakes, and ridges, is located high in the Cascades on the east flank of the great triangle formed by Mount Rainier, Mount Adams, and Mount St. Helens, with elevations ranging from 3,000 feet at Glacier Lake to 8,201 feet on Mount Curtis Gilbert. The wilderness derives its name from the bands of mountain goats that roam its high peaks. The Teton and Klickitat rivers drain the eastern side of the area, and streams of the Cowlitz River system feed from the western side. The alpine central portion of the wilderness lies above timberline.

The wilderness has approximately 95 miles of trails leading from dense forests and valleys up through broad meadows, ridges, and flower fields of lupine, heather, and phlox on up into the arctic-alpine mountain zone, with its barren rocky soils, rock-conglomerate slopes, snowfields, and glaciers. The Cascade Crest Trail winds through the heart of the wilderness.

Mount St. Helens and the Eruption of 1842

Mount St. Helens is situated on the geologically infant Rim of Fire that stretches from Mount Lassen in northern California northward along the crest of the Cascade Mountains to Alaska and the Aleutian Islands to Hawaii. It is the youngest volcano in the Cascades, about 5,000 years old, and like Mount Rainier and Mount Adams, it is a strato volcano, built up by alternating eruptions. Before its most recent eruption in 1980, Mount St. Helens was believed to have last erupted about 1842, when a violent explosion covered the earth with pumice cinders to a depth of

Goat Rocks, an alpine wilderness of rocky crags, meadows, and lakes

Huckleberry Fields of the Cascades

The huckleberry—not the insipid blueberry that east of the Rocky Mountains is called huckleberry—

Eruption of Mount St. Helens on May 18, 1980, with billowing plume that rose 60,000 feet into the atmosphere

10 to 20 feet. Tree trunks, rotting away in this cemented substance, left what is known as "tree wells," of which there were thousands on the south side of Spirit Lake before it was destroyed during the most recent explosion. It is believed that Spirit Lake was formed during the 1842 blast. The eruption buried the surrounding forest, dammed up a stream, and created a lake that no longer exists. During an eruption in 1200 B.C., ash clouds drifted as far north as the present side of Banff, Alberta, 500 miles distant.

Before its recent destruction during the May 1980 eruption, Spirit Lake commonly reached depths of 1,300 feet, and its true bottom had never been found. It was named by the Indians of the region, who interpreted the strange natural sounds of the volcanic peak as the haunting voices of ghosts. According to another legend, the area was the home of the *Siatcoes*, outcasts from other tribes, to whom were attributed ventriloquial and supernatural powers.

Mountain Beaver

Also known as the aplodontia, the mountain beaver is found in the moist forests of the Pacific Coast from California north through Washington. This dark-brown, beaver-shaped 12- to 17-inch rodent has small rounded ears and small eyes. It is believed to be the most primitive living rodent. It looks like a muskrat without a tail and is noted for its extensive system of runways, burrows, and stream-bank tunnels. During late summer and early fall, its presence is often indicated by small piles of hay along its runways.

Columbia River Gorge

The powerful Columbia—the great river of the West—cuts through the black basalt of the Cascade Range at the Great Gorge below Bonneville Dam and forms the boundary between Washington and Oregon. The forest lands that stretch south from the ancient Indian and fur-trade era water route of the Columbia River and the Great Gorge form one of Oregon's most scenic areas. The 900-foot slopes of the Great Gorge, which portray about 30 million years of geological history, and the sheer cliffs, picturesque waterfalls, and V-shaped upper valleys of Tanner Creek, Eagle Creek, and Hermann Creek, are encompassed within the 52,000-acre Eagle Roadless area.

Horsethief Lake Indian Village Site

Horsethief Lake State Park lies at the upper end of the Long Narrows where the Columbia River has sliced through the Columbia basalts. This area developed as a famous fishing ground and became the gateway between the two distinct regions of the Oregon country—the coastal and lower river tribes from the west and the dry plains tribes from the east. These distinctive groups mingled, traded, and absorbed each others' cultures, leaving behind in their campsites and burial grounds a wealth of artifacts. Although some of the ancient Indian mounds have been inundated by the Columbia River, many are accessible to the public in the state park, and pictographs and petroglyphs can be seen on the smooth basalt cliffs bordering the river. The site is five miles northeast of The Dalles in Klickitat County, Washington.

Historic Features Along Oregon's Skyline Trail

The Oregon stretch of the Pacific Crest National Scenic Trail begins at the Columbia Gorge above Bonneville Dam. From the time it climbs out of the Columbia River Gorge, it follows the Cascades through Oregon for 420 miles at altitudes from 4,000 to 7,100 feet. It winds southward high on the flanks of Mount Hood, past Mount Jefferson, Three-Fingered Jack, and Mount Washington. After passing the Belknap craters and the Three Sisters, the trail goes through a beautiful lake region, including Waldo, Odell, Crescent, and Diamond lakes. Farther south, it traverses Crater Lake National Park, along the uppermost crest to Fourmile Lake on the side of Mount McLoughlin, and then across Lake of the Woods Highway 140 into California near the southern end of the Cascade Range.

The trail, also known as the Oregon Skyline Trail, uses some routes first followed by animals and later by Indians, whose folklore still clings to mountain peaks and fields where they gathered olallie (huckleberries) to dry for their winter supply of food. Early trappers and trailblazers also found their way over the Cascade summits, leaving several roads that are still in use today. Barlow Pass was the first wagon road across the Cascades into the Willamette Valley. Developed by Samuel K. Barlow in 1845, it enabled the immigrants to avoid the dangerous and expensive raft trip down the Columbia River from The Dalles. Santiam Pass was first crossed in 1859 by Andrew Wiley, who explored an old Indian trail up the Santiam River and worked his way farther each year on his hunting expeditions from the Willamette Valley.

McKenzie Pass was named for the river explored in 1811 by Donald McKenzie, a member of Astor's Pacific Fur Company. It was opened to travel in 1862, when Felix Scott and a party of 250 men chopped their way through the forest, building the road for their 106 ox-drawn wagons as they traveled. They crossed the divide by what is known as the Old Scott Trail, two to three miles to the south of the present route.

The Dee Wright Observatory in the pass is a memorial to a trail builder and mountain guide who, with a few Indians, drove a pack train from the Molalla Valley along the crest of the Cascades over the route later developed as the Skyline Trail. For 24 years he was a forest service packer. Eleven windows spaced at intervals in the lava walls each frame a mountain peak. Peak names and distances are carved into the window frames. The lava flow, one of Oregon's most recent, came from Belknap Crater.

Mount Hood

The perpetually snowcapped volcanic cone of 11,245-foot Mount Hood, the state's highest mountain, dominates the crest of the Cascades, south of the Great Gorge of the Columbia. North of Crater Rock, numerous mountain fissures still emit steam and hy-

Lava Window at the Dee Wright Observatory, a memorial for a mountain guide and trail builder, at McKenzie Pass

Rich farmlands in the Hood River Valley

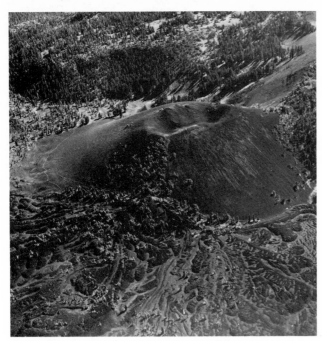

Yapoah Crater in the Three Sisters Wilderness. A portion of the Pacific Crest Trail winds around its base.

drogen sulfide gas. On clear and windless days these gas emissions, or fumaroles, are visible from as far away as Portland. Numerous glaciers, such as the Zigzag, White River, Newton Clark, Eliot, Coe, Ladd, and Reid glaciers, cling to its precipitous slopes.

McLoughlin House National Historic Site

The aid to American settlers in the Oregon country given by Dr. John McLoughlin, chief factor of the Hudson's Bay Company, won him enduring acclaim. His house is one of the few remaining pioneer dwellings in the region which once encompassed Oregon, Washington, Idaho, and part of Montana. Illustrative of Dr. McLoughlin's control over the area is the fact that during his administration, 1824–1846, there were few Indian outbreaks. He not only carried out his responsibilities associated with the fur-trading industry, but he also developed agriculture, husbandry, and export markets. The house has been restored to its original condition. The house is in Oregon City, at McLoughlin Park, between 7th and 8th streets.

McKenzie Lava Fields

Oregon's McKenzie Lava Beds, a portion of the region's most extensive flow, are near McKenzie Pass of the Cascade Range in the Deschutes National Forest. The igneous deluge, which many geologists believe took place within historic time, covered thousands of acres with a jagged sea of lava. Three layers of lava are in the bed. The earliest, the gray andesite of an ancient flow, is scored by glaciers and strewn with volcanic dust, cinders, and debris of the second disturbance. Over it are heavy sheets of black or burnt umber lava of the most recent flood. Along the backbone of the mountain in the center of the lava field is Belknap Crater, rising to 6,872 feet, from which these billions of tons of lava cascaded down the mountain in two congealing torrents. They formed many of the beautiful mountain lakes, numerous falls along the McKenzie River, and the large number of cinder cones, ridges, and buttes that dot the area.

Mount Washington and the Belknap Volcanic Cones

The 7,802-foot Mount Washington, which rises sharply above the lava-strewn plains, dominates a desolate country of great beauty. The mountain is a

Mount Hood volcano on the "Rim of Fire"—on clear days its gas emissions, or fumaroles, are visible from a great distance

Lava beds near McKenzie Pass

vivid example of a dissected volcano whose ancient ice flows denuded the summit, leaving only the most resistant lava fillings. The area adjacent to Mount Washington has experienced more recent volcanic activity than any other part of the Cascade Range. The lava sheet surrounding the Belknap Cones, commonly referred to as a black wilderness, is one of the largest in the United States. Belknap Crater, located near the center of the McKenzie Lava Beds, is a cinder and ash cone built up to an elevation of 6,872 feet. The volcanoes of the Northwest, including those in the Mount Washington area at McKenzie Pass, are part of the Rim of Fire that circles the Pacific Ocean. Seventy million years ago Oregon was covered by a shallow sea dotted with volcanic islands. As the sea gradually withdrew, the continent emerged in the form of volcanic eruptions, spreading vast flows of basaltic lava over eastern Oregon about 15 million years ago. The High Cascade peaks are less than 10 million years old, and the eruptions have continued to modern times. When hiking in the wilderness, don't attempt to walk on the lava flows, for the footholds are unstable and the rock is extremely sharp.

Broken Top, a remnant of an ancient volcanic explosion

Three Sisters and the Nation's Highest Crater Lake

Overshadowing the Pacific Crest Trail, the Three Sisters rise against a horizon broken by lesser peaks, tumbled foothills, and swelling ridges of the Cascades. Incredibly white and vast, they are pitted with glaciers, heaped with moraines, and slashed with a thousand small ravines and crevasses. Glacial melt clings to the higher levels of the great battered cones. Crusted snows that melt in summer send torrents down the slopes to water the forest and the broad, flower-grown meadows about the mountain's base. Geologists believe that the Three Sisters are the splintered remnants of an ancient Mount Multnomah, which was blown to fragments by volcanic gases during prehistoric times. On the crest of the South Sister is a small lake, cupped in an ancient volcanic pit, believed to be the highest crater lake in the United States.

Clear Lake and the Rim of Fire

Clear Lake, in the Cascade Mountains of the Deschutes National Forest, is a geological curiosity. It lies in a depression 2,000 feet deep and was formed by the damming of the old Santiam Valley by the great McKenzie Lava Flow on the volcanic Rim of Fire that stretches from northern California to Alaska.

Weather-beaten mountain hemlock growing in lava beds near the Three Sisters

It is fed by springs, the largest called Giant Spring, which gushes from the northeast shore. Clear Lake is the coldest in the Cascade Mountains, its temperature remaining a constant 41°F, the water of such crystal clearness that articles on the bottom, at a depth of 40 feet, can readily be distinguished. The lake is of so recent formation that tree trunks, well preserved and with bark still clinging to the trunks, stand on the sloping bottom.

White Heather

The lovely white heather was named cassiope by the naturalist-explorer John Muir, with whom it was a favorite. Found on high summits, this low-branching evergreen, with slim ascending stems often less than a foot high, is cloaked in an overlapping sheath of leaves arranged in fours. From the axils of the leaves, tiny bowls of white bloom, sometimes gently flushed like a pale pink lily, nod on graceful threadlike stems.

Purple Heather

The purple heather is one of the principal charms of mountain meadows and upper crests of the Western mountains. A low evergreen shrub, often growing in clumps several feet in width, it has numerous alternate leaves minutely serrated, which crowd the branches and are so nearly stemless that they seem

to sprout from the limbs themselves. The flowers are usually magenta pink, though variations occur.

Mount Newberry Caldera and the Glass Buttes

The awesome Mount Newberry Caldera is at the western end of the Harney High Desert, about 30 miles south of Bend, Oregon, and east of the crest of the High Cascades. The caldera at the summit of the ancient Mount Newberry volcano, which was once 20 miles in diameter at its base, rises about 4,000 feet above the desert plateau. The caldera is five miles long and four miles wide; two lakes, East and Paulina, lie within the crater. The slopes of the volcano are studded with about 150 small cinder cones that rise 200 to 500 feet above the ground. Mount Newberry was once 9,000 feet high and covered about 80 cubic miles in mass—greater than Mount Shasta and Shastina combined. About 20,000 years ago, Mount Newberry, a gently sloping shield volcano that slowly built up its height and mass through repeated oozing of thin layers of lava, collapsed inward of its own weight during a series of violent eruptions.

The jet-black Glass Buttes of southwestern Oregon, in the vicinity of Burns, rise 2,000 feet above the surrounding sagebrush flats. The mile-long buttes, formed by a rare volcanic byproduct that poured out of a vent or fissure long after Mount Newberry's collapse, are believed to be the largest obsidian outcropping in the world. This volcanic substance, formed from rapid cooling of the lava, fractures to form sharp edges. It furnished the Indians with material for their arrowheads and spear points, skin scrapers, axes, chisels, and other implements. At this spot are the one-time arrowhead factories and tons upon tons of chipped obsidian left by the aboriginal Indian tribes and perhaps their predecessors. These buttes and the outcroppings in Yellowstone Park furnished the obsidian arrowheads for primitive Americans as far east as Ohio. The identifying characteristic of this obsidian is its varied coloring and its iridescence, reaching to a quarter of an inch in thickness. The Yellowstone obsidian occurs in two colors only, white and black, and it is opaque. The glistening ebony and iridescent blocks of the Glass Buttes, cubistic in outline, are sometimes as large as houses.

Engelmann Spruce

Engelmann spruce is usually found above 9,000 feet elevation in the subalpine zone from the Rocky Mountains west to the eastern slope of the Cascade

Range and into northwestern California. This large tree of the Western mountains reaches heights of up to 150 feet with a tapering, narrow, pointed crown, with thick, cinnamon-red to purple-brown bark and square-to-plumb needles, and with minutely hairy twigs. Its cones are cylindrical, from one to two-and-a-half inches long. It is known locally also as balsam, white and mountain spruce, silver spruce, and Arizona spruce.

Crater Lake

Crater Lake is located in southern Oregon on the crest of the Cascade Range, a chain of snow-capped mountains that stretch from Mount Garibaldi in British Columbia to Lassen Peak in northern California.

This part of the country was covered more than 60 million years ago by shallow tropical seas. As the land began its upward movements, the seas were forced westward. The climate became more temperate, and after thousands of years, redwood forests covered much of eastern Oregon. About 50 million years ago, at the time land upheavals were taking place, volcanic activity was beginning, which has continued at intermittent stages down to recent times with the eruption of Mount St. Helens to the north.

After several million years of volcanic activity, the earth began to buckle in a north-south line. This

Towering Engelmann spruce found above 9,000 feet on the dry eastern slope of the Cascades

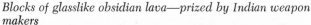

Blocks of glasslike obsidian lava—prized by Indian weapon makers

Crater Lake, 1,932 feet deep at its deepest point, created during the destruction of the Mount Mazama volcano 6,600 years ago

buckling, or upheaval, was the beginning of the formation of the Cascade Range. The growing mountain range soon blocked moist Pacific Ocean air from reaching the land to the east, causing it to become arid, which was the beginning of the area known today as the Oregon Desert.

Early volcanic eruptions in the Cascade Range produced gently sloping shield volcanoes. Later, about 1 million years ago, more violent eruptions took place which formed larger composite volcanoes such as Mount Shasta, Mount Hood, and Mount Rainier. Most of these larger mountains stopped their volcanic activity, but one 12,000-foot volcano, referred to as Mount Mazama (named by members of the Mazama Club, a northwest climbing club who made the trip to Crater Lake in September 1896), continued its eruptions until it finally destroyed itself 6,600 years ago.

The last stage of Mount Mazama was devastating. Volcanic gases that had built up within the mountain were allowed to escape. This had the same effect as occurs when a bottle of soda is shaken up. As the gases in the bottle escape, liquid is forced out in the form of foam. The escaping gases in the volcano forced out a huge quantity of molten lava, called pumice.

So much molten material was forced from Mount Mazama that a huge cavern began to develop. After the violent activity subsided, approximately 6,000 feet of the mountain had collapsed. The upper half had collapsed within itself, forming a 4,000-foot basin. Geologists call a basin formed in this manner a caldera. Even though Mount Mazama had collapsed, volcanic activity still continued, and the larger cinder cone, known today as Wizard Island, was built from the floor of the caldera—actually, a volcano within a volcano.

The last volcanic activity in the park ended between 1,000 and 2,000 years ago. As the ground in the caldera cooled, rainwater began to collect. Since there are no inlets or outlets, all the waters in the lake are collected from rain and snow falling directly into the basin. The amount of precipitation falling into the lake is equaled by that which evaporates and seeps into the ground.

Crater Lake is 1,932 feet deep at its deepest point. The great depth and pure, unpolluted water cause the lake to become a large prism. As the sun's rays penetrate into the water, wavelengths are absorbed, leaving only its deep blue color. The blue is then reflected to the surface, giving the lake its true blue color. When the sun's rays are blocked by the clouds, the blue is not quite so intense.

The first recorded discovery of Crater Lake by white men occurred on June 12, 1853, while a party of prospectors led by John W. Hillman searched the Southern Cascades for the "Lost Cabin" goldmine. While climbing the slopes of Mount Mazama to get a better view of the region, Hillman discovered Crater Lake.

Oregon Grape

The Oregon grape of the lower mountain forests has bright yellow flowers and glossy green leaves. The stem is thick, the root a yellowish hardwood used by the Indians in concocting stomach medicine and spring tonics. In autumn the fruit, a small, blue, rather bitter grape, is used in making jelly. The plant grows in shaded places, often near large rocks. It is conspicuous in fall, when, after other dense growth is gone, a single leaf may present an array of orange, brown, and red.

Rogue River Pioneer Sites and Wildlife Habitats

The historic Rogue River, named by the early French trappers *la Rivière Aux Coquins*, the River of Rogues, flows from its headwaters near Crater Lake

Unusual lava formations on the Pacific Crest Trail

Ponderosa pine near the Rogue River Trail, named by the early lumbermen because the heavy tree will barely float in water

in the Seven Lakes Basin of the High Cascades and carves its way west for 200 miles along a wild, scenic course to the Pacific.

The observant traveller along the remote stretches of the Rogue may see great blue herons with their six-foot wingspread, common mergansers, belted kingfishers, water ouzels, cliff swallows and their mud-walled nests, ospreys, bald eagles, pileated woodpeckers, blue and ruffed grouse, California quail, and waterfowl. Rogue River country is also inhabited by black-tailed deer, Roosevelt elk, black bear, otter, raccoon, and rattlesnakes.

Vegetation along the river includes some botanical rarities. Trees include Oregon ash, bigleaf maple, Pacific madrone, Oregon white oak, western red cedar, Port Orford cedar, Pacific yew, canyon live oak, golden chinquapin, tan oak, Oregon myrtle, Douglas fir, western hemlock, grand fir, and sugar pine. Brewer spruce, knobcone pine, and pitcher plants are found in remote areas. Side streams are lined with rhododendrons, azaleas, Pacific dogwood, Oregon grape, salal, salmonberry, and a variety of ferns.

The Rogue River Trail follows the wild middle portion of the river. Grave Creek, the starting point, was named for the death of a young girl who was passing through with her family in 1846. The Indians dug up her body, stripped it of its clothing, and hung

it over the branches of a tree as a mute, terrible warning to the white invaders. The beginning of the trail is very rocky. Old cabin sites and unusual rock formations occupy the banks. Hikers can stop to watch boats being lowered down treacherous Rainie Falls. After Tyee Rapids, a primitive campsite appears at Russian Creek. Tyee Bas was once a famous gold diggings. In the early days, some 300 Chinese took a million dollars in gold dust here. Deer and other wildlife stop to feed here, and interesting animal tracks can be detected in the soft sand. Bronco Creek, a few miles farther, was originally named Jackass Creek in 1855 because of the loss of a pack mule as some men were trying to evade a band of Indians. Battle Bar is named after the skirmish that occurred during the Rogue River Indian War of 1855–1856. Winkle Bar, a mile downstream from Battle Bar, is a stretch of rolling water named for pioneer prospector William Winkle and is the site of Zane Grey's famous summer steelhead fishing camp —now owned by the president of Levi Strauss Company. The Rogue River Ranch, at Mile 23, is managed by the Bureau of Land Management and provides emergency aid. The first white man to settle in the area built a cabin just a short distance from here in 1880.

Mule Creek Canyon was named in the summer of 1852 when a company of soldiers from Fort Oxford

Eroded lava pinnacles at Crater Lake

Volcanic Domes and Hoodoos

The Gearhart Mountain area contains some of the oldest volcanic domes in southern Oregon's western Lake County. Gearhart Mountain, at 8,364 feet, is the highest and oldest. After the original volcanic material cooled and moistened, glaciers carved out a large amphitheater known as the Head of Dairy Creek. Today its impressive headwalls tower over a primitive area of mountain meadows and springs. Three miles from the southeast entrance to Trail 100 lies the Dome, with its massively eroded cliffs 300 feet high stretching westward from the 7,380-foot dome for almost a mile. A half mile from the same trailhead are the stark sentinel-like hoodoos (columns of rock in fantastic shapes) of the Palisades.

The Abert Rim

The Abert Rim, along the east side of Lake Abert, is the largest and most exposed geologic fault in North America, rising nearly 2,500 feet above the lakeshore, with a 640-foot vertical lava cliff at the topmost part. When the explorer Fremont saw Abert Lake in 1843, during his search for the mythical Buena Ventura River that was supposed to flow from Klamath Lake into San Francisco Bay, it was 50 square miles of water. In years when rainfall has been below normal, however, it has been completely dry.

Oregon Caves in the Siskiyou National Forest

The Oregon Caves are located 50 miles south of Grant's Pass, Oregon, in the Siskiyou National Forest of southern Oregon. The caves, sculpted out of an ancient limestone seabed, lie within a natural transition zone between two forest types: a mixed forest of broadleaf and conifer trees, where tall Douglas firs and a few pines tower above low broadleaf trees and shrubs, and a high-elevation conifer forest, dominated by giant Douglas firs, white fir, Port Orford cedar, and incense cedar. Along the Big Tree Trail is an old Douglas fir estimated to be 1,200 to 1,500 years old.

The fractured-marble formations in the subterranean caverns include the parachutelike flowstone draperies in the Paradise Lost Cave, rimstone formations resembling waves on the sea, the Grand Column formed by a fused stalactite and stalagmite, the flowstone cascade at Niagara Falls, calcite deposits at the Petrified Garden, an underground stream at the River Styx, and the eerie Passageway of the Whale.

tried to open a trail along the Rogue. A member of the party later related that a Lieutenant R. S. Williamson rode a mule named John. When the mule was turned loose to graze along the stream, it wandered off and was not found despite a thorough search. The men promptly named the stream John Mule Creek, but the name was later shortened. The story has a happy ending: years later, Lieutenant Williamson found his mule in the possession of an Indian at Siletz. Downriver from Mule Creek you can overlook the famous Coffee Pot, a churning whirlpool of crosscurrents. Brushy Bar was the site of a large goldmining operation around the turn of the century. In 1905 a fire burned all summer long, and the resultant vegetation was, for a time, low brush, hence the bar's name. Flora Dell Creek offers a trailside pool which is perfect for a restful swim.

The trail ends at the site of a historic Indian burial ground. Trenches, once built in the forest as fortification against the Indians, are still intact.

Saw-Whet Owl

The saw-whet owl is a small species, usually found in pine forests or in rock clefts. It is dark grayish brown, spotted with white. In daylight, the saw-whet stays close to the tree trunks; during the night, its noiseless wings carry it along the edges of open meadows and alpine parks in search of mice. At the first sign of spring, the male's mating call echoes through the conifers—a monotonous, low, scraping note sung in quick succession like the sound of a saw being filed.

The Southern Cascades

The southernmost Cascade Mountains in northern California are made up of a line of volcanoes broken by basins, sags, and valleys. The Pitt River flows west through this portion of the range from the Great Basin into the Great Central Valley of California.

The Southern Cascades are dominated by Mount Shasta, one of the most striking of the Cascade volcanoes, which was last known to be active in 1786, and, 80 miles to the southwest, by the volcanic plug dome known as Mount Lassen, which rises 2,500 feet above the floor of a badly shattered former volcano and is about one and a half miles in diameter.

To the west and north, the Mount Shasta lavas abut against the Klamath Mountains of the Coast Range and merge on the east with the lava beds of the Modoc Plateau. To the south, Mount Lassen forms the approximate dividing line between the volcanic Cascades and the massive granite fault-block range of the Sierra Nevada.

Lava Beds of the Southern Cascades

The Lava Beds National Monument and the volcanic Medicine Lake Highlands are located along the southern tip of the Cascades northeast of Mount Shasta in the Great Basin Desert country of the Modoc National Forest. The lava beds were formed centuries ago by a group of volcanoes erupting masses of lava

Lava tube near Mount Lassen, formed when outer layers of a flowing river of lava cooled while the molten inner part flowed on

that cooled into a landscape of vast lava flows, cinder buttes, ice caves, and spatter cones. A variety of wildlife can be seen within the area, including bighorn sheep, which were reintroduced in 1971. The Medicine Lake Highlands to the south of the lava beds is an area of moderately sloping to steep mountains. They have numerous glass flows, lava caves, tubes, chimneys, cones, and craters and forests of sugar pine and red and white fir with an understory of bitterbrush, manzanita, and snowbrush. The Burnt Lava Flow Virgin Area is on the southern flanks of the highlands. This 9,000-acre area is a spectacular flow of jumbled black lava surrounding islands of 10 to 60 acres each on three old cinder cones cloaked by virgin stands of pine and fir.

Juniper-clad foothills common on the eastern slope of the Cascades

Great Basin sagebrush plains near Mount Shasta

Mount Shasta—Largest of the Cascade Volcanoes

The great double cone of Mount Shasta is the largest of the Cascade volcanoes, composed of Shastina (12,330 feet) on the west and Shasta (14,162 feet), the main peak, on the east. The mountain rests on a base 17 miles in diameter and is often shrouded at its upper levels by unusual cloud formations, rapid and violent storms, dazzling light displays, and the rare alpine glow of winter evenings. Five perennial glaciers, Whitney, Bolam, Hotlum, Wintun, and Konwakiton, hug the slopes above 8,500 feet. The glaciers form the headwaters of the McCloud, Shasta, and Sacramento rivers.

On the lower slopes of Mount Shasta, plant life common to the High Sierra overlaps with plants common to the North Cascades, creating unique subspecies, such as the beautiful and fragrant Shasta lily, Shasta daisy, and Shasta red fir. Manzanita and snowbrush have covered the old scars from the logging days. Wildlife in the Shasta area includes black bear, bobcat, pine squirrel, chipmunk, porcupine, mountain quail, and speckled grouse.

Weaverville Historic Gold Rush District

Weaverville is one of the best preserved gold-rush towns in the Shasta-Trinity counties area. In the mid-19th century it was the supplier of staple foods, tools, equipment, and clothing for miners and prospectors in a large portion of northern California. Saloons and a courthouse made Weaverville the entertainment and political center of Trinity County. Structures within the district include frame two-story residences, churches, brick commercial buildings, lodge halls, and a frame-and-brick Chinese joss house. Often there was separate ownership of upper and lower floors of the same building, and the second floor was reached by a circular iron stairway from the sidewalk. Worthy of mention are the brewery (1855), now the Chamber of Commerce Information Center; Larkin's Store, Moon Lee's Store, and the Old Fire House, all with tamped earth walls; the New York Hotel (1859); Trinity County Courthouse (1856); the Congregational Church (1891); and the Chinese temple (1874). The district flanks both sides of Weaverville's Main Street in Trinity County, California.

Historic Sites Along California's Pacific Crest Trail

In California, the proposed trail starts south of Observation Peak at the California-Oregon border, in the Siskiyou Mountains. When finished in this state, the trail will cover 1,660 miles, range in elevation from 500 to 13,200 feet, and end at International Border at Mexico, two and a half miles east of Tecate. Much of the trail, however, has not been completed. At some points where the completed trail ends, the route transfers to other trails or rural roads, but elsewhere the incomplete portions are unmarked.

The trail passes by many points of natural beauty and historic interest. South from the northern starting point of the trail is Grizzly Peak, where an early rancher shot and wounded a grizzly who nearly mauled him to death. Peter Lassen, a Danish pioneer, had a trading post just below the peak, which was the homeland of the last Yahi Indian. (Aboriginal Indians inhabited Pit River, Mount Shasta, and Lassen Peak, east of the trail.) Further south, the trail passes through the magnificent land of the Feather River, which includes one of the highest falls in the country. Gold Lake in the Plumas National Forest was once rumored to be the source of all placer gold. On the ascent to Carson Pass is a spectacular view of Lake Tahoe. The Yokuts Indians inhabited the region of the Mono Craters and Mono Pass before the arrival of Spanish missionaries in 1770. Further on lie the wildflower meadows of the Tuolumne River and the High Sierra wilderness of Yosemite National Park. The Mohave Desert lies to the southwest, a barren wilderness that defeated many who challenged it to reach the Pacific Ocean farther west. The trail moves on through Whitewater Canyon along the Whitewater River, at 1,185 feet, the lowest elevation of the entire trail within California. The San Jacinto Wilderness is another former Indian domain, steeped in the legends of the Soboba tribe. The Indians sang in their dance houses near San Jacinto Peak, praying to the Great Spirit for successful hunting.

French Gulch Historic District

French Gulch was founded in 1852 in an area previously prospected for gold. Placer mines dotted the surrounding countryside, and scars of the mining operations are visible. Important buildings still standing along Main Street are Franck's Store (1867), the Gartland Cabin (c. 1856—the oldest building in French Gulch), the Odd Fellow's Hall (1860s), Feeny Hotel (1887) and St. Anne's Catholic Church (c. 1900). The district is along both sides of French Gulch Road in Shasta County.

Lassen Volcanic National Park— Southern Terminus of the Cascades

Lassen Volcanic National Park, known as the "sweathouse of the gods," encompasses 100,000 acres of rugged coniferous forest surrounding lava-devastated acres of sheer, jagged cliffs, fumaroles, boiling lakes, great, weirdly shaped rocks, and bubbling mud pots, named in honor of pioneer Peter Lassen, a Danish immigrant who settled in California in the 1830s. The park is dominated by 10,487-foot Mount Lassen, an active plug-dome volcano situated at the southern tip of the Cascade Range that is still active. Evidence of the activity is visible in the beautifully symmetrical cinder cone, active hot springs, steaming fumaroles, and sulfurous vents. Other major features include the otherworldly scenery of the Devastated Area, littered with debris of trees destroyed by "The Great Hot Blast" of 1915, and the great mudflows, and Chaos Crags, a wild disarray of magnificent piles of pointed blocks surrounded by enormous banks of sharp talus reaching 1,000 feet high. Lake Helen, named for Helen Tanner Brodt, the first white woman to climb Lassen

Peak, lies within the crater rim of ancestral Mount Tehama, once the dominant volcano of the region.

Mount Lassen Volcano

The great mass of Lassen Peak began as stiff, pasty lava forced from a vent on the north slope of a larger extinct volcano known as Tehama. The lava was squeezed up to form a rough, dome-shaped mass, plugging the vent. After this plug dome was formed, Lassen Peak was calm for a long period. Beginning on May 30, 1914, eruptions occurred intermittently for more than seven years. With the eruption on the night of May 19, 1915, known as "The Great Hot Blast," a fiery mushroom-shaped cloud of fumes, ash, and volcanic debris rose more than five miles above the crater.

Sierra Nevada— The Range of Light

The Sierra Nevada, called the Range of Light by naturalist John Muir, and the Snowy Sawtooth Mountains, or *Sierra Nevada*, by the Spanish explorers, is a fault-block range carved out of a massive block of granite that had been uplifted and tilted to the west millions of years ago. Its massive ramparts form a continuous barrier that forms the nation's longest single mountain range, sweeping for 400 miles in a great arc of granite, snow-capped peaks and pinnacles, alpine lakes, and barren domes from near Mount Lassen at the southern end of the volcanic Cascade

Mount Lassen, the southernmost peak of the Cascade Range, dominating an area of volcanic chaos

Range southward to the Tehachapi Mountains and
the Mohave Desert.

Like the Cascades, this formidable range has been
pierced by only one river—the Pitt. The Sierra Nevada
is flanked by two great depressions, the Central Valley
of California on the west—noted for its vegetable
fields, vineyards, and orchards fed by the streams that
flow down the tilted western slope and through the
foothills—and the arid sagebrush country of the Great
Basin to the east.

A Land of Contrasts—The Eastern and Western Slopes

The glacier-scarred eastern and western slopes of
the Sierra Nevada are a land of contrasts. The bold
east front of the range has the appearance of a giant
staircase formed by a series of benches or "shoulders"
separated from each other by steep ridges. It rises
11,000 feet above the Great Basin Desert of Owens
Valley, higher above its surrounding countryside than
any other mountain front in the United States. A striking feature of the eastern slope is the absence of
foothills and scarcity of large streams and alluvial
fans, because of the great amount of frost-created rock

*Thirteen-thousand-foot cliffs of Temple Crag in the Pali-
sades Glacier Area—the southernmost glacier in the United
States and largest in the Sierra Nevada*

*Bold eastern slope of the Sierra Nevada abruptly rising 11,000 feet above the Great
Basin Desert in Owens Valley*

debris that mantles the upper slope of the front and absorbs the melting snow in spring.

In contrast to the sheer east front of the Sierra Nevada, the western slope rises gently across a belt 70 miles wide west of Lake Tahoe at the rate of about 100 feet per mile through the foothills up to the crest of 13,000- to 14,000-foot peaks. The western slope is cut by hundreds of valleys. When viewed from a distance, it looks like a plateau.

As the moisture-laden prevailing winds sweep up the long western slope of the Sierra, they create a dense north-south forest that includes the giant sequoia, ponderosa and sugar pine, golden and black oak, broad-leafed maple, incense cedar, and California laurel. Their moisture gone, the dry winds blow down the precipitous eastern slope, producing the arid sagebrush country and desert in the Great Basin between the Sierra and the Rockies. The drier eastern slopes are carpeted by stands of lodgepole and ponderosa pine, fir, Jeffrey pine, gnarled bristlecone, and tamarack.

Mount Whitney on the right and Whitney Pinnacles on the skyline to the left. Mount Whitney, at 14,495 feet, is the highest point in the continental United States.

Granite Domes of the High Sierra

One of the most striking features of the Sierra are massive helmetlike domes of granite that have been formed by layer on layer of granite, somewhat like an onion skin. As wind, rain, and forest erosion wear away the rock shells—a phenomenon known as exfoliation—the next layer expands and loosens the layer below. In vivid contrast to the horn peaks of Wyoming's Teton Range and the rock spires of the Wind River Range, the weathered domes of the Sierra Nevada exist on a scale found nowhere else. The domes are especially dramatic in Yosemite and Sequoia national parks and the Dome Land Wilderness.

Wind-stunted Jeffrey pine atop Sentinel Dome in Yosemite National Park

The Dome Land Wilderness takes in 62,206 acres at the southern end of the Kern Plateau between the South Fork and the main Kern River. Erosion and weathering have left the area strewn with oddly shaped rock outcroppings, giving the appearance of a dome land. Back-country trails lead to the "roughs" of the South Fork of the Kern River, White Dome and Church Dome. The vegetation on the lower slopes is light, consisting mostly of pinyon pine, mixed conifer, sagebrush, and rabbit brush.

From Giant Sequoias to Arctic Tundra— High Sierra Life Zones

Southward of California's Lake Tahoe lies the characteristic forest of the Sierra Nevada. Here, at an average elevation of 3,500 feet, is found the sequoia. Unlike the redwood, the sequoia, or "big tree," does not form great belts of continuous forest but stands in about 35 isolated groves, scattered from the American River to the Tule on the western slope of the Sierra. These trees are among the oldest living things in the world—some of them have been shown by ring counts to be more than 4,000 years old. In diameter they average from 15 to 20 feet; their average height is about 250 feet. The big tree is bulkier than the redwood, with cinnamon-colored bark and foliage similar to that of its coastal cousin.

The two trees, with the ginkgo tree and the marestail, are survivors from a flora that was nearly

Dense stand of juniper in the foothills of the Sierra Nevada's plateaulike western slope

destroyed in the glacial era. In Miocene times, sequoias of various species were common over much of the Northern Hemisphere. In spite of their great age, the "big trees" are not dying out, but rather are increasing with the aid of the reforestation work of the National Park Service and U.S. Forest Service.

The sequoia of the Sierra Nevada are found on the edge of the transition and Canadian zones, usually close to stands of fir. Below it, in the transition zone, stretch extensive forests of yellow and sugar pine, incense cedar, golden and black oak, California laurel and broad-leafed maple. In this Sierran forest, the most dominant wildflowers are penstemons, gilias, mariposa, tulips, pussypaws, mimulus, wild forget-me-nots, tiger and leopard lilies, buttercups, and the ubiquitous lupines.

As the Sierra hiker moves up into the Canadian zone, a change is immediately noticeable. The ponderosa (yellow) pine gives way to its relative, the Jeffrey pine. Higher still, mountain pines and red firs and lodgepole pines dominate the forest. Brushy areas are covered with dwarf manzanita and ceanothus. The understory in the fir forest is dominated by the brilliant snowplant and cancerroot. This is also the home of the unique Sierra puffball. Some of the more conspicuous birds are the blue-fronted jay, Sierra junco, western chipping sparrow, Sierra grouse, and the Townsend solitaire. Among the animals you are most likely to see are the mountain weasel, yellow-haired porcupine, snowshoe rabbit, golden-mantled ground squirrel, Sierra chickaree, and several species of chipmunks.

Just below the timberline of the Sierra is the Hudsonian forest zone. With the Canadian zone, it shares the lodgepole pine, which is the dominant tree here. Usually associated with or above the lodgepole are the whitebark, foxtail, and silver pines. These latter trees, with the mountain hemlock, form the stunted and twisted growth of the timberline. Birds become more scarce in this zone, though mammals are commonly sighted. The California pine grosbeak, mountain bluebird, white-crowned sparrow, alpine chipmunk, Sierra marmot, Sierra cony, pine marten, Sierra least weasel, and wolverine are dominant in this region.

Above the treeline is the alpine zone, a treeless area stretching from an elevation of about 10,500 feet to the summits of the highest peaks. Here are found the Sierra primrose, yellow columbine, alpine buttercup, and shooting star. Only one species of bird is

Golden-mantled ground squirrel often sighted in the open forest of the Canadian zone

native to the zone, the Sierra rosy finch; but many others are visitors, notably flocks of migrating hummingbirds, and, in summer, gray and white Clark nutcrackers. The principal mammals are visitors from lower elevations; the Sierra cony, however, is often found in these heights, and the Sierra whitetailed jackrabbit makes its home here. The Sierra Nevada bighorn sheep are seen occasionally in the White Mountains east of Owens Valley and in some of the southeastern ranges. A small band is protected in the Mount Whitney area, survivors of those described by the naturalist John Muir, which in his day ranged along the Sierra crest to the vicinity of Sonora Pass.

The mule deer, coyote, and mountain lion range through all the zones, as do a number of birds, notably the blue-fronted jay, the Sierra junco, the redshafted flicker, certain hawks, and some of the sparrows.

Alpine Chipmunk

The small, grayish, four-inch alpine chipmunk is found only among the talus slopes and cliffs of the

A brown Traill's flycatcher and young in nest on a lodgepole pine

Old foxtail pines on a boulder-strewn crest of the High Sierra, similar in appearance to the ancient bristlecone pines in the White Mountains at the edge of the Great Basin Desert, some 50 miles east

Sierra Nevada range from the timberline to 8,000 feet elevation. It has dark stripes on the sides of its face and a tawny body.

Alpine Wallflower

The alpine wallflower is an attractive yellow tundra plant, with close relatives in the parks of lower altitudes. It is found throughout the Western mountains. The fragrant yellow blossom emerges first, leav-

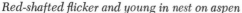
Red-shafted flicker and young in nest on aspen

ing the less important business of stem growth until later. It is a member of the mustard family.

Summer Weather at High Elevations in the Sierra Nevada

Night temperatures are often in the low 30s during the summer, with the possibility of dropping into the 20s. The backpacker should have a sleeping bag that is not bulky or heavy but that will keep him warm enough to get a good night's sleep. The daytime temperatures in the high country often vary widely, even to becoming quite warm. Summer weather in the High Sierra is remarkably pleasant by mountain standards. However, you can expect often violent thunderstorms, so a good waterproof jacket and a lightweight groundcloth or some plastic that can be rigged for a tent should be included.

Old Sacramento Historic Gold Rush District

The river port of Sacramento emerged during the California gold rush of 1849 as the interior distribution and transportation center for the gold mines in the Mother Lode country of the Sierra Nevada. In the 1860s, when the mining frontier moved eastward into Nevada, Idaho, and Oregon, Sacramento became the transportation gateway to most of this inland empire. The original business district has a larger number of buildings dating from the gold rush period than any other major city on the Pacific coast. Included among

Glacial erratics common throughout the Sierra Nevada

these are banks, express buildings, hotels, offices, restaurants, saloons, and stores.

Mother Lode Historic Mining District at Columbia

A well-preserved gold-mining camp of the California Mother Lode region, a long, narrow, 120-mile strip of land seamed with gold in the Sierra foothills, Columbia was phenomenally productive until about 1860. Because the town has been continuously occupied and maintained since its inception, a large number of the original buildings have survived. Today most of Columbia's historic section is included within the boundaries of a state historical monument. Evidence of mining is visible outside the town, and rock, pits, and hummocks show where the earth was washed away from the gold-bearing rock.

The district is four miles northwest of Sonora on California Highway 49.

Granite crags of Seven Gables Peak in the John Muir Wilderness, framed by the trunk of a dead whitebark pine

Dutch Flat Historic Gold-Rush District

Dutch Flat is an unspoiled classic gold-rush town founded in 1851. It was the site of rich hydraulic mining from 1854 to 1882 and was the key point on the Dutch Flat–Donner Lake freight wagon route linking the silver mines of Nevada with California. There are 45 frame dwellings in the district. Several notable structures are the Dutch Flat Hotel (1852), the General Store (1854), and the Dutch Flat School House (1898).

The historic district is in Dutch Flat at Main and Stockton streets in Placer County, California.

La Grange Gold Dredge

Mining at La Grange began as a hand operation in the 19th century. It became more mechanized, until hydraulic equipment was introduced in the early 1900s. The La Grange gold dredge is a significant and unusual remnant of the California gold industry. It stands as high as a two-story house and is an intricate combination of metal superstructure, conveyor belts, and cables anchored by a 72-ton stud. Using a 92-ton bucket chain and 12-cubic-foot buckets, the dredge dug to a depth of 75 feet in a semicircle around the stud. Inside the dredge was a gold refinery. Gold-laden rocks and soil were washed down in a revolving drum separating the large materials from the fine ones. The latter were sifted over a drain board, and

the gold was finally extracted by the addition of mercury. The dredge no longer operates.

The dredge is south of La Grange in Stanislaus County, California.

Old Auburn Historic Mining District

Auburn was an 1849 mining camp located between the northern and southern mines of the Sierra Nevada. It became the county seat of Placer County in 1851. Today, aside from the paving of streets and the laying of sidewalks, old Auburn remains largely unchanged from its appearance in the late 1800s. A fire ravaged the town in 1855, and most buildings date from the post-fire rebuilding. Among the extant structures are the American Hotel, the Old Post Office, the Union Bar, the Placer County Courthouse (1897), Lawyers Row (1855), and the Chinese joss house, a house of worship in the Chinese settlement area.

Auburn is in Placer County, California.

Sutter's Mill in the Mother Lode

John Marshall, a foreman for John Sutter, discovered gold at Coloma while inspecting a sawmill trace. Two years later, the resulting California gold rush of 1849 precipitated the establishment of California as a state. The town of Coloma, which grew up around the gold discovery site at Sutter's Mill, was the first white settlement in the foothills of the Sierra Nevada. A cluster of dilapidated buildings and structures still stands. Archeological investigations in 1947 established the dimensions and structural details of the ruined mill and recovered many artifacts. Sutter's Sawmill has been reconstructed near the original mill site.

The town is seven miles northwest of Placerville on California Highway 49.

John Muir Trail—A Wilderness Footpath in the High Sierras

The John Muir Trail winds for most of its 212-mile length along the western slope of the High Sierras through some of the most stunning alpine country on the continent. The great arc of the High Sierra Crest forms a continuous strip of remote, sparkling, jewel-like lakes and soaring, snowcapped peaks, extending from Yosemite Valley to the massive, 14,000-foot peaks dominated by Mount Whitney in Sequoia National Park. From Yosemite, the trail passes through the Minarets Wilderness, winds on past the Devil's Postpile National Monument and through the vast John Muir Wilderness in the Sierra National Forest, and enters the Sequoia National Park area, dominated by the Great Western Divide. The trail and numerous spur trails provide access to literally thousands of trout lakes, many of which hold thriving populations of golden trout, that lie in remote lake basins on both slopes of the High Sierra, including the Granite area in the Minarets Wilderness of the Sierra National Forest, the Upper Bishop Creek area in the John Muir Wilderness area of the Inyo National Forest, and the Mono Creek area, French Canyon and Humphreys Basin area, and Bear Creek area—all situated in the John Muir Wilderness in the Sierra National Forest. Wildlife that may be sighted by the sharp-eyed wilderness traveller includes deer, the shrill-voiced cony, marmots, coyotes and weasels, and the tracks of the buff-colored pine marten. A few bands of bighorn sheep are occasionally sighted along the east slope of the Sierra Crest from Convict Lake to Mount Whitney. Grouse and mountain quail are found throughout the timbered areas.

Foxtail pines at Lone Pine Lake in the John Muir Wilderness—a timberline tree found only at isolated locations in the High Sierra

Bighorn sheep, occasionally sighted among the high crags of the Sierra crest

ness of vision, the bighorn is equaled or surpassed only by the pronghorn antelope. A sudden alarm will often send a spooked ram galloping across the terrain at over 35 miles an hour.

Hawley Lake Indian Petroglyphs in the Northern Sierra Nevadas

The Hawley Lake site is one of the largest petroglyph areas in the northern Sierra Nevada. More than 500 different designs have been carved into a large exposed section of bedrock. The carvings include track forms of deer, bear, elk, and man; abstract forms, such as circles, wavy lines, and grids; as well as cupules, vulvaforms, anthropomorphs, and animals (mountain sheep and lizards). Stylistically, the petroglyphs appear to be related to a greater tradition of rock art found from this region through the Great Basin and possibly as far south as Texas. The petroglyphs were pecked, rubbed, and scratched into the rock surface. A lack of associated midden sites suggests that this was strictly a ceremonial or religious center.

The petroglyph site is west of Gold Lake in Sierra County, California.

Big and Little Petroglyph Canyons

The Big and Little Petroglyph Canyons comprise probably the most spectacular petroglyph area in the entire Western United States. More than 20,000 petroglyphs of a varied and complex nature are located here. There is evidence that the carving of the designs covers a long period of time and represents at least two cultural phases. A large array of geometric and naturalistic forms appear, including mountain sheep, mountain lions, deer, and hunters.

The canyons, located at the China Lake Naval Ordnance Test Station, are accessible to the public.

Meadow Lake Indian Petroglyphs

Petroglyphs near Meadow Lake are the most abstract yet found in the Sierra Nevada and represent an extreme style, in contrast to more naturalistic elements at other area sites. A total of 390 pecked design units cover a series of seven major panels, and isolated units are scattered over an area of 500 feet on glacially smooth granite bedrock and large boulders. Design elements are abstract curved lines, concentric circles, dots, and three naturalistic stick figures.

The site is near French Lake in Nevada County, California.

High Sierra Bighorn Sheep Area

The California Bighorn Sheep Zoological Area contains two management units surrounding Mount Baxter and Mount Williamson along the eastern slope of the High Sierra Crest in the John Muir Wilderness, due north and south of Onion Valley and the Kearsarge Pass. The California bighorn is occasionally seen on the rugged peaks and ridges in the area above the timberline. The bighorn is brown to grayish-brown, with a creamy white rump. The male has massive, broomed horns that spiral back, then out and forward to complete an arc. The sheep are extremely alert and seldom wander far from steep escape routes. In keen-

Lake Tahoe

Lake Tahoe, nestled among the towering Sierras on the state's western boundary, is one of the West's premier trout waters. The lake is 21½ miles long and 12 miles wide and has a delightfully irregular rocky shoreline thickly forested with evergreens. With the peaks of the High Sierras in view above the trees, the lake is a brilliant blue-green, owing to its great depth—1,776 feet at one point. It is the tenth deepest lake in the world and the second clearest in the U.S. The lake lies in a depression between two faults whose outlet was dammed by volcanic action and glacial

North End of Lake Tahoe—the tenth deepest lake in the world, reaching a depth of 1,776 feet

debris, capturing the runoff from rain and snow.

First recorded knowledge of the lake is in the report of Fremont's expeditions. When Fremont was encamped at Pyramid Lake near the mouth of the Truckee River in 1844, Indians made a drawing of the Truckee River, which they represented as issuing from another lake in the mountains three or four days distant, in a direction a little west of south. Fremont then crossed the Sierras over Carson Pass and saw Lake Tahoe, which he later called Mountain Lake. The name of the lake was changed many times, and finally the name Tahoe was put together from several Indian words.

Lake Tahoe Outlet Gates and Gatekeeper's Cabin

The gates were first built in 1870 to control the outflow of water from Lake Tahoe to the Truckee River and parts of Nevada. Control of these gates resulted in the Tahoe water war between lakeshore owners and downstream Truckee River water users. The dispute, which lasted two decades, was settled in 1910. The gatekeeper's cabin was built to house a recordskeeper who measured the amount of water discharged downstream.

The outlet gates and cabin are on U.S. Highway 89 at the mouth of the Truckee River near Tahoe City in Placer County, California.

The Donner Camp

At Donner Camp in the High Sierras a California-bound group of emigrants, led by Captain George Donner, was caught by two early winter storms. Marooned in deep snow, the party of 89 members built rude shelters of wagon tops and brush in their efforts to survive. Seven of the 15 who set out for help reached the California settlements, and on February 19, 1847, the first relief party arrived at the camp. Only 45 survived the winter ordeal. The fate of the Donner party epitomizes the hardships and dangers endured by pioneers of the overland migrations. A monument to the pioneers stands on the site which is now the Donner Memorial State Park.

The campsite is located 26 miles west of Truckee on U.S. Highway 40.

Walker Pass

Joseph Reddeford Walker served as one of the chief guides of Captain B. L. E. Bonneville's fur trapping expedition to the Rocky Mountains in 1833. On July 24, Walker left Bonneville's fort with a trapping party and started west to explore and trap in the country beyond the Great Salt Lake. They traversed the Sierra Nevada into California and on to the Pacific Coast. During the return journey in 1834, Walker discovered the 5,248-foot-high pass that has since borne his name. In 1843 Walker led the first emigrant wagon train into California through this pass.

The pass is 60 miles northeast of Bakersfield on California Highway 178.

Devil's Postpile—A Lava Pillar

The Devil's Postpile National Monument, in the eastern Sierra Nevada near Mammoth Lakes, occupies a rectangular area about two and one-half miles long by one-half mile wide, extending along both sides of the Middle Fork of the San Joaquin River, similar to the vertical columns of Devil's Tower in Wyoming. Thousands of blue-gray basaltic columns 40 to 60 feet high rise above the turbulent water and form a wall of nearly perfect prisms. An easy trail leads to the top of the columns, where glacial action has polished the surface to resemble tile inlays arranged in a honeycomb pattern. Also within the national monument, two miles down the river trail from the Devil's Postpile, are the lovely Rainbow Falls. Here the Middle Fork of the San Joaquin River drops 140 feet, its foamy white waters contrasting dramatically with the dark basaltic cliffs. The name of the falls stems from the rainbows that appear around noon on a clear day.

The monument is reached via California Highway 203, which leads west from U.S. 395 and the Mammoth Lakes Ranger Station.

The 40-foot bluish-gray basalt columns of Devil's Postpile formed between 100,000 and 200,000 years ago

Rainbow Falls cascading 140 feet into the Middle Fork of the San Joaquin River near Devil's Postpile

Yosemite National Park

This 1,189-square-mile national park lies thousands of feet above the arid Great Basin Desert in the heart of the Sierra Nevada in eastern and central California and contains the greatest concentration of natural grandeur along the entire 400-mile length of the Sierras. The park is bisected from east to west by Yosemite Valley to the south and the Grand Canyon of the Tuolumne to the north—both gouged down thousands of feet into solid rock when great rivers of ice advanced through Yosemite during the Ice Age.

The spectacular, glacier-carved, U-shaped trough of Yosemite Valley was first explored, accidentally, on March 25, 1851, by Major James D. Savage and Dr. L. H. Bunnell when, leading the Mariposa battalion in an expedition to capture the warring Miwok Indians, they stumbled upon the primeval valley spread out before them, cut by the winding waters of the Merced River. While camping on the banks of the Merced that night, they named the valley Yosemite, from *Uzumati*, the Miwok Indian word for grizzly bear, one of the tribal totems. Afterward, Bunnell's book, *Discovery of Yosemite*, spread the fame of the valley's natural wonders far.

Yosemite Valley lies at 3,985 feet altitude and is seven miles long, with an average width of one mile. It was carved out of the granite slopes of the High Sierra by stream erosion and massive glacial action. The level, parklike floor is sunk 3,000 feet below the rim of the park, and the once-famed trout waters of the Merced River meander through the green meadows and forests, dominated by immense granite domes and rock masses which form a sheer wall surrounding the valley. The valley was once the home of the Miwok Indians, who called it *Ahwahnee*, meaning deep grassy valley.

Yosemite's Glacier-Carved Valley

The incomparable valley, as Yosemite has been called, is probably the world's best-known example of a glacier-carved canyon. Its leaping waterfalls, towering cliffs, rounded domes, and massive monoliths make it a preeminent natural marvel.

Yosemite Valley is characterized by sheer walls and a flat floor. Its evolution began when alpine glaciers ground through the canyon of the Merced River. The ice carved through weaker sections of

Glacier-carved El Capitan in Yosemite Valley

Early morning view of Yosemite Valley—named after the Miwok Indian word Uzumati, *meaning grizzly bear*

granite, plucking and scouring rock but leaving harder, more solid portions—such as El Capitan and Cathedral Rocks—intact and greatly enlarging the canyon that the Merced River had carved through successive uplifts of the Sierra Range. Finally, the glacier began to melt, and the terminal moraine left by the last glacier advance into the valley dammed the melting water to form Lake Yosemite, which filled the newly carved U-shaped valley. Sediment eventually filled in the lake, forming the flat valley floor you see today. This same process is now filling Mirror Lake at the base of Half Dome.

In contrast to the valley's sheer walls, the Merced Canyon outside the park is a typical river-cut, V-shaped canyon, for the glaciers did not extend this far. Back from the rim of the valley itself, forested slopes show some signs of glacial polish. But for the most part, these areas also were not glaciated.

Yosemite Valley is a mosaic of open meadows sprinkled with wildflowers and flowering shrubs, oak woodlands, and mixed-conifer forests of ponderosa pine, incense cedar, and Douglas fir. Wildlife from monarch butterflies to mule deer and black bears inhabit these communities. Around the valley's perimeter waterfalls, which reach their maximum flow in May and June, crash to the valley floor. Yosemite, Bridal Veil, Vernal, Nevada, and Illilouette are the most prominent of these falls, some of which have little or no water from mid-August through early fall.

Bodie Ghost Town Historic District

Bodie is one of the most significant mining ghost towns of the West because of its more than 100 surviving buildings. Its history was typical of the strike, boom, and decline cycle of Western mining communities. The discovery of an extensive mineral zone in the

1870s precipitated the boom, and the town grew from a few shacks to a population of more than 10,000. Total output of the Bodie mines up to the end of World War II has been estimated at $70 million.

The district is seven miles south of Bridgeport on U.S. Highway 395, then 12 miles east via secondary road.

Mono Lake

To the southeast of Yosemite at a 6,409-foot elevation in the Great Basin Desert country lies Mono Lake, covering 87 square miles. The lake is the third-largest natural body of water in California, formed more than 20,000 years ago by descending Sierra Nevada glaciers. Its blue waters are so impregnated with alkaline materials that nothing lives in its briny depths but one small species of saltwater shrimp and tiny black-fly larvae. In *Roughing It*, Mark Twain tells a tale of a dog that hit a running speed of 250 miles an hour after taking a swim in the lake. Two large volcanic islands dot the lake's surface: Paoha, the larger, with its hot spring, and Negit, an old volcanic crater, with a rookery for sea gulls, or "mono pigeons," that have flown inland from the Pacific. South of the lake are the 20 Mono Craters, forming a crescent-shaped range and resembling gigantic ash heaps.

Mono Craters and Jeffrey Pines

The ancient volcanic ridges, craters, cinder pits, basalt formations, coulees, caldera, and obsidian domes of the eerie Mono Craters are located in the arid Mono Lake Basin on the eastern slope of the Sierra Nevada Range in the Inyo National Forest.

A self-guiding automobile route provides access for a rare closeup view of a primeval volcano- and glacier-shaped landscape. Oh! Ridge is a remnant of an ancient volcano, which was covered by a glacier after its eruption. As the glacier melted, it dropped boulders called erratics. East of Oh! Ridge is a low ridge of glacial debris, a moraine marking the terminus of the last glacial advance. The red cinder pits here are lavas from the Oh! Ridge volcano, which flowed into icy ponds formed by the melting glacier. The water caused the rocks to rust and trapped steam-formed air pockets, causing the rock lava to explode into the red cinder you see today.

The bowllike depression, known as the Devil's Punchbowl, represents the first stage of eruption to occur in the Mono Craters. The escaping volcanic material built up a cone around the vent, creating a bowl of granitelike ryholitic lavas. Near the Devil's Punchbowl is a "blast pit" formed by several craters which destroyed an obsidian dome. The second stage of eruption that formed obsidian domes is illustrated by

Bodie Ghost Town in Owens Valley, with more than 100 surviving buildings from the gold-rush era

Moro Rock—a typical helmetlike granite dome of the High Sierra at Sequoia National Park

Wilson Butte to the south of the main craters. It was formed by rhyolite, which poured up through the vents and eventually filled the blast pits. Rhyolite is a fine-grained volcanic glass, which contains black bands of obsidian, used by the area Indians to make arrowheads. Interspersed between the 9,000-foot-high Mono Craters are large barren flats that were once glacial lakes formed at the time of the eruptions and the long arms of coulees, formed by the slow-moving, semifluid lava. The Southern Coulee is mined by the U.S. Pumice Supply Corporation for its pumice, a lightweight porous obsidian used for a wide variety of commercial purposes, from building stone to a toothpaste ingredient.

The highly porous soils created by the pumice sands from the Mono Craters are the natural habitat of the Jeffrey Pine, a relative of the ponderosa pines found along the western slope of the Sierra Nevada. The Jeffreys, which reach maturity in 100 to 200 years, can be easily identified by the vanillalike odor of their bark, the incurved barbs of bracts on their cones, and their fascicles of three needles.

Sequoia and Kings Canyon National Parks

Sequoia and Kings Canyon national parks on the western slopes of the southern High Sierra, rise on the east more than 11,000 feet above the desert floor of Owens Valley and slope gently westward along its broad western flank to the Great Valley of California. They preserve, like nearby Yosemite, a spectacular landscape of U-shaped glacial troughs, cirques, hanging valleys, and glacial lakes. But the more conspicuous features in the southernmost portion of the Sierra Nevada are the scores of helmet-shaped granite domes, such as Fin Dome, Moro Rock, Tehipite Dome, and Beetle Rock; steep-sided avalanche chutes near Mount Whitney, Kern Canyon, and Bearpaw Meadow; and the Crystal, Paradise, and Palmer caverns. A majestic arc of cloud-weathered High Sierra peaks—dominated by Mount Whitney (14,494 feet), the highest point in the contiguous United States—bounds the area on the east, sloping down to the foothills of the Sierras on the west. The Great Western Divide, a jagged granite ridge, bisects the Sequoia from north to south. Situated between the Great Western Divide and the High Sierra crest are hundreds of remote alpine lakes and streams, the awesome Kaweah Peaks, the 3,000-foot walls of the Kern River Canyon, and the Chagoopa, Bighorn, and Boreal plateaus, formed by the glaciers of the Ice Age. West of the Great Western Divide in the 4,000- to 8,000-foot elevations of the foothills are the groves of giant Sierra redwoods, *Sequoia gigantea*, living relics of "The Age of the Dinosaurs."

Giant Sequoia—The Big Trees

Giant sequoias occur in 75 groves scattered between 4,500 and 7,000 feet on the west slope of the Sierra Nevada. Some groves contain only a few trees, others several thousand. The sequoias are not isolated from other trees, but grow in association with white fir, sugar pine, ponderosa pine, and incense cedar. What makes them stand out from the others is their unusual size.

The giant sequoia and its relative, the coast redwood, are the last surviving members of a group of trees that flourished over much of the world 100 million years ago, during the Mesozoic era, "The Age of the Dinosaurs." Fossil evidence shows the giant sequoia and its relatives once grew in places such as Australia, Antarctica, and Greenland, as well as throughout the western part of North America. These trees belong to an ancient family, *Taxodiaceae*, which include other closely related living species, such as the dawn redwood, native only to China, the bald cypress of the southeastern United States and Mexico, and the Japanese cedar of Japan.

Although not the oldest living things—a distinction held by the bristlecone pine—giant sequoias are the largest. Outstanding individuals measure some 30 to 35 feet in diameter and tower to heights of 250 to 300 feet above the forest floor. Near the base of these giants, the bark is 12 to 18 inches thick; the bark on the limbs, however, is very thin. This soft, fibrous bark is difficult to burn and protects the growth layer from the periodic lightning-caused fires that are a natural part of the ecology of a sequoia grove. The water-based, tannin-rich sap also helps to ward off the effects

Ancient Indian "grain mill" on the Kaweah River in Sequoia National Park

of fire. But the intense heat from debris accumulated at the trees' base and the effect of repeated fires can break the bark. Thus, burn scars and blackened, hollow trunks of some older yet healthy trees attest to the numerous fires that have burned through the groves, as well as the trees' ability to withstand their effects.

The fires prepare the way for the perpetuation of this species. Giant sequoias sprout from seeds so small and light they look like flakes of oatmeal. A one-ounce package would contain about 7,000 seeds. The seeds are produced in cones high in the branches of the trees. A cone takes two years to develop and, although the size and shape of a chicken's egg, contains some 200 to 300 seeds. Though most trees shed their seeds when they are mature, the sequoias retain the green, seed-bearing cones alive on the tree for up to 30 years. Outside forces, such as insect larvae, the Douglas squirrel, and fire, are required to help the tree disperse its seed. The energy held in the seed is sufficient only to produce a tap root about one inch long.

Giant sequoias are found only on the western slope of the Sierra Nevada

Sequoia, or "big tree," a living relic of a group of trees that flourished over much of the world 100 million years ago

High Sierra from Whitney Pass

If this tiny root fails to reach mineral soil, it will be unable to transport the nutrients necessary to keep the tree sprout alive. Fire prepares the seed bed by burning off the duff that collects on the forest floor, sometimes to depths of several inches.

Sequoia saplings can grow to their maximum height in several hundred years. At maturity, the cone-shaped trees begin to grow out, the bark thickens, the lower limbs are lost, the trunk begins to form the shape of a huge column, and the crown becomes rounded, and then craggy with large limbs. The wood of the giant sequoia is hard and brittle. Upon hitting the ground, the trees frequently shatter into irregular pieces.

The Mariposa Grove in Yosemite contains the oldest known and fifth largest sequoia, the Grizzly Giant, believed to be 2,700 years old. Some of the most striking specimens of big trees are found in Sequoia National Park's Giant Forest and King's Canyon's General Grant Grove and Redwood Mountain Grove, a 2,500-acre forest that contains thousands of giant sequoias.

Golden-Mantled Ground Squirrel

This chipmunklike ground squirrel burrows near boulders, logs, and trees in the high mountain country, chaparral and open coniferous forests of the West. This commonly sighted rodent has a coppery head and a black-bordered white stripe running down the side of its back. This common campsite nuisance is from six to eight inches long.

Mount Whitney—The Highest Peak in the Lower United States

Mount Whitney was named by the noted geologist Clarence King in honor of Professor J. D. Whitney, leader of the California Geological Survey party that in 1864 measured the peak at 14,494 feet—the highest peak in the continental United States, outside of Alaska. In 1871 King made the first attempt to scale Mount Whitney, but, confused by storm clouds, he unwittingly climbed Mount Langley (14,042 feet) to the south. In 1873 W. A. Goodyear climbed Mount Langley, discovered King's marker, and published accounts of King's mistake. King responded by rushing west from New York and climbing the true Mount Whitney on September 19, 1873, but lost the honor of making the first ascent by four weeks. On August 18, 1873, a party of three mountaineers had reached the level, three-acre summit and given the mountain the name of Fisherman's Peak. Nevertheless, King's original name for the great peak remained on the map.

10. Pacific Coast

THE narrow, rugged Pacific Coast forms an almost uniformly straight coastline of sheer vertical cliffs, rocky headlands, sea stacks, and arches carved by the awesome force of the sea. Unlike the jagged, sandy Atlantic shore, the Pacific Coast has few sand spits or barrier beaches. This land of rock—broken at Puget Sound, the Golden Gate of San Francisco Bay and Monterey Bay—is uplifting from the sea. This 2,000-mile-long coast is paralleled by a complex system of mountains known as the Coast Ranges that occasionally reach down to the pounding surf. Inland are the great valleys or troughs that sweep down through Washington, Oregon, and California.

Within this contrasting land of giant cliffs, pounding surf and wild, log-strewn beaches, glacier-studded mountains, rain forests, and arid chapparal are the famous Oregon Dunes and Olympic and Redwood national parks.

Forest Zones of the Pacific Coast

The great forests of the Pacific Coast sweep southward from Alaska, nurtured by mild temperatures and abundant moisture carried in by the ocean winds and summer fog. This coastal forest, more than 2,000 miles long, has several distinct zones, each characterized by a dominant tree species.

The northern Pacific Coast is dominated by the western hemlock, stately Sitka spruce, and western red cedar. Although a humble tree compared to the towering Sitka spruce, the western hemlock is the most abundant tree in the northern region. Farther south, along the Coast Ranges in Washington and Oregon, the forests are dominated by the majestic Douglas fir, which often reaches heights of 200 feet, diminishing in the southwestern corner of Oregon, where it is replaced by the giant coastal redwood forests, which

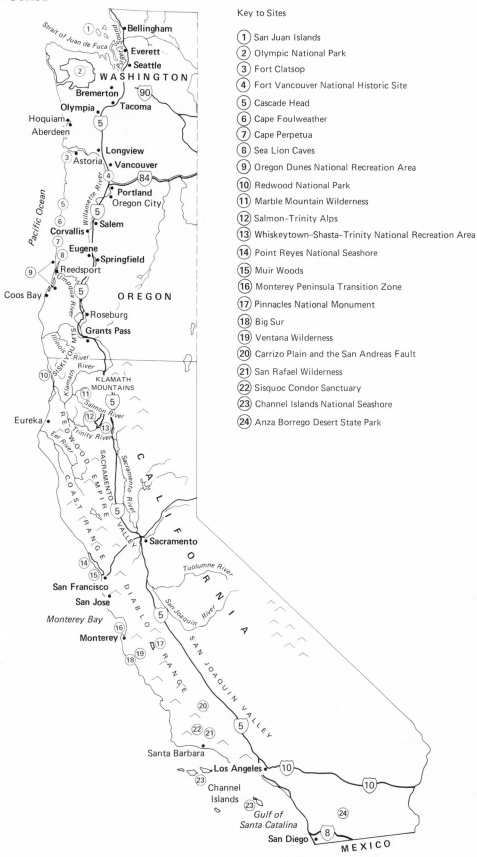

Key to Sites

1 San Juan Islands
2 Olympic National Park
3 Fort Clatsop
4 Fort Vancouver National Historic Site
5 Cascade Head
6 Cape Foulweather
7 Cape Perpetua
8 Sea Lion Caves
9 Oregon Dunes National Recreation Area
10 Redwood National Park
11 Marble Mountain Wilderness
12 Salmon-Trinity Alps
13 Whiskeytown-Shasta-Trinity National Recreation Area
14 Point Reyes National Seashore
15 Muir Woods
16 Monterey Peninsula Transition Zone
17 Pinnacles National Monument
18 Big Sur
19 Ventana Wilderness
20 Carrizo Plain and the San Andreas Fault
21 San Rafael Wilderness
22 Sisquoc Condor Sanctuary
23 Channel Islands National Seashore
24 Anza Borrego Desert State Park

Pacific coast countryside

Dense coastal forest in the fog belt

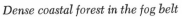

Western red cedar

Abalone shellfish, a favorite food of the endangered sea otter

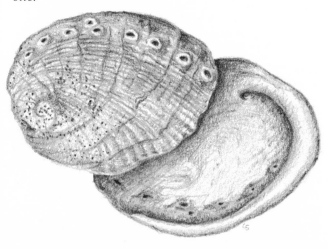

stretch southward along the fog belt of northern California to San Francisco.

South of the Redwood Empire is the land of the chaparral, where the annual precipitation decreases markedly, particularly during summer. This semiarid region of desertlike evergreen scrub forest is dominated by the dense, crooked limbs of the manzanita.

Plant Life of the Pacific Northwest Seashores

The most conspicuous of the marine plants of the Pacific Northwest seashores are numerous algae, varying from blue-green to brown and red. The most common of this group is the floating kelp, with its brown-bulbed whip. The sea rose, rarest and most complex of the red algae, is found in its branched form, native to the western coast of Asia. Two species of eelgrass grow here: one in exposed tidal waters, the other in protected marshes. Marine lichens and fungi of various kinds are common along the coast.

In summer the windswept sand dunes are colored by the blossoms of sturdy plants, including the delicately fragrant yellow and pink abroma or sand verbena and the saltbush with pale, scurvied leaves. Sand strawberries, beach pea, and blue, yellow, and purple lupine advance on the dunes, wherever some slight protection is afforded by driftwood or rock or hummock of solid earth. Fennel, spurrey, ruppia, willow, and the yellow-blossomed ragweed grow in profusion around the salt marshes. Above the dunes and beaches along the littoral runs a narrow band of Sitka spruce, also known locally as the tideland spruce.

Abalone

The abalone is a large mollusk, nearly a foot in length, commonly sighted along tidal rocks and crevices. It is noted for its muscular foot, which secretes a mucus that gives it a powerful suction to withstand the powerful waves, and it is prized for its inside layer of mother-of-pearl or glistening nacre rich in rainbow tints. Its shell is shaped like a broad, shallow bowl with a row of small oval breathing holes along one side. Its flesh is of high commercial value.

Sitka Alder

The Sitka alder is a small deciduous shrub from 5 to 15 feet high or a small tree up to 30 feet tall and eight inches in diameter. It has yellowish-green oval

Old-growth Douglas fir, a dominant tree along the coast in Washington and Oregon

leaves speckled and shiny above, and its sticky, orange-brown twigs when young becoming light gray with maturity. The Sitka alder is often a spreading shrub with numerous stems forming thickets in marshes, along streams, on landslides, and in clearings from sea level to the alpine zone above the timberline. It also becomes a small tree with many trunks. This pioneer species is common from Alaska south to western Montana and northern California. It follows disturbances such as landslides, logging, or glacial retreat. Sitka spruce often becomes established at the same time. It thrives with overhead light but is intolerant of shade and disappears from the stand when overtopped by Sitka spruce. Its wood produces good fuel and is commonly used for smoking fish in Alaska.

Salmonberry

The salmonberry, a thicket-forming deciduous shrub, is two to seven feet high, with green compound leaves, light-brown bark, and zigzag, light brown twigs with scattered sharp, weak spines or prickles. It is found from Alaska south to northwestern California, forming dense thickets in moist, lowland forests, clearings, and along streams. Its raspberrylike, orange to dark red conelike fruits make good jelly but are rather seedy for jam. They are favored by bears in fall; in spring the new leaves and twigs are browsed by deer, moose, and mountain goats.

Red Alder

Also known as the western alder, the red alder is common from Alaska southward to southern California and locally east to northern Idaho. It is common on stream bottoms with rich, rocky, moist soils and along beaches where streams enter the sea. On landslides it forms almost impenetrable thickets, often with Sitka alder. Its wood is used in smoking meat and fish and for wood carving. This small- to medium-sized deciduous tree is 20 to 40 feet tall, with a straight slender trunk and dark green, double-toothed oval- or elliptical-shaped leaves and dark red twigs with light dots, and gray bark.

Red Huckleberry

The red huckleberry is a tall, 3- to 10-foot-high shrub, also known as red whortleberry, has small leaves and red berries and is commonly seen in openings along roadsides and in cutover forest land in the Pacific coastal forests. Its berries are sour but with

Sitka spruce, commonly found along the northern reaches of the Pacific coast

good flavor and are used for jelly. Its green twigs are often browsed by deer, elk, and mountain goats in fall and winter, and the berries are eaten by blue grouse and bears. Its range extends from southeastern Alaska south along the coast to central California.

Bearberry

In Alaska the bearberry appears as a low trailing or matted shrub, although in California it becomes a tall shrub and an important feature in the chaparral vegetation. In Alaska it is also known as kinnikinnick and mealberry. In the northern forests it is usually sighted under aspen stands and elsewhere in open spruce stands or on dry rocky bluffs. It often forms pure mats several yards in diameter. Its mealy and dry berries are almost tasteless when raw but palatable when cooked. The dry leaves were occasionally used as a substitute for tobacco. As the name indicates, the berries are commonly eaten by grizzly and black bears. Its range extends from Alaska east across Canada and south to the mountains of Georgia and California.

Salal

Salal is a common undershrub of western red cedar, Alaska cedar, spruce, and hemlock forests in Alaska and south along the coast to California. In Alaska it forms an almost continuous cover in some stands. The stiff evergreen leaves and hairy flowers and twigs make this plant easily recognized. Its spicy berries are eaten by grouse and other birds, but rarely by humans. It is reported that the Pacific Northwest Indians gathered its fruit, a purple berry that appears in May and June.

Devil's Club

Devil's club, a large deciduous, spiny shrub with several thick stems and very few branches, is from 3 to 10 feet high and is found from south-central Alaska east to Montana, southern Oregon, and Idaho. Its numerous sharp spines are painful and can fester

when imbedded in the skin, making this a dangerous shrub to be avoided. This handsome plant with bright red berries and a beautiful mosaic of large leaves arranged to catch the maximum amount of filtered sunlight at the forest edge is common in ravines and openings, forming impenetrable thickets in coastal and floodplain forests, especially under alder and on good Sitka spruce sites. In spite of their spines, the young shoots are browsed by deer and elk in early spring and summer. The Alaskan Indians sometimes brew tea from its bitter bark as a tonic. Years ago the stalks were used by the Indians of Southeast Alaska for beating suspected witches to obtain confessions. On old Alaska homesteads people would nail the devil's club stalk over their door or window to protect the house from evil influences and bad luck.

Rusty Menziesia

Also known as skunkbrush and fool's huckleberry, rusty menziesia is a loose-spreading deciduous shrub 6 to 10 feet high with slender, widely forking paired branches and small yellowish red flowers. It is a common shrub in undergrowth of the coastal spruce and hemlock forests, often found under a dense canopy, in openings, on cutover forest land, and especially on

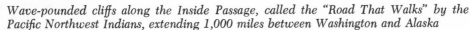

Wave-pounded cliffs along the Inside Passage, called the "Road That Walks" by the Pacific Northwest Indians, extending 1,000 miles between Washington and Alaska

well-drained slopes in association with blueberries. It also grows in the southern part of Alaska's boreal forest region among white spruce and paper birch stands. Because of its leaf and flower size and shape it is sometimes confused with the huckleberries, but its fruit is not a berry. Its range extends from Alaska south to northern California and eastward to eastern Washington.

Inside Passage of the Pacific Northwest

The fabled Inside Passage, called the Road that Walks by the Indians of the Pacific Northwest, is a series of sheltered waterways stretching for 1,000 miles between Seattle and its northern terminus at Glacier Bay, Alaska. This historic passage, once travelled by the powerful Coast Indian tribes in their cedar dugout canoes, winds through a maze of islands flanked by the rugged Coastal Mountains and thick rain forests, broken here and there by beautiful fjords and quaint fishing villages. The myriads of islands that you see are actually the summits of mountains that were submerged during the last Ice Age. Powerful tides that sometimes attain a speed of more than 10 miles per hour, fog, and layers of mist are frequently encountered along the route. The passage is 80 miles across at its greatest width. Natural barriers to the powerful coastal winds and storms are provided by Vancouver Island off the British Columbia mainland in the south and by the Alexander Archipelago along Alaska's southeast Panhandle in the north. Heavy rainfall is common along the waterway. As one travels northward up the passage, glaciers become more numerous, culminating in the 20 major glaciers, some thousands of feet thick, and numerous lesser ones that have their origin in the snowfields of the peaks surrounding Glacier Bay.

San Juan Island National Historic Park

San Juan Island National Historic Park commemorates the events that led to the peaceful settlement of the Oregon Territory boundary dispute in 1872. The Oregon Treaty of 1849 failed to settle the conflict concerning the water boundary between Vancouver Island, British Columbia, and the Oregon Territory of the United States. The situation reached a climax in the "Pig War of 1859," when hostilities almost began. The Treaty of Washington in 1871, which settled the dispute, marked the first time in United States history that there was no boundary quarrel with

Britain. All that remains of the American camp now are the foundations of several buildings. The British camp contains a two-story log blockhouse, a commissary, barracks, and other related buildings.

San Juan Island lies in the San Juan Archipelago made up of a maze of islands and tide-washed rocks in the northern waters of Puget Sound and the southernmost part of the Strait of Georgia. The archipelago forms the southernmost extension of the Inside Passage and is part of a submerged mountain range.

Seattle's Pioneer Square and the Klondike Gold Rush Historic Park

The first settlers, C. D. Boren, Arthur A. Denny, and William N. Bell, claimed land on the site of present-day Seattle in February 1852. This area now constitutes most of the central business district and waterfront. The new town was named for a friendly chief of the Duwamish Indians. In March 1853, Henry L. Yesler began operation of a steam sawmill at the corner of 1st Avenue and Yesler Way; lumbering was to become Seattle's principal industry. Pioneer Square–Skid Road (so called because logs were skidded along it enroute to the sawmill) and the surrounding neighborhood constituted the heart of the growing city for more than 50 years. In the 1890s, the district was the

Landscape at San Juan Island

English blockhouse at San Juan Island—site of the "Pig War of 1859" between Great Britain and the United States

"Canals" of Puget Sound

Like the drowned coast of the northern Atlantic, the Puget Sound area of Washington's Pacific Coast was pushed down under the awesome weight of the Ice Age glaciers and "drowned" by the rise of the sea level caused by the melting ice cap. This postglacial flooding has created a coastal maze of inlets, or canals, as they are called locally, in the lowland valley system that once drained through the Straits of Juan de Fuca, near present-day Tacoma.

Puget Sound, which reaches depths of 600 to 1,000 feet, marks the southernmost limit of the ice sheet on the Pacific Coast. North of the sound, the coastal countryside was carved and shaped by the glaciers of the Ice Age; the rocky shoreline to the south was shaped by the tremendous force of the ocean.

Point Wilson Lighthouse

Any ship that leaves or enters Puget Sound is warned of the sandy shore off Point Wilson by the Point Wilson Lighthouse. In clear weather there is no problem, but a fog signal is necessary in bad weather. The old oil lantern has been replaced by electricity, and a modern foghorn has been installed. The light tower itself is octagonal. The lighthouse is on a point of land between Juan de Fuca Strait and Admiralty Inlet.

Fort Nisqually Granary on Puget Sound

Fort Nisqually, the first permanent white settlement on Puget Sound, was originally located at Du-

major gateway for stampeders headed north to Alaska and the Yukon during the Klondike Gold Rush. The district is now part of the Klondike Gold Rush National Historic Park. It was here the *Portland* landed back in 1897 with the 68 prospectors who launched the Klondike Gold Rush. A fire swept the city in 1889, destroying most of the docks and other business establishments. Rebuilding took place, and one architect —Elmer H. Fisher—left his mark on the new downtown area. His work, coupled with the new building restrictions (only brick, stone, and iron could be used), produced a homogeneity of style and construction that is evident today in the historic district. Structures worthy of notice are the Pioneer Building, the Maud Building, the Maynard and Mutual Life buildings, and the Smith Tower Annex.

Earthworks of the American Camp at San Juan Island in the northern waters of Puget Sound

pont, 15 miles south of Tacoma. The fortified trading post served as a communication and supply center for the Hudson's Bay Company posts on the coast of British Columbia. The granary and factor's or agent's house were the only original buildings remaining in 1934, when they were moved to their present site. The one-story granary, measuring 20 by 31 feet, was constructed in the Canadian post-on-sill method, a type of log construction widely used by fur traders, missionaries, and settlers of the Pacific Northwest before 1846. It is the oldest extant frame structure in the state. The granary is in Tacoma, Washington at Point Defiance Park.

Wawona, three-mast schooner at Seattle used in Pacific Coast lumber and cod-fishing trade

Wawona Three-Mast Schooner

The *Wawona* was built in Fairhaven, California, for the lumber firm of Dolbeer and Carson. The three-masted schooner was constructed entirely of wood and is powered by sail alone. She was engaged in the Pacific Coast lumber trade until 1914, when the Robinson Fisheries Company of Anacortes, Washington, purchased her for a fishing vessel. Her last cod fishing cruise was in 1946, and, after unsuccessful attempts to use the ship as a cruise boat and a cattle boat, she was purchased by a private group to be part of a maritime museum. The *Wawona* is 156 feet in length, 36 feet in beam, and 12.3 feet in depth. The schooner is at the Seattle Police Harbor Dock, at the foot of Densmore Street in Seattle.

Great Coastal Valleys

East of the Coast Ranges along the Pacific shoreline are a great series of lowland troughs called valleys. The northernmost of these great natural troughs include the Willamette Valley in Oregon and Cowlitz Valley, Upper Chelalis Valley, and Puget Sound Trough in Washington. These northern valleys are flanked on the west by the Coast Ranges and foothills of the Olympic Mountains and on the east by the volcanic, snow-capped peaks of the Cascade Mountains. The southernmost of these structural troughs are formed by the Great Valley of California, which lies between the California Coast Ranges on the west and the ramparts of the Sierra Nevada and Southern Cascades on the east.

Olympic Coast—a land of rain forests, high cliffs, and wild, log-strewn beaches

Foothills of the plateaulike Coast Range

Cliffs and Sea Stacks of the Olympic Peninsula

The awesome shoreline of Washington's Olympic Peninsula is dominated by great cliffs, quarried during the past million years by the relentless pounding of the sea. These massive cliffs, which often plunge for more than 250 feet in a sheer drop to the crashing breakers, are eventually eroded into the myriad caves, arches, and sea stacks—former arch pillars. The colorful rock fragments that are smashed from the cliffs and eroding pillars are scraped, splintered and polished into beach pebbles that are remarkable for their extraordinary smoothness.

Olympic National Park

Olympic National Park forms a 1,400-square-mile wilderness in the center of the Olympic Peninsula. The park is dominated by the massive, glacier-studded Olympic Mountains and rain forests of giant Sitka spruce and western hemlock that tower above a junglelike forest floor of ferns, moss, and shrub thickets. The rocky headlands and beaches along the park's 50-mile-long Pacific Coast area are noted for their massive piles of driftwood, tidal pools, and off-shore islands and sea stacks. This remote back-country region is inhabited by Roosevelt elk, black-tailed deer, and black bear.

Wave-eroded sea stack, a common sight along the Olympic Peninsula shoreline

Beach landscape at Olympic National Park

Olympic Mountains

The Olympic Mountains arise in their splendid confusion about the center of Olympic National Park, encircled by a belt of evergreen forest 50 miles wide and more than 200 miles in circumference. Here are no ordered ranges, but instead a vast pile of rugged rock and snow-covered knifelike peaks, varying in elevation from 3,000 to 8,000 feet, the height of Mount Olympus. In places the mountain slopes drop almost vertically for more than 3,000 feet, and from the tops of these sheer stone cliffs flow hundreds of milky waterfalls fed by melting snows.

More than 50 glaciers with approximately 36 square miles of ice and snowfields drape the peaks, among them some of the largest and best-formed glaciers in the United States outside of Alaska. One of the most interesting is the Blue Glacier, which is really a clear blue. Here the climber on Mount Olympus, making his way over the rugged terminal moraine, may observe, wherever the bedrock is exposed, deep grooves in the striated surface, the marks of the glacier when it filled the valley to a lower altitude. At higher points, the hiker can view the broadly sweeping curves of the medial and lateral moraines and lines of flow in the ice, the curves of the glacier high in the cirques or ice pockets near the summit. Above the glaciers are the sheer cliffs, knife-edge crests, and jagged pinnacles of rock.

Glaciers of Olympic National Park

There are about 60 glaciers crowning the peaks of the Olympic Mountains, most quite small in contrast to the great rivers of ice in Alaska. The most prominent glaciers are those on Mount Olympus, which cover approximately 10 squares miles. Beyond Mount Olympus are the glaciers of the Bailey Range, Mount Carrie, Mount Christie, and Mount Anderson.

True glaciers are structurally three-layered bodies of water. The top layer is snow; the middle, mixed snow and ice; and the bottom layer is of pure ice. Crevasses or deep cracks in the glaciers form as the ice is subjected to uneven flow over the alpine terrain. Another prominent feature is the bergschrund, which is a crevasse-like opening at the head of the glacier where the ice has been pulled away from the mountain wall.

The rate of glacial flow is variable, and the Olympic glaciers are "slow-moving" in contrast to some in Alaska, which move at the rate of several hundred feet a day. There is not a rapid melting back or advance of the Olympic glaciers today. Forward surges in glacial flow often occur after a number of very heavy winter snowfalls and cool summers, but such activity has been relatively infrequent with the glaciers in recorded time.

The climate influencing Olympic glaciers is wet

and temperate. The average annual precipitation is about 200 inches, with most of the moisture coming in the form of snow. The snow nurtures the glaciers in the accumulation zone or at the origin of the ice. Most of the melting occurs near the snout of the glaciers. A vigorous glacier will be maintained by a heavy accumulation of snow in the winter and only average melting during summer. The freezing point for late spring and early fall precipitation is the critical factor in the glacier's gain or loss.

The movement of glacial ice has produced striking geological features in the Olympic Mountains. The lake basins, U-shaped valleys, and jagged peaks are the products of massive glacial erosion that occurred thousands of years ago when the year-round climate was significantly colder. This erosion process continues today, but on a much smaller scale. As the glaciers advance and retreat, rock is plucked, transported, and deposited by moving ice. The deposition of rock results in medial, lateral, and terminal moraines. In many cases, a glacially created bowl or cirque at the head of a valley will be dammed by a terminal moraine to create a lake basin.

Access to the Olympic glaciers is by trails and cross-country routes. The most visited glaciers in the park are the Blue and Anderson. From the Hoh Rain Forest, an upriver hiking trail leads 18 miles up to the snout of Blue Glacier. Anderson Glacier can be reached by hiking the Dosewallips River Trail for 11 miles, or from the west side by the East Fork of the Quinault River Trail for 16 miles.

The Olympic Rain Forests

Within a 50-mile radius of Olympic National Park is found one of the heaviest rainfalls in the United States and the driest area on the Pacific Coast, outside of southern California. The finest example of the magnificent rain forests are found in the lower valleys of the western slopes of the Olympic Mountains, where great stands of Douglas fir, western hemlock, western red cedar, and silver fir grow to gigantic size and height. Here, warm air currents strike against the colder reaches of the Olympics, and the precipitation is unusually heavy; most of the annual 144 inches falls as snow and during the winter rainy season. These conditions create an almost tropical luxuriance in both trees and thick undergrowths of Oregon grape, red huckleberry, salmonberry, salal, vine maple, wild strawberry, buttercup, Solomon's seal, trillium, dainty yellow violets, and hundreds of ferns, including western sword, bracken, and deer fern.

The fallen trunks of enormous trees become nourishment for seedlings that take root upon them, and thus new trees continually replace the old. Great tangles of green moss hang from the towering trees,

Hoh Rain Forest in Olympic National Park, where the warm, moisture-laden air currents of the Pacific strike against the cold reaches of the Olympic Mountains, creating one of the heaviest rainfall areas in the United States

Sword fern, a common plant of the rain forest floor

try. Scattered bands of elk are often seen cooling themselves on the vast snowfields on hot summer days, and bands of elk, sometimes numbering 15 to 60, are commonly seen wandering at some river bottom or crossing alpine meadows.

Olympic Marmot

The Olympic marmot, a close relative of the hoary marmot, is found only in the high slopes of the Olympic Mountains of Washington's Olympic Peninsula. It is a brown, drab-colored animal from 18 to 21 inches long.

Port Gamble Historic Lumbering District

Port Gamble was one of the earliest and most important lumber-producing centers on the Pacific Coast. Still an active sawmill town, it exemplifies the mid-19th-century company-owned town. Still standing are some Greek Revival cottages, New England boxlike houses, Victorian houses, a church, a community center, and the company store. The sawmill and docks were rebuilt in 1926.

and the ground in some places is an almost impenetrable wall of rotting trunks, vine maple, and other junglelike growth. In some spots the carpet of moss is easily six inches deep, soft as the richest rug.

Roosevelt Elk

One of the principal reasons for establishing the original Mount Olympus National Monument in 1909 was to ensure the protection for the largest remaining herd of Roosevelt elk, native to Washington's Olympic Peninsula. It is estimated that there are more than 3,000 of the magnificent deer within the boundaries of the park. In the winter they browse and forage in the lower valleys and along the waterways; in the summer they follow the melting snowline into the high coun-

Mima Mounds of Southwest Washington

Located in the Chehalis River valley in southwest Washington, the old Mima Mounds, from one to seven feet in height and from eight to 50 feet in diameter, crop up on several prairielike areas of glacial outwash. These unusual gravel and silt mounds are of unknown origin, but theories have been proposed, ranging from creation by glacial action to the work of pocket gophers.

Herd of Roosevelt elk native to the Olympic coast; on hot summer days they may be sighted cooling themselves on the high snowfields

Hecla Head Light in Oregon's Siuslaw National Forest, one of a string of lighthouses on the rocky Pacific headlands

Coast Ranges and Sand Dunes of the Pacific Northwest

The low-lying, plateaulike Coast Range of Washington and Oregon stretches for 250 miles from the Willapa Hills south of the Olympic Mountains, southward to the Klamath Mountains. The range averages about 50 miles in width and reaches its highest point at Marys Peak, 4,097 feet high. The range is cut by a series of westward-flowing rivers such as the Chehalis, Columbia, and Willapa and is bordered on the west by a narrow coastal plain of wild sand dunes and drowned rivers. An unusual feature is a series of lakes behind the dunes, especially along the Oregon coast between Coos Bay and Sea Lion Point (the only known mainland sea lion rookery in the world), that

were formed by the damming of tidal rivers by the extensive plant-anchored sand dunes.

Fort Clatsop National Memorial

Captains Meriwether Lewis and William Clark wintered here and built Fort Clatsop in 1805–1806, following their epoch-making journey from the Mississippi River to the Pacific Ocean. Their expedition supplied the most detailed published knowledge of the American Northwest available at the time and generated interest in Oregon which led to occupation of the vast territory. Named Fort Clatsop after a local Indian tribe, the site was near the ocean, hunting grounds, timber, and friendly natives. Nothing of the

Coast Range of Washington and Oregon, stretching for 250 miles and flanked on the west by narrow coastal plain of dunes, forests, and lakes

original fort has survived, but a replica following Clark's floor plan dimensions was constructed in 1955.

The replica of the original fort is 4.5 miles south of Astoria.

Fort Astoria

Launched by John Jacob Astor, an influential figure of the American fur trade, Astoria represented, both initially and later, an important American claim to the Oregon country. Astor's bid to break the British fur trade monopoly in the Northwest was initially successful. However, the War of 1812 and the failure of supply ships to arrive forced Astor to sell the post in 1813. Although most of the site has been obscured by the modern city, one small plot of ground remains, featuring a reconstructed blockhouse. The blockhouse is at 15th and Exchange streets in Astoria.

Fort Vancouver National Historic Site

Founded by the Hudson's Bay Company during the winter of 1824–1825 as a fur-trading and supply depot, Fort Vancouver for the next 20 years was the most important settlement in the Pacific Northwest from San Francisco Bay to the Russian outposts in Alaska. From establishment of the first fort in 1824 until 1849 this stockaded fur-trading post was headquarters for all activities of the Hudson's Bay Company west of the Rocky Mountains. It was the seat of British political authority for the Pacific Northwest, an area now comprising British Columbia, Washington, Oregon, Idaho, and western Montana. After the boun-

Fort Clatsop, built in 1805 by the Lewis and Clark expedition after their epic overland journey from St. Louis to the Pacific

Army House at Fort Vancouver, once the major fur-trading post of the Hudson's Bay Company west of the Rockies

Tillamook Head on the Oregon Coast—the westernmost point reached by Lewis and Clark. They made salt here by boiling sea water, but their permanent camp was at Fort Clatsop.

The Oregon Dunes, the most spectacular stretch of dune landscape on the Pacific coast

dary settlement with Britain in 1846 the post declined. In 1849 the site became a United States Army camp, and it is still partly used as such. Little remains of the original post.

The Oregon Dunes

The Oregon Dunes, which extend inland for about 2 and a half miles and for 40 miles in length along the Pacific, from Heceta Head on the north to Coos Bay on the south, forms the most spectacular stretch of dune landscape on the Pacific Coast. Behind the dunes are dense coastal forests and lakes.

Sea Lion Caves

The enormous wave-carved cave near Florence, Oregon is the winter rookery of the arctic Stellers. During summer, they inhabit rocky islands off the coast of Alaska. The main cavern at the Sea Lion Caves is a multicolored 1,500-foot-long chamber.

Steller's Sea Lion

The Steller's sea lions are a significant feature of the rocky Pacific Coast. Their range extends from the Bering Sea south along the Alaskan Coast to the Channel Islands in California. The sea lion, although awkward on land, is an extremely agile swimmer. Unlike seals, they can bend their hind flippers forward and under, which provides them with a great amount of control and maneuverability in the sea. On shore they are usually sighted basking on rocks or moving at a lumbering gallop. Although they appear slow and sluggish, they are capable of climbing steep rock bluffs and of leaping as much as 16 feet from a ledge to the surf. They are not generally alarmed by the approach of humans while in the sea but will take flight when approached on land.

Steller's sea lion males average 1,500 to 2,000 pounds, and up to 10 feet in length. The females are markedly smaller. Their coloration ranges from black or dark gray to yellowish to dark brown. They have a layer of oily, spongy tissue between the skin and body, which acts as an insulator. The thickness of this layer of blubber varies with the temperature of the seasons and available food supply of squid, crustaceans, and other marine animals. They breed in the Bering Sea in July and off Oregon and California in the summer. The mating of one bull to a harem of females takes place after the birth of a pup, which is born singly 12 months after the rut. A visitor to the famous Steller's sea lion rookery near Florence, Oregon, will enter a world of frenetic sounds and activity: the screaming gulls wheeling overhead, the roar and crash of the surf, the whine of the pups, and the deep barks and grunts of the lumbering bulls. The most northerly breeding ground of the smaller California sea lion lies just south of the Monterey Peninsula.

Trinity Alps in northern California—part of the legendary Bigfoot country

Klamath Mountains—Bigfoot Country

The sprawling Klamath Mountains straddle the northwestern California and southwestern Oregon boundary in the heart of the legendary Bigfoot Country. This rugged mountain range, which more resembles the Sierra Nevada than the coastal ranges to the south, reaches heights of 9,000 feet above sea level and embraces the Salmon-Trinity Alps Primitive Area and Marble Mountain—dominated by the white marble cap, some 700 to 1,000 feet thick, of Marble Mountain —formed by marine organisms deposited when the area formed the bottom of an ocean. Steep, V-shaped valleys have been cut through the range by the powerful Klamath, Trinity, and Salmon rivers, which have their headwaters in the remote peaks.

To the north are the high Siskiyou Mountains and the Red Buttes country—named after two red-rock horn mountains that dominate a broad high country of barred red desertlands, snow-capped crags, and forested valleys. The Siskiyous—inhabited by the rare wolverine—embraces dense montane forests with tall stands of white and noble fir, white-barked Brewer spruce, Alaska cedar, yew, Douglas fir, and western hemlock, broken by meadows of colorful lilies, pitcher-plant beds, Pacific dogwood, coneflower, and pink deershead orchid.

California coast countryside

The California Coast

The beautiful California coast is dominated by rocky headlands that jut out into the Pacific where the Coast Range Mountains meet the sea and by inlets and bays where the valleys meet the coast. Elsewhere the seaward slopes of the Coast Ranges are notched by wavecut terraces that reach up to 1,500 feet above sea level. The Golden Gate of San Francisco, the largest break in the rocky Pacific coastline south of Puget Sound, is a passage through the rocks that leads to a series of large bays.

Redwood National Park

Redwood National Park takes in 58,000 acres of spectacular redwood forest country in northwestern California, just south of the Oregon line. The park's rocky coastal headlands are inhabited by sea lion colonies, and migrating whales are often sighted offshore. In addition to the stands of towering redwoods, the park's natural features include windswept dunes, rocky bluffs and high seashore cliffs, and salt marshes. The Redwood Highway (U.S. 101) cuts through the heart of the park's redwood forests.

Redwood Empire and the Fog Belt

The stately coast redwood grows along the Pacific Coast from Monterey County, about 125 miles south of San Francisco, north as far as the southwest corner of Oregon. The heaviest concentration, however, lies in a narrow fog belt less than 35 miles wide along the California coast from the Russian River to the Oregon border. The largest known diameter of the coast redwood is 20 feet; its maximum known age is about 2,200 years, and the tallest tree, located in Redwood National Park, has a height of 367 feet. While coast redwoods grow taller than the giant sequoias, they have a much smaller circumference and total volume and do not live as long. The trees usually found growing in association with the coast redwood are Douglas fir, white fir, western hemlock and sugar pines, and a mixture of hardwood species such as tan oak and madrone.

The coast redwoods are rarely found above the 3,000-foot elevation and never far from the belt of coastal fogs, which serve as a substitute for rainfall during the dry season. It is the most distinctive botanical feature of the northern California coastline. The largest groves of coast redwoods are protected in the Redwoods National Park. The famous Avenue of the Giants along the Redwood Highway stretches

Redwood grove in the narrow northern California coastal fog belt

south for nearly 100 miles from Eureka.

Despite the redwoods' size, its cones are smaller than those of any other western evergreen, usually less than an inch in length. Its densely shaded understory is made up of delicate wildflowers such as trillium and ozalis and ferns such as ladyfern and sword fern. An unusual characteristic of the redwood is the giant, boulderlike jumbles of burls at its base. These lumpy root growths reach six feet in diameter and are known to contain buds. Repeated fires in redwood forests sometimes result in hollowed-out trees known as "goosepens," which were used by early pioneers to house poultry.

Redwood cone and needles

Giant redwood, one of the most distinctive features of the northern California coast, growing to heights exceeding 300 feet

Coastal Scrub

Lying between the log-strewn beach and the towering redwood forest is a dense, matlike plant community known as the coastal scrub. It is made up of a low tangle of coyote brush, currant, salal, blue blossom, silk tassel, and poison oak, all knitted together by the thorny Himalayan blackberry vine. This coastal scrub forest is broken here and there by grassy prairies where wildflowers, such as white seaside daisy, yarrow, yellow mustard, purple lupine, and the tall, white-headed cow parsnip, grow in desertlike conditions created by the warm drying winds and

Redwood coastal prairie and elk herd

Dune grass and coastal hills at Redwood National Park—the rocky headlands here are inhabited by sea lion colonies, while migrating whales are often sighted offshore

constant exposure to the afternoon sun. The coastal prairies are also the habitat of the rufous and Allen's hummingbird.

Forest Floor of California's Fog Belt

California's redwood forests of the Coast Range extend from the Oregon border on the north to the coastal canyons below Monterey on the south and as far as the inner limit of the summer fogs on the east. Beneath the giant redwoods, watered by the fog they have trapped and precipitated, is an extraordinarily luxuriant growth.

Sword ferns, woodwardia ferns, alumroot, fringe-cups, barrenwort, fetid adders tongue, trillium, and fritillaria carpet the floor. In almost impenetrable thickets grow huckleberry, Oregon grape, rhododendron, azalea, California buckthorn, salmonberry, elder, and wild currant. The trees most commonly found growing in association with the redwoods are the broad-leafed maple, madrone, tanbark oak, California laurel, and the Douglas fir, usually in separate stands.

Point Reyes National Seashore

The pale gray cliffs, wild beaches, and Douglas fir and bishop pine forests of the Point Reyes Peninsula lie to the north of San Francisco and westward

Redwood forest floor, watered by the fog trapped beneath the giant redwoods, nurturing a thick growth of ferns, shrubs, and wildflowers

from the San Andreas Fault. During the massive San Francisco earthquake, the Point Reyes Peninsula was thrust 16.4 feet northwestward. The major features of the area include the tule elk range, where, after an absence of more than 100 years, a small, free-roaming herd has been returned to this wilderness; gray whale migrations, which pass Point Reyes on their southward migration from December to February; Earthquake Tail along the San Andreas Fault; Kule Loklo, a replica of an aboriginal coast Miwok Indian Village; the Point Reyes Bird Observatory; and the sea lion overlook at the often fog-shrouded Point Reyes Light. The trail systems wind through three types of terrain: the pasture lands of Pierce Point, the chaparral ridges and California laurel valleys to the east and west of Limantour Road, and the meadowlands in the southeast end of the park.

First Pacific Coast Salmon Cannery Site

Here William and George Hume and Andrew Hapgood successfully perfected the canning techniques that led to the development of the multimillion-dollar Pacific Coast salmon canning industry. The cannery was situated on a large scow anchored in the Sacramento River offshore from the cabin in which they lived. By 1923 the Pacific Coast canneries had produced more than 8 billion pounds of canned salmon. Today nothing remains of either the cabin or the cannery scow.

The site is on the Sacramento River, opposite the foot of K Street, in Sacramento.

Pacific Salmon

The annual migrations of Pacific salmon up the great coastal rivers and streams of Washington, Oregon, and northern California are one of the great natural phenomena of the Pacific Coast region. All five species of the Pacific salmon—the chum, Chinook or king, silver or coho, red or sockeye, pink or humpback—often travel immense distances to spawn in fresh water over a gravel bottom in the exact streams where they were born. Their spawning nests are known in the region as "redds." Chinook salmon, for example, that have spent a year or more feeding off the extreme western coast of Alaska will journey more than 2,000 tortured miles to the Columbia River, travel over innumerable dams via fish ladders, and swim up through the churning gorges and chasms of the Snake River and on up into the high-country tributaries in Idaho's Rocky Mountains to spawn

Rugged cliffs at Drake's Bay in Point Reyes National Seashore, where Sir Francis Drake is believed to have stepped ashore in 1579 on his journey around the world in the Golden Hind

Pacific salmon during spawning run up a coastal river—chemical imprinting makes it possible for them to return to the streams of their birth, often a hazardous journey of thousands of miles

where they were born and die. They seek out their ancestral waters by means of their extraordinary olfactory sense.

East Brother Island Light Station in San Francisco Bay

The East Brother Island Light is situated on a small, rocky island at the north end of San Francisco Bay. Three wooden buildings comprise the lighthouse group: a turreted light tower with living quarters, a boathouse–engine room, and a combination shop and storage building. Except for the addition of bathrooms and the modernization of the kitchen units in the main building, all three structures are unchanged. Automated in 1969, the light itself is a 1,000-watt bulb magnified into 18,000 candle power visible for 13.5 miles. It serves as a navigational aid to ships entering and leaving San Francisco Bay, at the Oakland docks, and far up San Pablo Bay. The original foghorns were 12-inch, coal-fired steam whistles, replaces by electrically air-powered diaphones and now activated by a fog detector—a stroboscopic sensor.

California's Monterey Peninsula —A Transition Zone

California's beautiful Monterey Peninsula, like Cape Cod on the Atlantic Coast, forms a biological

Point Reyes Light, site of a sea lion rookery; gray whales may be seen from here during their annual migrations

transition zone for Pacific Coast animal and plant life of the north and south regions. It is the southern limit of the endangered arctic sea otter and the northern limit of the California sea lion. The peninsula is the natural habitat of the torrey pine, the rarest tree in North America, and of the moss-draped Monterey cypress, which is found only on the rocky headlands along the Bay of Monterey. This twisted, weather- and wind-gnarled tree numbers only about 10,000 and is found no more than a mile inland from the coast. The mature stands of cypress are draped by a

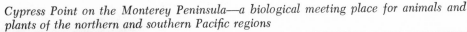

Cypress Point on the Monterey Peninsula—a biological meeting place for animals and plants of the northern and southern Pacific regions

Monterey cypress that provides nesting materials and resting platforms for a host of sea birds

mosslike lichen that smothers its leaf growth, eventually killing the tree. The dead, bleached ghost trees furnish nesting materials and resting platforms for a host of sea birds.

John Muir Ranch National Historic Site

This ranch at Martinez was John Muir's home from 1880 until his death in 1914, and it was there that his most important contributions to conservation and literature were made. Through his many published writings Muir established himself as an authority on the glaciers and mountains of the West and made a major contribution to the forest conservation movement in the United States. He was the first to verify the origin of Yosemite Valley by glacial erosion. His estate consisted of 800 acres on which the Martinez Adobe (Muir's home from 1880 to 1890) and a large Victorian-style house were situated. The two buildings stand today on a portion of the original site. The ranch is at 4440 Alhambra Avenue in Martinez in Contra Costa County, California.

Chaparral—the Pygmy Forest

The chaparral forest, a uniquely Western habitat of low, broadleafed, evergreen shrubs broken here and there by open, barren areas or by low creeping vegetation, occurs on the windswept coasts and the hot, dry hillsides of California and Arizona. California's great chaparral belt, often referred to as the "pygmy forest," was the home of the now-extinct California grizzly and is still the haunt of the endangered California condor, the largest flying bird in the North American hemisphere.

The chaparral forest is the habitat of the Digger pines, blue and scrub oaks, California buckeyes, manzanita, greasewood, certain kinds of yucca, and a host of other shrubs. Some of its dominant species

Yucca and chaparral—a low Western forest of the windswept coast and dry hillsides, once inhabited by the California grizzly and still the haunt of the endangered condor

A branch of manzanita, a member of the heath family and a dominant plant of the coastal chaparral

Townsend Chipmunk

The large, dark six-inch Townsend chipmunk is found only in the humid coniferous forests and adjoining chaparral of the Pacific Coast region. It has a dull gray or yellowish stripe along its sides and back. It is most commonly sighted feeding on the forest floor and the nearby chaparral.

San Andreas Fault and Pinnacles National Monument

The infamous San Andreas Fault is a zone of numerous faults that extends for 600 miles north of San Francisco southward to the top of the Gulf of California, where it disappears beneath the surface of the Imperial Valley. The fault is easily observed from the air and was the cause of the disastrous San

Rare California condor—a living relic of prehistoric times and the largest bird in the United States, with a wingspan up to 11 feet

of birds are the California jay, Steller's jay, California thrasher, bush tit, Anna hummingbird, bell sparrow, house finch, dusky poorwill, valley quail, mourning dove, and yellow-billed magpie. Among the dominant animals are the brown-footed woodrat, brush rabbit, antelope, and ring-tailed cat.

The chaparral is a region rich in flowers. The California poppy is especially abundant here. In the spring it colors hills and fields and roadsides with great masses of brilliant orange. The most common plant of the chaparral is the lupine, which varies from the dwarf kinds in the High Sierra to the arborescent varieties growing close to the ocean. Its pea-shaped flowers range from white through pale yellow, pink, and lavender to deep blue and purple.

California Condor

The largest of the American vultures, the California condor has a wingspread up to 11 feet. This giant black bird has an almost naked head, yellow or orange when seen at close range, and an orange-colored curved beak. An endangered species, it is estimated that there are about 30 pairs in existence from California's Monterey County to Los Angeles County to rugged mountains south of the San Joaquin Valley. This prehistoric remnant once ranged throughout the American Southwest. The Sisquoc Condor Sanctuary is in the San Rafael Wilderness area of the Los Padres National Forest in the Coast Range.

Six-hundred-mile-long San Andreas Fault at the Carizzo Plains, formed about 24 million years ago when two moving tectonic plates—large pieces of the earth's crust supporting the continents—collided against each other

Francisco earthquake of 1906, when the land just west of the fault shifted as much as 21 feet to the north. Geologists report that the block to the east of the fault is moving slowly southward, building up awesome pressure that will result in a future earthquake.

The stark, jagged pinnacles and spires at Pinnacles National Monument are the remnants of an ancient volcano formed some 23.5 million years ago and carved by rain, wind, frost, and heat. About the time this ancient volcano was formed, two moving tectonic plates—large pieces of the earth's crust that support the continents—glanced off each other. One, known as the Pacific plate, thrust itself under the western edge of the continent alongside the North American plate, gouging a long, narrow sliver from the continent and creating a huge 600-mile-long rift known as the San Andreas Fault, which ran through the ancient volcanic rocks. As the Pacific Plate slid to the north, the Pinnacles rock section on top of it also moved 195 miles north of its original location and is still moving at an average rate of one and a half inches a year. The high peaks and slopes of the Pinnacles area have the only complete example of Coast Range chaparral in the national park system, composed chiefly of greasewood and scattered, low-lying thickets of manzanita, buckbrush, toyon, and hollyleaf cherry.

Great Valley of California

The Great Valley of California, one of the largest valleys in the world, is 400 miles long, bordered by the Klamath Mountains on the north and the arid

Tehachapi Mountains on the south and is about 50 miles wide, stretching from the Sierra Nevada on the east westward to the Coast Range. The fertile northern floodplain section, known as the Sacramento Valley, is a low-lying area, broken only by the Maryville Buttes and the hilly, terracelike red lands. The more arid and southern San Joaquin Valley section of the Great Valley is dominated in the south by the domelike Kettleman Hills and braided streams that create numerous island-like tracts.

Maryville Buttes

Rising up to heights of 2,000 feet from the fertile lowlands floodplain of the Sacramento Valley are the eroded, striking peaks of the Maryville Buttes. These volcanic formations lie in the center of the valley and are about 10 miles in diameter.

Transverse Ranges of Southern California

The complex transverse ranges of southern California—which include the Santa Cruz, Santa Ynez, San Gabriel, and San Bernardino mountains—unlike the other north-south ranges of the state, rise in an east-west direction.

Brown pelican, a bulky, dusky-colored bird noted for its great bill and plunging dive, living in colonies on the rocky islands off southern California

Wave-carved rock arch at Anacapa Island, a roosting place for hundreds of brown pelicans

Marine Terraces

One of the most striking features of the southern California coast are eroded marine terraces that reach heights of up to 1,300 and 1,700 feet around San Diego, La Jolla, and on San Clemente and Santa Catalina islands, offshore from the Palos Verde Hills. These steplike terraces, which reach inland as much as 10 miles, were formed during the Pleistocene era and raised to their present altitudes with the uplifting of the coast.

The Channel Islands

The eight Channel Islands rise out of the Pacific off the coast of southern California. Five of these cliff-fringed isles have been set aside as the Channel Islands National Seashore—Anacapa, Santa Barbara, San Miguel, Santa Cruz, and Santa Rosa. Anacapa, the closest island to the mainland, is actually a chain of three separate islets, almost five miles in length. East and Middle Anacapa islands are the smallest and consist of rolling plateaus almost entirely surrounded by 90- to 300-foot-high cliffs. One of the most unusual plant features on Anacapa also grows on the other Channel Islands; this grotesque-looking plant, called giant corcopsis, or tree sunflower, reaches heights of 10 feet in some of the sheltered canyons. In early spring, each plant grows several large yellow flowers. On a clear day the islands often look like a green and yellow table from the distance. The ocean cliffs are the habitat for myriads of western gulls, scoter ducks, cormorants, and brown pelicans. The pelicans, nearly exterminated along the California coast just a few years ago, use the slopes of West Anacapa as their only large rookery on the West Coast of the United States. Other features on the Anacapa chain include massive Arch Rock, the 600,000 candlepower Anacapa Light, and Indian Water Cave.

Wild San Miguel Island, the westernmost of the Channel Islands, is completely exposed to the wind and storms of the North Pacific. Because of its isolation, three of the five major sea bird colonies in southern California live here relatively undisturbed. Cormorants, snowy plovers, gulls, guillemots, and auklets all breed on San Miguel and nearby Prince Island. Point Bennett is a major rookery for elephant seals and northern fur seals. This harsh but beautiful island, dotted here and there by rose mallow, wild buckwheat, and live-forever, is also inhabited by the San Miguel Island fox, red-tailed hawks, barn owls, and peregrine falcons. Beneath the blowing sands are barren fossil forests of wind-carved caliche.

The towering cliffs and canyons of Santa Barbara Island, with its hundreds of offshore pillars, blowholes, coves, and caves, lie 38 miles west of San Pedro Harbor in Los Angeles. The island is the breeding ground of California sea lions, harbor seals, and huge elephant seals, noted for their large, proboscis-like noses—which are inflated during mating season—and weights of up to 6,000 pounds. Today there are only remnants of the giant coreopsis thickets that once covered much of Santa Barbara Island.

Elephant seals on a rocky beach at Santa Barbara Island. These seals weigh up to 6,000 pounds and are noted for their proboscis-like noses, which become inflated during mating season.

PART TWO

Eastern United States

11. New England Woods and Trails —Northern Appalachians

The New England states and the Northern Appalachians offer some of the most beautiful and wild country east of the Rocky Mountains. Beyond the pastoral New England valleys, with their quaint farms, fields, and stone walls, are vast tracts of mixed hardwood and conifer forests, alpine lakes and ponds, and wild northwoods rivers.

The ancient, eroded peaks of the Appalachian chain and the Adirondacks are among the oldest mountains in the world and form the roof of the region. The beautifully wrinkled landscape first began to rise from the ancient Precambrian foundation some 450 million years ago, forced upward from the pressure of the merging continents of North America and Africa. These ancient peaks once soared higher than the present-day Himalayas. After the great platelike land masses of Africa and North America drifted apart, forming the Atlantic Ocean, the Northern Appalachians gradually were eroded over millions of years by wind, water, frost, and the awesome force of the ice sheets.

New England's Arctic Islands

Evidence of the four glacial ages that have occurred in the past 3 million years is scattered throughout the New England countryside. Rounded hills, U-shape valleys, and layers of glacial till attest to the mighty earth-shaping forces of the glaciers, particularly the last one, which retreated from the area about 10,000 years ago. Nowhere is the former presence of the glacier more apparent, however, than on the tops of New England's highest peaks. On the exposed, rocky summits of Mt. Mansfield and Camel's Hump in Vermont, Mt. Washington and other high peaks in New Hampshire's White Mountains, and Mt. Katahdin in Maine, thrive communities of plants whose home range lies far to the north in the windswept reaches of the arctic tundra. These small patches of arctic plants are arctic islands perched high above the deciduous forests of the lowlands and the coniferous realm of New England's uplands and mountain slopes.

As the ice sheets began to creep down from the

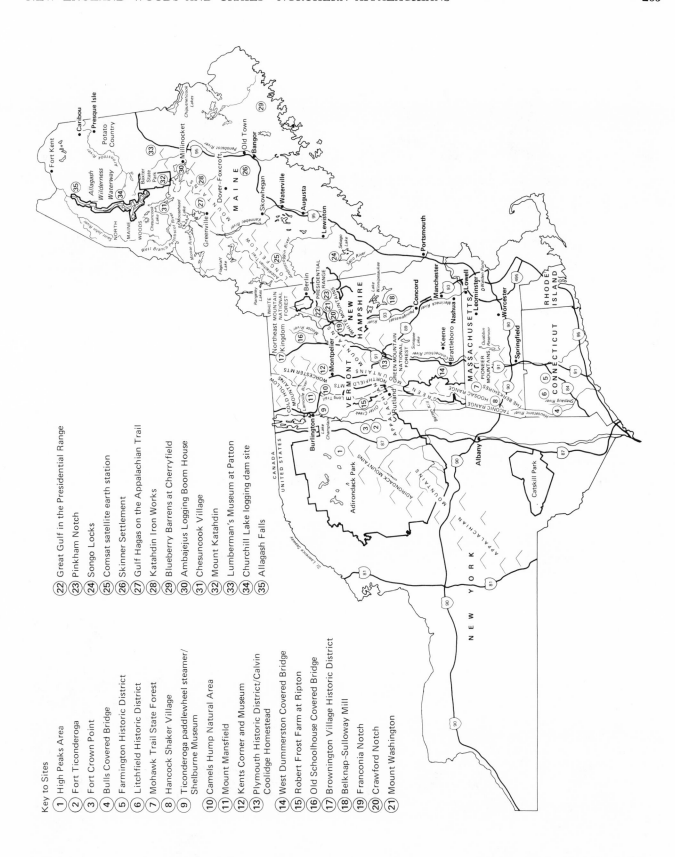

Key to Sites

① High Peaks Area
② Fort Ticonderoga
③ Fort Crown Point
④ Bulls Covered Bridge
⑤ Farmington Historic District
⑥ Litchfield Historic District
⑦ Mohawk Trail State Forest
⑧ Hancock Shaker Village
⑨ Ticonderoga paddlewheel steamer/
   Shelburne Museum
⑩ Camels Hump Natural Area
⑪ Mount Mansfield
⑫ Kents Corner and Museum
⑬ Plymouth Historic District/Calvin
   Coolidge Homestead
⑭ West Dummerston Covered Bridge
⑮ Robert Frost Farm at Ripton
⑯ Old Schoolhouse Covered Bridge
⑰ Brownington Village Historic District
⑱ Belknap–Sulloway Mill
⑲ Franconia Notch
⑳ Crawford Notch
㉑ Mount Washington

㉒ Great Gulf in the Presidential Range
㉓ Pinkham Notch
㉔ Songo Locks
㉕ Comsat satellite earth station
㉖ Skinner Settlement
㉗ Gulf Hagas on the Appalachian Trail
㉘ Katahdin Iron Works
㉙ Blueberry Barrens at Cherryfield
㉚ Ambajejus Logging Boom House
㉛ Chesuncook Village
㉜ Mount Katahdin
㉝ Lumberman's Museum at Patton
㉞ Churchill Lake logging dam site
㉟ Allagash Falls

Above timberline on Mount Washington, highest point in the eastern United States at 6,288 feet, where the greatest wind velocities in the world—up to 231 m.p.h.—have been recorded on its summit

climate moving farther to the south. When the glaciers retreated for the last time 10,000 years ago—just yesterday in the long sweep of geologic time—some of the arctic plants did not accompany them on the entire journey. They paused on the summits of a few New England peaks, where they are found still today.

These plants are called arctic-alpine species because of the alpine areas they recently have colonized. The plants have maintained their foothold in these high places because the climate on the tops of New England's highest peaks is almost identical to the eastern Canadian Arctic. Winters are long and severe, with snow depths of 150 inches or more not uncommon. The growing season in the summer is a brief few months with frosts possible at any time. Precipitation in the form of snow, rain, and fog is an almost constant event, and winds constantly buffet the mountains. The highest wind ever recorded, 231 miles per hour, was witnessed by the staff of the weather observatory on the summit of Mt. Washington in 1931.

The arctic-alpine plants are ideally suited to their harsh mountaintop home. To avoid the persistent winds, most of the plants keep a low profile, like the black crowberry, which rises only a few inches above the surrounding terrain. Many of the plants are evergreens also, allowing them to avoid expending energy in the spring on new leaf production, as deciduous species must do. As soon as the ice and snow have melted in the spring, the evergreens can go to work on completing the important processes of flowering and fruiting in the short period of suitable weather.

north millions of years ago, they scoured the earth beneath them, uprooting trees, plants, and soil along the way. But the vegetation didn't succumb entirely. The slow advance of the ice allowed much of the vegetation to adapt to the cooling climate that preceded the glaciers. The plants of the north migrated steadily southward, one step ahead of the glaciers' advance. When the ice sheets retreated, the process was reversed and the plants began to return to the north again, the cold-adapted species hugging the shadow of the ice mass and plants used to a warmer

Mount Chocorua in the White Mountains, dominating the countryside for 1,200 square miles in northern New Hampshire and part of eastern Maine

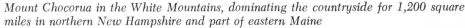

A rural New England village

The Lapland diapensia flowers for a brief 10-day period, so early in the spring that most mountain-goers have never seen the showy white flowers of the plant. They only see the bright green, cushionlike tufts of the diapensia that cover patches of barren ground above treeline.

The thick waxy leaves of the mountain cranberry are an adaption that provides added protection from the drying effect of the constant winds on the open ridges of New England's mountains. The tiny mountain sandwort, a native of Greenland and Labrador, has adapted well to the limits of mountain life; it thrives anywhere there is the barest covering of soil, turning the two-mile summit ridge of Mt. Mansfield into a sea of white-petaled flowers during the months of June and July. Another edge that some of the arctic-alpine species take advantage of is the ability to reproduce vegetatively by means of runners underground, a slower but more dependable method of propagation than sexual reproduction by means of pollen.

New England's high peaks are outposts then for unusual species of arctic plants, reminders of a time when ice masses thousands of feet thick covered the landscape. The plants are hardy, indeed they have to be to survive the rigors of the elements. The only pressure they can't stand is the constant pounding of human feet, which has become a problem in recent years as outdoor recreation has grown in popularity. To protect the plants, Ranger-Naturalists have been stationed during the summer months on most of New England's summits that harbor arctic-alpine vegeta-

tion. With the reminder that careless footsteps can destroy in a moment what nature has taken thousands of years to create, the impact of hikers on the fragile arctic-alpine vegetation has been reduced.

Glacial Lakes and Ponds of the Northern Appalachians

The remote, mirrorlike lakes and ponds that dot the high country of New England are largely the result of the great Pleistocene Ice Sheet which once covered the region and disrupted the normal drainage patterns. The rock debris dropped by the melting ice dammed many of the streams to form lakes, and in other instances, mountain glaciers gouged out basins in the valley bottoms forming deep lakes. Numerous kettle ponds were formed by the melting of isolated ice blocks buried under gravel.

Sugarbush Country

If you drive through Vermont, New Hampshire, or Maine in March or early April, you undoubtedly will see large groves of sugar maples with sap buckets hung like Christmas decorations from their trunks. These orchards of maples are known locally as the sugarbush. Without a sugarbush, there is no sap; without sap, no maple syrup and sugar.

Maple sap can be turned into edible syrup at any time from the first spring thaw until the leaf buds burst. The best, or first-run, syrup is made before the buds begin to swell. The longer the time between the first thaw and the swelling of the leaf buds, the more sap and syrup.

Dotting the sugarbush country of New England are the quaint sugarhouses, usually small rectangular wooden buildings with boards hanging loose on their sides and roofs in none-too-good condition. Each windowless structure has a large solid swinging door at one side and two holes cut just below the peak of the roof at each end to allow for escaping steam. The sugarhouses are sheds used for the boiling operations that turn the sap into fine-grade maple sugar. Against the sugarhouses are placed the storage tanks, usually on the north side to keep the sap cool, near an elevation from which sap can be poured from the gathering tubs or run in by pipe.

Common Trees of Northern New England

The most striking feature of the northern New England countryside is its great forests. Along the granite-bound lakeshores and waterways are stands of majestic white pine, also called the masting pine, because in Colonial times the larger trees of the once-vast virgin forests were marked for masts for the British Royal Navy. These great pines, with their large, 5-to-11-inch cones, have been known to reach

Maple sap buckets—a common sight during early spring along rural roads in New England's sugarbush country

An old white pine in the Maine woods, also called the masting pine, because in Colonial times the larger trees were used as masts for ships of the British Royal Navy

heights of 240 feet and diameters of 6 feet at the base. Pitch pine is often found in large tracts along the north country lakes and cold, meandering muskeg streams. The tall, straight, pyramidlike hemlock, once a valuable source for tanning fluid, is plentiful along the upland ridges and gorges. The beautiful white, or canoe, birch is common along the waterways, where it is found in nearly pure stands covering considerable areas. Red oak, which grows to heights of 150 feet, is found in all areas except the upper reaches of the north country.

The yellow birch is the region's largest native birch. Its loose bark was prized by the oldtime woodsmen as tinder for starting campfires. In the valley woodlands there are abundant stands of sugar, or rock, maple, particularly in the famed sugarbush areas of Vermont, New Hampshire, and Maine. The symbol of the northwoods country is the tamarack, known locally by its Indian name of hackmatack. On the dry hillsides and slopes red spruce, the most common of the region's conifers, grows to heights of 100 feet. It is valued as the principal wood used for paper pulp and spruce gum. White spruce, called skunk spruce by the oldtime loggers because of the pungent odor of its foliage, is also common throughout the region. Balsam fir, grown commercially on tree farms for the

Snow-laden spruce in the Adirondacks—the southernmost tip of the ancient Canadian Shield

Christmas tree trade, grows wild in the damp woods and swampy areas. Its wood, which has no flavor, was once used for making butter tubs. White cedar, with its reddish-brown bark and bluish cones, grows in dense stands in boggy areas. Other commonly sighted trees are the pyramid-shaped red cedar, large-toothed aspen, ironwood, common beech, hornbeam—also known as the water beech—black and white ash, red maple, moosewood, and the graceful white elm. The region's oldest and most valuable trees are the white oaks, with their light-gray bark, which live up to 600 years. Their acorns were used as food by the Indians.

New York's Catskill Mountains

New York State's Catskill Mountains, like the Adirondacks, are not mountains in the sense of being folded structures. Their separate peaks are heights of land between the valleys of a deeply dissected plateau. As the streams that drain the area tend to form straight valleys through the plateau, the mountain peaks have a tendency to form more or less continuous ranges. The lakes of the Catskills are few and small, except for the large manmade reservoirs.

The Adirondacks

The famous Adirondack Mountains, which occupy the northern portion of New York State, are made up of great masses of rocks. Because of their resistance to erosion, they tend to retain their altitude. At the close of the Ice Age, dams of glacial debris were left at the southernmost portions of the mountain valleys, streams were backed up, and the hundreds of blue lakes of the Adirondacks were formed on north-northeast to south-southwest lines. The tallest mountains, the High Peaks, lie about 25 miles west of Lake Champlain. The Adirondacks, which form the southern tip of the ancient rock-bound plateau known as the Canadian Shield, or Laurentian Upland, reach their highest elevation at Mount Marcy (5,344 feet), known to the Indians as *Tahawus*—The Cloud Splitter. Lake Tear-of-the-Clouds lies at the base of the mountain and forms the highest lake source of the Hudson River. On the east, the mountains terminate abruptly at Lake Champlain; on the south and north, they run out in fingerlike ridges; on the west, they end in a peneplain with only minor hills. On the northwest, the Adirondack rocks form a low ridge, which runs north and crosses the wide St. Lawrence River, in which it forms the Thousand Islands.

Barracks at Fort Ticonderoga on Lake Champlain. The fort was captured from the British by the Green Mountain Boys under Ethan Allen in 1775.

The Adirondacks are named after the Iroquois Indian name for the Montaignais, which means "bark eaters."

Fort Ticonderoga

Located at the junction of Lake Champlain and Lake George, Fort Ticonderoga was the key to both Canada and the Hudson River valley in the 18th century. Built by the French and originally named Fort Vandreuil, it was captured by the British in 1759 and renamed Ticonderoga. During the American Revolution, it changed hands many times, first coming into American possession on May 10, 1775, when a small force of Green Mountain Boys under Ethan Allen defeated its British defenders.

The fort, which has been largely restored, is two and a half miles south of Ticonderoga on New York Highway 22.

Fort Crown Point at Lake Champlain

Fort Crown Point, in its ruined but unaltered state, is considered one of the best existing architec-

tural and archeological examples of 18th-century military engineering in the United States. Included in the Crown Point Reservation are the ruins of Fort Crown Point, Fort St. Frederic (a post built and occupied by the French from 1731 to 1759), and the sites of 18th-century French and English villages.

Construction was started on the British fort in 1760 after the capture of the site from the French during the French and Indian War. The fort was called Crown Point or Fort Amherst, after General Lord Jeffrey Amherst, commander of the British forces that drove the French army from the shores of Lake Champlain. Disaster struck the new fort in 1773. The powder magazine blew up, and the entire fortress was damaged by fire. Reconstruction began, but before the work was completed, the Revolution broke out, and the fort was never rebuilt. The post played a minor role in the Revolution as an outpost of Fort Ticonderoga. Eventually the entire area of the fort reverted to pasture and orchard. The moat, wall, most of the stonework, and the five great bastions which extended from the corners are still largely intact, although overgrown with vegetation. Inside are the well-preserved remains of two of the three original two-story stone barracks. The fort is at the Crown Point Reservation, west of the south end of the Lake Champlain Bridge and New York Highway 8.

Snowshoe Hare

This large-footed, orange-eyed hare turns white in winter and dark brown in summer and is found in the coniferous and mixed forest regions of the northern United States from Alaska to Maine. It is the common prey of owls and goshawks and hides in thickets and brushy areas during the day. It feeds at night on twigs, bark, and frozen meat of carrion.

Block House at Fort Ticonderoga

New England Connecting Barn

The New England connecting barn is an excellent example of continuous architecture, common in the New England states. It allowed farmers to accomplish their chores in winter without going outdoors.

Connecticut Barn

The Connecticut barn is made with fieldstone for the lower livestock area with a wagon shed at a right angle. It is common along the wide farmlands of the Connecticut River valley.

Connecticut's Farmington Historic District

Farmington was settled in 1640 and grew rapidly as a distribution point for West Indian products (rum, sugar, molasses) brought by ship to Middletown and carted overland. Business flourished, and the population included tinsmiths, silversmiths, hatters, leather workers, and manufacturers of muskets, buttons, and carriages. Today the historic district, composed of 115 houses predating 1830, harmoniously blends the domestic architecture of four centuries in a relatively small area. The focal point of the community is the

The large-footed, orange-eyed snowshoe rabbit, a favorite prey of the goshawk, wears a white coat in winter and a brown one in summer.

meetinghouse (1771), probably the only original Congregational church in the state with its entry at the side. Two other noteworthy structures are the Union Hotel (c. 1830), a Greek Revival building, and the John Hart House (c. 1740). The historic district is at Farmington in Connecticut's Hartford County.

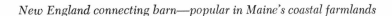

New England connecting barn—popular in Maine's coastal farmlands

Bull's Covered Bridge over the Housatonic River

Bull's Bridge is one of only a few public highway-covered bridges extant in Connecticut. Built on the Town lattice-truss principle, probably in the 1870s, the bridge has been reinforced by additional interior trusswork. The roof is shingled in wood, the sides are sheathed with vertical planking, and the seams are covered by battens. The bridge is about three miles southwest of Kent, Connecticut, in Litchfield County on Bull's Bridge Road.

The Bronson Windmill at Fairfield

The Bronson Windmill, with its large wooden tank, an 80-foot tower, and an underground cistern, is an unusual example of American agricultural engineering. It was the principal water source for the Verna Dairy Farm. Horizontal sheathing covers the framing of the octagonal tower up to the eaves and is then finished with shingles of uniform width in a fish-scale pattern. Squared shingles cover the roof. Above the roof is a circular gallery with a railing from which rises the four-sided tapering timberwork with a cross-braced octagonal platform supporting the axle, crank, and metalwork of the wind-powered wheel. The wooden mill blades, still in good condition, are stored in the tower.

The windmill is at 3015 Bronson Road in Fairfield, Connecticut.

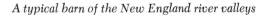

A typical barn of the New England river valleys

A typical New England general store at Old Sturbridge Village, Massachusetts—a representative town of central New England as it might have appeared in the early 1800s

Connecticut's Litchfield Historic District in the Old "Northwest Frontier"

Litchfield is one of New England's best surviving examples of a late 18th-century town. It served as an outpost and trading center on Connecticut's northwest frontier until the late 1700s. The present streets remain the same as the original ones shown on early maps. The four main thoroughfares, stretching toward the cardinal points of the compass, became known as North, South, East, and West streets. At their intersection was the central common, now called The Green, which was the focal point of the town. Litchfield today has a total of 15 frame houses that were erected in the last half of the 18th century. Also situated in this same area are three structures that were built between 1800 and 1828.

Mohawk Trail in the Berkshires

The Mohawk Trail led from the valleys of the Hudson and Mohawk rivers in New York to the valleys of the Deerfield and Connecticut rivers in Massachusetts. Before the permanent incursions of the white settlers, the Mohawks journeyed over the trail to their fishing and hunting grounds. During the French and Indian War, the trail was one of the principal routes of the French and Indians in their expeditions against the English settlements in western Massachusetts. Although most of the trail is no longer extant, this four-mile section of its course along the shores of the Cold River is preserved in its natural setting.

The Mohawk Trail is in the Florida and Savoy vicinity of Berkshire County in Massachusetts.

Hancock Shaker Village in the Berkshires

The Shakers, or United Believers in Christ's Second Appearing, were a religious group founded in England by Mother Ann Lee in 1747. Approximately 18 Shaker communities, distinguished by successful communal living and fruitful agricultural and industrial activity, had been founded in the northeastern and midwestern United States by 1825. The Shaker community near Pittsfield, organized in 1790 and finally dissolved in 1960, reached it high point during the three decades preceding the Civil War. Eighteen remarkably preserved buildings remain from the early period and are now the property of Shaker Community, a nonprofit corporation that maintains them as a memorial to the sect. They illustrate the communitarian life and distinctive architecture and furnishings of the Shakers. The most unusual building in the village is the Round Barn, built in 1826 to house 52 cattle and the hay to feed them. The barn measures about 270 feet in circumference, and it is believed to be the first round barn built in the United States. To date, nine of the buildings have been carefully restored and refurnished.

The village is on U.S. Highway 20, Hancock Turnpike, five miles south of Pittsfield, Massachusetts.

Green Mountains of Vermont

Vermont's Green Mountains, which once soared up higher than the present-day Himalayas, are the oldest mountain range in New England, about seven times as old as the Rockies, which were uplifted some

Old New England farmhouse in the Berkshires. This two-story house in Old Sturbridge Village was a rarity in its time.

60 million years ago. This ancient range, which forms the north-south backbone of the state, was formed during the Taconic uplift about 450 million years ago, when the uplifting Berkshire and Green ranges heaved off great waves of rock, creating the Taconic Range to the west.

Following the series of violent upheavals that formed the range during the shifting of the continental plates—which began when North America and Africa were drifting together to the period when the land masses drifted apart to form the Atlantic Ocean—the mountains were ground down and carved by successive ice ages that began more than a million years ago, creating the present-day remnants of this once-mighty range, a land of rolling hills, pastoral U-shape valleys, drumlins, glacial erratics, and stone-studded fields.

The Long Trail

Vermont's Long Trail winds for 262 miles along the crest of the Green Mountains from the Massachusetts boundary north to the Quebec border. This high-country trail passes through some of New England's finest wilderness areas, alpine tundra, and bog forests. More than 100 spur trails branch off from the main route and provide access to such areas as the Glastenbury Mountain Wilderness Area, the largest remaining primitive area in southern Vermont; the vast wetlands and beaver ponds of the Stamford and Woodford Plateau; Stratton and Bourne alpine ponds; Mt. Mansfield and Camel's Hump alpine tundra areas; and the Willoughby Cliffs Arctic flora on the rocky western slope of Mt. Pisgah.

Shaker round barn, built in the shape of a circle to "keep the devil from hiding in the corners." It represents the early American influence of religion on everyday architecture.

Vermont's ancient Green Mountains, about seven times as old as the Rockies, once towered higher than the present-day Himalayas

Mountain Laurel

Mountain laurel is an attractive pink or white flowered shrub common in cleared areas and in rocky and sandy soil from Maine westward to Indiana and south to Florida and Louisiana. It is also known as big-leaved ivy and poison laurel, because its green parts contain a poison, most commonly eaten by sheep, that causes intense salivation and paralysis.

Wind-stunted red spruce, growing to 100 feet tall on the low hillsides and mountain slopes

Glacial Till—An Ice Age Legacy

The low, rounded, oval hills common throughout the New England countryside, known as drumlins, were formed when the melting glaciers dumped compact deposits of sand, clay, and boulders over much of the region. Elsewhere the ice sheet scattered great numbers of boulders, some of immense size, such as Vermont's Green Mountain Giant near Whitingham, which is 40 feet long, 25 feet high, and 125 feet in circumference; and New Hampshire's Madison Boulder, three miles north of Madison, which is 7,650 tons. Many of these glacial "erratics" form so-called rocking, or balanced, stones, and in some places they form boulder trains that extend miles from their glacial source in the direction of the advance and retreat of the ice sheet.

Robert Frost's Homer Noble Farm

Winner of four Pulitzer prizes and author of 11 volumes of poetry, Robert Frost is one of 20th-century America's most distinguished poets. In the fall of 1940, he purchased the Homer Noble Farm in the Green Mountains. Living and writing there in the summer and fall months until his death in 1963, Frost produced five volumes of poetry. *A Witness Tree* (1942) brought him his fourth Pulitzer Prize in 1943. Additional honors during this period included his

participation in the inauguration of President John F. Kennedy in 1961, a medal awarded by Congress in 1962, and numerous fellowships and honorary degrees. The cabin which he occupied at this farm contains a number of Frost's personal belongings.

The farm is located one mile north of Vermont Highway 125, three miles east of the village of Ripton. Access is by appointment only.

Plymouth Historic District

Plymouth retains the bucolic atmosphere of 19th-century rural Vermont. The village is also distinguished as the birthplace of President Calvin Coolidge. The town is made up of fifteen frame buildings that date from the 1840s or later. Some of the significant structures are the Coolidge Birthplace (c. 1840); the Coolidge Homestead, where young Calvin Coolidge grew up; the Plymouth General Store, owned and operated by John Coolidge, the president's father; the Wilder House (c. 1830); the Brown House, a New England farmhouse built in 1868; the Plymouth Blacksmith Shop; the Plymouth church (1840); the Plymouth Cheese Factory, which is still operative;

and the Plymouth schoolhouse.

The village of Plymouth is in Windsor County, Vermont.

The *Ticonderoga*—The Lake Champlain Paddle-Wheeler

The *Ticonderoga* is the only extant and basically unchanged side-paddle-wheel lakeboat in the United States. From 1906 to 1953 the steamboat plied the waters of Lake Champlain as an excursion boat. The steel-hulled vessel is 120 feet long, with a beam of 57.5 feet. Its exterior has been restored, and the elaborate interior has been refurbished. The *Ticonderoga* is at the Shelburne Museum in the town of Shelburne in Chittenden County, Vermont.

Old Schoolhouse Covered Bridge

The Old Schoolhouse Covered Bridge is the only one in the state with covered walkways on both sides. The rectangular vehicle entrances are flanked by three-quarter arches at the eave line which support

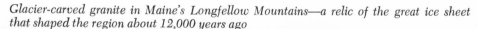

Glacier-carved granite in Maine's Longfellow Mountains—a relic of the great ice sheet that shaped the region about 12,000 years ago

A typical New England meeting house built in 1747

projections of the roof. It stands as built.

The covered bridge is on South Wheelock Road in Lyndon in Caledonia County, Vermont.

West Dummerston Covered Bridge

This is the longest covered highway bridge within the state and is the only known example of the work of master carpenter Caleb B. Lamson surviving in the county. Built in 1872, it consists of two arches resting on a central pier and extends a total length of 280 feet. The structural support consists of two flanking timber Town lattice trusses sheathed with flush boards. Around 1942 the bridge deck was strengthened to accommodate heavier traffic.

The bridge is at Dummerston Center Road and Vermont Highway 30.

Kent's Corner—A 19th-Century Crossroads

Kent's Corner is a relatively unspoiled 19th-century crossroads hamlet that includes the Kent Tavern, built in 1837; the sawmill with its entire hydraulic system intact; and several houses and barns surrounding the crossroads. Numerous foundations for earlier houses and buildings once associated with the hamlet remain.

Kent's Corner is at Calais in Washington County, Vermont.

Vermont's Brownington Village Historic District

Chartered in 1780, this village became an important stop on the stage route between Greensboro, Vermont, and Stanstead, Quebec, in 1791. In 1823 it became the seat of the county grammar school. The pivotal structure in the district is the frame Greek Revival Congregational Church, erected in 1841. Across from the church is the Samuel Read Hall House, a two-and-a-half-story frame house with fan-lighted entranceways on two sides, reminiscent of Connecticut Valley architecture. Also in the district is Prospect Hill, a natural outcropping affording a spectacular panoramic view of the surrounding countryside. The district is at Hinman and Brownington Center roads in Orleans County, Vermont.

Coyotes of New England

The eastern coyote, known in Maine as the brush wolf, is larger in size than its fabled western relative. It reaches weights of up to 50 pounds or more. The eastern coyote slowly trekked its way eastward over the last eighty years or so, spreading from Michigan and Ontario (where it interbred with the Ontario timberwolf, which accounts for its size), into New York State, Vermont, New Hampshire, and Maine.

White Mountains of New Hampshire

The White Mountains, known to the Algonquin Indians as *Waumbeck Methna*, or White Rock, domi-

Covered bridge over a New England stream

A beautiful stand of white birch near Pinkham Notch in the Presidential Range. Also known as canoe birch, the tree commonly grows along New England lakes and streams.

Painted trillium, one of the most attractive woodland flowers of New England, easily identified by the splash of pink at the center of its white flower

nate the landscape for 1,200 square miles in the northern half of New Hampshire and a portion of eastern Maine. The great Presidential Range forms the crown of the White Mountains, sweeping in a great arc from northeast to southeast along a crescent-shape crest of 4,000- to 5,000-foot peaks, culminating at 6,288-foot Mt. Washington. This glacier-carved range, with its granite ridges, narrow valleys, ravines, and cirques, has some of the most awesome alpine weather conditions in the world. Temperatures routinely reach arctic severity and there are days when the gales on Mt. Washington average 120 miles per hour with recorded wind velocities up to 231—the highest ever recorded.

With 46 peaks over 4,000 feet, the White Mountains dominate the White Mountain National Forest, a land area larger than the state of Rhode Island. The Appalachian Trail traverses the crest of the range and provides access to remote glacial tarns, cirques, cols, bogs and, above timberline, to boulder-studded islands of arctic tundra with their dense mats of dwarf black spruces, alpine plants, and lichens.

Alpine Plants of the Presidential Range

A number of arcticlike alpine plants are found on the higher slopes of New Hampshire's Presidential Range, as well as on Maine's Mt. Katahdin and Vermont's Mt. Mansfield. Above the timberline are odd-shaped and ancient gnomelike spruces, and here and there scrub birches and mountain alders bent and matted by the fierce mountain gales. Labrador tea, frequently mingled with large patches of bilberry below the timberline, is said to be the flowering plant

Cog Railroad and "lawns" on Mount Washington. The steam engines of the railway, completed in 1869, climb for 3½ miles to the "top of New England" on a trestle known as Jacob's Ladder.

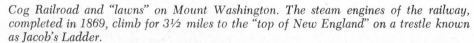

that grows nearest the North Pole. Here and there in the frigid alpine heights are found large mats of Greenland sandwort and beds of three-toothed cinquefoil, bearberry, willow, moss campion, and alpine azalea. Arctic rushes, sedge, and primitive lichens thrive on the summits. On the summit of Mt. Chocorua in the Presidential Range, lichens grow so thick that a heavy rain will change the color of the summit when the lichens change from a brownish gray to green.

The summits of the highest peaks in the Presidential Range were once islands where Arctic fauna were left by the receding ice of the last glacial period. Many of the insects found on these summits are of the same species as those found in the European Alps. Peculiar to New Hampshire, however, are a wingless grasshopper, the White Mountain fritillary, and the White Mountain butterfly. The latter has a sluggish flight and seldom rises more than two or three feet from the ground because of the strong winds that sweep over the peaks. Its caterpillars feed on sedges growing above timberline.

Felsenmeer—Boulder Fields of the High Peaks

The eerie, lunarlike areas of Felsenmeer—German for a "sea of rocks"—on the high peaks of the northern Appalachians were formed during the severe climate that followed the last Ice Age. These huge boulder fields were formed by the cracking action of frost, which broke apart the bedrock of the ancient summits into jagged rock piles. Remnants of this phenomenon, known as rock glaciers, are slowly scraping

their way down the valleys, continually eroding the heights of the summits.

Treeline of the Northern Appalachians

Because of the arcticlike weather conditions near the summits of the northern Appalachians, where subzero temperatures occur regularly and winds up to 100 miles are recorded every month on Mt. Washington, for example, the treeline ends at approximately half the height it does in the Rocky Mountains. Along the Appalachian Trail, as it winds over the high peaks of Maine and New Hampshire and along Vermont's Long Trail, the hardy, stunted, subalpine trees reach up to about 5,200 feet in the shelter of the lee slopes and up to about 4,800 feet on the wind-whipped northern and western slopes. At the edge of the treeline, stunted communities of black spruce, white birch, and balsam fir grow in windblown mats, often a century old, that reach heights of three to four feet in the lee coves and up to a foot in the severe exposed areas.

"Lawns" of the White Mountains

The flat, severely frost-eroded areas near the summits of the White Mountains, where waving patches of sedge grow in the soil formed in the rock fields, are believed to be remnants of an ancient erosion surface that was pushed up above the New England Upland during the uplifting of the range. These rocky lawns, thought to have been formed during the Cretaceous

Great Gulf on the eastern rim of the Presidential Range, the largest of New England's rocky, glacier-carved bowls, or cirques

Maine's Longfellow Mountains, the ancient eroded hills of the northern Appalachians that culminate at Mount Katahdin

Whiskey jack, also known as the gray jay and Canada jay, a joyous, noisy camp thief that has long been a welcome companion of the northwoods loggers

period, are found at heights of 1,000 to 1,200 feet above the level of the surrounding New England Upland. The stone stripes found on the lawns in the Presidential Range were formed by the eroding force of frost.

Gulfs of the Northern Appalachians

The rock-strewn glacial cirques of New Hampshire's White Mountain Range and Maine's Katahdin Range are known locally as gulfs. These U-shape bowls were formed about 12,000 years ago during the last Ice Age, when huge amounts of snow accumulated in the leeward ravines, where it was packed down by its own weight to form glaciers and carve the amphitheaterlike gulfs.

The most prominent glacial cirque in the northern Appalachians is New Hampshire's Great Gulf, a designated wilderness area that covers 5,552 acres along the eastern rim of the Presidential Range in the White Mountains. Boulder-rimmed Spaulding Lake, a mountain tarn, lies in the bowl of the Great Gulf.

Notches of the White Mountains

The wide valleys, or notches, in the White Mountains, such as Pinkham Notch and Crawford and Franconia notches, were created by the moving ice sheet of the last Ice Age. The ice sheet ground off the sides of many of the former stream-carved V-shape valleys, changing them to the broad U-shape cross-section of glaciated valleys you see today.

Indian Pipe

This 10-inch plant droops to form a pipe shape when in blossom but later becomes erect when its fruit is fully formed. Its stems, which are pinkish-white when young and black when old, grow in clusters from its spreading, matted masses of roots. It is a common sight in moist, shaded woodlands from Maine to California and Washington.

Whiskey Jack of the North Woods

The gray jay, also known as the whiskey jack, moose hawk, camp robber, or Canada jay, is a commonly sighted denizen of the coniferous forests of northern New England and the Great Lakes. This tame, fearless bird, which looks like a giant chickadee, is a constant companion of campsites in the north woods, where it will make away with just about anything it can carry off—from a slice of bacon to a chunk of morning-caught trout, to a bar of soap or pouch of tobacco. A joyous thief, the gray jay, with it's whistlings, chucks, squalls, and screams, has long been a welcome companion of north country loggers and trappers.

New Hampshire's Belknap–Sulloway Mill

A survey of the architecture of textile mills carried out by Old Sturbridge Village indicates that the Belknap-Sulloway Mill may be the oldest surviving structure of its type in the area. Built on a small scale,

Appalachian Trail footbridge in the Longfellow Mountains

the mill is representative of rural manufacturing operations. A wooden mill of the Meredith Cotton and Woolen Manufacturing Company preceded this structure. Situated on the banks of the Winnepesaukee River, the mill is brick and wood. The present cupola appears to be a reproduction of the original. Inside very little has been changed. Ceilings are open on each floor revealing the joisted flooring of the level above. The mill site formed the nucleus for present-day Laconia.

The mill is on Mill Street in Laconia in New Hampshire's Belknap County.

Maine's Mountains and the Appalachian Trail

The ancient eroded hills that form Maine's portion of the Appalachian Range extend northeastward from the thick spruce forests at Mahoosuc Notch in the White Mountains to Old Speck, Saddleback, Sugarloaf, and Bigelow mountains, culminating at Mt. Katahdin, a monadnock that rises 5,268 feet above a lake-dotted forest plain in the heart of the Maine Woods. Scoured by the glacial sheets of the Ice Age, these summits rise like sentinels above seemingly endless forests, wild rivers, and granite-rimmed, mirror-like lakes, from the Rangeley lakes to island-dotted Moosehead Lake, the largest in New England.

The Appalachian Trail, a 2,000-mile wilderness footpath, begins at Mt. Katahdin and follows the crest of the Appalachian Range southwestward through New England to Georgia. The extremely rugged Maine portion of the trail winds through the Maine Woods for 280 miles, with spur trails providing access to remote ponds and wilderness areas, including the spectacular Gulf Hagas, where the West Branch of the Pleasant River roars through a slate gorge in a three-mile-long series of rapids and falls.

The terrain of the state of Maine, the largest of the New England states, might best be described as a broad plateau running from the western boundary to the northeast across the Rangeley and Moosehead Lake regions, gradually sloping eastward toward the Penobscot River basin and northward to the wide St. John River. Toward the southeast, the plateau slopes gradually to sea level. Occasional mountains rise from the plateau to heights of 5,000 feet in the central and western part of the state. Mount Katahdin, for example, which rises to 5,267 feet, appears as high as some of the peaks in the Rockies, which rise from a plateau 5,000 to 7,000 feet above sea level.

Spread over the land surface is a remarkable system of eskers, or kames, known locally as horsebacks or hogbacks. These are long ridges of gravel deposited by the receding glaciers of the last Ice Age. They extend from one mile to 150 miles in length. In many cases the state's road network follows their course.

Arnold Trail to Quebec

American strategy in the early months of the Revolutionary War was designed to cut off British troops in Canada under Sir Guy Carleton from other forces in the colonies. George Washington ordered 34-year-old Colonel Benedict Arnold to lead an expedition northward through Maine to attack Quebec City. General Richard Montgomery led a second group of men simultaneously against Montreal. The route through Maine was regarded as the shortest and most direct to Quebec. Arnold headquartered at Fort Western in Augusta, departing from there on Septem-

Beaver—the sound of its powerful tail slapping the water is often heard on the high-country ponds and streams

ber 25, 1775. His march from Fort Western to Quebec took 45 days and covered 180 miles. Ultimately the expedition proved unsuccessful because Quebec was too heavily garrisoned. The Arnold Trail follows the Kennebec River, past Wyman and Flagstaff lakes along the Dead River and Chain of Ponds to Quebec, Canada.

Skinner Settlement at Corinth Village

The Skinner Settlement arose from the arrival of Daniel Skinner as the first permanent settler in 1793. Skinner opened a tavern in his log dwelling shortly after arriving in the area, and the town began to develop. Principal structures include the Daniel Skinner Farmstead, a one-and-a-half-story Cape Cod farmhouse, a 40-by-60-foot barn, and various outbuildings; the General Isaac Hodsdon Farmhouse, a one-and-a-half-story Cape Cod house with five fireplaces around a central chimney; the Skinner tavern, a one-and-a-half-story Cape Cod structure with a connected el and small barn; and the Hodsdon General Store, a two-story frame structure with a cross-gabled roof. In addition to these major structures, there are several supporting structures including five other farms or homesteads.

The village is three and a half miles west of East Corinth in Penobscot County, Maine.

Maine's Shrubs and Wildflowers

Most brilliantly colored flowers and blossoming shrubs common to Maine's northern temperate zone can be found along the coast rather than in interior regions. Mountain cranberries grow abundantly in the Mount Desert region, the Cranberry Isles, and the large bog cranberry is widely distributed in marshlands over the state. Among the more widely distributed species of the Mount Desert region are American wood anemone, New England aster, seaside aster, swamp aster, wild bergamot, American bittersweet, black-eyed Susan, bluet, tall meadow-cup, clover, sweet clover, white ox-eye daisy, and dandelion. Others are blueflag, Canada goldenrod, salt marsh goldenrod, fragrant goldenrod, blue-eyed grass, orange hawkweed, false heather, hepatica, and Indian pipe. Familiar are jack-in-the-pulpit, Joe-pye, seaside knotgrass, sea lavender, and wild lily-of-the-valley. The most common wayside lilies are the Canada lily and American turk's cap. Mayflower, the trailing arbutus, ushers in the spring. Of the many orchids native to Maine, the best known are arethusa, common and yellow lady-slippers, rose pogonia, and the small

Raven—common to the wild areas of New England, often sighted soaring like a hawk above coniferous forests and rocky coasts

purple and white orchids.

Devil's paintbrush grows in profusion in fields. Other bright flowers are the scarlet pimpernel, the sea or marsh pink, the swamp pink, pitcher-plant, and the rare pokeweed. Best known of the wild roses are the swamp rose, meadow rose, and wild brier rose. Purple trillium and painted trillium, yellow violet, common purple violet, blue marsh violet, and sweet white violet, the giant sunflower, sweetbrier, woodbine, and yellow wood-sorrel are all commonly found.

Blueberry Barrens of Eastern Maine

Near the quaint village of Cherryfield in eastern Maine's Washington County are vast blueberry plains, or barrens as they are called locally, that cover a 200-square-mile plateau, where a large percentage of the nation's blueberries are grown. Slow meandering streams wind through the low blueberry bushes, which in mid-June are covered with inverted bell blossoms. The blueberry harvesting begins in August and lasts through September. The Downeasters work from dawn to sundown raking, winnowing, and boxing the berries to be trucked to the canning factories. The virgin spruce that once covered the barrens was cut in the early 1800s, and the blueberry bushes quickly covered the sandy soil. The land is burned over every three years to stimulate new growth.

Blueberries on the barrens of eastern Maine

Mt. Katahdin—Sentinel of the Maine Woods

Far to the north of Maine's lobster and dory country rises Mt. Katahdin, like a sentinel in the wilderness, dominating the smoke-colored hills, forests, lakes, and wild rivers of the north Maine Woods. Katahdin is actually a range of peaks—more than 46 rise above 3,000 feet—preserved within the wilderness boundaries of 200,000-acre Baxter State Park. The often cloud-shrouded peaks of Mt. Katahdin are a perfect example of a monadnock, an isolated remnant of a former highland that rises above a plain. From its base Katahdin embraces several life zones: vast boulder fields on the Hunt Spur; a high, bleak plateau known as the Tableland about a mile from the top; a giant glacial cirque known as the Great Basin rimmed by a treacherous mile-long ridge known as the Knife Edge; upward dotted by mirrorlike glacial tarns; past the treeline to a windswept land of alpine tundra.

Alpine Flora of Mt. Katahdin

Maine's massive Mt. Katahdin, a monadnock rising above a forest plain, is the highest point in the state. At 5,267 feet, it is the first point in the United States upon which the rising sun shines. Alpine flora grows on the arcticlike upper reaches of Katahdin. Often stunted, wind-blown mountain white birch and mountain alder are found there, and among the more hardy plants in the alpine zone are Lapland diapensia, alpine bearberry, Greenland starwort, lance-leaved painted-cup, alpine trailing azalea, alpine holy-grass, narrow-leaved Labrador tea, blue spear grass, Lapland rosebay, and fir club moss.

Katahdin Ironworks

Moses Greenleaf discovered iron ore on Ore Mountain in 1843. Two years later, the Katahdin Ironworks was incorporated. The works operated, except for the years 1858–1863, until 1890, smelting surface limonite into large ingots or pigs. From 1873 to 1890 200 workers were employed, and the complex included two large boarding houses, a town hall, a school, post office, company store, and two farms. Only one of the 14 original charcoal kilns, or beehives, and the tower of the blast furnace remain.

The Ironworks is five miles north of Brownville Junction on Route 11, then six miles on a gravel road in Maine's Piscataquis County.

Moose of the Maine Woods

Often standing as high as seven feet at the withers and reaching weights of up to 1,800 pounds, the moose is a common sight along the lakes and rivers of the Maine Woods. The state's moose population—numbered in excess of 16,000—is the largest in the United States outside Alaska. This majestic symbol of the north country, which favors succulent water plants, was described by the famous northern explorer David Thompson as "the noblest animal in the forest."

Fiddleheads—New England's Gourmet Greens

Fiddleheads, unopened fronds of the ostrich fern, are harvested during the spring run-off in Maine, New Hampshire, and Vermont along the moist forest floors and stream banks. When boiled, these fast-growing greens are a local favorite. For centuries Maine's Indian tribes have prized the ferns as both food and medicine.

Songo Lock at Sebago Lake

Songo Lock, located between Long Lake on the north and Sebago Lake on the south, was originally built in 1830 of stone masonry with two wooden gates, each in two sections. During the 1830s and 1840s the canal enabled farmers, lumbermen, manufacturers, and merchants to ship and receive goods from Portland cheaply, swiftly, and efficiently. With the coming of the railroads in the mid-19th century, however, traffic on the canal declined steadily until it ceased entirely in the late 19th century. In 1911 the lock was rebuilt by the Sebago Improvement Company, which increased its length and width, replaced the original

Mount Katahdin, a mile-high monadnock—an isolated rock mass rising above a forested plain. Known to the Indians as "The Great One," it's the first point in the continental United States upon which the morning sun shines.

gates with iron gates, and faced the stone masonry with concrete. The lock is in constant use from late spring through the fall.

The lock is south of Naples, one mile off Maine Highway 114 in Cumberland County.

Northwoods Logging Camp

Throughout the north country regions of New England and the Great Lakes states, logging operations may be seen in progress, although not as extensively as some years ago. The northwoods were once

the domain of rugged lumberjacks, many of French-Canadian origin, who were supposed to "sleep in trees and even eat hay if it was sprinkled with whiskey." These were the legendary woodsmen of the Maine Woods, known locally as "moosetowners" and "Bangor Tigers," who never took off their red flannels from the time they hit camp in the fall until they came out in the spring; who never shaved; who chewed great chunks of tobacco and who could roll off a lusty, hair-raising stream of profanity.

Real bean-hole beans were important in the feed of lumber camps. Pots full of pork and beans were kept all night over rocks placed in the ground and brought to white heat. These were eaten with biscuits made by the camp cook, or cookee, who rose or fell on the quality of his output.

Logging today is an efficient, highly mechanized industry. Tractors, hauling logs over well-built roads, have replaced the oxen and the river drive. The keen spirit of competition has gone from the river drivers who once prided themselves on their strength, speed, and agility. Theirs was the job of following the drive of logs down the river to untangle the jams. Crawling across the logs in their calked boots until the key log was found and loosened, and then making their way back to shore as the logs started again, was no feat for the timid.

Ambajejus Boom House—The River-Drive Days

The Ambajejus Boom House is one of the most significant sites connected with the Penobscot lum-

Moose in Maine, where the nation's largest moose population outside Alaska roams

White-tailed deer on a Maine lake

bering industry in the 19th century. There has been a boom house on the site since 1835, although the present one-and-a-half-story shingled structure was erected about 1907. Near the Penobscot's mouth are two islands which were used as anchoring points for booming the logs driven down the river. Once collected the boom was towed down the chain of lakes to the North Twin Dam, where they were then sluiced to the Great Northern paper mills at Millinocket and East Millinocket. The boom house was used until 1971, when the drives ended due to practical and conservation reasons.

The boom house is about 11 miles northwest of Millinocket on Ambajejus Lake on the West Branch of the Penobscot River.

Chesuncook Village in the Maine Northwoods

Chesuncook Village is representative of the Maine Woods settlements which attracted people to the lumbering industry and then dwindled when the lumbering techniques changed. The village predated by a few years the heavy logging which began in the area around 1856. Today the village consists mostly of one-and-a-half-story frame houses and several buildings which were owned by the Great Northern Paper Company and used until 1971 in connection with the West Branch log drive. Although the village is nearly deserted during the winter, the Chesuncook House (1863), visited by Thoreau during his canoe trip down

Remote Chesuncook Village, visited by Henry David Thoreau during his canoe trip down the West Branch of the Penobscot River. He wrote of his experience in the classic Maine Woods.

The Allagash Wilderness Waterway flowing through historic logging country of the North Maine Woods

Screech owl—a small, mottled denizen of the lakeshores, woodlands, and old orchards, fearless in defense of its nest

the West Branch Penobscot River, the most notable structure in the village, still caters to the needs of canoeists and sportsmen in the area.

The village is on the northwestern shore of 20-mile-long Chesuncook Lake in Piscataquis County, Maine.

Allagash and St. John Wilderness Waterways

The vast logging country of the 2.5 million-acre North Maine Woods Tract, once the hunting grounds of the Abenaki Indians inhabited by herds of woodland caribou, wolves, and wolverine, is slashed by two of the last remaining wilderness rivers in the north-

The 14-foot-high Allagash Falls. The Allagash, from the Indian word for bark cabin, was the first river in the Northeast designated as a National Wild and Scenic Waterway.

eastern United States: the Allagash and St. John.

The Allagash, Indian for "bark cabin," rises in a series of lakes above prong-shaped, 20-mile-long Chesuncook Lake and flows north for 92 miles through a historic logging region to its confluence with the St. John River. Several historic remnants of the great logging era of the virgin white pine forest are still visible along its course: old wooden logging dams, the abandoned Eagle Lake and Umbazooskus Railroad, with its two rusting locomotive hulks, and the wooden remnants of a former 6,000-foot-long log tramway on the piece of land dividing Eagle and Chamberlain lakes, south of the 40-foot Allagash Falls.

The Allagash, the first river in the Northeast to be protected under the National Wild and Scenic Rivers System, is protected from logging for 400 to 800 feet back from both banks.

But more remote is the St. John, a big, often treacherous wilderness river, reminiscent of those in northern Canada, which flows from its headwater ponds in the most distant corner of Maine for 450 miles into the Bay of Fundy, making it the longest river in the Northeast next to the St. Lawrence. The upper St. John flows through a series of churning rapids and island-dotted channels, looping north through remote logging country, spiked here and there by giant, solitary white pines that tower like lonely spires above the spruce and fir forest and past remnants of former logging camps and bridges before it loops east to form part of the United States–Canada boundary.

Osprey nest high up on a dead snag above a Maine pond

Osprey—The Fish Hawk of the Northern Lakes and Streams

The large, long-winged osprey is a common sight hovering over the lakes of northern New England in search of trout, smelt, or landlocked salmon. When it sights a fish near the surface, it plunges feet first into the water, seizing the fish in its powerful talons.

12. Rocky Shore

THE shoreline of Maritime Canada and the United States south to Cape Cod is a land of fog, violent "Nor'easters," lighthouses, and rustic fishing villages. It is predominantly rocky, in vivid contrast to the vast stretches of wide sand beaches reaching almost unbroken from New York to the southern tip of Florida.

The granite-bound coast of Maine is a glacier-carved world of endless fascination, with a maze of offshore islands, headlands, steep-walled cliffs, and mountains. Cadillac Mountain on Mt. Desert Island rises to an elevation of 1,532 feet above the sea—the highest mountain on the Atlantic seaboard north of Rio de Janeiro in Brazil. The low-lying southern extremity of the Maine shore from the Cape Elizabeth area south to Cape Cod in Massachusetts is a land of salt marshes, dunes, sandy beaches, and rocky promontories.

The building of the ancient coastal mountain ranges and the melting of the glaciers about 10,000 years ago created the rounded granite masses, the drowned shoreline following up and down the jagged deep valleys, and mountains sloping abruptly into the sea broken by north-south valleys. As the glaciers melted and the water level of the sea rose, it eventually created a submerged coastline that appears today as though it had been combed down into the sea. As one moves southwestward from central Maine along the New England coast toward Cape Cod, the rate of submerging land is slower and salt marshes and sand beaches become more common.

Drowned Coast of New England

New England's drowned coast, with its hilly fingers of granite reaching into the sea and deep tidal rivers, was formed during the last Ice Age. The pressure from the weight of the great ice cap caused the mountain ranges to be submerged under the ocean. With the retreat of the glaciers, the submerged land rose slightly and exposed the formerly submerged mountain summits, which today form the coast's offshore islands. This beautiful rockbound coast is dotted with quaint fishing villages and natural harbors.

Key to Sites

1. St. Croix Island National Monument
2. Moosehorn National Wildlife Refuge
3. Acadia National Park
4. Rockport Historic Kiln Area
5. Penobscot Marine Museum
6. Bath Historic District
7. L.L. Bean Store; Maine Coastal Desert
8. Portland Head Light
9. Rachel Carson National Wildlife Refuge
10. Grand Banks Schooner Museum at Boothbay Harbor
11. Salem Maritime Historic District

Labrador Current

The incredibly rich sea life of the northeast Atlantic coast is a direct result of the Labrador Current, a massive flow of icy, oxygen-rich water that flows down from a long channel between Greenland and Canada. Its silica-rich waters support a staggering population of one-celled microscopic diatoms. The diatoms in turn provide the foundation of an active food chain that sustains a myriad of ocean life forms from lobsters, to cod, to seals, to whales. During Colonial times lobsters and Atlantic salmon were so abundant off the New England coast that they were harvested by the wagonload.

The Labrador Current is a recurrent process that actually begins in the warm tropical waters of the Equator. There the warm expanding waters cause the surface level of the Atlantic to rise slightly, forcing the equatorial waters to run "downhill" toward the North and South poles. As the equatorial current moves northward, it cools off, contracts, becomes heavier and heavier as it moves north, and increases its capacity to hold oxygen and carbon dioxide. In the northernmost latitudes, the extremely frigid, heavy waters descend to the ocean floor and, in a never-ending cycle, flow southward again as the Labrador Current.

Coastal lighthouse shrouded in fog created by the meeting of the frigid waters of the Labrador Current and the warm waters of the Gulf Stream

Fog Banks

Anyone who has spent a summer on one of Maine's coastal islands knows what it is like to walk through a closed foggy world where one can barely see ten yards ahead. Except for the comforting honk of the distant foghorns, it's an eerie, lost sensation.

The giant fogbanks that lie off the coast of Maine and Canada's Maritime Provinces are caused by the meeting of the frigid Labrador Current and warm Gulf Stream off the coast of Nova Scotia. The farther up the coast one moves from Maine, the thicker the fogbank, as the warm moisture-laden summer air reacts with the cold Labrador Current and condenses into a thick fogbank. With a slight change in the wind the fogbank will move closer and closer to the coast, eventually turning it into a gray ghostly world.

The moisture-rich fogbanks create magnificent, lush coastal woodlands with thick carpets of bayberry, ferns, lichen-covered rotting stumps, green tufts of pincushion and haircap moss, and dense stands of spruce and pine draped with gray strands of old-man's beard.

Maine's Coastal Deserts

During the thousands of years of the Ice Age, the weight of the glacier depressed New England below its former level. As water from the melting ice poured into the ocean, its level rose, and it flooded the coastal lowland up into the larger valleys. The receding flood left a layer of sand over the clays along the coast, creating sand plains. In some places along Maine's coast, notably at Freeport and Leeds, this sand, freed of vegetation and blown by the wind, has formed so-called deserts.

Forest Edge of the Rocky Shore

Along the rugged drowned coast of New England, forest plants are often found only a few yards from the high-tide mark. Along the rocky shore of Maine's Mt. Desert Island at the granite-bound edge of the woods are found the pale gray thickets of bayberry, often only a few strides landward from the tidal pools, with their low-branching gnarled stems and clusters of bunchy pale gray berries. Here and there are patches of prickly pasture juniper with shaggy evergreen leaves and white-flecked blue-gray berries, as well as low-growing thickets of raspberry, lowbush blueberry, evergreen bearberry, and dwarf, heathlike mats of black crowberry, a common plant of Newfoundland and Labrador.

Coastal Acadian forest and mountains—a meeting place of northern and temperate Gulf Stream climates, creating a range of habitats similar to a Newfoundland shore, a New Jersey pine barren, or a summit in North Carolina

Sea Stacks

The reddish gravels washed down to the coast from the ancient Appalachian Mountain ranges were buried and formed red conglomerates that have been sculptured by waves and wind into caves, arches, and isolated, oddly shaped sea stacks. Eventually the force of the sea will collapse the stacks, forming new ones as the waves pound the slowly receding coast.

Basalt Columns

The chimneylike columns of basalt occasionally seen along the rugged north Atlantic coast were formed by the rapid cooling of lava some 175 million years ago. Exposed to the eroding effects of the frost and sea, the columns are broken by the roots of trees that grow in pockets of soil that collect in the cracks and crevices.

Common Beach Plants—Zone Between Forest and Sea

Beyond the rocky, high-tide level are the bright green clusters of glasswort and sea blite; the reddish

Just beyond these colorful thickets and open fields of small pioneer spruce, cinnamon fern, Indian paintbrush and goldenrod is the spruce forest. The moist, shady spruce woods are a maze of lichen-spotted trunks, with beds of lady ferns, bracken, and polyody fern, and a needle-covered forest floor of pincushion and haircap mosses, mushrooms, and lichens.

Wind Pruning

When the prevailing offshore winds along the rocky coast are unhindered by natural obstacles, they create a phenomenon called "wind pruning." The constant force of the winds trims the tops of bushes and shore trees in a flat horizontal plane ascending from the gnarled, stunted bushes at the edge to the shore, which receives the full force of the winds, to the full-grown trees a few hundred feet landward.

Galls or Burls

Burls or galls are enormous bulges from the trunks of forest trees. These protective tumorlike growths are caused when an insect or fungus gets under the bark.

Rugosa, or wrinkled rose, common along the seashore thickets of the rocky coast

orach, with its arrowhead-shaped leaves; the flat, broad blades of cordgrass; and the primitive colorful pioneers, the lichens, coating the rocks.

On the uppermost edges of the beach, beyond the narrow high-tide zone, are the thick growths of tough, resilient colonizers—beach pea, seaside goldenrod, the parasitic common dodder, mullein, curlal dock, and ragweed.

Tidal Pools

The fascinating plants and animals of the shallow tidal pools trapped among the rocks between high and low tide are never exposed to the drying effects of the wind and salt and receive more sunlight per day than they would if they lived below the low-tide level. Among the most common inhabitants of the tidal pools are the sea anemone, limpets and chitons, crumb-of-bread sponge, and tangled, fluted threads and cellular sheets and tubes, and cloudy masses of numerous green seaweeds.

Salt Marshes of New England

The high, northern salt marshes of the New England shore are dominated by salt hay (*spartina patens*), which unlike the pure meadows of tall, coarse cordgrass of the mid-Atlantic tidal bays is low-growing, with thin wiry stems and blades that form a springy turf of swishing mats. Until the early 20th century salt hay of the northern marshes was mowed

to feed the livestock of New England farms. In autumn the feltlike mats of salt hay decay, the cordgrass dies, and the straw floats off on the tides forming windrows along the marsh margins.

The salt hay mats prefer high elevations that are not submerged by the flow of the tide for as long a period each day as cordgrass, which grows nearer water along the marsh shore and creeks. Closer to the woodlands on the landward margins of the marsh, the salt content of the soil is reduced and vegetation includes seaside plantain, a thick, grasslike, low-growing herb that replaces the salt grass as one of the dominant plants.

The salt marshes and their low-tide mud flats are rich in a variety of life, including clams and quahogs, razor clams, and the burrowing clam worm, lugworm, and blood worm. The northern salt marshes are also the feeding grounds of mink, raccoons, muskrat, and hundreds of species of waterfowl, waterbirds, and shorebirds ranging from great blue herons to the snow goose to terns to willets, gyrfalcons, and gulls.

Maine's Sandy Coast

Unlike the hilly, granite-bound coast of much of northern New England, the western portion of the Maine coast from Cape Elizabeth westward to the Piscataqua River is a gentle rolling sand plain dominated by white sand beaches and numerous large salt marshes, low hills, and cool sphagnum bogs. It includes the vast stretches of marshlands in the Rachel Carson National Wildlife Refuge.

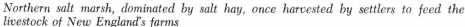

Northern salt marsh, dominated by salt hay, once harvested by settlers to feed the livestock of New England's farms

Portland Headlight at Cape Elizabeth, Maine

Cape Elizabeth's Portland Headlight

Portland Headlight is one of the four lighthouses in existence whose construction was authorized by President Washington. It has never been rebuilt. John Nichols and Jonathan Bryant, local masons, built the 72-foot tower of random stone rubble. The present keeper's quarters replaced the original quarters which were built in 1816. It is a two-and-a-half-story frame building finished in clapboards and shingles with a combination gabled and hipped roof.

The lighthouse is located at Portland Head off Shore Road.

Bath Historic District and Iron Works

The area known today as Bath was first settled in the 17th century, but not until 1781 did it become a town. From the 1820s through the late 19th century shipyards lined the waterfront and Bath ships played an important role in West Coast and Far East trade. During this prosperous period, many fine houses and churches were constructed, including the Greek Revival Patten-Smith House (c. 1820); the Italianate Larrabee-Newell-Simpson House (1850); and the Greek Revival Swedenborgian Church (1843). During World War I, the Bath Iron Works produced four Navy destroyers, and during World War II one-fourth of all the Navy's destroyers were built there.

Penobscot Marine Museum

The Penobscot Marine Museum commemorates the age of sail and steam and Maine's period of seagoing prosperity. Searsport was a leading port in the mid-19th century, with as many as eight shipyards in operation at once. The entire Penobscot Bay area from Wiscasset to Calais shared in the maritime trade and its profits, and today Searsport ranks second to Portland as a Maine port city. Included in the museum are four buildings: the Searsport Town Hall (1854), a one-and-one-half-story Greek Revival brick building; the Captain Merithew House (mid-19th century), a two-and-one-half-story gable-roofed brick dwelling; the Nickeis-Colcord-Duncan House (1860), a frame, clapboard-sheathed structure; and the Fowler-True-Ross House (1825), also frame, gable-roofed, and two and one half stories high. All contain objects relating to sea trade and shipbuilding. The museum is located on Church Street in Searsport.

Rockport Historic Kiln Area

Lime produced in the state of Maine was shipped all over the United States during the late 19th and early 20th centuries. Maine lime was used to build the Capitol in Washington, D.C. The coastal towns of Thomaston, Rockland, Rockport, and Camden were the chief producers. Kilns were employed to process quarried limestone. Prior to the Civil War most kilns were made of stone and used wood as fuel. Later coal and coal gas replaced wood, which led to the development of iron kilns. Competition from other lime-producing states eventually forced the Rockport kilns out of business.

Seven kilns remain on the site, located on Rockport Harbor at the mouth of the Goose River.

A "Down East" fishing village harbor and wharf on Mount Desert Island

Acadia National Park and Mt. Desert Island

When Samuel de Champlain discovered Mt. Desert Island in 1605, he named it "Isle des Monts Deserts" because of its barren, glacier-scoured mountaintops. The island and its glacier-formed mountain range, with eight peaks over 1,000 feet high, form a portion of Acadia National Park, a 54-square-mile preserve along the drowned coast of eastern Maine that includes the remote Isle au Haut. The park contains an interesting variety of flora and fauna of the rocky Atlantic shore. Among its fascinating geological formations is the Thunder Hole, near Newport Cove, a tidal cavern noted for its 40-foot high spouts of water. Nearby Cranberry Isles were the sites of battles between Indians and Vikings more than 1,000 years ago.

Somes Sound Fjord of Mt. Desert Island

Somes Sound, which reaches for seven miles into Mt. Desert Island like a narrow arm, was gouged out to a steep-walled depth of 150 feet by the massive Ice Age glacier that once buried Mt. Desert under a mile of thick, jagged ice fields. The Sound, the only true fjord on the Atlantic northeast coast in the United States, was once a river valley reformed by the glacier and flooded by the sea.

Acadia National Park's Big Heath

In the vicinity of Ship Harbor, in the southern part of Mt. Desert Island, is the Seawall Bog, or the Big Heath, an extensive coastal sphagnum mat with sheep laurel and leatherleaf and stands of stunted black spruce on and around the bog. It is the breeding site for Lincolna sparrows and the summer home of common yellowthroats and palm warblers.

Indian Relics of Mt. Desert Island

Three tribes of Indian peoples successively occupied the islands and mainland of Maine's Acadia National Park. The oldest group left relics and tools that were made some 6,000 years ago. They were enterprising fishermen, for in their refuse heaps the bones of tuna have been found. Tuna are fish of the pelagic waters, the open sea, that must have been pursued by these aboriginal tribes in sea-going canoes.

Another group, the ancient Red Paint People, lived there as long as 3,000 years ago. They made pottery and slate tools, and sprinkled their dead with red and yellow ochre, traces of which have been found in ancient gravesites.

Some thirty Red Paint graves have been recorded in Maine, all but two along stream banks or on the coast. Most of the graves contained knives, spear-points, sinkers, adze blades, fire-making tools, slate pendants shaped like whales' tails, and sharpening stones. No one has ever unearthed sites of their villages. We do not know where these people came from, how long they existed, or why they disappeared. One theory is that they inhabited regions of the Maine coast now sunk beneath the sea, and that their villages were borne away by a tidal wave. Geological discoveries of the sinking of the Maine coastal level seem to bear out this hypothesis.

At the time the first Europeans arrived, the Abnaki Indians occupied the Maine coast. They were forest Indians, skilled in the use of birchbark. It was they and their kin who taught Europeans to build that useful craft, the birchbark canoe. In summer the Abnaki left their permanent mainland villages and came to Pemetic, their name for Mt. Desert Island. They fished and gathered shellfish and travelled to the cranberry bogs on the outlying Cranberry Isles. For hundreds of years they continued this way of life, as deep-shell heaps discovered near the island's tidal flats testify. Then the Europeans arrived. By the 1840s the Abnaki wigwams had vanished from Acadia.

Life Zones of Acadia National Park

Acadia is a crossroads of land and sea, of northern and temperate zones, of mountain and valley, of lake and forest. Each of these distinct environments forms a specific life zone for different plant and animal species. Approximately 50 species of mammals and 275 species of birds inhabit the park during the course of the year. More than 500 kinds of flowering plants and numerous types of mosses, lichens, and lesser plants adorn its hills and valleys. Its water zones, both marine and freshwater, swarm with billions of organisms from microscopic algae to whales.

The Sea

Life patterns in the sea are determined primarily by temperature and depth. The Gulf of Maine, which is the marine environment of Acadia, is cold and shallow—two conditions that make for an abundance of marine life. A marine animal familiar there, one noted for its voracious appetite, is the American lobster, which lives on the ocean bottom, inshore in summer, but in deeper, warmer water in winter. Well armed for attack or defense, it hunts by stealth and speed, depending much more on chemical senses and touch than on sight. Living fish—flounders and other bottom feeders—are its principal prey. But crabs, other lobsters, and clams, which it digs out efficiently, are also

part of its diet. In turn sharks, cod, and other bottom-feeding fish prey on the lobster. People, with their baited traps, are the lobsters' greatest enemy. Commonly sighted mammals of the Gulf of Maine include the harbor porpoise, whales, and harbor seals.

Tide Zone

This zone is located between the tide lines along the 44 miles of rocky shorelines in Acadia, which are noted for their cliffs, boulder beaches, and tide pools. Twice daily the tide zone is alternately exposed to air and covered by water. Strong wave action brings food and oxygen. Because of this the living population is more dense there than in any other zone of the sea, with members of the brown, green, and red algae families predominating. Abundance of life does not mean that life is easy in the tide zone. It is a rigorous environment. Living things must function in both air and water. They must withstand the full force of the waves. And because of its great profusion, life is fiercely competitive.

A major problem for the tide zone animals is ex-

A tidal pool at remote Isle au Haut

posure to the air. They die if they dry out. The barnacle has solved this problem by developing a tight-closed shell. Within this bastion, it is bathed in a few drops of captive sea water, so that it can remain out of water 95 percent of the time. Barnacles are found at the highest levels of Acadia's tide zone. Other living organisms are less resistant to drying and remain at lower levels of the tide zone. This is why there are definite stratas of life along the shoreline: barnacles in one band, rockweed in another, and so on.

Sea snails are among the most common tide-zone animals in the park. They are instructive of the way marine organisms have made the transition to life on land. Three species of periwinkles found at Acadia illustrate this beautifully. The smooth periwinkle keeps close to the low-tide line and is submerged most of the time; the common perwinkle lives where high tide comes only a brief period each day, but it must still deposit its eggs in the sea; the rough periwinkle bears its young alive and can remain out of the water for weeks at a time, and is found along the higher bands of the zone.

Acadian Forest Zone

The forests of Mt. Desert Island have a special quality. Here the northern coniferous and temperate deciduous forests meet and overlap, bringing to the island an exceptional variety of trees, shrubs, and herbaceous plant life. There are places in the park that could be a Labrador shore, a pine barren in New Jersey, or a mountain summit in Tennessee.

Three mature forest types—spruce and fir, northern hardwood, and a mixture of the two—make up most of the forest growth within the park. Another major but transitory type is the shrub and sapling growth which has pioneered into the 10,000 acres of parkland burned in 1947. About 1,500 plant species are found in the park, but the majority of these are not common. The shrub oak, for example, is found on Acadia Mountain but nowhere else in the park. Among the dominant tree species are eastern white pine, pitch pine, red spruce, white spruce, eastern hemlock, balsam fir, northern white cedar, quaking aspens, big tooth aspen, gray birch, white birch, American beech, pin cherry, red maple, striped maple, and northern red oak.

Wildflowers are plentiful beginning in early spring, when trailing arbutus, or mayflower, blossoms. The procession of flowers continues until autumn, when the witch-hazel scatters its seeds from the bloom. The spring display of rhodora in the open wetlands is matched only by the autumn colors that inflame Acadia's deciduous plants.

The forests support approximately 50 species of mammals, including raccoon, mink, beaver, snowshoe hare, and white-tailed deer. After the great fire of 1947 which destroyed 10,000 acres of mature park forest, the deer population shot up as the burned-over areas were replaced by shrubs and saplings. But as the deer population overtook the natural food supply, eating more than the browse plants could produce by new growth, the harsh winter seasons brought near-famine conditions. This ecological imbalance had no solution except starvation. To avoid this the park service removed the deer to restore the balance.

Mt. Desert Island and Its Eroding Shore

Acadia National Park, located chiefly on Mt. Desert Island, is a land of mountains, forests, lakes, and seashores. Forest-covered granite mountains descend to the ocean's edge; Somes Sound, a fjord, almost bisects the island, and small glacial lakes dot the valley. Three-meter-high tides reveal four different life zones populated by plants and animals best adapted to a specific zone.

Lashing waves, sudden in their violence and relentless in their persistence, are only the most obvious of the forces that have created and shaped this land. The land offers but temporary resistance to rain, wind, frost action, chemical reaction, and the pounding waves of a tireless sea.

Out of Acadia's dim past, traced back by geologists some 400 million years, comes a story of forces that alternately built up and tore down the landscape.

Lush growth of ferns on the Acadian forest floor

Mount Desert Lighthouse with Cadillac Mountain in background

Ancient streams and seas eroded highlands and deposited sediments, which later became layers of rock. Millions of years passed. Deposition, erosion, uplifts, depression, and invasions of molten rock followed one another. Mountains sank beneath the sea only to be replaced by new land forms heaved upward by the unstable earth. About 275 million years ago a great pool of molten rock began to undermine the earth's crust above it. In time this crustal roof collapsed, and the molten rock rushed upward to fill the space. This intrusive rock cooled slowly, to become the coarse-grained pink granite that formed the Mt. Desert Range—a nearly continuous ridge of pink granite running east and west.

About one million years ago, a thick layer of ice formed over eastern Canada. As the weight of the ice increased at the center, the edges of the layer flowed outward, molasseslike. When the ice cap finally reached Mt. Desert Island, the solid east-west barrier of the granite range lay directly across its course. As pressure from the north mounted, the ice sheet heaved itself up and finally over the crest of the range. It sought out stream courses, widened them, and carved the U-shape valleys seen today. Rock debris in the grip of the ice sheet worked like a giant sheet of sandpaper and rounded off the north slopes. Once the ice covered the ridge, it moved onward, tugging at the south face of the mountains. This powerful quarrying action, aided by cracks and faults in the rock, created the steep cliffs and giant steps on the southerly faces of the mountains.

The Mt. Desert Range was buried to depths of up to 5,000 feet. Under this gigantic glacial load the land yielded. When the massive ice cap finally melted, the once unbroken ridge emerged as a line of separate peaks broken by the deep valleys now occupied by lakes and the Somes fjord.

Even today Acadia is being shaped by geologic forces, primarily the sea. Each wave sets in motion a new sequence of events. Nature's grindstone, the sand and rocks of the shoreline, swirl and rub against the land. Caves and chasms along the shore are cut a little deeper. Cliffs are undermined and eventually collapse into the sea. What it erodes from one shore, the sea may deposit on another. Sand Beach is actually a sandbar built by the waves across a longer cove. The section of the cove closed off by the sandbar is now a lagoon. One day piled high and steep by the waves, the next washed broad and flat, Sand Beach is an excellent place to observe short-term geological change.

Back from the sea other kinds of erosion take place. Streams cut into the rocks. Frost cracks them. Chemicals dissolve them. Pounded by the sea, eroded from within, Mt. Desert Island is slowly wearing away. Ironically the forces that are destroying this land and bringing it down to the level of the sea are the very ones that have created its beauty.

Damariscotta Indian Oyster Shell Heaps

Artifacts and shells unearthed by archeologists during the past 100 years indicate that these oyster shell heaps are probably 2,000 years old. Owing to ecological changes oysters have not lived in this area for over 300 years, and in recent times commercial interests have disturbed the heaps in the process of converting the shells into lime. Some loss has been caused by tidal erosion. Estimates for the total area of the shell heaps (as great as 5 million cubic feet) place them among the largest in the world.

The shell heaps are located on the Damariscotta River north of Damariscotta.

Maine's Cranberry Isles

The beautiful Cranberry Isles, just west of Mt. Desert Island in Acadia National Park, are named for the vast cranberry marsh spreading over 200 acres on Great Cranberry Island, where birds rare to this latitude nest. Leach's petrel, seldom seen except in the pelagic waters, lays its eggs there. Colonies of herring gulls and common terns have their rookeries along the rocky cliffs and shores.

Tidal Bores of Moosehorn National Wildlife Refuge

The tidal bores at the Moosehorn National Wildlife Refuge on Cobscook Bay in eastern Maine often exceed 20 feet and are the largest in the United States, with the exception of Alaska's Cook Inlet.

St. Croix Island National Monument

In 1604 on St. Croix Island the French attempted to found a permanent settlement in the New World. The expedition had a complement of 120 men, but during the extremely severe winter of 1604–1605, one-third of the party died. After this experience the settlers moved in 1605 to Port Royal, Nova Scotia. From St. Croix the French explorer Samuel de Champlain set out in 1604 on his explorations of the coast of Maine. The settlement plan included a fort, storehouse, blacksmith shop, meeting hall, kitchen, and bake shop, plus houses and a chapel.

This historic island is in the St. Croix River on the international boundary near St. Croix Junction in Maine's Washington County.

Fishing Villages of Maine's Coastal Islands

Maine's quaint coastal fishing villages, with their green dories and stacks of lobster pots and net-drying racks, have long supplied some of the state's most important exports. Captain John Smith, who carefully noted the variety of fish found there, established fishing villages at Monhegan Island in 1614. It is thought that Basque, Portuguese, Spanish, and Breton fishermen were taking rich cargoes of codfish from these waters at the time Columbus discovered America.

Abandoned lighthouse at St. Croix Island—discovered by the French explorer Samuel de Champlain in 1604

Mañana Island, which lies adjacent to Monhegan, has unusual four-foot long scratches on its ledges that have been used to support the belief of those who think that Norsemen visited the island about 1000 A.D.

During summer fishing smacks unload cargoes of green lobsters along the waterfronts of Monhegan Island and the isles of Casco and Penobscot bays. Most of the lobsters caught average about 10 to 11 inches in length, which is considered the standard market size; but occasional prodigies turn up. The largest lobster caught along the Maine coast, taken in Casco Bay in the late 1800s, weighed 36 pounds. As lobsters increase in size, their hard shells split up the back and are sloughed off, to be replaced by new ones. During the time of these periodical sheddings, the lobsters take refuge in crevices under stone or in the heavy eel grass. Though unwieldly in appearance, the lobsters move rapidly, by preference backward. The large anterior claws, used to crack clams, are strong enough to take off a man's finger.

Lobster Country

The lobster is perhaps the most famous trademark of the rocky New England seashore. In Colonial times lobsters were so abundant along the New England coast that farmers used them for fertilizer and an occasional lobster up to five or six feet long was not uncommon.

These creatures of the ocean bottom can live up to depths of 1,000 feet and are most often sighted along the shore hiding among the kelp and rocks at low-tide mark. There, usually at night, they try to locate a fiddler crab, worm, or mollusk, or a small lobster by probing with their long antennae, aided by the thousands of tiny hairs on their bodies that act as sensing mechanisms. Each lobster has two claws: one claw with white rounded humps used to crush its prey and another claw with sharp points used to cut and tear. If an appendage is lost, a healing mechanism seals the opening and prevents it from bleeding to death. If one of its original claws is lost, it is replaced with a regenerating one.

The green molting lobster that hides in the rocky crevices at low tide develops a new shell over every part of its body within its old shell. At the proper time the molting lobster bends itself into a "V," splitting the old shell open at the back of the carapace, and pulls itself out of its old shell, front and tail ends first. When free of its old shell, it increases in size, its new, soft shell covering every appendage, from the surface of its eyeballs to its antennae and the tiniest hairs. The lobster stays in hiding until the new tissues harden and returns to its hunting life among the rocks and weeds of the ocean floor, 50 percent larger than it was before the molt.

By the end of its first year, a lobster will have molted about 15 times and be one inch long, after which it grows and molts more slowly. At the age of

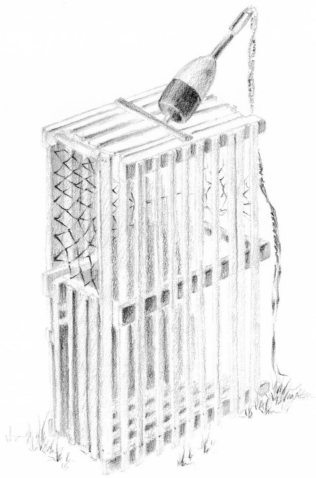

Lobster pot and buoy

Setting lobster pots off the Maine coast

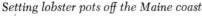

five, it will molt once a year and weigh one pound. Estimates of the ages of the giant lobsters caught along the rocky New England shores in former times vary from 50 to 100 years and over. It's entirely possible that a monster lobster living today in the depths off the Maine coast was alive during the Civil War.

Lobster Pots and Buoys

The stacks of sun- and salt-bleached lobster pots stacked high beside the wharves of New England's coastal fishing villages are moved out to sea in the fishermen's dories with the seasons, following the on- and offshore movements of the lobsters. Their set location is marked by means of a painted, top-shaped buoy attached to the submerged pot, usually at depths of 50 to 100 feet.

The lobster pots have been developed by trial and error over many generations. Typically they are designed as a rectangular box made of wooden slats about three feet long with a funnel of netting leading in at each end, terminating in a four-and-a-half- to five-inch hole. The voracious scavenger crawls through the hole to get at the bait fastened to the floor in the interior of the trap. Usually a ripe cod head or trash fish is used as bait.

One of the most popular designs in the lobster pot and dory country of the rocky New England coast is the "parlor" pot, which is divided by netting into a parlor and a kitchen area where the bait is. The rate of escape from parlor pots is lower than most other designs. The pots are connected to a top-shaped wooden buoy, painted in the fisherman's colors, by a long tethering line or warp. The fisherman's string of pots is known as his set, which he hauls up to check daily (weather permitting). Each pot has a trap door in the top, which allows the fisherman to reach in and pick up his catch by its back. The lobster is then held down on the dory's coaming while a small peg is stuck into the joint of the large claw.

Maine and Massachusetts have strictly enforced laws that forbid keeping lobsters that have a carapace (the area between the back and the tail) less than three and three-sixteenths inches long. Maine also has a large-size limit that requires that all lobsters with a carapace over five inches be thrown back to protect the breeding stock.

Birds of Maine's Coastal Islands

The islands off the Maine coast, isolated by strong tides and frequent curtains of fog, form one of the great rookeries of North American seabirds. Green Island, six or seven miles out from Cliff Island in Casco Bay, is a renowned breeding place for American herring gulls. In years past the herring gulls have decimated nesting colonies of double-crested cormorants on the Penobscot Bay islands. Inland great numbers of herring gulls breed on Gull Island in Moosehead Lake, and many others on the islands of the Rangeley lakes. The black guillemot breeds on many of the offshore islands and the American merganser is common along the coast during winter. Also a common visitor to the coastal islands is Leach's petrel, the northern raven, great black-billed gulls, and double-crested cormorants on the Penobscot Bay islands.

American eider ducks, the largest of Maine's sea ducks, are seen frequently near the outer islands in January. Merrymeeting Bay is one of the most important way stations for the Canada goose in spring, where they gather in great numbers from early March until the middle of May. The common tern breeds on most of the state's grassy outer islands as do the roseate tern, and puffins, known as the sea parrot, especially "down east" in the Bay of Fundy on Canadian-owned, treeless Machias Seal Island. Razor-billed auks inhabit the same island. A colony of the rare laughing gull is found in Penobscot Bay and a large breeding ground for the great blue heron is found on Bartlett's Island near Bar Harbor. Black-crowned night herons and the osprey or fish hawk are frequently seen along the coast.

Many of the islands are uninhabited or have lighthouses only and are accessible only to experienced navigators.

Island Hummocks

Many of the rugged, often fog-bound wilderness islands off Maine's rocky Atlantic coast have large treeless grassy plateaus that consist of large hummocks of grass broken everywhere with holes created by puffins, herring gulls, razorbills, great black-backed gulls, common eiders, Leach's storm petrels, and Arctic terns, who use the islands as nesting grounds.

Maine's Puffin Colonies

The puffin is related to the now-extinct great auk. Efforts have been made in recent years by the National Audubon Society to restore the once-great nesting colonies of puffins on the remote wilderness islands off the Maine coast, especially on Eastern Egg Rock in Muscongus Bay and at Matinicus Rock, a giant mass of granite rising 60 feet above the high-tide mark, one of eight islands comprising the Matinicus Archipelago south of Rockland. Known as the clown of the sea, this silly-looking aclid has a short,

Puffins—the sea parrot, related to the extinct great auk, which nest on remote, rocky islands off the Maine coast

stocky, stub-winged figure, brilliant red and yellow triangular bill, and an unusual call that sounds like *Hey, Al.* Its range in North America extends from Greenland south to Maine. Puffin nesting rookeries have a barren otherworldly appearance with seemingly countless mounds of dirt piled all around from the digging of their burrows, guarded by scores of these comical creatures, and mounds of matted grass and rocks covered with patches of grayish guano. A powerful swimmer and diver, the puffin can travel underwater at top speed harvesting up to 28 fish in its sawtooth bill without losing others it has already caught. Outside of man, its most common enemy is the black-backed gull, who will fly into a group of puffins, appear to go to sleep, lulling them off guard, and then strike an inattentive bird, carrying it off.

Life Zones of the Rocky Shore

The life zones are indicated by horizontal bands of color along the rocky shore and are best seen during low tide at exposed areas where the land slopes deeply downward into the water.

Spray Zone

The spray zone of the rocky shore appears as a gray or black stain just below dry land and above the high-tide line. It receives its link with the sea from the spray of waves and is populated by the blue-green algae, among the earth's most ancient plants. They are protected from the drying effect of the sun and wind by gelatinous sheaths. A black lichen that looks like a tar spot also grows in this zone.

Periwinkle Zone

Immediately below the primitive black bank of algae is the periwinkle zone. This zone is formed by the hordes of dark, small snails—rough and smooth periwinkles, the largest of which are seldom more than half an inch long—that live at the upper limit of the monthly high-tide zone and move up to browse on the film of blue-green algae. These indicators of the northern rocky coast are gastropods with single spiral-shape shells, and can endure prolonged exposure to air, like most land snails. The rough or common periwinkle gives birth to live young.

Barnacle Zone

The barnacle zone of the rocky shore is formed by a whitish horizontal band of acorn-shape northern rock barnacles that cling tenaciously in colonies to the

Periwinkle—a commonly sighted snail of the tidal zone, usually seen clinging to beach rocks and wharf pilings

wave-pounded rocks. Exposed to the air twice daily during low tide, they feed on tiny plant organisms washed in with the high tides.

Rockweed Zone

The rockweed zone is just below the gleaming white zone of barnacles. It is a broad yellowish-brown zone, a fertile, rubbery world formed by rockweeds or sea wracks that cover the intertidal rocks, chiefly in high-tide pools. The rockweed zone is inhabited by a host of crabs, snails, mussels, and dog whelks. Rockweeds are commonly used by New England fishermen to pack lobsters and clams for shipment.

Irish Moss Zone

The reddish Irish moss zone at the lower intertidal pools is dominated by the flattened blades of Irish moss, tufted red weed, and green sea lettuce, which provide a welcome relief to hikers from the slippery tangles of rockweeds on the upper tidal zone. These flattened mats are inhabited by a myriad of starfish, rock and green crabs, and sea urchins. Also common in this zone are dulse, which look like deep red sassafras leaves, and laver, a reddish tissuelike plant that grows singly or in small groups.

Reddish, flattened mats of Irish moss at low tide

Kelp Zone

The kelp zone is the lowest intertidal zone of the rocky northern shore, at the very threshold of the sea. It is dominated by the wide blades and straplike fingers of horsetail kelp, which gently sway with the ebb and flow of the tidal movements. This dark brown, yellowish life zone is the habitat of sea anemones, marine worms, starfish, jellyfish, crabs, the prickly green sea urchins, and sea cucumbers.

Knotted Wrack

Knotted wrack is a brown seaweed that is a common sight covering the intertidal rocks just below the bank of rockweeds along the rocky, boreal coast from Long Island Sound north through Maine. The long fronds of this slippery olive-colored weed have numerous knots, which are air bladders placed along the narrow, ribless branches that also have rabbit-eared one-to-two-inch branchlets.

Sea Lettuce

Sea lettuce is a commonly sighted shallow-water seaweed found from the boreal, northern beaches south to the tropics on exposed rocks, to quiet, brackish pools. It forms a translucent, light green sheet that is often ruffled along the edges.

Northern Rock Barnacle

The familiar northern rock barnacle is a creature of the rocky, northern coast from Maine south to Delaware, where it competes with the blue mussel and rockweeds on boat bottoms, wharf pilings, and intertidal rocks. It is generally replaced southward by the ivory barnacle. A relative of shrimp, barnacles feed on small organic matter floating in the water. Its shell is firmly anchored to a rock, wharf piling, or boat bottom by a cement it secretes.

Common Periwinkle

The often sighted common periwinkle snail of the tide zone is seen on beach rocks and wharf pilings from Cape May, New Jersey, northeastward through Maine. It had a solid shell, reaching lengths of up to one inch, with a glossy yellow, red, black, or brownish coloration with dark bands. It feeds on plant life with a tongue twice its body length. Its eggs are laid in masses on rocks and weeds. They are able to go for long periods without food or water. The rough periwinkle, noted for its taller spire, lives on a higher band of the tide life zone and produces its young live instead of laying aquatic eggs.

Gulls of the Rocky Shore

The most conspicuous gulls of the New England coast are the common herring gull and its larger companion and relative, the great black-backed gull. Called the minister by fishermen, the black-backed gull has a wing span up to five feet and preys on small ducks, shellfish, fish, and the eggs and young of other gulls. White-bodied, with black wings and back, it nests in mixed colonies with the ever-present herring gull, often on offshore islands during the spring and early summer.

New England's Gray Seal Colonies

A small colony of gray seals lives on Nantucket Island off the Massachusetts coast. Larger ones live on the islands around Maine's Grand Manan Island,

Herring gulls, the common "seagull" sighted along the coast. It often drops clams and mussels on the rocks to crack the shells and get a quick meal.

where they can be seen in summer sunning themselves on the rocky cliffs and isolated beaches. Its primary habitat is the Canadian Maritime provinces. The gray seal is also called a horsehead because of the long sloping nose of the adult male.

Bracken

Bracken is a common fern of the Atlantic coast, often sighted in the open woods and stream banks. Its young fronds, known as fiddleheads, from their shape, are partially covered with silvery gray hair and are a local delicacy in Maine, where they are gathered with enthusiasm in early spring. They are often sighted in the rich coastal woodlands along with cinnamon fern, huckleberries, beds of blue flag, and wild roses.

Seashore Lichens

The bright splashes of color on the rocks, stumps, and woodland floor near the rocky shore are the primitive crusts of lichens. Among the rocks just above the high-tide mark are found the small gray or black crusts of crustose lichens and the orange splotches of *Xanthoria*, the most common lichen of the rocky coast.

Farther inland, among the moist, thick seashore woodlands, are found the gray-green smears of parmelia on the tree trunks, pale brown strands of old-man's beard or usnea moss hanging from the spruce boughs, the red-capped British soldiers sprouting up from the rotting, dead timber, and miniature gardens of tiny gray goblet lichen. On the glacial boulders and rock ledges grow large greenish mats of another lichen known as rock tripe.

Starfish of the Low-Tide Zone

Along the low-tide zone of the rocky shore three types of starfish are often sighted: the small, fragile brittle stars, which move by means of their long flexible arms; the voracious orangish-purple five-armed common starfish; and the bristly sea urchin, often camouflaged by the small pieces of seaweed and shell debris it places on its back. Both the common starfish and sea urchin move by means of hundreds of tubelike feet with suckerlike discs attached to the tip. The common star and brittle star both have the power to regenerate their arms, which provides them with the means to escape anything that grasps it by its arms.

Old-Man's Beard

Old-man's beard is an unusual lichen made of branching, radiating fibers, often green to straw-colored, and found in forests and woodlands hanging on bark and branches of living or dead trees. Its fruit is shieldlike with a light disk.

Crabs of the Rocky Shore

The commonly sighted crabs of the Irish moss and kelp zones along the rocky shore are the green crab, rock crab, and Jonah crab. They are constantly on the move along the shoreline in search of food. The ill-tempered green crab is the most common New England shore crab as far north as Nova Scotia's Bay of Fundy. The yellowish rock crab and its larger, rougher relative, the Jonah crab, with which it is easily confused, are common among the rocks, tide pools, and crevices in jetties. They are often caught in lobster pots.

Glacier-carved bluffs on the Maine coast

Mussel Beds of the Intertidal Zone

The large black areas in the Irish moss and kelp zones are usually massed numbers of the dark blue mussels that have seeded down and attached themselves to the rocks or other mussels by means of a web of strong threads which they secrete, known as byssus.

Kelp

Kelp is a leathery, brown seaweed and is the dominant plant of the rocky shore at and below the low-tide mark. A mature kelp may be several feet long and weigh as much as 25 pounds. They anchor themselves to the sea bottom by a cluster of bladelike branches that radiate outward from a powerful single stalk that can withstand the force of the breakers against the rocks.

Harbor Seal

Common place names along the Maine coast—Seal Harbor, Seal Island, Seal Cove—attest to a once-large population of harbor seals. Although shy of people, their sleek bobbing heads are often seen in the waters among the jagged granite rocks of Maine's coastal islands and Canada's Maritime Provinces, where they breed in large rookeries among the colonies of puffins, Arctic terns, and razor-billed auks. Evolved from an earlier land ancestry, their limbs are only partly modified as flippers. Much of their time is spent basking on the rocks and slopes of the offshore islands.

Moon Jellyfish

The most common jellyfish of the rocky shore are the moon jellies, which grow to a width of about six inches and drift inshore around the end of August in the scores of thousands as they become enfeebled by the increasingly colder water temperature and resemble little mounds of Jell-O. Their stings are gentle and they can be handled with little hazard.

Sea Cucumbers

Sea cucumbers are odd creatures of the kelp zone and tidal pools and are related to starfish. They may be up to a foot or more in length with rows of small tube feet. They have a leathery, flexible surface and

Derby Wharf Lighthouse at Salem Maritime Historic District, Massachusetts, built in 1871

feed on organic debris by means of the moplike tentacles around their mouths.

Cormorants

The long-necked gooselike black birds flying over the shore are most likely double-crested cormorants (derived from the Latin name *corvus marimus*, meaning "sea crow") and locally called shags. These expert fishermen are related to the pelican and have orange throat pouches and tufts on their crowns, which are seldom visible. Cormorants nest in spring on the rocky offshore islands and migrate in large, V-shape flocks. Unlike geese they are silent during flight.

Massachusetts' Salem Maritime National Historic District

Founded in 1626, Salem owed its beginnings to its seaboard location 20 miles northeast of Boston, Massachusetts. As early as 1643 fish, lumber, and provisions were being shipped from Salem to the West Indies in exchange for sugar and molasses. During the Revolutionary War and the War of 1812, the port aided the American cause as a privateering center. Derby Wharf was the center of this activity. On any given day a dozen vessels—schooners, brigs, and ships—alongside the wharf might be loading tea, fish, or timber bound for Boston, Kingston, or Savannah or unloading silk, iron, or pepper from Kronstadt, Bombay, or Sumatra. As a fishing village, haven for privateers, and mercantile center, Salem was the embodiment of its exotic motto: "To the farthest port of the rich East." Near Derby Wharf is the customs house where Nathaniel Hawthorne worked as Surveyor of the Port of Salem from 1846 to 1849. The building, its occupants, and the surroundings are described in the introduction to *The Scarlet Letter* (1850). The Derby House, built in 1761, and the Hawkes House, constructed in 1780, also recall the seaport's zenith.

13. Mid-Appalachian Mountains

IN striking contrast to the high, wind-swept peaks of the northern Appalachians and the Adirondacks, the central Appalachians, which stretch from New Jersey south through Pennsylvania to northern Virginia, consist of long parallel ridges separated by a series of narrow, deep valleys. These uniform ridges, or hogbacks as they are called locally, resemble a series of great waves upon the land, familiar to anyone who has driven through the tunnels along the Pennsylvania Turnpike. Within this region of "the Endless Mountains," as it was known to the early colonists who settled here in what was then the western frontier, the bold escarpments of the Catskill, Pocono, Allegheny, and Cumberland mountains form the longest and most nearly continuous topographic feature in the United States.

Geologically, the oldest part of this region is the Piedmont Plateau. This land originally was part of a chain of lofty mountains stretching from a more extensive land mass in the north that was eventually worn down by running water. To the west was a vast bay with its western shore in what is now Ohio, its northern shore the Canadian Shield, and the ancient Piedmont Mountains its eastern boundary. In this great bay were deposited the dead animals and plants of the Paleozoic era, forming the almost unbroken bituminous coal fields of western Pennsylvania. During a series of violent upheavals, which exerted enormous pressure against the old rock formations of the Piedmont Plateau, a series of subparallel chains that we know today as the Alleghenies was formed.

The great coal deposits of western Pennsylvania were formed at a time when the entire Appalachian region from New York to Alabama was covered with vast forested swamps. In the shallow waters plants grew, died, and settled to the swamp floor. This layer upon layer of rotted plant life was compacted into peat, which later changed into coal, which eventually changed the face and history of the nation from an agricultural to an industrial society.

Within this land of endless mountains are the crossing at the Delaware River where Washington led the Revolutionary troops to their victorious march on Trenton, Valley Forge, remnants of the great hard-

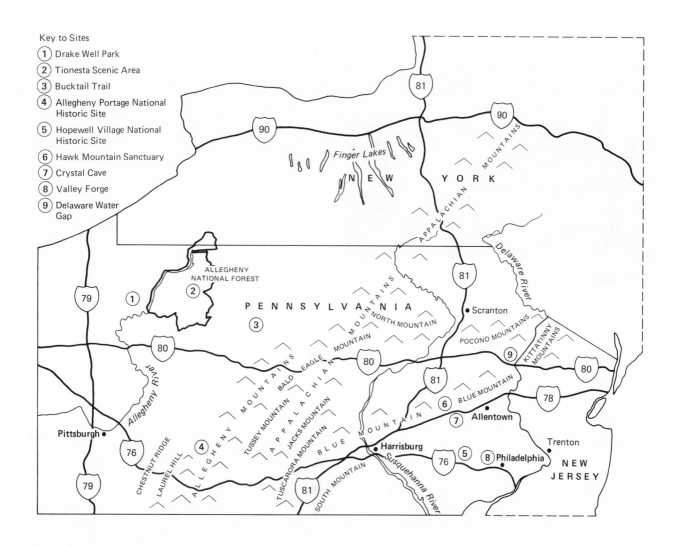

Key to Sites
1 Drake Well Park
2 Tionesta Scenic Area
3 Bucktail Trail
4 Allegheny Portage National Historic Site
5 Hopewell Village National Historic Site
6 Hawk Mountain Sanctuary
7 Crystal Cave
8 Valley Forge
9 Delaware Water Gap

Ridges and valleys of the Mid-Appalachian region—called "The Endless Mountains" by the early colonists

that rise abruptly from the Allegheny Plateau in the center of the state. Geologists believe that the lake valleys once contained southward-flowing rivers backed up by dams of glacial debris formed during the Ice Age, and that the postglacial drainage was forced to seek the northward course it now takes. Tributary streams, rushing down from steep slopes, have cut glens and formed waterfalls. Taughannock Falls, near the head of Lake Cayuga, plunges 215 feet, making it the highest waterfall east of the Rocky Mountains.

Allegheny Mountains

The front range of the Allegheny Mountains, part of the ancient Appalachian Mountain chain, stretches from southern New York across western Pennsylvania to West Virginia. Though neither as high nor as rugged as the Adirondacks of New York or the Great Smokies of North Carolina and Tennessee, the Alleghenies consist of beautiful rolling hills and northern hardwood forests.

wood forests that fed the charcoal furnaces of Colonial America, the Civil War battlefield at Gettysburg, and the site of the nation's first oil well.

Allegheny National Forest —Land of the Northern Hardwoods

The Allegheny National Forest encompasses 495,000 acres of mixed northern hardwood forests, fields, bogs, streams, and the rolling hills of the ancient Allegheny Plateau in northwest Pennsylvania. The northern hardwood forests of the region are composed primarily of beech, birch, and maple. Several stands of virgin "climax" forest, composed primarily of great stands of eastern hemlock, are found in the Heart's Content and Tionesta areas. This magnificent evergreen is usually found in wet areas and along streams and gorges; it can be easily identified by its flattened needles, which are arranged in two rows, and a striped underpart. Its inner bark yields most of the materials formerly used to tan leather in the Northeast and Canada, and in the 1800s whole forests were cut down for the bark alone. Its seeds are eaten by woodland birds and squirrels and twigs provide browse for white-tailed deer, red squirrels, and snowshoe rabbits.

Finger Lakes

The glacier-formed Finger Lakes of New York State lie in north-south valleys dotted with vineyards

A hemlock ravine at the Heart's Content Natural Area in the Allegheny National Forest, a 120-acre stand of virgin forest left uncut when the surrounding area was logged over in the late 1920s

Gray squirrel of the Appalachian woodlands

Limestone Caves of the Great Appalachian Valley

A large number of caves are concentrated in a sweeping arc from Pennsylvania to Virginia in the warped and folded limestone beds of the Great Appalachian Valley, which lies between the hard quartz and granite Appalachian ridges on the west and the Blue Ridge on the east. Within this great arc are found some of the most beautiful and famous caves in North America: Crystal and Indian Echo in Pennsylvania and the Shenandoah, Luray, and Virginia caverns in Virginia. The warping and folding of the earth's crust that created the mountain ranges also created strikingly beautiful caves in the ancient limestone layers.

Crystal Cave, in a limestone ridge about 20 miles southwest of Allentown, Pennsylvania, was first explored in 1873. It has yielded important artifacts of prehistoric man and animal life. Discoveries in this remnant of a prehistoric forested swamp have included bone fragments of the woodland reindeer and bison, teeth of the peccary and great beaver, as well as a bone fishhook, harpoon head, five bone awls, a bone needle, spearhead, fragments of a knife, and bits of brown baked pottery.

Drake Oil Well

The wooden derrick and museum located three miles southeast of Titusville on Pennsylvania Highway 36 mark the site of the world's first oil well, drilled by Edwin L. Drake in the summer of 1859. An oil boom soon followed and Titusville became the oil producing center of the United States for the next quarter of a century.

Allegheny Portage Railroad National Historic Site

The Allegheny Portage Railroad was built to carry canal boats over the forests of the Allegheny Mountains and link the eastern and western divisions of the Pennsylvania Canal, a 395-mile waterway between Philadelphia and Pittsburgh. This canal, built between 1826 and 1834 to transport raw materials, farm products, and manufactured items between the Ohio River valley and the eastern seaboard, was the main Pennsylvania transportation line west for more than two decades until the railroad made it obsolete.

This 36.69-mile railroad, situated near Johnstown, Pennsylvania, consisted of a series of ten inclined planes, five on each side of the mountain, 901-foot-long Staple Bend tunnel, and long level stretches. At the top of each plane a stationary steam engine provided power to a seemingly endless hemp rope moving up one track and down the other, to which the ascending or descending cars were attached. In between the planes were stretches of nearly level track over which the cars were initially transported by horse and later by steam locomotives.

The Lemon House, built about 1831 near the summit of Allegheny Mountain, was a tavern and rest stop for passengers. Today it serves as the visitor center. Other features here include the flat level

Farmlands in the Great Appalachian Valley

Lemon House at the Allegheny Portage National Historic Site. Built in 1830, the Lemon House served as an inn and tavern along the railroad. In the foreground are remains of the stone "sleepers," or railroad ties.

planes, stone culverts, stone railroad ties, engine house foundations, the Shew Arch Bridge, and the Staple Bend Tunnel.

The historic site is located near Cresson on U.S. Highway 22 in the Front Range of the Allegheny Mountains.

Hopewell Village National Historic Site

Hopewell Village, located 10 miles northeast of the Morgan Interchange on the Pennsylvania Turnpike, is a microcosm of the industrial enterprise of Colonial, Revolutionary, and 19th-century America. This iron-making village manufactured a wide variety of cookware and other iron products for a growing nation. Stoves were its major product and many different types were manufactured, among them the famous "Franklin fireplaces" for combined heating and cooking, which were produced in the casting house.

The molded or cast iron articles produced at Hopewell Village were the end products of a relatively simple process. The raw materials needed—iron ore, limestone, and hardwood forests for charcoal—were all readily available in the area. Miners dug the ore from nearby open pit mines and washed it in the streams. Teamsters hauled it to the furnace.

Hopewell's prosperity reached its zenith in the mid-1830s. Except for a brief boom during the Civil War, the rural manufacturing community, with its time-honored methods of charcoal smelting, became increasingly obsolete with the development of new smelting methods utilizing hotter-burning anthracite coal and heated air blasts that could produce high-quality iron more rapidly and at less expense. New ironworks were generally located near the growing urban markets, since they no longer needed vast hardwood forests for fuel. One by one the rural charcoal furnaces closed down. Hopewell's last attempt to remain competitive, with the construction in 1853 of an anthracite coal furnace, failed to halt the decline. In 1883 the furnace "blew out" for the last time.

This iron-making village site includes the restored ruins of the old furnace, an office/store, a barn, the blacksmith shop, spring house, tenant houses, charcoal hearth, coaling shed and charcoal house, casting house, water wheel, and blast machinery.

Gettysburg Civil War Battlefield

At the battle of Gettysburg, from July 1–3, 1863, the Confederate soldiers of General Robert E. Lee's

Double tracks at Allegheny Portage—built in the 1820s to carry canal boats over the mountains

Army of Northern Virginia were pitted against 88,000 men in General George G. Meade's Army of the Potomac. The combined losses of both armies were 51,000 men killed, wounded, or captured in the bloodiest battle ever fought on the North American continent. The defeat for the South marked the turning of the tide in the eastern theater of the Civil War. Near the battlefield site is Gettysburg National Cemetery.

The waterwheel. Water from Lake Hopewell, 1,200 feet upstream, flowed through the West Head Race to turn this wheel, which powered the blast machinery.

The waterwheel, furnace, and casting house at Hopewell Village. From 1845 until its final blast, Hopewell produced only pig iron.

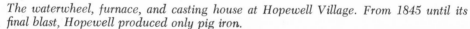

Cornwall Iron Furnace

The Cornwall Iron Furnace, located at Cornwall, Pennsylvania, is an example of the charcoal furnaces that produced most of the nation's iron until 1865. This ironworks made pig iron from 1742 to 1883. Charcoal-making was an exacting process. Woodcutters chopped 25 to 50 cords of hardwood billets from the surrounding hemlock forests for each circular hearth in the woods. The hearth was simply a round, level area 10 to 40 feet in diameter, cleared of debris, roots, and stumps. From April to November, skilled colliers stacked the billets at an angle against a central wooden chimney. They covered the rounded, cone-shaped structure with thin "lapwood," or sticks, over which they spread layers of leaves and dust to keep out excess air. Finally, they filled the chimney from

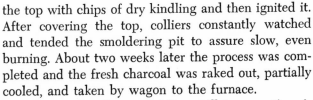

Red-tailed hawk above Kittatinny Ridge—thousands upon thousands of hawks and eagles funnel past this spot during their annual migration

the top with chips of dry kindling and then ignited it. After covering the top, colliers constantly watched and tended the smoldering pit to assure slow, even burning. About two weeks later the process was completed and the fresh charcoal was raked out, partially cooled, and taken by wagon to the furnace.

The nearby Cornwall Mine, still in operation, is the oldest continually used iron mine in the United States. It is also the nation's deepest open-cut mine. Just east of the furnace is Miner's Village, a group of two-family houses constructed in the 1860s.

Hawk Mountain on the Kittatinny Ridge

Kittatinny, the easternmost of the great ridges of the mid-Appalachians, borders the Great Appalachian Valley, which extends southward from New York into Georgia and is the ancestral migration route for hawks and eagles. At Hawk Mountain, near Drehersville, Pennsylvania, the broad Kittatinny Ridge forms a high, narrow spur reaching up nearly 2,000 feet. Beginning as early as August 20th, the annual migration gets underway, with bald eagles and ospreys in the vanguard, funneling down from Canada and New England past this narrow spot on their ancestral highway. By mid-November, tens of thousands of golden eagles, broad-winged hawks, northern goshawks, Cooper's hawks, sharp-shinned and red-tailed hawks glide by, riding the invisible air currents on nearly motionless wings.

Valley Forge

Of all the places associated with the War for Independence, none conveys the suffering, sacrifice, and ultimate triumph of the American cause more than Valley Forge. Valley Forge is the story of an army's epic struggle to survive against terrible odds, against hunger, disease, and the unrelenting forces of nature. During the bitter winter of 1777, when Washington's army struggled into camp at Valley Forge, tired, cold, and ill-equipped, it was lacking in much of the essential training for consistent success on the battlefield. On June 19, 1778, after a 6-month encampment and training led by Friedrich von Steuben, one-time member of the elite General Staff of Frederick the Great of Prussia, this same army emerged to pursue and defeat the British Army at the Battle of Monmouth in New Jersey.

Today Valley Forge contains extensive remains and reconstructions of major forts and lines of earthworks, the Artillery Park, Washington's Headquarters, and the Grand Parade grounds, where General von

Steuben rebuilt the army and where news of the French Alliance was announced on May 6, 1778.

Delaware Water Gap

The beautiful Delaware River Water Gap lies between the Kittatinny Ridge in New Jersey and the Pocono Mountain Plateau in Pennsylvania. At the gap, the Delaware has cut a bold gash through an ancient trough, exposing the stumps of ridges formed during the original uplift of the Appalachian Range. Several other rivers that flow through the great parallel ridges and narrow valleys of the mid-Appalachian region form dramatic water gaps. The Potomac forms a striking gap at Harpers Ferry, West Virginia, and the Susquehanna has eroded gaps out of six deep ridges in a distance of only 40 miles.

The Delaware Water Gap is part of a 70,000-acre national recreation area that takes in 35 miles of the long, narrow Delaware River valley and includes the Pocono Environmental Education Center, Dingman Falls on the eastern flank of the Pocono Plateau, and the Peters Valley Craft Village.

Washington's Crossing of the Delaware

General George Washington's crossing of the Delaware on Christmas night, 1776, for the raid against British troops in Trenton, New Jersey, was a turning point in the struggle for American Independence. Despite its almost legendary associations, it was a realistic and carefully planned effort to revive a waning cause. By taking the offensive, Washington gave the nation and the army a taste of victory at the Revolutionary War's lowest ebb. Washington's Crossing State Park on the Delaware River, between Yardley and New Hope, Pennsylvania, preserves the site of the embarkation of Washington's main force. It contains a number of stone farmhouses and the Ferry Inn, which occupies the site of the original ferry house.

Delaware River Water Gap at Tocks Island

14. Sandy Shore

THE vast, sandy shore of the Atlantic coast begins at the glacier-formed transition zone between Cape Cod and Staten Island—with its rocky shore interspersed with sand beaches which increase in number as one moves southward—and extends south to the broad, white beaches that stretch almost unbroken to Florida.

Travelling from the salt spray, the pounding surf, and the picturesque rocky shore of New England to the vast sandy beaches, barrier islands, and rhythmic breakers of the sandy shore, there is a marked change in the coastland's natural features and beach life.

South of Cape Cod the Atlantic coast has a sandy outer shore with barrier islands broken by shifting inlets and the mouths of large sounds and estuaries. The intertidal zone of these sandy beaches is dominated by burrowing animals, from various amphipods and minute flatworms that live in the water between the grains of sand to ghost crabs and beach fleas.

In the protected bays and lagoons of the sandy coast eelgrass and widgeon grass compete with sea lettuce and red seaweeds. The grasses provide a habitat for a wide variety of species, including bay scallop, killifish, blue crab, sticklebacks, and pipefish. The next zone above the seagrasses includes the lower mud and sand flats, dominated by clam worms, soft clams, horseshoe crabs, and quahog. At a still higher level the salt marshes take over. At the lowest level of the salt marsh, tall cordgrass often forms a solid wall mingled with half-buried ivory barnacles, mud crabs, ribbed mussels, and rockweeds among the roots. At high levels this tall cordgrass wall gives way to a mosaic of short cordgrass, glassworts, fiddler crabs, marsh snails, and sea lavender. At the uppermost level of the salt marsh are found beach fleas, crickets, ants, and earwigs. On the open sandy beaches the foreshore and back beach areas are dominated by migrants such as the mole crab, coquina clam, beach fleas, and ghost crabs. Above the high storm-tide line are the dry, shifting primary dunes, dominated by beach grass, beach pea, and sea-rocket.

Shoreline Features of the Sandy Coast

Like the submerged valleys of New England the drowned rivers of the middle Atlantic coast are evidence of the rising sea. This was caused by the melting of the glaciers during the last Ice Age, creating a ragged, complex shoreline.

The estuaries of the Atlantic sandy shore divide this coastal region into numerous broad peninsulas,

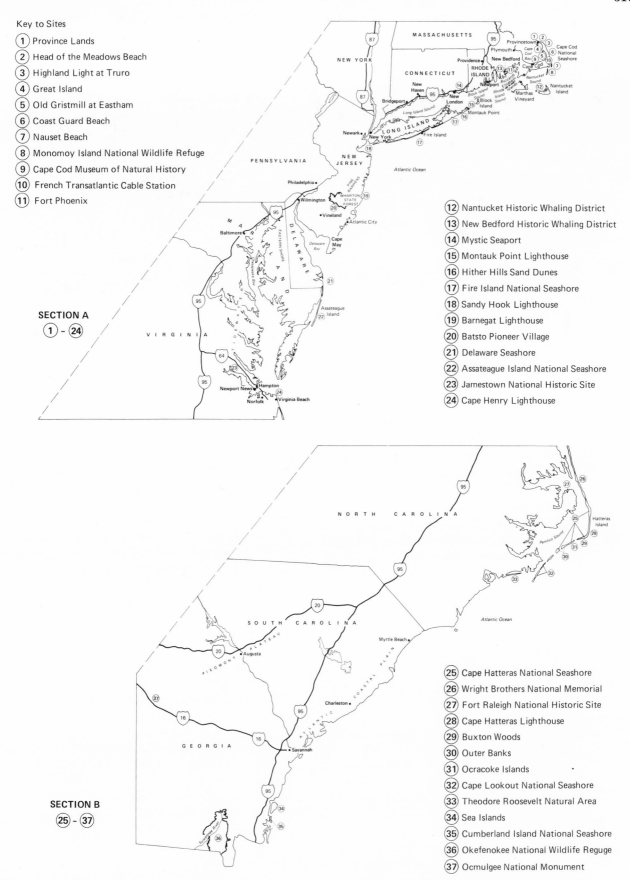

Key to Sites

(1) Province Lands
(2) Head of the Meadows Beach
(3) Highland Light at Truro
(4) Great Island
(5) Old Gristmill at Eastham
(6) Coast Guard Beach
(7) Nauset Beach
(8) Monomoy Island National Wildlife Refuge
(9) Cape Cod Museum of Natural History
(10) French Transatlantic Cable Station
(11) Fort Phoenix

(12) Nantucket Historic Whaling District
(13) New Bedford Historic Whaling District
(14) Mystic Seaport
(15) Montauk Point Lighthouse
(16) Hither Hills Sand Dunes
(17) Fire Island National Seashore
(18) Sandy Hook Lighthouse
(19) Barnegat Lighthouse
(20) Batsto Pioneer Village
(21) Delaware Seashore
(22) Assateague Island National Seashore
(23) Jamestown National Historic Site
(24) Cape Henry Lighthouse

SECTION A

(1) – (24)

(25) Cape Hatteras National Seashore
(26) Wright Brothers National Memorial
(27) Fort Raleigh National Historic Site
(28) Cape Hatteras Lighthouse
(29) Buxton Woods
(30) Outer Banks
(31) Ocracoke Islands
(32) Cape Lookout National Seashore
(33) Theodore Roosevelt Natural Area
(34) Sea Islands
(35) Cumberland Island National Seashore
(36) Okefenokee National Wildlife Reguge
(37) Ocmulgee National Monument

SECTION B

(25) – (37)

Wind-swept dunes along the sandy shore

islands, and inlets, with offshore bars especially common along the northern part. The most common and distinctive features of the region are the wide sandy beaches, wave-cut cliffs, dunes, and sandbars. Offshore bars and barrier islands are especially conspicuous along the New Jersey coast and south of Chesapeake Bay. The shoreline from Cape Henry, Virginia, southward to Cape Fear, North Carolina, is protected by a string of barrier islands unequaled anywhere in the world.

Life Zones of the Sandy Shore

Exposed Shore

Although the long, wide, sandy shore facing the open sea may appear barren, it does sustain life. Sheltered by the wet sand and stones it provides a habitat for minute plankton, beach fleas, and sand hoppers. The wrack line separating the sloping, exposed sands from the upper beach is composed of blackened rockweed, sea lettuce, dulse, Irish moss, straw from saltwater grass, and a tangle of surf clams, shells, driftwood, starfish, sponges, egg cases of skates, gull feathers, and spider crabs washed up by the surf. Sanderlings are often seen scurrying along the wet sand feeding on the minute creatures that live buried here, and blackback gulls and herring gulls scavenge along the wrack line.

Upper Beach

Between the debris of the wrack line and the foremost sand dunes is the dry upper beach, reached only by storm waves and unusually high tides, which wash up the shells of the ten-ridged neptune, waved whelk, slipper limpet, and knobbed whelk often found there. The plants are hardy, salt-spray resistant pioneers that also must endure the drying effects of the sun and wind. The seaside goldenrod has adapted to this harsh environment by developing a waxlike coating on its fleshy leaves which helps retain moisture. The seaside spurge avoids the harsh, drying rays of the sun with its tiny leaves, which offer minimum exposure. During the high summer days the thin leaves of beachgrass curl up to avoid the ceaseless glare of the sun.

Beach Sand and Pebbles

The sand grains of eroded translucent quartz that make up the beaches along the Atlantic coast help determine the character of the beaches. Coarse grains of sand are usually found along narrow cliff-lined beaches, while lighter fine-grained sand is found along the flat, wide beaches south of Cape Cod. As the waves recede they deposit the fine-grained sand farther off-shore, forming a wide, firm, gently sloping beach. The older the sand, the smoother the grains—the result of ages of wind erosion.

The beach pebbles formed from angular glacier-plucked granite, quartz, and felsite debris have been brought down from the north over the course of thousands of years. They have been polished and given their angular shape and their edges by constant exposure to wind-driven sand, unlike the pebbles of the rocky northern shore which are well rounded and polished by the grinding and jostling of countless thousands of tons of rock in the surf.

Sand Dunes

Wild, wind-rippled dunes are among the beautiful sights along the Atlantic coast. These little deserts, which retain little moisture, and in summer reach temperatures of 150 degrees and above, are created when an obstacle such as driftwood, a tuft of beach grass, or a rock captures wind-blown sand grains. Over several seasons they may build dunes as high as 150 feet. If a dune remains motionless long enough, it may become anchored by patches of fast-growing beach grass, dusty miller, bayberry, and beach plum. In most cases, however, the dunes march crosscountry in the direction of the prevailing offshore winds, over-

Sanderlings, usually seen at the edge of the surf, scurrying behind retreating breakers to feed on tiny fish and mollusks

Fishing dory among the dunes on Montauk Point, at the scenic tip of New York's Long Island that juts into the Atlantic.

powering everything in their path, invading forests, filling salt marshes and small kettle ponds.

Sand-Dune Life

A sand dune anchored by clumps of beach or dune grass is quickly invaded by hardy pioneer plants with taproot systems and leaves tolerant to the cease-less salt spray. The most commonly sighted dune plants are the beach pea, with its underground stems and lovely violet flowers, seaside goldenrod, the dusty miller, identified by its powdery leaves and spikes of golden flowers, and clumps of wild, salt-spray rose, with its beautiful pink flowers.

Growing behind the foremost dunes is a zone of low-growing shrubby plants such as beach plums and poison ivy. The next zone of plant life is usually made up of low-spreading mats of bearberry with their red berries and beach heather, or poverty grass, with its small yellow flowers that bloom in June, broken here and there by patches of gray-green reindeer moss.

The plants of the dunes provide shelter and food for Fowler's toads and the harmless hognosed snake, sand dune locust, pale wolf spiders, digger wasps, and a host of birds.

Beach Grass—The Dune Builder

The dominant plant of the Atlantic beaches, the long, thin drooping blades of beach grass, also known as marrane grass, flourish in sand a few feet above the high-tide mark. The long, narrow stems run beneath the surface forming clumps of blades every foot or so, anchoring the wind-blown sand and stabilizing the beach. With the steady accumulation of sand, the grass grows higher, forming thick mats and building banks held together by its wiry stems that often rise to heights of 30 feet above the high-water mark. Following the building of the anchored sand bank, other plants begin to grow among the clumps of grass— seaside goldenrod, poison ivy, beach plum, salt-spray rose, bayberry, and finally, on the older dunes, oak, pitch pine, cedar, and loblolly pine.

Beach Pea

Beach pea is commonly sighted on the foremost dunes colonized by beach grass and is identified by tendril-like leaves, a violet flower in summer, and leaflets that fold together in the sunlight.

Salt-Spray Rose

A hardy inhabitant of the foremost dunes, the salt-spray rose has floppy pink flowers and bright scarlet red fruits, or hips, growing in summer in clumps.

Beach Heather

Beach heather is a low-growing, yellow-flowered, sand-loving plant, locally known as poverty grass. It thrives on the hot, dry dunes above the extreme high-tide mark, where it grows in cushionlike hummocks.

Beach Flea

The wet sand near the high-tide mark is the home of those sand-colored shrimplike creatures known as beach fleas that come up to forage on the surface when the waves have retreated. These hopping fleas, with pale-blue crossed eyes, can leap several feet in any direction.

Quahog, or Hard-Shelled Clam

The hard-shelled clam is a common bivalve with a thick, strong shell with a broad, oval shape. The inside shell has a purple stain at the rear and a toothed inner margin. It is found along sandy beaches and bays from the Gulf of Mexico to Cape Cod. Commercially it is known, according to its size, as the littleneck, cherrystone, or chowder clam. The south-ern quahog is larger and rarely stained purple on the inner shell. The false quahog is smaller and lacks the purple stain and has a smooth inner margin.

Longshore Current

The beautiful, broad beaches along the Atlantic coast were built by the strong, sand-filled, longshore currents, whose waves hit the beach at a diagonal, carrying enormous quantities of sand from the eroded uplands. When the shoreline curves away from the sea, the longshore current builds up a sandbar, which grows into a sandspit with the incessant deposits of sand and eventually into a dune-covered beach and finally into a peninsula.

Swash Marks

Swash marks are the common, long interlacing curves on the beach that mark the farthest limits reached by the forward surge of the waves. These dark swash markings contain marine debris washed up by the tides—seaweeds, shells, mussels, clams— that provides forage for sandpipers, gulls, and terns.

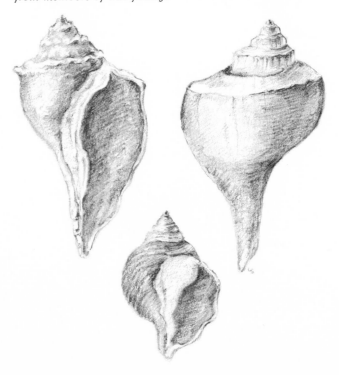

Shells of waved, channeled, and knobbed whelks, commonly found on sandy beaches from Cape Cod south to Florida. Ancient civilizations extracted royal purple dye from members of this family.

Barrier island at Cape Hatteras, one of a string of narrow offshore islands stretching from the Gulf of Mexico to New Jersey

Cusps

Cusps are long, low curving mounds of sand, set at regular intervals on the beach, formed when waves have been breaking on the beach at right angles.

Beach Pinholes

Beach pinholes are found just below the high-water mark, caused when the swash of a wave flows and recedes over dry sand and the air trapped beneath escapes upward, forming the pinholes. When the remaining air below tries to escape with the next swash, it creates small domes of wet sand.

Beach Rills

Beach rills are odd marks on the beach that look like miniature river systems with their mouths facing the sea, caused when water that has covered the beach drains with the falling tide.

Ripple Marks

Ripple marks are common beach markings that are parallel troughs and ridges caused when wind or water passes over an obstacle in the sand, turns downward, and scoops out a trough, forming a ridge. The ridge in turn forces a swash or wind to scoop out another trough beyond it.

Winter Berm

The steep, clifflike stretches of beach, known as berm, are created by the powerful winter waves that push their debris beyond the level reached by the summer tides. The onshore winds are much stronger in winter and the waves are higher, steeper, and in more rapid succession.

Jetties

The jetties that dot the Atlantic shore like stout fingers of stone were built to combat beach erosion and preserve navigable inlets. The most commonly sighted type of jetty is called a groin—a short jetty of massive stones built at right angles to the shore. They act like dams, catching the sand and widening the beach on the side from which the sand flow comes.

Tidal Flats

The protected, life-rich tidal flats, which merge with the lower part of the sandy beach, extend to the farthest limit of the low tide, varying in places from a 100 yards to 2 or 3 miles. Compared to the widely fluctuating temperatures of the beach, the tidal flats provide a stable environment inhabited by sand shrimps, periwinkles, lobsters, barnacles, calico crabs, sand worms, moon snails, mussel beds, skates, horseshore crabs, tiny purple-hued gem shells, clams, and sea snails, including the channeled whelk and knobbed and waved whelk.

Barrier Islands

The incredibly beautiful barrier islands, a typical formation of the sandy shore, form only along sandy coasts that slope gently down to shallow water. The barrier islands are formed by the action of the waves, which break, scoop up sand like a bulldozer, and hurl it forward, creating a submerged ridge which eventually grows into a narrow island. Between the barrier islands and the Atlantic mainland are shallow lagoons and salt marshes, which are slowly being filled in by the action of storms, eventually joining the islands with the mainland.

The Atlantic coast, from Florida northeastward to Virginia, is protected by a string of often wild, desolate barrier islands—from Cape Canaveral to Virginia's Hog Island—that form a primeval world of tall shifting dunes, beach grass, scattered myrtle bushes and loblolly pines, great colonies of sea birds, shallow salt marshes, and wooded ridges.

Eelgrass

Eeelgrass is a slender, pale-green ribbonlike plant that grows submerged in shallow bays and estuaries along the middle Atlantic coast. A primary link in the source of a food chain for a variety of sealife, from shrimp and bay scallops to weakfish, eelgrass was once almost extinct from a fungus or bacterial disease, but has made a strong recovery, as have the scallops and weakfish. These submarine grass meadows provide cover and food for small periwinkles, algae, pipefish, seahorses, shrimp, sea anemones, hermit crabs, plumed worms, clams, and blue mussels. It is the primary winter food of the brant.

Salt Marshes of the Sandy Shore

The vast, flooded, salt-marsh flatlands of tall cordgrass that stretch for seemingly endless miles behind the barrier islands of the Atlantic coast are among the region's most fascinating natural features.

Controlled by the lifeblood of the ebbing and flowing tides, the salt marsh is a quiet, seldom-explored world dominated by the tall, waving meadows of cordgrass at its upper levels and along its edges by thickets of marsh elder, and samphire, rushes, and marshmallow. The tides wash in the sand and silt that are anchored by the marsh grasses, whose rotting roots and stems build up thick layers of peat—some more than 20 feet deep—up to the normal levels of the high tide. As the land height rises beyond the margin of the salt marsh, the low vegetation abruptly gives way to bayberry bushes and tall stands of loblolly pines and cedar trees.

The basic building block of the salt-marsh life chain is the cordgrass (and salt hay in the higher northern marshes). As the veritable food factories of cordgrass die and decay, it is broken down by fungi and bacteria, producing a thin film of protein-rich detritus, which is in turn consumed by swarming masses of small marsh creatures such as insects, marsh periwinkles, fiddler crabs, mud crabs, blue crabs, oysters, billfish, mussels, and shrimp.

These small marsh creatures in turn support thriving populations of raccoons, great blue herons, striped bass, white egrets, ducks, roseate spoonbills, clapper rails, laughing gulls, boat-tailed grackles, seaside sparrows, and stilt sandpipers.

Pond Holes of a Salt Marsh

Pond holes are the odd grass-free pools of shallow water that dot the waving seas of cordgrass and salt hay in the coastal salt marshes. It has been suggested that they are miniature remnants of ancient lakes. The bottoms of the pond holes are carpeted with thick mats of green algae, dotted by thousands of small oxygen bubbles, which occasionally float the entire mat up to the surface.

Cordgrass and Salt Hay

Cordgrass, also known as thatch, is one of the dominant plants of the salt marshes of the middle Atlantic coast. The extensive root system of cordgrass, which forms seemingly endless acres of tall, gently swaying green coastal windrows, anchors the silt and creates thick layers of peat as its old roots die and prevents the otherwise fragile marsh from eroding. A close relative of cordgrass, *Spartina patens*, dominates the salt marshes of the northeast Atlantic coast. The low-growing patens, with its thin wiry stems and blades, is known along the New England coast as salt hay and was mowed for hay until the early 1900s. This dominant plant of the high-lying northern marshes forms a finlike mat that will support a human's weight.

Cape Cod Coastal Transition Zone

Narrow, hook-shaped Cape Cod, with its wind-swept sand dunes, stunted forests of pines and oaks, salt meadows, marshes and kettle ponds, and quaint New England fishing villages, is a key geological and biological transition zone, like the Olympic Peninsula on the Pacific coast. The Cape presents a natural, elbow-shape barrier to the mixing of the warm Gulf Stream from the south with the cold Labrador Current from the north. It forms a natural dividing point between the glacier-formed rocky coast on the north and the low-lying wave-formed sand beaches of the Atlantic Coastal Plain to the south, and between the sea plants and animals of the Atlantic boreal region of the northern rocky coast and those of the sand beaches of the Atlantic temperate zone to the south. On the rocky northern shore of Cape Cod, for example, the periwinkles of the rocky coast are common, while on the sandy southern shore the sea roach of the sandy coast is commonly sighted.

Landscape of Cape Cod

The peninsula of Cape Cod reaches into the Atlantic for 65 miles in the form of an arm bent upward at the elbow, ending at the salt-sprayed dunes of the pond-dotted, fist-shaped Province Lands. It owes its origin to the glacier of the last Ice Age and was reshaped by the erosion of the wind and sea. Near here are numerous islands of the same origin— Martha's Vineyard, Nantucket, and the 16 Elizabeth islands. The glacial outwash plains of Martha's Vineyard and Nantucket are now broad grassy heaths and plains. The southern side of the deltalike plain of Cape Cod has been cut along high cliffs by the surf and waves. Here the plain is covered with a growth of pitch pine and scrub oak barrens, dotted by Ice Age kettle ponds, fringed by forests of Atlantic white cedar, where huge chunks of ice remained before melting. Much of the forearm of the Cape is a bleak grassy country, while the outer end at the Province Lands is a beautiful region with long sand beaches, tall dunes, ponds, and salt meadows.

Cape Cod National Seashore

The northernmost of our national seashores on the Atlantic stretches for 40 wind-swept miles along the great outer beach on the forearm of Cape Cod, from Chatham Light on the elbow of the Cape to Long Point Light in Provincetown Harbor, and 14 miles of bay beach and salt marshes backed by a tall ridge of sand dunes.

The Great Beach

The Great Beach of Cape Cod, formed as a result of the Ice Age which ended a mere 10,000 years ago and smoothed off by the sea, forms a continuous stretch of sand, constantly shifted by the action of the offshore currents and storm waves, south and north from Provincetown to the tip of Monomoy Island, broken only by inlets at Orleans and Chatham.

The Cape has several microclimates created by the tides and water temperature: at the broad tidal

Cordgrass of the salt marshes

Windmill on Cape Cod—a distinctive feature of New England's seashore fishing villages

flats and salt marshes along Cape Cod, the mean range of the tide is ten feet; on the southern sandy shore of the Cape, the mean range is two feet. In similar fashion the water temperature on the north shore is ten degrees cooler than that on the south shore.

Cranberry Bogs of Cape Cod

Patches of low-growing wild cranberries are found in the valleys between the dunes of the northernmost Province Lands of Cape Cod, where these natural bogs are occasionally covered by a fine sifting of sand. Ocean breezes maintain a moderate climate and the dunes protect the cranberries from the violent storm winds. With the decline of the shipping industry and the decline of fish prices after the Civil War, these fields of "red gold" became an integral part of the Cape Cod landscape. Although the cranberry industry on the Cape has declined, the area still produces about 10 percent of Massachusetts' crop. A remnant of the once-vast cultivated boglands that dotted the Cape during the 1800s is found at the Pamet Cranberry

Coast Guard Beach at Cape Cod. The Cape forms a natural transition zone between seashore life of the rocky, glacier-carved shore to the north and the low-lying sand beaches stretching south to Florida.

Beach grass

Bog at Truro. Forests have reclaimed much of the bog since it fell into disuse, but a small patch of cranberries has been preserved to re-create an historic landscape that is part of Cape Cod's heritage.

Cape Cod Museum of Natural History

The fascinating museum of Cape Cod's Natural History is located off Highway 6A in West Brewster and offers a wide variety of exhibits, field trips, and classes for children. The museum maintains nature trails through a salt marsh and seashore highlands.

Fort Phoenix at Buzzards Bay

Following the Battle of Concord and Lexington a British ship was sent into the waters of Buzzards Bay in search of food supplies. As a result the Americans constructed a fort on this site to protect the harbor at Fairhaven from future enemy incursions. The structure was completed by 1777. On September 5, 1778, over 4,000 British troops under the command of General Grey landed on the western shore of the harbor, marched across to Fairhaven, and destroyed the fort which at that time was deserted. Immediately after Grey's attack the local militia rebuilt the fort, hence its name Fort Phoenix. The horseshoe-shape fort consists of outer and inner walls, between which

sod and earth form a parapet. Exterior walls are constructed of brick. A cement covering was added to the walls in 1950.

The fort is at Fort Phoenix State Park south of U.S. Highway 6 in Fairhaven, Massachusetts.

Indian Relics of Cape Cod

The Nauset Indians, who were living in the Cape Cod area in 1600, were of Algonquin stock. It is not known exactly how long they were living there, but it is believed from 3,000 to 5,000 years. They were primarily farmers and fishermen, supplementing their diet with game. Beans, corn, and squash were raised, and succotash was the principal dish into which any meat available was tossed. Shellfish were used extensively.

Their houses were of the Massachusetts beehive type, simple structures built of saplings tied together and covered with sedge grass. Beds were crude, slightly raised bunks, with animal skins or grass-covered padding. In summer they wore little and covered their bodies with a heavy grease. Winter wear consisted of animal skins. Arrowheads, scrapers, knives, stone axes, and harpoon heads were made in profusion. Shell heaps, known as kitchen middens, are located along the Cape Cod shores and help tell something about their way of life.

Indian Rock, located at the top of Skiff Hill, was

used by the Indians as a community grinding stone to sharpen bone harpoon heads and fishhooks and stone axes. There were originally four such rocks in the vicinity of the Nauset Marsh.

Cape Cod's Offshore Islands

Cape Cod's offshore islands—Nantucket, Martha's Vineyard, and the Elizabeth group—and the Cape itself were formed when the retreating glacier of the last Ice Age deposited great moraines that marked the farthest visible southerly advance of the ice sheet. The passage of time and the subsequent erosion of these great ridges and bluffs of boulders, clay, and stones by wind and water created the landscape and form of the present-day Cape and offshore islands. Martha's Vineyard, off the southern coast of Cape Cod, is about 20 miles long from east to west and 10 miles across at its greatest width, surrounded by broad sand beaches and dunes. The vegetation of the low-lying, flat eastern end consists primarily of scrub oak and a few stands of pitch pine. Toward the western end open grass heaths and rolling hills terminate in the multi-colored clay cliffs at Gay Head. A series of freshwater and brackish ponds dot the southern side of the island, protected by narrow strips of dunes.

The scrub-oak barrens of Martha's Vineyard were the last remaining habitat of the heath hen, which became extinct in the early 1930s. Gay Head is the winter habitat of Atlantic puffins, razorbills, black guillemonts, northern gannets, and a host of other seashore birds.

Low-lying Nantucket Island, a historic New England whaling center, lies off the southern coast of the Cape. Moving inland from the clay bluffs and sand beaches of its southern and western ends are broad grass heaths, dotted elsewhere by small patches of pitch pine and scrub oak, small ponds, and tidal flats. Nearby tiny Muskeget Island, a bird sanctuary, is noted for its large population of herring gulls and great black-backed gulls.

Monomoy Island, site of the national wildlife refuge, is a long barrier sand beach protecting extensive dune formations, hollows, ponds, and salt marshes. Extending for about 10 miles from near the elbow of the Cape, it is the habitat for great numbers of transient oceanic and land birds.

French Transatlantic Cable Station

This one-story frame house was the American terminus of the first direct Atlantic cable laid for

Wave-eroded cliffs at Montauk Point on the eastern tip of Long Island

3,173 nautical miles between the United States and Brest, France. The cable line was the work of a French firm, *La Compagnie Française du Telegraphe de Paris a New York*, and originally terminated in Eastham. The terminal was moved to Orleans in 1891, but the cable was not direct (running by way of the island of St. Pierre near Newfoundland) until 1897. The communication line was extended to New York in 1898. A Wheatstone Bridge was operated in the test room of the station. This was an apparatus designed to locate breaks in the line by measuring the resistance to outgoing signals. An artificial line duplicated the cable and allowed for simultaneous sending and receiving of signals. Inactive during the German occupation of France in World War II, the cable system was abandoned totally in 1959.

The station is located in Orleans on Cape Cod at the southeast corner of Cove Road and Route 28.

Nantucket Historic Whaling District

The American whaling industry originated on Nantucket Island. By 1748 Nantucketers owned 60 ships, and the island retained supermacy in the industry for another 100 years. On Main Street, between Centre Street and Monument Square, are numerous houses associated with this era. Notable among them are the Three Bricks, a row of houses built between 1833 and 1837 for the three sons of a wealthy whale oil merchant.

New Bedford's Historic Whaling District

New Bedford began whaling in the 1760s and by the 1840s was America's major whaling port. Although the industry began to decline in the late 1850s, the town had a whaling fleet until 1925. The wealth and commerce produced by whaling are evident in the historic district, where a number of public and private buildings from its whaling era still stand. Prominent among these are the Old Bank (1831) at the foot of William Street; the Customs house (c. 1835) at Second and William Streets; and the Mariner's Home (1790) on Johnny Cake Hill.

Square-rigged Whaler at Connecticut's Mystic Seaport

The *Charles W. Morgan* at Connecticut's Mystic Seaport is the last of the 19th-century wooden whaling vessels. Owned principally by a New Bedford whaling merchant of the same name, she sailed in pursuit of whales off the New England coast for almost 80 years. Constructed of live oak and pine, she is a typical square-rigged whaler of the period. The *Morgan*, which has been restored, is 105 feet overall and has a 27-foot beam.

Long Island

The glacial forces that created Cape Cod molded the coast southward to Long Island and Staten Island. The glacial moraine that formed the northeast and south forks of Long Island continued westward to Staten Island and marks the most southerly advance of the glaciers on the Atlantic coast, dividing the narrow, rocky beaches of New England from the wide, sandy beaches of New Jersey and the Middle Atlantic States.

The shape of Long Island was formed by two end moraines deposited by the glaciers of the Ice Age: one at the south, known as the Ronkonkoma, and one at the north, known as the Harbor Hill moraine. These moraines created the forks at the eastern end of the island, terminating at Montauk Point on the south and at Orient Point on the north. South of the Ronkonkoma Moraine the land is a flat, sloping outwash plain. If the glacial debris were somehow magically swept off the island, its total area would be about one-fourth what it is today and its maximum elevation would be only 250 feet, as opposed to the 400-foot heights that exist near its western end.

Montauk Point Lighthouse

Beyond the wild, wind-swept sand dunes at Hither Hills, at the easternmost tip of Long Island, is the famous Montauk Point Lighthouse, one of the earliest built by the federal government. The massive octagonal tower is built of cut stone and rises 108 feet above the steep, rocky cliffs at Montauk Point overlooking the waters of Block Island Sound and the Atlantic. Its location on this major sea approach to the New York Harbor has made it a landmark for ocean navigation for more than 170 years. Designed by John McComb, the lighthouse, operated today by the U.S. Coast Guard, was authorized by President George Washington in January 1796.

Sunken Forest at Fire Island

Fire Island's primeval sunken forest is a maritime wilderness that embraces 75 acres of tangled, dark woodlands, bogs, and salt marshes near the

Boardwalk nature trail through Fire Island's primeval Sunken Forest

island's western end. It is a world of creeping stunted pitch pines, ghostly salt-bleached dead timber, clumps of beach grass and cushionlike hummocks of beach heather, salt-trimmed holly and sassafras trees, treacherous bull-brier thickets, steep ridges of prehistoric sand dunes, wet meadows of great reeds and glasswort, flanked by high, virgin sand dunes on its seaward side, which gives the forest the appearance of being sunken. Looking down upon the forest from the top of one of the tall dunes, it has the appearance of a miniature world, where the salt-sculptured trees, which actually reach to heights of 35 feet, look like small bushes.

The stunted trees of the forest are the effect of constant coating of salt spray from the pounding surf on the seaward side of the island. The tiny crystals of salt kill the growth of most of the seaside vegetation and stunt the growth of the trees in the interior areas, creating an even, salt-clipped canopy of green, broken here and there by ghostly, bleached skeletons of trees that lost their battle with the salt.

Tough salt-resistant plants inhabit the seaside margin of the forest just below the dunes. Here, among the dwarf pitch pines and clumps of beach grass, are ground-hugging mats of bearberry, seaside goldenrod, and hummocks of beach heather.

A nature trail begins at the eastern end of the Sunken Forest near the National Park Service ranger station at Sailor's Haven.

Sandy Hook Light

The tall white lighthouse at Sandy Hook, New Jersey, is the oldest standing light tower in the United States. Originally called the New York Lighthouse, it has served the shipping world with relatively few interruptions since its construction. The original tower of the Sandy Hook Light is octagonal with massive masonry walls. The tower rises 85 feet above the ground and 88 feet above the water.

Barnegat Lighthouse

Barnegat Lighthouse was one of four such structures erected along New Jersey's coastline from Sandy Hook to Cape May. The 163-foot tower housed a

16,000-candlepower light which was operative until replaced by an offshore lightship in 1927. A spiral staircase extends to the top of the brick and iron tower, and the windows below the light level were set at compass points and used at lookouts. George Gordon Meade, who directed the work, later commanded the Union forces at Gettysburg (July 1863).

The lighthouse is at the northern tip of New Jersey's Long Beach Island.

New Jersey's Coastal Pine Barrens and Batso Pioneer Village

The stark pine barrens of southern New Jersey mark the beginning of the great Piney Woods region, which stretches from a narrow band and follows the broadening Atlantic coastal plain through the south for more than 100 miles to the west of the Mississippi Delta. These pure desolate stands of pine are dominated by shortleaf pine in the north, longleaf pine along the southern coast, and loblolly pine in the interior, interspersed throughout the southern coastal regions with cypress, sweetgum, magnolia, red bay, tupelo, and live oak.

The Pine Barrens of New Jersey cover nearly 650,000 acres of vast, sandy plains filled with stunted, eerie dwarf forests of pines, great swamps, ponds, and bogs, broken by the meandering, tea-colored waters of the Batso, Mullica, Wading, and Oswego rivers. More than 80 species of birds nest in the Barrens, including bald eagles, great blue herons, Cooper's hawks, and great horned owls. The Batso Trail winds through the heart of the Pines, running parallel to the twisting course of the Batso River as it flows through the Lebanon and Batso state forests.

Batso Village in Burlington County is a unique iron-industry community that has undergone little or no change since its period of peak activity in the early 1800s. The iron furnace, built in 1766, was used to cast iron until the 1850s, when the iron industry declined and glass became the village's principal product. A mansion, erected in several stages between 1790 and 1880, the store, grist- and sawmills, blacksmith shop, and several workers' houses have been renovated.

Chesapeake Bay

No place along the middle Atlantic coast provides a better example of the drowning of the lower reaches of a river than does Chesapeake Bay. This shallow, marsh-lined, 3,000-square-mile estuary was once the

Spray-pruned "dwarf" forest on Fire Island

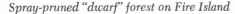

Pioneer-era village blacksmith shop

peregrine falcon, known locally as the duck hawk; wide-spreading loblolly pines, patches of gray-barked bayberry bushes with their waxy, greenish-gray fruit that provides food for birds and browse for the exotic sika deer, introduced on the island by a Boy Scout Troop in 1923; forest glades of salt-bleached pines and oaks, and salt-marsh meadows; and a herd of wild ponies, descended from the herds of Colonial times that grazed and destroyed the natural cover of many of the barrier islands along the southern Atlantic coast.

Jamestown Island—First Permanent English Settlement in America

Jamestown is the site of the first permanent English settlement in the United States. The town that grew up here, which has long since disappeared, was the capital of the colony of Virginia during its first century of development from 1607 to 1698. In 1619 the first meeting of the House of Burgesses was held here. It was the first representative legislative assembly in the New World. Among the historic figures associated with the colony's early years were Captain John Smith, John Rolfe, and his Indian wife, Pocahontas. With the exception of the old church tower, which dates from the 1640s, there are no remains of the settlement above ground. Archeological excavations have uncovered foundations of houses and public buildings, remains of streets, and small artifacts.

mouth of the Susquehanna River. After the melting of the glaciers during the last Ice Age, the sea rose for a distance of about 175 miles upstream, swallowing the lower reaches of great rivers—the Potomac, Dames, and Rappahanock—that were once tributaries of the Susquehanna, but today flow directly into the bay.

Assateague Island National Seashore

Assateague Island, a 37-mile-long nearly roadless coastal wilderness, straddles the Maryland-Virginia boundary. Its forests and meadows of long stretches of wild driftwood-littered beaches and dunes are the home of 275 different kinds of birds, including both permanent local species and migratory visitors such as long-legged shore birds—plovers, curlews, and sandpipers; colonies of seabirds, among them terns, laughing gulls, and black skimmers that nest among the dunes and clumps of beach grass in summer;

Abandoned lifeboat station on Assateague Island National Seashore—a barrier island of forests, meadows, high dunes, and wild, driftwood-littered beaches

Jamestown National Historic Site—the first permanent English settlement in America

Cape Henry Lighthouse at Virginia Beach

The oil-burning lamps of Cape Henry Lighthouse, which stands at the entrance to Chesapeake Bay, were first lighted in October 1792. The first lighthouse to be erected by the federal government, it was in constant use until a new tower was erected nearby in 1881. The 90-foot-high stone building is faced with hammer-dressed stone. Though no longer in operation the lighthouse remains a landmark.

North Carolina's Outer Banks and Cape Hatteras National Seashore

Unlike the other barrier islands of the Atlantic coast, which hug the shoreline, the Outer Banks curve out to sea, forming a narrow eastward-pointed chain of islands that stretches for 175 miles from Cape Lookout to the Virginia border. Behind the Outer Banks is Pamlico Sound. The Cape Hatteras National Seashore portion of the Outer Banks includes Bodie Island, Pea Island, Hatteras, the largest island in the chain, and Ocracoke Island, a 70-mile stretch of seashore wilderness between Whalebone Junction and Ocracoke Inlet. Offshore are the treacherous Diamond Shoals, which extend for 12 miles out to sea and are littered with the skeletons of ships wrecked by savage storms or destroyed by enemy torpedoes during two world wars.

The seemingly endless beaches of the national seashore are a wave-pounded world of tall dunes ornamented with clumps of beach grass and the tall, golden, swaying stems of sea oats, inlets, high hills and forests, marshes and fresh-water ponds, dwarf palmettoes and cedar trees, hollies, hummocks of small oaks, and bayberry bushes.

Stretching south of Ocracoke for 60 miles are the barren, uninhabited Cou Banks and the Cape Lookout National Seashore.

Buxton Woods of the Outer Banks

One of the finest examples of how the Atlantic coast must have looked in pre-Colonial days is found at Buxton Woods on the southernmost end of Hatteras Island in the Outer Banks. It contains 3,000 acres of oaks, dwarf palmettos, ironwood, dogwood, loblolly pines, and yaupon—a southern holly bush with light gray bark and bright red berries—that grows in tall stands and wild thickets along the crests and slopes of old sand dunes broken here and there by fresh-water ponds and marshes. The woods and pond margins are inhabited by a variety of wildlife including white-tailed deer, raccoons, cottonmouths, diamond-back terrapin, the exotic nutria, and mink, muskrat, and river otters.

Lighthouses at Cape Hatteras and the Outer Banks

The history of the Outer Banks is so full of stories about ships in distress and shipwrecks that this section of the North Carolina coast has become known

Statue of Pocahontas near the old church on Jamestown Island

U.S. Weather Bureau Station and beach at Cape Henry, Virginia

as the Graveyard of the Atlantic. A combination of conditions extremely hazardous to ships is responsible for this grim epithet. Here the Gulf Stream and the northern Labrador Current used as shipping lanes come very close to Diamond Shoals—the shallow sandbars that extend about 16 miles into the Atlantic from Cape Hatteras. Ships taking advantage of these northward and southward-flowing currents are forced to follow a narrow channel or run aground on the shoals. This situation is further complicated by the fact that at sea it's sometimes very difficult to recognize landmarks along the low sand dunes of the cape. Other factors such as bad weather and poor navigation also can contribute to the problem.

Today three lighthouses within the Cape Hatteras National Seashore—and a Texas Tower out on Diamond Shoals—guide mariners along this treacherous coast. The Cape Hatteras Lighthouse is the tallest in North America, and with its distinctive candy-striped pattern it has become the most popular landmark in the area. More importantly it serves as a primary navigational aid visible both day and night for a distance of 20 miles out to sea.

Fort Raleigh National Historic Site on Roanoke Island

Fort Raleigh National Historic Site is the scene of Sir Walter Raleigh's ill-fated attempts to establish an English colony in America. The first settlement,

1585–86, failed because of hardships and trouble with Indians. The "Lost Colony" settlement of 1587 was the birthplace of Virginia Dare, first child born of English parents in the New World. War with Spain isolated the colony until 1591, by which time the colonists had disappeared. Their fate was never determined. Among the men who figured in the history of the settlements were "sea dogs" Sir Richard Grenville and Sir Francis Drake. Based on historical and archeological evidence, Fort Raleigh was reconstructed in the early 1950s.

The site is located four miles north of Mantso on U.S. 158.

Wright Brothers National Memorial at Kitty Hawk

At Kitty Hawk, North Carolina, on December 17, 1903, Orville and Wilbur Wright changed the technical complexion of the 20th century. Orville Wright's 12-second flight was the first in which a machine carrying a man had raised itself by its own power and had sailed forward without reduction of speed. The Wright Memorial Shaft on Kill Devil Hill commemorates the flight, and markers nearby indicate the take-off and landing spots. Two wooden structures nearby are reconstructions of the Wrights' 1903 camp based on research and photographs. On display in the visitor center is a reproduction of the Wrights' 1903 airplane.

Ghost Crab

Ghost crabs are busy little crabs that are a common sight above the intertidal zone on ocean beaches from the Delaware south through the Caribbean, where they often are seen scurrying into the wash of the broken surf to wet their gills or to forage for bits of food. This swift-footed, sand-colored crab has a squarish-shape shell, similar to the marsh crab.

Sassafras Trees

One of the dominant trees of the Atlantic shore, the sassafras is highly salt tolerant and usually forms short, dense thickets, identified by its cinnamon brown, deeply furrowed bark, rubbery twigs, and mitten-shape leaves up to four inches wide and six inches long. Its young roots make a delicious tea with sugar flavoring. The fall foliage of the sassafras is a magnificent display of reds, yellows, and oranges.

Holly Trees

A dominant evergreen along the forest edges of the wild coastal dunes, which reaches heights of 100 feet in the moist interior woodlands, the seaside holly is noted for its smooth trunk and scores of upswept, crooked branches and flat crown, trimmed by the salt spray and ocean winds.

Bull and Cat Brier

The fierce, black-berried vines of the bull brier inhabit the thick undergrowth of the wild seaside

Beached freighter at the Outer Banks—"the graveyard of the Atlantic"

Wild ponies on Ocracoke Island—descendants of horses that swam ashore from a wrecked Spanish galleon

forests along the Atlantic coast. The tangles of bull brier dominate the open, sunlit parts of the forest. Its leather-tough vines form impenetrable thickets and bear large, sharp, curving thorns.

The more forgiving cat brier is also a denizen of the sunny areas of the dark interior forest. Its thorny vine bears large blue berries in spring and brilliant, reddish-orange leaves in fall.

Codium

Codium is a common sea plant often found washed up on beaches with round, spongelike fronds and shaped like a many-branched candelabra.

Cumberland Island and the Sea Islands of Georgia

Georgia's Sea Islands are part of the great string of barrier islands that extends parallel to the Atlantic and Gulf coasts from New Jersey to Texas and protects the mainland from the waves and winds of the open ocean. These barrier islands are no more than sandy bars in some places, but along Georgia's coast they form the Sea Islands, one of which has been

Cape Hatteras Lighthouse—the tallest in the nation

protected as the Cumberland Island National Seashore.

Cumberland Island is 16 miles long and 3 miles wide at its widest point. This low-lying island has only an occasional dune rising 50 feet above sea level. In the interior of the island is a dense canopy of widely spreading live oaks laced with woody vines and Spanish moss, as well as dense stands and tangles of willow oak, laurel oak, magnolia, holly, red bay, and long-leaf, slash, pond, and loblolly pines. Beneath the trees are the chartreuse fans of the palmetto. The ponds and sloughs scattered throughout the island are inhabited by alligators, mink, and otter.

Along the white sand beaches you will often see starfish, whelks, cockles, swallowlike terns, sanderlings, black skimmers, and white pelicans. Behind the beach, sea oats and viny plants trap the wind-whipped sand, gradually building up dunes. The wild dunes are the landmarks for female loggerhead turtles that come ashore annually to lay their eggs.

The island is separated from the mainland by several miles of salt marsh, river, and sound. In the salt marsh, dominated by waving fields of cordgrass known as Spartina, life varies with the high and low tides. When the tide is in, the mosquitofish swims by, and ducks paddle and dive for fish. When the tide is out, fiddler crabs climb out of holes and scuttle across the mud flats, oysters are exposed, and long-legged wading birds—great blue herons, Louisiana herons, snowy and American egrets—stalk their prey.

The island, the largest and most southerly off the Georgia coast near St. Marys, was inhabited as early as 4,000 years ago by the Missoe and Sassafras Indians. They lived on shellfish and wild game, and their control of the island and its waters was undisputed until the arrival of the Spanish.

Hercules' Club

Hercules' club is also known as devil's walking stick. It grows in dense thickets with straight stems and half-inch long, needle-sharp spines that inflict painful wounds on the unsuspecting coastal hiker. They are particularly common on the wild southern barrier islands.

Sea Rocket

The many-branched sea rocket, identified by its fleshlike leaves and purplish-white flowers, grows just above the high-tide mark, where it is often found along with sandwort and the sand-hugging seaside spurge.

Fort Raleigh—site of Sir Walter Raleigh's "Lost Colony," an ill-fated attempt to establish an English colony in America

American holly. Highly resistant to salt spray, this is a common tree in the seashore forests.

Sand dollar, often found washed up on the beach at low tide

Sand Dollar

The white, disc-shape skeletons of the sand dollar, a close relative of the sea urchin, are often found among the tufts and tangles of beach drift along the sandy Atlantic shore.

Okefenokee Swamp—"Land of the Trembling Earth"

Okefenokee Swamp, derived from the Seminole Indian word meaning "land of the trembling earth," spreads across about half a million acres of the Atlantic coastal plain in the southeastern corner of Georgia. The great swamp is a land of primitive beauty that was once a shallow ocean sound, cut off during the Pleistocene era, a half million to a million years ago, by a 100-mile-long sandbar now called Trail Ridge.

Today a large part of that ancient depression is choked with a moist expanse of moss-covered cypress trees, tupelos, white and golden water lilies, and quivering "houses"—clumps of bushes and trees with an undergrowth of smaller plants formed when swamp gases produced by decaying vegetable matter forced masses of plant growth up from the bottom of the water—all surrounded by a mosaic of lakes, islands, and prairies. The overflow from the low-lying swamp pours into two outlets: the fabled Suwannee and St. Marys rivers. The St. Marys flows along the southern boundary of Georgia for about 100 miles before it empties into the Atlantic. The Suwannee River meanders through the quiet cypress forests of Florida, emptying into the Gulf of Mexico.

The eastern portion of the swamp is dominated

The snowy egret inhabits salt marshes, swamps, and shallow coastal bays. This small white heron was nearly slaughtered to extinction for its elegant plumes, used to decorate women's hats.

Palmettos (below), common on the barrier islands from North Carolina to Florida

Indian ceremonial earthlodge at Ocmulgee

by open marshlands, called "prairies," dotted with what appear to be countless floating islands of pines and cypresses. The western portion is a land of trees—bald cypress, magnolia, and red bay—beyond which slowly flow wide, meandering stretches of open water—the headwaters of the Suwannee River.

Portions of the swamp have been protected as the Okefenokee National Wildlife Refuge and the Okefenokee Swamp Park.

Ocmulgee Indian Ruins on Georgia's Atlantic Coastal Plain

The Ocmulgee National Monument near Macon, Georgia, where the Ocmulgee River passes from the red clay land of the rolling piedmont to the sandy flat lands of the coastal plain, represents a zone where many important historic and prehistoric cultures overlapped. The Swift Creek Indians settled here about A.D. 1250 but were driven out by the Macon Plateau Indians about 1350. It was the Macon Plateau tribe who built the huge Temple mounds, the fortified village, ceremonial earth lodge, and two lines of ditches you see today, and cultivated the surrounding fields. The 40-acre tract south of Ocmulgee was occupied by the Lamar Indians from 1350 to 1500; they probably represented the first arrival of the Creek Indians. These inhabitants built mounds and lived inside a stockaded village in the swamps. Burials of the historic Creek Indians on the middle section of the plateau are preserved exactly as they were found.

Alligator at Okefenokee. Adults may reach weights of up to 500 pounds and lengths of 9 feet.

15. Southern Appalachian Highlands

THE beautiful Blue Ridge and Great Smoky mountains form the southern anchor of the Appalachian chain. The chain rose up from the sea some 200 million years ago to heights that rivaled the present-day Rockies and stretched in an unbroken chain from Newfoundland to Alabama.

Unlike the craggy, glacier-carved peaks of New England, the Southern Appalachian highlands were untouched by the glaciers of the Ice Age. Their lofty, rounded peaks include more than a score of peaks higher than New Hampshire's Mt. Washington. The peaks of the Great Smokies, with their cloud-filled gaps, foggy coves, and mist-shrouded slopes were rounded off over millions of years by wind, rain, and frost.

Blue Ridge Mountains

Considered by many to be the most beautiful and dramatic portion of the ancient Appalachian chain, the Blue Ridge Mountains extend for a distance of 550 miles from southern Pennsylvania south to north-eastern Georgia and include the spectacular Great Smoky Mountains and the highest peaks east of the Rocky Mountains.

The Blue Ridge region is divided into two natural parts by the Roanoke River, the southernmost stream to flow eastward through the mountains: the northern Blue Ridge and the southern Blue Ridge. The northern Blue Ridge, with peaks that reach up above 4,000 feet elevation, never exceeds 14 miles in width and narrows to form a single ridge that rises 1,200 feet above the Great Valley on the west and 2,000 feet above the Piedmont on the east. One of the distinctive features of the northern region are the numerous wind gaps, remnants of ancient streams that once flowed eastward through the mountains, as the Potomac, James, and Roanoke rivers do today.

The southern Blue Ridge, south of Roanoke, Virginia, broadens into a dramatic mountain upland that reaches a width of 80 miles near Asheville, North Carolina, and forms a dramatic cluster of high peaks along a frontal scarp along the Tennessee–North Carolina boundary that makes up the Unaka and Great Smoky mountains. Here 46 peaks exceed 6,000 feet

Key to Sites

1. Cumberland Gap National Historic Park
2. Linville Gorge and Caverns
3. Mount Mitchell
4. Davy Crockett Tavern at Morristown
5. Shining Rock Wilderness Area
6. Great Smoky Mountains National Park
7. Carl Sandburg Home
8. Joyce Kilmer Cove Forest
9. Historic Traveler's Rest

10. New Echota—restored capital of the Cherokee Nation
11. Mabry Mill on the Blue Ridge Parkway
12. Peaks of Otter Recreation Area
13. Grand Caverns
14. Big Meadows
15. Luray Caverns
16. Thunderbird Museum and Archeological Park
17. Skyline Caverns

18. Harpers Ferry National Historic Site
19. Chesapeake & Ohio Canal National Historic Park
20. New River Gorge
21. Cranberry Glades
22. Cass Scenic Railroad
23. National Radio Astronomy Observatory
24. Seneca Rocks
25. Smoke Hole
26. Dolly Sods Wilderness Area

Blue Ridge farmlands

Graybacks

Giant sandstone boulders, known locally as graybacks, are a common sight in the forests and on the slopes of the Southern Appalachians. Often found isolated near forest trails or in groups of boulder fields, the graybacks are a legacy of the awesome power of frost action, which originally pried them loose from the summits. Slowly, over thousands of years, they moved down the slopes, pulled by gravity and the successive freezing and thawing of the forest floor.

The Piedmont—Foothills of the Blue Ridge

The gently rolling hills of the Piedmont Plateau east of the Blue Ridge form what can be called the foothills of the Southern Appalachians. The Piedmont, the least mountainous portion of the Appalachian highlands, is an ancient erosion surface that rises above the lowlands of the Coastal Plain to the east and lies as much as 1,800 feet below the high peaks of the Blue Ridge to the west. A few isolated granite domes that have survived millions of years of weathering rise above the undulating landscape. Stone Mountain in Georgia, for example, is an ancient granite dome that stands 650 feet above the surrounding Piedmont and is about one and a half miles long.

altitude, culminating at Mt. Mitchell, the highest peak in the eastern United States at 6,684 feet, and Mt. Le Conte, which rises a mile above the town of Gatlinburg, Tennessee, some 6 miles to the west. From near Blowing Rock, North Carolina, the great frontal mountains of the Blue Ridge slowly decrease in elevation from 4,000 feet to 1,000 feet near Gainsville, Georgia. Unlike the river-pierced northern section the southern Blue Ridge is not cut through by a single stream.

Climate of the Southern Highlands

The Southern Appalachian highlands, swept by the warm, moisture-laden prevailing winds from the Gulf Stream, receive more precipitation than any place in the United States except the Pacific Northwest. This tremendous amount of snow and rainfall, in some areas of the Great Smokies almost 100 inches, has created a lush and complex forest environment, with over 100 native species of trees, and life zones that vary from fertile coves to wind-swept high-peak fir forests and dun-colored grass balds.

Wind Gaps of the Northern Blue Ridge

One of the most striking features of the northern Blue Ridge Mountains are the water gaps created by the James and Potomac rivers and the ancient wind gaps at Manassas Gap, Ashley Gap, and Snickers Gap. The former streams that once flowed through these wind gaps were captured, or pirated, at their headwaters by the meandering Shenandoah River, a tributary of the Potomac, which flowed southward along a weak rock structure west of the Blue Ridge.

The Fall Line

The Southern Appalachians, from the Blue Ridge southwestward through the Great Smokies and Natahala mountains, rise west of a boundary called the Fall Line, named by the early pioneers of the region, that connects the places on the map where rapids and waterfalls made upstream travel by boat impractical, if not impossible. Most of the region's major cities—Richmond, Raleigh, Columbia, and Augusta—were founded at these upstream points along the Fall Line. Rising to the west of the Fall Line are the low foothills known as the Piedmont and beyond, the crest of the Southern Appalachians.

Cumberland Gap—Route of the Warrior's Path and Daniel Boone's Wilderness Road

At historic Cumberland Gap, where the western wall of the ancient Appalachian Mountains in westernmost Tennessee and Virginia opens into the Bluegrass region of Kentucky, four natural features combine to open the way through the Appalachians—

*High peaks rising above a sea of mist created by the moisture-rich prevailing winds
from the Gulf Stream that sweep over the southern Appalachians*

the gap or notch at Cumberland Mountain cut by Yellow Creek; the Middleboro Basin, a large flat area formed by the impact of a meteor or the collapse of a huge underground bubble; Yellow Creek Valley; and the "narrows," a gap that crosses Pine Mountain and opens into the Bluegrass country of Kentucky.

These four features form a natural doorway through the mountains, long used by the Indians to reach the buffalo hunting grounds of Kentucky. The gap was also an important feature on the ancient Warrior's Path, a trail used by generations of raiding Indians, that led south from the Potomac River across the gap and north to Ohio. In 1775, Daniel Boone and 30 men marked out the Wilderness Trail from Cumberland Gap into Kentucky. Emigration began immediately, and by the end of the Revolutionary War some 12,000 people had crossed into the new territory, opening the first American Western frontier.

Cumberland Gap National Historical Park contains more than 20,000 acres in Kentucky, Virginia, and Tennessee.

Hensley Pioneer Settlement at Cumberland Gap

The Hensley Settlement, situated on an isolated plateau on Brush Mountain in Cumberland Gap National Park, thrived for nearly five decades as a community of 12 scattered farmsteads. It was established about 1904 by Sherman Hensley, who, with his family, constructed the buildings here, mostly of hewn chestnut logs with shake roofs. They also split rails for fences. In the decades after 1925, the settlement

Pioneer split-rail fence at the Hensley Settlement

Cumberland Gap—nature's doorway to Kentucky's Bluegrass country and to Daniel Boone's Wilderness Road

Grassy bald and heath barren of purple rhododendron. The heath barrens of the highlands, also called "plains" or "hells," are densely covered with low-growing shrubs and dotted with stunted, flagged spruce, shaped by the prevailing westerly winds.

reached a peak population of about 100 people. During the late 1940s the settlement was abandoned. Since 1965, the National Park Service has restored three of the farmsteads with their houses, barns, fences, and fields, as well as the schoolhouse and cemetery.

Balds of the Southern Appalachians

Although there is no true timberline in the Southern Appalachians, not all of the high ridges and mountains are completely forested. Some of the summits are marked by treeless areas called balds. These balds are among the most noted of southern vegetational communities, similar to the lawns of New England's White Mountains and high grassy tracts in the Bighorn and Beartooth mountains in the Rockies. Their history is vague, but at least a few are recorded in pre-European Indian lore. Fire and high, cold winds are the most commonly cited causes for their creation. Following pioneer settlement of the highlands in the early 1800s, grazing livestock further increased the size of the balds.

Balds are of two distinct types, grassy and heath; both are characterized as areas of extreme exposure. Grassy or smooth balds occur primarily within high-elevation deciduous forests. Ranging from garden to pasture size the open fields contain herbs, grasses and sedges, such as bald oat and autumn bent, along with numerous weed species introduced with domestic grazing. Among the typical grass balds are Russell and Spence fields within the Great Smokies National Park and the extensive, almost meadowlike balds crowning Roan and its satellite mountains on the Tennessee–North Carolina border.

Heath, or wooly, balds are usually found where there are high-peak spruce-fir forests, although they can extend well below them. As the name implies, they are dominated by members of the *Ericaceae*, or heath family, such as rhododendron, mountain laurel, azalea, and blueberry. Depending on the exposure the shrub understory varies from 3 to 10 feet in height, forming tangled, almost impenetrable stands called hells by the highlanders. The heath balds reach their flowering peak in mid-June at Gregory's Bald in the Smokies, famous for its flame azaleas, and at Roan Mountain, the site of the largest continuous stand of rhododendron in the world.

With the establishment of the national parks and national forests and the end of livestock grazing within their boundaries, the balds are slowly shrinking in size. Whether the forest will cover the balds completely, ending the dazzling floral displays and grassy vista points, will be settled only with the passage of time.

Ancient Cove Forests of the Southern Appalachians

Ancient cove forests occur at altitudes below 4,500 feet in areas where the soil is deep and loggers have either bypassed or spared virgin stands of trees. Within the Southern Appalachians, the best examples are Linville Gorge and Joyce Kilmer Memorial Forest, both in North Carolina, and the untouched hardwood stands of the Great Smoky Mountains. Areas logged only once also will return to mature hardwood forests, but it will be some time before the trees approach the size of those within the untouched stands.

The cove forests culminate in either of two types, hemlock or hardwood, depending upon the soil and microclimate conditions. Eastern hemlock is common along streambanks and on lower slopes to approximately 4,000 feet. In previously disturbed areas, maple, beech, and birch may also be interspersed along with extensive stands of Rosebay and Catawba rhododendron. Where the hemlocks exist in pure groves, undergrowth may be virtually nonexistent. In Linville Gorge the hemlock trunks climb massively to the sky, with only a few strands of light penetrating

through the dense canopy. The trees were old before the first settlers saw them, already saplings when Columbus discovered America. The hemlock forests were in some ways fortunate since their wood was less valuable than that of the hardwoods, and many stands were spared or allowed to recover after only a single cutting.

Hardwood forests thrive in drier, richer soils than hemlocks, reaching the peak of their development within the cove and bottom valleys of the Southern Appalachians. A mixed deciduous forest is the usual culmination, dominated by white and red oak, American beech, sugar maple, yellow poplar, black cherry, basswood, yellow buckeye, cucumber magnolia, and silver-bell. Most of these trees reach record heights within the Great Smoky Mountains National Park.

In former years the list also would have included the American chestnut. With its cascade of white blossoms crowning the treetops in spring, *Castanea dentata* was one of the dominant and most useful trees of the eastern climax forest. But now only bleached remnants remain. A fungus, *Endothia parasitica*, was accidentally introduced, first in New York City in 1904, then rapidly spread throughout the entire East during the 1920s and 1930s. The fungus penetrates the tree through any small wound, infecting the cambium layer of the bark, stopping the flow of sap and literally strangling the tree.

The chestnut was valued by the Indians and then the early settlers. The nuts, along with acorns, were a principal wintertime food, eaten roasted, boiled, or

Wayah Bald Tower in the Nantahala Mountains of North Carolina

Ruffed grouse nest and eggs, in the mountain forests of the southern Appalachians, a favorite habitat of these upland birds

ground into paste and baked into bread. The settlers prized not only the nuts for food but also the rot-resistant wood of the trees for building cabins, making shingles, and splitting rails for fences. With the loss of the chestnut, an important member, not only of the ancient cove forests but also the entire eastern deciduous forest, was lost.

High Peak Fir Forests

At elevations above 5,000 feet the upper ridges and peaks of the Southern Appalachians are dominated by Canadian-zone vegetation. Since the temperature drops 2.25°F for every 1,000-foot increase in height, a walk or drive up one of the high mountains is the botanical equivalent of travelling 1,000 miles north to Canada along level ground. Accompanying the increase in altitude is an increase in moisture because the rising humid air is forced into the colder elevations where the water vapor condenses and falls as rain. The climate becomes similar to that encountered much farther north, resulting in Canadian-like islands among the southern forests.

Because of their resistance to cold and desiccation (which occurs in the winter when the available water is locked up in ice and snow), conifers outcompete the deciduous trees at this height, with red spruce and Fraser fir commanding the forest community. The two can be separated with only a little expertise. The spruce is larger, with needles that are green on both sides, and scaly bark; the Fraser fir, on the other hand, has needles that are green on top but have white stripes below, and the bark is smooth. Although the Fraser fir is the true balsam of the Southern highlands, both it and the red spruce were called balsams by the

settlers. To differentiate between the two, Fraser firs were known as he-firs, while the red spruces were called she-firs. In most stands both Fraser and red spruce are present, although the proportion of fir increases in the higher elevations and moister sites, while the percentage of spruce increases toward lower elevations and drier sites. On many of the peaks, especially Mt. Mitchell, the Fraser fir is on the decline because of the wooly aphid, a parasite that first entered New England from Europe in the early 1900s and rapidly spread to the southern mountains.

The conifer forests are often so dense that shrubs and other plants are totally absent from the understory. However where aphids, fire, or windfalls have created gaps, a rich shrub layer quickly appears, with rhododendron, scarlet elder, gooseberry, and blueberry flourishing amid luxuriant ferns. Yellow birch, pin or fire cherry, American mountain ash and mountain maple follow in secondary succession. In time though the firs once again will prevail. It is only on the north slopes, with the constant pruning of the wind and ice, that a true understory forms, consisting of yellow-green mosses, wood sorrel, and shrubs such as winterberry and *Viburnum*.

Ravens were at one time common on the higher mountaintops, but they decreased in number with pioneer settlement and have only recently become

Flame azalea blooming in many hues, from deep yellow to deep red

Barred owl in the high-country forest

Mountain meadows and rock outcroppings above 5,000 feet

reestablished. The high country is also the range of the red squirrels, known as boomers because of their noisy chatter and vigorous actions. Both animals are more typical of the north country and reinforce the sense of geographic dislocation—a taste of Canada in the American South.

Brown Mountain Lights

Brown Mountain lights are mysterious natural lighting effects, named for the mountains where they have been sighted. They are rare glowing lights that

occur at night in the gaps and valleys of the Southern Appalachians. Well authenticated by area naturalists and scientists, these ephemeral natural phenomena glow for a few brief moments then fade away, light up again far away, then disappear again. Authorities believe they are caused either by electrical charges in the moisture-rich atmosphere or by phosphorescence.

Great Smoky Mountains

The Great Smoky Mountains, named for the smokelike haze and fog that often shroud the slopes

Rugged Pisgah Mountains of North Carolina

of the high peaks, are the most dramatic subdivision of the Blue Ridge segment of the Southern Appalachian highlands. The most massive mountain range in the eastern United States, the oval-shape Great Smokies rise for about 70 miles on an almost east-west line between North Carolina and Tennessee. In the eastern portion of the range 16 peaks, crowned by Mt. Le Conte, exceed 6,000 feet, and to the west is the land of the grassy, mysterious balds.

The high-country trails and roads of the Great Smoky Mountains National Park wind through a seemingly endless sea of billowing peaks and valleys and provide access to ancient cove forests, high-peak fir forests and heath balds, old pioneer artifacts, and mountain streams bordered by dense forests and thickets of flame azalea, purple rhododendron, paw-paw bushes, and dogwoods.

Coves of the Great Smoky Mountains

One of the most striking features of the Great Smoky Mountains are the oval-shape, smooth-floored valleys, known locally as coves. Rarely larger than 10 miles in area, the coves are especially common along the northwest slope of the Great Smokies and are believed to be "windows" in the ice sheet that covered the area during the last Ice Age.

Forest Zones of the Great Smokies

The mist-shrouded forests of the Great Smokies have a history that stretches back far beyond the successive ice ages, when the vast ice sheet forced plants south, where most of the Southern Appalachian forest remained untouched. The lush rain forests of the Smokies are the home of more than 130 tree species, 1,400 different kinds of flowering herbs, 2,000 species of fungi, and about 350 species of mosses and related plants.

Below 4,500 feet elevation are the ancient, sheltered cove forests, remnants of the prehistoric circumpolar forest, that covered the globe with deciduous trees before the descent of the ice ages. Here tulip trees grow to 200 feet tall and hemlocks to 100 feet, and the silver-bell, which grows elsewhere as a shrub, reaches an awesome size, with trunks 12 feet around. Below the oval-shape coves are the Piedmont forests of the foothills, dominated by sweet gum, red birch, persimmon, and holly, as well as oaks and hickories.

Stretching above the ancient cove forests are the northern hardwood forests, characterized by giant stands of sugar maple, beech, buckeye, and yellow birch. Near the highest limit of the northern hard-

Wood thrush and young

Pipsissewa, a plant of the pine groves, also known as Prince's pine

woods, at about 6,000 feet, the trees become gnarled and widely spaced, forming what the native residents call the Orchards. Above 6,000 feet are the high-peak fir forests, a land of dense stands of red spruce and Fraser fir similar to the north country forests of southern Canada.

Tulip Trees

Gray-barked tulip trees, with their elegant pale green leaves and sun-colored blossoms, are one of the dominant trees of the Southern Appalachian forest. This magnificent tree, the tallest hardwood in North America, reaches ages of more than 300 years and towers more than 200 feet in height in the sheltered coves, and is found outside the southern mountains only in China.

Silver-Bell Trees

Another distinct tree of the ancient cove forests of the Southern Appalachians is the silver-bell tree. Occasionally reaching heights of more than 100 feet in the coves, their clusters of white flowers color the green forest.

Cades Cove Pioneer Area of the Great Smokies

On the western end of the Great Smokies, surrounded on all sides by high mountains, lies Cades Cove, a pioneer settlement preserved by the National Park Service. The cove was formerly part of the territory ruled by the Cherokee chief, Abram of Chilhowee. Nearby Abrams Creek and Abrams Falls are

Tulip tree, with its sun-colored blossoms, towering to more than 200 feet in sheltered coves

named after him. The cove itself is traditionally said to be named after Abram's wife, Kate.

The first settler of the cove, John Oliver, entered one year before the Treaty of 1819 ceded the land from the Cherokees. Most of the cove's pioneers arrived via the traditional route of immigration from Pennsylvania down the Great Valley of Virginia to northern Tennessee and North Carolina. The majority of the settlers of Cades Cove, like most pioneers in the Southern Appalachians, were Scotch-Irish, who actually were not Irish but Presbyterian Ulstermen who came seeking the open country of the highlands. Families like the Olivers, Gregorys, Shields, and Cables married young and had many children; they lived in one- or two-room cabins, following the mountain philosophy of "do it yourself or do without." Sturdy, self-sufficient farmers, the settlers of Cades Cove grew corn, cabbage, beans, squash, and pumpkins. Barter was the chief means for securing other necessaries, though some obtained cash by selling apples, nuts, animal hides, and distilled spirits. The area was famous for the high quality of its liquor, which included both fruit brands and whiskey.

The cove was not as isolated as sometimes presented; there were three organized schools, regular deliveries of mail, and occasional trips to Maryville and Sevierville. Social functions centered around work and church-going. House raisings, quiltings, corn shuckings, and bean stringings were festive gatherings where stories and news were exchanged. Religious revivals were enthusiastically received for their social as well as spiritual benefit.

Pioneer-era cabin at Cades Cove

Beehives at Cades Cove

By the 1850s Cades Cove supported 685 people in 132 families, but the land was beginning to show signs of exhaustion—even marginal slopes were cleared and farmed. By 1865, due to Civil War casualties and emigration westward, the population had dwindled to 275. It increased to 750 in the early years of this century. In the 1920s, when the park was formed, the cove slowly emptied, signaling an end to 100 years of close-knit community life.

Today an 11-mile loop road follows the periphery of the cove. Many of the original cabins, especially those with the finest axework and construction, have been preserved, allowing a glimpse into highland life of the 19th century. The John Cable grist mill, a general store, and two Baptist churches whose adjoining

The Cable Mill at Cades Cove Pioneer Area

graveyards are dotted with simple hillside stones also remain. A few descendants of the original families still reside in the cove, under Park Service permit, keeping cattle, repairing cantilever barns, and tending bee gums (hollow gum trees in which bees build their hives). In all details the settlement is maintained as faithfully as possible to its original state.

Whether viewed from within or from any of the vantage points surrounding it such as Rich Mountain, Spence Field, or from majestic Thunderhead, Cades Cove is the essence of pastoral serenity, a long look backward.

Rhododendron Hells

The beautiful rhododendron grows thick and wild throughout the Southern Appalachians in dense, twisted thickets known as hells to the local mountain folk. These thickets, formed by the tough, sinuous trunks of the rosebay rhododendron, with their leathery, dark-green leaves, present almost impenetrable barriers to the hiker who wanders off the high-country trails.

Brinegar Pioneer Cabin and the Blue Ridge Parkway

The Brinegar Cabin is a well-preserved example of the construction used by the early settlers in the 18th century, as well as that used by settlers of more remote regions in later times. A one-story log cabin, it consists of two rooms, one in the main block and one in the shed addition. The interior is lighted by one tiny window beside the large stone chimney plus a slightly larger window and central entrance. To the northwest of the house is a frame outbuilding which

Brinegar Pioneer Cabin on the Blue Ridge Parkway

ancient, narrow valleys and coves of the Craggies, the Pisgahs, and the Balsams of North Carolina to the Great Smokies.

Linville Gorge in North Carolina's Pisgah National Forest

The spectacular Linville Gorge in the Grandfather District of the Pisgah National Forest was carved out over thousands of years by the Linville River. The water sliced its way through the Linville Mountains, creating a 1,700-foot-deep chasm as it wound its way south from its headwaters at Grandfather Mountain into the Piedmont to its confluence with the Catawba River. Along its course through the Gorge, the river drops 2,000 feet in 12 miles. The gorge has been preserved within a 7,600-acre wilderness area, noted for its unspoiled rarity of native flora and fauna, including the largest stand of virgin hemlock in the East.

probably served as a dairy.

The cabin is at mile 238.5 on the Blue Ridge Parkway, near Whitehead, North Carolina.

The Blue Ridge Parkway extends for 469 miles through the Southern Appalachian Highlands. From Shenandoah National Park for 355 miles, the parkway follows the crest of the Blue Ridge Mountains, the eastern rampart of the Appalachians. Then, skirting the massive Black Mountains, it weaves through the

Shining Rock Wilderness

North Carolina's Shining Rock Wilderness is a 13,600-acre wild area in the Pisgah National Forest. The area is dominated by Shining Rock Mountain, a natural outcropping of white quartz that rises to a 6,000-feet elevation above the surrounding forest.

Oconalufte Valley Pioneer Farmstead in the southern portion of the Great Smoky Mountains National Park in North Carolina. The Mingus Grist Mill here operates daily, grinding corn just as it did in the 1800s.

Linville Gorge

The New River—A Geological Antiquity

The inappropriately named New River, the only Appalachian highland stream that flows westward across the Ridge and Valley and Appalachian Plateau regions, is one of the oldest rivers in the eastern United States, flowing along the same course it followed in prehistoric times. The wild, turbulent river flows from its headwaters near Blowing Rock, North Carolina, down a steep gradient, then flows across the Ridge and Valley region and enters the Appalachian Plateau and plunges through one of the deepest

Summit of 6,000-foot Shining Rock Mountain, whose white quartz rock is visible for miles

gorges in eastern North America—the New River Canyon. Near Gauley, West Virginia, it merges with the Gauley River to form the Kanawha River.

Glades of the Southern Appalachians—The North Country Islands

The lush bogs of the Southern Appalachians, known locally as glades, are the home of plant and animal species commonly associated with the north country of New England and the Upper Great Lakes, species such as weasels, beaver, black spruce, sundew, pitcher plant, cranberry, and bog rosemary. Like those found far to the north, the bogs of the Southern Appalachians are the remnants of lake basins gouged out by the Ice Age glaciers and are in the transition to becoming dry land.

One of the region's most spectacular sphagnum bogs is the Cranberry Glades area in West Virginia's Monongahela National Forest. Once known as the Wilds of Pocahontas, it covers 53,000 acres and contains the southernmost extension of north country flora and fauna pushed southward by the glaciers of the last Ice Age.

High on the Allegheny Plateau, adjacent to the Monongahela National Forest, are the north country sphagnum bogs, heath mats, and spruce forests of the Dolly Sods area. These large open areas of heath and bog meadows, with their windblown red spruces and beaver dams, are similar in appearance to the Canadian tundra thousands of miles to the north.

Henry Clay Furnace

The Henry Clay Furnace was one of the earliest and most important in the Virginia (now West Virginia) iron-smelting industry. Low-grade native ore was employed, and the resulting iron was utilized chiefly by the cut-nail industry. Built by Leonard Lamb for Tassie and Bissell between 1834 and 1836, the Clay Furnace may have continued to operate until 1868, when all the Cheat River ironworks ceased production. Externally the furnace resembles a truncated pyramid. The base is 30 feet square, and the original height was approximately 34 feet. Ore, limestone, and charcoal were charged into the top of the furnace from a tramway which ran to the ore pits. The cold blast furnace was run by steam and produced about four tons of pig iron every 24 hours. Near the furnace was a water pit for cooling the melt. At peak activity, the furnace complex employed about 200 men digging ore, making charcoal, and smelting iron, and a community of almost 500 people grew up close by. The

Named for the Indian tribe that inhabited the Monongahela National Forest area, Seneca Rocks tower nearly 1,000 feet above the Potomac River. They are mere stumps of a once magnificent mountain formed 275 million years ago, inhabited today by stunted table mountain pines and the hardy mats of silvery whitlowwort, alumroot, mosses, and lichens.

furnace is southeast of Cheat Neck in Cooper's Rock State Forest in Monongalia County, West Virginia.

Harpers Ferry National Historical Park in the Blue Ridge Mountains

Harpers Ferry, situated on a point of land at the confluence of the Shenandoah and Potomac rivers in West Virginia and dominated by the Blue Ridge Mountains, was a tiny wilderness village founded in the early 1700s. The first settler here was Peter Stephens, a trader, who arrived in 1733 and set up a primitive ferry service at the junction of the two rivers. By the mid-19th century, after the construction of the Chesapeake and Ohio Canal and the Baltimore & Ohio Railroad, it was a town of some 3,000 inhabitants, an important arms-producing center, and a transportation link between east and west. In October 1859, John Brown's raid jarred the peaceful settlement, and the civil war that followed 17 months later was to destroy the town's economy. Brown's objective was to liberate the slaves by violence and set up a stronghold of free Negroes in the Appalachian Mountains. Because of the town's geographical location and its railway system, Union and Confederate troop movements through the town were frequent, and soldiers of both armies occupied the town intermittently throughout the war. The

Harpers Ferry—for years following the devastation of the Civil War, empty buildings stood in silent desolation as nature reclaimed once-active industrial sites.

Mather Gorge on the old Chesapeake and Ohio Canal

largest military operation against Harpers Ferry occurred prior to the Battle of Antietam in September 1862, when General Thomas J. "Stonewall" Jackson's Confederate corps seized the town and captured the 12,700-man Union garrison.

During summer, conducted walks, demonstrations, and short talks by historians will help you understand the old armory complex, the blacksmith shop, the ruins at Virginius Island, and John Brown's raid.

Chesapeake and Ohio Canal

In 1828, after the settled frontier was extended beyond the Allegheny Mountains, the Chesapeake and Ohio Canal Company was organized to build a canal up the Potomac River valley to provide easy communication between east and west. The final link between Dam No. 6 at Great Cacapon and Cumberland, Maryland, was completed in 1850. A series of 74 locks, constructed at a cost of $22 million, raised the water from sea level at Georgetown to 609 feet at Cumberland, more than 184 miles away. The completion of the faster and less expensive Baltimore & Ohio Railroad made the canal obsolete. However, canal boats carrying flour, coal, grain, and lumber were used here until 1924, when a serious flood put the "Old Ditch"

out of business. The canal towpath, followed by the mule teams that pulled the canal boats, is unobstructed and follows the entire length of the canal.

Shenandoah National Park— Heart of the Northern Blue Ridge

Shenandoah National Park extends for 80 miles along the heart of the northern Blue Ridge Mountains in northwestern Virginia. The park covers 331 square miles and contains 60 peaks ranging in elevation from 3,000 to 4,000 feet along the crest of the ridge. The spectacular 105-mile Skyline Drive Parkway winds near the crest of the ridge, flanked to the east by spur ridges with deep coves above the tree-covered foothills of the Piedmont and on the west by the beautiful fields and farms of the Shenandoah Valley, cut by meandering streams.

The bulk of the park is covered by hardwood forests broken here and there by meadowlands and old fields. At the highest elevations, stands of hemlocks, firs, spruces, and pines are dominant. This northern Blue Ridge forest is noted for its luxuriant undergrowth of rhododendrons, mountain laurel, and flame azalea. Two areas of interest between Thornton Gap and Swift Run Gap on Skyline Drive are the high-

Virginia's Humpback Covered Bridge

country woodlands at Skyland, 41 miles south of Front Royal, and the open fields at the Big Meadows area, in the central section of the park.

Virginia's Humpback Covered Bridge

The Humpback Bridge was built in 1835 as part of the James River and Kanawha Valley Turnpike. It is the oldest remaining covered bridge in Virginia and the only one of its type in the country. Constructed of hand-hewn oak timbers and held together with locust pins, the bridge has no middle support. The center floor and roof are eight feet higher than the bridge ends, and the discrepancy produces the peculiar humped appearance. Both ends of the bridge are supported by high stone foundations.

The bridge is eight-tenths of a mile southwest of the intersection of U.S. 60 and County Route 651 near Covington, Virginia.

Mabry Mill at Mile 176.1 on the Blue Ridge Parkway. This mountain road passes through a region rich in the history of the late 1700s, when the Blue Ridge marked the edge of the western frontier.

16. Gulf Coast and the Florida Shore

ABOUT one million years ago the present shoreline of the Gulf of Mexico was formed when
a massive island joined with the mainland
of North America, forming the Florida Peninsula. At the Straits of Florida the vast mud flats,
marshes, deltas, and sand beaches of the Gulf Coast
meet the string of gemlike coral-built Keys and America's southernmost coast of the Atlantic Ocean.

Most of the Gulf Coast is protected by barrier
islands that form a sweeping arc from 140-mile-long
Padre Island off the oil fields and refineries of the
Texas Gulf country through Louisiana's Sabine Shoals
to Deer Island and the barrier reefs of the Gulf Islands National Seashore that begin in the Mississippi
Sound down to the great mangrove forests of the Ten
Thousand Islands and the Florida Keys. The lagoons
they shelter from the often violent Gulf storms form
a portion of the Intracoastal Waterway—a sailing
route that stretches from New Jersey to Mexico.

The Gulf of Mexico is a virtually enclosed sea.
Except for a few openings on the eastern edge of the
Gulf between the islands of the Antilles, it is completely encircled by land. The great river-built deltas
on the coast have been created by countless tons of
earth washed down from the Central Prairies and
Great Plains by the Mississippi, Rio Grande, the

Brazos and Colorado of Texas, the Chattahoochee, and
others.

Unlike the Atlantic, with its powerful currents,
the currents of the Gulf are weak and incapable of
transporting the awesome loads of river-eroded soils—
some carried from as far away as the Rocky Mountains of Montana, the Black Hills, Dakota Badlands,
and the Minnesota northwoods—out to sea. This results in the piling up of sediments at the mouths of
the rivers that empty into the Gulf and the forming
of great, triangular-shaped bulges known as deltas.

From the mud-washed deltas to the semitropical
coral reefs off the southern coast of Florida, the warm
waters of the Gulf create an incredibly diverse habitat for wildlife and marine animals—from the moss-
draped cypress swamps and hammocks to coral reefs
to sawgrass glades and mangrove forests.

Big Thicket Region of the Texas Coastal Plain

The twelve portions, or units, of the Big Thicket
National Preserve in southeastern Texas cover a 50-
square-mile area with a wild, primeval tangle of ferns,
oaks, pines, hollies, and orchids—a remnant of an
ancient forest that once spread across the gently roll-

354

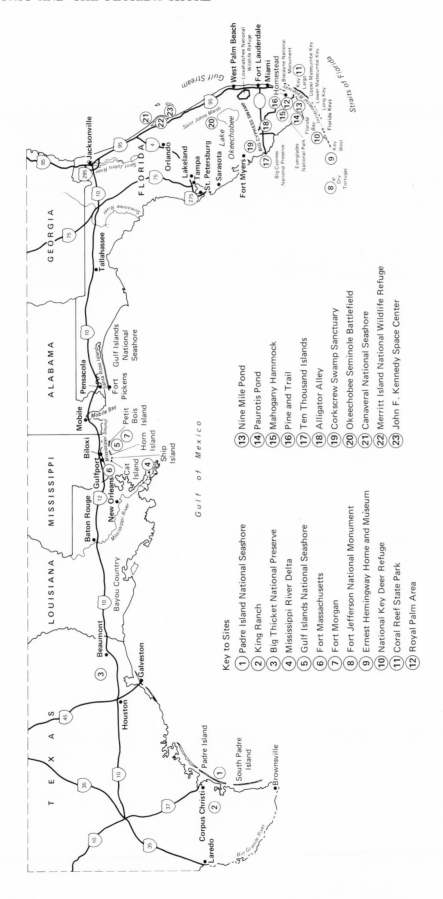

Key to Sites

① Padre Island National Seashore
② King Ranch
③ Big Thicket National Preserve
④ Mississippi River Delta
⑤ Gulf Islands National Seashore
⑥ Fort Massachusetts
⑦ Fort Morgan
⑧ Fort Jefferson National Monument
⑨ Ernest Hemingway Home and Museum
⑩ National Key Deer Refuge
⑪ Coral Reef State Park
⑫ Royal Palm Area
⑬ Nine Mile Pond
⑭ Paurotis Pond
⑮ Mahogany Hammock
⑯ Pine and Trail
⑰ Ten Thousand Islands
⑱ Alligator Alley
⑲ Corkscrew Swamp Sanctuary
⑳ Okeechobee Seminole Battlefield
㉑ Canaveral National Seashore
㉒ Merritt Island National Wildlife Refuge
㉓ John F. Kennedy Space Center

Shrimp boat beached on the coast—a testimony to the force of the Gulf storms. Shrimp boats are a common sight along the barrier islands. Shrimp hatch in the open Gulf, but by the time they are juveniles they reach the estuaries inside the barrier islands, where they grow to be adults before returning to the open sea.

ing hills. The Turkey Creek Unit takes in a 7,800-acre floodplain community. The Beech Creek Unit is noted for its stands of beech, magnolia, and loblolly pine, while the Hickory Creek Savannah Unit is noted for its open long-leaf pine forest and wetlands.

Elsewhere within the preserve is the undeveloped 25,025-acre Lance Rosier Unit, where one of the first oil wells in Texas was drilled in the mid-1860s. Along the course of the Neches River are dense cypress sloughs, bluffs and hammocks, acidbog baygalls, floodplain hardwood forests, and abandoned channel lakes. On the northern edge of the thicket is the Alabama and Coushatta Indian Reservation.

King Ranch on the Texas Coastal Plain

King Ranch is one of the best known cattle enterprises in the Southwest. It was founded by Richard King, who purchased a Spanish land grant of 75,000 acres on Santa Gertrudis Creek in 1852. By the middle of the 20th century, the ranch included 1,225,000 acres covering most of four counties. The largest ranch in the United States, it is still in operation and renowned for developing the Santa Gertrudis, a breed of large cattle which thrives in warm climates. The

present brick house and most of the other buildings date from 1912. The ranch is near and in Kingsville.

Padre Island National Seashore in the Texas Gulf

First known as the White Island, Padre Island stretches for 113 miles along the Texas Gulf from Corpus Christi on the north almost to Mexico on the south, separated from the mainland by Laguna Madre, a shallow lagoon with a maximum width of 10 miles. From Gulf to lagoon, the island consists of a wide sand beach and outer dunes, where senna and croton shrubs grow along the borders and railroad vines reach 20 feet and more across the sand, blending their purple flowers with the yellow blossoms of evening primrose. On the grassy flats of the island's interior are meadowlarks, marsh hawks, great horned owls, and in winter sandhill cranes. Nearer the lagoon stands of seauvium form thick islands of vegetation where they have anchored small dunes.

This great barrier island, built by wave action, is famous as a graveyard for ships driven ashore by the fury of the Gulf storms. The most famous of these disasters occurred when a 20-ship Spanish treasure fleet ran into a hurricane and broke up on shore. Of some 300 survivors only two lived through the bloody Karankawa Indian attacks and the hardships of the march down the coast to Mexico.

Spindletop Oil Field

The tapping of the Spindletop Oil Field by the Lucas Gusher opened the Texas Gulf Coastal Plain to commercial development and marked the beginning of the modern petroleum industry. By 1922 Texas was the third largest oil-producing state in the country, and by 1927 it was the largest. After the gusher "blew in" on January 10, 1901, a geyser of petroleum flowed uncapped for six days at an estimated rate of 75,000 barrels a day. The site is marked by a granite monument, near which are storage tanks built in 1901, a well pump, and a replica of a wooden derrick.

The oil field is three miles south of Beaumont on Spindletop Avenue in Jefferson County, Texas.

The Louisiana Coast—A Land of Cheniers and Bayous

Louisiana's 1,500-mile-long coast on the Gulf of Mexico is fringed by a wide, flat treeless plain dominated by marshes of sedge, grass, and rushes and dotted by a mosaic of seemingly endless, shallow salt-water lakes, crazy-built bayous in ancient river beds, and quaint lagoons that reach in from the Gulf. Except in the Mississippi Delta area the marshes are bordered near the sea by sand and shell barrier beaches running parallel to the coast. These beaches rise to a crest and are covered by stands of moss-draped live oaks on their inner slopes. Sand and shell ridges rise above the marshlands. They are remnants of former barrier beaches called chenieres because of the oaks found growing there.

In addition to the cheniers such as Pecan Island and Grand Cheniere in southwest Louisiana, several salt domes, or "land islands," a mile or more long rise above the surrounding marshes. Five distinct surface mounds known as the "Five Islands" extend from 10 miles west of New Iberia to the mouth of the Atchafalaya River. They reach their maximum elevation of 196 feet at Avery Island. They are among the most famous of the hundreds of salt domes in the Gulf region.

Cypress Forests of the Bayous

The dramatic, moss-draped cypresses achieve their most vivid effect along the shores of the bayous, swamps, and lakes near the Gulf Coast. The traveller in this region occasionally will sight a "ghost" forest of towering, bleached cypresses, killed by the inroads of salt water. The cypress is readily distinguished by its feathery green foliage, flared trunk, and "knees," a part of the root system that pushes itself above the water for air. Spanish moss, or long moss, a seed-producing plant of the pineapple family, with minute, lilylike, straw-colored flowers, drapes the cypresses and live oaks of the Gulf Coast. An air-feeding plant that reproduces by division, it merely uses the tree as an anchor.

Amistad Dam straddling the U.S.–Mexico boundary on the lower Rio Grande River, which flows for 2,200 miles from its headwaters in the Colorado Rockies into the Gulf of Mexico

Sand dunes at Padre Island National Seashore

Great Mississippi Delta

The coast of the Gulf of Mexico from northern Florida to Texas was created by immense cargoes of silt washed down from numerous rivers in the heartland of the nation into the Gulf, constantly expanding the boundaries of the land. The Mississippi, the Father of Waters, carries more than 400 million tons of sediment each year into its mouth and has been pushing the coastline out into the Gulf at an average rate of 300 feet a year, forming one of the major deltas of the world. Some of this earth-building debris is carried out by the weak currents of the Gulf, which is virtually an enclosed sea, but most settles at the mouth, forcing the Mississippi to branch into a mosaic of channels and minor deltas.

The bayou-dotted Delta of the Mississippi has a surface area of about 12,000 square miles and is constantly being added to and anchored by water plants such as the water hyacinth, which thrives in the tide-washed mudflats. Introduced from Brazil, these plants, with their orchidlike blossoms, can double the area covered by their leaves within a mere three weeks, shutting out all sunlight from the water, anchoring the mud and debris washed down by the rivers, and creating a biological desert as well as choking navigable waterways.

Inland the countless shallow, mud-choked bayous of the Delta form a lazy, meandering maze. Derived from the Choctaw Indian word meaning a "sluggish stream," many of the bayous have been completely cut off from the Mississippi by the shifting mud of the Delta.

Mississippi Valley Alluvial Plain

The Mississippi River alluvial plain sweeps southward along the river from Arkansas sloping gradually about 2½ inches per mile to sea level at the Gulf of

Mexico, where it forms a broad, beltlike landscape with an average width of 50 miles. Narrow near southern Arkansas, it widens considerably below Baton Rouge, where it swings southeastward to its mouth at the Mississippi Delta. Bluffs rise to 300 feet elevation, walling the alluvial plain on the east and west, sloping away from the valley on each side.

Along the Mississippi and its natural outlets are ridges known as natural levees. The rich bottomlands broken by meanders, cutoffs, and crescent-shape oxbow lakes make up the frontlands of black, sticky clay formed from the silt and mud washed down the ancient floodplain. Behind the frontlands are backlands of fine silt and shallow swamps and deeper, permanent cypress-tupelo swamps that serve as catch-basins for overflow and rainfall.

The immense alluvial floodplain formed by the Mississippi and Yazoo rivers extends northward from, as one local wag put it, "Catfish Row in Vicksburg to the lobby of the Peabody Hotel in Memphis"—a region dominated by rich farmlands, plantation towns, meandering streams, lakes, sloughs, and cutoffs.

Gulf Islands National Seashore

The sandy string of barrier islands that lies parallel to the mainland and makes up the Gulf Islands National Seashore stretches from West Ship Island

Sand dunes and salt marsh on the Gulf Islands—part of the string of barrier islands stretching along the Atlantic coast from Texas to New Jersey

in the Mississippi Gulf eastward for 150 miles to the far end of Santa Rosa Island in Florida. These wind-swept islands buffer the mainland of the Gulf Coast from storms. They harbor a wide variety of coastal life ranging from sea oats on the dunes to palmetto, slash pine, and scrub live oak, all of which grow behind the dunes. On the sound side of the barriers are large areas of salt marshes inhabited by alligators, great blue herons, ospreys, and brown pelicans. On the mainland itself are the bayous and forests of hardwoods and loblolly pine.

A few areas of the mainland have been included in this Gulf Coast preserve. Among them are the Old Spanish Trail in the Davis Bayou of Mississippi; the Naval Live Oaks near Gulf Breeze, Florida; historic Fort Barrancas near Pensacola and Fort Pickens on Santa Rosa Island, both in the Florida Gulf.

Florida's Biscayne National Park and Coral Reefs

Biscayne National Park, one of the nation's largest marine preserves, encompasses three distinct biological systems: Biscayne Bay, an important nursery area for fisheries between the Upper Florida Keys and the mainland; the undeveloped upper Florida Keys with their natural vegetation; and the coral reef, found exclusively in the southern part of the United States.

The Biscayne reefs, which continue southward into the southern Florida Keys, lie in waters no deeper than 40 feet. These limestone reefs owe their existence to groups of animals and plants that deposit calcium around themselves as a protective shell. The reefs are made up of coral both living and dead, which build on top of the limestone houses of their ancestors in moving salt water no deeper than 200 feet and warmer than 70 degrees. The world of the coral reef is in-

Stand of cypress. Note the "knees" in the foreground, through which the tree breathes.

Fort Pickens on Santa Rosa Island, one of several forts established in the 1820s to develop Pensacola Bay into a major naval base. The only action Fort Pickens saw came during the Civil War.

habited by colorful porkfish, urasse, queen angelfish, and neon gobies. Sponges, sea "grasses," hard corals, and plantlike sea feathers and sea whips cover the bottom.

The Florida Keys

In the waters off the southern Florida coast, low islands or coral reefs are called keys, an English modification of the Spanish word *cayo*, meaning "small island." Key Largo, some 30 miles long and less than 2 miles wide, is the northernmost of the chain of limestone and coral islands that make up the Florida Keys and extend in a sweeping arc to Key West, more than 100 miles out in the Gulf of Mexico.

The northern, or upper, half of this barrier chain, stretching from Biscayne Bay down to Loggerhead Key, is made of an ancient coral reef on the edge of the peninsula plateau, which drops off rapidly into the depths of the Gulf Stream, or the Florida Current. The southern half formerly consisted of a single large limestone island, which was raised above the sea

during the first Pleistocene era and was later partly submerged. The keys are noted for their sandy, shell-strewn beaches and are surrounded by a shallow sea famous for its green, occasionally purplish color and an aquatic terrain consisting of coral patch reefs and turtle grass. Many of the upper Keys have low, wet areas blanketed with mangrove thickets and junglelike uplands where silver palms, coconut palms, mahoganies, gumbo limbos, wild tamarinds, and other tropical West Indian hardwoods grow in rank profusion. There are no pines on the upper Keys; on the lower Keys, pines are common.

Little is known about the aboriginal inhabitants of the Keys. The Arawak and Caribee tribes are believed to have been the first in the region, based on the discovery of pottery in the many mounds along the Keys. These tribes were driven out by the powerful seafaring Calusa, who had at least two villages on the Keys at Cuchiyago and Guarungunve, in which they accumulated gold from wrecked and pillaged ships.

The old shipping routes of Spain and England passed close to the Keys, and in later years schooners trading along the coast picked their way through these waters. Strong currents and high winds, storms and violent hurricanes, and the ever-present reefs and shoals made passage through the Florida Straits a risky business at best.

Mangrove Forests of the Ten Thousand Islands

While corals grow off the wave-lapped Keys facing the Atlantic, dense thickets of red, white, and black mangroves rise on the Gulf side from the tide-washed flats of Florida's lower coast. With their exposed vertical roots, mangroves give the impression of a forest marching on stilts. They grow from floating seeds shaped like elephant tusks that anchor on the shallow mud flats. Their aerial roots collect tide-washed earth and debris, gradually forming small, then large islands and building up the shoreline back of the trees. Among the world's greatest mangrove forests are those extending north from Key West to the wild, partially submerged Ten Thousand Islands area of the Everglades region. Made up of elongated shell bars, some only 4 feet wide, the islands along the Shark River estuary support mangroves that reach heights of 80 feet with trunks 7 feet around.

Mangroves occur where southward creeping glades waters and salt waters meet.

Fort Jefferson in the Gulf of Mexico

During the first half of the 19th century, the United States began a chain of seacoast defenses from Maine to Texas. Fort Jefferson, the largest of these, was once the key to the control of the Gulf of Mexico because of its strategic location. Commerce from the Mississippi Valley to the Atlantic passed through this vital area. The fort was active during the Civil War, Spanish-American War, and World War I. The Lincoln conspirators were confined here for several years. The fort's massive ruins provide eloquent testimony to its former strength as a guardian of the southernmost coastlines of the United States.

The massive brick citadel of old Fort Jefferson—a New World Gibraltar—is situated on Garden Key in the Dry Tortugas archipelago, 70 miles west of Key West.

Southern bald eagle in the Everglades—the immense nests or aeries of this endangered species may be seen in the tall slash pines.

Everglades—A River of Grass

Until 1842 the Everglades were an unexplored, mysterious region known only to the Seminole Indians who found sanctuary there from invading whites. It forms a vast 50-mile-wide river of grass that covers 2,100 square miles of flat low-lying terrain—an area larger than the state of Delaware—with thousands of freshwater sloughs and channels that nowhere reach an elevation higher than 10 feet above sea level. The interior sawgrass country consists of open prairies, or glades, of sawgrass that reach heights of 12 feet and often stretch for hundreds of miles as far as the eye can see. During the wet season this river of grass flows inches per mile, dropping a total of 15 feet over

The black anhinga, or "snakebird," is a common sight in the Atlantic and Gulf Coast swamps, where it is often observed swimming with only its long, snakelike neck and head visible above the water.

its course before emptying into the Gulf of Mexico.

At the high elevations are numerous, often dome-shape tree islands made up of thick tangles of bay, holly, and magnolia overgrown with countless vines, enclosed by the sea of sawgrass. Elsewhere, rising above the sawgrass, are dense, junglelike hammocks and higher elevations of pinelands on the limestone bed of the ancient sea that underlies the region. The region is bordered on the south and west by great mangrove swamps in the tidal flats and saltwater shallows.

The Everglades National Park encompasses eight natural life zones, or ecosystems, dependent on the balance between flood and fire, fresh and salt water, rainy season and drought. Freshwater sloughs such as the Shark River and Taylor Slough are the main channels bringing glades water into the park. Acting as reservoirs, sloughs help plant life and animals such as deer, opossum, raccoon, and otter survive the dry season. The Anhinga Trail offers good views of Taylor Slough wildlife. Alligators, fish, water snakes, and a wide variety of birds including anhingas, American coots, and purple gallinules, migrate here in winter. The Shark Valley observation tower, just off the Tami-ami Trail in the northern section of the park, looks out over expanses of slough and freshwater prairie.

The Pinelands

Long Pine Key Nature Trail off the road east of the Pa-hay-okee Trail, winds for seven miles through typical pinelands habitat. The pinewoods are found only in elevated areas of bare limestone outcrops. Along the trail at Pinelands slash pine appears to grow right out of the limestone. The trees root in "solution holes," dissolved potholes in the underlying limestone. The pines would not reproduce and survive without fire, which destroys competing vegetation and exposes mineral soil for seedlings. The pine country has an understory of saw palmetto, rough-leaf velvet-seed, and short-leaf fig.

Cypress Forest

The road over the glades toward Florida Bay passes through the cypress forest, an open area of scattered, stunted pond cypresses, which grow where marl or lime muds build up in solution holes.

The Glades

The Pa-hay-okee Trail boardwalk leads to an elevated platform overlooking typical glades that give the national park area its name. More than 100 species of grass may be seen from this trail, including muhly grass, coinwort, three-awn grass, Everglades beard-grass, love-vine, and arrowhead. Sawgrass, not a true grass but a sedge, is also prominent. These flat prairies are inhabited by pigmy rattlesnake, red-winged blackbirds, and Cape Sable sparrows.

Bald cypress attains ages of up to 600 years.

Hardwood Hammock

The Gumbo Limbo Trail leads to the hardwood hammock, which usually sits about three feet above the surrounding landscape and requires protection from fire, flood, and salt water. Hardwood hammocks do not need extensive roots because a fungus recycles nutrients from the shallow soil to the trees. The Mahogany Hammock Trail passes paurotis palms and some of the largest mahogany trees in the continental United States.

Mangrove Forests

The mangrove forest occurs where southward-creeping glades waters meet salty water. The mangroves, which can be viewed from the Hell's Bay Canoe Trail or West Lake Mangrove Trail, act as nurseries for small marine animals, and their leaves are building blocks for many food chains. Their debris-catching root systems act as effective land builders. Least tolerant of salt water are the buttonwood mangroves; closer toward the shore are the tangles of red, white, and black mangroves.

Coastal Prairie

A number of salt-tolerant plants such as yucca, cactus, and agave, normally associated with desert country, grow on the coastal prairie. They are best viewed from the West Lake and Bear Lake canoe trails. A few hardwood hammocks grow here on old Indian shell mounds but are stunted by the high level of salt in the soil.

Coastal Waterways

The wilderness waterway winds through estuaries and an island-dotted Caribbean marine habitat. The waterway serves as spawning grounds and nurseries for fish, water birds, sea turtles, corals, blue crab, stone crab, and lobster.

Hammocks

Hammocks are circular, islandlike stands of hardwoods and shrubs surrounded by pine woods or glades of sawgrass and spike rush. In the hardwood hammocks tangled vines of rattan, wild grape, and Spanish moss grow on the cabbage palms, magnolias, and oaks. The tropical hammocks that grow on the limestone ridges of southern Florida are made up mostly of trees of West Indian origin: fiddlewood, Madeira, paradise tree, gumbo limbo, and coco plums.

The brilliant-pink roseate spoonbill, often mistaken for a flamingo, is usually sighted fishing for shrimp and small fish in the mangroves along Florida Bay and the Gulf Coast.

Prairies

The prairies of south-central Florida are vast, open, relatively dry grass-covered areas with scattered growths of saw palmettos, scrub oaks, and clusters of cabbage palmettos, broken by tracts of flatwoods, marshes, and hammocks. The most famous of Florida's prairies is the Kissimmee Prairie, which extends from the Orlando vicinity southward to Lake Okeechobee. The prairies are a prime habitat for grasshopper sparrows and sandhill cranes.

Pine Woods

The open pine forests of the South are of two kinds: the flatwoods, low-lying areas of gallberry, myrtle, rosemary, and dense thickets of saw palmetto dominated by slash and longleaf pines; and the rolling, high pinelands with open stands of longleaf pines and sparse undergrowth.

Alligators

Gator holes and nests—mounds of plant debris mixed with mud and up to four feet high and eight feet long—are common along the coastal rivers and

Alligator—"the keeper of the Everglades." It uses its feet and snout to weed out the dense vegetation in limestone sinkholes. Without this constant weeding action, the rooted water plants would choke out the freshwater fish that live in the swamp pools.

swamps of the South from the Carolinas south through Florida and west through the Gulf Coast to the Rio Grande in Texas. The adult alligator may reach lengths of up to 15 feet and weigh up to 500 pounds. Common throughout the sloughs and swamps of the Everglades, the gator catches its prey with its viselike jaws or by stunning it with a blow from its powerful tail. During dry season the alligator often uses its long snout to dig out gator holes to reach water that seeps up from the region's porous limestone bedrock, creating miniature oases for other wildlife.

Big Cypress Swamp—A Subtropical Wilderness

Big Cypress Swamp covers 2,400 square miles of subtropical Florida due north and west of the Everglades National Park. Not a true swamp, the land consists of sandy islands of slash pine, mixed hardwood hammocks, wet and dry prairies, marshes, and estuary mangrove forests.

Rainfall is the lifeblood of this national preserve, falling to the northeast in the lakes of the Kissimmee basin, moving slowly southward to Lake Okeechobee, then draining at the rate of about two inches per mile through Big Cypress into the Everglades and the Gulf of Mexico. The area is about one-third covered with cypress trees, mostly dwarf pond cypress at the edges of the wet prairies and along the sloughs. A few great bald cypresses, some attaining ages of up to 600 years, that escaped the logger's ax earlier in the century, border the ponds festooned with air plants. Sometimes at a considerable distance from the buttressed trunk of the cypress are the knees, a part of

the root system used to aerate the tree. Spanish moss, a member of the pineapple family, is the most conspicuous of the air-growing plants. In contrast to the bright green of the new cypress foliage are the colorful orchids, including the fragrant, narrow-petaled spider orchid, with its large white flowers; the shell orchid and chintz orchid, noted for its odd, mottled flowers; and great orchids, sometimes reaching enormous size. One specimen found in the nearby Everglades was estimated to be 500 years old and was so large four men were needed to lift it.

Corkscrew Swamp

At the heart of the Big Cypress Swamp National Preserve is the Corkscrew Swamp Sanctuary, which contains the last remaining stand of virgin bald cypress in Florida. A mile-long boardwalk trail passes through several habitats of the region: flatwoods of slash pine and saw palmetto; treeless prairies of grasses and sedge; and a dense subtropical forest dominated by pond cypresses and magnificent stands of bald cypress. The domes of pond cypress grow in shallow depressions often rising 80 feet above the surrounding dwarf cypress forest. The ponds in the center of the cypress domes are created by deeper sinkholes, or "solution holes," in the region's limestone

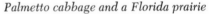

Palmetto cabbage and a Florida prairie

Green tree frog—the male's peeping call may be heard up to one mile away

floor. The sanctuary is also the state's most important rookery for the endangered wood stork.

Wood Storks of the Cypress Swamps

The large white and black, heronlike wood stork, or as it is known locally, the ironhead, is found in the cypress swamps and waterways of the Gulf Coast and Florida during breeding season, when it nests in large colonies in trees. Half as tall as a human, it feeds on fish, crayfish, and other aquatic animals that it snaps with its long, downward-curving bill.

Alligator Alley

This aptly named 84-mile stretch of Florida Highway 84, which goes straight across the southern portion of the state, traverses vast unspoiled areas of the eastern Everglades and western portions of the Big Cypress Swamp. Parking turnouts offer viewing sights to observe the variety of wildlife and natural features of the sloughs and swamplands. Commonly sighted birds include herons, egrets, northern harriers, and red-shouldered hawks in the cypress swamps.

Lake Okeechobee Seminole War Battlefield

On the northern shore of Lake Okeechobee on Christmas Day, 1837, Zachary Taylor won a decisive victory over a band of Seminole and Mikasuki warriors. This victory, which occurred only a few months after General Thomas S. Jessup had inspired Indian resistance by having Osceola and other chiefs seized under a flag of truce, proved to be the turning point in the Second Seminole War.

The battlefield location is well established and is located four miles southeast of Okeechobee on U.S. Highway 44.

Palm Trees

The Florida peninsula has 15 native palm trees, the majority of which are palmate or fan-flared and only two, the royal and coconut, bear pinnate or feather leaves. Only the cabbage palmetto grows naturally throughout the state. The beautiful royal palm grows wild on the wetlands near the coast, and the coconut palm is common on the Florida Keys to Key West. Its presence on the Keys is attributed to the buoyancy of the coconut, which drifted up from the

West Indies and took hold on the reef, where it grows along with small palms, mostly of the thatch variety.

Palmettos, with their giant root systems, grow in thick mats throughout the state. Most are yellowish-green in color, but one species stands out as a bright blue on the high sand dunes along the Atlantic coast.

Cape Canaveral and the Merritt Island National Wildlife Refuge

Cape Canaveral and the Kennedy Space Center are on Merritt Island, part of a long barrier island, with the Atlantic Ocean on the east and the waters of Mosquito Lagoon and the Indian River—a great 130-mile-long lagoon—on the west. A portion of this bar-rier island, which lies off the eastern Florida coast between Jacksonville and West Palm Beach, has been preserved as the Canaveral National Seashore and the Merritt Island National Seashore.

Several drives and hiking trails on the lagoon side of the national wildlife refuge provide access to pine flatlands, marshes and uplands, a hardwood hammock, and Turtle Mound, a prehistoric Indian midden. Wildlife at the refuge and national seashore includes several kinds of gulls and terns, among them the royal tern, laughing gull, least tern, herring gull, and ringbilled gull. Commonly sighted wading birds in the refuge are the great blue heron, green heron, Louisiana heron, snowy egret, white and glossy ibis, and wood stork.

Among the endangered species at the refuge is the Southern bald eagle. Their large nests—some

Seminole ceremonial village in the Everglades

Cape Canaveral on Merritt Island off the eastern Florida coast

reaching 6 feet in diameter and more than 10 feet thick—may be seen in the tall slash pines along the refuge roads. Today about five pairs are successfully raising their young each year. The refuge is also a prime habitat of the American alligator. About 4,000 lurk in the refuge, where they may be seen basking along the freshwater canals and waterways.

Loggerhead and Green Sea Turtles

The large tractorlike tracks on the sand beaches of the subtropical coast leading from the water to the edge of the sand dunes and back to the ocean are those of giant sea turtles. The loggerhead and green sea turtles come ashore during summer nights to lay their eggs at the base of sand dunes and return to the sea. Found off the subtropical regions of the Atlantic coast, the loggerhead and green sea turtles range north to Cape Cod during summer. The green sea turtle, with its horny, shieldlike shell and paddle-shape limbs, reaches weights up to 850 pounds, while the loggerhead may weigh up to 450 pounds.

Pelican Island National Wildlife Refuge

Pelican Island, located off the east-central coast of Florida in the Indian River, was once the only nesting site of brown pelicans on Florida's Atlantic coast. With the flourishing millinery trade at the turn of the century and the demand for their large wing feathers, the brown pelican was threatened with extinction. As a result of this slaughter, President Theodore Roosevelt declared the island the first of what are today more than 330 units of the national wildlife refuge system.

Anhinga—The Water Turkey, or Snake Bird

One of the most unusual birds of the bayous, seacoast, and swamps of the South is the glossy, greenish-black anhinga, also called the water turkey or snake bird. It is often sighted perched on low vegetation drying its wings after diving for fish or swimming with only its head above water, which gives it the name *snake bird*.

17. Central Prairies

THE heartland of the United States is a vast plain, which owes its remarkable levelness to deep glacial deposits of soil and gravel. The fertile corn and grain fields of the central prairies form the breadbasket of the nation, extending eastward from the 100th meridian to the eastern woodlands and ancient hills of Ohio.

The region owes its rich crop-producing soils chiefly to the four great glaciers that covered most of the area during the Pleistocene period, the last of which retreated only 25,000 years ago.

As the glaciers ground their way into the region, at an estimated rate of one mile in 10 years, they carried along the coarse and fine rock particles scraped up from the land over which they passed. The glaciers began to melt and retreat as slowly as they had advanced, and they left boulders and fine clay, known as till, behind them. Streams that flowed out from beneath the successive melting glaciers poured immense deposits of sand and gravel in valleys and on top of the till, which together with the sand and gravel is known as drift.

Before the central prairies were cultivated into seemingly endless mosaics of fields, pastures, and farms, the prairie grass grew as high as the wheels of the settlers' prairie schooners and covered the entire region. It seemed a limitless sea of tall-grass prairie mixed with hundreds of species of wildflowers, including cream-flowered paintbrush, lemon-and-orange-colored gromwell, yellow stargrass, prairie lilies with orange cups, and countless roses.

Today, despite decades of tillage, the virgin bluestem grasslands may be seen in a few patches along railroad rights-of-way, by old country roads, and in state-protected parks and preserves.

The East-Facing Escarpment Along the 100th Meridian

A low, east-facing escarpment, roughly along the 100th meridian, extends intermittently as hills or ridges southward from North Dakota to the Coteau des Prairies in South Dakota to the Flint Hills of Kansas and on into Oklahoma and Texas. West of the 100th meridian, the colors of the landscape change from green to brown in the High Plains country where rainfall diminishes.

368

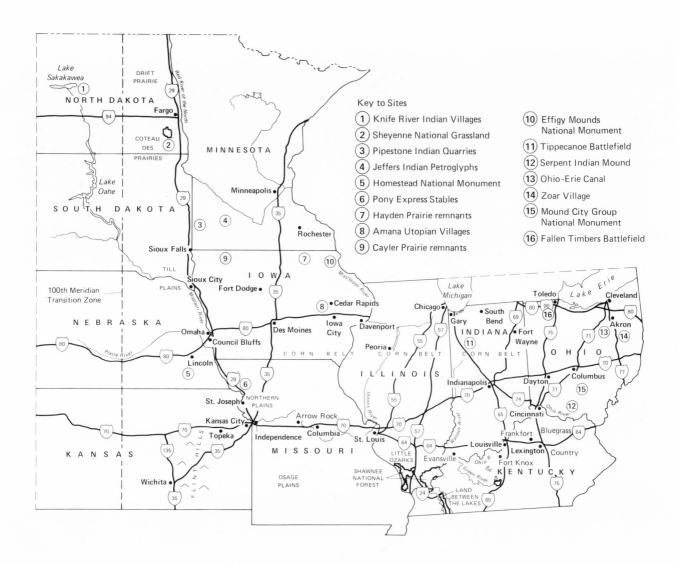

Key to Sites

1 Knife River Indian Villages
2 Sheyenne National Grassland
3 Pipestone Indian Quarries
4 Jeffers Indian Petroglyphs
5 Homestead National Monument
6 Pony Express Stables
7 Hayden Prairie remnants
8 Amana Utopian Villages
9 Cayler Prairie remnants

10 Effigy Mounds
   National Monument
11 Tippecanoe Battlefield
12 Serpent Indian Mound
13 Ohio-Erie Canal
14 Zoar Village
15 Mound City Group
   National Monument
16 Fallen Timbers Battlefield

Pipestone Quarries of the Plains Indians in southwest Minnesota. George Catlin, who travelled among and painted the American Indian from 1829 to 1838, visited the quarries in 1836. His pipestone samples were the first to be studied. Today pipestone is called catlinite in his honor.

In southeastern Kansas, for example, the average annual rainfall is 40 inches; at the western border of the state in the treeless High Plains, average annual rainfall decreases to 15 inches. Wind velocities also decrease: In the eastern third of the state winds are about the same as those in the eastern part of the nation as a whole, while the western third of Kansas is one of the windiest inland spots in the nation, noted for its "dust storms" during the dry season in winter or early spring.

Eastern Kansas is tall-grass country, where Indian grass covers the valleys, little bluestem and sideout gramma grow on the uplands, and sloughgrass borders the streams. On the arid High Plains to the west, short grasses—buffalo, blue gramma and hairy gramma—dominate the landscape.

Drift Prairie of North Dakota

The Drift Prairie of North Dakota is a rolling, fertile plain of finely ground rock, sand, and gravel deposited by the glaciers of the Ice Age. It is bounded on the north by the wooded Pembina Mountains, which rise sharply above the valley floor, and on the south by the rolling glacial moraines of the Coteau des Prairies. The prairie varies from 70 to 200 miles in width between the Pembina Escarpment on the east and the hills of the Missouri Escarpment on the west, broken here and there by low ridges, small lakes, and shallow coulees. Devil's Lake, the largest in the state, lies in the northern section of the prairie.

Ancient Lake Agassiz and the Red River Valley

The fertile, flat Red River valley, which forms the boundary between North Dakota and Minnesota, was once the floor of glacial Lake Agassiz. It is flanked on the west by the 300-foot-high hills of the Pembina Escarpment, which marks the beginning of the glacier-formed Drift Plain country. Farmlands dot the landscape of the valley, and during the fall, the northern portion is aflame with highbush cranberry, known to the Indians as *Pembina*.

Lake Agassiz, which existed some 10,000 years ago and covered an area larger than the present Great Lakes, was formed by the melting of the Wisconsin Ice Sheet. Named in honor of Louis Agassiz, who first theorized that drift was formed by land ice, the sole existing remnant of this vast inland sea in the United States is Lake of the Woods in northern Minnesota.

Pipestone Indian Quarries in the Upper Mississippi Valley

The great Pipestone Quarry of the Plains Indians, preserved today as a national monument, lies in the upper Mississippi River valley in southwestern Minnesota. Indians of many tribes travelled as much as a thousand miles by foot to reach the sacred red pipestone quarry. The quarries, which were first used more than 400 years ago by ancestors of the Oto and Iowa Indians, yielded a soft red clay stone that was fairly easy to craft into T-shaped bowls. Both the clay bowls and wooden stems into which they were placed were often elaborately decorated with paints, feathers, and metal inlays. The pipes were greatly revered and were used to show intentions for war and peace, to seal agreements and treaties, to strengthen alliances, or to solemnize an occasion. To many tribes, the pipe was an altar and the smoke was an incense that carried their prayers to the Great Spirit. Because pipes were used to seal treaties, all ceremonial pipes came to be known as peace pipes.

The national monument, which also preserves a small section of virgin prairie and houses the Upper

Corn stalks in an Iowa field

Midwest Indian Cultural Center, is located near the city of Pipestone, Minnesota.

Jeffers Indian Petroglyph Site

Due east of the ancient Pipestone Quarries on the plains of southwestern Minnesota is the Jeffers Indian petroglyph site, thought by experts to contain the finest examples of Indian carvings in the Plains region. The figures, carved on an outcropping of Sioux quartzite by the Dakota Indians, are sticklike representations of human figures and animals common to the Central Plains—turtles, bison, rattlesnakes, fish, and birds. The carvings were made with a round, pointed tool and a chisel-like instrument.

The site is located near the town of Jeffers in Minnesota's Cottonwood County.

Coteau des Prairies

The Coteau des Prairies, a plateaulike escarpment that lies chiefly in South Dakota and southern North Dakota, lies between the Missouri Escarpment and the Missouri River and marks the eastern boundary of the Great Plains, which extend west to the Rocky Mountains. The irregular rolling landscape of the Coteau des Prairies is dotted with old lake beds. West of the Missouri River it is known as the Missouri Slope, where erosion has formed the colorful yellow, gray, and blue buttes and mesas of the "badlands" that rise abruptly from the landscape.

Knife River Indian Villages Historic Site on the Missouri Slope

The Knife River Indian Villages National Historic Site lies within the 100th meridian transition zone between the Central Prairies and the High Plains near Stanton, North Dakota. This site preserves the remaining artifacts—the earth-covered lodges, cache pits, and burial grounds—of the main stronghold of the Hidatsa Indians, who were well established here by the 13th century.

By the late 15th or 16th centuries, the small villages with rectangular houses had evolved into larger, more compact, and sometimes fortified villages with circular earth lodges. The biggest of these villages had more than 100 lodges. By 1800, more people probably lived along the Missouri River in North Dakota than live in the same area today.

In October of 1804, the Lewis and Clark Expedition stopped at the three Hidatsa villages on the Knife River. They wintered through April of 1805 at Fort Mandan, a few miles below the Knife River villages. There Toussaint Charbonneau and his Shoshone wife, Sacajawea, joined the expedition.

Dissected Till Plains of Eastern Nebraska

The eroded glacial moraines and farmlands of eastern Nebraska, a strip averaging 70 miles in width paralleling the Missouri River, is part of the Dissected Till Plain. The rich, yellow-gray earth of the Loess Region in the southwestern half of the state covers a triangular area of about 42,000 square miles, underlain by thick wind-blown loess deposits, formed after the melting of the glaciers.

In the eastern half of the state, where rainfall is heavier than in the arid short-grass country of the western tablelands and High Plains, are the rolling

Greater prairie chicken once found from the Atlantic west to the Rocky Mountains

tall-grass prairies and broadleaf forests of oak, basswood, sycamore, and hickory of the Missouri bluff and bottomlands.

Homestead National Monument

Homestead National Monument, a T-shaped quarter section of prairie and woodland near Beatrice in southeastern Nebraska, is located on the claim of Daniel Freeman, one of the first applicants to file under the Homestead Act of 1862, which made it possible for settlers to claim farms up to 160 acres by paying a minor filing fee. To become full owner, a homesteader was required to build a house, live on the land, and cultivate it for five years. Later acts made homesteads easier to get. Legitimate settlers, however, often found themselves competing with speculators, claim-jumpers, and railroads for their land.

The monument, which commemorates the influence of the homestead movement on American history, includes the Palmer-Epard homestead cabin, erected in 1867 and later moved here; the site of the Freeman cabin and later buildings; the graves of Freeman and his wife; and 90 acres of tall-grass prairie.

Palmer-Epard Cabin at Homestead National Monument built in 1867. The tools and furnishings in it are typical of those used by the Nebraska pioneers

Kansas's Flint Hills Country—The Bluestem Belt

The famous Flint Hills region of Kansas is also known as the Bluestem Belt. It lies east of the low plains of the Great Bend Prairie in the central portion of the state that merges into the flat, treeless High Plains to the west. The rich, fertile silt deposits of the rolling, wooded Flint Hills, broken here and there by limestone cliffs, extend along the 100th meridian south from Oklahoma north to Nebraska, forming the great Break in the Plains and the rich grazing region of bluestem grasses. The Great Bend Prairie is flanked on the north by the Smoky Hills and Blue Hills and on the south by the eroded cliffs bordering the Cimarron River, known as the Cimarron Breaks.

The tall-grass prairies of eastern Kansas are winter wheat country; winter wheat is sown in the fall and germinates before frost. Spring wheat is grown north of Kansas, where the climate is too harsh for the young plants to survive the frigid winter.

Red Glacial Boulders of Northeastern Kansas

The ice cap of the glacial age reached down into northeastern Kansas, though not into the rest of the state. It left in its path deposits of glacial till and boulders of red quartzite ripped from their original hills in southeastern Minnesota and South Dakota and carried south by the glacier along the Mississippi Valley.

Flora of the Missouri River Country

Along the yellow-gray, loess-covered bluffs and mounds of the Missouri River as it flows southward through its great valley in Nebraska, Iowa, Kansas, and Missouri, plants from the western and southwestern plains mingle with those of the tall-grass prairie. With the bluestems are western plants and grasses, such as mesquite, buffalo grass, Spanish-bayonet, red locoweed, prairie trefoil, and Indian breadroot, or pomme de prairie.

Glacial Prairies of Missouri

A great expanse of level land, known as the Glacial, or Northern, Plains, extends across Missouri north of the Missouri River and the Ozark Highlands. As the glaciers ground south to the Missouri River, beginning about one million years ago, they transformed the landscape into rolling prairie lands with wide, shallow stream valleys. They deposited a rich drift soil of finely ground shale, limestone, and sand-stone, as well as boulders and fragments of granite and quartzite. Decayed animal and plant remains have given this soil a rich black color that forms part of the Corn Belt.

A typical example of this drift prairie left by the melting glaciers is the rich farmlands of the Black Prairie in the northeastern portion of the state. In north-central Missouri are the eroded parallel north-south divides and wide, shallow valleys of the Rolling Prairie that resemble the ridges of a washboard. The Flat Prairie to the northeast has only a thin veneer of glacial drift, broken here and there by a few low hills left by the ice sheet.

The yellow or buff-colored loess-covered hills and bluffs along the Missouri and Mississippi rivers were created by vast dust storms that occurred after the melting of the glaciers.

Tower Rock in the Mississippi River

Standing 80 feet above the normal water level, Tower Rock dominates the Mississippi River at a point 150 feet from the Missouri shore. Formed of eroded limestone, the rock supports a growth of grasses and shrubs on its summit. The rock was known to the Indians before the time of Columbus, and it posed a serious navigational hazard to early river travellers. Before the advent of steam power, river boats could not ascend beyond this point because of whirlpools and the threat of rocks. They had to be towed around the cape on the Illinois side.

Tower Rock is one mile south of Wittenburg, Missouri, in the Mississippi River.

Osage Plain of Western Missouri

The flat unglaciated prairies of western Missouri, known as the Osage Plain, are an eastern extension of the Great Plains. The monotony of the landscape is broken by low, rounded hills, which slope steeply near the Ozark Highlands.

Pony Express Stables at St. Joseph

On April 3, 1860, the first Pony Express rider left St. Joseph, Missouri, bound for Sacramento, California. The freighting firm of Russell, Majors, and Waddell had organized the Pony Express in an effort to publi-cize the central route to California (along the Platte River through Nebraska to Bridger Pass, Wyoming) and to obtain the government contract to carry mail to the West Coast. Eighteen months later the Pony Express was put out of business by completion of the transcontinental telegraph line. The stables were sub-sequently sold and passed through several hands be-fore becoming a museum in 1959. The original one-story wooden stable building was redone in 1888 by incorporating brick walls into the extant structure. The facade is highlighted by six applied pilasters. All win-dows are segment arch headed, and three semi-continuous string courses unify the exterior.

The stables are located at 914 Penn Street in St. Joseph, Missouri.

Arrow Rock and the Santa Fe Trail

Arrow Rock was the starting point for traders from Old Franklin and Boon's Lick who opened the Santa Fe Trail. It commemorates the beginning of the Santa Fe trade. Even before then traffic was so great that by 1817 a ferry crossing the Missouri River was in operation. Both of William Becknell's pioneering Santa Fe expeditions of 1821 and 1822 were organized here. The rock cliff of Arrow Rock, remains of the old ferry road, and the Santa Fe Spring used as a rendez-vous point are preserved in Arrow Rock State Park.

The site is at Arrow Rock State Park in Missouri's Saline County.

Corn Belt—The Great Central Prairies

Seen from the air the vast, rolling corn- and grain-fields of Iowa, Illinois, and Indiana in the central heartland of the continent appear as an intricate grid of squares and rectangles, where farm fits snugly against farm and between them is nothing but the straight line of a fence or road or meandering, wooded river valley.

Stretching eastward from the treeless, short-grass prairies of the Great Plains to the woodlands of the East—from eastern Kansas and the Break in the Plains to Ohio—is the great Corn Belt, the tall-grass prairie, where native grasses once grew more than six feet tall in vast waving fields of glacial till left behind by the ebb and flow of the great ice sheets, enriched by prairie grasses over thousands of years.

Iowa is wholly within the prairie region. Striking changes in the landscape are found only in the north-east, where cliffs rise 300 to 400 feet above the Mississippi and tree-covered hills reach westward, and in the west, south of the mouth of the Big Sioux River, where a line of moundlike bluffs sweep up from the floodplain of the Missouri to heights of 100 to 300 feet.

Illinois marks the transition zone from the wood-

An Ice Age esker between the prairie and woodlands in Iowa's loess hills country

lands of the East to the treeless plains of the West. The early pioneers found almost half the state in forest, with prairies of waist-high grasses running in great fingers between the rivers and streams.

The central till plain of Indiana is bordered on the north by the northern lake country, and on the south by hills and lowlands. It merges on the east with the level, central-plain farmlands of Ohio.

Big Bluestem

Big bluestem, which grows up to heights of six feet, once covered the region of the United States known as the Tall-Grass Prairie and was one of the principal grasses that helped produce the black soils of the Midwest Corn Belt. This native plant ranges from Maine west to Wyoming, Utah, and Arizona. A vigorous, tough bunchgrass acts as a soil anchor against wind and water erosion. The flowers that blossom at the tip of its erect stems often branch into three parts and resemble a turkey foot. Except for small virgin patches, usually along abandoned railroad tracks, little of the nation's original tall-grass prairie remains.

Iowa's Amana Utopian Villages

Of the utopian societies that flourished in the 19th century, the Amana Society has been the most durable. Historically an outgrowth of a persecuted German religious minority group, "The Community of True Inspiration," the sect emigrated first to New York State and subsequently to Iowa, founding the village of Amana in 1855. During the next seven years five other villages were established, and the town of Homestead was purchased to gain access to a railroad. In 1859 the community was incorporated under the laws of Iowa as the Amana Society. In all of the villages there are buildings built in the 1850s, 1860s, and 1870s, primarily two-story houses. Many of the mills, shops, and factories also remain, a number of which are still in use. The villages are at Middle Amana in northeastern Iowa County.

Effigy Mounds National Monument

Along the high bluffs and lowlands in the upper Mississippi River valley are numerous prehistoric Indian burial mounds of a type unique in North Amer-

Prairie windmill in the corn belt—the "breadbasket of the world"

ica. Though different groups of prehistoric Americans built burial mounds at various times and places, only in southern Wisconsin and adjacent areas in Iowa, Illinois, and Minnesota were they built in the shape of bears and other animals.

Effigy Mounds National Monument was established to preserve the earth mounds found in northeastern Iowa. Within the monument's borders are 191 known prehistoric mounds, 29 in the shape of bear and bird effigies and the remainder conical or linear-shaped.

The monument area is divided into two parts by the Yellow River. The Fire Point Group to the north contains the monumental Great Bear Mound, which is 137 feet long and about 3 feet high. To the south are the effigies of the Marching Bear Group, containing an alignment of 10 mounds in the shape of marching bears, each about 3 feet high and 80 to 100 feet long, as well as three bird effigies and two linear mounds. The mounds provide valuable information on the burial customs of prehistoric people who were of the Middle Woodland, Late Woodland, or Late Hopewellian cultures.

The monument is three miles south of Marquette, Iowa, on State Highway 13.

Illinois Bottomland Forests and the Little Ozarks

In the extreme southern portion of Illinois, along the wet bottomlands of the Ohio and Mississippi rivers, are almost semitropical forests of sweet gums, cypresses, and other trees usually associated with the South. One of the region's finest examples of bottomland forest, known locally as the levee, are the stands of cypress and sweet gum found in the Little Ozarks (an eastern extension of the Ozark Highlands) at the Crab Orchard National Wildlife Refuge. The refuge, like the surrounding countryside of the Little Ozarks, has a mixed terrain of upland forests, open farmlands, and wet bottomland forests, inhabited by a wide variety of wildlife, including shorebirds, great egrets, and herons.

The Little Ozarks and the wildlife refuge are located east of Carbondale.

Great Prairie Chicken Sanctuaries of Illinois

The Great Prairie chicken, which once ranged over the virgin grasslands of Illinois, is found today only in areas where farming has ceased, particularly in the southeastern portion of the state, where old pastures and fields of redtop grass lie idle during the nesting season at the Chauncey McCormick and Ralph E. Yeatter prairie chicken sanctuaries. This chicken-like bird, noted for its striking courtship dance and booming call, was once found on the undisturbed prairies from Wyoming to the Atlantic coast. Its eastern relative, the heath hen, became extinct.

Bald Eagles of the Mississippi

The greatest concentration of bald eagles outside of Alaska occurs during midwinter along Illinois's portion of the Mississippi River. The birds migrate there to feed on the large populations of gizzard shad found along the ice-free areas above and below the system of locks and dams constructed after the 1930s.

Illinois Iron Furnace in the Shawnee National Forest

The Illinois iron furnace is the only remaining furnace of the completely native iron industry in Illinois. The furnace consists of a central brick tower 8 feet in diameter and 40 feet high, surrounded and supported by a square tower of irregular limestone blocks, 30 feet square at the base tapering to 22 feet square at the top. On the north and south are arched recesses leading to the lower part of the tower. Molten metal flowed out of these recesses into molds to make pig iron. Rebuilt and enlarged in 1856, the furnace continued operating until 1861. Seven years later it was reactivated and ran until 1883.

The furnace is located near Rosiclare, Illinois.

Saline Springs in the Shawnee National Forest

The site consists of 306 acres surrounding the actual springs, used in aboriginal times by native animals, in pre-Columbian times by the indigenous Indian tribes, and in modern times as a commercial source of salt and a location for industry. Indian salt-manufacturing at the spring consisted of evaporating salt water in shell-tempered clay basins 3 to 5 feet in diameter and about a foot deep. The residual crust of salt that was left in the basin was then scraped away. More modern methods were utilized in the 19th century when wood-burning furnaces were used. As the wood supply ran out near the spring, timbers were hollowed and bound together, and the salt water was piped to a source of burnable wood. More than 100 miles of these pipes were being used by 1875.

Cedar trees and eroded iron rocks at Illinois' Shawnee National Forest

Early iron furnace

The springs are 3.5 miles southeast of Equality, Illinois, in the Shawnee National Forest.

Tippecanoe Battlefield

William Henry Harrison's November 7, 1811, victory at Tippecanoe Battlefield destroyed the Shawnee Chief Tecumseh's plans for a confederation of northern and southern Indian tribes to block westward expansion. The battle of Tippecanoe sparked agitation for war against Britain, for the settlers believed that British aid had enabled the tribes to harass the settlements beyond the Appalachians. In June of 1812 war was declared against Britain.

The battlefield is seven miles northeast of Lafayette, Indiana, on State Highway 225.

Michigan's Tail-Grass Prairie Remnants

The early 1800s saw waves of immigrants spread into southern Michigan, settlers from the East and South looking for a place to put down roots, familial as well as agricultural. The bold pioneers in their covered wagons followed routes laid out along old Indian trails, routes that took them through dense forests, oak openings, and wide open grasslands such as many had never encountered in their home state or homeland. These grasslands were Michigan's tall-grass prairies, and for some of the spirited settlers, the prairies were the reason they had ventured so far. The prairies held a promise—the promise of deep, fertile soil and bumper crops of wheat and corn.

But the pioneers must have had mixed emotions as their wagons came to rest on the solid turf. They knew that prairie soil was fertile, but they also knew that exposing that soil was an exacting task. The tangled roots of the 10-foot grasses and other teeming prairie plants made the sod almost impenetrable. A bull plow and up to four teams of cattle, when they were available, were used for "breaking up," as the pioneers called the initial splitting of the sod. Some hardy settlers made breaking up their profession, getting $5 a week for their toil. Michigan's prairies were not large compared to the natural meadows that stretched for mile after mile in the center of the continent from Ohio to Kansas and Nebraska. Southern Michigan lay on the northwestern rim of this vast grassland system. But Michigan's prairies were no less

striking than those farther to the south and west. The dominant plant of the prairies, the big bluestem grass, grew in such luxurious abundance that a steady wind turned the prairies into waving seas. Under the big bluestem grew a host of other prairie plants whose names—poverty oat grass, hairy puccoon, sleepy catchfly, prairie shoestring—are as colorful as the plants themselves as they flower from spring through fall.

Michigan's prairies drew no less respect than the midcontinent prairies either. Often prairie names came before village names, and directions were given with reference to the location of prairies, indicating their prominence in the frontier culture. "He plowed the first furrow" was a saying that symbolized the settlers' perseverance and hard work. The saying can still be seen on tombstones of the period. The prairies, with their promise of agricultural abundance, lured people to the Midwest. It is no small irony that this lure was also the eventual undoing of the prairies. For as more settlers came, more prairie was turned to plowland and the natural meadows began to disappear. With the completion of Michigan Central's railroad line through southern Michigan in 1950, the area was opened up even further to residential, commercial, and industrial endeavors. The prairies diminished. But

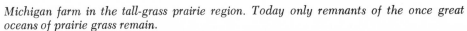

Michigan farm in the tall-grass prairie region. Today only remnants of the once great oceans of prairie grass remain.

Dandelion—a member of the sunflower family that is a common prairie wildflower

not all the prairies succumbed to the pressures of an expanding nation. For the railroads, while they provided ready access to those who wished to dismantle the wilderness, also provided a way to preserve part of it. The railroads took a 100-foot strip of land for the track right-of-way, land which often had never been disturbed, and in many cases, still hasn't today. In this manner strips of prairie along the tracksides were preserved. The railroad companies also unwittingly used a sound ecological strategy to maintain these strip prairies by burning the tracksides periodically to control the brush. This simulated the natural fires that are needed to perpetuate the prairie ecosystem.

In addition to the strip prairies along the railroad lines, remnants of the original prairie also exist along the fencerows, backroads, and out-of-the-way places of southern Michigan, small examples of the magnificent grasslands that the settlers encountered as they crested the gentle hills and surveyed their new home. A number of these prairie remnants have been preserved by local, state, and national conservation groups that have realized the value of preserving this little-known part of Michigan's natural heritage. The Sauk Indian Trail Prairie Plant Preserve is a small trackside prairie in St. Joseph County near White Pigeon. The quarter-acre preserve, containing species such as the yellow cornflower, prairie shoestring, and stiff goldenrod, is owned by the Michigan Nature Association. The same organization has also

preserved the Rattlesnake Master Preserve in St. Joseph County near Centreville. This three-acre mixed prairie and open woodland harbors the little bluestem, poverty oat grass, and bush clover. The Michigan Nature Association has preserved a sizeable prairie, the 100-acre Newaygo Prairie, near the town of Newaygo (Newagyo County). Newaygo Prairie is an excellent example of the dry sand prairies that once covered much of Newaygo County. Plants on the preserve include the prairie smoke (a state-threatened species), needle grass, and prickly pear cactus.

Ohio and Erie Canal

The Ohio and Erie Canal was part of a thousand-mile canal network that connected Lake Erie to the Ohio River and gave access to New York, Pennsylvania, and Indiana canals. For 20 years the system accelerated the growth of population, industry, and commerce, but eventually it could not compete with the greater speed, flexibility, and lower costs of the railroads. The one-and-a-half-mile section, which includes locks 37 and 38, also includes the aqueduct over Tinkers Creek, a mill, and a house, all dating from the period of canal use.

The canal is located at Valley View Village in Ohio's Cuyahoga County.

The Great Serpent Mound

The Great Serpent Mound, built by either the Adena or Hopewell peoples, is situated on a high, crescent-shape hill. Conforming to the curve of the hill and occupying its summit is the serpent, its head resting near the top and its body winding back down a slight slope for 1300 feet. This earthen snake effigy site was one of the first areas in the United States to be set aside because of its prehistoric interest and scientific value. Following excavations in 1886, the site was purchased by Harvard's Peabody Museum, and in 1900 it was deeded to the Ohio Historical Society.

The Serpent Mound is five miles northwest of Locust Grove, Ohio, on State Highway 73.

Fallen Timbers Battleground

General "Mad Anthony" Wayne's victory over the Indians in Ohio and their Canadian militia allies here on August 20, 1794, established United States sovereignty in the Old Northwest and opened the Ohio country to settlement. The resulting Treaty of

Mound City Indian Earthworks in Southern Ohio—a 2,000-year-old cemetery that has yielded artifacts made of Great Lakes copper, chunks of volcanic glass from a site in Yellowstone National Park, shark teeth from the Chesapeake Bay area, mica from the Great Smokies, seashells from the Gulf Coast, and silver from Ontario

Greenville in 1795 cleared the way for settlers who occupied the area during the next decade.

The Battlefield is two miles west of Maumee on U. S. Highway 24.

Ohio's Zoar Historic District

The village of Zoar was settled in 1817 by a group of Separatists from Germany. Although founded primarily as a religious community, Zoar soon began operating on a communal basis so the settlers could pay their debts and ensure some measure of eco-nomic security. The village contained a church, a bakery, a tin shop, a blacksmith shop, a store, a furniture shop, weaving and sewing houses, a pottery, several mills, a brewery, a large decorative garden with greenhouses, and residences. Under the leadership of Joseph Baumeler (Bimeler), the community prospered in agriculture and industry, and Baumeler reinvested all profits in society enterprises. At his death an economic decline began, and this, coupled with waning idealism and internal dissension, finally caused the dissolution of the colony in 1898. Several structures have been torn down, but the nucleus of the village remains intact. A number of the early log houses still stand, as do the bakery, the tin shop, the garden and greenhouse, the sewing house, and Baumeler's residence.

Zoar is in Ohio's Tuscarawas County.

Mound City Group Indian Burial Grounds

Mound City Group National Monument in southern Ohio was primarily a ceremonial center for the disposal of the remains of prehistoric Hopewell Indians. The territory we today call southern Ohio was the principal center of different Indian groups during a period of seven hundred years or more, from 200 B.C. to A.D. 500, extending from Michigan to southern Florida and from Kansas to the East Coast connected by a network of trails spanning the continent. The Hopewell peoples are best known for their artistic achievements and their practice of erecting mounds of earth over the remains of their dead. The significance of their burial mounds, such as those found at Mound City, was that they established and perpetuated a system of rank distinctions as a visible reminder and demonstration of the power of individuals and families, much like those found in medieval Europe or aboriginal Hawaii. Excavations of these mounds have yielded much information about the Hopewellian burial customs, and many artifacts typical of the Indians' culture have been found in the graves. The burial site consists of a rectangular earth enclosure within which are located 24 earth mounds.

The national monument is four miles north of Chillicothe, Ohio, on State Highway 104.

18. Ozarks

THE low mountains and hills of the Ozark Highlands are the only extensive elevated area between the Rocky Mountains in the West and the Appalachians in the East. The Ozarks cover a 55,000-square-mile area, bounded by the Kansas and Oklahoma prairies on the west, the Missouri River on the north, the Arkansas River on the south, and the Mississippi River on the east.

The hills of the Ozarks, shaped over the ages by spring-fed rivers and streams, reach their highest elevations at Taum Sauk Mountain in southern Missouri, which rises 1,772 feet above sea level, and in the Boston Mountains in the Arkansas Ozarks, which crest at 2,578 feet. The secret to the region is its beautiful waterways, which have carved through an ancient uplifted seabed of limestone and dolomite that traps the rainfall into a great underground reservoir, creating spectacular springs, caverns, sinkholes, and rugged bluffs.

Two national forests dominated by pine, hickory, maple, and oak embrace the hills, scenic spring-fed waterways, and valleys of the region: the Ozark National Forest in northern Arkansas and the Mark Twain National Forest in southern Missouri.

The Ozark Biological and Climatic Transition Zone

Similar to the Black Hills of South Dakota, the Ozarks are a land of vivid contrast and transition. The southeast boundary marks the beginning of the fertile flatlands of the hot southern Mississippi Embayment country. The Missouri River boundary on the north marks the southernmost advance of the Ice Age glaciers. The low-lying western boundary in Oklahoma marks the beginning of the Great Plains that sweep westward to the foothills of the Rocky Mountains.

These three climate zones have created unusually diverse habitats for plants and animals ranging from grasses of the High Plains country to great stands of water tupelo, normally found in the great semitropical swamps of the Deep South, which encircle the Ozarks' sinkhole bogs.

Ozark Hills and the Ancient Rivers of Lava

Sometime between 1.2 and 1.5 billion years ago, the Ozark region underwent a series of volcanic erup-

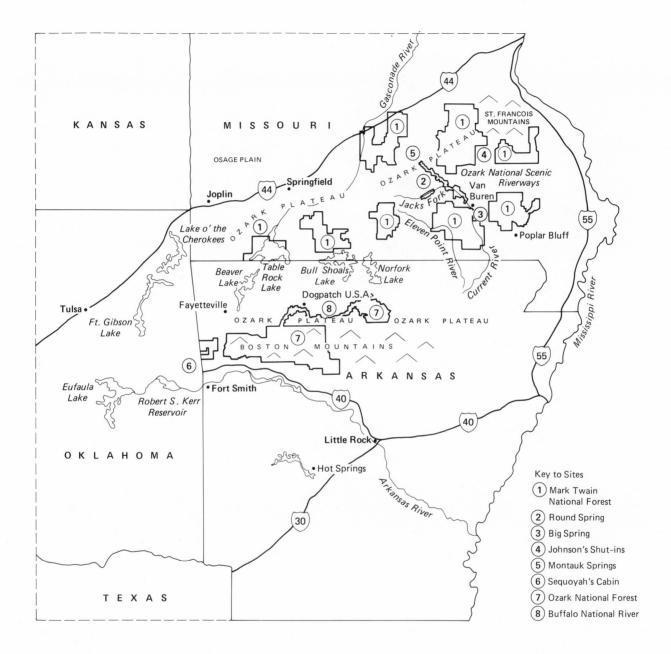

Ozark Highlands, where the Eastern Woodlands and the Great Plains meet. The white birch of the north country, the beech tree of the Eastern Woodlands, wayter tupelo of the Deep South, roadrunners of the Southwest, and lichens characteristic of Arctic tundra all find niches here.

literacy. The syllabary, completed in 1821, has 86 characters, each of which represents a syllable. The giant sequoia trees of California's Sierra Nevada were named in his honor, and he is acclaimed on the doors of the Library of Congress as one of the world's alphabet inventors. His frontier cabin of hewn logs has undergone minor restorations.

Glades—Miniature Prairies in the Ozarks

The open, grass-covered meadows, known locally as glades, that open on the rolling, wooded hills are among the most beautiful features of the Ozark countryside. These miniature prairies are isolated pockets of the arid High Plains and Great Plains that sweep eastward from the rain-shadow region of the Rocky Mountains. Surrounded by the Ozark woodlands the glades are inhabited by plant species common to the short-grass prairies to the west—prickly pear, prairie rose, and a variety of hardy prairie grasses, including waving patches of big bluestem that reach upward to heights of five or six feet. The only tree that has been able to carve a dominant niche in these prairie pockets is the shallow-rooted eastern red cedar, a small, gnarled species of juniper.

tions that produced lava flows and a huge mass of molten rock that cooled and hardened underground. The region was then uplifted, creating a landscape of low peaks and knobs. Some 525 million years ago seas buried the ancient hills, creating layers of limestone from the dead marine life and sandstone from the sea's floor and beaches. Then about 380 million years ago, the last of the seas receded and a major uplifting occurred, creating the Ozark dome and the low hills of the Ozark Plateau, which reaches its crest in the St. Francois Mountains, where the ancient volcanic granite and rhyolite rocks, formed more than one billion years ago, are exposed.

Sequoyah's Cabin in Oklahoma's Ozark Foothills

Sequoyah's cabin is situated on the westernmost edge of the Ozark Plateau on Oklahoma Highway 101 in Cabin State Park near Akins. By his invention of the Cherokee syllabary, Sequoyah, an American Indian, teacher, and scholar, gave the Cherokee Indians, who had been driven west from the Great Smokies to Oklahoma along the Trail of Tears, the gift of

Ozark back-country barn and farmlands

Caverns of the Ozarks

The Ozarks are famous for their dark underground caverns, carved over eons by the dissolving action of water on the porous and soluble limestone bedrock of the region. Hundreds of Ozark caves—many as yet unexplored—dot the water-carved countryside of the ancient Ozark dome from southern Missouri into northern Arkansas. Blanchard Springs Cavern in north-central Arkansas is one of the region's most spectacular caves, with its giant rooms, treelike stalagmites, and stalactites hanging like icicles from the domelike ceilings. Maintained by the U.S. Forest Service, the cavern is open to the public. The caverns of the Ozarks form a dark, watery habitat for the Ozark blindfish and a blind species of salamander found nowhere else in the world.

The Collapsed Caverns of Missouri's Grand Gulf

Located a few miles north of Arkansas' Mammoth Springs, the Grand Gulf is a spectacular chasm that winds for a mile through 120-foot-high walls. Grand Gulf was formed when erosion ate away the ceilings of a chain of caverns, creating a great natural gorge. An underground channel connects the collapsed caverns of Grand Gulf with Mammoth Springs.

Cave opening in the Ozark hills. Relics and skeletons of prehistoric bluff dwellers have been found in several similar locations.

Great Springs of the Ozarks

The Ozarks form one of the country's great aquifers. The meandering, interconnected rivers of the region have carved through the limestone and dolomite, exposing the underground water table, and forming several of the largest natural springs in the United States: Big Springs near the Current River at Van Buren, Missouri, for example, gushes nearly one billion gallons of sweet spring water a day; and Round Spring, located in a collapsed water-eroded cave, pours out more than 300 million gallons a day. No one

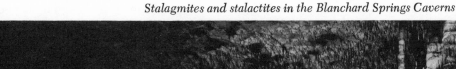

Stalagmites and stalactites in the Blanchard Springs Caverns

Spring-fed Ozark waterway

has been able to determine the exact number of springs in the region, but most are small, producing less than a million gallons a day. Several, such as Blue Spring at the headwaters of the Eleven Point River in Missouri's Oregon County, have colorful hues, created by the interaction of the sunlight with mineral particles in the water.

The Current River, which rises from a dozen springs in a parklike area at Montauk Springs in the Missouri Ozarks, is, next to the Snake River in Idaho, the largest spring-fed river in the nation. The springs at the headwaters of this wild and scenic river produce above 45 million gallons of water a day and make up 60 percent of the Current's total volume.

Old gristmill at Greer Springs

Sinkholes

The tremendous amount of precipitation that has created the scenic Ozark waterways and giant springs and carved out the hundreds of caverns has also created the region's numerous sinkholes. In many cases these have been formed by the collapsing of a cave's ceiling, eaten away by the mildly acid underground water. Often the Ozark sinkholes are connected by underground channels to area springs, or they become plugged, forming shallow, boglike ponds dominated by a ring of giant-trunked water tupelo trees, also known as swamp gum.

Shut-Ins—The Gorges of the Ozarks

The gorges along the winding waterways of the Ozarks, known locally as shut-ins, were formed where the rivers carved their way through the hard, ancient remnants of Precambrian lava that cooled 1.5 billion years ago. Upstream and downstream from the shut-ins are the wider river valleys, where the water eroded the less resistant beds of Paleozoic sedimentary rocks.

Wild and Scenic Rivers of the Mark Twain National Forest

Missouri's wild and scenic rivers—the Current and its tributary, the Jacks Fork, and Eleven Point—rise from springs in the hills of the Ozark Plateau, surrounded by the woodlands and glades of the Mark Twain National Forest. Like most Ozark streams they flow through an ancient world of limestone and sandstone bluffs, caverns, rock outcroppings, sinkholes, and remote, wooded hollows.

The beautiful, spring-fed Current River (see "Great Springs of the Ozarks") flows for about 140 miles from its headwaters at Montauk Springs past colorful bluffs, numerous caves, and several large sinkholes—Burr Oak Basin and the Sunkland—to the flatlands of northern Arkansas where it joins the Black River.

The enchanting Eleven Point National Scenic River rises in the national forest, fed by several large springs, and flows swiftly along its wooded course through the unspoiled Irish Wilderness and on past Greer Crossing, an Osage Indian and pioneer ford, and within sight of the old Greer Mill on a knoll south of the crossing, which was once powered from a watermill at the beautiful Greer Spring.

Paddlefish of the Ozark Waterways

The bluish-gray paddlefish of the Osage River, which is a tributary of the Mississippi that flows out of the short-grass prairies of Kansas to form the northwestern border of the Ozarks, is a remnant of prehistoric times, named for its odd-looking snout. The paddlefish, which grows to weights of 100 pounds and more, has only one living relative, found in the Yangtze River in China.

Buffalo National River

The wild and scenic Buffalo River, named for the herds of bison that once grazed along its banks, rises from its headwaters high in the Boston Mountains of the Ozark Plateau in northwest Arkansas and flows for 148 miles along its ancient course through Lost Valley and past huge canyonlike limestone and sandstone bluffs and meanders out into the Springfield Plateau to its confluence with the White River, which eventually joins the Mississippi. This primeval water-

Pioneer cabin near Big Bluff on the Buffalo River

way is marked along its route through the ancient Ozark hills and woodlands by little valleys, towering multicolored bluffs, cascades, caverns, and remote rural hamlets with such colorful names as Bug Scuffle and Lick Skillet. The riverbank life zone is a lush green world of ash, sycamore, willow and witch hazel, wild azalea, moss-covered boulders, flowering dogwood and leatherwood shrubs, inhabited by great blue heron, river otter, beaver, wild turkey, black bear, and whitetail deer.

Mark Twain's Birthplace Cabin

Samuel Langhorne Clemens was born in a two-room cabin on November 30, 1835. The Clemens family lived in the Florida, Missouri, area until November 1839, when they moved to Hannibal. The cabin is constructed of native red oak clapboard siding with log sills, studs, and joists. The pine floor is original, although some alterations have been made to other portions of the building. Previously located one-quarter of a mile north, the cabin was moved to its present location in 1930.

The cabin is at Mark Twain State Park south of Florida, Missouri, on State Highway 107.

Ozark Iron Furnace

Pig iron production by means of charcoal-heated blast furnaces was an important Missouri industry during the late 19th century. William James, son of Thomas James, who founded the Maramec Iron Works, organized the Ozark Iron Company in 1872. The new ironworks were constructed only 50 feet from the Atlantic & Pacific Railroad (now the St. Louis–San Francisco), near a main transportation artery rather than the ore supply. Once in operation, the hot blast furnace produced 30 tons of pig iron per day. Various setbacks plagued James until he was forced to declare bankruptcy in 1877. The furnace operated once more in 1883–1884. Constructed of sandstone blocks, the furnace stack is pyramidal in shape and about 40 feet high. There are three arched openings at the furnace base. The east opening provided egress for the molten metal, while the other two conducted hot blasts into the furnace. West of the furnace stack is a similar stone structure which is believed to have supported the boilers and the hot blast heating chamber equipment. Also on the property are the remains of a two-and-one-half-story brick building believed to have been the company store.

The furnace is near Newburg in Missouri's Phelps County.

19. Great Lakes

THE glacier-scarred countryside surrounding the shores of the Upper Great Lakes—Superior, Michigan, and Huron—embraces the ancient Canadian Shield uplands of northern Minnesota, Wisconsin, and Michigan, vast evergreen forests, thousands of sky-blue lakes, brawling wild rivers, great lowland areas of bogs, and tea-colored muskeg streams. There are incredibly wild and scenic granite cliffs, bays, coves, and countless rocky islands scattered along the rugged, wave-pounded shores of the Upper Great Lakes. In the southern regions of the states, glacial deposits have formed gently rolling plains, crossed here and there by wide valleys. The Upper Great Lakes have a significant influence on the climate of Minnesota, Michigan, and Wisconsin, absorbing heat from warmer air and warming the colder winds. In the summer, prevailing westerly winds are cooled by the lake waters. Summers are often hot, with sudden storms and foggy conditions along the coastal areas. Sudden squalls can turn the coastal waters into a frothing sea of whitecaps, occasionally smashing small boats against the towering, cliff-lined shores.

Origin of the Great Lakes

In preglacial times the land now filled by the massive Great Lakes basins was a rocky lowland drained by an ancient river system that flowed eastward into the Gulf of St. Lawrence. The massive ice sheets of the Wisconsin Ice Age rearranged this river system and scooped out five great basins along its valleys. During the early phase of the Ice Age small lakes lay against the ice wall at the north. These were forerunners of the present-day lakes: Lake Duluth was the original Lake Superior; Lake Chicago was what became Lake Michigan; Lake Saginaw evolved into Lake Huron; Lake Nicolet became Green Bay; Lake Maumee became Lake Erie; and Lake Iroquois, Lake Ontario.

After the melting of the massive ice sheets the Great Lakes covered a much greater area than they do today, including what are now the cities of Detroit and Chicago. Up until 10,000 years ago, when the ice retreated and the St. Lawrence River became the outlet to the Atlantic, the Great Lakes sought outlets along the ice margins through the Finger Lakes into

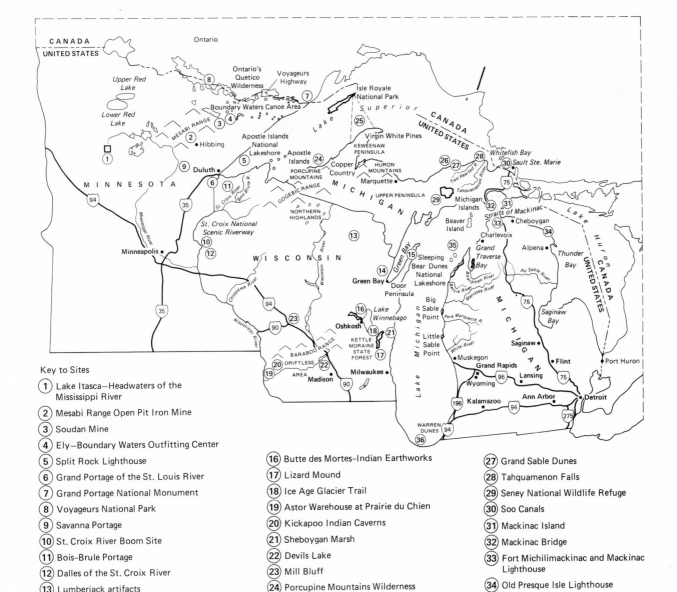

Key to Sites

1. Lake Itasca—Headwaters of the Mississippi River
2. Mesabi Range Open Pit Iron Mine
3. Soudan Mine
4. Ely—Boundary Waters Outfitting Center
5. Split Rock Lighthouse
6. Grand Portage of the St. Louis River
7. Grand Portage National Monument
8. Voyageurs National Park
9. Savanna Portage
10. St. Croix River Boom Site
11. Bois-Brule Portage
12. Dalles of the St. Croix River
13. Lumberjack artifacts
14. Copper Culture-Oconto Indian Mounds
15. Eagle Rock Lighthouse
16. Butte des Mortes-Indian Earthworks
17. Lizard Mound
18. Ice Age Glacier Trail
19. Astor Warehouse at Prairie du Chien
20. Kickapoo Indian Caverns
21. Sheboygan Marsh
22. Devils Lake
23. Mill Bluff
24. Porcupine Mountains Wilderness
25. Isle Royale Ferry
26. Pictured Rocks
27. Grand Sable Dunes
28. Tahquamenon Falls
29. Seney National Wildlife Refuge
30. Soo Canals
31. Mackinac Island
32. Mackinac Bridge
33. Fort Michilimackinac and Mackinac Lighthouse
34. Old Presque Isle Lighthouse
35. Manitou Islands
36. Indiana Dunes National Lakeshore

A north-country waterway

the Susquehanna River; across the broad valley of upper New York State into the Hudson; and from Lake Michigan along the Des Plaines and Illinois rivers; and from Lake Superior along the St. Croix River into the Mississippi.

With the retreat of the ice sheets and the removal of their crushing, depressing weight the land surrounding the Great Lakes tilted upward to the north and northeast several hundred feet. This uplift is still going on at a rate of a couple of inches a year. It is estimated that in about 2,000 years the waters will flow out to the Atlantic not through the St. Lawrence in the uplifted east, but in the south through the Chicago River and into the Mississippi.

Lake Superior—Longfellow's "Shining Big-Sea Water"

Lake Superior, the northernmost of the Great Lakes and the largest body of fresh water in the world, is about 360 miles long, 160 miles wide at its maximum, and covers approximately 32,000 square miles. It reaches a depth of 1,302 feet about 13 miles northwest of Caribou Island at the eastern end of the lake. At 602 feet above sea level it forms the top step in a staircaselike chain of lakes that drops to Lake Huron via the rapids at Sault Ste. Marie, from Lake Huron into Lake Erie and Lake Ontario, and finally plunges over Niagara Falls to the St. Lawrence River. The massive cliffs along the Superior shoreline were exposed after the retreat of the ice cap and by the

uptilting of the land when it was released from the awesome crushing pressure of the ice sheet. The cliffs were then exposed to erosion from the wind and pounding waves. The waves have carved these great sandstone cliffs into a maze of arches, caverns, pinnacles, natural bridges, and spires that rival those of the Canyonlands in Utah. (See the section "Pictured Rocks of Lake Superior—A Storied Coast," later in this chapter.)

The Great Lakes Shoreline and Natural Features

Impressive facts only begin to describe the enormous body of water that dominates the interior of the North American continent. The Great Lakes as a unit comprise the largest body of fresh water in the world —about one-fifth of the globe's fresh surface water. The Great Lakes and their connecting waters form the longest water transportation route in the world, the 2,300-mile St. Lawrence Seaway, along which Great Lakes trade plys its way to and from the Atlantic. Just as impressive as the lakes themselves are the 9,400 miles of Great Lakes' coastline that the United States shares with Canada. The coastline is so extensive that when the St. Lawrence Seaway connected the Great Lakes to the Atlantic in 1958, Congress declared it the fourth coast of the United States. The Great Lakes stretch almost forever, endlessly the same, like oceans. In contrast, the coastal lands that rim the lakes are marked by an almost endless diversity, from the rugged and inaccessible coastline of Lake Superior in northern Michigan to the great urban and industrial centers of Detroit, Chicago, Cleveland, and Buffalo. Great Lakes coastal environments represent a rich variety of natural, commercial, recreational, ecological, industrial, and aesthetic resources. These coastal environments can be broken down into four primary types: bluff, sand dunes, wetlands, and low coastal plains.

Bluffs are certainly one of the most spectacular of all Great Lakes coastal types. Curiously enough, they are the most durable and the most fragile. Erodible bluffs are composed of unconsolidated materials, such as sand and gravel, that are highly unstable under attack from the sometimes awesome waves produced by fierce Great Lakes storms. Ranging in height from 10 to 300 feet, erodible bluffs are changing shape almost constantly, and their faces are usually devegetated owing to the frequent erosion. Nonerodible bluffs, by contrast, are the most stable shoreline in the Great Lakes. The bedrock or rock rubble of which they are composed can withstand the constant pounding of waves fairly well. In some cases thousands of years of wave action has carved

Wind-swept dunes during a Great Lakes storm

the cliffs, particularly those made of softer rock like sandstone, into fascinating shapes. At Pictured Rocks National Lakeshore near Munising in northern Michigan, the roar of the waves against the sculpted cliffs is so great that the Indians used to regard the area as the home of the gods of thunder.

Sand Dunes

Shifting sand dunes are a common sight along the Great Lakes shorelines wherever the prevailing winds blow inland. These windswept dunes form an unusual habitat for cacti from the arid Southwest and pines from the frozen Canadian north. Both are adapted to survive the hot sun and drying winds:

The Palisades along Minnesota's north shore of Lake Superior

the thick-skinned leaves of the pines and the thick, fleshy stems of the cacti allow them to conserve moisture and hold evaporation to a minimum. (See Sleeping Bear Dunes below.)

Many think of sand dunes as a seacoast feature, but along the Great Lakes shoreline rise some of the most impressive and diverse sand dunes in North America. Windblown and constantly changing, the dunes extend in many places several hundred yards from the shoreline and rise to a height of 300 feet. Some dunes are ancient, formed centuries ago and now covered over by a seemingly stable community of trees and shrubs. Others are being shaped today as windblown sand meets an obstacle such as a piece of driftwood or a clump of beach grass around which a mound and eventually a dune forms. Though most dunes are ever changing, some retain their shape long enough to become landmarks and even legends. The famous Sleeping Bear, a tree-covered dune perched atop a bluff along the Lake Michigan coast near Frankford, Michigan, has held its shape long enough to be the subject of a Chippewa legend about a mother bear who lay down along the coast to wait for her two cubs who had floundered during the long and exhausting swim across the lake's endless waters.

Coastal Wetlands

In many ways wetlands are the most important and unappreciated of the coastal environments that rim the Great Lakes. Despite their seeming tranquility and unassuming character, wetlands are complex and dynamic ecosystems that provide immeasurable benefits to all living things—including humans. Wetlands are those areas where the water table is at, near, or above the land surface for a significant part

The Lake Michigan shoreline

Glacial Features of the Great Lakes Countryside

The countryside surrounding the Upper Great Lakes is a land of glacier-gouged lakes, end moraines, outwash plains, kettle ponds, eskers, kames, and drumlins formed during the advance and melting of the great ice sheets during the ice ages of the last one million years. The thousands upon thousands of lakes in the northwoods country were created by the damming up of rivers by glacial debris, and some have been carved out of the ancient bedrock. The kettle ponds in bowl-shape depressions in glacial till or outwash were formed when a buried block of ice melted. Kames, such as those found at Kettle Moraine State Forest in Wisconsin, are cone-shape hills of debris deposited by the melting glacier in a small hole in the ice or as a small fan-shape deposit at the edge of a stagnating block of ice. The long, winding eskers were created by stream-borne debris flowing under the ice sheet or in a crevice. They vary in length from thousands of feet to a couple of miles and in height from 10 to 100 feet. Fields of drumlins—low, elongated, oval-shape hills, such as those found near Fond du Lac at the southern end of Lake Winnebago in Wisconsin—are steeper on the side from which the ice came. Outwash plains are gently sloping layers of sand and gravel washed down from the front of the melting ice sheet.

of the year—for long enough periods of time to sustain a community of aquatic vegetation. Marshes, the most common wetland type along the Great Lakes, provide spawning sites for many species of fish and act as nurseries for young fish. Waterfowl depend on wetlands for nesting and breeding and for staging and stopover points during their semiannual migration journeys. Wetlands provide direct benefit for humans also by acting as water-storage basins during times of flooding. They recharge underground aquifers that we draw on for water supplies, and they provide ecologically and aesthetically diverse environments for study and recreation.

The Plains

Coastal plains are the most common shoreline type along the Great Lakes and are characterized by relatively low elevations only a few feet above lake level and flat or gently rolling topography. Coastal plains are, in many places, former lakebeds themselves, remnants of the ancestral lakes that were created thousands of years ago by the meltwaters of the Wisconsin Glacier that now have gradually subsided to their present levels. The coastal plains have historically been places where people have chosen to settle. Native and immigrant Americans chose protected bays in these lowland areas for their fishing villages. Later, as the Great Lakes developed into a thriving shipping and industrial region, a few villages developed into major cities, like Detroit and Chicago. In addition to providing suitable space for these cities to become established, the low coastal plains also provided fertile agricultural lands to support the expanding populations that became the backbone of these great urban and industrial centers.

The Great Canadian Shield and Boundary Waters Canoe Area of Minnesota

The fabled waterways of the Boundary Waters Canoe Area (BWCA) in northern Minnesota take in more than one million acres of the Superior National Forest. Set aside in 1926 to preserve its wilderness character, the Boundary Waters area stretches for approximately 200 miles along the great chain of lakes that forms the United States–Canadian boundary adjoining Ontario's Quetico Provincial Park on the north. This land of thousands of interconnected lakes and streams, dense evergreen forests, bogs, stark rock outcroppings, and lakeshore cliffs straddles the vast rock-ribbed Canadian Shield and is flanked on the south by the ancient iron-ore deposits of the Mesabi and Vermillion mountain ranges. At one time the mountains towered over the landscape, only to be worn down over the ages by the great ice sheets to form a landscape of low, rounded hills and forested valleys dotted by 5,000 glacial lakes, ranging in size from a few acres to 70 square miles.

The great V-shaped Canadian Shield (also known as the Precambrian Shield because of the age of its

Beaver pond and house. The den, surrounded by deep water, has an underground entrance and a large, well-ventilated, dry room protected by sticks and mud-plastered walls.

A wave-eroded shore in the Canadian Shield country

ancient crystalline rocks, some estimated at 2.7 billion years old) covers nearly half of Canada, stretching southward from the Arctic Circle to areas west and south of Lake Superior in northern Michigan, Wisconsin, and Minnesota. Called "the land of the flat stone" by the Norse explorer Leif Ericson, the great shield forms a classic north-country landscape of low-lying spruce and jack pine forests, muskeg bogs, and seemingly endless chains of oddly shaped lakes and wild rivers.

Great glaciers ground across the area three times during the Ice Age, creating the northwoods landscape you see today. Outcroppings of this ancient shield, part of the earth's original volcanic crust, which are known as greenstone are found at the northwoods outfitting village of Ely, east of Disappointment Lake, and on the north shore of Knife Lake. The Ely greenstone outcropping is estimated to be 2.7 billion years old.

The Boundary Waters country was first explored by the French Canadian voyageurs and explorers commissioned by the Hudson's Bay Company, who blazed the original portages that were later worn deep by centuries of use. In the spring of 1732, Sieur de la Verendrye and the members of his expedition paddled their birchbark canoes down the boiling rapids and along the shorelines of the Boundary Lakes, establishing fur trading posts along the border lakes.

The great chain of boundary lakes—including island-dotted Lac La Croix, Basswood, Saganaga, Gunflint, and Crooked lakes—was once the scene of savage battles between the Sioux and Chippewa

Moose swimming across a north-country lake

Indians over the spoils of the fur trade. Scores of the canoe-country lakeshores contain Indian petroglyphs, and several ancient Indian dams built with huge glacial boulders are found where such boulders are naturally scarce.

The area's forests of balsam, aspen, tamarack, white spruce, and canoe birch contain about half of the nation's remaining timber wolf population as well as large populations of moose, black bear, deer, red and gray fox, bald and golden eagles. Wolves usually

Golden eagle of the lake-dotted forests—easily identified by its chocolate or yellow head, seven-foot wingspan, and wide-spread, upcurved wing tips in flight

live in packs of 2 to 12, but they are shy and secretive and are rarely sighted, although you might see their tracks in winter. The evergreen forest mantle is broken by stark rock outcroppings along the Laurentian Divide—a height of land that divides the waters flowing northward into Hudson Bay from those flowing into Lake Superior. Hundreds of varieties of wildflowers brighten the forest floor in spring and summer, including trillium, wild rose, wild iris, and daisies.

Loon, or Great Northern Diver —Symbol of the Northwoods

The long, mournful cry of the loon piercing the quiet of the night is the symbol of the Great Lakes northwoods. The Chippewa and Cree Indians say that the cry, which also resembles a wild, maniacal laugh, was that of a slain warrior who had been forbidden entry into heaven. The goose-size loon, or great northern diver, can dive as much as 300 feet below the surface and swim faster than most fish. When frightened, these denizens of the forested lakes and rivers can swim submerged with only their thick, pointed bills out of the water, and are practically invisible if the wind is forming a ripple on the lake.

Indian Pictographs of the Boundary Waters Canoe Country

Native American Indians have long been present in the Boundary Waters Canoe Area. For the modern visitor the most intriguing remains of their rich heritage are the rock paintings, or pictographs, scattered throughout the canoe country. These mysterious signs and drawings are vivid reminders of the native people who once paddled their birchbark canoes throughout the BWCA.

Pictographs can be seen almost always at water's edge within reach of a canoe, on vertical rock faces and cliffs that sometimes rise over 100 feet high. The artists mixed a paint, orange-red in color, from fish or animal oils and crushed iron oxides, and used their fingers to apply the paint to rock face.

Individual pictographs range in shape from realistic representations of animals to simple canoe figures to handprints and human figures. Some are mystical or supernatural in character, such as the horned human figure and pipe-smoking moose on the Basswood River site. Usually pictographs appear in clusters, but occasionally a single one decorates a cliff face.

Researchers have had trouble pinpointing the age of the pictographs. Some estimates say they are nearly 1,000 years old; some pictographs, such as the Darky Lake site where a man appears to shoot a rifle, suggest a more recent time, following contact with white men. To confuse the matter, some experts believe that the pictographs were painted continuously throughout

Common loon—the great northern diver

such a time span.

Much of the intrigue over the BWCA's Indian pictographs stems from the mystery of their origin. Not even modern Indians know with certainty the identity of the artists, the meaning of the pictographs, or why the artists painted them. Whatever their origin, the pictographs add immeasurably to the mystique of the Boundary Waters Canoe Area.

Voyageurs Highway of Northern Minnesota

The presence and influence of the French-Canadian *voyageurs* is still felt in Minnesota's north country. The voyageurs provided the vital link in the fur trade of the 18th and 19th centuries. Paddling their fragile birchbark canoes across thousands of miles of water wilderness, the canoemen linked Montreal with Minnesota's beaver and canoe country and beyond to the arctic reaches of the Northwest Territories. In their canoes and on their backs, the voyageurs transported valuable beaver furs, supplies, and trading goods of the fur empire.

One of the existing strategic trails used by the voyageurs, well known both in Quebec and the courts of Europe, was Grand Portage at Lake Superior. The stockade at the lake served as the crucial midpoint rendezvous on the voyageurs' route. The nine-mile portage trail rises from the shores of Superior and runs northwest around savage rapids and waterfalls to the Pigeon River and the canoe country beyond. The tough canoemen carried furs and goods across this path, trudging with several 90-pound packs on each trip.

Many lakes throughout the canoe country bear names bestowed by the voyageurs. Knife Lake, called by the voyageurs Lac des Couteaux, received its name from the sharp pieces of slate found along its shores.

Great blue heron nests—a typical heron colony may include more than 150 nests, often used for many years

Lac La Croix—lake of the cross—once possessed two large wooden crosses, erected by missionaries, on islands at the western end.

Other portage trails still in use were travelled by the voyageurs. The Height of Land Portage, where the Laurentian Divide separates the drainage basins of Lake Superior from Hudson Bay, was one of the most famous. Here novices were initiated as North Men, in the words of one voyageur-to-be, "by sprinkling water in my face with a small cedar bow." He was also made to promise never to allow a new hand to pass by this spot without a similar initiation that "stipulates particularly never to kiss a voyageur's wife against her own free will."

The canoe country bore witness to voyageurs paddling their canoes over the long decades of the fur trade, singing their lively *chansons* across the lakes along their route. The lifeblood of a commercial empire travelled along with them past the pine-clad shores and tumbling rapids. It was an empire described by one historian as held together by nothing stronger than birchbark. The portion of their route between Lake Superior and Lake of the Woods is still a highway through the Minnesota north country, nearly unchanged since the days of hardy French paddlers.

Mesabi Range Open Pit Iron Mine

In the ancient Mesabi Range of Minnesota's North Country is the immense iron-ore output of the Hull-Rust-Mahoning Open Pit Iron Mine—the largest in the world. It enabled the United States to become the world's leading manufacturer of steel. The mine was also among the first to be worked by open-pit or strip-mining techniques. This site contains not one mine but more than nine open pits operating from what appears to be a single hole in the ground. It is more than 1.5 miles wide, 3 miles long, and 534 feet deep at one point.

The mine is located in the Hibbing vicinity at Third Avenue East in Minnesota's St. Louis County.

Mountain Iron Mine in the Mesabi Range

The opening of the Mountain Iron Mine in 1890 revealed that Minnesota's Mesabi Range possessed the world's largest deposits of iron ore. Production from this mine made Minnesota the nation's largest supplier of iron ore. During its period of operation the mine yielded more than 48 million gross tons of ore. After operations were discontinued in 1956, the mine quickly filled with water. However, because the

Great horned owl—the "winged tiger" of the forests

Fisher—the deadly enemy of the porcupine

Vermillion River Gorge, a sluiceway through the ancient granite of the Canadian Shield

water height is relatively low in the crater, the dimensions of the open pit are readily discerned. At the end of Missable Avenue in the town of Mountain Iron, visitors will find an observation platform, telescopes, and a vicinity map offering interpretation.

The mine is located north of the village of Mountain Iron in St. Louis County.

The Soudan Mine

The opening of Minnesota's oldest and deepest underground mine began the development of one of the richest deposits in the United States. Active until 1962, its peak year was 1892, when the Soudan Mine shipped more than 568,000 long tons of high-grade iron ore. A number of original buildings survive: the engine house, drill shop, crusher house, and dry house.

The mine is at Tower-Soudan State Park near Tower in St. Louis county.

Split Rock Lighthouse on Lake Superior's North Shore

Congress authorized the construction of the Split Rock Lighthouse in 1907, five years after Minnesota's Mesabi Iron Range had been in operation. Cargoes of iron ore, as well as the iron deposits in the lake basin, caused the compass needles on ore-carrying ships to deflect greatly from true north. Thrown off course, ships frequently ran aground in the shallows of the rocky coastline. The lighthouse was built as a navigational aid. The construction itself was a feat of engineering and logistics, since there were no roads in the region, and men and materials had to be transported by ship and hauled up the face of the 124-foot cliff. The site is located on a 7.6 acre tract that includes the octagonal brick light tower, still housing the original two-paneled lens manufactured in Paris, an attached service building, fog-signal building, fuel-storage sheds, and frame dwellings. There have been no major changes at the site in the past 60 years, even though the lighthouse is no longer in operation.

The lighthouse is about 20 miles northeast of Two Harbors on U. S. Highway 61 in Lake County.

Grand Portage National Monument—The "Great Carrying Place"

Grand Portage is on the western shore of Lake Superior in northeastern Minnesota. It was the most important shipping and distributing center of the late 1700s for operations of the North West Company of Montreal, Canada. The "great carrying place" was a nine-mile trail between the log post on the lake shore and a point above the unnavigable falls and rapids of the Pigeon River. This strategic portage, used by

Grand Portage National Monument—the "Great Carrying Place" of the voyageurs

Indians before the advent of white men, connected the Great Lakes with the interior network of waterways to western Canada and served as a principal route for explorers, missionaries, fur traders, and military expeditions. A hewn-timber building with stockades, blockhouses, and a "great dining hall" has been reconstructed on the excavated site of the once-great depot and trading post.

Grand Portage is 38 miles north of Grand Marais in Cook County, Minnesota.

Grand Portage of the St. Louis River

The streams and lakes threading the landscape of Minnesota were the highway of the fur trade. One of the most important of these was the complex of lakes and streams connecting the Great Lakes with the Mississippi River. The route began at the mouth of the St. Louis River near present-day Duluth and ended at Big Sandy Lake and the Mississippi, some 70 miles to the west. Traders going between these two major points often followed smaller streams and negotiated several difficult portages, one of which was the Grand Portage—a rugged nine-mile trip along a stretch of the St. Louis River.

The Grand Portage is west of Duluth in Jay Cooke State Park off Minnesota Highway 210.

Northern Bogs—Remnants of the Ice Age

Bogs of the northwoods are nature's eerie deceivers. From a distance the sedges, shrubs, and small trees of the bog look like they stand on solid ground. But step into a bog and you'll discover the deception, as the "earth" beneath you trembles and a slightly pungent liquid begins to seep into your shoes. Stand in one place long enough and you may be submerged up to your knees. You've discovered that the seemingly solid surface of a bog is actually a permeable mat of vegetation floating on a body of water below. If this isn't strange enough, the silence of the bog contributes to the eeriness, as animals that thrive a short distance away do not venture into the bog. Many plants, too, halt their progress at the edge of a bog, giving way to a unique community of plants that have adapted to the bog's limiting environmental factors. Unusual plants, such as the sundew and pitcher plant, solve the problem of nutrient deficiencies by snaring and digesting small insects with ingenious trapping devices.

Like many of nature's creations, a bog has a life of limited duration. Bogs are one stage in a sequence of events, known as succession, that transforms open

The "Witch Tree" at Grand Portage—an old landmark along the voyageurs highway

ponds and lakes into solid ground. The bog is the middle stage in this process—it has one foot in the aquatic world and one foot in the terrestrial.

Many northern bogs owe their origin to an event that took place around 10,000 years ago, when the glaciers that covered the northern half of the continent retreated to the Arctic regions where they had originated. The glaciers were earth sculptors on a grand scale. They scraped mountains bare, gouged out valleys, and deposited sediments hundreds of feet thick. They left water-filled depressions where a large chunk of ice had broken off from the main sheet, formed a pocket for itself, and melted as the climate warmed. Most of the northern tier of states, in particular North Dakota, Wisconsin, and Minnesota, are dotted with these isolated lakes and ponds. Most of the lakes lie in a northeast-southwest direction indicating the path of the retreating glacier.

Because of the way they were formed glacial lakes and ponds lack water inlets or outlets. They depend on rainwater and evaporation. This makes them acidic, nutrient-poor environments. Under these conditions, and because the temperatures that occur in most northern bogs are cool, decomposition is retarded and the buildup of organic matter takes place at a faster rate. The edges of the lake begin to migrate inward, providing a substratum for more vegetation and a source of more organic matter. A thin mat of tangled vegetation develops and spreads the margins of the pond even farther inward toward the center. The mat is composed primarily of sphagnum moss, a water-loving plant that thrives in the nutrient-poor environment of the bog. As the sphagnum and other plants that use it for a substratum become more dense, hardy shrubs like leatherleaf, Labrador tea, and bog laurel gain a foothold and in turn are followed by trees such as larch and black spruce. Like the front lines of an advancing army this succession of plants advances, eventually closing in on itself, sealing the pond forever. In time a thick forest replaces the former bog.

In some areas the bog succession has run its full course and the only way to tell that a bog once existed is to bore below the surface, a technique that scientists use to study the climatic history of an area. Because so little decays in a bog, the layers of partially decomposed sphagnum moss or peat are a storehouse of information about the changes in climate and surrounding plant communities that have occurred since the last Ice Age. From the layers of peat that are the trademark of northern bogs, scientists retrieve well-preserved pollen grains and other ancient plants. In areas where the ice retreated more recently, it is possible to observe all stages of bog succession at one glance. The stagnant, tea-colored water of the bog pond is surrounded by a floating mat of sphagnum, sedges, and shrubs, which in turn is encircled by a forest of tamarack and black spruce.

Bog Rosemary

Bog rosemary is a small evergreen shrub, one to two feet tall, commonly found in bogs, coastal and boreal forests, and in wet sedge tundra from Alaska east across Canada and south to Washington, New Jersey, and Minnesota. This early flowering shrub contains a strong poison, andromedontoxin, which causes vomiting, dizziness, diarrhea, and cramps. It has reddish-purple stalks and dark green leaves.

Labrador Tea

Labrador tea is a resinous, three-foot-tall evergreen shrub known to the early explorers as muskeg tea. It has numerous branches with alternately thick and leathery leaves, and a densely wooly underpart with its margins rolled under. Labrador tea is a common shrub of the black spruce and birch forests and bogs, where it is conspicuous for its fragrant white flowers clustered at the ends of its twigs. It is also abundant near the treeline in open white-spruce stands, where it blooms profusely from mid-June to mid-July, often alongside bog rosemary and leatherleaf. In old bogs it is usually the dominant plant along the bog borders. Its range extends throughout Alaska east across Canada and south to New Jersey, Minnesota, Ohio, and Washington.

Wild Cranberry

Wild cranberry is a slender, creeping, vinelike plant with red fruit, found in cold peat-bog formations from Maine westward to Washington and Alaska. Its flowers are nodding pink bells, up to six on a twig, which bloom May through July. It is also known locally as crowberry, sourberry, and moss melon.

Leatherleaf

Leatherleaf is a profusely branched shrub of the northern bogs and swamps. It reaches heights of up to four feet, with thick, leathery, oblong-shape leaves. Leatherleaf, also known as Cassandra, is a staple food of snowshoe hares and sharp-tailed grouse.

Common Cattail

The common cattail is a frequently sighted marshland species. It reaches heights of up to six feet and forms extensive stands throughout temperate North America. Its stalks, which end in the two familiar spike-shape "cat tails," are used by muskrats in constructing their houses and serve as nesting platforms for redwing blackbirds, long-billed marsh wrens, and yellow-headed black birds.

Wild Rice

Wild rice is known to the American Indians who threshed the standing plants into their canoes as *Manomin*. The early French explorers knew it as the

Cattails

sunspot activity. At full intensity the aurora will cover the entire night sky with erratic, shifting curtains of brilliant white light and dancing, curved bands of green or rose. The legends of the Chippewa Indians say that far up in the northern skies the fur of a celestial deer was stroked by a mystical hand, activating sparks and creating the phenomenon they observed. Several explorers and North Men have told in their journals of being able to actually hear the brilliant aurora whisper and crackle during its dance across the winter night sky of the far north.

Voyageurs National Park

Like the Boundary Waters Canoe Area to the east, Voyageurs National Park lies in the southern portion of the Canadian Shield along the old voyageurs highway in the great Boundary Waters lake chain. The park is a north country wilderness dominated by more than 30 lakes, ranging from huge Kabetogama Lake to tiny kettle ponds, that were gouged out by the glaciers of the Ice Age. Between the lakes and adjacent rocky knobs and ridges of the Kabetogama Peninsula stretch bogs, marshes and beaver ponds. The nests of osprey, great blue heron, and eagle are scattered throughout the park. Its water-dominated landscape is also inhabited by timber wolves, beavers, kingfishers, loons, mergansers, and cormorants.

The voyageurs, Indians, and lumberjacks gave this region most of its place names, such as Grassy Portage, Lake Kabetogama, and Cutover Island. It is interesting to note that the park's place names are predominantly water related. The ancient sediments that comprise the shield represent some of the oldest rock formations exposed anywhere in the world. Younger rock formations do not appear here. Perhaps they never existed, but more likely glaciation simply removed them. At least four times in the past million years, continental glaciers—ice sheets two miles thick—bulldozed their way through the area. They removed previous features leaving mostly level, pockmarked rock up to 2.7 billion years old. Hundreds of ponds, lakes, and streams now nestle in the depressions, and some rock surfaces in the park still bear the scrape marks from the giant glaciers. The glaciers gouged out the lake and river beds and set the stage for the vast evergreen forests.

wild oat. Wild rice grows in shallow waters along streams, marshes, and lakes from the mouth of the St. Lawrence River westward through the lake country of the Canadian Shield, south to Kansas and Virginia, around the Gulf Coast to Louisiana. It grows to a height of nine feet with long, flat green leaves that curve backward. The wild rice grows in loose, open clusters at the top of the stalk. The rice grains are bluish-black, sheathed in papery hulls that have to be rubbed off to expose the grains. Wild rice beds are an important source of food for a variety of north-country wildlife, including waterfowl, marsh birds, muskrat, deer, and moose.

Aurora Borealis—The Northern Lights

The northern lights are a luminous meteoric phenomenon appearing at night in the northern hemisphere. They are caused by electrically charged particles from the sun that are diverted toward the earth's magnetic poles where they collide with gases in the atmosphere and change their electrical charge. Displays are most frequent around times of greatest

St. Croix River Boom Site

The St. Croix Boom Site was the earliest and longest-lived of the major log storage-and-handling areas in Minnesota. From 1840 to 1914 it served as the terminal point for the log drives of the white-pine lumber industry down the St. Croix River. Here millions of logs were sorted, measured, and rafted to sawmills downriver. During its existence it handled over 15.5 billion feet of logs. There are no remains of the log boom, but the general setting is unimpaired.

The boom site is three miles north of Stillwater on the St. Croix River in Washington County.

Itasca State Park— Headwaters of the Mississippi

Lake Itasca is the official source of the Mississippi River. The headwaters were first discovered by Indian agent, author, and geologist Henry Rowe Schoolcraft, who visited the upper river as a member of Governor Cass's exploration party in 1820. In 1836 French scientist Joseph N. Nicollet surveyed and mapped the entire Itasca basin. Evidences of prehistoric habitation have been found in sites within the park, and there is one bison kill site. The park, which contains remnants of Minnesota's primeval "Big Woods," was established in 1891 and structures from that period are the Theodore Wegman Cabin (1893) and the Douglas Lodge (1905, Clarence H. Johnston, Sr., architect).

The park is 21 miles north of Park Rapids off U. S. Highway 71 in Clearwater County, Minnesota.

Wild rice on a north-country lake

Vermillion River Falls and northwoods at Voyageurs National Park—one of the last remaining habitats of the eastern timber wolf

Lake Itasca Indian Bison Site

At this site archeologists have found the only evidence in Minnesota linking man with the extinct bison *occidentalis*, which was much larger than the modern buffalo. Indians dried the meat for food, dressed the hides for clothing and shelter, and fashioned piercing and scalping tools from the bones. These nomadic hunters are believed to have wandered about in groups of less than 12 families. Archeologists date the kill site between 7500 B.C. and 5500. Hunters probably drove the animals into a swampy area where they could be killed with primitive weapons.

Savanna Portage

The Savanna Portage was one of the most important avenues of communication between the upper Mississippi Valley and the Great Lakes during the days of the fur trade in Minnesota. It has been described in the journals of traders, travellers, and missionaries who penetrated the region between 1763 and 1850. Some of the earliest written references to the portage routes were left by Jean Baptiste Perrault. David Thompson, a Scottish surveyor, and Dr. Alexander Wolcott, a surgeon, travelled the route with the expedition of Governor Lewis Cass in 1820. Today the six-mile portage is marked by guideposts and flags along its full length.

The portage is in Savanna Portage State Park near McGregor in Aitkin County, Minnesota.

Wisconsin's Gogebic Range— A Precambrian Ridge

Certain ridges and monadnocks in the Midwest are remnants of the early landscape. These more resistant metamorphic rocks stood above the ancient plain much as they do now. The 80-mile-long Gogebic Range in northern Wisconsin is an outstanding example of a Precambrian ridge. The quartzite Barron Hills, the Flambeau Ridge, and Rib Mountain are prominent. The latter, rising 1,940 feet above sea level, is the highest known outcrop in the state.

The Ice Age Scientific Preserve and Wisconsin's Kettle Moraines

If you fly over the countryside surrounding the Upper Great Lakes, you'll notice that certain distinctively shaped hills and ridges occur repeatedly, and in patterns that rule out the possibility of random distribution. These recurring landforms are mementos of the Wisconsin Ice Age, the most recent major episode in the earth's geological history. The great sequence of events that did so much to shape the landscape of the northern half of North America spanned perhaps 1,500,000 years. The Wisconsin stage, the latest series of glacial advances and retreats, began possibly 70,000 years ago and ended only 10,000 years ago. In fact, we can't even be certain that we are not still in the Ice Age, merely enjoying a warm period between two glacial advances.

Devil's Lake in the Ice Age National Scientific Preserve— an ancient gorge dammed during the Ice Age

This knowledge, strangely, is only about a century old. Until the mid-19th century no one could account satisfactorily for drumlins, eskers, kames, kettles, moraines, or other common features of the countryside. It was the great Swiss naturalist Louis Agassiz who developed the bold new theory of continental glaciation.

The Ice Age Scientific Preserve consists of nine separate units located across the state of Wisconsin from Lake Michigan on the east to the St. Croix River on the Minnesota-Wisconsin border. Each unit possesses features significant in the history of the glaciation of the Great Lakes region. Four units are existing state parks or forests: the Kettle Moraine State Forest, and Devils Lake, Mill Bluff, and Interstate parks.

Kettle Moraine

First among the Ice Age units from the standpoint of variety, abundance, and magnitude of its glacial features is the northern unit of the Kettle Moraine State Forest, located 50 miles north of Milwaukee. The famous 120-mile-long Kettle Moraine was formed as the ice of the Green Bay lobe and Lake Michigan lobe came together. Blocks of ice buried within the deposited material melted to form the numerous kettle ponds that dot the surface and give the rugged moraine its name.

The Kettle Moraine unit also contains some of the world's finest examples of moulin kames—conical hills formed when debris is washed by streams into holes in the glacial ice. Many of the moulin kames here are further accentuated because they rise from a broad, flat plain deposited by sediments that washed together between the two moraines.

One of the most striking features of the Kettle Moraine Ice Age Unit is the Parnell Esker—a long, winding ridge formed by water running beneath the ice sheet.

The Campbellsport Drumlin

The long, rounded hills of the Campbellsport Drumlin Ice Age Unit are located six miles west of the Kettle Moraine. Like much of southeastern Wisconsin's farmlands, the unit is dotted with elongated, rounded hills known as drumlins, which tend to lie parallel to the direction of movement of the glacial ice. Scientists have identified nearly 5,000 drumlins in the state.

Sheboygan Marsh

The large Sheboygan Marsh, once the site of glacial Lake Sheboygan, is located 19 miles west of a

A small kame—a conical hill formed from the sand, gravel, and rocks carried by the melting water that ran along the surface of the ice sheet and cascaded off the glacier's face

town with the same name. As the ice of the Green Bay lobe moved southeasterly it caused the formation of a large basin. Glacial Lake Sheboygan was formed in the basin by water from the melting glacier. Sediment carried by the Sheboygan River following the glacier's retreat gradually filled the basin, leaving a large marsh overlying 100 feet of river-washed debris.

Two Creeks Buried Forest

During an interglacial period, a forest of spruce, hemlock, and associated plants grew along the shore of Lake Michigan. Later, a period of glacial advance covered and preserved the forest in a layer of glacial clay, sand, gravel, and boulders, which was uncovered by erosion. Radiocarbon dating shows that this forest was alive 11,850 years ago. Water-deposited materials show that twice after the ice retreated, the land was covered by waters about 100 feet above the present-day levels of Lake Michigan.

Cross Plains in the Wisconsin Driftless Area

The Cross Plains Ice Age Unit provides striking evidence of the ice sheet's farthest advance into the Driftless Area—an "island" covering nearly 10 million acres in Minnesota, Iowa, Illinois, and Wisconsin that was never covered by ice. At Cross Plains, where the glacier's advance stopped, the end moraine is relatively thin and rests on bedrock. Nearby are sculptured limestone outcroppings that would have been destroyed had glacial ice covered them. The high bluffs, cliffs, and well-drained river valleys of the Driftless Area are in marked contrast to much of Wisconsin's topography.

Devils Lake

Beautiful Devils Lake is one of the most dramatic examples of the force of continental glaciation in the Great Lakes region. Devils Lake, located in the Baraboo Hills 20 miles from the Wisconsin Dells, is a biological transition zone where remnants of plants now associated with the north country are found in cool, sheltered areas, while on the dry, high bluffs prairie species grow.

Millions of years before the Ice Age, the ancient Wisconsin River cut an 800-foot deep gorge through the quartzite of the preglacial Baraboo Range. Later, the ice of the Green Bay glacier lobe spread around these hills, damming both ends of the narrow gorge

Kettle pond at the Chippewa Moraine

Dalles of the St. Croix River

The narrow gorge, or dalles, of the St. Croix River, the westernmost of the nine Ice Age Units, lies 62 miles northeast of Minneapolis, in Interstate Park, and attests to the tremendous erosive force of the glacial meltwaters. During the Ice Age, the St. Croix River drained a vast inland sea known as glacial Lake Duluth, which flooded southward down the St. Croix River valley into the Mississippi.

At St. Croix Falls, the river cut a narrow, sheer-walled gorge through layers of sandstone and Precambrian lava. The water roaring through the gorge created giant whirlpools. Scientists believe that the Lake o' the Dalles, located within this Ice Age unit, was once a gigantic whirlpool. Large potholes up to 16 feet deep were carved by rocks and boulders caught in the torrent.

Apostle Islands National Lakeshore of Lake Superior

The wave-carved cliffs of the Apostle Islands National Lakeshore were called the Twelve Apostles by French explorers, who counted only a dozen on first sighting the archipelago. They lie off the Bayfield Peninsula in northern Wisconsin, which juts into the waters of Lake Superior like a giant thumb pointing toward Canada.

Originally there were probably eight or nine additional islands, now reduced to rocky shoals scattered throughout the archipelago. All of the islands bear evidence of the effects of repeated glaciation and wave erosion. Each is composed of red sandstone bedrock blanketed by a layer of glacial till—rocks, clay, and

with ice and moraine debris, creating Devils Lake Basin. Melting water pouring off the two glacial fronts poured tons of sediments into the basin, filling the gorge. Today, Devils Lake lies atop 325 feet of this glacial debris and its morainal dams form broad hills at either end of the ancient gorge. The massive glacier forced the Wisconsin River to its present-day course nine miles to the east.

Mill Bluff

The towering rocky buttes of the Mill Bluff Ice Age Unit, which rise above a flat terrain two miles east of Camp Douglas, were once small sandstone islands in a now-extinct glacial lake, known as glacial Lake Wisconsin. This lake eventually covered 1,150,000 acres to a depth of 60 to 80 feet. The waves and currents of the lake eroded sandstone from the bluffs of the outlying Driftless Area, depositing tons of glacial sediments into the lake. Some stacks of hardened sandstone, however, did not erode as rapidly. Today they survive as islands rising from the flat plain that marks the old lake bed. The bluffs were used as landmarks by Indians, early explorers, and pioneers.

Chippewa Moraine

The Chippewa Moraine Ice Age Unit, located six miles north of the town of Bloomer, is a woodland of jumbled glacier-deposited hills dotted with more than 300 kettle lakes, ice-walled lake plains, ponds, and marshy pools.

A Lake Superior tugboat towing a log boom

boulders. Along the shores of many of the Apostles, wave action has produced intricate, sometimes grotesque carvings in the 10- to 60-foot cliffs fringing the coastlines. The interior landscapes are characterized by unspoiled white sand beaches, thick evergreen forests, and marshes, the habitats of deer, mink, beaver, muskrat, and many species of migratory waterfowl.

The earliest inhabitants of the region were called the Mound Builders, a group of prehistoric Indians who lived near the shores of Lake Superior some 12,000 years ago. More recently, shortly before the discovery of America, Ojibway or Chippewa tribes built a settlement on Madeline Island, the largest of the Apostles. They dubbed the area *Monigwunakauning*, meaning "home of the golden-breasted woodpecker," because of the thousands of birds that stopped on the island during their annual migrations.

Brule-St. Croix Portage from Lake Superior to the Mississippi

This portage between the Brule and St. Croix rivers was used by explorers, fur traders, travellers, settlers, and missionaries from the late 17th through the mid-19th centuries. Daniel Greysolon, Sieur de Luth (Du Luth), is credited with being the first white man to use the portage (1680). For the next two hundred years it was one of the most heavily travelled routes between Lake Superior and the Mississippi River.

This historic portage is about three miles northeast of Solon Springs in Brule River State Forest in Douglas County, Wisconsin.

Wisconsin's Butte des Morts and Indian Earthworks

The Indian earthworks in Wisconsin made by prehistoric southern migrants are of two structural types. Conical or round heaps, found singly or in groups, are common throughout the state. Butte des Morts—Hill of the Dead—near Neenah is one of the best known. Platform mounds, rarest of the mound types in Wisconsin, exist today only at Aztalan. These earthworks, flat-topped squares of pyramids, their sides sometimes terraced, were strikingly like constructions of the great Mexican and Central American civilizations that antedated mound civilizations of Wisconsin. They are held by some as evidence for the theory that ancient peoples of Mexico and Central America and those of the Midwest are culturally linked.

Far more mounds were erected for burial than for ceremonial purposes. Custom called for deposition of objects with the dead, and the mortuary mounds—some of them the accumulated pilings resulting from a number of community funerals widely spaced in time—are sites of mass findings. Occasionally they yield rare pieces, such as effigy pipes and the three clay portrait masks unearthed in 1936 at Rice Lake, the only pieces of their kind found in North America.

Eagle Bluff Lighthouse in Green Bay

The Eagle Bluff Lighthouse, built in 1868, marks the east passage from Green Bay to Lake Michigan. Still in use today, the light has been converted to electricity. The light tower and keeper's house is two stories high with a gabled roof. At the gable ends are ornamental finials that extend from the top level of the second-story windows through the roof; near the lower end of each finial is a horizontal supporting crosspiece attached to the verge boards forming an interesting piece of Gothic Revival ornament. The light tower is square and oriented diagonally to the keeper's house. The cupola containing the light is decagonal. Restoration work was undertaken in 1961–1963 using the original plans.

The lighthouse is three and a half miles north of Fish Creek on Shore Road in Peninsula State Park in Wisconsin's Door County.

Oconto Copper Culture Burial Mound

The Oconto Site, which dates from 5,000 to 4,000 B.C., is a prehistoric burial ground where implements of the Old Copper culture have been found in association with human burials. The site provided what is thought to be an accurate date for the culture. If so, the Old Copper Complex may represent the earliest use of metals in the world, even though their use by these people later died out.

The burial mound is at Oconto in Copper Culture State Park in Wisconsin's Oconto County.

Astor Fur Warehouse at Prairie du Chien

French, British, and American occupation of Prairie du Chien shaped the settlement and development of the Old Northwest. Among the town's historic buildings is the Astor Warehouse, one of the American Fur Company's principal establishments. This stone building, built about 1835, recalls the Astor empire and Prairie du Chien's prominence as a fur trading center.

Wisconsin's Lizard Mound State Park

During prehistoric times southern Wisconsin was occupied by a group of Indians who constructed low earthworks, three to four feet high, in conical and linear forms and resembling birds and animals. As a result of this practice the Indians are identified as belonging to the Effigy Mound culture. The mounds were used for burials and have yielded tools and weapons of bone, wood, stone, and occasionally copper. Apparently these people lived in small bands and fished, hunted, and farmed. There are 31 extant mounds in the park which vary in length and shape but are about three and one-half feet high. Lizard Mound is the most outstanding and measures 250 feet in length.

The park is three miles northeast of West Bend on Wisconsin Highway 144, then about a half mile east on County Route A in Washington County.

Michigan's Upper Peninsula and the Porcupine Mountains

Michigan's geologically ancient Upper Peninsula, bounded on the north by the frigid waters of Lake Superior and on the south by the beautiful Straits of Mackinac—an important fur trade route on the old voyageurs' highway connecting lakes Huron and Michigan—is a glacier-carved land of great coniferous forests, wild, meandering north-country rivers, bogs, winding eskers, moraines, iron- and copper-rich mountains, and rugged, wave-pounded shorelines where

The large, stocky red-tailed hawk

Michigan's Upper Peninsula countryside

giant sand dunes alternate with towering cliffs. The Upper and Lower peninsulas of the state are connected by the 5-mile-long Mackinac Bridge, called locally "Big Mac," which spans the Straits of Mackinac, site of the historic fur-trade capital of Mackinac Island, known to the Indians and voyageurs as *Michilimackinac*, or the "great turtle," because of its appearance as it rises from the Straits.

The eastern portion of the Upper Peninsula, the setting for some of Hemingway's Nick Adams stories and Longfellow's *Song of Hiawatha* is dominated by the low-lying jack pine and spruce forests and swamps of the Hiawatha National Forest and north-country rivers such as the fabled Big Two Hearted and Tahquamenon, bordered on the north by sandstone tablelands and on the south by rolling limestone hills. Along the often fogbound eastern shoreline of Lake Superior are the glacier-formed cliffs of Pictured Rocks National Lakeshore, the Grand Sable Dunes, and ancient Indian burial grounds at Grand Island.

The abandoned Point Iroquois Lighthouse at the mouth of the St. Marys River provides views of Canada, Lake Superior, and oceangoing freighters, known locally as "salties," plying the lake and river.

The interior of the eastern and central portions of the Upper Peninsula are dominated by bogs and wet lowlands with mats of black spruce, tamarack, sedges, and cedar alternating with sandy uplands covered with stands of red, white, and jack pines. Woodland caribou, once native to the region, have vanished. The old northwoods logging country is a naturalist's delight, with large populations of Canada jays, beavers, otters, pine martens, boreal chickadees, pine siskins, bald eagles, deer, black bear, and sandhill cranes, especially in the Seney National Wildlife Refuge west of Hiawatha National Forest in the Great Manisitque Swamp.

The landscape of the Upper Peninsula, which extends 320 miles from east to west changes dramatically in the rugged, mountainous northwestern area, where ancient iron- and copper-rich mountain ranges culminate at the 2,000-foot elevations of the Porcupine Mountains. Westward of the Keweenaw Peninsula mining country, the Lake Superior shoreline becomes dramatically precipitous, with sheer, towering rock cliffs that serve as nesting sites for northern ravens.

The Porcupine Mountains Wilderness State Park, which lies within the rugged Canadian Shield, takes in 58,000 acres of remote lakes and wild rivers, giant stands of virgin pine and hemlock, and beautiful cascades, including Shining Cloud, Traders, Greenstone, and Trappers falls along the shoreline of Lake Superior. Called locally "the Porkies," these ancient peaks reach heights of 2,023 feet. They were named by the Chippewa Indians because their shape resembled crouching porcupines. To the south of the range are the lake-dotted expanses of the Ottawa National Forest and the Gogebic Iron Range.

Isle Royale of Lake Superior

Isle Royale, cliff-bound and copper-lined, is the largest island in Michigan waters. It lies like a battle-

Rock Harbor Lighthouse at Isle Royale, built in 1855 as a beacon for ships during the copper mining era

The Isle Royale archipelago in Lake Superior, inhabited by a large population of moose and timber wolves, is made up of more than 200 islands and countless "rocks"

ship at anchor in the northwestern part of Lake Superior. Nearer the Canadian shore than the American, the island is within a right-angle turn of the international boundary, a turn that marks a deviation from the centerline placement of the boundary on all lakes and connecting waters between the Atlantic seaboard and western Lake Superior.

Isle Royale is 44 miles long and between 3 and 9 miles wide. Its surface is broken by parallel ridges from which rise Mt. Franklin, Mt. Lookout-Louise, and several other lava peaks. Strewn among the peaks are sea stacks such as Monument Rock, marked by terraces and pitted with caves. Similar markings at approximately the same elevation on the mainland of Canada and the United States indicate that Lake Superior was once much larger than it is today.

The surrounding waters are studded with innumerable atoll-like reefs and small islands. Government lighthouses are maintained on Rock of Ages, at the southwestern tip of the island, on Menagerie Island in the south, and on Passage Island in the east, one of the most important lights on Lake Superior. At the western entrance to Rock Harbor stands a lighthouse that was last used in 1858. Only a thin mantle of soil cover and glacial debris covers the ledge rock of the island, which is made up of a series of ancient lava flows with interbedded conglomerate and sandstone. These all dip southeastward into the lake, from which they again emerge on Keweenaw Point, the northernmost reach of the Upper Peninsula.

The island today is protected as a national park.

Michigan's Keweenaw Peninsula —The Copper Country

The copper mines of Michigan's Keweenaw Peninsula, the northernmost portion of the Upper Peninsula jutting out into the frigid waters of Lake Superior, are often referred to as the Treasure Chest of Michigan. They have produced billions of tons of high-grade copper. The copper abounds as pure metal in the ancient Copper Range, a series of northward tilted lava flows and conglomerates. The ore bodies, which extend for thousands of feet horizontally and have been mined down to depths of more than a mile, dip downward to the north under Lake Superior and emerge again at Isle Royale.

Thousands of years before the arrival of the white explorers and settlers, aboriginal Indians had worked extensively the surface deposits throughout the region. From old Indian pits—some mere holes, others open mines 500 feet long—that scar the terrain north of the old mining village of Mass City, tons of pure copper and some silver were laboriously extracted by the primitive fire-and-water and stone-hammer methods.

Some believe that the pits were created by the Vikings of the 10th and 11th centuries, who made occasional expeditions to the Great Lakes for cargoes of copper, rather than by the native Indian tribes. This view is not in harmony with the fact that the mining was done by late Stone Age methods, whereas the Vikings lived in an Iron Age culture. Some archeologists are convinced that the Phoenicians, noted for their bronzeware, worked the mines 20 centuries before the Christian era.

Stannard Rock Lighthouse

The Stannard Rock Lighthouse is moored on a sandstone shoal about 45 feet long and 30 feet across extending several miles off Keweenaw Peninsula. For many years the shoal went undiscovered until Captain Charles C. Stannard nearly wrecked his ship on it in 1835. By the 1860s the shipping traffic in the lake created an increased need for a warning light off this shoal. The lighthouse was erected on top of the pier formed by a rock-filled coffer-dam tied to the shoal. The light was automated in 1962.

Indian Copper Mines

The ancient Indian copper mines of Michigan's Lake Superior region and Isle Royale are a unique contribution to American archeology. The Indians

Stannard Rock Lighthouse

Pictured Rocks National Lakeshore—the sound of crashing waves against sheer cliffs led the Chippewa Indians to call the area "home of the gods of thunder."

were made aware of the existence of the metal by masses of float copper carried south by the glaciers and left lying on the surface. Sometime in the remote past an unknown tribe began to mine the native copper in Michigan's Upper Peninsula. They dug pits in the ground and separated the copper from stone by hammering, by the use of wedges, and possibly by the use of fire. Thousands of hammers have been found in and about old pits, some grooved for hafting. Copper from these mines was widely distributed throughout the country, and it is probable that numerous tribes made pilgrimages to the Upper Peninsula to get supplies of the precious metal.

Isle Royale in Lake Superior was probably the first place in North America where copper was mined, but it seems unlikely that any vast quantities of the metal were transported across Lake Superior in frail prehistoric craft. The Isle Royale deposits were worked by alternate applications of fire and cold water, causing the rock to crack, so that small particles of copper could be pounded out with stone hammers. Fragments of these crude tools have been found near the mines, the only prehistoric implements that have been found on the island. The many theories concerning the identity of these ancient miners range from Indians to the roving Norsemen.

Pictured Rocks of Lake Superior —A Storied Coast

The Lake Superior shoreline is rugged and remote, a rim of spectacular sandstone cliffs, rock and sand beaches, and gravelly bluffs that have remained essentially untouched since the retreat of the last glacier. Past centuries have seen some changes worked by human and natural forces, though. The Chippewa Indians located their summer camps along the lakeshore in bays that provided attractive sites for fishing and protection from the often rough waters of the lake. In the 1800s, with the discovery of iron, copper, and the "green gold" of the magnificent white-pine forests, pioneers and settlers arrived from the East, and the area thrived for the better part of a century. But the seemingly abundant natural resources did not prove to be inexhaustible. Today the old fishing villages, lighthouses, and blast furnace remains blend with field, lake, and forest to tell a story of the region's brief prominence. Nowhere is this story better told than in the Pictured Rocks area along the Lake Superior coast in the eastern part of Michigan's Upper Peninsula. The natural and cultural diversity of the area led to the creation of the Pictured Rocks National Lakeshore in 1972.

An old miner's cabin at Pictured Rocks

The best way to experience the story the Pictured Rocks region has to tell is to journey some 40 miles along the lakeshore from Grand Marais to Sand Point. Once a thriving commercial fishing and lumbering town, Grand Marais is now a small village, protected from Lake Superior by a horseshoe-shape bay. Just west of Grand Marais are the Grand Sable Dunes, among the finest examples of perched dunes in the United States. Four miles long and a mile wide, the dunes sit atop the Grand Sable Banks. The bluffs are composed of ancient lakebed sands and glacial till. At Sable Falls, the waters of Sable Creek cascade down a gorge cut through this sand and gravel before joining Lake Superior. To the west of the dunes is Au Sable Point, a triangular lakeward projection covered with coniferous trees and bog vegetation.

Century-old Au Sable (literally "by the sand") Light Station still operates at the tip of the scenic point, a vivid reminder of the important role played by the U. S. Lighthouse Service in early Great Lakes shipping. (The Light Station is on the National Register of Historic Places.) Despite the sweeping beacon of the lighthouse, some ships still met an unlucky fate in the often storm-churned waves of Lake Superior. Several shipwrecks lie in the shallow waters west of Au Sable Point, their weathered ribs dissecting the waves that break upon the nearby shore.

A chapter of Michigan's great white-pine logging era was written here too. On the eastern edge of the escarpment above Au Sable Point are the remains of a 400-foot log chute cut through the sand and gravel where, in the 1890s, massive pine logs cut in the plains to the south were slid down into Lake Superior and

towed inside giant log booms to the mills of Grand Marais. The vast gravel outwash area of the Kingston Plains testifies to the dedication and vigor of the logging crews. Some areas of the plains reforested naturally after logging, while other areas have been replanted with red and white pine. But large parts of the Kingston Plains have changed little since the late 1800s when the loggers cut the towering pines, some of which had stood for more than four centuries. Repeated fires have swept the barren stump fields and sterilized the soil so that regeneration of the original vegetation has proceeded at a very slow pace.

West of Au Sable Point begins a long, straight stretch of shoreline known as Twelve Mile Beach. The pebbly beach and 30-foot sandy bluff behind it are broken only occasionally along their length by the lowland areas of Beaver Basin and the mouths of Seven Mile and Hurricane creeks. Just back from the beach, near its eastern end, is an inspiring 40-acre stand of pure white birch, a rare vegetative occurrence that most likely resulted from the logging and subsequent fires that occurred in the area in the late 1800s.

At the western end of Twelve Mile Beach begins the unique geologic formation that has given the area its name. Varying in height from less than 50 feet to almost 200 feet, the Pictured Rocks are sheer cliffs of sandstone deposited 500 to 600 million years ago during the Cambrian period. The horizontal bands of red, yellow, and brown sandstone have been streaked vertically by water dripping down the smooth face of the rock, a multihued pattern best viewed by boat from a lake-level vantage point. In places the colorful stratification of the soft sandstone cliffs has been contorted into caves, arches, stacks, and other strange formations by constant wave action. The crashing of Lake Superior's waves through these grottos led the Indians to regard the area as the home of the gods of thunder. The Pictured Rocks trail follows the top of the cliffs high above Lake Superior, providing expansive views

A red fox

Thimbleberry near Miner's Castle

of the lake's endless waters. Along the landward side of the Pictured Rocks are diverse vegetative communities—stands of virgin northern hardwoods, red and jack pine groves, and bogs and marshes.

The Sand Point area is the western terminus for the journey and also the headquarters for the Pictured Rocks National Lakeshore. Again cultural and natural history merge here almost as one. Munising Falls is one of the most accessible of the many waterfalls of the lakeshore, so accessible in fact that it is possible to walk into the hollow behind the tumbling waters of the falls. Directly adjacent to the falls, and at one time intimately associated with them, are the remains of the Schoolcraft Iron Furnace (also on the National Register of Historic Places). In the 1870s iron ore from the Marquette Range to the west was fashioned into pig iron. Several dozen kilns were built in the hardwood forests of the surrounding area to produce charcoal to fire the blast furnace. The pig iron produced was loaded at the port of Munising at the head of nearby South Bay, where iron carriers began a difficult journey through the inland seas of the Great Lakes, through islands, straits, and reefs frequently masked by storms and fog. Along the way the carriers passed shorelines like Pictured Rocks, where natural and cultural history unfolded like the pages of a visual anthology.

Plant Zones of the Pictured Rocks Lakeshore

The beautiful forests of Michigan's Upper Peninsula are primarily a transition between the northern hardwoods and the boreal, or spruce-fir, forests. This northern hardwood and conifer forest is dominated by sugar maple with mixtures of white and yellow birch, beech, ash, basswood, and elm. The conifers, when present, are generally white pine and hemlock, and on some sites, jack pine, red pine, spruce, fir, tamarack, and arbor vitae. The true boreal forest is not common, but there is enough mixed with birch, aspen, and mountain ash to give the feeling of the northwoods.

The upland soils of glacial till, clay, and sand support stands of sugar maple, beech, and yellow birch. Areas of outwash and well-drained sands are forested with pine. Upland areas are more poorly drained and have a greater abundance of hemlock and red maples.

The boggy areas are generally coniferous, with arbor vitae, black spruce, tamarack, and balsam fir dominant. Leather leaf and other bog shrubs are common along the pond margins. Alder thickets are common along the stream banks.

Several areas within the Pictured Rocks National Lakeshore of Lake Superior are of more than passing interest for botanical reasons. Sand Point, northeast of Munising, juts out into Lake Superior for over one-half mile from the sandstone bluffs, an extension of the Pictured Rocks escarpment. It is roughly triangular in shape and is composed entirely of lake-transported sand deposits. Four small bog ponds are located about in the center of the triangle and are connected with wet areas at the base of the bluffs. The wet areas are fed by small streams running from the face of and over the top of the cliffs.

White and red pine grow in open stands on sandy

Cedar swamp forest

ridges between the boggy area and the beach. A rich carpet of reindeer moss grows on the forest floor. The combination of dry, sandy, low ridges, boggy areas, and wet, heavily vegetated bluffs makes this a fascinating area for the naturalist.

In the embayed areas of Miners Basin and Chapel Basin, red pine and jack pine grow back from the shore, and inland these are mixed with aspen and birch as well as with balsam fir, arbor vitae, black ash, white spruce, mountain maple, and elm. The steep slopes have a rich collection of trees, understory shrubs, and ground-cover plants.

Au Sable Point, another roughly triangular area containing ancient beech ridges and swales, is covered with mostly coniferous forest and swamp vegetation. Inland about one-half mile is a sandy bench up to 100 feet tall. Another half-mile inland is another 100-foot-high bench connecting with the top of the Grand Sable Banks. The benches are covered with stands of northern hardwoods.

On the inland approach to the beautiful Twelve Mile Beach area, there is an extensive, almost pure stand of white birch, a truly breathtaking spectacle. Nearby in the Grand Sable Dunes area there are several isolated stands of jack pine growing on flat areas composed of old lakebed deposits. Some of the dunes are active; others are at least partly stabilized with American beachgrass, sand cherry, and other hard-dune plants. Dune forests grow in a narrow line along the leeward edge of the dunes west of Grand Sable Lake.

American Green Alder

American green alder is also known as mountain alder and green alder. It is common in thickets on gravelly slopes and floodplains from Alaska south to Oregon, Michigan, New York, and in the high mountains of North Carolina. This spreading shrub is from 3 to 13 feet tall. Its leaves have short, slender, dark red-brown petioles with oval-shape or elliptic blades. The blades are usually a shiny yellow green above and pale green beneath with tufts of whitish hairs in the vein angles. Its twigs are smooth and dark, brownish red with many light dots. It flowers during May and June, with its conelike fruit maturing in July. The alder twigs make up an important part of the winter food of wildlife. In fall and winter its nutlike seeds are eaten by many songbirds.

Crowberry

Crowberry is a low, creeping evergreen heatherlike shrub that reaches six inches high. It forms dense mats in arctic-alpine tundra, moist rocky slopes, and muskegs and spruce forests. Its range extends from Alaska south to California and east in the alpine areas to Maine, New York, and Michigan. The edible, shiny, bluish-black or purple berries are reported to be excellent in pies. In winter Alaskan Eskimos gather the fruits under the snow. The berries serve also as fall and winter food for grouse, ptarmigan, and bear.

Prickly Rose

The prickly rose is also known as the wild rose. It is a spiny, many-branched shrub one to four feet high, common in shaded undergrowth of deciduous and spruce forests, with aspen on old burns, and in thickets, bogs, and along the roadside from Alaska across Canada and south to Idaho, New Mexico, West Virginia, and Minnesota. The reddish edible fruit is known as rose hips, or rose haws, and is rich in vitamin C. The fruit is gathered in the fall when hard. The juice is extracted by boiling and is mixed with other fruit juices or used in jellies or syrups. Jams, marmalades, and catchup are prepared from the pulp after the seeds and skin are removed by sieving. Its flavor is improved by adding a tart fruit or juice such as cranberry or highbush cranberry. It is possible that a tea may be made from the leaves. Rose hips are eaten by grouse and other birds during fall and winter.

Grand Sable Banks and Dunes of Lake Superior

In the eastern section of the Pictured Rocks National Lakeshore of Lake Superior are the Grand Sable Dunes and Banks—the result of ancient lake, glacial,

Grand Sable Dunes of Lake Superior

and wind activity. Grand Sable Banks is the exposed part of a glacial deposit extending five miles along the present Lake Superior shore and rising to 275 feet above the lake level. Perched on top of the banks are the Grand Sable Dunes, covering an area of five square miles and rising 80 feet higher than the banks. The sand was blown into great dunes at the edge of an ancient lake, known as Lake Nipissing, which preceded Lake Superior. Sand was blown up into ridged rows from successive beaches of the ancient lake. The dunes in general are actively moving inland from their original location. The prevailing winds off Lake Superior continue to erode the banks, adding material to the dunes.

The Tahquamenon Falls

The Tahquamenon, sometimes called the dark or golden river, flows through marshy lowlands, past densely wooded ridges, and between towering rock cliffs as it makes its way through Lake Superior State Forest and neighboring Mackinac State Forest in the eastern portion of the Upper Peninsula and then flows into Lake Superior's Whitefish Bay. The river figures prominently in Longfellow's epic poem *Hiawatha*, where it marks the watery grave of Kwasind, the friend of Hiawatha who is killed in a mighty battle with the scheming otters. Between the towns of Newberry and Paradise are the legendary Tahquamenon Falls, known as the Little Niagara, tumbling down the face of a 40-foot cliff. Six miles downstream from

the Big Falls are the Cataracts, or Lower Falls, from which point the river broadens over wide ledges, then swirls through impressive stretches of thundering rapids, until it finally comes to rest in Lake Superior.

Bay Furnace in the Marquette Iron Range

Concentrated efforts to mine the Marquette Iron Range were under way by the 1850s. Furnaces and charcoal kilns were built throughout the region, one of which, located west of Munising, was operated by the Bay Furnace Company. A settlement grew up around the furnace known as Onota, or Bay Furnace. In full operation by 1870 the furnace was supplied by two separate sets of six charcoal kilns. The town contained two-story frame dwellings, log houses, a store, a school, blacksmith and wagon shops, and eventually a church. Suddenly in May 1877 a flaming holocaust developed from scattered fires and devastated the town. Bay Furnace was never rebuilt, and the massive sandstone furnace ruins are all that remain of the once booming community.

The furnace site is northwest of the hamlet of Christmas off Michigan Highway 28 in Alger County.

Kingston Plains

The rolling Kingston Plains, once the site of a virgin pine forest near Munising in Michigan's Upper Peninsula, is typical of logging country areas that have long been cut and burned and are now open country. As far as the eye can see is a grass- and bracken-covered plain dotted by stark, gray stumps, broken here and there by a stand of young pines or lake basin. The plains are a habitat for a wide variety of birds, including eastern and western meadowlarks, upland sandpipers, and sandhill cranes.

Michigan's Mackinac Island—The "Great Turtle"

Mackinac Island, the bottleneck of the Great Lakes, lies in the Mackinac Straits. The straits connect Lake Huron on the east with Lake Michigan on the west. The island rises from the straits on six terraces. Geologic evidence in the rock formations suggests that in ancient times the island was entirely covered by an inland sea. As the waters receded the rocky limestone pinnacle emerged, until the Great Lakes reached their present levels. The action of the sea wore away the less resistant parts of the rock, resulting in such natural wonders as Arch Rock, Scott's Cave, Chimney Rock, and the Devil's Kitchen. The eastern and southern shores of the island were once overshadowed by huge limestone cliffs, some portions of which gradually broke away, while others softened, making possible the growth of pine and cedar forests.

The island was called *Michilimackinac*—the great turtle—by the Indians, who believed it had risen from the Straits of Mackinac through supernatural causes. Time and usage shortened the term to Mackinac. Because of its strategic position in the straits, the island successively became a natural gathering place for nomadic Indians, a refuge for tribes fleeing before the conquering Iroquois, and a key fur-trade center and battleground between the Americans and the British. The Americans won the battle for the island and gained a monopoly of the fur trade. The headquarters of John Jacob Astor's American Fur Company was based here in 1817. At Fort Mackinac, still standing, palisaded curtain walls connect two-story blockhouses of squared logs elevated on a secure masonry base of local stone. The dwellings, churches, and storehouses were also constructed of logs, placed horizontally and chinked with clay.

Fort Michilimackinac on the Straits of Mackinac

Fort Michilimackinac was strategically located on the south shore of the Straits of Mackinac, the crossroads of the Upper Great Lakes. Erected by the French, the post was surrendered to the British in 1762 during the French and Indian War. It was the only British garrisoned outpost on the Great Lakes until near the end of the American Revolution. In 1781 the post was moved to Mackinac Island. The site of the original fort has been established by archeological investigation, and the stockade has been reconstructed. Its museum exhibit includes current on-site archeological operations.

The fort is at Mackinaw City near the Mackinac Bridge at the end of U. S. Highway 31.

Agency House of the American Fur Company

John Jacob Astor organized the American Fur Company in April 1808. Less than 10 years later, after failure of his Astoria venture, Astor sent Robert Stuart and Ramsay Crooks west to manage fur trade operations in the Great Lakes area. Eventually Stuart be-

White pine—prized tree of the logging era

came head of this operation, which totally dominated the economy of Mackinac Island. He remained in his post until 1834, and shortly thereafter the fur trade operations shut down. The Stuart House, originally an agent's residence, has been restored. It was one of four structures forming the nucleus of the fur-trade empire (agency warehouse, trading post, and clerks' quarters). It is a two-story frame building with a gable roof containing dormers. Many of the window panes date from construction as do the wooden cross and Bible doors and the fanlight above the main entrance. A kitchen and storage rooms were located in the basement, and agency clerks were housed on the second floor.

The agency house is at Market Street on Mackinac Island.

Indian Dormitory at Mackinac Island

On March 28, 1836, a treaty was signed between the Ottawa and Chippewa nations and the United States government. It effected one of the largest Indian land cessions ever while providing for the reservation of various tracts to be held in trust for the Indian nation. Article Seven of the treaty called for construction of a dormitory for the Indians visiting the post. Plans for the building were drawn up under the supervision of Indian agent Henry Rowe Schoolcraft. By the 1850s a dormitory was no longed needed, and the building was converted to a school for the Indian children. During the mid-1860s the dormitory served as a teaching facility for the city of Mackinac Island and continued as such for over 90 years. In 1964 the structure was purchased and restored by the Mackinac Island State Park Commission.

Mackinac Point Lighthouse

Mackinac Point Lighthouse is a round tower connected to a service building, both of which are made of light brick and rest on high foundations of stone. The light station was established in 1890 on the Straits of Mackinac, a main crossroads for shipping on the Great Lakes. The lighthouse was not completed until 1892. It was discontinued in the late 1950s.

The lighthouse is at Michilimackinac State Park near Mackinaw City.

Old Presque Isle Harbor Lighthouse

Because Presque Isle Harbor was used frequently by the coastal shipping trade and was the only safe haven between Detroit and Michilimackinac, this site was chosen for the location of a lighthouse. The lighthouse is a circular tower 30 feet tall, 18 feet in diameter at the base, and 9 feet at the top. The walls are 3 feet thick at ground level, tapering to 20 inches at the top. They are stone on the lower two-thirds and brick on the top. Adjacent to the tower is the two-and-a-half-story brick lightkeeper's dwelling. In 1871 a taller light was built at the top of Presque Isle to replace this structure.

The Golden Age of White Pine

To some it was a forest primeval, overwhelming in its vastness and mysterious in its depth, a tangled wilderness full of danger and the unknown. To others the great pine woods were a haven of solitude, a place of peace and grandeur unequaled on the North American continent. But to all the great expanse of towering pine trees that in the early 1800s stretched from Maine through New York and Pennsylvania to western Minnesota and up into Canada must have seemed endless and unlimited in its potential for supplying wood. The pine woods of the northern forest belt could never be exhausted, or so it was thought. But one factor was not considered—the tremendous thirst of an expanding nation for lumber to build houses, factories, fences, and fleets of sailing ships.

White-pine logging began with the first settlers in New England. When the forests of the Northeast had been largely depleted, the pioneers began to cut their way westward. Some land was cleared for farms and the wood used for shelter or fuel. In other places the timber was harvested and sent down the waterways to sawmills. When they reached the Midwest, the pioneers must have stood in wonder at the pines that towered 150 to 175 feet above the rolling plains. Some of these giants had begun to grow more than 300 years earlier, long before the Pilgrims sighted Plymouth Rock, and they still stood firm, their lacy tops sweeping the clouds, the bark of their five-foot-diameter trunks dark gray and deeply furrowed with age.

The Golden Age of Michigan Pine began in 1840, only three years after the state was admitted to the Union, and continued until the turn of the century. Millions of acres of virgin pine were cut by timber companies that had acquired land from the federal government at the bargain price of $1.25 per acre. Modest amounts of timber were cut during the first decade of logging because of the near total lack of mechanization. But with the coming of the railroads and the development of new tools and logging methods in the 1850s, the logging industry stepped into

White pine cone

volume of each log and stamped each one with a log mark to indicate ownership. Then the logs sat, frozen in the ice and snow, until the spring thaw set them free to float downstream. Back at camp the services of the tinker, blacksmith, filer, and perhaps most importantly, the cook, ensured that the shanty boys could keep up the dawn-to-dusk pace six days a week for the better part of seven months.

Log marks were to Michigan what cattle brands are to the grazing states. First used by Queen Anne's Surveyor General to mark the finest pines of New England for use as masts, they gave order to a romantic industry that would have been chaos without them. Thousands of log marks were used over the years, each one officially registered by the company it symbolized. When the ice went out on the rivers and the logs began to float downstream, not even the rough-and-ready jam crews, whose job it was to keep the logs moving, could keep them separated by ownership. So they were floated en masse until they reached the mouth of the river on one of the Great Lakes—Superior, Michigan, or Huron. There the sorting and rafting men used the distinctive log marks to steer the logs of each company into separate booms, enclosures made by long, squared timbers chained together. Then the whole boom was towed to a sawmill, often located near the river mouth, but sometimes some distance away down the lake in one of the great mill towns like Saginaw, Muskegon, Menominee, or Manistique. From ice to thaw the logs were hauled out of the woods and piled along the stream banks; during the rest of the year the great log drives coursed the rivers.

At the height of the white-pine era, around 1873, more than 1,600 sawmills operated in Michigan. With the development of mechanization from the two-man gang saw to the water- or steam-powered circular saw, these mills put out billions of board feet of lumber per year. (A board foot is a piece of wood one

full swing. Each fall, as frost settled on the prairies and farms of southern Michigan, trains began to pull out of Bay City, Muskegon, Detroit, and Grand Rapids carrying Mexicans, English, Canadians Germans, Swedes, French, Poles, and Indians bound for the lumbering camps in the central and northern parts of the state. The camps were primitive assemblages of makeshift shanties where a mixture of languages, nationalities, religions, personalities, and temperaments came together in a melting pot of raw American society.

Collectively they were known as shanty boys, the term "lumberjack" being of relatively modern origin. But separate names applied to each of the numerous tasks involved in getting the pine out of the woods and to often distant lumber mills. Choppers and sawyers began the process, felling the trees, trimming the limbs, and cutting the trunks into logs, usually 16 feet in length. Then the swampers and skidders took over, hauling the logs out of the woods with a team and chain to the nearest trail where they were piled at intervals. Loaders and deckers helped the teamsters load the logs onto sleighs for transportation to the banking grounds—the banks of feeder streams and rivers, where the scalers and stampers recorded the

Relic from the golden age of the white pine—a water tank on a sleigh, used to ice down logging roads

Wooded Empire Dune at Sleeping Bear National Lakeshore

foot long, one foot wide, and one inch thick.) By the 1890s the lumber companies were actually running out of pinelands to cut, something that had seemed almost impossible only 30 years earlier. The Golden Age of Michigan Pine was coming to a close. By government estimates, from 1840 to 1900, 161 billion board feet of white pine had been cut in Michigan, enough to floor the entire state with one inch pine boards and still have an ample supply in reserve.

Fires repeatedly swept across the barren stump fields left in the wake of the lumbering era. But now much of Michigan is reforested and modern logging practices ensure that the timber is being harvested at a sustainable pace. It's difficult to imagine the dimensions of the original pine forests; small vestiges were spared the logger's axe and have now received protected status, like the Estivant Pines at the very tip of northern Michigan's Keweenaw Peninsula. Elsewhere, beneath the second- and third-growth evergreen forests that now cover much of the northern half of the State, enormous moss-covered stumps are all that is left to attest to the time when the shanty boys cut the big pines, a time when the name of Michigan was synonymous with white-pine lumbering.

Sleeping Bear Dunes of Lake Michigan

Told and retold through the centuries by the Chippewas is the tale of a mother bear and her two cubs trapped by a forest fire on the western shore of Lake Michigan. To escape the fire the bears set out to cross the broad lake, the older bear out front breaking through the waves and the two cubs swimming behind. The lake was wider than they had thought, and for two days and nights they swam seeking the eastern shore. Their small reserves of energy waning, the cubs lagged behind, and when the exhausted mother bear finally pulled herself up onto the eastern shore, the cubs were nowhere to be seen. The mother bear climbed to the top of a bluff to wait in vain for her offspring, but they never emerged from Lake Michigan's waves. The great spirit Manitou took pity on the bear and transformed her, so that today she can still be seen as the Sleeping Bear, a solitary, tree-covered sand dune that overlooks the clear blue lake below. The cubs, having died from the effort, can still be seen as the two islands, North and South Manitou, that lie several miles offshore.

Modern geologic theory tells a different tale about the origin of the sand dunes that are the central feature of Sleeping Bear Dunes National Lakeshore on the northeastern coast of lower Michigan. Several times in the past 10 million years continental glaciers, vast sheets of ice up to a mile thick in places, crept down from the Arctic to cover an area of North America as far south as southern Illinois, Indiana, and Ohio. Like a giant earth-moving machine, the glaciers carried along with them soil and rock debris scoured from the land they passed over. As they melted back the glaciers deposited this debris, or till, as thick ridges, loose mounds, or as an even covering over the landscape. These glacial deposits, known as moraines, are a prominent feature of the Sleeping Bear area today and are one of the reasons why so many come from so far to see this area.

The most dramatic example of glacial moraines are the bluffs that tower over the shoreline of Lake Michigan. Atop one of these bluffs rests the Sleeping Bear Dune, actually a relatively thin cap of sand deposited by the wind and gradually covered over by a dense stand of evergreens, once vaguely resembling a sleeping bear. But time and the forces of erosion—wind, rain, and gravity—have been at work on the Sleeping Bear Dune so that it no longer resembles the one that inspired the Chippewa legend. The dune has been cut in half; a valley of sand now divides two tree-clad ridges. Some may regret the change, but it's a change that illustrates vividly the dynamic character of the Sleeping Bear Dunes National Lakeshore. Wind, wave action, and the process of succession are constantly reshaping the dunes, headlands, beaches, and bays of the Lakeshore.

Human settlement has shaped the area too. Abandoned fields and orchards attest to a time when the area was an important agricultural community. The dramatic landforms of the area and the way they have been altered by human and natural forces led to the designation of the Sleeping Bear Dunes National Lakeshore in 1970. When all authorized lands have been acquired by the National Park Service, the Lakeshore will contain some 70,000 acres. (Acquisition was 60 percent completed by October 1980 and is expected to be fully completed by the end of 1981.)

Sand dunes are not the only interesting feature of Sleeping Bear Dunes National Lakeshore, but they are one of the most impressive. Several types of dunes are found at Sleeping Bear, the two most common being the beach dune and the perched dune. Beach dunes are formed at lake level as onshore winds carry beach sand inland. These dunes occasionally grow to considerable height but more commonly form the low, rolling dunes most people think of as sand dunes. Perched dunes differ from beach dunes primarily in their location; they sit atop headlands often several hundred feet above the level of the lake. The Sleeping Bear Dune is an example of a perched dune that was covered by vegetation and is now undergoing erosion. No dunes are completely stable; most are constantly being moved by the prevailing winds, particularly those that lack a protective covering of vegetation. Ghost forests, stands of weathered tree trunks that have been partially submerged by shifting sand, attest to the movement of dunes.

Without stabilizing vegetation, a process called

Cedar logs on the dunes

saltation causes dune sand to move. Grains of sand, set in motion by the wind, collide with each other, bounce into the air, and are driven downwind as they fall. When they land they produce a chain reaction by striking other grains, so that on windy days a hazy zone of moving sand is visible a foot or two above the ground. Because of the dynamic nature of the dunes, they are excellent places to witness the process of primary succession, the colonization of barren ground by communities of plants. Beach grass is the first to become established. Then sprawling mats of bearberry and juniper cover the sand, giving way eventually to stands of cottonwoods. Finally, given enough time and little disturbance, a climax beech-maple forest may develop.

People come to Sleeping Bear Dunes National Lakeshore to see the famous Sleeping Bear, to climb and play in the other pure sand dunes of the area, to gaze from the glacial headlands out over the clear waters of Lake Michigan. But the dunes environment is only one of many at the Lakeshore. Groves of aspen and lush beech-maple forests exist in the shadow of the barren, desertlike sand dunes. Elsewhere stands of pine dot the landscape and cedar swamps, and even a few secluded quaking bogs of sphagnum moss can be found. The Lakeshore's varied habitats support a diversity of wildlife, including white-tailed deer, red fox, bobcat, and over 220 species of birds. Fish in the area's lakes and streams include rock bass, bluegill, perch, pike, rainbow trout, and the aggressive coho salmon, introduced into Lake Michigan at the Platte River just south of Sleeping Bear in the 1960s.

One of the best ways to observe the wildlife of Sleeping Bear is to journey by boat to North or South Manitou islands, which have recently become part of the Lakeshore. The islands are richly endowed with natural and cultural features, including Lake Michigan's oldest lighthouse, which guarded the treacherous

Manitou Passage from a point of land on South Manitou Island for a century until it was abandoned by the United States Coast Guard in 1958. The solid structure still stands, a monument to the area's importance as a shipping route.

Because deer have never found their way to South Manitou, the 5,000-acre island supports a remarkably diverse flora, including five species of trillium, a host of jack-in-the-pulpit, and the rare green spleenwort. The prize of the island is a 110-foot white cedar, whose 206-inch girth makes it the largest white cedar in the world. Along with the cedar in the Valley of the Giants are found national-record specimens of common elder, red-berried elder, and mountain maple. Plants are not the only abundant form of wildlife, however—179 species of birds have been recorded on the island at one time or another, and the northeast corner of the island is a major nesting colony for herring and ring-billed gulls. Abandoned farmsteads, a one-room schoolhouse, and an old cemetery tell of the agricultural community that once thrived on South Manitou.

North Manitou also once supported an active community, centered around the logging operations on the 15,000-acre island. But deer have replaced people as the island's primary residents, and the buzz of loggers' saws has given way to the solitude that is the island's primary attraction. Backpacking is the best and only way to fully explore the island's diverse environments.

Kingbird and nest, common in orchards and woodland borders

In the fall warmed lake water moderates the arrival of the season's cold air masses moving southward from Canada, allowing vegetation to mature before the first frost. Another effect of Lake Michigan on the Sleeping Bear region is increased cloudiness in late fall and early winter. The cold winter air mixing with warmer, moist air from the lake often results in snow, rain, and fog nine months of the year.

Great Lakes Climate

Extreme seasonal temperature variations and a fairly even annual distribution of precipitation are typical of the Upper Great Lakes region, which is near the center of the North American continent. Climatic conditions in the Sleeping Bear Dunes region, however, are strongly influenced by Lake Michigan, which has a stabilizing effect on air temperatures. Because of the prevailing westerly winds, winters are mild and summers cooler along the shoreline than in the interior areas. This moderating effect on air temperatures and the fact that air drainage patterns form microclimates, or air pockets, near the shore, result in a greater amount of mild, pleasant weather.

In spring cool Lake Michigan water tends to level temperature extremes along the shoreline, reducing the incidence of frost damage. During summer, when the main storm track moves northward into Canada, the difference in temperature between land and water areas frequently results in a lake breeze during periods of easterly winds, cooling temperatures during hot weather.

Vegetation Zones

Because of its diverse geological character the Sleeping Bear region exhibits a wide variety of plants associated with dune, forest, plain, meadow, swamp, and aquatic habitats. The processes of plant succession and adaptation are clearly demonstrated at various sites throughout the region.

The effects of timber cutting after the arrival of settlers in northwest Michigan in the mid-19th century are apparent today. Where infertile soils forced the abandonment of farming, trees either regenerated or were replanted, resulting in scattered second-growth forests.

Plant succession in the region begins on the barren, sandy beach and climaxes in the beech and maple forest farther inland. The following series is typical of the succession in the lakeshore area.

Beach and Active Dune Zone

Beyond the beach, where wave action makes plant growth impossible, only a few plants can grow:

White-tailed deer

American searocket, seaside spurge, and beach pea. Several grasses grow adjacent to this zone and act to stabilize the wind-blown sand.

Heath Zone

The dominant plant species of the heath zone include shrubs such as sand cherry, common and creeping juniper, buffalo berry, bearberry, chokecherry, and an occasional cottonwood tree, as well as flowering plants such as dune wormwood, false heather, and evening primrose. This plant zone is commonly found inland from the beach and on morainal bluffs and plateaus.

Stabilized Dune Zone

The stabilized dune zone includes a group of plants that could not exist without the improved conditions provided by the heath. Red, white, and jack pines are often scattered throughout this zone, resulting in a clumping of vegetation. Solitary trees are surrounded by low juniper and other shrubs, all ringed by masses of bearberry, mosses, and creeping juniper.

Open Woodland Zone

The open woodland zone is dominated by red oak mixed with conifers from the heath dunes. Bracken fern, smooth aster, and cow wheat are often found growing beneath the oaks. On poor soils aspen stands are found, dominated by largetooth and quaking aspen.

Hardwood Forest Zone

The inland hardwood forest zone is a climax forest dominated by beech and maple forests. Commonly found on morainal hills, the dominant species of this zone are sugar maple and beech, mixed with basswood, ironwood, black cherry, red oak, and white ash. Hemlock and yellow birch are found in moist areas of the forest. Plant succession in old abandoned fields will eventually climax in the beech and maple forest. Apple trees and black locust have been introduced and have established themselves in some of the old fields.

Another successional series characteristic of the Sleeping Bear Dunes begins near or in the water of inland ponds and lakes. These plant zones can be divided into the lake and pond zone, swamp and bog zone, and aspen and birch zone.

Lake and Pond Zone

Species found in the shallow areas of lakes and ponds include cattails, arrowgrass, water smartweed, and bullrush. Spearmint, marsh pea, sedge, bugleweed, and other species are found near the water's edge.

Cedar Swamp Zone

The dominant plant species in the cedar swamp is white cedar, mixed with yellow birch, balsam, fir, and tamarack in damper areas. Where the trees grow close together there is little vegetation; where they do not, they are interspersed with American elm, black ash, and green ash.

Lily pads in a bog pond

South Manitou Island Lighthouse, built in 1871. The island had the only natural harbor north of Chicago, 220 miles to the south. The light beckoned to the wood-burning steamers needing to refuel for either north- or southbound voyages.

Black Spruce and Quaking Bog Zone

In the black spruce and quaking bog zone, black spruce trees mixed with tamarack occur in clumps and in open spaces that are usually filled with Canada blueberry, leatherleaf, bog rosemary, swamp laurel, and others. A thick mat of sphagnum or other mosses, mixed with sedges, extends over the water in the quaking bog.

Aspen and Birch Zone

The stands of aspen, yellow and white birch, and white cedar are the dominant species in the aspen and birch zone.

Wildlife Habitats

With the exception of birdlife, wildlife species on the islands of the Sleeping Bear Dunes region are relatively few compared with those found on the mainland along Lake Michigan. The distinct and isolated island populations offer opportunities for studying distribution, adaptation, and evolution. The introduction of white-tailed deer on North Manitou Island illustrates the detrimental effect that an introduced wildlife population can have on an environment. The deer have heavily browsed the area, altering the vegetation so that it differs significantly from that of South Manitou Island.

White-tailed deer, raccoon, white-footed mouse, and porcupine are common species in most areas of the national lakeshore. Other common species include snowshoe hare, cottontail rabbit, red fox, woodchuck, striped skunk, and mink. Two species of flying squirrel and all three species of the eastern tree squirrel—red, gray or black, and fox—are present. The eastern chipmunk is common in most forest areas, and the 13-lined squirrel is found in open meadow areas. Bobcat, gray fox, otter, badger, coyote, and beaver are present but are rarely seen in the vicinity of Sleeping Bear Dunes.

Birdlife is abundant and varied, with particular species often associated with lake areas, hardwood forests, shore bluffs, morainal plateaus, and sand dunes during the summer months. Species associated with specific habitats of the lakeshore area are as follows:

Morainal Plateau and Active Dunes

The morainal plateau and active dunes include the vesper sparrow, horned lark, goldfinch, and marsh hawk.

Hardwood Forest

The hardwood forest is the habitat of the red-eyed vireo, red start, and ovenbird.

Lake, Marsh and Swamp

The lake, marsh, or swamp is the habitat for numerous shorebirds, like grebes, great blue herons, ducks, and loons.

Common winter residents include the pine grosbeak, chickadee, crossbill, and pine siskin. The herring and ring-billed gull colonies on South Manitou Island are some of the oldest rookeries on the Great Lakes, although foxes have reduced the rookery population to the point that the gulls may abandon the site. Bald eagles and peregrine falcon are occasionally sighted in the Sleeping Bear area, as are osprey, piping plover, sharp-shinned hawk, Cooper's hawk, red-shouldered hawk, marsh hawk, American kestrel, and yellow-throated warbler.

Thirty-two species of reptiles and amphibians are found within the Sleeping Bear Dunes. The eastern massasauga is the only poisonous snake in the region and is seldom seen.

Pioneer Artifacts of the Sleeping Bear Dunes

There are numerous historic sites and structures found throughout the Sleeping Bear Dunes National Lakeshore that are culturally significant. They represent the historical themes of navigation, logging, agriculture, and the turn-of-the-century resort era. The lifesaving stations at Sleeping Bear Point, South Manitou Island, and North Manitou Island are all in good states of repair.

Two lighthouses were located within Sleeping Bear Dunes area, one on North Manitou Island and the other on South Manitou Island. The only remaining structures on North Manitou that were associated with the lighthouse are a barn, two privies, and a collapsed boathouse north of the lighthouse. The rest of the complex has been claimed by Lake Michigan. The South Manitou Lighthouse was one of the first lighthouses constructed in the Sleeping Bear region.

Other historic sites consist mainly of former towns, docks, and sawmills. On the mainland these are the former towns of Aral, Port Oneida, Good Harbor, and North Unity; the remnants of docks at Aral, Glen Haven, Port Oneida and Good Harbor; and the site of D. H. Day's sawmill. On South Manitou Island there are the sites of the old dock and the sawmill near the cemetery. On North Manitou Island there are sites of several logging camps and docks as well as the site of the old logging town of Crescent City. The only physical remains of these sites are numerous surface and subsurface archeological materials: old dock pilings, foundations of the sawmill operations at Aral, Crescent City, and South Manitou, and a few old buildings at one of the logging camps on North Manitou.

Several remnants of logging-period structures remain in Glen Haven. Logging was an important aspect to life there, although the community was not a sawmill town in the conventional sense because of its diverse economy. The Sleeping Bear Inn was originally a boardinghouse for loggers, and the old D. H. Day store was the company store for Day's employees, many of whom were engaged in his lumbering operation. Glen Haven's association with logging, along with its ties to maritime and agricultural history, make it one of the few towns of its kind in Michigan.

Most of the old structures on the national lakeshore are related to agriculture, but many of the farms of historical significance are in private ownership. Only on North and South Manitou Islands will the national park own all the farms, most of which are deteriorating, although they are still historically and architecturally interesting.

Bird of Fire—The Kirtland's Warbler

On a summer afternoon in 1903 a Michigan ornithologist pushed his way through a stand of scrubby pines on a sandy terrace above the valley of the Au Sable River. He searched for a bird he'd never encountered in the wild, a warbler that had been idenified for the first time in Ohio 50 years earlier, but about which little was known, including where the bird nested. Norman A. Wood had never heard the bird sing either, but when "a new song, so rich, loud, and clear" suddenly rang through the pines, he knew right away the bird he sought was nearby. Guided by the bird's beautiful song Wood eventually caught a glimpse of the warbler and a few hours later discovered the bird's nest on the ground beneath a pine tree. That day Wood became the first person to look for and find the nest of the Kirtland's warbler, a species named for Ohio naturalist Jared P. Kirtland of Cleveland, near whose farm the first Kirtland's warbler was collected in 1851.

Since that triumphant day near the turn of the century hundreds of nests of the Kirtland's warbler have been located but none outside of a 60-mile radius of the spot where Wood made his discovery. This fact begins to tell the story of the Kirtland's warbler, for the songbird is one of the rarest members of the wood warbler (*Parulidae*) family and is included on the United States List of Endangered and Threatened Species. The rarity of the Kirtland's warbler is the bird's most noted distinction. The 1980 census of the bird estimated the population to be 484 individuals, a figure determined by doubling the number of singing males counted on the breeding grounds in the spring. The warbler's song, variously described as "wild and clear," "liquid," and "the most beautiful of any warbler," and the unusual curiosity of the bird are two other singular characteristics. But the most in-

Kirtland's warbler—the "bird of fire"

triguing feature of the bird, and the ultimate reason it is so uncommon, is its relationship to its environment. For nesting and breeding the Kirtland's warbler has a very strict set of habitat requirements—dense stands of young jack pine at least 80 acres in size growing on a porous, nutrient-poor soil known as Grayling sand. These stringent requirements are met in a nine-county area in the northern half of lower Michigan around Mio, the entire breeding range of the Kirtland's warbler.

Another environmental factor, one normally considered an enemy of most living things, plays a key role in the life cycle of the Kirtland's warbler: fire. The scrubby jack pines the bird depends on for shelter and nesting cover in turn depend on the periodic recurrence of fire to complete their life cycle. Normally sealed shut by a sticky resin, the cones of the jack pine open to release their seeds only when fire sweeps through the tree's barren environment. Just as importantly the fire also prepares the ground for germination of the released seed. Lightning-caused fires were common in presettlement days on the sandy outwash plains the jack pine prefers, allowing large tracts of the two-needled pine to flourish in the Great Lakes region. Though probably never abundant, the Kirtland's warbler most likely reached its population peak long before we began keeping records of the bird, in the centuries following the retreat of the last glacier, which left large expanses of sandy till ideal for the pioneering jack pine. But because of the natural process of succession, these sandy barrens are no longer as abundant as they once were, and the range of jack pine has consequently been reduced. Modern

forest management techniques have reduced jack pine habitat also by curtailing fire, the crucial link in the tree's reproductive cycle. With fewer stands of jack pine the population of the Kirtland's warbler has declined dramatically in the past 80 years.

Though the relationship between the "jack pine bird" and its environment isn't completely understood, it is known that the Kirtland's warbler breeds almost exclusively in pure stands of jack pine 8 to 25 years of age. Apparently the branching pattern during this stage of the short-lived tree is ideal for the ground-nesting bird, providing the right amount of overlap to conceal the nest below. When the tree gets much older, the shaded-out lower branches begin a process of self-pruning, taking away the warbler's cover and causing the bird to abandon the habitat. This dependency on jack pines of a particular age best illustrates the narrow ecological niche the Kirtland's warbler has evolved to fill.

One species does compete with the Kirtland's warbler, however, and the conflict is another important factor in the scarcity of the warbler, especially since the turn of the century. The brown-headed cowbird is a brood parasite, a species that somewhere along its evolutionary journey lost the inclination or ability to build its own nest and raise its own young. The female cowbird lays her eggs in the nests of other species, leaving the duties of parenthood to the host. For the Kirtland's warbler, this brood parasitism is a serious problem, as the cowbird eggs hatch first and then the larger cowbird chicks take most of the food brought to the nest. The warbler chicks simply cannot compete. It is thought that this problem is a relatively new one for the Kirtland's warbler, as the brown-headed cowbird, normally a species of open fields and grasslands, extended its range into the forests of northern Michigan only after the white man opened these forests with his settlements.

Together the brown-headed cowbird and the loss of jack-pine habitat have been devastating to the Kirtland's warbler, to the point where the bird, in the mid-1970s, was barely maintaining a viable breeding population. This led to the establishment of a program to protect and develop habitat for the endangered species, sponsored by the U. S. Fish and Wildlife Service, the U. S. Forest Service, and the Michigan Department of Natural Resources. Under the program jack-pine stands are harvested and the areas burned to prepare the ground for jack-pine seedlings, which are planted by hand. The program ensures that jack-pine stands of suitable age are available for the warbler to nest in. The second part of the program entails the removal of the brown-headed cowbird from selected areas of the Kirtland's warbler habitat. The parasitic bird is captured in traps, using seed bait and

Indiana Dunes National Lakeshore lies along old Indian routes between the Great Lakes and the Mississippi River. The Indians followed the Calumet Beach Trail, hunting and gathering food during summer.

live decoys, and then taken from the area.

Aided by this two-pronged management approach the population of Kirtland's warblers is slowly rebuilding from the precarious levels of the mid-70s (total population in 1974: 334 individuals). The long-range goal of the Kirtland's Warbler Recovery Team is to maintain a population of about 1,000 pairs. This should be a large enough population to assure the bird's continued success.

During the summer months naturalists give guided tours of the jack-pine barrens around Mio where the yellow-breasted bird of fire makes its summer home. The warbler's curiosity usually brings it out of the jack-pine cover, making it easy to catch a glimpse of the rare bird. If not, the fluid notes of its song indicate its presence. Birders from around the country come to see the Kirtland's warbler, a species that seems to be gaining ground in the struggle against extinction.

Indiana Dunes of Lake Michigan

Similar to Michigan's Sleeping Bear Dunes, the Indiana Dunes stretch for 25 miles along the Lake Michigan shoreline between Gary and Michigan City, Indiana, less than 50 miles from Chicago. At the close of the Ice Age about 10,000 years ago, the landscape at Indiana Dunes National Lakeshore was covered with spruce and fir forests now found in Canada. As the glaciers retreated, the climate warmed and the forests crept northward. But some arctic plants, such as bearberry, persisted, while plants formerly forced south by the glaciers reappeared. The high dunes, hot and dry like deserts, now provided homes for southern dogwood, plains flowers, and prickly pear cactus. The older dunes there may be forested with pine or oak, but the moist, protected ravines harbor beech-maple forests. The ponds tend to lie between the foredune and pine dune zones. Marshes and tamarack and cranberry bogs are usually found farther inland. Both wetlands are dying ponds that will eventually become meadows and then forests. The Indiana Dunes are inhabited by a wide variety of migratory shorebirds—plovers, sandpipers, sanderlings—and summer residents such as cedar waxwings, red-shouldered hawks, prairie warblers, and green herons.

Hoosier Prairie nearby is the largest remnant of original prairie in Indiana. It contains more than 300 native plants, many of which are rare in the state.

Picture Credits

The following photographs used in *The Great American Countryside* are reproduced with the permission of the U.S. Geological Survey (*USGS*), National Park Service (*NPS*), and the U.S. Forest Service (*USFS*). Part One, Chapter 1—"Great Plains": *NPS* photographs of Missouri River paddlewheeler, Missouri River ferry, Devil's Tower, Little Missouri River, bison herd, Little Missouri badlands, agate fossil beds, paddlewheel steamer, Scotts Bluff, Chimney Rock, Fort Larned, old stage station, adobe church on the Santa Fe Trail; *USFS* photographs of crested wheat, Medicine Rocks, honeycombs, Missouri River Breaks, Dark Butte, Black Hills, Needles area, Inyan Kara Mountain, rock outcroppings, South Dakota badlands, river-carved flats, red-tailed hawk, prairie dog, badger, forb, farmstead, eroded rock formations, high plains, pioneer homestead, volcanic dikes, antelope, sod house, Texas high plains, sharp-tailed grouse. Chapter 2—"Southern Rockies": *NPS* photographs of Fort Union, Pecos Pueblo, Indian kiva, Bandelier National Monument, Great Sand Dunes, alpine lake, Capulin National Monument, Maroon Bells, Florissant Fossil Beds; *USFS* photographs of the tundra zone, rock formations, prickly pear cactus, Red Rocks, coyote, Front Range, ponderosa pine, glacial valley, wind timber, ptarmigan, marmot, Flat Tops, aspens, San Juan Range, Great Wall, juniper, Chinese Wall, Garden of the Gods, mountain pass, alpine fir, beaver dam, Pawnee Buttes. Chapter 3—"Great Gap in the Rockies": *NPS* photographs of Fort Laramie, Oregon Trail markers, South Pass City, Custer and Crow scouts, Battle of Little Bighorn; *USFS* photographs of eroded rock formations, sagebrush flats, sage cocks, grasslands, pioneer ranch, working cattle ranch, Bighorn Canyon, old Army fort, sage hen. Chapter 4—"Middle Rockies": *NPS* photographs of sheepeater Indian wickiup, Grand Tetons, coyote, Teton Range and sagebrush flats, hay meadows, elk herd in Jackson Hole, whiteface cattle, corral, glacier-carved valley, Douglas fir, Hayden Valley, white pelicans, Specimen Ridge, sequoia stump, Grand Canyon of the Yellowstone, Firehole River and geyser basin, Jupiter Terrace, sprinkler wagons at Yellowstone National Park; *USFS* photographs of a Rocky Mountain canyon, Wasatch Mountains, Uinta Mountains, Flaming Gorge Dam, Great Wall, glacial valley, rock field and tundra, trees at timberline, mountain pass, Ramshorn country, Paternoster lakes, talus slopes, night hawk, beaver pond, Western larch, columbine, ptarmigan, ranch, Shiras moose, Hoodoo Basin, Absaroka Range, Beartooth Plateau, Beartooth glaciers, young sparrow hawks. Chapter 5—"Northern Rockies": *NPS* photographs of the Great Divide, bighorn sheep, Lewis Overthrust, Nez Percé National Historical Park; *USFS* photographs of homestead ranch, female grizzly, Chinese Wall, krummholz, Sawtooth Range, pioneer marker, field of lupine. Chapter 6—"Cactus and Sagebrush": *NPS* photographs of Death Valley, pupfish, charcoal kilns, rhyolite ghost town, Death Valley Salt Pan, roadrunner, Golden Spike ceremony, saguaro cactus, organ pipe cactus, coatimundi, Casa Grande, Fort Bowie, Chiricahua National Monument, Gila Cliff Dwellings, Gran Quivira Ruins, White Sands, Carlsbad Caverns, Capitan Reef, El Capitan, Mariscal Canyon; *USFS* photographs of basin and range landscape, Great Basin Desert, Mohave Desert, south-facing slopes, Great Salt Lake, Wheeler Peak, Fort Rock, yucca plant, big sagebrush, bristlecone pine, juniper, desert bighorn sheep, Sonoran Desert landscape, saguaro forest, Lake Mead, Boulder Dam, barrel cactus, Roosevelt Dam, Weaver's Needle, sotol and octillo plants, javelina, prickly pear cactus. Chapter 7—"Canyons and Mesas": *NPS* photographs of the Yampa River, roadrunner, Wupatki Ruins, Keet Seel Ruin, four-stick hogan, Walnut Canyon National Monument, Montezuma Castle, Tuzigoot Ruins, Canyon de Chelly, Navajo pictograph, Petrified Forest, Monument Valley, Navajo Bridge, Pipe Spring, slickrock country, White Cliffs, Bryce Canyon, Capitol Reef, Needles at Canyonlands, Green River at Dinosaur National Monument, Hovenweep Ruins, Long House and Cliff Palace at Mesa Verde; *USFS* photographs of mesa and canyon country, San Rafael River, Grand Mesa, Lizard Head. Chapter 8—"Snake River Country": *NPS* photographs of Craters of the Moon, spatter cones; *USGS* photograph of Dry Falls of the Grand Coulee; *USFS* photographs of Grand Canyon of the Snake River, coyote, The Island of the Crooked River, Palouse Hills, Seven Devils Range, Box Canyon of the Snake, Idaho sand dunes, old hotel, Columbia Basin lava, Snake River Breaks. Chapter 9—"Rim of Fire and Range of Light": *NPS* photographs of active glacier world, Ross Dam, bald eagle, Diablo Dam, wildflower meadow at Mt. Rainier, alpine meadow, Mt. Rainier glacier field, Crater Lake Pinnacles, lava tube, Mt. Lassen, Jeffrey pine, Devil's Postpile, Rainbow Falls, El Capitan, Yosemite Valley, Moro Rock, Indian grain mill, sequoias; *USGS* photographs of Mt. St. Helens and the eastern slope of the Sierra Nevada; *USFS* photographs of Crater Mountain, Mt. Baker, abandoned mine, homestead ranch, Indian paintbrush, sawtooth peaks, South Cascades Glacier, Jefferson Park, black bear, rhododendron thicket, Franklin grouse, mountain goats, Mt. Adams, Little Mt. Adams, Goat Rocks, Dee Wright Observatory, Hood River Valley, Broken Top, mountain hemlock, obsidian lava, Engelmann spruce, ponderosa pine, Abert Rim, lava formation, juniper foothills, Great Basin landscape, Temple Crag, Mt. Whitney, Sierra foothills, golden-mantled ground squirrel, foxtail pines, Traill's flycatcher, red-shafted flicker, glacial erratics, Seven Gables Peak, Lone Pine Lake, Lake Tahoe, Jeffrey pine, view of High Sierras. Chapter 10—"Pacific Coast": *NPS* photographs of Fort Vancouver, San Juan National Historical Park, Olympic coast, sea stack, Olympic beach landscape, Blue Glacier, Hoh Rain Forest, sword fern, Roosevelt elk, Fort Clatsop, Oregon Dunes, redwoods, Redwood National Park, prairie and elk herd, redwood forest floor, sea gulls, Point Reyes Light, Drakes Bay, Pinnacles, Channel Islands, Anacapa Island, elephant seals; *USGS* photograph of the San Andreas Fault and Carizzo Plains; *USFS* photographs of a coastal forest, Douglas fir, Western red cedar, Sitka spruce, Inside Passage, coastal foothills, Hecla Head Light, Coast Range,

Tillamook Head, Trinity Alps, sea birds, Cypress Point, chaparral, California condor.

In Part Two, Chapter 11—"New England Woods and Trails": *NPS* photographs of Grant's General Store, old New England farmhouse, village meeting house, Appalachian Trail, logging camp, Allagash River, Allagash Falls, Fort Ticonderoga; *USFS* photographs of Mt. Chocorua, Mt. Washington, white pine, snow-laden spruce, snowshoe rabbit, Green Mountains, red spruce, Maine mountains, cog railroad, Great Gulf, raven, white-tailed deer. Chapter 12—"Rocky Shore": *NPS* photographs of Mt. Desert Island, Ironbound Point at Acadia, Isle au Haut, fishing village, Acadian forest, Mt. Desert Lighthouse, Irish moss zone, St. Croix Island Lighthouse, Derby Wharf; *USFS* photographs of a coastal forest, salt marsh. Chapter 13—"Mid-Appalachian Mountains": *NPS* photographs of Lemon House, Allegheny Portage Railroad, Hopewell Village, waterwheel, Delaware Water Gap; *USFS* photographs of ridges and valleys, Heart's Content Area, Allegheny Front Range, farmlands. Chapter 14—"Sandy Shore": *NPS* photographs of a barrier island, windmill, Montauk Point, boardwalk nature trail, Fire Island dwarf forest, pioneer-era blacksmith shop, Assateague Island, Jamestown Island, Cape Henry, Outer Banks, wild ponies, Fort Raleigh, Cumberland Island, Ocmulgee Earthlodge. Chapter 15—"Southern Appalachian Highlands": *NPS* photographs of Cumberland Gap, Hensley Settlement, flame azalea, Cable Mill at Cades Cove, Oconalufte Valley, Harpers Ferry, Mather Gorge, Mabry Mill; *USFS* photographs of spruce tree, farmlands, high peaks, grassy bald, Wayah Bald Tower, ruffed grouse nest, red spruce, barred owl, mountain meadows, Pisgah Mountains, wood thrush, Seneca Rocks. Chapter 16—"Gulf Coast and the Florida Shore": *NPS* photographs of Padre Island, shrimp boat, Fort Pickens, Shark River estuary, green tree frog, Seminole ceremonial village, Cape Canaveral; *USFS* photographs of cypress stand, palmetto cabbage. Chapter 17—"Central Prairies": *NPS* photographs of the Pipestone Quarries, Ice Age esker, early iron furnace, Mound City earthworks; *USFS* photographs of a prairie windmill, cedar trees, prairie farm. Chapter 18—"Ozarks": *NPS* photographs of Ozark National Waterway, Buffalo River bluffs, Eleven Point River, Buffalo River, pioneer cabin; *USFS* photographs of the Ozark highlands, stalagmites, cave opening. Chapter 19—"Great Lakes": *NPS* photographs of wind-swept dunes, Great Lakes shoreline, sand dune, kettle pond at Ice Age National Preserve, wave-eroded shore, Voyageurs National Park, Grand Portage, "Witch Tree," Vermillion River Falls, Devil's Lake, kame, Apostle Islands, tugboat, Isle Royale, Rock Harbor Light, Pictured Rocks, old miner's cabin, thimbleberry, buried forest at Sleeping Bear Dunes National Lakeshore, Empire Dune, gulls, cedar logs, South Manitou Lighthouse, Indiana Dunes; *USFS* photographs of the Palisades, Basswood River, beaver pond, moose, golden eagle, great blue heron, great horned owl, fisher, northern hardwoods, red-tailed hawk, white spruce, red fox, red pine, cedar swamp, Grand Sable Dunes, logging tank, kingbird, white-tailed deer, lily pads.

Index